Using PC Tools™ 8
Special Edition

WALTER R. BRUCE III

Revised for Version 8.0 by

MARK CHAMBERS

SALLY NEUMAN

KATHLEEN PAQUETTE

JUDY PETERSON

HILDE WEISERT

RICK WINTER

Using PC Tools 8, Special Edition

Copyright© 1993 by Que® Corporation

Library of Congress Catalog No.: 92-82062

ISBN: 1-56529-103-4

95 94 93   4 3 2

Interpretation of the printing code: the rightmost double-digit number is the year of the book's printing; the rightmost single-digit number, the number of the book's printing. For example, a printing code of 93-1 shows that the first printing of the book occurred in 1993.

Screens reproduced in this book were created using Collage Plus from Inner Media, Inc., Hollis, NH.

This book is based on PC Tools for DOS, Version 8.

Publisher: Lloyd J. Short

Associate Publisher: Rick Ranucci

Operations Manager: Sheila Cunningham

Book Designer: Scott Cook

Production Team: Claudia Bell, Julie Brown, Jodie Cantwell, Paula Carroll, Laurie Casey, Jeanne Clark, Tim Cox, Heather Kaufman, Bob LaRoche, Joy Dean Lee, Loren Malloy, Caroline Roop, Linda Seifert, Susan Shephard, Greg Simsic, Tina Trettin, Johnna VanHoose

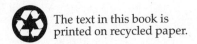 The text in this book is printed on recycled paper.

CREDITS

Title Manager
Walter R. Bruce III

Acquisitions Editor
Sarah Browning

Product Directors
Timothy S. Stanley
Steve Schafer

Production Editors
Tracy L. Barr
Joy M. Preacher

Editors
Elsa Bell
Barb Colter
Jane A. Cramer
Kelly Currie
Susan M. Dunn
Lori A. Lyons
Gregory R. Robertson

Technical Editors
N.J. Naclerio and Associates
David Wolfe

Editorial Assistants
Betsy Brown
Jill Stanley

Composed in *Cheltenham* and *MCPdigital* by Que Corporation

Walter R. Bruce III is the author of many Que books including *Using PC Tools 7.1*. He has written several instructional texts for use in intermediate and advanced workshops on using popular microcomputer software packages. He has also led workshops on the use of computer software for government and private-industry clients from coast to coast.

Mark Chambers has been a PC software technical writer and bulletin board system operator for over five years. He and his wife Anne live in Columbia, Missouri, with their daughter, Erin.

Sally Neuman is a System Integrator in Longview, Washington. She provides complete business integration services to the construction, legal and financial, engineering, and wood products industries, with special emphasis on small business automation. She also is a system operator for ZiftNet, providing technical support for DOS and windows environments and hardware configuration issues.

Kathleen Paquette is a technical writer in the computer industry. She has worked with the Peter Norton Group of Symantec, Candle (a mainframe manufacturer), and Ashton-Tate. Kathleen is the author of *OS/2 Featuring the Presentation Manager* and is a regular contributor to Ashton-Tate's *Quarterly* magazine.

Judy Peterson is a WordPerfect instructor and resource staffperson for the Leon County (Florida) School Board Vocational Program. In her own business, Judy is a lawyer, computer software consultant, and trainer for businesses and individuals in the Tallahassee area.

Hilde Weisert is a writer and instructional designer specializing in high technology for business and education. In her consulting work, she focuses on human factors in software design, end user documentation, and training, as well as expert use of word processing, graphics, utilities, and hypertext applications. Hilde is also a published poet.

Rick Winter is a senior partner at PRW Computer Services. He has trained more than 1,500 adults on personal computers and is the coauthor of *Q&A QueCards*. Rick also is the revision author of *1-2-3 Release 3.4 QuickStart, 1-2-3 Release 2.4 QuickStart, 1-2-3 for DOS Release 2.3 QuickStart*, and *1-2-3 for DOS Release 3.1 QuickStart*. Other technical editing projects include Que's *1-2-3 for Windows QuickStart*, quick reference guides for WordPerfect 5.0 and dBASE IV, and on-line help for WordPerfect 5.0, Symphony, and DisplayWrite 4.

ACKNOWLEDGMENTS

Trademarks

All terms mentioned in this book that are known to be trademarks or service marks have been appropriately capitalized. Que cannot attest to the accuracy of this information. Use of a term in this book should not be regarded as affecting the validity of any trademark or service mark.

PC Tools 8 is a trademark of Central Point Software.

CONTENTS AT A GLANCE

Introduction 1

I Using the Desktop

1 Navigating the Desktop 23
2 Controlling the Desktop 55
3 Using the Desktop as a Program Manager 89
4 Working on Files...133
5 Locating and Viewing Files 171
6 Working on Disks 201

II Using the System Utilities

7 Protecting Your Data with Central Point Backup 259
8 Speeding Up Your Hard Disk with Compress 311
9 Obtaining System Information 333

III Using the Recovering and Security Utilities

10 Recovering Damaged or Deleted Files.........................367
11 Recovering Damaged or Formatted Disks 403
12 Editing a Disk with DiskEdit.......................................435
13 Securing Your Data with PC Secure and Wipe 459
14 Protecting Your System with CP Anti-Virus 485

IV Using the Desktop Manager

15 Navigating the Desktop Accessories 525
16 Using PC Tools Notepads...559
17 Using PC Tools Clipboard 599
18 Using the Outliner..615
19 Using PC Tools Databases 625
20 Managing Your Appointment Schedule 673
21 Automating Your PC Using PC Tools Macros.............719
22 Using the Calculators 749

V Communicating by Modem, Fax, or Local Area Network

    23 Using PC Tools Telecommunications 789
    24 Using Electronic Mail 845
    25 Sending and Receiving Fax with Fax
           Telecommunications 863
    26 Controlling a PC Remotely with CP Commute 881

Appendixes

    A Installing and Configuring PC Tools 909
    B Using PC Tools from within Microsoft Windows 933

    Index 947

Introduction 1

    What Is PC Tools? 1
        PC Tools Desktop 2
        The System Utilities 3
        The Recovery and Security Utilities 4
        The Desktop Accessories 6
        The Communication Utilities 6
        Windows Support 7
    What's New in PC Tools 8? 8
    What Should Your System Have? 11
    Who Should Read This Book? 12
    What Is in This Book? 13
        Part I, "Using the Desktop" 13
        Part II, "Using the System Utilities" 14
        Part III, "Using the Recovering
           and Security Utilities" 15
        Part IV, "Using the Desktop Manager" 16
        Part V, "Communicating by Modem,
           Fax, or Local Area Network" 17
        Appendixes 18
    Conventions Used in This Book 19

I Using the Desktop

1 Navigating the Desktop **23**

    Starting PC Tools Desktop 24
    Using PC Tools Desktop Menus 27
        Using Pull-down Menus 28
        Using Function Key Commands 30
        Using Drag-and-Drop 32
    Understanding the PC Tools Desktop Windows 33
        Moving between Windows 35

Logging On to a Different Disk
and Rereading the Tree 36
Moving, Resizing, Zooming,
and Hiding the Windows 36
Turning Off the Background Mat 37
Moving a PC Tools Desktop Window..............37
Resizing a Window 38
Zooming or Maximizing a Window 39
Hiding a Window 40
Moving around the Screen 41
Using Dialog Boxes 42
Message Dialog Boxes 42
Command Dialog Boxes 43
Using Option Buttons 45
Using Option Check Boxes 46
Using a List Box 46
Using a Text Box 47
Using Command Buttons 47
Getting Help from PC Tools Desktop 48
Using the Help Menu 48
Using the Context-Sensitive Help Facility 50
Closing PC Tools Desktop 52
Chapter Summary 53

2 Controlling the Desktop 55

Configuring the Desktop 56
Redefining the Function Keys 58
Setting Confirmation Preferences 60
Customizing the Screen Display..............................62
Modifying the File Display 64
Filtering the File List 66
Using Speed Search 68
Using Your Own Text Editor 69
Toggling Quick Run 70
Customizing the Pull-down Menus 71
Switching to Version 6 or Version 7 Menus 71
Switching to Shorter Menus 72
Using the Menu Editor 72
Moving and Adding Menu Commands 73
Editing a Menu Item 75
Adding DOS Commands or Applications
to the Desktop..76
Saving the New Menu Scheme 77

Protecting the Configuration with a Password 78
Modifying the Window Layout 79
  Toggling between Dual Lists and One File List 80
  Displaying the Menu Window 82
  Displaying the View Window 83
  Toggling Individual Windows 84
  Hiding All Windows 85
Using the DOS Command Line 86
Changing How Desktop Returns from DOS 87
Chapter Summary 87

3 Using the Desktop as a Program Manager 89

Accessing the Menu Window 90
Understanding the Menu Window 92
  Launching Programs from the Menu Window 94
  Changing the Configuration
    of the Menu Window 95
Building a Menu Window System 96
Adding and Editing Program Groups 100
  Creating a New Group 102
  Adding a Description to a Program Group 104
  Modifying Program Group Properties 106
  Deleting a Program Group 106
Adding and Editing Program Items 107
  Specifying a Program Title 108
  Specifying Program Commands 108
  Specifying a Start-up Directory and Password 109
  Indicating Command Parameters
    with Keywords 109
  Adding Pause after Exit 112
  Adding a Description to a Program Item 112
Adding Advanced Program Item Information 113
  Adding a User Prompt 113
  Specifying File Associations 114
  Adding Keystrokes 114
  Selecting Advanced Execution Control 116
  Editing a Program Item 117
  Deleting a Program Item 117
Changing an Item's Position or Program Group 117
Saving the Changes to the Menu Window 118
Importing Direct Access Menus 119
Using the Task Switcher 120
  Configuring Task Switcher To Run at Startup 120
  Running Applications with Task Switching 122

Switching between Tasks 124
Closing an Active Task 125
Scheduling Programs with the Scheduler 125
Configuring the Scheduler To Run at Startup 126
Adding a Scheduled Event 127
Changing the Schedule 130
Customizing the Calendar 130
Preparing for Scheduled Events 131
Chapter Summary 132

4 Working on Files 133

Selecting and Deselecting Files 134
Selecting Single Files 135
Selecting Multiple Files 136
Using the File Select Filter 136
Deselecting Files 137
Running Programs and Launching Files 137
Copying and Moving Files 139
Copying Files 139
Moving Files 142
Compressing and Uncompressing Files 143
Looking for Discrepancies 145
Comparing the Contents of Two Files 146
Verifying a File 148
Modifying Files 149
Renaming Files 149
Deleting Files 150
Undeleting Files 151
Using Wipe To Clear Files 152
Using the File Editor 153
Using the Hex Editor 157
Viewing Files in the File Edit Screen 157
Editing Files on the Sector Edit Screen 159
Changing File Attributes, Date, and Time 161
Changing File Attributes and Dates from DOS 163
Encrypting and Decrypting Files 164
Printing 165
Printing Files 165
Printing Directories 168
Chapter Summary 169

5 Locating and Viewing Files 171

Locating Files with FileFind 172
Starting FileFind 172

Locating Files by File Name 174
Locating Files by Using Predefined
    Search Groups 176
    Adding a Search Group Entry 178
    Editing a Search Group Entry 178
    Deleting a Search Group Entry 179
    Using a Search Group Entry 179
    Adding Filters 180
    Filters on a Stand-alone System 181
    Filters on a Network 182
    Using the Specified Filters 183
    Selecting Drives and Directories 183
    Finding Duplicates 185
Searching Files for Text 187
Looking at Files with View 189
    Displaying the View Window 189
    Understanding the PC Tools Desktop Viewers ... 192
    Moving around the View Window 194
    Understanding Viewer Function Key
    Commands 196
Chapter Summary 199

6 Working on Disks **201**

Preparing a Disk 202
    Formatting a Disk 202
    Running PC Format from the
    DOS Command Line 208
    Making a Disk Bootable 211
    Renaming a Disk Volume Label 212
    Copying a Disk 212
    Obtaining Disk Information 215
Preparing an Emergency Disk 216
    Creating a New Emergency Disk 217
    Updating after a Configuration Change 218
    Testing the Disk 219
Looking for Discrepancies after Copying 219
    Comparing the Contents of the Two Disks 219
    Comparing the Contents of Two Directories 221
    Verifying a Disk 221
Searching a Disk 223
Using the Tree List Window 225
    Understanding the Tree List Window 226
    Selecting a Different Disk and
    Refreshing the Tree 227

Navigating the Tree 228
Collapsing and Expanding Branches 228
Configuring the Tree List 233
Maintaining Directories in PC Tools Desktop 234
Adding a Directory in PC Tools Desktop 235
Renaming a Directory in PC Tools Desktop 237
Deleting a Directory in PC Tools Desktop 237
Undeleting a Directory 238
Moving a Directory in PC Tools Desktop 239
Moving or Copying a Directory
    with Drag-and-Drop 240
Modifying the Attribute Byte in
    PC Tools Desktop 241
Using the DM Directory Maintenance Program 242
Changing the Tree Data Display in DM 245
Changing the Volume Label in DM 246
Adding a Directory in DM 247
Renaming a Directory in DM 247
Deleting a Directory in DM 248
Copying a Directory Branch in DM 249
Moving a Directory Branch
    (Prune and Graft) in DM 250
Printing the Tree 251
Modifying the Attribute Byte in DM 252
Displaying Network Rights in DM 253
Exiting from the Directory Maintenance
    Program 254
Sorting a Directory 254
Chapter Summary 256

II Using the System Utilities

7 Protecting Your Data with Central Point Backup 259

Starting Central Point Backup 260
Answering Initial Configuration Questions 261
Examining the Express Backup Window 266
Performing a Full Backup from the Express
    Backup Window 269
Performing a Selective Backup 272
Specifying the Drive To Back Up 274
Choosing Specific Directories 276
Selecting Files 278
Starting the Backup 278
Comparing and Restoring Data 280

Selecting a Backup Set and Destination 281
Starting the Compare Operation 283
Performing a Restore Operation 285
Reconfiguring CP Backup 287
Changing the Backup Device 288
Changing the Backup Speed 289
Changing the User Level 290
Saving the Configuration Changes 291
Scheduling Backups 291
Setting Backup Options 294
Setting Procedural Options 297
Changing the Backup Method 297
Creating a Backup Report 298
Compressing Backup Files 299
Verifying Data 299
Selecting Media Format 300
Formatting Backup Media 301
Correcting Errors 301
Virus Detection 301
Saving a Copy of the Backup History File 301
Protecting Duplicate Files 302
Timing the Backup 302
Setting Selection Options 302
Including Subdirectories 302
Including Files 303
Excluding Files by Attribute 304
Including Files by Date 305
Setting Display Options 305
Choosing Sort Options 306
Changing the Display Format 306
Saving the Setup 306
Creating a Setup File 306
Using a Setup File 307
Using Tape Tools 308
Using CP Backup Command Line Parameters 308
Chapter Summary 310

8 Speeding Up Your Hard Disk with Compress 311

Checking for File Fragmentation with FileCheck 312
Starting Compress 314
Analyzing Your Disk 317
Analyzing Disk Allocation 317
Analyzing a File 319
Showing Files in a Map Block 321

Using Compress Options 322
   Selecting the Compression Technique................322
   Choosing an Ordering Method Option 324
      Specifying Directory Order 326
      Placing Files First 326
      Specifying Unmovable Files 327
   Sorting Directories 328
   Printing a Report 329
Running Compress 330
Command Line Options 331
Chapter Summary 332

9 Obtaining System Information **333**

Displaying General System Information 334
   System Type 336
   Operating System 337
   Video Adapter 338
   I/O Ports 339
   Keyboard/Mouse 340
   CMOS Information 341
   Network Information 342
   Software Interrupts 345
   Hardware Interrupts 347
Displaying Disk Drive Information 348
Displaying Memory Information 350
   Conventional Memory 351
   Extended Memory 352
   Expanded Memory 353
   Device Drivers 354
Running Benchmarks 354
   CPU Speed Test 355
   Disk Speed Test 355
   Overall Speed Test 356
   Network Performance 357
Displaying System Files 357
Printing an SI Report 358
System Information Command Line Options 359
Mapping Files, Disks, and Memory 359
   Mapping a File 360
   Mapping a Disk 361
   Mapping Memory 363
   Using MI.COM 363
Chapter Summary 364

III Using the Recovery and Security Utilities

10 Recovering Damaged or Deleted Files...................367

Using FileFix...369
  Selecting Files To Repair 370
  Repairing Database Files 371
    Repairing R:BASE Files 372
    Repairing Paradox Files 373
    Repairing dBASE Files......................................374
    Repairing dBASE File Headers 376
  Repairing Spreadsheet Files 379
  Repairing WordPerfect Files 380
  Quitting FileFix 382
Using Undelete To Recover Deleted Files 383
  Starting Undelete 384
  Finding Deleted Files 387
    Finding Files by File Name 387
    Finding Files by Using Predefined
      Search Groups 390
    Scanning Free Clusters for Deleted Files 391
  Selecting Files To Undelete 394
  Undeleting Files 395
    Using the Automatic Method 396
    Using the Manual Method 397
    Using the Create-File Method 399
  Undeleting a Directory 400
  Undeleting Files on a Network...............................400
  Purging Delete Sentry Files 401
  Quitting Undelete 402
Chapter Summary 402

11 Recovering Damaged or Formatted Disks 403

Using Mirror 404
  Saving System Information to
    the Mirror-Image File 405
  Saving the Partition Table, CMOS Data,
    and Boot Sector 407
Using the Emergency Disk 409
Using Unformat 412
  Recovering from an Accidental Format
    by Using the Mirror-Image File 412
  Recovering from an Accidental Format
    without Using the Mirror-Image File 416

Checking for Problems with FileCheck 419
Using DiskFix 422
   Repairing a Disk 424
   Scanning the Disk Surface 426
   Revitalizing a Disk 429
   Configuring DiskFix 431
   Exiting DiskFix 432
Using DiskFix from the DOS Command Line..............433
Chapter Summary 434

12 Editing a Disk with DiskEdit 435

Starting and Configuring DiskEdit 436
Using the DiskEdit Editors 440
   Using the Directory Editor 440
   Using the File Allocation Table Editor 444
   Using the Partition Table Editor 445
   Using the Boot Record Editor 447
   Using the Hex Editor 448
   Displaying and Mapping Objects 449
   Marking, Copying, and Pasting Objects 451
Repairing Disks and Data with DiskEdit 453
Displaying Memory Information 456
Exploring Command-Line Options 457
Chapter Summary 457

13 Securing Your Data with PC Secure and Wipe 459

Starting PC Secure 460
   Entering the Master Key.......................................461
   Examining the PC Secure Screen
     and Its Functions 463
   Selecting Options 464
     Choosing the Type of Encryption 465
     Compressing Files 465
     Using One Key Per Session 466
     Taking Additional Precautions 466
     Saving the PC Secure Configuration 468
   Encrypting Files..468
     Selecting Individual Files................................469
     Selecting Entire Directories 470
   Decrypting Encrypted Files and Directories 472
   Exiting from PC Secure 473
Encrypting and Decrypting Files
   from the DOS Command Line 473

Using Wipe To Clear a File or Disk 475
    Wiping Files 476
    Wiping Disks 479
    Configuring Wipe 480
Wiping Files from the DOS Command Line 481
Chapter Summary 484

14 Protecting Your System with CP Anti-Virus 485

Scanning with Express 486
    Searching for Viruses 488
    Running Detect and Clean 490
    Changing Drives 490
    Switching to Full Menus 491
    Exiting from the Express Menu 491
Starting Central Point Anti-Virus Using Full Menus ... 492
    Choosing a File, Disk, or Directory To Scan 494
    Searching for Viruses Using the Long Menus 496
    Cleaning Viruses 496
    Immunizing Your Files 498
        Removing Immunization 498
        Setting Immunization Exceptions 499
    Setting Options 501
    Using Checklist Files and Checksums 503
    Setting Exceptions for Checksums 504
    Scheduling Automatic Detection and Cleaning ... 505
    Using the Activity Log and Infection Reports 507
    Using the Virus List 508
    Updating the Virus List 509
    Sending Network Notification Messages 509
    Changing Alert Messages 510
    Setting Passwords 510
    Exiting from Central Point Anti-Virus 511
Using Command Line Options with Anti-Virus 512
Defending against Viruses 513
    Installing VSafe or VWatch 514
    Configuring VSafe for Your Current Session 514
    Using Command Line Options with VSafe 516
    Using Command Line Options with VWatch 518
    Unloading VWatch from Memory 518
    Unloading VSafe from Memory 519
Using BootSafe 519
    Saving Your Partition Table with BootSafe 520
    Using BootSafe To Search
        for Partition Table Viruses 520

Using BootSafe To Restore a Partition Table 521
Using Command Line Options with BootSafe......521
Chapter Summary 522

IV Using the Desktop Manager

15 Navigating the Desktop Accessories 525

Activating PC Tools Desktop Accessories 526
Opening an Application Window 529
Using Desktop Accessories Menus 530
Using the Horizontal Menu Bar 531
Using Pull-down Menus 532
Using Shortcut Commands 532
Understanding Desktop Accessories Windows 534
Changing Window Colors 535
Moving, Resizing, and Maximizing Windows 537
Moving an Application Window 538
Resizing a Window 539
Maximizing a Window 540
Saving the Setup 541
Scrolling through a File 542
Closing a Window 543
Using Multiple Windows 544
Opening Another Window 544
Switching among Windows 545
Using Dialog Boxes 547
Getting Help from Desktop Accessories 547
Using Desktop Accessories Utilities 550
Selecting Hotkeys 551
Displaying the ASCII Table 552
Unloading Desktop Accessories 555
Returning to DOS 556
Chapter Summary 557

16 Using PC Tools Notepads 559

Opening a Notepads Window 560
Assigning a Default File Name Extension 562
Assigning a Default Directory 562
Creating a Notepads File 563
Loading an Existing Notepad 565
Examining the Notepads Window 566
Entering Text 569
Understanding Wordwrap 570

Using Auto Indent 572
Displaying Control Characters 573
Moving around the Notepad 574
Inserting and Deleting Text 575
Inserting and Deleting Characters 576
Inserting a File 576
Deleting All Text in a Notepads Window 577
Copying and Moving Text 577
Marking a Text Block 578
Cutting and Copying Text 580
Pasting Text 581
Using Spellcheck 581
Searching a Notepads File.......................................584
Finding Text 584
Finding and Replacing Text 585
Using the Tab Ruler 586
Printing a Notepads File 589
Setting the Page Layout 589
Creating a Header or Footer 591
Printing the File 592
Deleting a Notepads File 594
Saving a Notepads File 595
Choosing the File Format
and Making a Backup 595
Toggling Autosave 596
Saving the Setup 596
Exiting Notepads 596
Chapter Summary 597

17 Using PC Tools Clipboard 599

Understanding the Clipboard 600
Copying and Pasting Text 600
Copying Text to the Clipboard 601
Pasting Text from the Clipboard 603
Opening the Clipboard Window 606
Editing Text in the Clipboard 609
Printing from the Clipboard 611
Setting Playback Delay 612
Using the Clipboard 613
Chapter Summary 614

18 Using the Outliner 615

Opening an Outline Window 615
Editing an Outline 617

Creating Headlines 617
Promoting and Demoting Headlines 618
Collapsing and Expanding Headlines 620
Collapsing Headlines 620
Expanding Headlines 622
Saving an Outline 623
Printing an Outline 623
Exiting from an Outline 623
Chapter Summary 624

19 Using PC Tools Databases 625

Understanding Database Fundamentals 626
Creating a New Database: Defining
  the Database Structure 627
Naming a Field 628
Selecting Field Type, Field Size, and Decimals 629
Saving or Abandoning the Database Structure ... 632
Toggling between Browse and Edit Modes 633
Modifying a Field Definition 634
Adding Records 634
Correcting Mistakes and Editing Records 638
Saving or Abandoning a Field Entry 639
Exiting from or Displaying a New Record
  for Data Entry 639
Loading an Existing Database File 641
Modifying a Database Structure 642
Adding or Deleting a Field Definition 643
Modifying a Field Definition 643
Purging Records from the Database 644
Deleting and Undeleting Records 645
Packing a Database 646
Hiding and Selecting Records 647
Specifying Selection Criteria 648
Deleting a Database File 650
Sorting a Database 651
Searching a Database 654
Searching Fields 654
Using Goto To Search by Record Number 657
Using Form Files 657
The Default Form File 657
Custom Form Files 659
Printing a Database 664
Printing from Browse Mode 664
Printing from Edit Mode 666

Transferring and Appending Records 669
  Transferring Records 669
  Appending Records 670
Chapter Summary 671

20 Managing Your Appointment Schedule 673

Opening an Appointment Scheduler Window 674
  Loading a Schedule File 675
  Examining the Appointment
    Scheduler Window 676
  Loading Another Appointment Schedule 678
  Moving around the Appointment
    Scheduler Window 679
  Using the Mouse 681
Customizing the Appointment Scheduler 682
  Adjusting the Appointment Settings 682
    Setting the Work Days 683
    Setting Appointment Start Time,
      Stop Time, and Increment 683
    Setting Date Format and Time Format 684
  Assigning Holidays 685
Making a New Appointment 686
  Entering a Description and Assigning
    Appointment Type 688
  Setting the Appointment Starting Time
    and Duration 689
  Establishing Recurring Appointments 689
  Assigning a Type 690
  Setting an Alarm 691
  Attaching a Note 692
  Saving the Appointment 693
  Using Group Appointments 694
  Creating Local Groups 694
  Creating Network Groups 695
  Making Group Appointments 696
Deleting an Appointment 697
Editing an Appointment 699
  Editing the Appointment Dialog Boxes 699
  Adding a Note to an Existing Appointment 700
  Editing and Detaching a Note 701
Using Appointments 702
  Finding an Appointment 703
  Displaying the Next Appointment 705
  Finding Free Time 705
  Showing Time Usage 706

Using the To-Do List 707
    Creating a New Entry 708
    Editing an Entry 710
    Deleting an Entry 711
Printing 711
Saving the Schedule File 717
Exiting from Appointment Scheduler 718
Chapter Summary 718

21 Automating Your PC Using PC Tools Macros **719**

Defining a Macro 720
Understanding the Macro Editor Window 721
Understanding the Components of a Macro 722
    The <begdef> Command 723
    The Macro Key 723
    The Script 727
    The <enddef> Command 727
Typing a Macro 728
    Recording a Macro by Using Learn Mode 729
    Activating and Deactivating Macro Files 732
    Adjusting Playback Delay 734
Using Special Macro Techniques 735
    Using Macros for Printer Control 735
    Overriding an Active Macro 741
    Linking Macros 741
    Inserting System Date and Time 742
    Pausing a Macro 742
    Creating Fill-in-the-Blanks Macros 743
        Fixed-Length Blanks 743
        Variable-Length Blanks 743
Setting Smart Alarms 744
    Running a Program at a Preset Time 744
    Loading a File into a Notepad
        at a Preset Time 745
    Using Macros in the Appointment Scheduler 746
Chapter Summary 747

22 Using the Calculators **749**

Opening and Closing a Calculator Window 750
Using the Algebraic Calculator 750
    Toggling Wide Display 753
    Performing a Simple Calculation 754
    Performing Calculations
        by Using the Memory Register 756

Editing the Tape 757
Printing and Copying the Tape 758
Erasing the Tape 759
Using the Financial Calculator 760
Using the Financial Calculator Keypad 762
Performing a Simple Calculation 766
Understanding the Financial
    Calculator Registers 768
Performing a Financial Calculation 769
Using the Programmers Calculator 771
Using the Programmers Calculator Keypad 774
Understanding the Programmers
    Calculator Registers 777
Using the Scientific Calculator 779
Using the Scientific Calculator Keypad 780
Understanding the Scientific Calculator
    Registers 784
Chapter Summary 785

V Communicating by Modem, Fax, or Local Area Network

23 Using PC Tools Telecommunications 789

Opening the Modem Telecommunications
    Window 790
Examining the Telecommunications Window 791
Loading a New or Existing Phone Directory 792
Managing a Phone Directory 795
Creating an Entry 795
Specifying the Name 796
Specifying a Database 797
Specifying a Phone Number 798
Listing a Script File 799
Supplying User ID and Password 799
Setting Line Parameters 800
Selecting Terminal Emulation 802
Activating Flow Control 803
Choosing End-of-Line Processing 803
Selecting Duplex 804
Editing an Existing Entry 805
Deleting an Entry 806
Saving the Phone Directory 806
Connecting to Another Computer 807
Configuring Your Modem 807
Using an Entry To Dial a Phone Number 808

Understanding the On-Line Screen 809
Understanding the Alternate Keyboards 813
Using Manual Dial 814
Receiving a Call 816
Connecting during a Voice Call 817
Using a Direct Connection 818
Ending a Connection 819
Sending and Receiving Files 819
Selecting the Binary Transfer Options 820
Using the ASCII File-Transfer Protocol 821
Sending a File Using ASCII 822
Receiving a File Using ASCII 823
Using the XMODEM File-Transfer Protocol 824
Sending a File Using XMODEM 825
Receiving a File Using XMODEM 826
Using the ZMODEM File-Transfer Protocol 827
Sending Files Using ZMODEM 828
Receiving Files Using ZMODEM 829
Using the KERMIT File-Transfer Protocol 830
Sending Files Using KERMIT 830
Receiving Files Using KERMIT 831
Using Scripts To Automate Telecommunications 831
Creating a Script File 832
Understanding the Script Commands 833
Variables and Variable-Manipulation
Commands 834
Communication Commands 835
Program-Control and Branching
Commands 837
Display Commands 838
Looking at an Example 839
Using Autodial 841
Configuring Autodial 841
Dialing a Number from within Desktop
Databases 842
Dialing a Number from within Another
DOS Program 843
Chapter Summary 844

24 Using Electronic Mail 845

Understanding PC Tools' Electronic Mail 845
Setting Up Electronic Mail 848
Selecting an Electronic Mail Service 848
Specifying Directories 851

Creating an Electronic Mail Message 852
Sending Electronic Mail..854
Reading Electronic Mail 855
Using Electronic Mail's Scheduling Feature 858
    Scheduling Automatic Reading 859
    Scheduling Automatic Sending..........................860
Chapter Summary 861

25 Sending and Receiving Fax with Fax Telecommunications 863

Understanding What You Need 864
Configuring Fax Telecommunications 865
Examining the Send Fax Directory Window 868
Sending a Fax or File 869
    Selecting a File 872
    Including a Cover Page 873
    Sending the Message or File 874
Receiving Fax 875
Using the Fax Log 875
    Deleting an Entry or Aborting a Transmission 878
    Adjusting AutoUpdate 878
Chapter Summary 879

26 Controlling a PC Remotely with CP Commute 881

Starting Commute 882
Getting Set Up 882
    Selecting a Modem 884
    Selecting a COM Port 884
    Creating a Private Call List 885
    Creating a Give-Control List................................889
Connecting 891
    Preparing the Give-Control PC
      To Answer a Call..891
    Initiating the Call from the Take-Control PC 892
    Initiating the Call from the Give-Control PC 894
Running an Application on the Give-Control PC 895
    Starting the Application 896
    Running Windows on the Give-Control PC 897
Displaying the Commute Session Manager
    Window 898
    Accessing the DOS Command Line
      on the Take-Control PC 899
    Using the Chat Window 900

Transferring Files 902
Using the Advanced Options 904
Ending a Session 905
Chapter Summary 906

Appendixes

A Installing and Configuring PC Tools 909

Meeting Basic System Requirements 910
Running Install 911
Choosing an Installation Type 911
Continuing with Install 915
Creating an Emergency Disk 916
Configuring PC Tools Desktop and Desktop
Accessories 919
Selecting Startup Options 920
Setting Screen Colors 921
Configuring the Display 923
Configuring the Mouse 924
Configuring the Keyboard 925
Selecting Startup Programs 925
Setting Up RAMBoost 928
Setting Up DriveMap 929
Using Install Command Line Options 930
Summary 931

B Using PC Tools from within Microsoft Windows 933

Starting Windows 3.x 934
Running PC Tools Programs in Windows 936
Working with PC Tools Applications
under Windows 939
Commute 939
Compress 940
Data Monitor 940
DiskFix 941
PC-Cache 941
PC Tools Desktop 942
Scheduler 942
TSR Manager 943
Summary 945

Index 947

Introduction

You are about to become an expert with PC Tools 8, the most comprehensive yet easy-to-use set of software tools available for the personal computer. *Using PC Tools 8*, Special Edition, helps you decide when you need one of the PC Tools programs, which program to select, and how best to use it. Whether you use your personal computer for business or for personal use, for profit or for pleasure, you need PC Tools 8. This book shows you how to get the most from this powerful collection of programs.

What Is PC Tools?

The most current version of PC Tools is Version 8.0, produced and licensed by Central Point Software, Inc. As the name implies, PC Tools isn't one program but several. You can think of PC Tools as a workbench overflowing with practical software utensils. Some of the tools are business software applications specially designed to help you be more productive. Other tools significantly enhance your ability to use your other software. With still other PC Tools utilities, you can protect the data stored in your computer and, therefore, better protect the time and money you have invested and will continue to invest in your system.

All the PC Tools features are available through a consistent user interface designed to conform to modern graphical user interface (GUI) standards, with pull-down menus and access to all functions through the keyboard or mouse. Learning to use PC Tools, therefore, is relatively easy, and everything you learn about the PC Tools user interface will help you quickly learn future programs that also use this type of interface. You may notice that PC Tools 8 closely resembles the DOS Shell program included with MS-DOS 5.0. If you are familiar with the DOS Shell, you already know how to use many of the features of PC Tools Desktop utilities; the capabilities of PC Tools Desktop and PC Tools' other utilities, however, go well beyond the capabilities of DOS 5.0.

PC Tools 8 programs are accessible through Windows and can be installed as a Windows program group. Like PC Tools, Microsoft Windows uses a graphical user interface with full mouse support. Indeed, all PC Tools 8 programs look and feel similar to Microsoft Windows. PC Tools even provides some Windows-like functions in the DOS environment, such as the following:

- Moving text between DOS applications or Desktop Accessories windows using the Desktop Accessories Clipboard

- Running up to eight DOS applications simultaneously with the Task Switcher

- Using the graphic drag-and-drop method to copy, move, and launch files

PC Tools Desktop

PC Tools Desktop, 8.0's expanded version of PC Shell, is a group of utilities included in PC Tools. In Version 8.0, Desktop is the command center for almost all other PC Tools programs. For example, the Accessories menu includes the complete group of Desktop Accessories, such as Notepads, Appointment Scheduler, and Modem Telecommunications.

You can run Desktop as either a stand-alone or memory-resident program. Many Desktop features are separate stand-alone programs that can be run directly from DOS.

  NOTE Because PC Shell is renamed Desktop, the former Desktop Manager suite of programs is now known as Desktop Accessories. You can, however, still run PC Shell from DOS by using the PCSHELL command or the PCTOOLS command. Typing **desktop** still runs the Desktop Accessories, not PC Tools Desktop.

Desktop performs typical file- and disk-management functions usually available through the disk operating system (Microsoft MS-DOS or

IBM DOS). But with Desktop, you gain two important advantages. First, you can accomplish all the standard DOS file-related tasks, such as copying a file from one DOS directory or disk to another, comparing two files, renaming a file, or deleting a file, by choosing commands from a menu. You no longer need to remember archaic DOS command names and their cryptic syntax. You also can format a disk that can later be unformatted, compare disk contents, and rename disk volumes.

Second, you can perform operations that would be impossible using DOS. For example, you can search selected files or even an entire disk for specific data contents. You can define search groups that group files by any combination of file name, file name extension, file contents, or the order in which you select the files. You also can copy a floppy disk to another floppy with only a single pass, move a directory and all subdirectories in one step, and erase directories without first emptying them of all files. You can view the contents of files stored in an impressive number of different formats, including word processor formats such as Microsoft Windows Write, Microsoft Word, WordPerfect, DisplayWrite, and WordStar; spreadsheet formats such as Borland Quattro and Quattro Pro, Microsoft Excel, and Lotus 1-2-3; database management file formats such as dBASE and Paradox; and even PCX format in graphic or text display. (The graphic PCX file viewer makes Desktop an excellent graphics file manager.)

After you view a file, you can use Desktop to "launch" instantly the pertinent applications program with that file loaded.

The System Utilities

PC Tools also includes several system utility programs that often are sold as separate programs. (You may have purchased PC Tools just to get one of these indispensable utility programs.) CP Backup, Compress, and System Information are available from the Desktop Tools menu or from DOS.

With Central Point Backup (CP Backup), you can safely and quickly make a complete copy of all or any selected group of files on your hard disk. CP Backup can compress the data as it is backed up and, therefore, use fewer disks to make the copy. To ensure that the copy is good, you can have the program verify all data after it is written to the backup disk.

The utility program Compress performs an operation often described as *optimizing*, or unfragmenting, a disk. Compress rearranges the files so that each file's data is contained in a single contiguous area of the disk's physical magnetic surface rather than scattered in fragments across the disk's many sectors. As a result, you receive enhanced performance from the disk drive as it reads and writes to these unfragmented files and an increased likelihood that files deleted accidentally can be completely recovered. With this program, you can sort all the directories on disk simultaneously and diagnose and mark off potential errors on the surface of disks so that DOS doesn't use them to store data.

With Version 8.0's FileCheck program, you can check for disk fragmentation without having to start Compress. This program also spots any lost clusters and cross-links that may indicate disk maintenance by using the DiskFix program described in the next section, "The Recovery and Security Utilities."

The System Information (SI) program provides a wealth of key facts about your computer system. With SI, you can determine your computer's hardware configuration and memory configuration, AUTOEXEC.BAT and CONFIG.SYS file information, and disk performance and central processing unit (CPU) performance. If you are connected to a Novell network, you can display information about the network.

On 386 or 486 PCs with at least 1M of RAM, the new RAMBoost program complements your memory manager (Microsoft's HIMEM.SYS and EMM386.EXE, Quarterdeck QEMM-386, Qualitas 386MAX and BlueMAX, or Helix Netroom) by optimizing memory usage for your particular configuration.

The Recovery and Security Utilities

PC Tools protects against data loss, corruption, or misuse with a variety of powerful recovery and security utilities. Of those utilities described here, Anti-Virus, Undelete, Unformat, Build Emergency Disk, DiskFix, and FileFix are available from the Desktop Tools menu or DOS; PC Secure is available from the Desktop File menu or DOS.

Nothing is more frustrating to a PC user than losing an important data file because the file is damaged or accidentally deleted. PC Tools provides utilities that, in many cases, enable you to recover damaged or deleted files. The File Fix utility enables you to recover damaged data files created in dBASE, Lotus 1-2-3, or Symphony and, new in Version 8.0, in Quattro Pro, WordPerfect, Paradox, Excel, R:BASE, and FoxPro. The Data Monitor and Undelete programs used together enable you to recover files that you accidentally deleted from a disk.

The Mirror and Unformat programs are potentially the most important PC Tools 8 utilities. Working in tandem, Mirror and Unformat effectively protect your data stored on hard disks from accidental loss through inadvertent use of the DOS commands RECOVER and FORMAT. If, for example, someone in your office accidentally formats a hard disk protected by Mirror, you can use Unformat to restore the disk to the state it was in when Mirror was last run. Even when Mirror hasn't been used before the errant formatting of a disk, the Unformat program still might be capable of recovering the otherwise lost data. (**Note:** Unless the PC Tools program PC Format was used to format the disk, Unformat might not be able to restore an accidentally formatted floppy disk.)

The Build Emergency Disk program makes Version 7.1's installation-time opportunity to build or update a recovery disk available at any time, from Desktop or DOS. The emergency disk includes two things: the critical hard disk information needed to recover from a crash or boot failure and the PC Tools utilities (such as DiskFix, described next) needed to fix disk problems.

The PC Tools utility DiskFix, deceptively easy to use, can repair a multitude of hard or floppy disk problems. Using DiskFix, you can repair many errors in a disk's file allocation table, root directory, and subdirectories; you can scan a disk's surface for damaged sectors and move data to a safe location; and you can perform a nondestructive, low-level format of a disk including selecting the optimum interleave setting for a hard disk.

The full-featured Anti-Virus 1.4 program scans your disk (on request or at start-up) for over 1,300 viruses, including the nefarious stealth, polymorphic, and boot sector viruses and provides something life rarely offers in other contexts, permanent immunization (for files) against future attack.

PC Secure is a sophisticated encryption and decryption program capable of completely protecting any DOS data file from prying eyes. PC Secure (in PC Tools 8 packages shipped to the United States) uses the DES encryption system, which meets stringent federal government file-encryption standards. When you use PC Secure to encrypt a file, you assign a password to the file. Without the password, absolutely no one (including you) can convert the file back to a readable form. This high-security utility is indispensable when your nonremovable hard disk contains sensitive data and your computer is accessible by other users not authorized to view the data.

The Desktop Accessories

PC Tools Desktop Accessories (formerly just "Desktop") is a collection of business tools that provides many of the capabilities of full-fledged integrated applications such as Symphony, Framework, and Enable. Desktop Accessories includes a basic word processor—complete with a spelling-check program—for recording notes and writing correspondence; an outline processor for organizing your thoughts; a database manager for handling business and personal information; and a telecommunications program for facilitating voice, data, electronic mail, and fax communication. Also, Desktop Accessories includes an appointment scheduler to help you better manage your time and four powerful calculators: an algebraic calculator, a financial calculator, a programmer's calculator, and a scientific calculator. You can automate your use of the PC with the full-featured macro generator (keystroke recorder).

These handy business tools are doubly useful because they can be called from your other PC software applications or from the Accessories menu in PC Tools Desktop. Alternatively, you can invoke the Desktop Accessories program as a *stand-alone program*—the only program loaded in the computer's memory. Optionally, you can load it as a memory-resident program; then all the program's many functions are available at the press of a *hotkey*—a key or key combination that starts the memory-resident program—regardless of which program you are using.

The Communication Utilities

The Desktop Accessories' modem, electronic mail, and fax telecommunications programs and the Central Point Commute and DriveMap programs provide powerful tools for communicating with other computers in a variety of ways. The Accessories programs are available from Desktop's Accessories menu or by running Desktop Accessories standalone; Commute is available from Desktop's Tools menu or DOS; and DriveMap is available from Desktop's Configure menu or DOS.

If you have a modem, the Desktop Accessories' Modem Telecommunications program includes the features you need to transmit and receive one or a group of files (using ASCII, XModem, Kermit or, new in Version 8.0, ZModem protocols) and to send and receive electronic mail. The related E-mail program provides additional mail-specific features, such as sending mail from Notepads or Outliner and scheduling mail transmissions. Unlike some communications software, these utilities can be set for modems operating at speeds from 300 to 19,200 baud on any PC port. The program is preconfigured for accessing the commercial services MCI Mail, CompuServe, and EasyLink, plus Central Point Software's BBS (Bulletin Board Service).

If you have a CAS-compliant (Communicating Applications Specifications) fax board on your computer or in your Novell Netware Network, Fax Telecommunications enables you to send and receive facsimile messages. With the capability to send text files, add automatic cover pages, set up and use a fax directory, and schedule and log fax transmissions, the program takes much of the hassle out of fax communications.

True telecommunicating is made possible with the Central Point Commute program. Commute enables you to connect your PC to another PC by telephone (and modem) or over a Novell local area network (LAN) so that you can run DOS or Windows programs on the remote computer. With Commute, you can access from home the files, printers, and network servers located at your office. You also can easily transfer files between your computer and a remote computer.

A related program, DriveMap, provides another kind of communication, communication between two computers in the same office or home. (DriveMap's ancestor in earlier versions was DeskConnect; the new incarnation includes significantly enhanced functions.) DriveMap solves the problem of moving files between two PCs with incompatible drives. DriveMap also makes light work of the chores involved in changing computers, copying one system's hard disk to another at speeds up to 115,200 baud. To connect the computers, you need a null modem cable attached to their serial ports, a centronics parallel adapter for parallel cables attached to parallel ports, or a LAN connection.

As you can see, PC Tools has an impressive array of features. With this book as your guide, you can quickly learn to use all these tools to enhance your productivity and sense of security and to reduce your computer-related headaches.

Windows Support

Most PC Tools 8 programs can be installed to be used from the Microsoft Windows operating environment (Version 3.0 and later). The PC Tools installation program installs these utilities in a program group in the Windows Program Manager. You then can start every program from within Windows by selecting the appropriate program icon in the Program Manager.

Unlike Version 7.1, Version 8.0 makes its DOS orientation unequivocal, dropping much of Version 7's Windows-specific support. Gone are Central Point Launcher and special Windows versions of Undelete and CP Backup (although CP Backup—and Undelete in the Delete Sentry mode—can be used from within Windows). One program, Central Point Commute, has added features, such as special mouse and keyboard drivers, for working more efficiently with Windows.

PC Tools 8 does provide two Windows-specific utilities: the Central Point Scheduler for Windows and the TSR Manager. The Scheduler for Windows enables you to schedule unattended operation of Central Point Backup, Commute, Desktop EMail, or DiskFix and to use the Desktop Accessories Appointment Scheduler from within Windows. The TSR Manager adapts any PC Tools programs operating in terminate-and-stay-resident mode to work within the Windows environment.

What's New in PC Tools 8?

Since the introduction of PC Tools, Central Point Software progressively has added utilities and enhanced the original tools and interface. PC Tools 8, released in 1992, includes a number of significant enhancements to earlier releases. These features are summarized in table I.1.

NOTE   The Version 7.1 Windows versions of Central Point Backup, Central Point Launcher, and Undelete haven't been updated in Version 8.0; they, and the notion of extensive Windows-specific features, have been dropped from the program.

Table I.1 New Features in PC Tools 8

Category	Enhancement
General	Menu access (from Desktop) to almost all PC Tools programs
	Enhanced network support
	Capability to change, on the fly from Desktop, the program configuration and what programs load at startup, rather than having to run the separate PC Config utility
PC Tools Desktop	Completely customizable menus

Category	Enhancement
	36 user-programmable function keys
	Drag-and-drop mouse support for more operations, more graphically
	Selection numbers to help keep track of selected files
	Confirmation check before deleting hidden, system, or read-only files (can be turned off)
	More logical menu organization
	Expanded list of customizable features
	User choice of file editor
	DOS multitasking with the Task Switcher (stand-alone CPTask)
	Automatic, unattended execution of almost any operation with the Central Point Scheduler (stand-alone CPSched)
	Enhanced user-defined menu system for running applications, with capability to import Direct Access menus
	Capability to create or update an emergency disk (for full system recovery) at any time (stand-alone EDisk)
	Expunge command for deleting a nonempty directory
	Menu commands to zip and unzip files
Central Point Anti-Virus 1.4	Full-featured program for protection against 1,300 viruses, including stealth, polymorphic, and boot sector viruses, and unknown viruses
	Permanent file immunization (includes utilities CPAV, VWatch, VSafe, and BootSafe)
	Available from Desktop Tools menu or DOS
Central Point Backup	SCSI tape drive support
	Features for tape maintenance (formatting, erasing, and retensioning tapes)
	More options for scheduling and for specifying file include/exclude criteria

continues

Table I.1 Continued

Category	Enhancement
	Enhanced network support, including backup of Netware bindery and trustee information and network file selection by server/volume or letter of logical drive
	Available from Desktop Tools menu or DOS
Commute	Super VGA support
	Support for NetBIOS-compatible networks
	Enhanced speed
	Menus for easy file transfers
	Available from Desktop Tools menu or DOS
CPSched	New program to schedule automatic execution of many tasks in PC Tools or other applications
	Available from Desktop Tools menu or DOS
CPTask	New program for DOS multitasking of up to eight applications
	Available from DOS, or from Desktop by configuring applications in the menuing system to start up in task-switchable mode
DiskEdit	New stand-alone disk editing with separate editors for viewing and editing disk elements (including new directory, boot record, FAT, and partition editors)
	Available from Desktop Disk menu or DOS
DriveMap	Enhanced version of DeskConnect, with capability to edit, execute, and copy files on a direct-connected (null modem cable or LAN) PC, to establish peer-to-peer network drives, and to back up a laptop on a tape drive
	Available from Desktop Configure menu or DOS
EDisk	New program to build or update emergency disk
	Available from Desktop Tools menu or DOS
FileAttr and FileDate	New utilities for checking and changing file attributes and dates

Category	Enhancement
FileCheck	New program for checking disk fragmentation, lost clusters, and cross-links
FileFix	Support for repairing files in additional formats (WordPerfect, Excel, Quattro Pro, R:BASE, FoxPro, and Paradox)
	Available from Desktop Tools menu or DOS
NetMessage	New messaging utility for Novell NetWare networks
	Available from Desktop Tools menu or DOS
PC-Cache	Automatic Windows support and faster caching
RAMBoost	New program for automatic optimization of upper memory usage, complementing memory managers such as EMM386 or QEMM
Undelete	Support for DR-DOS and NetWare delete tracking methods
	Available from Desktop Tools menu or DOS
Desktop Accessories	Available stand-alone or from PC Tools Desktop
	Modem telecommunications file transfer with the ZModem protocol

What Should Your System Have?

For PC Tools to run as a single-user program, your system must have at least 512K of system memory (RAM). If you want to take full advantage of all the PC Tools features by running PC Tools Desktop and Desktop Accessories in memory-resident mode, your system must have 640K of system memory. Central Point Commute also requires at least 640K of system memory. PC Tools 8 is designed to be used from a hard disk. To install all PC Tools programs, you need about 9M of space on your hard disk. Your system must be running DOS Version 3.3 or later.

NOTE Substantial extended or expanded memory is necessary to make use of all the PC Tools programs that memory-resident can run in the background or pop-up with the press of a hotkey. If you use delete protection with the Delete Sentry method, your hard disk must have room to keep a backlog of hidden *erased* files. (You can specify the backlog duration and the maximum space to use.) These files aren't reported in the DOS DIR command, nor are they reflected in PC Tools' report of free space. CHKDSK does take them into account, so using Sentry means your DIR and CHKDSK figures will not match.

Although using a mouse is optional, the PC Tools user interface is designed to optimize use of a mouse. If you use an older mouse, you may need to obtain new driver software from the manufacturer before the mouse will work with all the PC Tools applications, particularly in memory-resident mode. PC Tools 8 supports these mouse drivers: Microsoft Version 6.14 or higher and Logitech/Dexxa Version 3.4 or higher.

For you to use PC Tools for modem telecommunications or electronic mail, your system should have a Hayes-compatible modem. To use the fax telecommunications feature, you first must install a Connection CoProcessor or SatisFAXtion Board from Intel, a SpectraFAX Personal Link board from SpectraFAX Corporation, or another 100-percent CAS-compliant fax board.

PC Tools 8 also can be installed on a Novell NetWare system using Version 2.12 or higher or on an IBM PC LAN server. (You must license a separate copy of PC Tools for every network workstation with access to the program over the network or alternatively obtain a site license.)

Who Should Read This Book?

Using PC Tools 8 is for you if you are a new PC Tools user and want to get the most from this feature-rich product. If you are an experienced user, this book helps you gain a clear understanding of the new features and enhancements introduced in PC Tools 8.

This book makes no assumptions about your background or experience with personal computers in general or PC utility programs in particular. All features are thoroughly explained and demonstrated. Numerous examples and screen shots help you quickly and confidently become comfortable with each of PC Tools' utilities. Wherever appropriate, helpful tips, cautions, and warnings are provided to let you know about tricks and shortcuts and to alert you to potential pitfalls.

Features that are new in PC Tools 8 are annotated with a Version 8.0 icon. These icons can help experienced PC Tools users locate the discussions about new features. If you are using an earlier version of PC Tools and haven't yet chosen to upgrade, these icons indicate that you can skip these sections.

What Is in This Book?

This book is divided into five major parts:

Part I	"Using the Desktop"
Part II	"Using the System Utilities"
Part III	"Using the Recovering and Security Utilities"
Part IV	"Using the Desktop Manager"
Part V	"Communicating by Modem, Fax, or Local Area Network"

This book includes two appendixes:

Appendix A	"Installing and Configuring PC Tools"
Appendix B	"Using PC Tools from within MS Windows"

The following sections preview topics covered in the individual chapters in each part of the book.

Part I, "Using the Desktop"

The first part of *Using PC Tools 8* covers PC Tools Desktop, the PC Tools program that contains many utilities normally associated with the disk operating system (DOS).

Chapter 1, "Navigating the Desktop," examines the aspects of PC Tools Desktop that are common to all the utilities in the program. This chapter shows you around the Desktop screen and describes how to use Desktop's windows, menus, drag-and-drop mouse features, and dialog boxes.

Chapter 2, "Controlling the Desktop," explains how to customize Desktop's function keys, display, menus and window layout, and how to use the DOS command line.

In Chapter 3, "Using the Desktop as a Program Manager," you learn how you can use Desktop's menu window and menuing system as a platform from which you can run all the other programs on your computer's hard disk. The chapter also describes the use of the Task Switcher, which you use to multitask DOS applications, and the Scheduler, which you use to execute PC Tools tasks or other applications automatically.

Chapter 4, "Working on Files," demonstrates how to use PC Tools Desktop to perform file-related operations. You learn how to copy, move, compress, compare, verify, rename, and delete files. This chapter explains how to launch a program automatically with a given file (or group of files, if the application supports it) loaded. Chapter 4 covers how to edit a file's contents (in text or hex mode) and its attributes and date. Finally, the chapter describes how to print the contents of a file or a listing of files in a directory.

Chapter 5, "Locating and Viewing Files," explains finding files by name or other search criteria, or by the files' contents using any text string. You also learn how to view files created by many popular programs, such as Lotus 1-2-3, WordPerfect, and dBASE IV.

Chapter 6, "Working on Disks," covers the disk-related functions in PC Tools Desktop. This chapter explains how to prepare a disk for use, prepare an emergency disk, look for discrepancies in disk contents or the list of files in two directories, and search a disk for particular data. Chapter 6 compares Desktop's two directory maintenance tools, the directory maintenance commands and the visual DM Directory Maintenance program, and describes how to use each one to add, rename, delete, copy, and move directories. Finally, the chapter explains how to sort a directory to order files by name, extension, date, size, or selection order.

Part II, "Using the System Utilities"

The second part of *Using PC Tools 8* discusses utilities likely to be critical to the protection and optimum performance of your computer system. CP Backup enables you to make backup copies of your system's hard disk. Compress enables you to rearrange the location of data on your hard disk to optimize hard disk operation. The System Information program provides useful technical data about the system, such as the operating system version, CPU type, video display type, number of serial and parallel ports, relative speed, and amount of memory (RAM) being used.

Chapter 7, "Protecting Your Data with Central Point Backup," explains the file archive bit, how to check for it, and how to use the DOS version of the hard disk backup program Central Point Backup. This chapter describes how to set the numerous backup options, specify whether to copy the entire hard disk or only certain files, and perform the backup. Finally, Chapter 7 explains how to use a backup copy of your hard disk to restore a damaged disk.

Chapter 8, "Speeding Up Your Hard Disk with Compress," explains how to check for file fragmentation using the FileCheck utility and how to solve any fragmentation problems with the Compress program. Compress rearranges the files on your disk so that every file is placed in a single, physically contiguous section of the disk. This operation results in faster access to files and also increases the likelihood that the Desktop Undelete command will be successful in recovering an erroneously deleted file.

Chapter 9, "Obtaining System Information," examines how to use the System Information program to obtain information, such as the operating system version, CPU type, amount of memory (RAM) being used, disk type and size, and partition table information. Chapter 9 also explains how to view a map of files, disks, and memory usage, and how to check the relative performance of your computer's CPU and disk drives.

Part III, "Using the Recovering and Security Utilities"

The third part of *Using PC Tools 8* teaches you how to use the utilities that enable you to recover lost data from damaged files, accidentally deleted files, damaged disks, and accidentally formatted disks. Part III also explains how to use PC Secure to safeguard sensitive files.

Chapter 10, "Recovering Damaged or Deleted Files," explains two tools for recovering files: FileFix for repairing damaged files (in Lotus 1-2-3, Symphony, dBase, WordPerfect, Excel, Quattro Pro, R:BASE, FoxPro, and Paradox formats) and Undelete for recovering erased files.

Chapter 11, "Recovering Damaged or Formatted Disks," discusses two other programs that work in tandem to protect your data. Mirror and Unformat enable you to recover from accidental formatting of a hard disk. This chapter shows you how to run Mirror every time you turn on your system to make a safe copy of your hard disk's file allocation table (FAT), enabling Unformat to recover completely from an accidental formatting of your hard disk. Chapter 11 explains using the emergency disk to start the computer when it will not boot and to reconstruct critical disk information. Finally, the chapter describes using the FileCheck utility to check for disk problems, and then solve them using DiskFix to repair damage to a hard or floppy disk.

Chapter 12, "Editing a Disk with DiskEdit," explains how and why to use DiskEdit to check or change otherwise inaccessible information on your hard disk, such as directory, boot record, FAT, and partition information.

Chapter 13, "Securing Your Data with PC Secure and Wipe," explains how to use file encryption to protect sensitive information, how to decrypt encrypted files, and how to eradicate any trace of files with Wipe.

Chapter 14, "Protecting Your System with CP Anti-Virus," describes using Central Point Anti-Virus 1.4 to protect against 1,300 viruses, including stealth, polymorphic, boot sector, and unknown viruses, and to immunize files permanently from future virus attacks.

Part IV, "Using the Desktop Manager"

The fourth part of *Using PC Tools 8* consists of seven chapters that describe how to use the various utilities included in PC Tools Desktop Accessories for everyday tasks such as taking notes, making outlines, managing information, using modem and fax communications and electronic mail, managing your schedule, and performing numeric and financial computations.

Chapter 15, "Navigating the Desktop Accessories," explains generally how to get around the Desktop. This chapter shows you how to use menus, the keyboard, a mouse, windows, and dialog boxes in Desktop Accessories. You learn how to obtain on-line help from Desktop and how to fine-tune the program by using the Accessories Utilities menu.

Chapter 16, "Using PC Tools Notepads," introduces you to Notepads, the basic word processor included in Desktop Accessories. The chapter describes how to open a Notepads window; how to create, edit, and save a notepad; and how to use Notepads features, including spelling checking, searching and replacing, and printing. Chapter 16 also teaches you how to copy or move text from one Accessories window to another and even from one DOS application to another (from a spreadsheet to a word processing file, for example).

Chapter 17, "Using PC Tools Clipboard," details the benefits of using PC Tools Clipboard features which enable you to cut and paste data from one program to another. This chapter instructs you on the methods of copying data from one program into the Clipboard and then explains how to insert that copied data into another program.

Chapter 18, "Using the Outliner," covers the Outlines module of Desktop Accessories. The Outliner is a handy tool for organizing ideas. This chapter shows you how to create, edit, save, and print an outline, with particular emphasis on collapsing and expanding outline headlines.

Chapter 19, "Using PC Tools Databases," explains how to use Databases, Desktop Accessories' database-management tool, to manage large amounts of information, such as a client list. This chapter describes how to define and modify a database structure, as well as how to use any existing dBASE files. You learn how to add data to a database file, edit data, create custom forms, sort data, search for specific data, and print information contained in a database file.

Chapter 20, "Managing Your Appointment Schedule," demonstrates how to use the Desktop Accessories' Appointment Scheduler to manage your time. This chapter shows how to use the Scheduler to maintain a daily appointment calendar, use the monthly calendar, keep track of an ongoing to-do list, and print daily, weekly, and monthly schedules and to-do lists. You learn how to schedule appointments for yourself and for a group of people who are users on the same local area network (LAN), and how to set "alarms" that will run a program, load a Notepads file, or activate a macro at a preset time.

Chapter 21, "Automating Your PC Using PC Tools Macros," shows you how to take some of the drudgery out of your work by using *macros*—recorded keystrokes—to automate repetitive tasks. This chapter describes how to create and edit macros, explains how to activate and erase macros, demonstrates a number of practical uses for macros, and provides several special macro techniques that can make macros even more useful.

Chapter 22, "Using the Calculators," covers how to use all four calculators included in PC Tools Desktop: the Algebraic Calculator; the Financial Calculator, which emulates the Hewlett-Packard HP-12C calculator; the Programmer's Calculator, which emulates the Hewlett-Packard HP-16C calculator; and the Scientific Calculator, which emulates the Hewlett-Packard HP-11C calculator.

Part V, "Communicating by Modem, Fax, or Local Area Network"

The fifth and last part of the book describes how you can use PC Tools 8 for communications. This part of the book describes the use of the Desktop Accessories Modem Telecommunication, Electronic Mail, and Fax Telecommunications features, as well as the Commute program for running programs and managing files on a remote computer.

Chapter 23, "Using PC Tools Telecommunications," discusses how to use the Modem Telecommunications module to connect your computer to other computers over the telephone line. This chapter explains how to work with phone directories, dial and connect to another computer, send and receive computer files, and use scripts to automate a connection. The chapter describes how to use communications in the background, for example, to send a file to another computer at the same time you are working on a spreadsheet. Chapter 23 also demonstrates the Autodialer, for dialing any phone number that appears in a Desktop Accessories database, or for dialing a number while you are using another application, such as a word processor or spreadsheet.

Chapter 24, "Using Electronic Mail," explains how to use Desktop's Electronic Mail module to send and receive messages on MCI Mail, CompuServe, or EasyLink.

Chapter 25, "Sending and Receiving Fax with Fax Telecommunications," describes how to use the Fax Telecommunications feature to send and receive facsimiles (fax) on computers with an internal fax board. The chapter explains setting up for communications, sending a fax or file, including cover pages automatically, and maintaining and using a fax directory and log.

Chapter 26, "Controlling a PC Remotely with CP Commute," teaches you how to use Commute for true telecommuting between home and office, or any two locations. This chapter shows how to run programs—including Windows programs—on another computer to which your computer is connected by way of modem, local area network, or direct cable. You also learn how to transfer files between two computers that are both running Commute.

Appendixes

Appendix A, "Installing and Configuring PC Tools," provides a guide to the installation and configuration process and step-by-step instructions and describes how to use the Install program to install PC Tools on your computer. This appendix lists files included in PC Tools, explains how to customize your PC Tools setup, and explains how to use the many PC Tools start-up parameters. Because your installation and configuration choices may have hidden implications, the chapter provides useful information about interactions between various PC Tools programs and other system functions, such as Delete Sentry and the DOS DIR command, and between memory-resident programs.

Appendix A also explains how to install and use the new RAMBoost utility to optimize memory usage. The configuration section covers how to customize the color, display, mouse, and keyboard operation of PC Tools programs, select programs to run at start-up, and set password protection for various options. Finally, the appendix covers using the new DriveMap program to share disk drives between a PC and laptop or two PCs.

Appendix B, "Using PC Tools from within Microsoft Windows," explains how to optimize the use of various PC Tools programs from Windows and how to use the two Windows-specific utilities, the Central Point Scheduler for Windows and the TSR Manager.

Conventions Used in This Book

The conventions used in this book have been established to help you learn to use the program quickly and easily. As much as possible, the conventions correspond with those used in the PC Tools 8 documentation.

For function-key commands, the function key is presented first, followed by the name of the command. For example, F1 (Help) means that you press the F1 function key to access the program's Help facility. For keystrokes separated by plus signs, such as Alt+F1, hold down the first key (Alt in this example) and press the second key (F1 in this example) to invoke the option.

PC Tools 8 enables you to use both the keyboard and the mouse to select menu items: you can press the letter that is highlighted on the menu option, or you can click the item by using the mouse. In most cases, the keys on the keyboard are represented as they appear on your keyboard (for example, G, Enter, Tab, Ctrl, Ins, and Backspace).

In this book, new or defined terms appear in *italics*; words or items that you type appear in **boldface**; and screen messages appear in a `special` font.

Using the Desktop

P A R T

1

O U T L I N E

Navigating the Desktop

Controlling the Desktop

Using the Desktop as a Program
  Manager

Working on Files

Locating and Viewing Files

Working on Disks

Navigating the Desktop

This chapter introduces the group of utilities in the PC Tools Desktop program. You can run PC Tools Desktop as either a stand-alone or memory-resident program. This program performs typical file- and disk-management functions normally available through the DOS operating system (Microsoft MS-DOS or IBM DOS). With PC Tools Desktop, you can copy a file from one DOS directory or disk to another, rename or delete a file, or compare two files. You can safely format or copy a disk, compare disk contents, and rename a disk volume. These operations are easy because you select commands from a menu rather than type commands at the DOS command line.

More significantly, with PC Tools Desktop you can easily perform operations that are impossible to perform through the operating system alone. For example, you can view contents of files stored in an impressive number of formats (such as 1-2-3 spreadsheet files, dBASE database files, WordPerfect word processing files, and so on). In Version 8.0, you can even delete a directory without first emptying it.

This chapter discusses the aspects of PC Tools Desktop common to all its utilities. The chapter shows you around the Desktop screen and describes how to use its menus and prompts.

After you become familiar with the information in this chapter, you will be ready to examine the other chapters in this part of the book. Chapter 2, "Controlling the Desktop," describes how to configure PC Tools Desktop. Chapter 3, "Using the Desktop as a Program Manager," teaches you how to use PC Tools Desktop as a *platform*—a menuing system or *DOS shell*—from which you can run all the other programs on your computer's hard disk. Chapter 4, "Working on Files," demonstrates how to use PC Tools Desktop to perform file-related operations. Chapter 5, "Locating and Viewing Files," explains how to use the FileFind and View programs, which can be accessed from the Desktop, to locate and view files. Chapter 6, "Working on Disks," covers the disk-related functions in PC Tools Desktop.

 PC Tools Desktop replaces PC Shell in previous versions, adding enhancements such as a Tools menu to access all PC Tools programs and complete *drag-and-drop* mouse control of many operations. The Desktop Manager is now named Desktop Accessories, available on the Accessories menu.

NOTE   If you are running PC Tools Desktop from DOS, you can still type the command **PCSHELL** to run Desktop. Typing DESKTOP does not run PC Tools Desktop; this command still runs Desktop Accessories.

Starting PC Tools Desktop

This chapter and the others in Part I assume that you have installed PC Tools on your computer by using Install (supplied with PC Tools) and have loaded PC Tools Desktop into memory as a terminate-and-stay-resident (TSR) program. PC Tools should be installed on your hard disk in the DOS directory C:\PCTOOLS. You should also have a Microsoft-compatible mouse attached to your computer.

See Appendix A, "Installing and Configuring PC Tools," for a complete discussion of using Install to install PC Tools and loading PC Tools Desktop as a TSR program. Appendix A explains how to run PC Tools Desktop as a stand-alone program and how to add special parameters to the start-up command.

To activate PC Tools Desktop from within any DOS program or from the DOS command line, press the hot key Ctrl+Esc. A *hot key* is a key or key combination that you press to immediately access an application. The Desktop hot key (Ctrl+Esc) is also a *toggle*, which means the same key combination switches into and out of Desktop. Therefore, when you want to exit Desktop, you press the hot-key combination again. Every time you turn on the computer, PC Tools Desktop displays the following message the first time you activate the program:

```
Analyzing drive d:

Reading directories
```

The message replaces *d* with the letter of the start-up disk drive. PC Tools Desktop reads the *directory tree*—the list of directories and files—on the default start-up disk. PC Tools Desktop keeps a copy of the tree in memory and updates the copy continually. Every time you exit from PC Tools Desktop, the program saves a copy of the directory tree to a file named CPS*d*.TRE, where *d* is the name of the disk drive. If you subsequently hot-key into PC Tools Desktop during the same work session, the program reads the directory tree file rather than the entire directory tree.

The keystroke combination Ctrl+Esc is the default hot key. You can change this hot key to another keystroke combination by using a special start-up command. See Appendix A, "Installing and Configuring PC Tools," for more about customizing this command and other PC Tools parameters.

While PC Tools Desktop is memory resident, the program occupies as little as 8K of RAM (*memory*, explained in Appendix A); however, when you press the hot key to activate PC Tools Desktop, the Desktop must make more room for itself in RAM. To make more room, Desktop temporarily suspends the currently running application and takes a snapshot of the RAM contents. The program then writes this RAM image to any expanded memory (compatible with LIM—*L*otus, *I*ntel, or *M*icrosoft) or extended memory your system might have. PC Tools Desktop writes to a disk file any portion of the RAM image that cannot fit in expanded or extended memory. Finally, PC Tools Desktop loads its program file into memory and displays the PC Tools Desktop screen (see fig. 1.1).

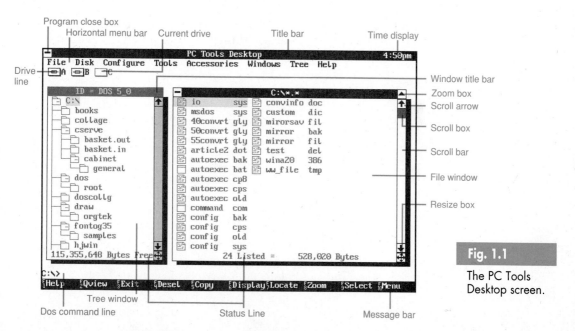

Fig. 1.1

The PC Tools Desktop screen.

NOTE Although PC Tools 8 works fine with only conventional memory, you can hot-key back into the DOS application more quickly if you have expanded or extended memory.

NOTE If your computer screen cannot display PC Tools' special graphics characters, your screen may look somewhat different from the screen shown in figure 1.1.

All memory-resident PC Tools 8.0 programs can be loaded safely into *reserved memory* (sometimes called *high memory* or *upper memory blocks*)—the portion of your computer's memory (random-access memory or RAM) between 640K and 1,024K. This technique provides more memory for use by your applications program but is available to you only if your computer and operating system software are capable of loading programs into reserved memory. Your computer's central processing unit (CPU) must be an Intel 80386 or 80486 or a compatible, and your operating system software must provide a method of loading programs into reserved memory. See Appendix A, "Installing and Configuring PC Tools," for more information about how to take advantage of this capability of your computer.

The top line of the PC Tools Desktop screen is the *title bar*. At the left end of the title bar, PC Tools Desktop displays the *program close box*, a minus sign enclosed in a box. You can *close* (or quit) Desktop by moving the mouse pointer to the close box and double-clicking (pressing and releasing twice in quick succession) the left mouse button (see the section "Closing PC Tools Desktop" near the end of this chapter for more information). PC Tools Desktop displays the program name in the center of the title bar and displays the current system time at the right end of the title bar.

NOTE PC Tools Desktop no longer displays the current user mode to the right of the close box because this version does not differentiate user modes as such. By default, the menus display all commands, as they did in Version 7.1's Advanced user mode. To display only less technical, more commonly used commands, you can configure the menu type to Short by using the Load Pull-Downs option on the Configure menu.

The second line of the PC Tools Desktop screen is the *horizontal menu bar*. The following section, "Using PC Tools Desktop Menus," describes how to select options from menus that appear on this line.

Just below the horizontal menu bar, PC Tools Desktop displays the *drive line*, which lists the drive letters of the disk drives in your computer and highlights the current disk drive. In figure 1.1, drive C is the current drive.

At the bottom of the screen, the *message bar* lists function-key commands. In the line above the message bar, PC Tools Desktop displays an optional DOS command line. This line, available for entering DOS commands, displays a prompt that indicates the current directory.

Between the drive area and the DOS command line, PC Tools Desktop divides the screen into several areas called *windows,* each headed by a *window title bar.* On the right side of each window is a *scroll bar,* which you *click* (press and release the mouse button) to move around the window.

Using PC Tools Desktop Menus

You can initiate virtually every PC Tools Desktop operation by choosing options from a series of menus. These PC Tools Desktop menus fall into two categories: the options on the horizontal menu bar and the menus these options lead to—*pull-down menus.* You can access a pull-down menu in one of two ways:

■ Move the mouse pointer to an option and click the left or right mouse button. The pull-down menu appears.

■ Press the Alt key to activate the horizontal menu bar. PC Tools Desktop highlights the first menu, File, and one letter in each of the other menu options. Press the key that corresponds to the highlighted letter in the menu option you want to select. To select **F**ile from the menu, for example, press Alt+F (refer to fig. 1.1). The File pull-down menu appears.

The menu options in PC Tools 8.0 differ from the menus in the versions PC Tools 7.1 and 6. Generally, changes in Version 8.0 make understanding the program and finding the functions you want simpler. For example, options that were on Version 7.1's obscurely named Custom List Configure menu, a submenu under the View menu, appear on the new Windows menu. The Windows menu shows at a glance which screen elements, such as the File window or the background mat, are on or off.

If you are familiar with the menus in either earlier version and don't want to take the time to learn the new menu structure, you are in luck. To use Version 7 or 6 menus, first select **C**onfigure from the horizontal menu bar; then choose **L**oad Pull-downs. PC Tools Desktop displays the Use a New Menu File dialog box listing pull-down menu choices. Select PC Shell Version 7- or Version 6-compatible menus, and then select the **O**K button. The horizontal menu bar and its associated pull-down menus switch to the selected menu type.

If you changed to Version 6 or 7 menus and want to return to the Version 8.0 menus, choose **L**oad Pull-downs from the **S**pecial menu. From the dialog box that appears, select the PC Tools Desktop Version 8 Menus, choosing either long menus, for all commands, or short menus, for basic commands.

> **NOTE** When you are using Version 6 or 7 menus, the horizontal menu bar changes to include the Special menu, on which you can find the Load Pull-downs option.

Using Pull-down Menus

When you select an option from the horizontal menu bar, PC Tools Desktop displays a *pull-down menu*, a list of options in that category. If you select **F**ile, for example, PC Tools Desktop displays the File pull-down menu (see fig. 1.2).

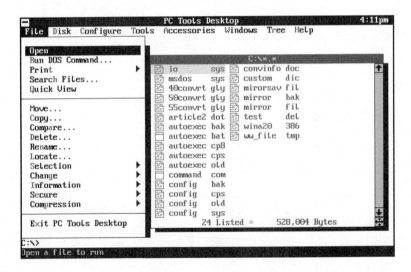

Fig. 1.2

The File pull-down menu.

You can use the following techniques to make selections from pull-down menus:

■ Move the mouse pointer to a horizontal menu bar option and click the left or right mouse button. A pull-down menu appears. Move the mouse pointer to the menu option of your choice and click.

■ Press and hold the Alt key to activate the horizontal menu bar. PC Tools Desktop highlights one letter in each of the menu options. Press the key that corresponds to the highlighted letter in the menu option you want to select. To access the File menu shown in figure 1.2, for example, press Alt+F; the File menu appears. Each item in the pull-down menu has a highlighted letter (**O**pen, for example). Press the letter that corresponds to the option of your choice.

■ Press and release the Alt key to activate the horizontal menu bar, use the left- or right-arrow keys to position the highlighted block on the menu option of your choice, and then press Enter. In the pull-down menu, use the up- and down-arrow keys to highlight an option and press Enter. This method sometimes is called the *point-and-shoot* method.

NOTE You can use any combination of these methods to select a menu option.

Although the point-and-shoot method requires the greater number of keystrokes (and, therefore, takes more time), it has an advantage when you are learning to use the program. As you move the highlighted bar to various menu options, the PC Tools Desktop message bar on the bottom line of the screen displays a short description of the highlighted option. When you activate the File menu, for example, the **O**pen option is highlighted (refer to fig. 1.2), and the message bar displays the following message:

```
Open a file to run
```

If you press the down-arrow key to highlight Search Files, this message appears in the message bar:

```
Search for text in the contents of selected files
```

If you are not sure which option you want to select, you can read the screen messages displayed in the message bar to make an educated guess. If you want a quick tour of the program, you can move through the menus to get an idea of what the various options do.

Some menu options do not immediately execute a command or change a setting but rather display another menu, referred to as a *submenu*, from which you can make further selections. By displaying an arrowhead to the right of the option name, PC Tools Desktop alerts you that a menu option displays a submenu. On the File menu, for example, an arrowhead appears to the right of the Print, Selection, Change, Information, Secure, and Compression options (refer to fig. 1.2). If you select one of these options, PC Tools Desktop displays a submenu.

If you choose **P**rint from the **F**ile menu, for example, PC Tools Desktop displays the Print submenu, which contains two options: Print Directory and Print File (see fig. 1.3).

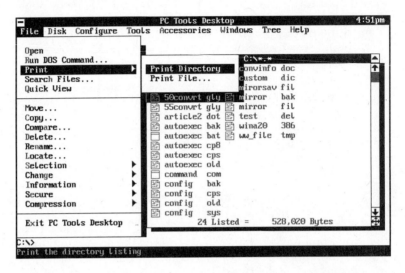

Fig. 1.3

The Print submenu.

The remaining chapters in Part I, "Using the PC Shell" describe the function of the options available on PC Tools Desktop pull-down menus.

Using Function Key Commands

When you display the PC Tools Desktop screen, the message bar contains a list of *function key commands*. Function key commands are shortcuts you can use to execute commonly used operations with a single keystroke. The commands in the list vary, depending on the current area of the PC Tools Desktop screen. When you first start PC Tools Desktop, for example, the message bar contains the following list of function key commands:

```
F1 Help F2 Qview F3 Exit F4 Desel F5 Copy
F6 Display F7 Locate F8 Zoom F9 Select F10 Menu
```

To execute a function key command, press the corresponding function key, or use the mouse (click once) to select the command in the message bar. If you want to view the contents of a file without using the function key commands, you must press Alt, select **F**ile to display the File menu, and then choose **Q**uick View from the menu. When you use the function key command, however, you press only F2 (Qview) and save two keystrokes.

Table 1.1 lists and describes the default function key commands available in PC Tools Desktop. In addition to using the function key commands, you can perform other operations with single keys. The basic keystroke commands are also listed in table 1.1.

Table 1.1 PC Tools Desktop Keystroke Commands Available in All PC Tools Desktop Applications

Key	Name	Function
F1	Help	Displays context-sensitive Help facility
F2	Qview	Displays contents of current file
F3	Exit	Exits current dialog box or closes PC Tools Desktop screen (same as Esc)
F4	Desel	Deselects all selected files
F5	Copy	Copies selected files
F6	Display	Activates Display Options dialog box
F7	Locate	Starts the FileFind utility for locating files
F8	Zoom	Toggles the current window display between full-screen and default size
F9	Select	Displays File Select Filter dialog box
F10	Menu	Toggles between the current window display and the Menu window
Alt	Menu bar	Selects horizontal menu option (used with highlighted letter in option)
Esc	Cancel	Exits current dialog box or closes PC Tools Desktop screen (same as Esc)
Ctrl+Esc	Hot Key	Returns to DOS application
Alt+space bar	System Control	Displays System Control menu
Ctrl+d	Read Disk	Makes drive d active (where d is any drive on your system) and reads drive d's directories
Ins	Dual Lists	Switches to a dual-lists display
Ctrl+Alt+d	Dual Lists/ Read	Switches to a dual-lists display and makes drive d active in second set of windows
Del	One List	Switches to a one-list display, with default window size and position

continues

Table 1.1 Continued		
Key	**Name**	**Function**
Tab	Tree/Files	Moves left to right, top to bottom, between windows
Shift+Tab	Tree/Files	Moves right to left, bottom to top, between windows

Version 8 triples the number of available shortcuts by combining Alt or Ctrl with a function key. If you press Alt, the message bar changes to display the Alt+function key commands. If you press Ctrl, the bar displays the Ctrl+function key commands.

With the exception of F1 (Help) and F3 (Exit), you can customize the function of any of these keys. Refer to Chapter 2, "Controlling the Desktop," for more information.

Using Drag-and-Drop

With the *drag-and-drop* method of directly manipulating files and directories, you accomplish tasks by using only the mouse. Drag-and-drop bypasses commands entirely, by enabling you to perform such tasks as copying or moving selected files or directories by dragging them to the new location. To execute a function on a particular file, you can even drag-and-drop a selected file to the appropriate function key. To view a file, for example, you can drag a file to the F2 (Qview).

Copying a file illustrates the basic drag-and-drop method. To copy a file to a different directory or drive, point to the file in the File window and press the left mouse button to select the file (do not release the button). Then *drag* (move the mouse while holding the button) the file to its new location. As you drag the file, a small rectangular box (called a *banner*) appears with the message Can't Drop Here. When you drag the file to a directory in the Tree window (a legitimate place to copy the file), the banner message changes to Copy 1 File. When the banner is next to the directory into which you want to copy the file, release the button. A Copy message box appears briefly. If you change your mind about copying the file, you have a second to select Cancel; otherwise, Desktop copies the file.

NOTE If the file is small, the message box may disappear (and the file may be copied) before you have time to click Cancel. Using the keyboard—pressing Esc or C for Cancel—is more reliable.

To move a file, follow the preceding steps, but press Ctrl and the left mouse button to select the file. When the file is next to a directory or drive icon, the banner message changes to Move 1 File.

For Related Information

▶▶ "Redefining the Function Keys," p. 58.

▶▶ "Running Programs and Launching Files," p. 137.

▶▶ "Copying and Moving Files," p. 139.

▶▶ "Moving or Copying a Directory with Drag-and-Drop," p. 240.

FROM HERE...

Understanding the PC Tools Desktop Windows

By default, the PC Tools Desktop screen displays two windows: a *Tree window* on the left, which lists the directory structure of the current disk, and a *File window* on the right, which lists the files in the current directory. Desktop also gives you options for displaying two other types of windows: the *View window*, which you use to view the contents of a file, and the *Menu window*, which you use to start applications programs.

PC Tools Desktop constructs every window from the same elements:

- A *title bar* identifies every window. In the Tree window, the volume label for the current disk appears in the title bar. In the title bar of the File window, the current disk and directory name appears.

- A *close box* appears at the left end of the active window's title bar, which is highlighted. Click the close box to close the window.

- A *zoom arrow*, the small box containing an upward-pointing triangle, is at the right end of the active window's title bar. When you click the zoom arrow, Desktop zooms the window to full-screen size. A downward-pointing triangle indicates that the window will be downsized when you click the zoom arrow.

- A *resize box* is in the bottom right corner of every window. To resize the window, point to the Resize box, hold down the mouse button, and drag the mouse in any direction.

■ A vertical *scroll bar*, a *scroll box*, and a *scroll arrow* are on the right side of each window. You can use the mouse and these features to move quickly around the window.

In addition to these standard window elements, PC Tools Desktop displays a *status line* at the bottom of the Tree and File windows. In each window, this status line displays information, such as the amount of storage space available on the current disk or the number of files contained in and space occupied by the current directory.

When you first hot-key into PC Tools Desktop (by pressing Ctrl+Esc), the Tree window is the active window. In this window, Desktop displays the directory structure of the current disk. A vertical line down the left side of the window depicts the disk's *root directory*, the "trunk" of the tree. Horizontal lines branch off to the right to indicate the disk's main subdivisions, its *directories* and *subdirectories*. PC Tools Desktop highlights the name of the current directory, the same name that appears in the window title bar in the File window. The status line in a tree window displays the storage space available on the current disk drive. The example in figure 1.1 shows 115,355,648 bytes of hard disk storage space available (one character of text usually requires 1 byte of space).

In the File window, PC Tools Desktop lists all files stored in the current directory. By default, Desktop can display three columns of files, with as many as 16 files per column. When the current directory holds more than 48 files, you must scroll the window to view the entire list of file names. At the bottom of the File window, Desktop indicates the number of files in the directory, as well as the storage space occupied by these files. The example in figure 1.1 shows 24 files, occupying 528,020 bytes of disk storage space, listed in the current directory.

In Version 8.0, you can display entries in the tree and file lists in upper- or lowercase letters. Lowercase is the default. To change the case, select **C**onfigure to display the Configure pull-down menu, and then select Display Options. Desktop displays the Display Options submenu. Select Upper Case.

The Tree and File windows appear by default; however, the View and Menu windows are hidden by default. To display the View window in full-screen size, you must use Desktop's Quick View feature. You can change the default view, however, to include the View window. If you want the View window to appear by default, select **W**indows from the horizontal menu bar to display the Windows pull-down menu. A check mark appears to the left of File Window and Tree Window, the windows that are currently showing. From the pull-down menu, select **V**iew Window. The View window occupies the lower half of the screen, and the Tree window and File window move to the upper half of the screen. This setup is useful when you want to view many files in succession (see fig. 1.4).

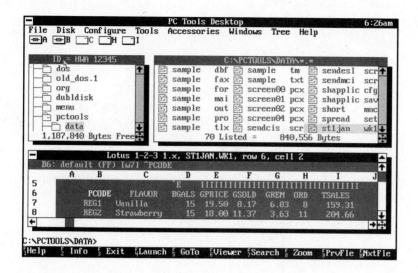

Fig. 1.4

The View window added to the PC Tools Desktop screen.

When displayed, the View window shows the contents of the *current file* (the file whose file name is highlighted in the file window) or, if one or more files are selected in the file window, the contents of the first file selected. PC Tools Desktop can display the contents of files created by more than 30 different DOS programs. In figure 1.4, for example, a 1-2-3 file appears in the View window.

To turn off the View window, repeat the process you use to turn the View window on. This time when you select **W**indows, the submenu displays a check mark next to View Window. Select the **V**iew Window option to turn it off. Desktop again hides the View window and returns the screen to its original configuration, the Tree and File windows side by side. For more information about the View window and the associated Quick View feature, see Chapter 5, "Locating and Viewing Files."

Moving between Windows

To move between windows, click the window you want to use, or press Tab or Shift+Tab until the title bar is highlighted at the top of the desired window. If you press Tab or Shift+Tab, Desktop includes the DOS line in the cycle.

If an action does not register, you probably are not in the current window. Check the screen to see which window's title bar is highlighted or whether your cursor is blinking at the DOS prompt, and then move to the desired window.

Logging On to a Different Disk and Rereading the Tree

You can use the mouse or the keyboard to log on to a different disk. Position the mouse pointer on the desired disk drive letter in the drive line and press either mouse button. Alternatively, press Ctrl+*d*, substituting the disk drive letter for *d*. While reading the list of directories and files on the destination disk, Desktop displays the message Reading system areas, followed by the message Reading directories. Then, in the Desktop windows, Desktop displays the files and directories from the new disk.

Occasionally, PC Tools Desktop is not aware that you altered the file or directory structure on the disk and, consequently, displays an inaccurate list of files or directories. To force the program to reread the directory tree, follow one of these procedures:

- Select **D**isk and select R**e**-Read Tree.
- Click the drive letter in the drive line.
- Press Ctrl+*d*, substituting the drive letter for *d*.

PC Tools Desktop reads the list of subdirectories and files on the current disk and displays an accurate file and directory list.

Moving, Resizing, Zooming, and Hiding the Windows

You can use the mouse or keyboard to control the size and position of PC Tools Desktop's windows. You can even hide some or all of the windows so that only the DOS command line and message bar remain.

By default, the PC Tools Desktop screen is 80 characters wide by 25 lines tall. If your computer's display adapter supports the EGA standard, you can use a command-line parameter at start-up to display 43 lines of text (see Appendix A, "Installing and Configuring PC Tools," for more about PC Tools Desktop's command-line parameters). When you use a VGA adapter, you can even display 50 lines. By default, the PC Tools Desktop windows occupy all but 7 lines of the PC Tools Desktop screen.

Turning Off the Background Mat

When you first start PC Tools Desktop, the program displays a solid
background, called the *background mat*, behind the PC Tools Desktop
windows. The background mat hides the DOS screen that appeared
when you hot-keyed into PC Tools Desktop. Because you may occasionally want to display a portion of the underlying DOS screen while you
work in PC Tools Desktop, the program enables you to turn off the
background mat and to move, resize, or hide one or more of the PC
Tools Desktop windows.

To turn off PC Tools Desktop's background mat, select **W**indows
from the horizontal menu bar. PC Tools Desktop displays the
Windows menu, which has a check mark to the left of the menu option **B**ackground Mat (see fig. 1.5). This check mark indicates that the
background mat is on. To turn off the background mat, select the **B**ackground Mat menu option. The next time you pull down the Windows
menu, no check mark appears beside Background Mat. Desktop removes the background mat and displays the underlying DOS screen in
the background.

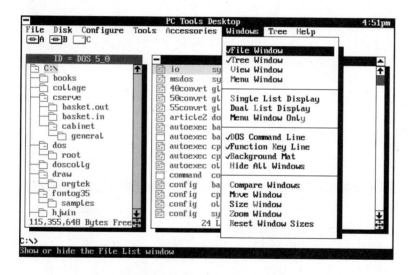

Fig. 1.5

The Background
Mat option
selected in
Windows menu.

Moving a PC Tools Desktop Window

With the background mat turned off, you can see the portion of the
DOS screen that appeared when you hot-keyed into PC Tools Desktop.
The portion of the DOS screen that you want to see, however, may be
hidden by a PC Tools Desktop window. PC Tools Desktop enables you

to easily move a window around your screen so that you can see any information in the DOS screen. You can move a window by using your mouse or the arrow keys on the keyboard.

To move a window by using the mouse, position the mouse pointer on the title bar of the window. (Be careful not to touch the close box, which is in the upper left corner.) Press and hold the left or right mouse button. Move the mouse in the direction you want to move the window. Desktop moves the window along with the pointer, a process called *dragging* (described in the earlier section "Using Drag-and-Drop"). Drag the window to the desired location and release the mouse button.

You also can move a PC Tools Desktop window by using the keyboard. Press Alt+space bar or click the program close box once. Desktop displays the System Control menu (see fig. 1.6).

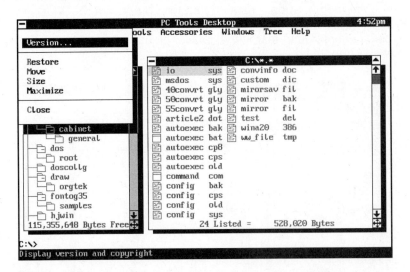

Fig. 1.6

The System Control menu.

From the System Control menu, select **M**ove. PC Tools Desktop displays a box prompting you to use the cursor-movement keys to adjust the location of the window. Use the arrow keys (←, →, ↑, and ↓) to move the window to the screen location you want, and then press Enter.

Resizing a Window

When you want to change the size or shape of a PC Tools Desktop window, you can use the mouse, the easiest method of making the change. Move the mouse pointer to the Resize box at the bottom right corner of the window. Press and hold down the left or right mouse button.

To make the window larger, drag the Resize box down and to the right side of the screen. The upper left corner of the window remains stationary, and the window expands diagonally downward. You can make the window smaller by dragging the Resize box up and to the left. When the window is the size you want, release the mouse button.

As an alternative to using the mouse, PC Tools Desktop enables you to resize the current window by using only the keyboard. You can also use this method to resize an application window for a program you run from the Tools or Desktop Accessories menu. Press Alt+space bar. PC Tools Desktop displays the System Control menu (refer to fig. 1.6).

From the System Control menu, select **S**ize. PC Tools Desktop displays a box prompting you to use the cursor-movement keys to adjust the size of the window. Use the arrow keys to move the lower right corner of the window until the window is the size you want, and then press Enter.

Zooming or Maximizing a Window

To display more information, you may want a window to fill the available space between the drive line and the DOS command line (or message bar, if you have toggled off the DOS command line). PC Tools Desktop enables you to easily *zoom* (maximize) the window to full size by using the mouse or the keyboard.

The easiest way to zoom the window to full size is with the mouse. Move the mouse pointer to the zoom arrow, which is in the upper right corner of the window border, and press the right or left mouse button. Desktop zooms the window to full-screen size. Figure 1.7 shows a File window zoomed to full size. Notice that the triangle in the zoom arrow points down.

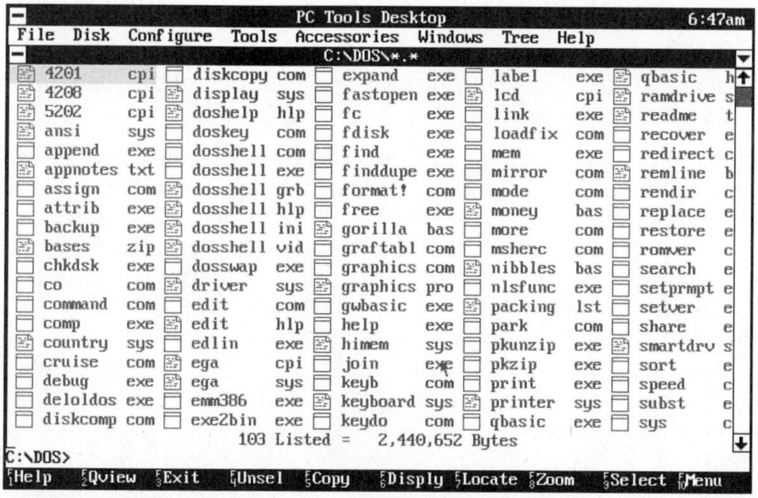

```
┌─────────────────────────────────────────────────────────────┐
│ ─                    PC Tools Desktop                 6:47am  │
│ File  Disk  Configure  Tools  Accessories  Windows  Tree  Help│
│ ─────────────────────── C:\DOS\*.* ──────────────────────────│
│ 4201    cpi  diskcopy com   expand   exe   label    exe  qbasic  h│
│ 4208    cpi  display  sys   fastopen exe   lcd      cpi  ramdrive s│
│ 5202    cpi  doshelp  hlp   fc       exe   link     exe  readme   t│
│ ansi    sys  doskey   com   fdisk    exe   loadfix  com  recover  e│
│ append  exe  dosshell com   find     exe   mem      exe  redirect c│
│ appnotes txt dosshell exe   finddupe exe   mirror   com  remline  b│
│ assign  com  dosshell grb   format!  com   mode     com  rendir   c│
│ attrib  exe  dosshell hlp   free     exe   money    bas  replace  e│
│ backup  exe  dosshell ini   gorilla  bas   more     com  restore  e│
│ bases   zip  dosshell vid   graftabl com   msherc   com  romver   e│
│ chkdsk  exe  dosswap  exe   graphics com   nibbles  bas  search   e│
│ co      com  driver   sys   graphics pro   nlsfunc  exe  setprmpt e│
│ command com  edit     com   gwbasic  exe   packing  lst  setver   e│
│ comp    exe  edit     hlp   help     exe   park     com  share    e│
│ country sys  edlin    exe   himem    sys   pkunzip  exe  smartdrv s│
│ cruise  com  ega      cpi   join     exe   pkzip    exe  sort     e│
│ debug   exe  ega      sys   keyb     com   print    exe  speed    c│
│ deloldos exe emm386   exe   keyboard sys   printer  sys  subst    e│
│ diskcomp com exe2bin  exe   keydo    com   qbasic   exe  sys      c│
│              103 Listed =    2,440,652 Bytes                     │
│ C:\DOS>                                                       │
│ ─Help  ─Qview  ─Exit  ─Unsel  ─Copy  ─Disply ─Locate ─Zoom  ─Select ─Menu│
└─────────────────────────────────────────────────────────────┘
```

Fig. 1.7

A File window zoomed (maximized) to full size.

Later, you may want to return the window to its previous size and position. Click the zoom arrow again. This time, PC Tools Desktop restores the window to its size and position before you maximized it.

You can use the keyboard to zoom and restore a window. To zoom the current window, press F8 (Zoom). To return the window to its original size, press F8 (Zoom) again. Alternatively, you can press Alt+space bar or single-click the program close box to display the Desktop System Control menu. From the System Control menu, select Maximize. Desktop expands the size of the window to completely fill the space between the horizontal menu bar and the DOS command line. To restore the window to its original size, display the System Control menu and select Restore.

Hiding a Window

Using the mouse or the keyboard, you can *hide* (turn off the display of) any Desktop window. Hiding windows is useful when you want to see all or part of an underlying DOS application. To hide a window by using the mouse, click the window close box in the upper left corner once; Desktop hides the window.

> **NOTE** Clicking any window close box except the program close box closes the window but does not close Desktop. Desktop closes, however, if you double-click the program close box.

To hide a window by using the keyboard, select Windows. Desktop displays the Windows menu, which lists the names of the four window types: File Window, Tree Window, View Window, and Menu Window (refer to fig. 1.5). Desktop displays a check mark to the left of the names of the currently displayed window types. To hide a window, select the corresponding menu type from the menu, toggling the window off. No matter how you hide a window, you must use the Windows menu to redisplay it. Select Windows, and then select the menu option that corresponds to the window you want displayed.

To hide all PC Tools Desktop windows at one time, select Windows, and then select Hide All Windows. Desktop hides all windows, as well as the horizontal menu bar and makes the underlying DOS application, if any, visible. To redisplay the hidden windows, press F10 (Menu); you also can select Windows from the horizontal menu bar and choose Hide All Windows again to toggle the windows on. To redisplay the horizontal menu bar, click the top line of the screen or press Alt.

For Related Information

▶▶ "Looking at Files with View," p. 189.

FROM HERE...

Moving around the Screen

You can move around the active window by using the mouse or the keyboard. Use the mouse to move the highlighted bar to a file name in the File window, making it the *current file*, or to a subdirectory in the Tree window, making it the *current directory*.

> If you're using the mouse, you can make the file or tree window active and select a file or directory simultaneously. Just point to the desired item and click.

T I P

If the file or subdirectory name you want is visible in the PC Tools Desktop screen, move the mouse pointer to the name and press the right mouse button. If a name is not visible, use the mouse and the window's scroll bar to scroll the file or subdirectory name into view. Click the up arrow to move the highlighted selection bar up through the list one line at a time. Click the down arrow to move the highlighted selection bar down through the list, line by line. You also can drag the scroll box up or down to scroll the entire contents of the window at one time.

You can also use the cursor-movement keys listed in table 1.2 to move the highlight around the active PC Tools Desktop window. The highlighted file or directory becomes the current file or directory.

Table 1.2 PC Tools Desktop Cursor-Movement Keys

Key	Cursor Movement
↓	Down one line
↑	Up one line
→	One column to the right
←	One column to the left

continues

Table 1.2 Continued	
Key	**Cursor Movement**
Home	To beginning of the current list
End	To end of the current list
PgDn	Down one screen
PgUp	Up one screen

Using Dialog Boxes

As you work with PC Tools Desktop applications, the program routinely displays messages and prompts in on-screen boxes called *dialog boxes*. Dialog boxes fall into three categories: message dialog boxes, command dialog boxes, and help dialog boxes. The following sections discuss the message and dialog boxes. The help dialog boxes are explained in detail in the section "Getting Help from PC Tools Desktop" later in this chapter.

Some menu options require you to provide certain information before the chosen command can be executed. Selecting one of these menu options does not immediately execute a command or change a setting but rather displays a dialog box. To alert you that a menu option displays a dialog box, Desktop displays an ellipsis (...) after the option name. Several File menu options—Run DOS Command, Search Files, Move, Copy, Compare, Delete, Rename, and Locate, for example—access dialog boxes.

Message Dialog Boxes

When you first activate PC Tools Desktop by pressing Ctrl+Esc, Desktop displays this message enclosed in an on-screen box:

    Reading system areas

The following message then replaces the first one:

    Reading directories

This box, which displays the words Analyzing drive *d* in its title bar (where *d* is the default start-up drive), is an example of a *message dialog box*. This type of dialog box informs you of the status of a PC Tools Desktop application window.

Some message dialog boxes also contain confirmation buttons. If you select **D**elete from the **F**ile menu, for example, Desktop displays a message dialog box, shown in figure 1.8, warning you that Desktop is ready to delete (erase) the current file and asks for your confirmation. PC Tools Desktop provides two options: Delete and Cancel, called *confirmation buttons*. The first option, Delete, is highlighted.

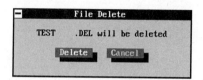

Fig. 1.8

A message dialog box with confirmation buttons.

To indicate your response, select the appropriate confirmation button. This action executes or cancels the operation and removes the dialog box from the screen. To confirm the deletion of the file listed in figure 1.8, for example, select the **D**elete button. To abort the deletion, select the **C**ancel button instead. In either case, PC Tools Desktop removes the message dialog box from the screen.

You can use any of the following three methods to select the appropriate dialog box confirmation button. These methods are similar to the methods used to select an option on the horizontal menu bar or a pull-down menu:

- Move the mouse pointer to the confirmation button you want and click the right or left button.

- Press Tab or Shift+Tab until the confirmation button you want is highlighted, and then press Enter.

- Press the letter corresponding to the letter highlighted in the word on a confirmation button. To select the **D**elete button, for example, press D. (***Note:*** You can press and hold down the Alt key and press the highlighted letter; however, in this case, pressing Alt is not necessary.)

To cancel the action, you can select the Cancel button to close the dialog box, or you can single-click the close box in the upper left corner of the dialog box, press Esc (Exit), or press F3 (Exit).

Command Dialog Boxes

When you select some commands in PC Tools Desktop, the program displays a *command dialog box* (or often just *dialog box*). Most dialog boxes in PC Tools Desktop fall into this category. Desktop uses command dialog boxes to request information. If you press F6 (Display) or select **Configure**, and then select File **Display** Options from the Display Options submenu, the Display Options dialog box appears (see fig. 1.9).

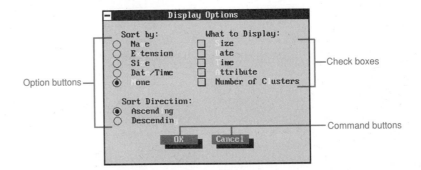

Fig. 1.9

The Display Options dialog box.

Figure 1.10 provides another example of a command dialog box, the Define Function Keys dialog box, displayed by selecting Define **Function** Keys from the **Configure** menu. A third example of a command dialog box, the File Select Filter dialog box, is shown in figure 1.11. You can display this dialog box by pressing F9 (Select) or by selecting **Selection** from the **File** menu and then choosing Select **Filter** from the submenu that appears.

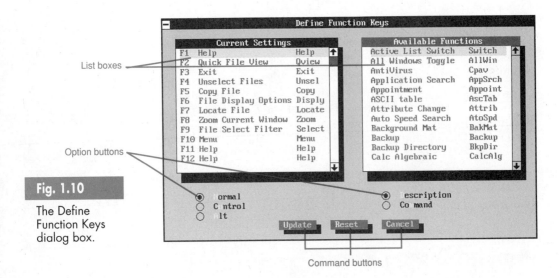

Fig. 1.10

The Define Function Keys dialog box.

Desktop command dialog boxes are made up of one or more of the following elements: text boxes, list boxes, option buttons, and command buttons. The Display Options dialog box contains option buttons on the left side, check boxes on the right side, and two command buttons across the bottom portion of the dialog box (refer to fig. 1.9). The Define Function Keys dialog box contains two list boxes side by side, two sets of option buttons below the list boxes, and three command buttons along the bottom (refer to fig. 1.10). The File Select Filter dialog box contains two text boxes and three command buttons. The following sections explain how to use each of these elements of a command dialog box.

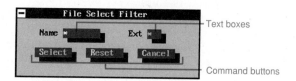

Fig. 1.11

The File Select Filter dialog box.

Using Option Buttons

Some command dialog boxes use *option buttons* for selecting command settings. Every option button is a circle followed by a command setting. Option buttons occur in groups, never one at a time. The option buttons operate like the buttons on a car radio (other programs that use dialog boxes even refer to these buttons as *radio buttons*).

In addition, the buttons in each group are mutually exclusive, meaning that only one button can be active at any particular time. When you select one button in a group, for example, any other button that was selected "pops out" or is canceled. A dot in the center of the option button indicates the active button. In Figure 1.9, the None option button is selected.

The easiest way to select a different option button is by using the mouse. Position the mouse pointer on the name or circle of the option button you want and press the left or right mouse button once.

You can also use the keyboard to select a different option button. Suppose, for example, that you want to use the Display Options dialog box to sort files by file name. First press Tab or Shift+Tab until one of the option buttons in the Sort By group of options is highlighted. Then use the up- or down-arrow key to move the highlighted bar to the new option—in this example, the Name option button. When you press Enter, Desktop selects the new option button, removing the dot from the None button and displaying it in the Name option button.

Using Option Check Boxes

Many PC Tools Desktop commands permit optional settings. Some dialog boxes enable you to select the command settings you want by "checking" the appropriate *check boxes*. A command dialog box can have any number of check boxes. Each check box is independent of the others, and the check boxes can be used in any combination.

A check box turns a command setting on or off. A setting is "checked" (or on) when a check mark appears in the box (see fig. 1.12). The setting is off when the box is empty. To toggle the setting on or off, click the setting name or its check box, or press the highlighted letter. Alternatively, you can press Tab or Shift+Tab until the desired command setting is highlighted, and then press Enter. Every time you click the setting or press Enter while the setting is highlighted, you toggle the setting on or off.

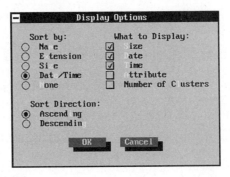

Fig. 1.12

The Display Options dialog box with the Size, Date, and Time check boxes selected.

Using a List Box

Some dialog boxes contain a *list box*, a scrollable list of available options from which you can choose. Because each list box has its own title bar and scroll bar, it resembles a Desktop window. The Define Function Keys dialog box in figure 1.10, for example, displays two list boxes, one entitled Current Settings and the other entitled Available Functions.

To select an item in a list box, use the mouse and scroll bar to display the item you want and then click it. You also can press Tab until the highlight is in the list box, press the cursor-movement keys to highlight the item you want, and then press Enter.

Using a Text Box

When you need to type information to complete an operation, PC Tools Desktop includes one or more *text boxes*. Desktop often provides a default value in each text box, but you can type a different value in the box.

To make an entry in a text box, press Tab or Shift+Tab until the box is highlighted. Alternatively, simply click the box. Backspace over the current entry and type another, or use the left- and right-arrow keys to move the cursor within the box, and then edit the current entry. Press Enter to accept the value in the text box.

The File Select Filter dialog box in figure 1.11, for example, includes two text boxes: the Name text box and the Ext text box. Each box contains an asterisk (*) as its default value. In the context of this particular dialog box, the asterisks cause Desktop to select, in the File window, all file names in the current directory. To limit which file names Desktop selects, you can type a file name specification in the two text boxes. To select all files that begin with the letter *B* and that have the extension TXT, for example, you type **b*** in the Name text box and **txt** in the Ext text box.

Using Command Buttons

After you make entries in text boxes, select the appropriate check boxes, and press the correct option buttons, you are ready to execute the command. To do so, select a command button. Command buttons execute (or cancel) the command you chose, using the information or criteria you specified in the dialog box.

Each command dialog box usually contains at least two command buttons—one to execute the command and close the dialog box, and another to cancel the command and close the dialog box. Some dialog boxes, however, contain more than two command buttons. In these boxes, choosing a command button executes its function, but does not automatically close the box. The Define Function Keys dialog box, for example, contains three command buttons: Update, Reset, and Cancel. Choosing **U**pdate or **R**eset executes the action but leaves the box open for more instructions.

When a command dialog box contains command buttons, you can select your operation by using one of the following methods:

■ Move the mouse pointer to the command button you want and click it, using the right or left mouse button.

- Press Tab or Shift+Tab until the desired command button is high-lighted, and then press Enter.

- Hold down the Alt key and press the highlighted letter in the command button you want.

T I P   Rather than select the Cancel button to close the dialog box, you can click once on the dialog box's close box, press Esc (Exit), or press F3 (Exit).

Getting Help from PC Tools Desktop

As you learn to use PC Tools Desktop, you may want to perform a task for the first time and need a few hints, or you may have performed the task in the past but have forgotten the precise steps. In addition to providing sophisticated help that is available through the Help menu, PC Tools Desktop provides a convenient, on-line, context-sensitive Help facility that is available at the touch of a key.

T I P   If you only need a reminder of what a certain menu option does, highlight the option and check the message line for a short description.

Using the Help Menu

You can access the PC Tools Desktop Help menu from the horizontal menu bar. Select **Help** to display the menu, shown in figure 1.13, which contains the following options:

- *Topics.* Choose this option to display the Help Topics screen, which lists broad Desktop topics in which you might be interested. The available topics include the following:

About PC Tools Desktop
Menu Commands
Function Keys
The PC Tools Desktop Window
Selecting Files
Using Command-Line Options
Using Help
Basic Skills
Getting Technical Support
Glossary
Index

■ *Index.* Choose this option to display an index for the Help facility.

■ *Keyboard.* Choose this option to describe the function key commands that have the same effect in all parts of Desktop.

■ *Commands.* Choose this option for an explanation of each option on the horizontal menu bar.

■ *About.* Choose this option to display a list of topics that describe many of the features of PC Tools Desktop.

■ *DOS Advice.* Choose this option to access the Advice system, an excellent troubleshooting guide that points you to the appropriate PC Tools utility to use for any problem, DOS error message, or CHKDSK error message.

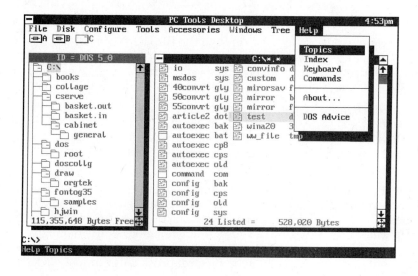

Fig. 1.13

The Help menu.

Using the Context-Sensitive Help Facility

The first function-key command listed in the message bar is F1 (Help); you can access an on-line Help facility by pressing the F1 key. In any PC Tools Desktop window, you can press F1 (Help) to immediately access pertinent on-screen documentation in a Help window. Figure 1.14, for example, shows the Help window for the tree list.

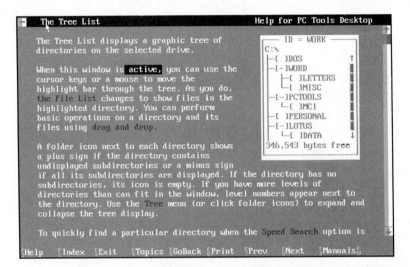

Fig. 1.14

The Tree List
Help window.

Every Help window accessed through the F1 (Help) key contains a description of the current menu, command, or operation you are performing. When you are in a PC Tools Desktop operation and press F1 (Help), Desktop displays a Help window specific to the operation.

Occasionally, the help information is several screens long. You can move between pages (screens) by using the PgUp and PgDn keys, the up- and down-arrow keys, or the mouse and vertical scroll bar. You also can press Home to move to the beginning of the Help window or End to move to the end.

Many PC Tools Desktop windows contain highlighted words called *hypertext links* (refer to fig. 1.14). These highlighted words are terms discussed more fully in another Help window. If you move through the Help window by pressing the cursor-movement keys, the highlighted bar moves from one hypertext link to another. To display the Help window that discusses the highlighted word, press Enter or just click the word.

At the bottom of every set of Help windows, PC Tools Desktop displays a solid line followed by a list of related topics. Each topic is a hypertext link to another help screen. To display the related Help window, you can highlight the link and press Enter, or you can click the hypertext link.

If an explanation uses terms or concepts you don't understand, you can follow the hypertext links to track down exactly the information you need, and then press F5 (Go Back) to return to where you started. To return to the PC Tools Desktop window, click the close box or press Esc (Exit) or F3 (Exit).

In addition to the general Help windows, PC Tools Desktop provides a Help index that lists all the available Desktop Help windows, not just the Help window related to the operation you are performing. To access the Help index, press F2 (Index) from any Help window or select Help from the horizontal menu bar and then select Index; Desktop displays the Help Index window. You can use the PgUp and PgDn keys, the up- and down-arrow keys, or the vertical scroll bar to scroll the contents of the window until you see a topic that interests you. Click the topic or use the highlighted bar to highlight the topic and then press Enter. Desktop displays the selected Help dialog box.

Table 1.3 lists other function key commands available in the Help windows.

Table 1.3 Help Window Function Key Commands

Key	Name	Function
F1	Help	Displays a list of topics related to basic PC Tools skills and using Help
F2	Index	Displays the Help Index
F3	Exit	Exits the Help window
F4	Topics	Displays a list of available help topics
F5	GoBack	Returns to previously displayed Help window, letting you retrace your steps
F6	Print	Prints a copy of the current help topic
F7	Prev	Displays the previous help topic in the Help file
F8	Next	Displays the next help topic in the Help file
F9	Manuals	Lists all the PC Tools help systems

Closing PC Tools Desktop

PC Tools Desktop provides several ways to close or exit from the program; you can use the mouse, keystroke commands, and menus.

To use the mouse to close PC Tools Desktop, choose either of the following two methods:

■ Move the mouse pointer to the program close box and double-click.

■ Click the program close box once. PC Tools Desktop displays the System Control menu, from which you select Close.

 NOTE   If you started Desktop with the hot key, exiting with the hot key leaves the program in memory, allowing a quick restart with the hot key. If you exit from Desktop by pressing Esc (Exit), F3 (Exit), or Alt+F4 (Close), or by selecting Exit PC Tools Desktop from the File menu, the program is removed from memory.

The keyboard offers three ways to exit from PC Tools Desktop:

■ Press Ctrl+Esc to hot-key back to the original DOS application. Desktop swaps the contents of memory to expanded memory (EMS), extended memory (XMS), or to disk (depending on the command-line parameters you used to start Desktop).

■ Press Esc (Exit), F3 (Exit), or Alt+F4 (Close) to exit from Desktop and to remove the resident portion of the program from your computer's memory. When you use any one of these keystrokes, PC Tools Desktop does not swap the contents of memory to EMS, XMS, or disk.

■ Select File from the horizontal menu bar, and select Exit PC Tools Desktop from the File menu.

Whichever method you use to exit Desktop, the Close PC Tools Desktop dialog box appears, confirming the closing of the program (see fig. 1.15). If you have made changes to configuration options, the Save Configuration setting is checked. If you do not want to save the changes, select Save Configuration to toggle the setting off. Select OK to close; if you decide to return to the program, select Cancel.

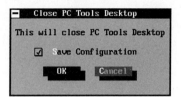

Fig. 1.15

The Close PC
Tools Desktop
dialog box.

If you started PC Tools Desktop as a memory-resident program, closing
Desktop does not completely unload it from your computer's memory
(RAM); consequently, you can always return with the hot key. If you
remove Desktop from memory, you cannot return with the hot key. For
information on removing the program from memory, see Appendix A,
"Installing and Configuring PC Tools."

Chapter Summary

This chapter discusses aspects of PC Tools Desktop common to all its
utilities. Now that you are familiar with the information in this chapter,
you are ready to read the other chapters in this part of the book. The
next chapter demonstrates how to configure PC Tools Desktop to best
suit your needs.

Controlling the Desktop

As you become more familiar with PC Tools Desktop and its many features, you may want to modify the manner in which the program operates or the on-screen appearance of the program. One of Desktop's greatest strengths is the extent to which it can be customized. At first, however, the array of alternatives can be overwhelming, and with Desktop's enhanced role in Version 8.0 as home base for Accessories and stand-alone PC Tools utilities, the number of choices is greater than ever.

This chapter focuses on the options that affect most Desktop users, pointing you to other chapters for more specialized configuration choices. In particular, this chapter teaches you how to change function keys, set confirmation checks, modify screen and file display, customize the pull-down menus, and change the layout of the Desktop windows. In addition to explaining how to change the program's configuration, this chapter shows you how to use the DOS command line from the Desktop.

Two pull-down menus, the Configure and Windows menus, contain most of the customization options. The Configure menu includes a mix of widely used functions and functions with more narrow applicability. The following section, "Configuring the Desktop," explains the widely used commands and refers you to the chapters in which you can find details on the other commands. Three related Configure menu options—Load Pull-downs, Edit Pull-downs, and Password—are discussed in a separate section, "Customizing the Pull-down Menus," later in this chapter. Commands on the Windows menu are applicable to general Desktop use and are covered in the section "Modifying the Window Layout" later in this chapter.

 Although some commands have been shifted between menus, generally the Configure menu replaces Version 7's Options menu, and the Windows menu replaces the View menu. New commands on the Configure menu enable you to change some settings, such as mouse and keyboard characteristics, that previously required running the PC Config program.

Configuring the Desktop

The PC Tools Desktop is a powerful organizer of all your hard disk programs. PC Tools can maintain files and directories as well as execute programs easily and quickly. Below is a list of some of the aspects of Desktop. The items in parentheses indicate the command term Desktop uses for the function listed. PC Tools Desktop enables you to perform the following tasks:

- ■ Change what the function keys do (Define Function Keys)
- ■ Set confirmation preferences (Confirmation)
- ■ Customize the screen (Display Options)
- ■ Modify the file display (Display Options)
- ■ Filter the file display (Display Options)
- ■ Use speed search to expedite your work with file lists (Speed)
- ■ Use your own text editor for viewing and editing files and directories (Configure Editors)
- ■ Run DOS commands and applications without first freeing up memory (Execution)

To change any of these settings, select Configure to display the Configure menu shown in figure 2.1.

The selections you make on this menu determine the configuration of PC Tools Desktop. When you finish setting up your configuration, select Save Configuration to save the new configuration to disk.

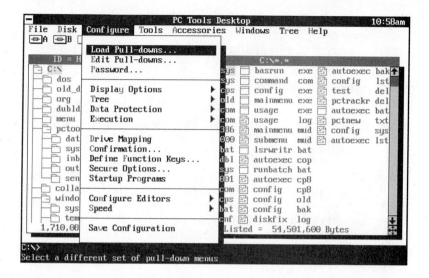

If you forget to save the changes you make to the configuration and attempt to exit from PC Tools Desktop, the program displays the Close PC Tools Desktop dialog box with the **S**ave Configuration check box already checked. Select the **OK** command button to exit from PC Tools Desktop, and all the changes to the configuration will be saved automatically. If you do not want to save the changes, be sure to click the **S**ave Configuration check box to remove the check mark before you exit.

For information on the Load Pull-downs, Edit Pull-downs, and Password options, see the section "Customizing the Pull-down Menus" later in this chapter. Following is a list of the more specialized options on the Configure menu and the chapters in which you can find additional information on them:

- *Tree*. Use this option to change the default directory for various operations and to configure the Tree display (see Chapter 6, "Working on Disks").

- *Data Protection*. Use this option to select a method for recovering files with Undelete (see Chapter 10, "Recovering Damaged or Deleted Files").

- *Execution*. This option accesses a submenu which contains Autodialer and Execution Passwords options. Use this option to set passwords for Tools programs (see Chapter 23, "Using PC Tools Telecommunications).

■ *Drive Mapping.* Replaces Version 7's DeskConnect. This TSR enables you to connect two computers via a serial or parallel port so that resources can be shared (see Appendix A, "Installing and Configuring PC Tools").

■ *Secure Options.* Use this option to set file encryption standards (see Chapter 13, "Securing Your Data with PC Secure and Wipe").

■ *Startup Programs.* Use this option to determine what PC Tools programs run at system startup (see Appendix A, "Installing and Configuring PC Tools").

■ *Speed.* This option accesses the Speed submenu, which contains the Keyboard Speed and Mouse Speed options. These two options enable you to determine how quickly a held down key repeats and the amount of time that will elapse before the key begins to repeat *(keyboard speed),* and how fast the mouse tracks across the screen *(mouse speed).* See Appendix A, "Installing and Configuring PC Tools."

Redefining the Function Keys

PC Tools Desktop displays a default list of function key commands in the message bar. If the functions you use most often differ from these functions, you can change the function keys to match your preferred functions.

To customize the function keys, display the Configure menu and choose Define Function Keys. PC Tools Desktop displays the Define Function Keys dialog box (see fig. 2.2).

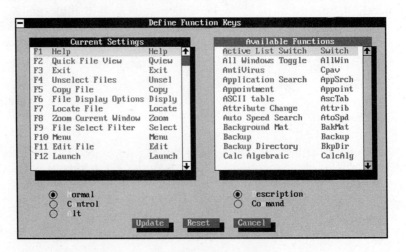

Fig. 2.2

The Define Function Keys dialog box.

If you specified a password during installation or by using the Password command when you customized the pull-down menus, you are prompted to enter the password when you attempt to change these definitions. No one can modify the function key list without the password. If you did not assign a password, the program does not prompt you to enter a password to edit the function key commands.

You can redefine the function of all the keys except F1 (Help) and F3 (Exit). If your keyboard includes F11 and F12 keys, you can define functions for them, but these function commands will not appear in the message bar. See Chapter 1, "Navigating the Desktop," for information about the default function key commands.

In addition to the normal function keys, Version 8.0 triples the number of available shortcuts by combining Ctrl or Alt with a key. These "shifted" keys appear in the message bar when you press and hold Ctrl or Alt.

To redefine a normal function key, follow these steps:

1. Select the key from the list in the Define Function Keys dialog box by clicking the line. Alternatively, highlight the line and press Enter.

   PC Tools Desktop activates the Available Functions list box, which appears on the right side of the dialog box.

2. Scroll through this list of functions and highlight the function you want to assign to the selected function key.

3. Press Enter.

   The function key setting changes to reflect the new choice of Desktop command. Continue this procedure to redefine any other function keys.

To redefine a Ctrl+function key or Alt+function key combination, select the Control or Alt option button under the Current Settings list box. Desktop switches the list to display the current settings for the Ctrl or Alt combination. You can redefine these keys just as you did the normal, unshifted keys. To return to the normal function key settings, select the Normal button; PC Tools displays the normal function key assignments.

After you redefine the desired function keys, select the Update command button at the bottom of the dialog box. PC Tools Desktop saves the changes and returns to the PC Tools Desktop screen, with the new list of normal function keys in the message bar. Until you change these commands again or reset them to the default settings, these commands appear in the message bar when you use PC Tools Desktop.

NOTE If you make changes and then select **C**ancel to exit the dialog box without saving the changes, PC Tools displays a System Configuration Warning box. Select **S**ave if you meant to save the changes; select **C**ancel to lose the changes.

To return to the original default function key settings, even after updating, display the Define Function Keys dialog box and select the **R**eset command button. Desktop restores the default settings. Select **U**pdate to save the change. Desktop displays the System Configuration Warning box to confirm the change. Select **S**ave to reset and return to the Desktop.

Setting Confirmation Preferences

Some operations that PC Tools Desktop enables you to perform are destructive in nature. For example, when you delete a file from a disk or copy a file to a directory that already contains a file of the same name, you destroy data on your disk. Unless you are using the Sentry feature, even PC Tools Undelete cannot recover data that has been replaced by other data.

Desktop's designers have built in a confirmation check for the potentially irreversible file or directory Delete and Replace commands. You can expand confirmation checks to encompass other potentially hazardous operations, such as copying or moving directories or files with the mouse. If, however, you're confident you will not make mistakes with commands such as Delete and Replace, you can turn off the confirmation check.

 PC Tools Desktop normally displays the system files that the DOS DIR command hides from its list. As useful as this feature can be, it also can lead to trouble if you mistakenly move, delete, or change a system file. Version 8.0 enables you to set confirmation preferences for protection in operations involving system files.

To change the confirmation requirements, select **C**onfigure to display the Configure menu, and then select **C**onfirmation. PC Tools Desktop displays the Confirmation Options dialog box shown in figure 2.3.

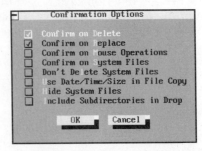

Fig. 2.3

The Confirmation Options dialog box.

The Confirmation Options dialog box displays these check boxes:

- *Confirm on Delete.* A check mark appears in this check box by default so that Desktop asks you for confirmation every time you delete a file. When this option is not checked, PC Tools Desktop deletes files, at your command, without asking for further confirmation.

> **CAUTION:** If you deactivate Confirm on Delete, turn on the Don't Delete System Files option to protect irreplaceable system files; otherwise, you may lose these files.

- *Confirm on Replace.* A check mark appears in this check box by default so that Desktop asks you to confirm every file replacement. When this option is not checked, PC Tools Desktop replaces files when you copy a file to a directory that contains another file with the same name, overwriting that file without asking for confirmation.

- *Confirm on Mouse Operations.* Check this box if you want Desktop to ask you for confirmation when you use a mouse to perform file copying or file moving. This box is not checked by default.

> **NOTE** By using the Date/Time/Size option described in the following list, you can limit the scope of Confirm on Replace and Confirm on Mouse Operations when the operation replaces a file. Turn on the Date/Time/Size option to limit confirmation checks to operations replacing files that match in date, time, size, and name.

- *Confirm on System Files.* Check this box if you want Desktop to ask you for confirmation when you attempt any operation that can change the content or location of a system file. Because a change to a system file can stop your system from working, this confirmation is a useful protection.

- *Don't Delete System Files.* This actually means, "Don't delete system files without asking." Check this box if you want Desktop to ask you for confirmation when you attempt to delete a system file.

- *Use Date/Time/Size in File Copy.* Check this box if, when you are copying a file that replaces another file by the same name, you want Desktop to ask for confirmation only if the date, time, and size of the two files are identical.

■ *Hide System Files.* Check this box if you do not want Desktop to display system files in the File window. Hiding system files ensures that no user of your system can move or alter them with PC Tools Desktop.

After you check the boxes you want, select the **OK** command button. PC Tools Desktop sets the new confirmations and removes the dialog box from the screen.

Customizing the Screen Display

You can customize the screen colors, change the screen size (in lines displayed), set the screen to blank out after a given length of time, and put a disk activity light directly on-screen if you do not have one on your computer. To change any of these settings, select Configure, and then select Display Options; the Display Options submenu shown in figure 2.4 appears.

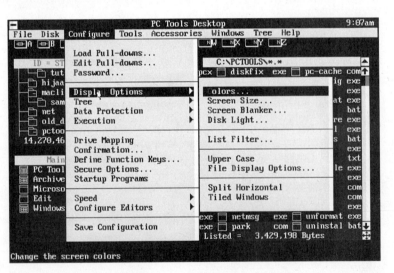

Fig. 2.4

The Display Options submenu.

The Colors command displays a dialog box in which you can change to a different preset color scheme or fine-tune the color (including highlighting) of any screen feature in the current scheme. The Screen Size command displays a dialog box containing a toggle between text and graphics mode and options that enable you to view more information by increasing the number of lines appearing on-screen. (When you *toggle* an option, you select the setting once to turn it on; to turn the option off, you select the setting again.) Your choices depend on the type of monitor you have.

> **NOTE** When you select the Colors or Screen Size option, Desktop runs the PC Tools PC Config configuration program. As PC Config settings, the color and screen size configurations apply to all PC Tools programs, whether they are run from Desktop or from DOS.

Refer to Appendix A, "Installing and Configuring PC Tools," for a complete discussion of PC Config and the Color and Screen Size options. (*Note:* In PC Config, the Display command is equivalent to the Screen Size option in Desktop. The numerous appearances of the word "display" on the Configure menu probably account for the use of "Screen Size" instead.)

The Screen Blanker and Disk Light options are actually features of the PC Tools Data Monitor program, but you may find them helpful in general. Use the Screen Blanker to prevent computer images from "burning in" a permanent image on your screen. You can have the screen go blank immediately when you press a hotkey or after a given number of minutes of inactivity.

> **NOTE** *Hotkey*, in PC Tools Desktop terms, is the highlighted letter in a command that, when pressed, actives that command. In the command File **D**isplay Options in the Configure menu, for example, the hotkey is D. Pressing D while the Configure menu is displayed activates the File Display Options command.
>
> Desktop's use of the term *hotkey* can be confusing. These keys are shortcuts for selecting menu commands, not for hot-keying between applications.

Activate the Disk Light option if you want an indicator of disk read-and-write access to appear on-screen. Use the Disk Light option if you want a "light" to appear in the upper right corner of the screen. This light shows the drive letter being accessed, with an *r* indicating a read operation or *w* indicating a write operation.

NOTE PC Tools displays the disk light from within text-based programs only; the light does not appear in Desktop if you are using a graphics display.

Refer to Chapter 10, "Recovering Damaged or Deleted Files," for details on these Data Monitor features.

Modifying the File Display

Using the File Display Options command on the Display Options submenu (refer to fig. 2.4), you can change the level of detail and the order of the file information in the File window.

By default, file and directory names appear in lowercase in Version 8.0. If you prefer the standard uppercase, from the Display Options submenu, select Upper Case. This command is a toggle.

PC Tools Desktop normally displays only the file name in the File window. If you want PC Tools Desktop to list other characteristics—file size, date, and time, for example—you can use the Display Options dialog box (see fig. 2.5). Press F6 (Display); alternatively, choose Display Options from the Configure menu, and then choose File Display Options from the submenu.

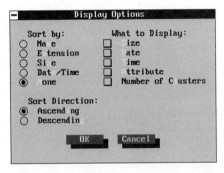

Fig. 2.5

The Display Options dialog box.

By default, PC Tools Desktop lists file names in the order they are stored on the disk. A sorted list, however, often is easier to scan when you are trying to find a particular file. You can select option buttons in the left portion of the Display Options dialog box to display files in several sort orders. Sort the list by file name, file name extension, file size, or date and time by selecting the appropriate option buttons.

You can sort in ascending order (A through Z and 0 through 9) or descending order (Z through A and 9 through 0) by selecting the appropriate option buttons. The default is ascending order.

The check boxes on the right side of the Display Options dialog box determine which file characteristics—in addition to the file name, which is always listed—appear in the File window. To add or remove characteristics, choose one or more of the check boxes by clicking the setting name or corresponding square box or by pressing the hotkey. Every option is a toggle. As you select characteristics, PC Tools Desktop places a check in each box.

After you select the display options, select the **OK** command button. The program returns to the PC Tools Desktop screen. The files appear in the new sort order, and the new group of characteristics appear in the File window with each respective file name. Figure 2.6, for example, shows the C:\PCTOOLS directory sorted in ascending order by file name, with file size, date, and time listed with every file name.

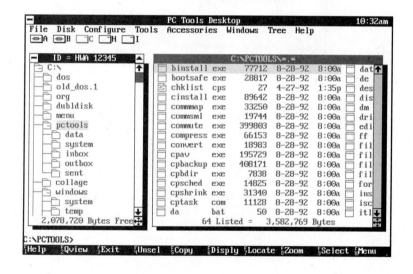

Fig. 2.6

Listing file size, date, and time, sorted by file name.

When you sort a directory listing by using the Display Options dialog box, PC Tools Desktop does not change the actual order used by the operating system for storing the files. See Chapter 6, "Working on Disks," for a discussion of how to sort and store a directory to disk in sorted order.

NOTE   If you display all characteristics, you must zoom the File window to full size to view the last column that lists the number of clusters occupied by each file. See Chapter 1, "Navigating the Desktop," for more information.

When you want to see the file characteristics for a particular file, PC Tools Desktop enables you to display that information without changing the file display options for all files. After highlighting the file you need more information about, display the File menu and choose Information; then choose File Information. PC Tools Desktop displays the More File Information dialog box, which lists file name, extension, path, attributes, date and time, size, clusters, and the starting cluster number (see fig. 2.7). The dialog box also lists the total number of files in the current directory (the same number displayed in the last line of the file list window).

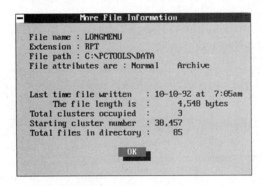

Fig. 2.7

The More File Information dialog box.

Filtering the File List

Normally, PC Tools Desktop displays in the File window all files in the current directory. Sometimes, however, you want the program to display a more limited group of file names in the windows. You may want to find a particular file name or to list a certain category of files (all spreadsheets, for example). You can limit the files listed in the File window by using the file list filter. Display the Configure menu and choose the Display Options command to display the Display Options submenu. Select List Filter to reach the File List Filter dialog box (see fig. 2.8).

Fig. 2.8

The File List Filter dialog box.

The File List Filter dialog box displays two text boxes: Name and Ext. Entries in these text boxes determine which files PC Tools Desktop lists in the File window. Use the Name text box for the DOS file name criterion and the Ext box for the file name extension criterion.

In entering criteria, you can use either or both of the DOS *wild-card* characters. The asterisk (*) takes the place of any string of characters, and the question mark (?) takes the place of any single character. By default, PC Tools Desktop displays an asterisk in every text box, causing the File window to list all files in the current directory.

When entries are complete, press the **D**isplay command button. The PC Tools Desktop screen returns, listing only the file names that meet the File List Filter criteria.

Suppose, for example, that the current directory is C:\PCTOOLS and that you want to display all files in the directory that have the EXE extension; follow these steps:

1. Display the **C**onfigure menu and select Display Options to access the Display Options submenu. Select List **F**ilter to display the File List Filter dialog box (refer to fig. 2.8).

2. Leave the asterisk in the Name text box and type **exe** in the Ext text box.

3. Press the **D**isplay command button. To return to the PC Tools Desktop screen without accepting the new File List Filter criteria, select the **C**ancel command button.

PC Tools Desktop returns to the PC Tools Desktop screen and displays in the File window only file names from the C:\PCTOOLS directory that have the EXE file name extension (see fig. 2.9).

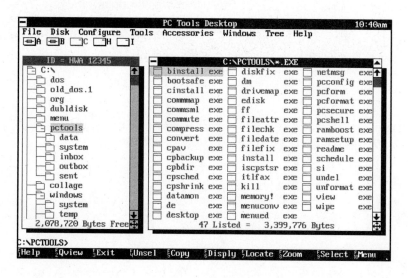

Fig. 2.9

File names with the EXE extension.

PC Tools Desktop continues to list files according to the most recent File List Filter criteria until you reset the criteria, change the current directory, or change the current disk drive. To reset the criteria, return to the File List Filter dialog box and select the **R**eset command button. Then choose the **D**isplay command button to return to the PC Tools Desktop screen.

T I P If a file list seems suspiciously short or a directory alarmingly empty, you probably set a filter that you forgot about. Check the File List Filter dialog box and reset the filter, if necessary.

Using Speed Search

With long file or directory lists, scrolling to find a particular name can be tedious. Using Desktop's speed search feature, you can skip instantly to a file by typing its initial letters. To use speed search to skip to a file, activate the File window by tabbing to it or clicking the File menu title bar. Type the first letter of the file name. Desktop displays the Speed Search dialog box and moves the highlighted bar to the first file that begins with a matching letter. Type as many letters as you need (up to eight) to highlight the file for which you are looking. Press Enter to close the dialog box. (Press Enter a second time to select the file.)

With the Tree window selected, you can use speed search in the same way to quickly find a directory or subdirectory.

T I P Speed search is activated automatically when you type while the File or Tree window is active. Handy as the feature can be, it also can be disconcerting if you think the DOS command line is active, attempt to type there, and instead bump into the Speed Search dialog box. If you encounter this obstacle often, reset Desktop to activate speed search only on demand. First turn automatic speed search off. Choose **C**onfigure and then **S**peed to display the Speed submenu. Choose **S**peed Search, toggling it off. Now, when you want to use the feature, press Ctrl+F2 to access the Speed Search dialog box at any time.

Using Your Own Text Editor

Using the Edit Text command (which you access by choosing Change from the File menu), you can do simple editing on text files such as AUTOEXEC.BAT. Previous versions of PC Tools used either a built-in editor, with limited capabilities (Version 6), or the Desktop Accessories Notepads, with enhanced word processing features such as printing options and a spelling checker (Version 7). In Version 8.0, the internal editor is again the default, but you can switch to Notepads or, if you have a favorite text editor, you can use that.

To change the editor, choose Configure and then Configure Editors to display the submenu. Choose File Editor. PC Tools Desktop displays the Configure File Editor dialog box (see fig. 2.10).

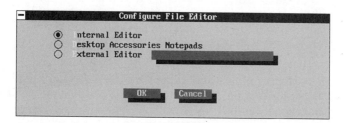

Fig. 2.10

The Configure File Editor dialog box.

To use Notepads as the editor, select the Desktop Accessories Notepads option button. To use a different program, select External Editor and type the program's name in the text box. Include the entire file name, such as PCEDIT.EXE, and any path information. For example, if the program PCEDIT is in the WP directory, type the following:

    C:\WP\PCEDIT.EXE

Although Notepads has more features than the internal editor, it cannot edit files greater than about 60K, the equivalent of 14 to 17 pages. (You can open a larger file, but Notepads truncates it.) The internal editor is only limited by the available amount of RAM. Even then, the internal editor can edit larger files by using temporary swap files on disk when RAM is low; doing so, however, slows the edit down. If you occasionally need to edit long files, you may want to stick with the internal editor.

T I P

For information on configuring and using the Disk Editor, a highly advanced program, see Chapter 12, "Editing a Disk with DiskEdit."

Toggling Quick Run

By default, when you instruct PC Tools Desktop to execute a DOS command or launch an application program, PC Tools Desktop first saves the contents of the computer's memory to a disk file, temporarily removes itself from memory, and executes the command or application. Although this process is intended to provide maximum memory to the command or program, it also causes a slight delay before the command or program is executed. In some cases, however, the command or program you intend to execute does not need a large amount of RAM. If you prefer that Desktop execute commands immediately without first freeing up the memory, you may want to try the Quick Run feature.

To toggle Quick Run on, choose Execution from the Configure menu, and then select Quick Run. PC Tools Desktop places a check mark to the left of the option and returns to the Desktop screen. The next time you instruct Desktop to execute a DOS command or to launch an application program, it does so immediately, without freeing up any memory.

PC Tools Desktop, running stand-alone with the Quick Run feature turned on, uses approximately 322K of RAM. With Quick Run turned off, PC Tools Desktop occupies only about 12K when it executes a DOS command or launches an application program. The memory that remains free for the DOS command or application varies, however, depending on the amount of RAM in your computer and the amount of memory used by other programs that you may have already loaded into memory.

To toggle off the Quick Run feature, select Quick Run again from the Configure menu's Execution submenu.

FROM HERE...

For Related Information

◀◀ "Using Function Key Commands," p. 30.

▶▶ "Sorting a Directory," p. 254.

▶▶ "Selecting Startup Options," p. 920.

▶▶ "Setting Screen Colors," p. 921.

▶▶ "Configuring the Display," p. 923.

▶▶ "Configuring the Mouse," p. 924.

Customizing the Pull-down Menus

With Version 8.0, you have greatly enhanced control over the pull-down menus. You can perform the following tasks:

- Switch to Version 6- or Version 7-compatible menus.

- Switch to abbreviated menus to screen out advanced utilities, such as DiskEdit and DiskFix (substitutes for Version 7's User Level option).

- Create your own variations on the menus, moving commands within and between the pull-downs and submenus and even adding any DOS command or application to a Desktop menu.

- Set a password to protect your configuration.

Switching to Version 6 or Version 7 Menus

If you are a veteran PC Tools user upgrading to PC Tools 8, you can continue using familiar menu commands and shortcut keys by loading Version 6- or Version 7-compatible menus.

To load the menu scheme for either version, display the Configure menu and choose Load Pull-downs. PC Tools Desktop displays the Use A New Menu File dialog box, shown in figure 2.11, which lists the available menu schemes. The default, PC Tools Long Desktop Menus, is selected. (*Note:* Each menu scheme is kept in its own file. The file for the long menu scheme is LONG.MNC. Menu files use the extension MNC.)

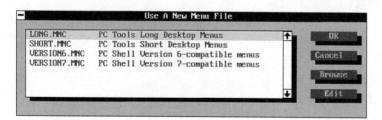

Fig. 2.11

The Use A New Menu File dialog box.

Select PC Shell Version 6- or Version 7-compatible menus from the list; then select **OK**. PC Tools Desktop closes the dialog box and puts the new menu file into effect. In Versions 6- and 7- compatible menus, the Load Pull-downs command is on the Special menu.

Switching to Shorter Menus

If you do not use advanced programs, you can reduce the clutter of the menus by selecting the short pull-downs. Access the Use a New Menu File dialog box and select PC Tools Short Desktop Menus. The short menu is a preconfigured set of menu commands that are most commonly used. Only the basic commands, tools, and accessories are available from the short menu.

Version 8.0 does not include an option to set user experience level, but switching between long and short menus serves a similar purpose.

Using the Menu Editor

If you find that a particular command is not where you expect it to be or if you want to execute DOS commands or applications directly from a PC Tools Desktop menu, you can create your own menu scheme. With Version 8.0's Menu Editor, you can move menu options within and between pull-downs and submenus; change the name, shortcut key, or bottom-line help for a menu item; and add your own DOS commands to a Desktop pull-down menu.

To use the Menu Editor, display the **C**onfigure menu and choose **E**dit Pull-downs. PC Tools Desktop displays the menu editor dialog box, shown in figure 2.12, with the current menu scheme—the scheme to be edited—appearing in the window title bar. In figure 2.12, for example, PCTD - PC Tools Long Desktop Menus appears in the title bar, indicating that the long menus will be edited.

T I P   To edit a menu scheme different from the one currently selected, select **M**ore from the Menu Editor dialog box to display the Menu Editor Options dialog box. Select **L**oad to switch to the other file; then select **OK** to return to the Editor. You also can skip to the Menu Editor immediately after loading a different menu scheme. (In the Use A New Menu File dialog box, select **E**dit.)

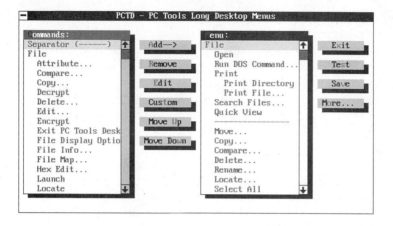

Fig. 2.12

The menu editor
dialog box.

On the left of the menu editor dialog box, the Commands list displays
every Desktop command available in the current menu scheme. So that
you can find commands quickly, the commands are grouped not only in
menu categories, such as File and Configure, but in functional categories, such as Communications and Directory. Because of this method of
grouping, some commands appear in two places. File Display Options,
for example, is listed under Configure and under File. Within a category,
all commands, whether they normally appear on a submenu or even on
a sub-submenu, are in one alphabetical list.

On the right, the Menu list displays the current menus. Submenu items
are indented, similar to their appearance in an outline.

The Menu Editor gives you the tools to be your own interface designer,
where the redesign can range from minor tweaking to a major overhaul.
If you find that the changes you make don't work out, you can always
revert to the original structure. In the menu editor dialog box, select
More to display the Menu Editor Options dialog box. Select Restore
Defaults. Desktop displays a warning that this action will destroy any
customizations. Select OK to restore the defaults, returning the menus
to the way they appeared when you installed PC Tools Desktop.

Moving and Adding Menu Commands

If a command you use often is buried on a submenu, you can move it up
a level. Suppose, for example, that you want to make the File Display
Options command available on the Configure menu, without going
through the Display Options submenu. In the Menu list of the menu
editor dialog box, scroll to the Display Options under the Configure
menu, and select File Display Options. Select the Move Down button

once; File Display Options moves down one position in the submenu. If you want to move the menu item off the submenu onto the Configure menu, between Display Options and Tree, select the Move Down button three more times.

With the Move Up and Move Down buttons, you can relocate a menu item anywhere in the menu structure. Similar to moving headings in an outline, when you move a command for a submenu, you move any commands under it.

In some cases, having a single command available in two menus can be useful. Instead of moving the menu item in the Menu list, you can select the command in the Command list and add it to the desired menu. Suppose, for example, that you want the List Filter command (currently on the Configure menu's Display Options submenu) available when you're using the File menu to work on files; follow these steps:

1. In the Commands list box, scroll to the Configure category and select List Filter.

2. In the Menu list box, identify the placement of the addition by highlighting the command that you want to appear *above* List Filter; for example, highlight Locate to add List Filter below Locate (see fig. 2.13).

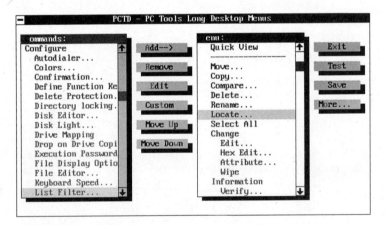

Fig. 2.13

Preparing to add the List Filter command to the File menu in the Menu list box.

3. Select the Add button; List Filter appears in the File menu in the Menu list box. (List Filter will not appear on the actual File menu until you save the new menu scheme, as described in "Saving the New Menu Scheme" later in this section.)

Editing a Menu Item

When you add or move commands, the hotkey you can press as a menu shortcut may be duplicated by a command on the same menu. List Filter and Locate, for example, both use the letter *L* as their menu hotkeys. With the Menu Editor's Edit button, you can revise a command's hotkey, as well as the command name and *bottom-line help* (the text—usually a short sentence indicating what the command does—displayed at the bottom of the screen when the command is highlighted).

To change the hotkey for List Filter, highlight List Filter in the Menu list, and then select the Edit button. Desktop displays the Edit Menu Item dialog box in which you edit the List Filter item (see fig. 2.14).

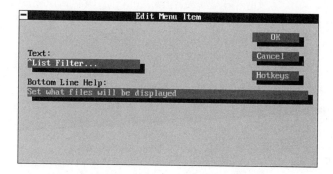

Fig. 2.14

The Edit Menu Item dialog box.

In the Text box, the caret (^) precedes the hotkey. In this case, the caret precedes the L, indicating that letter is the hotkey. To change the hotkey, delete the caret before L and insert the caret (press Shift+6) in front of a different letter. (Press Ins to toggle Insert mode on so that you do not type over existing characters.) To make sure the choice is unique, you can select the Hotkeys button. Desktop displays the Hotkeys message box showing which keys are available and which, if any, appear in the menu text. For List Filter, one key exists: F. Select OK to close the message box. In the Text box, type a caret in front of the F in *Filter*. Select OK to return to the Menu Editor.

Using the Edit Menu Item dialog box, you also can change an item's name or bottom-line help. If you make significant menu changes, you can test the effect of the changes before you save the new scheme. In the Menu Editor dialog box, select Test. Desktop switches you to the Desktop screen in a special test mode. In test mode, you can display the menus but not execute commands.

A dialog box appears at the lower right of the screen. The top button, Alternate Menu Scheme, toggles between the normal File menu and the altered version used when the menu window is active. The bottom button returns you to the Menu Editor. Examine the new menus, note any corrections you want to make, and then select the Return to Editor button to go back to the Menu Editor dialog box.

Adding DOS Commands or Applications to the Desktop

With the Menu Editor's Custom button, you can add any DOS command, including a command to run an application, to any Desktop menu. This feature is handy if you often use the DOS command line to execute a particular DOS command.

Suppose, for example, that you often run a short batch file, SERIAL.BAT, to switch from your default parallel dot-matrix printer to a serially connected laser printer. You can use the Menu Editor to make this a menu item by following these steps:

1. In the Menu list box, identify the placement of the new item by highlighting the command that should appear above it. To place the new item at the end of the File menu's Print submenu, for example, highlight Print File.

2. Select the Custom button. Desktop displays the Create Custom Menu Item dialog box shown in figure 2.15.

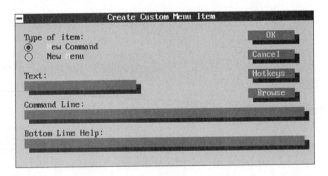

Fig. 2.15

The Create Custom Menu Item dialog box.

3. In the Text box, type the text for the menu item: **Switch to Laser**, for example.

4. In the Command Line box, enter the command just as you would from DOS, including any path specifications. To run the batch file SERIAL.BAT that resides in the DOS subdirectory, for example, type **c:\dos\serial**.

> **NOTE** You can use the Browse button to find and select the desired file and enter the required information automatically.

5. In the Bottom-Line Help box, enter a short description, such as **Use laser printer on serial port**.

6. Use the **H**otkey button to check available letters.

7. To use *L* as the hotkey, insert a caret in front of Laser in the Text box so that the entry reads `Switch to ^Laser`.

8. Select **OK** to return to the Menu Editor.

> To go beyond individual menu entries to a complete menuing system for launching other applications, use Desktop's Menu Window. See Chapter 3, "Using the Desktop as a Program Manager," for more information.
>
> **T I P**

Saving the New Menu Scheme

Whenever you make changes in the Menu Editor and want to lock them in, select the Save button. When all your changes are complete, select Save again, and then select Exit. Desktop displays a message box to confirm your leaving the Menu Editor. Select OK. (If you select Exit before saving changes, Desktop gives you a chance to save them with the **S**ave button or cancel them with **D**iscard.)

Desktop closes the Menu Editor and saves the new scheme, replacing the previous version of the menu file. Because Desktop keeps the default menu structure in a special file, PCSHELL.MNT, you can always restore the defaults even if you made changes to LONG.MNC, the default menu file. In the Menu Editor, select the More button, and then select Restore **D**efaults from the Menu Editor Options dialog box. Select OK to return to the Menu Editor dialog box, Sa**v**e to save the change, and Exit to return to Desktop.

To save the new scheme to a different file rather than replace the currently selected file, from the Menu Editor dialog box select More to display the Menu Editor Options box. Select Save As; Desktop displays a dialog box in which you can name the new file or accept Desktop's suggestion, MENU1.MNC. (If you save additional schemes, Desktop uses the next available number for the suggested name, such as MENU2.MNC.)

You can document revised menus—or any menu scheme on your system—by creating a report file. In the Menu Editor dialog box, select **Mo**re for the Menu Editor Options dialog box. Select **R**eport. PC Tools Desktop shows you the name of the report file it will create (MENU.RPT is the default). Leave the **S**hort option selected to print the menu items and hotkeys; select **L**ong to print bottom-line help also. If you are printing several different menu schemes, give each one a different file name. The default location is the DATA subdirectory under the PCTOOLS directory. Select **O**K to save the menu scheme to a file and return to the Menu Editor dialog box. Select E**x**it to close the dialog box. You can view or print the file from Desktop.

Protecting the Configuration with a Password

You can assign a password to make sure no unauthorized users use any Configure menu commands that change essential elements of your configuration. When you assign a password, that password will be required to execute the Load Pull-downs, Edit Pull-downs, Confirmation, Define Function Keys, and Configure Editors commands, as well as the Password command itself.

> **WARNING:** You must use the set password to change or remove password protection. If you forget your password, you may have to reinstall PC Tools from scratch to gain control of the configuration option. Choose a password that is personal to you and not something another person can figure out.

To set configuration password protection, display the **C**onfigure menu and select **P**assword. Desktop displays the Change Password dialog box (see fig. 2.16). In the New text box, type the word or character string you want to use (the character string can include up to eight characters) and press Enter. For confidentiality, Desktop displays only asterisks as you type. In the Confirm box, type the character string again. Select **O**K or press Enter to save the password. Be careful when entering a password. If your new and confirm passwords to not match, the password is not accepted.

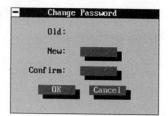

Fig. 2.16

The Change
Password dialog
box.

When you attempt to access any menu editing commands, PC Tools prompts you for the password. If you mistype the password, you are returned to the main Desktop display. You can attempt to enter your password as many times as necessary. PC Tools returns to the main display after each incorrect entry.

If you decide to remove the password, select the **P**assword command again. Desktop displays the Enter Password dialog box to verify that you are authorized to use this command. Enter the current password and press Enter. Desktop displays the Change Password dialog box. In the Old text box, type the current password, and press Enter. In the New and Confirm boxes, just press Enter, replacing the old password with nothing.

Modifying the Window Layout

By default, PC Tools Desktop displays the Tree window and File window, a good layout for basic file management activities. PC Tools Desktop also can display a Menu window, which contains programs you can run from the Desktop, and a View window, which shows file contents. You can add either window to the basic layout. With the Windows menu toggles, Desktop can display the various window types in almost any combination. Only the View window and the Menu window cannot be displayed together. The discussions that follow describe how to use the Windows menu, shown in figure 2.17, to control which windows are displayed in the PC Tools Desktop screen.

| NOTE | The new Compare Windows option, which you may want to use to check the results of file copying, is extremely useful in flagging unmatched files in two different directories. Although it appears on the Windows menu and is used with Dual List Display, this command is a file and directory management operation, not a windows layout option. Refer to Chapter 5, "Locating and Viewing Files," and Chapter 6, "Working on Disks," for details. |

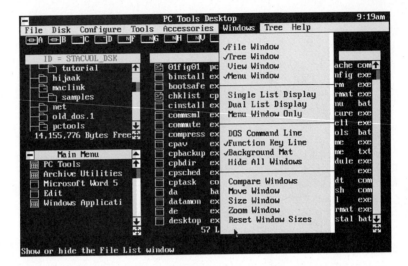

Fig. 2.17

The Windows menu.

Toggling between Dual Lists and One File List

By default, Desktop displays only one Tree window and one File window at a time. To see in one screen the directory tree of two disks or perhaps the file list of two directories, you can open a second pair of Tree and File windows. This dual list is similar to a split screen feature in word processing, enabling you to work on two disks or directories simultaneously.

To display two sets of PC Tools Desktop windows, press the Ins (Dual List) key or display the **W**indows menu and select Dual List Display. Desktop displays two pairs of PC Tools Desktop windows, each pair occupying one-half of the screen (see fig. 2.18).

While the layout is set to dual-list display, each pair of windows works independently of the other. You can scroll through one Tree window without affecting the other Tree window and through one File window without affecting the other File window. The highlighted directory in the upper Tree window determines the files that are displayed in the upper File window; similarly, the highlighted directory in the lower Tree window determines the files that are displayed in the lower File window.

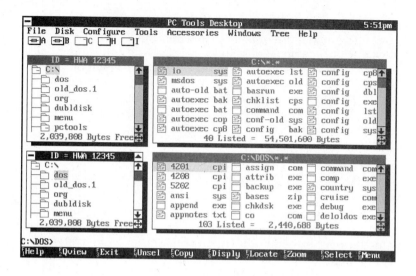

Fig. 2.18

The Dual List Display.

In addition, you can change drives in either set of windows independently. Use the mouse or press the Tab key to move to the set of windows whose drive you want to change. Press Ctrl+*d*, where *d* is the drive letter. PC Tools Desktop displays the new disk's directory structure in the Tree window and its file list in the File window.

As a shortcut, rather than pressing the Ins key to display two lists, you can press Ctrl+Alt+*d* and substitute the drive letter for *d*. In one step, this command opens a dual-list display and displays the directories and files for disks in the second set of windows.

T I P

In dual-list display mode, you use the standard window features to move between, resize, zoom, and move windows.

T I P

To return to the one-list display, press the Del (One List) key or display the **W**indows menu and select the **S**ingle List Display option. PC Tools Desktop displays the active Tree window and File window set.

NOTE The dual-list display cannot be used with the View or Menu windows. In fact, if the View or Menu window is open, selecting Single List Display or Dual List Display closes the window.

An important benefit of having a dual list display is that you can copy or move files much more quickly than with a single list display. To copy or move quickly in a dual list display, set one list to the source directory and one list to the target directory. Select the file to be copied or moved in the source directory, and then activate the copy or move command. Desktop asks whether you want to use the second path as the target. At this point select **Yes**. The selected files are copied to the second display directory.

Displaying the Menu Window

In addition to providing an alternative to using the operating system (DOS) to perform system chores, PC Tools Desktop provides a convenient method of running all the other programs on your system. A program that performs this function is sometimes called a *menuing program*. PC Tools Desktop's Menu window provides this capability.

PC Tools Desktop enables you to display the Menu window alone in the Desktop screen or with the Tree and File windows. When the Menu window is displayed alone, it becomes a top-notch menuing system complete with cascading menus. If you prefer, however, you can use the Menu window to launch programs from the same screen that displays the Tree window and the File window.

To display the Menu window with the Tree and File windows, select **W**indows, and then select **M**enu Window. Desktop displays the Menu window in the lower left corner of the screen, as shown in figure 2.19.

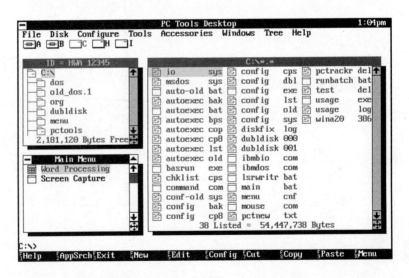

Fig. 2.19

The Menu, Tree, and File windows.

To display the Menu window alone, press F10 (Menu). The Menu window appears in the center of the screen. Press F10 (Menu) to return to the preceding PC Tools Desktop screen.

To turn off the Menu window, toggle it off on the Windows menu, or select any incompatible option on the Windows menu: Single List Display, Dual List Display, or View Window.

Chapter 3, "Using the Desktop as a Program Manager," contains a full discussion about how to use the Menu window to launch all the programs on your computer.

Displaying the View Window

The View window is used to display the contents of the *current file*, the file whose file name is highlighted in the File window, or the first selected file. By default, the View window is hidden, only to be displayed when you use PC Tools Desktop's Quick View feature. You can, however, change the default view to include the View window.

To display the View window full-time, select Windows, and then select View Window. The View window appears across the bottom of the screen, as shown in figure 2.20. This layout is useful when you want to view many files in succession.

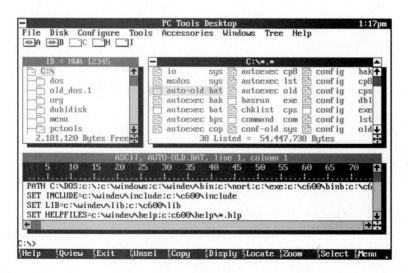

Fig. 2.20

The Tree, File, and View windows.

84

 NOTE You can move the View window to appear vertically on the right side of the screen, with the Tree and File windows stacked on the left. Display the **C**onfigure menu, and select Displa**y** Options to access the Display Options submenu. Select Split **H**orizontal, a toggle between horizontal and vertical window display.

The View window displays the contents of the current file or the first selected file, if one or more files are selected. Desktop can display the contents of files created by more than 30 different DOS programs.

To turn off the View window, toggle it off on the Windows menu, or select any incompatible option on the Windows menu: **S**ingle List Display, Dual **L**ist Display, or **M**enu Window.

Chapter 5, "Locating and Viewing Files," provides a more detailed discussion of the view window and the associated Quick View feature.

Toggling Individual Windows

You can change the layout by toggling windows on and off from the Windows menu. If a window is on, a check mark appears to its left in the menu, and selecting that option—or a mutually exclusive option—toggles it off.

The following windows and items can be toggled on or off from the Window menu:

- Select the **F**ile Window option to toggle on or off the File window.
- Select the **T**ree Window option to toggle on or off the Tree window.
- Select **V**iew Window option to toggle on or off the View window. This option is mutually exclusive with the **M**enu Window option.
- Select the **M**enu Window option to toggle on or off the Menu window. This option is mutually exclusive with the **V**iew Window option.
- Select the **D**OS Command Line option to toggle on or off the DOS command line at the bottom of the screen.
- Select the Function **K**ey Line option to toggle on or off the display of the function keys in the message bar.
- Select **B**ackground Mat to toggle on or off the background mat. (Refer to the discussion of the background mat in Chapter 1, "Navigating the Desktop.")

The default window "style" is *cascaded*, in which one window overlaps another. Every PC Tools Desktop window can be sized and moved independently, even though the windows overlap. The other window style is *tiled*, which means that one window cannot overlap another. You can zoom the windows to full size, but you cannot size or move them. You change the window type from the Configure menu. Display the Configure menu; then choose Display Options for the Display Options submenu. Select Tiled Windows to toggle between cascaded (the default) and tiled window style.

Hiding All Windows

Using the mouse or the keyboard, you can hide some or all of every PC Tools Desktop window. To hide a window by using the mouse, click the window close box in the upper left corner. To hide all PC Tools Desktop windows at one time, select Windows and then Hide All Windows. PC Tools Desktop hides all windows and the horizontal menu bar. This feature can be useful when you want to see the entire screen of an underlying application.

> **WARNING:** Although you can use Desktop commands with windows hidden, File menu commands work differently. Because the Tree and File windows cannot be used to select directories or files, Desktop displays a dialog box where you must type file specifications, just as you would in DOS.

To redisplay the horizontal menu bar, click the top line of the screen, using either mouse button, or press Alt. To redisplay the hidden windows, either press F10 (Menu) or select Windows from the horizontal menu bar and choose Hide All Windows.

For Related Information

▶▶ "Finding Duplicates," p. 185.

▶▶ "Comparing the Contents of Two Directories," p. 221.

FROM HERE...

Using the DOS Command Line

One of the most useful features of PC Tools Desktop is its *DOS command line*, a simulation of your operating system's command line. You can think of this optional line, displayed just above the message bar, as a window into the operating system. The DOS command line enables you to execute any DOS command from within PC Tools Desktop, just as though the cursor were at the actual DOS command line. Generally, you can use this handy feature to execute DOS commands that have no equivalent function in PC Tools Desktop and to access DOS from within any other DOS program by way of PC Tools Desktop.

Using the DOS command line is easy. While PC Tools Desktop is displayed, press the Tab key or Shift+Tab to make the DOS command line current. (If the command line is turned off, toggle it on from the Windows menu.) Type any valid DOS command and press Enter.

If you type **chkdsk** and press Enter, for example, PC Tools Desktop first saves to a temporary disk file a copy of the current contents of memory (RAM) and loads into RAM another copy of the operating-system command processor. The program then executes the command (CHKDSK in this example), displays the results on your screen, and prompts you to press any key or a mouse button to return to PC Tools Desktop.

 NOTE   Even with the DOS command line off, you can execute a DOS command. Select the **F**ile menu, and then select **R**un DOS Command. Desktop displays a dialog box in which you can enter the command. Enter the command here rather than in the DOS command line at the bottom of the screen.

Assuming that you are running PC Tools Desktop as a memory-resident program, the DOS command line gives you access to DOS from within any DOS program.

T I P   The DOS command line is useful for single operations. To execute several DOS commands in a row, you can avoid returning to the Desktop after each one by exiting to a DOS session. Select the **T**ools menu; then select D**O**S Session. Desktop exits to DOS and clears the screen. When you finish working in DOS, type **exit** and press Enter to return to the Desktop.

Changing How Desktop Returns from DOS

By default, whenever you execute a command from the DOS command line, PC Tools Desktop executes the command and then pauses, displaying a message to press any key or mouse button to reenter PC Tools Desktop. This pause lets you see the result of the DOS command before the PC Tools Desktop screen reappears. To clear the DOS (or DOS application) screen and return to PC Tools Desktop's screen, press any key. PC Tools Desktop pauses before returning to PC Tools Desktop's screen to give you a chance to read any messages.

If you do not need to see the results of DOS commands, you may prefer to have PC Tools Desktop return immediately to its screen after the command executes. Display the Configure menu, and then select Execution to access the Execution submenu. Notice that a check mark appears to the left of the Wait on DOS option. Select the option to toggle it off. PC Tools Desktop removes the check mark and closes the menu. The next time you execute a DOS command or program from within Desktop, Desktop returns immediately to the PC Tools Desktop screen at the end of the command (or program).

Chapter Summary

This chapter describes how to control the way PC Tools Desktop operates and looks by configuring the program to your preferences. In particular, this chapter teaches you how to tailor the function key list, set confirmation preferences, customize the screen and file displays, customize the pull-down menus, and control the layout of PC Tools Desktop windows. In addition to explaining how to change the program's configuration, this chapter shows you how to use the DOS command line in PC Tools Desktop.

Turn to Chapter 3, "Using the Desktop as a Program Manager," to learn how to use PC Tools Desktop as a program manager or menuing program, which makes launching applications programs that reside on your computer's hard disk easy.

Using the Desktop as a Program Manager

Besides being an excellent utility for performing operating-system functions, Desktop can provide a convenient method for running all the other programs stored on your computer. A program that performs this function is often called a *program manager, DOS shell,* or *menuing program.* In Desktop, the name for this function is the *Menu window.* You can use the Menu window as a program manager that provides quick access to an unlimited number of DOS application programs. If you have been using the Direct Access menu system (Version 5), Desktop can automatically convert those menus into its own Menu window format.

With the PC Tools Task Switcher, program management means not only accessing programs easily but actually running up to eight programs at the same time. You can work on multiple tasks simultaneously—without having to close one program before opening another—and switch between tasks with a keystroke. You can use the Task Switcher by itself or build it into your menuing system.

The Menu window organizes your tasks and simplifies running them. The Task Switcher makes carrying out tasks much more fluid than the usual DOS start-stop-start sequence. The new Scheduler helps you to turn over to PC Tools the actual performing of many housekeeping tasks. In Version 7.1, automatic scheduling was available for Central Point Backup and Commute. Now the Scheduler is a full-featured program that can automate running PC Tools utilities or other applications at daily, weekly, or other intervals. With a little planning, you can have routine chores—hard disk backup, disk compression, and disk maintenance, for example—occur unattended.

This chapter describes each of these management tools. First, you learn how to use the Menu window as a program manager. Desktop enables you to create any number of menus, referred to as *program groups*, on which you can list one or more *program items* for starting programs stored on your computer. This chapter explains how to define program groups and program items and how to use program groups and items to run application programs.

When you set up applications for the Menu window, you can associate specific file types with particular application programs, thus enabling Desktop to launch the correct program whenever you open an associated file in the File window. You can, for example, associate files that have the file name extension DOC with your favorite word processing program. Every time you open a DOC file in the File window, Desktop "knows" to load the word processing program into memory and then to load the selected DOC file into the program. This chapter describes how to use program items to create the association between file types and specific application programs. Refer to Chapter 4, "Working on Files," for a full discussion about how to open or *launch* programs from the File window.

After describing how to manage programs with the Menu window, this chapter explains using the Task Switcher, in conjunction with the Menu window or by itself, to run multiple programs simultaneously. Finally, this chapter shows you how to automate many regular computer chores using Version 8.0's Scheduler.

Accessing the Menu Window

Desktop enables you to display the Menu window in the Desktop screen with the Tree and File windows or to display the Menu window alone. When the Menu window is displayed alone, it becomes a top-notch menuing system complete with cascading menus. If you prefer, however, you can use the Menu window to launch programs from the same screen that displays the Tree window and the File window.

To display the Menu window alone, press F10 (Menu). Desktop displays the Menu window in the center of the screen, similar to figure 3.1. Press F10 (Menu) to return to the preceding Desktop screen.

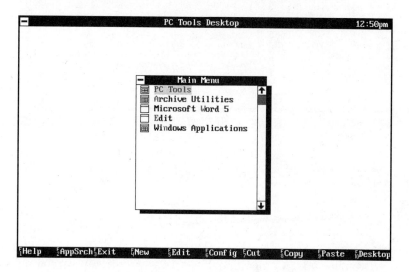

Fig. 3.1

The Menu window displayed alone.

If you want the Menu window to appear on the same screen as the Tree window and File window, display the **W**indows menu and select **M**enu Window. Desktop displays the Menu window in the lower left of the screen below the Tree window, with the File window at right (see fig. 3.2).

To remove the Menu window from the screen, display the **W**indows menu and select **M**enu Window again; the Menu window toggles off.

If you plan to use Desktop as a program manager, you can start the program by typing the command **pctools** and pressing Enter, or you can configure the program to display the Menu window at start-up by displaying the Menu window, as discussed in this section, and then selecting **C**onfigure and Save Configuration. Alternatively, just make sure the Menu window is displayed when you exit Desktop. When the Close Desktop dialog box appears with the **S**ave Configuration check box checked, select the **OK** command button. The next time you start Desktop, the Menu window appears on the Desktop screen.

```
┌─────────────────────────────────────────────────────────────────┐
│ ■                          PC Tools Desktop              12:51pm  │
│  File  Disk  Configure  Tools  Accessories  Windows  Tree  Help   │
│ ⊟A  ⊟B  ☐C  ☐H  ☐I                                                │
│ ┌──────ID = HWA 12345──────┐ ┌─────────C:\PCTOOLS\*.*──────────┐ │
│ │ ☐ dos                   ↑│ │☐ binstall exe ☐ dm       exe ☐ park     com↑│
│ │  ☐ dubldisk             ▓│ │☐ bootsafe exe ☐ drivemap exe ☐ pc-cache com│
│ │  ☐ menu                  │ │☐ cinstall exe ☐ edisk    exe ☐ pcconfig exe│
│ │   ☐ backups              │ │☐ commsml  exe ☐ ff       exe ☐ pcform   exe│
│ │  ☐ old_dos.1             │ │☐ commute  exe ☐ fileattr exe ☐ pcformat exe│
│ │  ☐ org                   │ │☐ compress exe ☐ filechk  exe ☐ pcmenu   bat│
│ │  ☐ pctools              ▼│ │☐ cpav     exe ☐ filedate exe ☐ pcsecure exe│
│ │  1,544,192 Bytes Free  ▓ │ │☐ cpbackup exe ☐ filefix  exe ☐ pcshell  exe│
│ └──────────────────────────┘ │☐ cpbdir   exe ☐ format   bat ☐ pctools  bat│
│ ┌─ ─Main Menu────────────▲┐  │☐ cpsched  exe ☐ install  exe ☐ ramboost exe│
│ │ ▦ PC Tools             ↑│  │☐ cptask   com ☐ iscpstsr exe ☐ ramsetup exe│
│ │ ▦ Archive Utilities     │  │☐ da       bat ☐ itlfax   exe ☐ readme   exe│
│ │ ☐ Microsoft Word 5      │  │☐ datamon  exe ☐ kill     exe ▨ readme   txt│
│ │ ☐ Edit                  │  │☐ de       exe ☐ memory!  exe ☐ schedule exe│
│ │ ▦ Windows Applicati     │  │☐ desktop  exe ☐ mi       com ☐ si       exe│
│ │                        ▼│  │☐ diskfix  exe ☐ mirror   com ☐ swapdt   com│
│ │                        ▓ │  │▨ diskfix  rpt ☐ netmsg   exe ☐ swapsh   com▼│
│ └──────────────────────────┘ │     60 Listed =    3,560,659 Bytes        │
│                              └────────────────────────────────────────────┘
│ ▤Help  ▤AppSrch▤Exit  ▤New  ▤Edit  ▤Config ▤Cut  ▤Copy  ▤Paste ▤Menu │
└─────────────────────────────────────────────────────────────────┘
```

Fig. 3.2

The Menu, Tree, and File windows displayed together.

Understanding the Menu Window

Items listed in the Menu window are in two categories: program items and program groups. A *program item* starts a specific software application on your hard disk; a *program group* is a collection of program items or other program groups—essentially, a menu. A program group that contains one or more other program groups is called a *parent group*.

Program groups enable you to group your applications programs by category. For example, you may create a Word Processing group, a Database group, and a Spreadsheet group. By default, the initial list of program items and groups, which you see when you first display the Menu window, are in the Main program group. The items on your computer that actually appear in the Main group depend on which applications programs are loaded on your computer when you run the PC Tools installation program (see Appendix A, "Installing and Configuring PC Tools"). The Main group probably includes another program group named PC Tools, which in turn includes program items and other program groups that run the various PC Tools programs.

Program groups and program items have two different icons to help you distinguish between them. The following icon appears to the left of program item names:

The following icon appears to the left of program group names:

Selecting a program item starts the selected program. Selecting a program group displays another menu that, in turn, displays a list of program items or program groups. The name of the parent group is listed as the first item on the menu with two dots to the left. This parallels DOS's representation of the parent directory with the two dot symbol.

When the display is Menu only, the second and subsequent group menus overlap the Main group's menu in a *cascading* pattern, as shown in figure 3.3. If the Menu window is displayed with other Desktop windows, selecting another program group causes the new group's menu to replace the preceding group's menu on-screen.

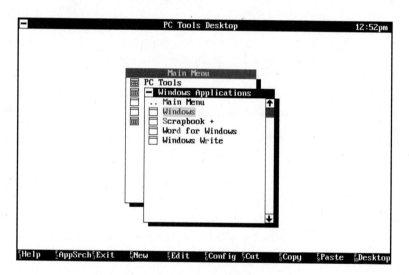

Fig. 3.3

A Windows
Applications
program group.

With the Menu window active, make selections by using any of the following three methods:

■ Move the mouse pointer to an option name (not the icon) and double-click the left button.

■ Desktop highlights one letter in each menu option. Press the key that corresponds to the highlighted letter in the name of the menu option you want to select. To select **A**rchive Utilities, for example, press A.

■ Press the up- or down-arrow key to move the highlighted menu selection bar to your choice, and press Enter.

To return to a parent group, such as Main Menu, select the parent group's name from the menu or press Esc.

When Desktop runs another program, Desktop initially blanks the screen and stores the contents of memory (RAM) to a file on the disk. Desktop then runs the specified application program. When you quit from this program, the cursor automatically returns to the Desktop screen.

Launching Programs from the Menu Window

Some programs listed in the Menu window are configured so that a data file opens with the program—a process often called *launching* the file. (**Note:** You cannot launch files with the display set to Menu window only. The File window must be showing so you can select the desired file.) You can launch files in any of three ways. The first two methods require the Menu and File windows to be open, as shown in figure 3.2. With the third method, the Menu window can be on or off.

To launch a program and file, first move the highlighted bar in the File window to the file you want to launch; then with the file highlighted, make the Menu window the current window and select the appropriate program from the Menu window list.

In Version 8.0, you can also use drag-and-drop if you configured the program item to accept dropped files (see the section "Adding Advanced Program Item Information" later in this chapter). Display the program item in the Menu window to be executed; then click and drag the file to the program item in the Menu window. If the program can operate on a group of files, as CP Backup can, you can select the group and drag it to the item.

When you begin dragging, Desktop displays the Can't Drop Here banner. When you move the pointer to a launchable Menu window item, the legend changes to Execute Program. (Compare this process to dragging the files into the Tree window, where Desktop assumes you want to copy them and changes the banner to Copy n Files.) When you release the mouse button, the menu item program is run with the selected file(s) loaded.

Alternatively—and even if the Menu window isn't showing—you can highlight the file you want to launch and press Ctrl+Enter, double-click, or select Open from the File menu. Desktop runs the associated program and opens the file. (Data file association is explained in detail later in this chapter in the section "Adding Advanced Program Item Information.")

To run programs from the Menu window *without* launching files, use the Menu window only display (press F10). Otherwise, if you select a program item with the Menu window and file window displayed, Desktop tries to open whatever file is highlighted in the File window. The message `Application filespecs do not match` appears. Select **I**gnore to run the program without loading the file. If you meant to open that file, select **R**un.

T I P

Changing the Configuration of the Menu Window

Desktop provides several configuration options to enhance the use of the Menu window as a stand-alone menuing system. For Menu window only mode, you can display a menu description panel. If you are setting the Menu window up as a menuing system for others and want to prevent their access to Desktop, you can disable the use of the F10 key from the Menu window only display.

To modify the Menu window configuration, make the Menu window current and press F6 (Config). Desktop displays the Menu Options Configuration dialog box, which contains the following options:

- *Disable F10 Switch to PC Tools Desktop* works when the display is set to Menu window only, and keeps a user from toggling to Desktop. When you choose this option, the Menu window functions as a menu system for inexperienced users, without letting them use any other PC Tools features.

- *Require a Path for Each Program Item* stipulates that path information must be included in the command used to run a menu item application.

- *Password Protect Configuration* sets a password for access to this dialog box and for editing or removing any program groups or items. If you set a password, you must use it the next time you want to change the menu configuration.

- *Display Item Information Panels* works when the display is set to Menu window only, and displays a description window showing the description of the highlighted menu item.

After you select the items you want to change and specify a password if desired, choose OK to save the new configuration.

Building a Menu Window System

You can build your Menu window system automatically, manually, or with a combination of the two. The easiest way to get started is to have PC Tools do an application search that scans your computer's hard disk or disks looking for popular applications programs that it "recognizes" and automatically places on menus. The following paragraphs describe this method. The manual method for adding groups and items or changing how they work is described in the sections "Adding and Editing Program Groups" and "Adding and Editing Program Items" later in this chapter. To add menus from Direct Access Version 5, see the section, "Importing Direct Access Menus" later in this chapter.

When you installed PC Tools, you were given the opportunity to search for applications. If you chose not to search during installation, Desktop prompts you to perform the search the first time you run Desktop. Choose **OK** to perform the search; choose **C**ancel if you decide not to search for applications.

If you are performing the first search or have added applications and want to perform a new search, you can execute the search without leaving Desktop. With the Menu window active, select **F**ile for the special File menu of Menu window commands. Select Application **S**earch. If this is the first search, applications are organized in program groups as described later in this section. If you have done a previous search, a new program group, **N**ew Applications, is added to the bottom of the Main Menu list. The search recognizes the more than 70 popular programs in the following list. You can reorganize items in the group following the steps described in "Changing an Item's Position or Program Group" later in this chapter.

Desktop searches your system files for programs it inherently recognizes, as shown in figure 3.4, and creates a program item/group for them. (If the item contains multiple programs, Desktop creates a program group for it.)

The programs Desktop recognizes are listed in the following:

Agenda	dBASE IV
Applause II	dBXL
Borland C++	DisplayWrite 4
Clipper	Epsilon
CompuServe Information	Excel
Manager (CIM)	FoxBase+
Copy II PC	Framework
dBASE III PLUS	Freelance Plus

Generic CADD
Grammatik III
Graphwriter II
Harvard Graphics
LetterPerfect
LHZ
Lotus 1-2-3 (Releases 1A,
    2.x, and 3)
Managing Your Money
Manuscript
Microsoft C
Microsoft Windows
Microsoft Word (4.0, 5.0,
    and 5.5)
Microsoft Works
Money Counts
Mosaic Twin
MultiMate
Multiplan
OnTarget
Option Board
PageMaker for Windows
PageMaker 3
PAK
Paradox 3
PFS: First Choice
PFS: First Publisher
PKlite
PKUnzip
PKxarc
PKZip
Power Point

PROCOMM
Professional File
Professional Write
Project for Windows
Q Edit
Q&A
Qmodem
Quattro
Quattro Pro
QuickBASIC
QuickC
Quicken
R:BASE
Reflex (1.0 and 2.0)
RightWriter
SuperCalc 5
Symphony
TaxCut
Turbo C
Turbo C++
Turbo Pascal
TurboTax
Ventura Publisher
VP Planner
Windows Write
WordPerfect
Words and Figures
WordStar
WordStar 2000
XyWrite 3+
Zoo

If the search finds any of these programs on your computer's disks, PC
Tools automatically adds the programs to the Menu window menus,
creating a *program item* for each application it recognizes. Where possible, the initial search places the application in one of the following 13
groups:

Archive utilities
Databases
Desktop publishing
Integrated software
PC Tools
Personal finance
Personal-information managers

Presentation graphics
Programming tools
Spreadsheets
Telecommunications
Window applications
Word processing

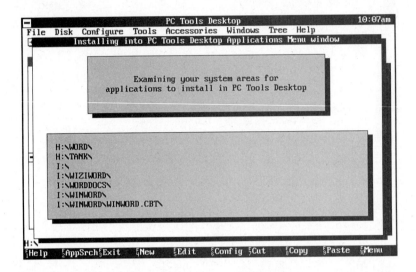

Fig. 3.4

Desktop performing an initial application search.

When the search finds more than one applications program from the same group, it creates in the Desktop Menu window a separate menu for the group. Each menu is called a *program group*. A Windows Applications group might contain, for example, such program items as Windows, Scrapbook, Word for Windows, and Windows Write (refer to fig. 3.3).

Program groups can contain program items, other program groups, or both. The initial Menu window displays the title Main Menu in its title bar (refer to fig. 3.1). The items and groups listed in this menu constitute the *Main program group*. All other program groups are subordinate to the Main program group.

The PC Tools program group itself contains six program items and the following six program groups (see fig. 3.5):

Recovery Tools

System Tools

File Tools

Disk Tools

Security Tools

Setup Tools

A program group that contains other program groups is a *parent group*. Table 3.1 lists the PC Tools utilities in the PC Tools group and in each of the six subordinate groups. (*Note:* Specifics may vary on your system, depending on the PC Tools programs you installed.)

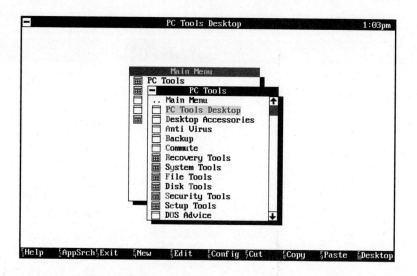

Fig. 3.5

The PC Tools program group.

Table 3.1 Program Groups Created by the Application Search

Groups	Items
PC Tools	PC Tools Desktop
	Desktop Accessories
	AntiVirus
	CP Backup
	Commute
	DOS Advice
Recovery Tools	DiskFix
	File Fix
	EDisk
	Undelete
	Unformat
System Tools	Program Scheduler
	System Information
	NetMessage
File Tools	FileFind
	View

continues

Table 3.1 Continued	
Groups	**Items**
Disk Tools	Directory Maintenance
	PC Format
	Compress
	DiskEdit
	DriveMap
Security Tools	PC Secure
	Data Monitor
	Wipe
Setup Tools	Install
	PC Config

Adding and Editing Program Groups

By creating your own program groups within the Main program group, you can easily organize your computer programs according to your personal work habits. You may divide your programs by software type, for instance, creating a word processing group, a database group, a spreadsheet group, and a graphics group, just as PC Tools application search does by default. Or you may decide to split programs into groups by subject matter, establishing a Productivity group, a Personal Management group, and a Games group.

When the Menu window is the current window in Desktop, the File menu switches to menu-maintenance commands (see fig. 3.6), and the message bar switches to menu-maintenance function keys. Table 3.2 lists the function keys and their uses. You can use these keys to add and edit program groups and program items. The discussions that follow explain how to use each of these commands.

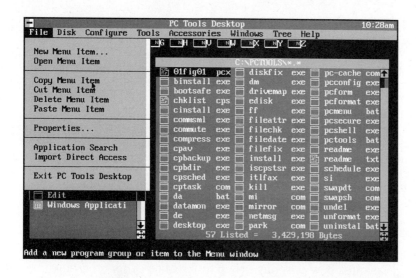

Fig. 3.6

The File menu
with the Menu
window active.

Table 3.2 Menu Window Function Key Commands

Key	Name	Function
F1	Help	Displays the context-sensitive Help facility
F2	AppSrch	Brings up the Search for Applications dialog box, which you use add programs to the Menu window
F3	Exit	Returns to the Desktop screen
F4	New	Adds a new program item or group to the menu
F5	Edit	Edits the highlighted program item or program group
F6	Config	Brings up the Menu Configuration options to customize Menu window appearance and operation
F7	Cut	Removes an item or group from the menu
F8	Copy	Copies an item or group
F9	Paste	Inserts on the current menu an item or group that has been cut or copied
F10	Desktop	Returns to Desktop screen (available from display of the Menu window only)
F10	Menu	Displays the Menu window only (available from Desktop)

NOTE With the display set to Menu window only, you must use the function keys; no pull-down menus are available.

Creating a New Group

When you create a new Program group, you are creating a file folder that will contain the actual Menu items to be executed. Program groups can be nested inside of other groups, or they can be placed directly in the main menu of the Menu window. The organization is up to you.

To add a new program group, follow these steps:

1. Display the Menu window by pressing F10.

2. Select the program group to which the new group will be added. To add a new program group to the Main program group, for example, press Esc until the Main group's menu is the current menu. When you want to add a program group to another program group, use the mouse or cursor-movement keys to make that menu group active.

3. When the program group you want is displayed, press F4 (New). Desktop displays the New Menu Item dialog box, which contains two option buttons: Group and Item (see fig. 3.7).

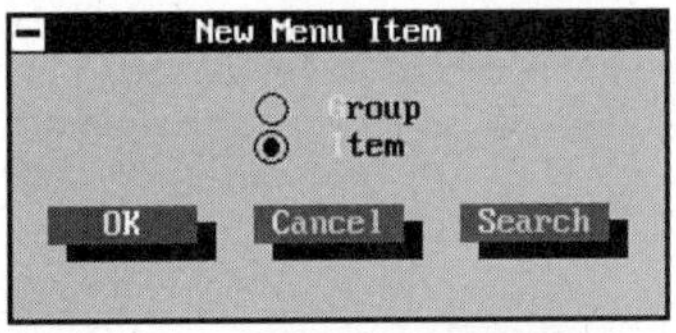

Fig. 3.7

The New Menu Item dialog box.

4. Select the **Group** option button, and then select the **OK** command button. The Program Group Information dialog box appears (see fig. 3.8).

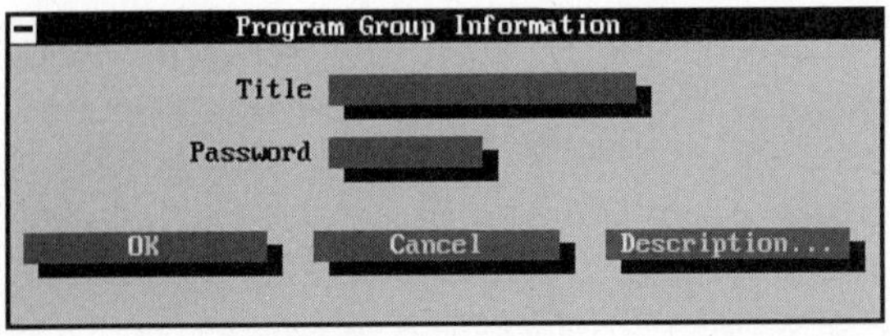

Fig. 3.8

The Program Group Information dialog box.

This dialog box contains two text boxes: Title and Password. You must type an entry in the Title text box, but you may leave the Password text box blank. All entries in the Program Group Information dialog box are referred to collectively as the program group's *properties*.

5. In the Title text box, type a program group title. The title, which can contain up to 20 characters including spaces, is the name, or menu option, that appears in the Menu window menu when the parent program group is displayed.

When you type the name, insert a caret (^) before the letter you want Desktop to highlight. This letter is the hotkey you use to select this new program group item from the current program group menu. If you duplicate the same hotkey for two programs in the same menu group, Desktop selects the first item in the menu when you press this hotkey.

If, for example, you are creating a program group for your database applications, you might type ^**Database Programs** in the Title text box. Later you can select this program group from the Menu window menu by pressing D.

The title you type in the Program Group Information dialog box appears not only in the Menu window menu but also in the Menu window title bar when the program group is selected.

6. After you type a title, you optionally type a password in the Password text box. This password can be as long as 10 characters, including spaces.

> **WARNING:** Using a password to limit access to a Desktop program group provides only minimal security. Any user with access to your computer can easily bypass Desktop and start programs from the DOS prompt. Passwords are useful for limiting access to young children.

7. Choose the **OK** command button to accept the entries you have made in the Title and Password text boxes and to return to the Menu window. Select **C**ancel to abandon the Title and Password entries and return to the Menu window without adding the new group. (See the following section to learn the purpose of the Description command button.)

After you select **OK**, Desktop adds the new program group item to the current program group. If you select the new program group item now, Desktop opens a Menu window menu so that you can add program items. The only item listed in the menu is the name of the parent group.

Adding a Description to a Program Group

When you add a new program group to a Menu window menu, Desktop gives you the opportunity to add a text description, which can be displayed in a description box next to the menu whenever the group's menu item is highlighted in the Menu window. The automatic application search adds such a description for each program item and program group it adds to the Menu window menus.

Descriptions help identify menus as you highlight through the items in the Menu window, but you can view descriptions only when the display is set to the Menu window only. To turn on the descriptions, press F6 to access the Menu Configuration Options dialog box. Select Display Item Information, and then choose **OK**. Desktop opens the *description window* to the right of the menu (see fig. 3.9).

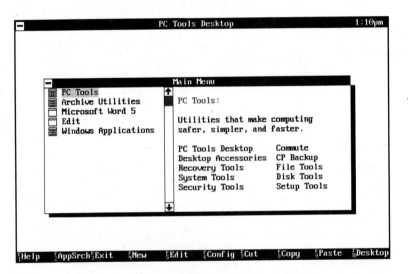

Fig. 3.9

The description window.

To add a description, first display the Program Group Information dialog box, as discussed in the preceding section, and then select the **D**escription command button. Desktop temporarily suspends itself and opens a File Editor window. Type the desired description in the window.

If, for example, you create a Database Programs group that includes dBASE IV and Paradox 3.0, the following description might be appropriate:

```
Database Programs:

Programs that help you compile and manage large amounts
of information.

    dBASE IV

    Paradox 3.0
```

After you type the description, press Esc (Exit), F3 (Exit), or Alt+F4
(Close). Alternatively, click the close box. Desktop saves the description and returns to the Menu window. Figure 3.10 shows the Main
program group with the new Database Programs group item and its
description.

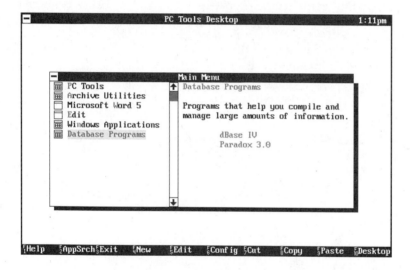

Descriptive text is normally black, but you can emphasize special text
with color by entering one of the following codes before the text. After
the emphasized text, enter the code for black to return the description
following the emphasized text to the normal nonemphasized color,
which in this case was black.

Code	Color
^I	Begin cyan text
^N	Begin black text
^B	Begin blue text

Many descriptions supplied by the application search use all three colors.

Modifying Program Group Properties

After you create a program group, you can change its name, command parameters, password protection, description, and other characteristics—its *properties*—through the File menu or the F5 (Edit) function-key command.

To modify program group properties, first select the Menu window. If the group that contains the properties you want to change is not included in the Main group, select the program group that includes the target group. Use the mouse or cursor-movement keys to move the selection bar to the name of the program group that contains the properties you want to modify.

Press F5 (Edit) or, if the display is not set to Menu window only, press F5 or display the File menu, and then select **P**roperties. Desktop displays the Program Group Information dialog box (refer to fig. 3.8).

Make any desired changes to the title, password, and description; then select the **O**K command button. Select **C**ancel to return to the Menu window without changing any of the program group's properties. See "Adding Advanced Program Item Information" later in this chapter for information on using advanced options such as those enabling file launching and drag-and-drop program execution.

Deleting a Program Group

If you reorganize menus or remove applications, you can remove any obsolete program groups. Display the Menu window that contains the program group you want to delete. Move the selection cursor to the name of the group to be deleted. Press F7 (Cut). If the display is not set to Menu window only, press F7 or select the File menu, and select **D**elete Menu Item. (*Note:* In Version 8.0, the Delete function key has been removed; therefore, you must use Cut.) If you used the Delete Menu Item command, Desktop displays the Delete an Item dialog box. Select the **D**elete command button to remove the program group; select **C**ancel to return to the Menu window menu without deleting the program group item.

Adding and Editing Program Items

Before you can run an applications program from the Menu window, the program must be added to a program group. Although the application search recognizes and automatically installs many of the most popular programs, the following situations can occur:

■ You install a program that the search does not recognize, or you install a program after doing a search.

■ The search installs a program in a manner that does not match your requirements.

■ The search installs an option you never plan to use.

Desktop provides ways, therefore, to add a program manually to the Menu window and to change or delete an item or group on the Menu window.

Adding a program item is similar to adding a program group. When you want to add a new program item to a particular group, make the Menu window current and display the program group to which the new program item will be added. To add a new program item to the Database Programs group, for example, press Esc until the title area of the Menu window displays the title Main Menu. Then use the mouse or cursor-movement keys to select Database Programs.

After the program group is selected, press F4 (New) or, if the display is not set to Menu window only, press F4 or select the File menu, and then choose New Menu Item. Desktop displays the New Menu Item dialog box (refer to fig. 3.7).

Select the Item option button, and then select the OK command button. The Program Item Information dialog box appears (see fig. 3.11). The dialog box contains four text boxes: Program Title, Commands, Startup Directory, and Password. You must type an entry in every Program Title and Command text box, but entries in the Startup Directory and Password text boxes are optional. All entries in the Program Item Information dialog box are referred to collectively as the program item's properties.

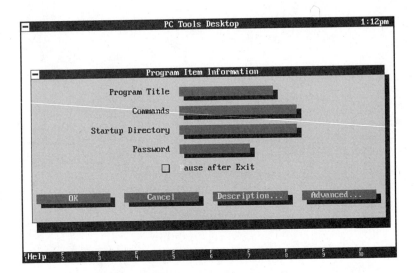

Fig. 3.11

The Program Item
Information
dialog box.

Specifying a Program Title

In the Title text box, type a program title consisting of up to 20 characters, including spaces. The title you enter appears as the menu option
in the Menu window when the parent program group is displayed.
When you type the name, insert a caret (^) before the letter you want
Desktop to highlight as the hotkey.

If, for example, you are creating a program item to start the database
program Paradox 3.0, you might type **^Paradox 3.0** in the Program Title
text box. Later, you can select this program from the Menu window
menu by pressing P.

Specifying Program Commands

Type the application program's start-up command in the Commands
text box. A start-up command can be as simple as the application
program's name. The start-up command for Paradox 3.0, for example,
is PARADOX.EXE.

Specifying a Start-up Directory and Password

Specify a start-up directory, if you choose, in the Startup Directory text box of the Program Item Information dialog box. The start-up directory is the name of the directory that should be current when Desktop issues the specified start-up command. The program does not have to reside in this directory if that information is specified in the Commands box or if the directory is in your path. (Some programs, however, must be started from their own directory.)

You can use the Startup Directory text box to specify the directory in which the files are stored. If, for example, your Paradox 3.0 data files are stored on your hard disk in the directory C:\DATABASE\PDOXDATA, include this directory's name in the Startup Directory text box.

After you type a start-up directory, you optionally can type a password in the Password text box. This password can contain up to 10 characters, including spaces.

> **WARNING:** Using a password in Desktop to limit access to a program provides only minimal security. Any user with access to your computer can easily bypass Desktop and start the program from the DOS prompt.

Indicating Command Parameters with Keywords

Many programs allow or require you to specify certain parameters on the DOS command line to control different aspects of the program's operation. Several PC Tools programs, for example, enable you to control how they operate through command-line parameters (see Appendix A, "Installing and Configuring PC Tools"). You can specify any desired parameters in the Commands text box, along with the start-up command.

If you are launching an application by selecting a file in the file list, the application may require path information for the selected file. Because the path may vary, Desktop provides a way to enter a general path variable (represented as <Path>) rather than placing a never-changing path in the command line. Desktop's *keywords* (replaceable command line parameters Desktop feeds to the executing program) can be used to insert several variables, such as path or drive, in the Commands text box.

T I P   If the DOS command line is on, click a Menu window program item once, and its command appears at the DOS prompt. This action can help you understand, by example, how to enter commands and use keywords. With the DOS command line active, you can modify the command to make a one-time change before running the program.

To insert a keyword, position the cursor in the text box at the location where you want the keyword to be inserted, and press F8 (Keyword). Desktop displays the Keyword List dialog box (see fig. 3.12).

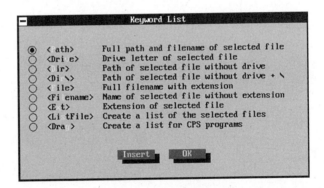

Fig. 3.12

The Keyword List dialog box.

Each word in the keyword list is a special replaceable parameter used by Desktop to pass information to the applications program. Table 3.3 lists the meaning of each code.

Table 3.3 Program Information Keyword List		
Keyword	**Availability**	**Meaning**
<Path>	2,3,5,7	Full path and file name of selected file
<Drive>	2,3,5,7	Drive letter of selected file
<Dir>	2,3,5,7	Path of selected file without drive

Keyword	Availability	Meaning
<Dir\>	2,3,5,7	Path of selected file without drive but with the backslash (\)
<File>	2,3,5,7	File name of selected file with extension
<Filename>	2,3,5,7	File name of selected file without extension
<Ext>	2,3,5,7	File name extension of selected file
<ListFile>	2,3,5,7	Create a file (in PCTOOLS\DATA) listing all selected files so that the application can operate on the group (use only with an application that can operate on a group of files)
<Drag>	2,3,5,7	The drag and drop counterpart of <ListFile>; also set the Accept **D**ropped Files option in the Advanced Program Item Information dialog box
<NL>	5	Start the next part of the user prompt on a new line
<DelayN>	7	Delay *N* seconds
<Typein>	7	Accept a variable-length user input (terminated by Enter) before executing the command

To insert a keyword into a text box, select the option button for the keyword and select the **I**nsert command button. (**Note:** Because the Keyword List dialog box stays open, you don't immediately see the keyword inserted.) To insert another keyword, select the keyword and again select **I**nsert. When all the needed keywords have been added, select the **O**K command button to return to the Program Item Information dialog box.

Suppose, for example, that you want your database program, Paradox 3.0, to run the Paradox Application Language (PAL) script contained in the current file (the file highlighted in the File window) at start-up. Add the keywords <Dir\> and <Filename> to the start-up command as follows:

    PARADOX.EXE <Dir\><Filename>

The numbers in the Availability column denote the text boxes in which you can use the keyword. Keyword lists are available in several text boxes (wherever you see F8 Keywrd in the message bar), but not all the lists are the same. The numbers in the Availability column of table 3.3

indicate in which text boxes each keyword is available. The number 2 in the column means that the keyword is available in the second text box—the Commands text box—in the Program Item Information dialog box. (*Note:* Text boxes 5, 6, and 7 are found in the Advanced Program Item Information dialog box, which is displayed when you select the Advanced command button.)

Adding Pause after Exit

The Pause after Exit check box in the Program Item Information dialog box determines whether the screen returns immediately to the Desktop screen when you leave an applications program that you started from the Menu window. By default, this check box is not checked, and Desktop returns immediately to the Desktop screen.

In some cases, however, the program you want to add to the Menu window displays information as the program terminates. You might not have an opportunity to read the information on-screen before it is replaced by the Desktop screen. Selecting the Pause after Exit check box in the Program Item Information dialog box pauses the screen after the applications program exits and displays the following message:

```
Press any key or a mouse button to re-enter Desktop
```

The CHKDSK.EXE program (a MS-DOS utility), for example, analyzes your hard disk and then displays a report. If you are adding CHKDSK.EXE to the Desktop Menu window, check the Pause after Exit dialog box in the Program Item Information dialog box to give you time to read the CHKDSK report.

Adding a Description to a Program Item

When you add a new program item to a Menu window, Desktop gives you the opportunity to add a text description. With the display set to Menu window only, this description can be displayed whenever the item is highlighted in the Menu window. The application search adds such a description for every program item and program group it adds to the Menu window. To view the description, see the "Changing the Configuration of the Menu Window" section earlier in this chapter.

The steps required to add a description to a program item are the same as those required to add a description to a program group. Refer to the "Adding a Description to a Program Group" section earlier in this chapter for more information.

Adding Advanced Program Item Information

In addition to the program title, start-up commands, start-up directory, and password, Desktop provides 10 more options for customizing the way it executes applications programs from the Menu window. Advanced options include those needed to set up file associations, to launch a program with a file, and to enable drag-and-drop for program execution.

When you are adding the program item, select the Advanced command button from the Program Item Information dialog box to display the Advanced Program Item Information dialog box (see fig. 3.13). The sections that follow describe the options available in the Advanced Program Item Information dialog box.

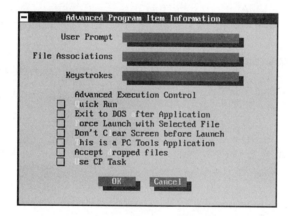

Fig. 3.13

The Advanced Program Item Information dialog box.

Adding a User Prompt

With the user prompt text box you can supply a prompt that appears before the application runs. A prompt is used to inform, instruct, or provide options to the user who must take some action before the program runs. Some programs, for example, do not run until you insert a *key* disk. Other programs need to make use of some peripheral device such as a printer or external tape-backup system.

To add your own prompt, type up to 69 characters in the User Prompt text box. You can use keywords—for example, <File> to insert the name of the selected file. Later, when you select this Menu window item from a menu, Desktop blanks the screen and displays your message and Press any key to continue. Desktop doesn't run the applications program until the user presses a key.

Specifying File Associations

Use the File Associations text box to enter a list of file specifications (wildcards allowed) that identify potential data files for the application. The conventional way to perform this task is to specify file extensions of a certain type. You can use the following entry in the File Associations text box for the Paradox 3.0 program item:

   *.SC

This file specification tells Desktop that all files having the file name extension SC are associated with the Paradox 3.0 program item. When you use any automatic launching method, such as the **O**pen command with a selected file, and the file has the SC extension, Desktop automatically starts Paradox.

FROM HERE...

For Related Information

▶▶ "Running Programs and Launching Files," p.137.

Adding Keystrokes

The Keystrokes text box is a "mini macro editor" with which you can make Desktop feed particular keystrokes into the program that has just been executed. This capability is handy if you constantly perform the same keystrokes once inside the program. After you open your word processor, for example, you may always open a data file or select a constant option. Using the Keystrokes text box, you can enter the keystrokes to perform these actions so that when Desktop executes your word processor from the Menu window, it also feeds the keystrokes to open a file or select a particular option for you.

For a displayable keyboard character, just type the character. For a nondisplayable character, such as Enter, a function key, or a cursor-movement key, first press F7 (LitKey), and then press the keystroke you want included in the macro. Desktop inserts a special code that stands for the keystroke. (The keystroke codes used in this text box are listed also in Chapter 21, "Automating Your PC Using PC Tools Macros.")

NOTE To use drag-and-drop to launch an application, include the <Path> keyword in the Keystrokes text box so that you can use Desktop to select a file to be handled by a program. If you use this procedure, Desktop feeds this selected file to the executed program. The program you are assigning the <Path> keyword to must be able to accept a command line file. The DOS Edit program does this very well. By typing EDIT filename.ext, the filename.ext file opens automatically.

You can use the F8 (Keywrd) function-key command to insert any of the keywords listed in table 3.3, with the exception of <NL>. (The keyword <NL>, which means New Line, can only be inserted in the User Prompt box. The <NL> code places whatever follows it on the next line down.)

The keyword <DelayN> can be used in the Keystrokes text box only. This keyword causes the macro to delay a set number of seconds. You must replace the letter N with a number in the format *nn.n* where each *n* is a positive integer and the entire number denotes a delay in seconds. Figure 3.14, for example, shows the entry for 1-2-3 that is added automatically by the application search. The entry in the Keystrokes text box includes the keyword <Delay2>. When you select **Lotus 1-2-3** from the Menu window menu, Desktop loads 1-2-3 and then pauses two seconds before executing the keystrokes stored in the Keystrokes text box. If the keyword were <Delay3.5>, the delay would be 3 1/2 seconds.

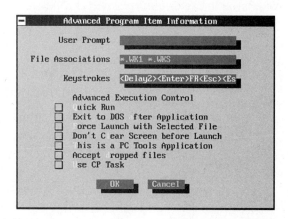

Fig. 3.14

The Advanced Program Item Information dialog box filled out for invoking Lotus 1-2-3.

The keyword <Typein> also is unique to the Keystrokes text box. This keyword causes the keystroke macro to stop executing until you press Enter. During the pause, you can type in any characters. After you press Enter, the keystrokes continue. For example, you might want the macro to pause while you type a file name and then continue and complete the macro keystrokes.

Selecting Advanced Execution Control

The Advanced Program Item Information dialog box lists seven additional check boxes, referred to collectively as the Advanced Execution Control options. By default, these features are not selected. Use the keyboard or mouse to mark the check box for each of the following options you want to include for the program item:

- *Quick Run.* Choose this option if you want Desktop to run the program without first freeing up all available memory. Invoking this option causes the program to load faster. Use this option only with small programs; otherwise, sufficient RAM may not exist for the program to load or run.

- *Exit to DOS after Application.* Choose this option to cause Desktop to exit to DOS rather than return to Desktop after you quit the application.

- *Force Launch with Selected File.* Choose this option to cause the current file name (or first selected file name) to be included as a command-line parameter. This option has the same effect as the keyword <Path> in the Commands text box in the Program Item Information dialog box. Leave this option off if the application does not accept a command-line file name at start-up.

- *Don't Clear Screen before Launch.* By default, Desktop clears the screen before running another program. Choose this option to prevent Desktop from clearing the Desktop screen before running the applications program. Check this option only if you lose characters on-screen when you start the other program.

- *This Is a PC Tools Application.* Choose this option only if the program is another PC Tools program. This option ensures fastest access to other PC Tools programs, without screen flicker.

- *Accept Dropped Files.* Choose this option to launch the application with drag-and-drop. The application must be able to accept a file name at start-up, and you must include the <Path> keyword in the Keystrokes text box so that it knows where to find the file or files. For applications that can operate on a group of files, also include the keyword <Drag> in the Commands text box.

■ *Use CP Task.* Choose this option if you are using the Task Switcher and want to run the application as one of the tasks. For this task to work, Task Switcher must be memory-resident, and Desktop must be started using the /S parameter. See the section "Using the Task Switcher" later in this chapter for more information on that feature.

After making any desired selections on the Advanced Program Item Information dialog box, select the **OK** command button to return to the Program Item Information dialog box. Select the **OK** command button in the Program Item Information dialog box to save the new program item and return to the Menu window.

Editing a Program Item

To edit a program item in the Menu window, highlight the item and press F5 (Edit). Desktop displays the Program Item Information dialog box. Make the desired changes and select the **OK** command button.

Deleting a Program Item

When you want to delete an entry, display the Menu window and highlight the item you want to remove. Press F7 (Cut) or, if the display is not set to Menu window only, press F7 or choose File to display the File menu, and select **Delete Menu Item**. (In Version 8.0, because the Delete function key has been removed, you must use Cut.) If you use the Delete Menu Item command, Desktop displays the Delete an Item dialog box. Select the **Delete** command button to complete the deletion operation, or select **Cancel** to abort the operation without deleting the item.

Changing an Item's Position or Program Group

Reorganizing items within and between program groups is as easy as cutting and pasting. Placing your most frequently used groups near the top of the group listing is convenient; you can find these groups more quickly. You can place groups and program items in any order you want. If the display is set to Menu window only, you can use the function keys to reorganize items. If the Desktop screen is displayed, you can also use the File menu commands. To move a group or program item from one place to another in the menu list, follow these steps:

1. Move the highlight to the item to be moved.

2. Press F7 (Cut) or select File and then Cut Menu Item. Desktop removes the item from the screen and places it in a buffer or "scratch pad" in the computer's memory.

3. Use the cursor-movement keys to move the highlight to the new location.

4. Press F9 (Paste) or select File and then Paste Menu Item. (The item is pasted just above the item you highlighted.)

To move an item to another program group, first make that group's menu active, and then highlight the desired location and paste. Desktop inserts the item at the new location. To place an item on more than one menu, use F8 (Copy) or select File and then Copy Menu Item; then paste. You can repeat these steps as often as necessary to produce the order you want for your groups.

> **CAUTION:** After using Cut, be sure that you do not select Copy instead of Paste. Doing so copies the currect selection to the buffer, overwriting the text you just cut.

Saving the Changes to the Menu Window

Any change on the Menu window is effective immediately but only for the duration of the current Desktop session. To make the changes permanent, you must save the changes to the Desktop configuration file. From the Desktop horizontal menu bar, select Configure, and then select Save Configuration. Alternatively, close the Desktop and make sure to check the Save Configuration check box in the Close Desktop dialog box.

Importing Direct Access Menus

If you have been using Direct Access Version 5 as a menuing system, Desktop can automatically convert those menus into the Desktop Menu window format, either at installation or later. Import Direct Access menus into the Desktop Menu window by doing the following:

1. Display the Menu window on the main Desktop screen with the File and Tree windows. Select the **Window** menu, and then toggle the **Menu** Window on. The Menu window appears in the lower left corner of the screen.

2. Make the Menu window active by tabbing to it or clicking the Menu window title bar.

   When the Menu window is active, the File menu changes to reflect file commands associated with the Menu window.

3. Pull down the **File** menu and select **Import Direct Access**.

   You are prompted to save your current configuration. You can save the current Menu window set, ignore the save warning and proceed with the Import Direct Access command, or cancel the operation.

4. Select **Save** or **Ignore** to continue the search; then select **OK** to confirm the search. (Select **Cancel** to return to the Menu window.)

   You hard drive is searched for any Direct Access menu. If found, these files are imported into your Desktop menu structure.

When the search is complete, Desktop adds the Imports program group to the Menu window. This group includes the Direct Access main menu and submenus, which you can reorganize as you want (refer to the section "Changing an Item's Position or Program Group" earlier in this chapter). (***Note:*** The conversion adds the menus to the Menu window configuration but does not alter the original Direct Access files.)

NOTE Desktop's Menu window system does not include a usage log. If you use the Direct Access log to track your time on various projects or programs, you may not want to change to Desktop's menus and lose that feature.

Using the Task Switcher

The Task Switcher makes possible working with up to eight programs simultaneously, switching between them without putting away any open files, or shutting down an application. Like MS-Windows (but with no frills), the Task Switcher simulates multitasking in the single-task DOS environment. The difference is that the application you leave is suspended until you return to it.

After the Task Switcher is loaded into memory, you access it the first time you want to run a program as a switchable task. Then you can leave the program without closing it by pressing Alt+Esc to return to the Task Switcher. To switch to the next task that is running, press Alt+Tab.

NOTE   You cannot switch out of PC Tools Compress, CP Backup, Unformat, or DiskFix because these programs operate at a disk-intensive level.

Task Switcher can be run at start up or as you need it from DOS. If you expect to make only occasional use of Task Switcher, you can run it as needed by typing **cptask** from DOS instead of running the Task Switcher at start-up.

NOTE   Task Switcher is able to put a task on hold and capture all information (the system image) about that task in a swap file. Depending on how you configure it, the swap file may be maintained on the hard disk or in extended or expanded memory. On disk, each task gets its own swap file, CPTASK.IM*, kept in the \PCTOOLS\SYSTEM directory. The required memory depends not only on the size of each application program but also on the size of any open data files. Expect to use about 600K of disk space or memory per active application.

Configuring Task Switcher To Run at Startup

If you did not select the Task Switcher as a Startup Program when you installed and configured PC Tools and want to use the Task Switcher consistently, select **C**onfigure from the horizontal menu bar; then from the Configure pull-down menu, select Startup Programs. PC Config (the configuration program) presents a list of PC Tools programs that can be run automatically each time you turn on your computer. Select Task Switcher by placing a check mark next to it in the list. PC Config displays a dialog box, shown in figure 3.15, in which you can review and modify the following aspects of Task Switcher:

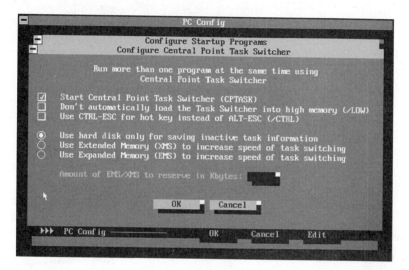

Fig. 3.15

The PC Config dialog box used to review and modify Task Switcher.

■ *Start Central Point Task Switcher* must be checked for the Task Switcher to be loaded into memory (leave this box checked).

■ *Don't Automatically Load the Task Switcher into High Memory (LOW)* loads the Task Switcher program itself into conventional memory regardless of any high memory on your system.

■ *Use CTRL+ESC for Hot Key instead of ALT+ESC (/CTRL)* changes the hot key used to pop up Task Switcher. If Alt+Esc is used by one of the applications you want to run with Task Switcher, you can check this box to use Ctrl+Esc instead.

If you need to rule out both key combinations, you can select a combination of Alt and any function key by running Task Switcher with a special parameter. You must run CPTASK from the DOS prompt or modify the CPTASK line in your AUTOEXEC.BAT file (use the Desktop's Change command on the File menu). After typing **cptask**, type a space and the parameter /**Fn**, where *n* is the number of the function key you want to use. For example, the command CPTASK /F2 activates the Task Switcher by pressing Alt+F2.

T I P

The option buttons determine where Task Switcher stores its *swap files*—the information it captures about a task when you switch to another task. By default, the hard disk is used, but choosing extended or expanded memory can speed up multitasking. If you select one of these options, you must specify the amount of memory, at least 800K.

Choose **OK** to save the new configuration. PC Config informs you that the new configuration information will be added to your AUTOEXEC.BAT and CONFIG.SYS files. Choose **OK** to update the files, putting the command line, CPTASK, in your AUTOEXEC.BAT file. Finally, PC Config tells you that you must reboot the computer for the changes to take effect. Select **R**eboot to put the Task Switcher into memory now; choose E**x**it to wait until the next time you reboot the computer.

When the Task Switcher loads into memory, it displays a message reporting the amount of free memory, any extended or expanded memory used, and the current hotkey.

NOTE When CPTASK is in memory, you can remove it (and all tasks in progress) by typing **cptask /u** at the DOS prompt or pressing Alt+Esc to access the Task Switcher menu and then choosing Unload. The Task Switcher asks you for confirmation. Select **U**nload to proceed. Generally, unload the Task Switcher only after exiting from other tasks individually. This step ensures that any data in use is saved properly.

Running Applications with Task Switching

If you are using the Menu window to run applications, you can easily begin automatic task switching through your menu system. If you are not running applications with the Menu window, you can use the Task Switcher any time you are about to run an application, from the DOS prompt or from another application. In either case, the Task Switcher must be memory-resident.

To start an application with task switching from the Menu window, first do the following:

1. Start Desktop with the /RS parameter by typing **pctools /rs** at the DOS prompt and pressing Enter or by including the command in your AUTOEXEC.BAT file.

2. Edit the menu item (refer to "Adding and Editing a Program Item" earlier in this chapter for additional information). In the Advanced Program Item Information dialog box, if **Use CP Task** is not checked, select it and **OK** twice to save the new setting. (***Note:*** The application search may have already set this as the default.)

Now, running the application from the Menu window engages task switching. You can run additional applications by returning to the Menu window by pressing Alt+Tab, or you can start additional applications from the Task Switcher window.

To start an application from the DOS prompt or another application, press the hotkey Alt+Esc (if you changed the hotkey, press the new hotkey instead) to access the window shown in figure 3.16.

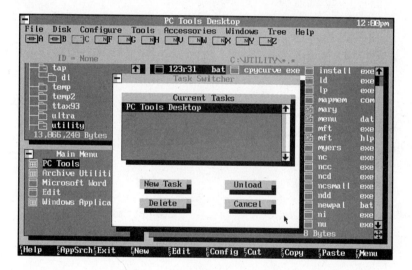

Fig. 3.16

The Task Switcher window.

The window lists tasks that are currently running. If you started from the DOS prompt, the window lists DOS prompt. If you started from an application, the window lists the application name. To start the new application, select **New Task**. The Enter Task to Run dialog box appears (see fig. 3.17).

Fig. 3.17

Task Switcher's Enter Task to Run dialog box.

In the text box, type the command needed to run the program (you do not need to type an extension). Include path information if the program's directory is not in your AUTOEXEC.BAT path statement. As with many PC Tools file selection dialog boxes, you can select the **B**rowse button to find the desired directory and program file. If the program accepts command-line parameters, such as a file name, you can include them. For example, if WordStar is in the WS directory, to start the program with the file CH01.REV loaded, type the following:

C:\WS\WS CH01.REV

Each time you want to start another application without closing the current one, access the Task Switcher window and add the new task. When you have at least two tasks running, you can switch between them, as explained in the next section.

Switching between Tasks

You can press Alt+Tab to cycle through active tasks in the order in which they are listed in the Task Switcher window. Alternatively, you can select a task from the task list. Press the Task Switcher hotkey, Alt+Esc, to select from or add to the task list. To switch to another active task, highlight the task and press Enter. Alternatively, you can double-click the task.

NOTE   If not enough memory exists to create the necessary swap file, you cannot use the hotkey to get out of the application. Instead, Task Switcher beeps. In this case, you must quit the application in the conventional way.

T I P   Task Switcher stores a program in a temporary swap file when you switch from it to another program. Save all data files of an operating program before you switch to another program to protect your data in the event that something prevents you from returning to it. (Certain programs can cause Task Switcher to crash, and power outages do happen.)

Closing an Active Task

The safest way to close an active task is to exit the program by using the standard exit procedure. If you still want to delete a running program out of the Task Switcher, select the task from the list of current tasks, and select **D**elete. Task Switcher asks for confirmation. To confirm, select **D**elete again. Task Switcher closes the task.

> **CAUTION:** Deleting a running program is highly discouraged because swap files may not be deleted, taking up valuable hard drive space; unknown data files may not get saved; and the actual program file may become corrupted and unusable. The preferable option is to quit the program in the normal way.

Scheduling Programs with the Scheduler

The new Central Point Scheduler remedies one of the worst computer management headaches: remembering to routinely perform disk and file management tasks. The Scheduler is ideal for people who, working under tight deadlines or on multiple projects, often put off tedious file backup and disk maintenance chores for spare time that never comes.

With Version 8.0, to solve your computer housekeeping problems forever, you only need your good intentions and about 30 minutes—time you use to make a housekeeping plan and program the Scheduler to execute the plan. As in Version 7.1, you can schedule Commute sessions and, if you have a tape drive, unattended backups. With Version 8.0, you now can also schedule unattended virus checks, DiskFix sessions, or disk compression. In addition, the Scheduler works with any application, not just PC Tools programs.

Although scheduled events interrupt whatever program is running, Scheduler displays a 15-second advance warning box before running the scheduled event. If you're in the middle of a task, you can cancel the event; if not, you can let the schedule proceed. After an event is complete, the suspended program resumes.

NOTE   The Scheduler programs *events* (the running of any executable command that can be entered at the DOS prompt) to occur automatically. Any parameters a program accepts can be included (up to 64 characters). PC Tools includes other automatic-programming facilities with more specialized functions. In Desktop Accessories, Electronic Mail allows sending and receiving mail at specified times, and Fax Telecommunications allows sending a fax on schedule.

Configuring the Scheduler To Run at Startup

Although you can program the Scheduler without it running, scheduled events will not take place unless the Scheduler is memory-resident. If you did not select the Scheduler as a Startup Program when you installed and configured PC Tools and you want it installed each time you turn on your computer, do the following:

1. Select **C**onfigure; then from the Configure menu, select Startup Pr**o**grams.

    PC Config (the configuration program) presents a list of PC Tools programs that can be run automatically each time you turn on your computer.

2. Select Program Scheduler by placing a check mark next to it.

3. Choose **O**K to save the new configuration.

    PCConfig informs you that the new configuration information will be added to your AUTOEXEC.BAT and CONFIG.SYS files.

4. Choose **O**K to update the files, putting the command line, CPSCHED, in your AUTOEXEC.BAT file.

    PC Config tells you that you must reboot the computer for the changes to take effect.

5. Select **R**eboot to put the Scheduler into memory now, or select E**x**it to wait until the next time you reboot the computer.

Instead of loading CPSCHED at boot up, you can run CPSCHED from DOS when you know events are scheduled to occur. For most users, however, this action defeats the purpose of setting up the Scheduler once and then forgetting about it.

NOTE You can remove CPSCHED from memory by typing **kill** or **cpsched /u** at the DOS prompt.

Adding a Scheduled Event

You can add any events you want to the Scheduler. Scheduler can run anything you tell it to, not just PC Tools programs. Keep in mind that the program you set up as an event must run without user input. The purpose of Scheduler is to run programs unattended. To add an event to Scheduler, perform the following steps:

1. From the Desktop menu, select **T**ools to access the menu of PC Tools programs (see fig. 3.18). From the Tools menu, select Pro- gram **S**cheduler.

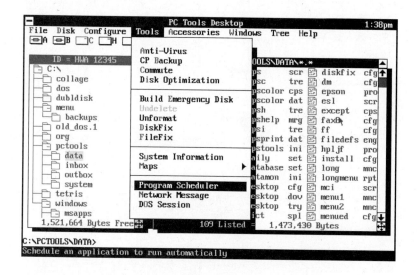

Fig. 3.18

The Tools menu.

NOTE If you are programming CP Backup or Commute events, select the program first from the Tools menu; then run the Scheduler from the program. This way, the Schedule or Edit an Event dialog box is customized with an extra option for a CP Backup Setup file or a Commute Script file.

The Program Scheduler window, shown in figure 3.19, includes a monthly calendar (with the cursor on today's date) at left and a list of scheduled events at right. You can use the calendar to change or check a date. Move by day with the left and right arrow keys, by week with the up and down arrow keys, by month with the PgDn and PgUp keys, and by year with Ctrl+Right arrow key (forward) or Ctrl+Left arrow key (backward). As in the Desktop display, Tab moves between windows, from the calendar to the events list and back.

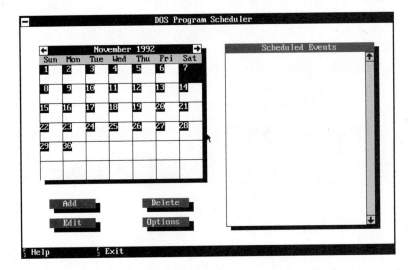

Fig. 3.19

The DOS Program Scheduler window.

2. Select the **A**dd button to put an event on the calendar. The Scheduler displays the Schedule or Edit an Event dialog box (see fig. 3.20). The currently selected date in the monthly calendar is the default date.

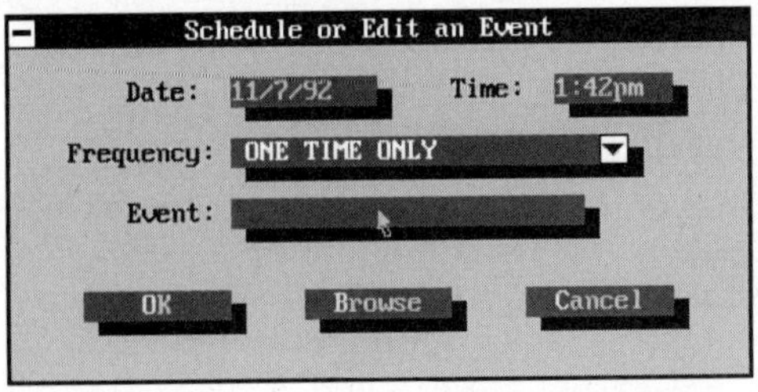

Fig. 3.20

The Schedule or Edit an Event dialog box.

3. The date in the date box determines the date of a one-time-only event or the starting date for a regularly scheduled event. If the current day, 11/7/92, for example, is a Saturday, a weekly event will occur every Saturday. Type in a different date, if desired, in the format MM/DD/YY.

4. In the Time box, type the time of day for the event to occur, in the format HH:MM. Add *a* or *p* for A.M. or P.M. (the *m* is added automatically), or use 24-hour format. For example, for two o'clock in the afternoon, type **2:00p** or **14:00**.

   Make sure to schedule any back-to-back events at sufficiently long intervals to complete each task.

5. For Frequency, press Enter or click the Frequency box to select from any of the following intervals:

   ■ *DAILY* schedules the event to occur every day, seven days a week. An example might be file backups during a crash project for which you cannot risk losing a single day's changes.

   ■ *ONE TIME ONLY* schedules the event to occur at the selected date and time only. This feature is useful for some nonroutine event you might otherwise forget about.

   ■ *WORKDAYS ONLY* schedules the event to occur Monday through Friday. You can define different days as workdays using Scheduler Options, described in the section "Customizing the Calendar" later in this chapter.

   ■ *WEEKLY* schedules the event to occur every week at the selected time, on the same day of the week as that of the selected date, starting with that date. To select a different day, change the date.

   ■ *MONTHLY-FIXED DAY* schedules the event to occur on a given date every month, such as the first of the month.

   ■ *MONTHLY-FIXED WEEKDAY* schedules the event to occur on a given day of the week every month, such as the first Tuesday.

   ■ *BIWEEKLY* schedules the event to occur every other week, on the selected weekday.

6. Specify the event in the Event text box. Unlike programming an application in the Menu window, no extension is required; you only need the command to be entered at the DOS prompt. To run the batch file CONVERT.BAT, for example, type **convert** (with any necessary path information).

7. To select the program from any file on your system, select the **B**rowse button to find the desired directory and file. After the program name, you can include any desired command-line options of up to 64 characters. To optimize the hard disk with full compression, for example, type **compress /cf**.

8. After you complete the event set up, choose **OK** to add the event to the list of Scheduled Events. Each event is described with two lines—the first showing the name of the program, the second the schedule. In the monthly calendar, an icon appears on every day an event is scheduled to occur.

9. After you add all the events you want to schedule, select **E**xit. Scheduler seeks confirmation that you want to save the changes in the schedule.

10. Choose **OK** to save the changes and return to Desktop.

Changing the Schedule

To reschedule an event or change a program instruction, select Pro-gram **S**cheduler again from the **T**ools menu. Skim through the calendar until the event you want to change appears in the Scheduled Events list. Highlight the event (either line of the description, the program, or the scheduled time) and select the **E**dit button, press Enter, or double-click the event itself. Scheduler displays the Schedule or Edit an Event dialog box, where you can make any desired changes. Choose **OK** and then **E**xit to save the changes.

To delete an event from the Program Scheduler dialog box, select the event and choose the **D**elete button.

 For repeating events, you can select any occurrence to edit or delete the overall event.

Customizing the Calendar

You can change two aspects of the Scheduler: what days are consid-ered workdays and what events are listed in the Scheduled Events list. Unless you customize the calendar, workdays are considered to be Monday through Friday, and the events list shows the current day's events only.

To change days or events, from the Program Scheduler window select **O**ptions. Scheduler displays the Scheduler Options dialog box (see fig. 3.21). On the left, the current workdays are checked. Select or unselect workdays to match your work week. On the right are the options for what events appear in the list. Select **M**onthly to see the current month's entire event roster without having to skim day by day through the calendar. Select **A**ll to list every event. Choose **OK** to save the changes.

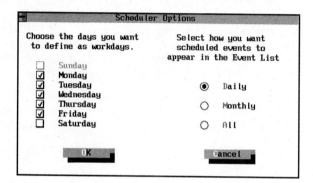

Fig. 3.21

The Scheduler Options dialog box.

Preparing for Scheduled Events

For scheduled events to occur, the computer must be on and the Scheduler memory-resident. Refer to "Configuring the Scheduler To Run at Startup" earlier in this chapter if you have not already set the Scheduler to run automatically. For scheduled events to execute successfully, there must be no obstacles, such as a drive door open, when files are to be copied. Optionally, remove any execution password to run Central Point Anti-Virus, DiskFix, or Compress unattended.

NOTE If a dialog box comes up during an automatic backup, the default response is chosen. For example, a tape backup offers a choice of erasing the tape or appending the backup files to the existing information. The default is Append. Refer to Chapter 7, "Protecting Your Data with Central Point Backup," for details on using Central Point Backup.

Chapter Summary

This chapter describes how to use three powerful program management tools: the Menu window, Task Switcher, and the Scheduler. You learned how to use the Menu window as a program manager, defining program groups and program items and using them to run application programs. You learned how to associate specific file types with particular application programs, thus enabling Desktop to launch the correct program whenever you open an associated file in the File window. In addition, you learned how to run several programs simultaneously by using the Task Switcher from the Menu window or on its own. Finally, you learned how to use the Scheduler to automate routine chores such as hard disk backup, compression, and disk maintenance.

Chapter 4, "Working on Files," contains a a full discussion about how to open or launch programs from the File window and how to perform such chores as copying, moving, renaming, and deleting files.

Working on Files

Whether you more often use a spreadsheet program, a word processor, a database program, or some other PC-based software, you invariably work with computer files. This chapter explains how to use PC Tools Desktop to perform file-related operations—some that your computer's operating system (DOS) can perform and other operations unique to PC Tools Desktop.

Most of the menu options described in this chapter are on PC Tools Desktop's pull-down File menu (see fig. 4.1). You can apply most of the File menu commands to a selected file or to a group of selected files. As a result, the first thing you learn in this chapter is how to *select* or *make current* the file or files on which you want Desktop to operate.

This chapter explains how to use Desktop's many file-related commands to look for file discrepancies, make changes to files, and print file contents. Commands described in this chapter include Open, Print, Move, Copy, Compare, Delete, Rename, Change, Secure, Select All, and File Compression with PKZip. This chapter also explains the Verify command on the File menu's Information submenu.

In Version 8.0, the critical file rescuing command, Undelete, appears on the Tools menu rather than the File menu.

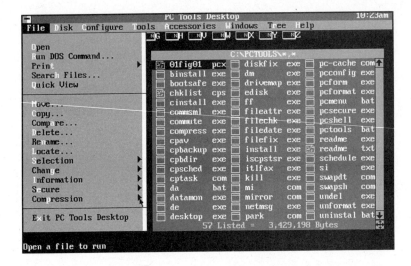

Fig. 4.1

The Desktop
File menu.

For information about other File menu commands, see Chapter 5, "Locating and Viewing Files," and Chapter 2, "Controlling the Desktop." Briefly discussed in this chapter, Undelete is fully explained in Chapter 10, "Recovering Damaged or Deleted Files."

Selecting and Deselecting Files

Some of Desktop's file commands operate only on the *current* file—the file highlighted in the File window. Other commands operate on the current file or on all *selected* files. You can have any number of files selected at any particular time. When one file is selected, Desktop displays the file name in high intensity and replaces the file icon with the number 1 for the first selected file. As you select additional files, Desktop numbers them in the order selected and displays their file names in color (or its counterpart on your monitor).

T I P

You can use file selection as a tool to rearrange the file list according to some order other than the usual sort options (name, date, size, or extension) available from the Display Options dialog box. Select files in the order in which you want to list them, and then use the Sort Directory command on the **D**isk menu to sort them by selection order. You also can use this method to group selected files in the File window.

Do not confuse a current file with a selected file. In Desktop, the file highlighted by the highlight bar is the *current file*. The current file is the object of any applicable file command—unless you have selected a file. Only one file at a time can be current. A *selected file*, on the other hand, is a file you have specifically tagged, using any of the selection methods described in later sections of this chapter. You can select multiple files.

If you choose a command when files are selected, the command operates on the selected file or files (depending on the type of command you choose). Single-file commands, such as Quick View, operate only on the first selected file. Multiple-file commands, such as Copy, operate on all selected files. For single-file operations, you can either select the file or make it current (if no other files are selected). For multiple-file operations and for using drag-and-drop to copy, move, or launch files, you must select the files.

Selecting Single Files

Use one of the following procedures to make an individual file current or to select a file:

- Use the mouse or cursor-movement keys to make the Tree window current. Type the first letter of the directory name you want to be current. Desktop opens the Speed Search dialog box, which displays the letter you typed in a text box. In the tree list, Desktop moves the highlighted bar to the first directory name that begins with the letter you typed. Type the second, third, and fourth letters (and so on) of the file name until the highlighted bar rests on the name of the directory you want to use. For details on Speed Search, refer to Chapter 2, "Controlling the Desktop."

    Press Tab or click the File window to move the highlighted bar to that window. Use the Speed Search feature to move the highlighted bar to the file name you want to make current. Press Enter to select the file.

- Using the mouse, scroll the Tree window until you find the name of the directory that contains the files you want to select. Click this directory name.

    Scroll the File window until the name of the file you want to select appears. Point to the file name. Press the left mouse button to select the file and move the highlighted bar to the next file; press the right button to make the file current without selecting it.

Selecting Multiple Files

Use one of the following procedures to select multiple files:

- To select multiple files in the order that they appear in a Desktop window, move the pointer to the first file you want to select. Then, while holding down both mouse buttons, drag the pointer over the files until you reach the last file you want to select. After all the appropriate files are selected, release both mouse buttons.

- To quickly scroll down through the entire directory and select files, hold down both mouse buttons and move the pointer into the lower edge or right edge of the window border. PC Tools Desktop scrolls the window, marking files, until you release a mouse button. Hold both mouse buttons until all appropriate files are selected. To scroll up quickly through the entire directory and select files, perform this same technique, except place the pointer in the upper edge or left edge of the window border.

- To select all files in the current directory, choose **Selection** from the **File** menu, and then from the submenu, choose **Select All**.

- Make the Tree window the active window, and use the cursor-movement keys to move the highlighted bar to the directory that contains the files you want to select. Press the Tab key to activate the File window. Use the cursor-movement keys to move the highlighted bar to the file you want to select. The file name is highlighted. Press Enter to select the file and move the highlight to the next file.

Using the File Select Filter

In addition to the methods explained in the preceding section, you can use the File Select filter to select a group of files in one step. To display the File Select Filter dialog box, shown in figure 4.2, press F9 (Select) or choose **Selection** from the **File** menu. Then choose Select Filter.

Use the Name text box to specify a DOS file specification and the Ext text box to specify an extension. The entries in these two text boxes determine which files Desktop selects in the File window. Desktop enables you to use DOS *wild-card* characters; the asterisk (*) takes the place of any string of characters, and the question mark (?) takes the place of any single character. By default, PC Tools Desktop displays an asterisk in both text boxes.

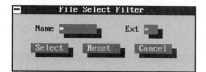

Fig. 4.2

The File Select
Filter dialog box.

After you finish making entries in the two text boxes, press Enter (with the cursor in the Ext text box) or choose the **S**elect command button. PC Tools Desktop returns to the Desktop screen and, in the File window, lists as selected only the file names that meet the File Select Filter criteria. To return to the Desktop screen without accepting the new File Select Filter criteria, choose the **C**ancel command button in the File Select Filter dialog box. Choose **R**eset to return the entries in the two text boxes to their default values.

You can select files in two different locations by switching to a dual list display (choose Dual **L**ist Display from the **W**indows menu). In each Tree window, select the directory you want to use.

T I P

Deselecting Files

To deselect a single file, simply "select" the file again. The file is removed from the selection list. To deselect all selected files in one step, press F4 (Desel) or choose **S**election from the **F**ile menu; then choose **D**eselect All from the submenu. To use the mouse to deselect all selected files, click any directory name in the Tree window.

Running Programs and Launching Files

Chapter 3, "Using the Desktop as a Program Manager," discusses how to build Menu window program lists. That chapter also describes how to use the Menu window to start a program and load a file into the applications program—a process called *launching* the file.

After you define a Menu window item for a particular applications program, you can launch a single file or—if the application can operate on a group of files, as CP Backup can—a group of files. You can launch the file or files in any of three ways. The first two methods require that the Menu and File windows be open. (If necessary, make the appropriate choices from the **W**indows menu to open the Menu window or File window.)

With the third method, the Menu window can be on or off, but you can launch only a single file whose extension is associated with an applications program. (Chapter 3, "Using the Desktop as a Program Manager," describes how to associate file names with applications.) First move the highlighted bar in the File window to the desired file or select the desired group of files; then do one of the following:

- Make the Menu window the current window and select the appropriate program from the Menu window list. The program runs and loads the file or group of files.

- In Version 8.0, you can also use drag-and-drop. Click and drag the file to the program item in the Menu window. Alternatively, if the program can operate on a group of files, you can select the group and drag it to the item. When you begin dragging, Desktop displays the Can't Drop Here banner. When you move the pointer to a launchable Menu window item, the legend changes to Execute Program. When you release the mouse button, the program is run with the selected file(s) loaded.

> **NOTE** With these two methods, if the name of the file or files has not been associated with the selected application, Desktop displays a dialog box with the message Application Filespecs do not match. To proceed and launch the file, choose **R**un. To run the program with no file loaded, choose **I**gnore.

- Alternatively—and even if the menu window is not showing—you can use one of the file open methods from the File window. *Open*, in Desktop terms, launches a single file into its associated application. (If an executable application file is selected or current, choosing **O**pen from the **F**ile menu runs that application without launching a file.) To launch a file with the open method, press Ctrl+Enter, double-click the file, or select **O**pen from the **F**ile menu. Desktop runs the program and launches the file.

NOTE If you try to open a file that has no association or is not an executable file, Desktop displays the message Extension is not EXE, COM, or BAT, and no application associations found. Click **OK** to clear the box and select a different file, or associate the file with an application.

When you exit the application, you return to the Desktop window from which you launched the file or files.

For Related Information

◀◀ "Specifying File Associations," p. 114.

FROM HERE...

Copying and Moving Files

The most common file-related function probably is copying files from one disk or directory to another. Your computer's operating system, DOS, provides this function in the COPY and XCOPY commands (DOS 3.3 or later). Desktop's **C**opy option, however, provides the capabilities of COPY, XCOPY, and much more.

A common task for many PC users is to copy one or more files from one storage location to another location and then to delete the original files. The final result is that the files are *moved* from the first location to the second. Desktop offers such a capability with its **M**ove option.

The following sections describe how to use Desktop to copy and move files.

Copying Files

With Desktop, you can copy one or more files within a directory, between directories, or between disks by using one of several methods. The quickest and easiest method to learn and use, regardless of the type of copy operation, is the dual file-lists display method, in which you display two sets of Desktop Tree and File windows.

The dual file-lists method of copying files with Desktop involves the following five steps:

1. Make the *source* drive and directory (which contain the files you want to copy) the current drive and directory.

2. To switch to a dual file-lists display, press Ins (Dual Lists). Figure 4.3 shows an example of a dual file-lists display, with I:\TEMPORG displayed in the top pair of windows and B:\ (an empty disk in the B drive) displayed in the bottom windows.

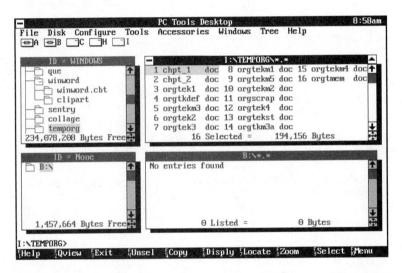

Fig. 4.3

Using the dual file-lists display.

3. Use the mouse or the cursor-movement keys to make the target drive and directory the current drive and directory in the second set of windows. (When you copy a file within the same directory, this step is not necessary.)

4. Use the cursor-movement keys or mouse to make current the first set of windows and select the files you want to copy. Note in figure 4.3 that all files in I:\TEMPORG are selected, as indicated by the message (16 selected, in the example) that appears at the bottom of the window.

5. Press F5 (Copy) or choose Copy from the File menu; then answer OK to the message

   Confirm using Second Path as the Target. *pathname*

   where *pathname* is the name of the other window's drive and directory, the *second path*.

Alternatively, to copy using the drag-and-drop technique, drag the source file to the destination File window. While you drag the file, you see the message Can't Drop Here. When the pointer reaches the File window, the message changes to Copy ... Files. Release the mouse button to complete the copy operation.

When you copy to the same directory, you are prompted for a new file name. Enter the name and extension and then choose Continue. You cannot use the drag-and-drop method to copy files within a directory.

No matter which copy technique you use, Desktop displays the Copy dialog box and reports the name and destination of every file as it is copied.

Sometimes the name of a source file is the same as a file name in the target directory. When this problem occurs, Desktop displays in the Copy dialog box the name of the file to be copied, the message File already exists, and the following command buttons (see fig. 4.4):

- *Replace All.* Replaces the file in the target directory that has the same name as a source file and replaces any other files that may have names duplicating source file names in that directory. Desktop replaces files without the need for further confirmation. Use this option when you are deliberately overwriting old versions with new.

- *Replace File.* Replaces the file in the target directory with the source file that has the duplicate file name but stops and asks for confirmation before replacing any other duplicates.

- *Skip File.* Skips the file whose name is listed in the Copy dialog box and proceeds with the next selected file.

- *Skip All.* Copies only files that don't have duplicate file names in the target directory.

- *Cancel.* Cancels the copy procedure and returns to the PC Tools Desktop screen.

You can limit the confirmation check to appear only if the file you're replacing is exactly the same version of the file (matching in date, time, size, and name). From the Configure menu, choose Confirmation, and in the Confirmation Options dialog box, choose Use Date/Time/Size in File Copy. *Note:* Because files matching in name only will be overwritten, use this feature with caution.

T I P

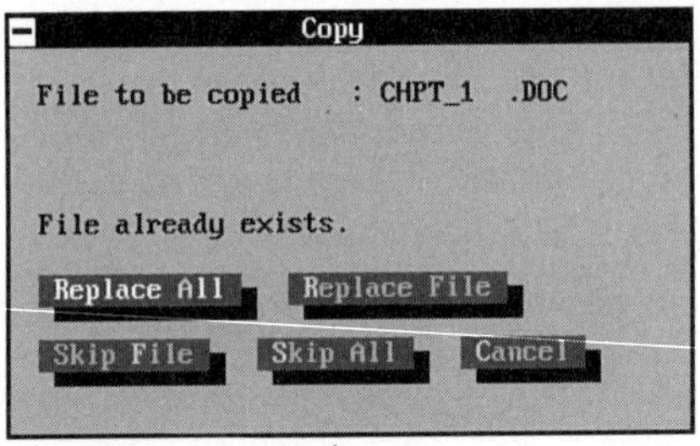

Fig. 4.4

The Copy dialog
box.

Moving Files

When Desktop moves a file, the program actually copies the file from
one storage location to another and then deletes the file from the original location. The procedure for moving one or more files with PC Tools
Desktop, therefore, is nearly the same as the procedure used for copying files.

When you want to move one or more files, you use many of the same
steps as you use to copy files, as explained in the following steps:

1. Make the source drive and directory (which contain the files you
   want to copy) the current drive and directory.

2. To switch to a dual file-lists display, press Ins (Dual Lists).

3. Make the target drive and directory the current drive and directory in the second set of windows.

4. Make current the first set of windows and select the files you want
   to copy.

5. Choose **M**ove from the **F**ile menu; alternatively, you can hold
   down the Ctrl key and drag the selected files to the target directory. Desktop displays the following warning:

   ```
   Please confirm the move operation.
   Source file(s) will be deleted.
   ```

6. Choose **OK** to proceed with the move. PC Tools Desktop asks you
   to confirm whether you want to use the Second Path (the current
   directory in the other set of windows) as the target for the move.

7. Choose **OK**. Desktop copies the selected files from the source disk
   and directory to the target disk and directory and then deletes the
   selected files from the original source directory.

   Figure 4.5 shows the result of moving the selected files from
   I:\TEMPORG to B:\.

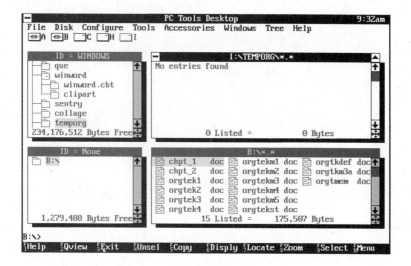

Fig. 4.5

The result of a
move operation.

Compressing and Uncompressing Files

File archiving is the general term for removing files from active use and storing them, often in a compressed format. Desktop provides an excellent utility for file archiving, PkZip, and its unarchiving partner, PkUnzip. Periodically *zipping* files (archiving them with Zip) is part of good file management; zipping files frees your hard disk for current projects but keeps the old files safe.

Zipping files has also become the method of choice for easily and economically moving large files or a large group of files via disk or modem. You can zip one or more selected files, all the files in a directory, or all the files in a directory and all of its subdirectories.

If you are zipping less than an entire directory, select the desired files. If you are zipping a directory (and, optionally, its subdirectories), make that directory current in the tree list. To compress the files, choose the File menu and then Compression. From the Compression submenu, choose Zip Files. The Compress File Settings dialog box appears (see fig. 4.6).

In the Name for ZIP File text box, type the name for the new zip file, including any drive specifier or path. To create the zip file FIGURES.ZIP on drive B, for example, type **b:figures.zip**. (Although Desktop does not require the conventional ZIP extension, using it helps identify your compressed files.) Next, select what you want to zip: Selected Files Only (the default), All Files in Current Directory, or All Files in Current Directory and Subdirectories.

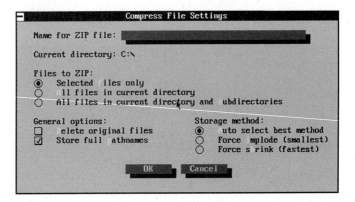

Fig. 4.6

The Compress
File Settings
dialog box.

Change the storage method, if desired. Zip can store files in one of two
ways: *imploding* (for the greatest compression) or *shrinking* (for the
fastest compression). Depending on the type of file, one or the other
method may have little advantage. For example, imploding a binary file
may produce a smaller result than shrinking it, but only by a slight margin. By default, Desktop chooses the best method based on the type of
file (**A**uto Select Best Method). Alternatively, you can choose Force
Implode or Force **S**hrink.

You can also change the information Desktop stores with the files and
whether it erases the originals after zipping them. By default, Desktop
stores the pathnames of the original files. When you unzip these files,
they will be restored to their original locations on your system. If this is
not desirable—for example, you are transferring files—uncheck the
Store Full **P**athnames option. If you are archiving or moving the files,
check **D**elete Original Files to remove them after zipping. If you are
duplicating the files or zipping them as a backup, leave this box unchecked. When your choices are complete, choose **OK**. Desktop zips
the files, creating the new file where specified and, if you selected Deleting Original Files, removing the originals.

NOTE   Files that are unzipped with Desktop can be restored to
their original paths or to any specified directory.

Using Unzip, you can uncompress all files or only selected files. To
uncompress zipped files, first select the file to unzip or make it current.
Choose the **F**ile menu and then Com**p**ression. From the Compression
submenu, choose **U**nzip Files. The Uncompress File Settings dialog box
appears with the current or selected file identified as `File being
unzipped` (see fig 4.7).

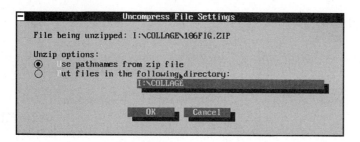

Fig. 4.7

The Uncompress
File Settings
dialog box.

To unzip the files to their original location (if they were zipped with
pathnames stored), choose **OK**. To put the files elsewhere, choose **P**ut
Files in the Following Directory and type the desired directory; then
choose **OK**.

Desktop presents the Extracting Files dialog box naming the first file
about to be extracted. To uncompress files selectively, choose **E**xtract
to uncompress the file or choose **N**ext File to skip this file and go to the
next. Continue in this way through the file list. Alternatively, to
uncompress all files in the zip file, choose Extract **A**ll.

After Desktop has unzipped the specified files, you can delete the zip
file or keep it for backup.

Desktop's Unzip command has no option for listing files in a zip file
(the PkUnzip -v option). The View window, however, provides a
viewer for zipped files, which shows a complete file list for any zip
file. To view the list of files in a zip file, make the file current and
press F2 (Qview).

T   I   P

Looking for Discrepancies

Whenever you use electronic media—such as your computer's disk—
to store information, you always risk the chance that some portion of
the data will be damaged. Two File menu options, Compare and Verify
(which is on the Information submenu), can help you determine
whether such problems have occurred, as explained in the following
sections.

Comparing the Contents of Two Files

With the Compare option, you can compare the contents of two files that should be identical. This command is most useful when you have made a copy of a file and want to determine whether the copy contains any discrepancies. You can use Compare to compare files with the same name, files with different names, and even multiple pairs of files.

> **T I P**
>
> Compare enables you to check a backup file against the current version of the file. For example, you can compare CH01.BAK with CH01.DOC to see any changes.

As with the Copy and Move options, the Compare option is easiest to use from a dual file-lists display. The following steps summarize the procedure required to perform the comparison:

1. Make current the drive and directory that contain the original files.

2. Press Ins (Dual Lists) to display a second set of Desktop windows.

3. In the second set of windows, make current the drive and directory that contain the target files. Every file in this directory is referred to as a *Compare To* file. **Note:** When you compare files within the same directory, this step is not necessary.

4. Return to the first set of windows and select the files you want Desktop to use as originals—referred to as the *1st File(s)*. Desktop compares these files with the Compare To files.

5. Choose Compare from the File menu. Desktop displays the File Compare dialog box, shown in figure 4.8, which prompts you to choose whether to compare files with matching or different names.

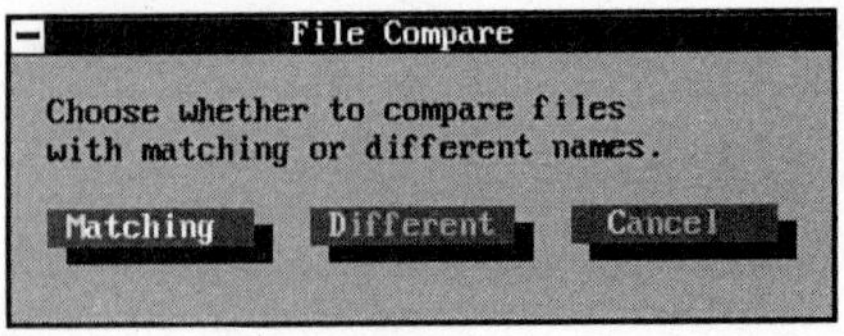

Fig. 4.8

The File Compare dialog box.

```
┌─ ─────────── File Compare ───────────
│  Choose whether to compare files
│  with matching or different names.
│
│   Matching       Different        Cancel
```

Select from the following command buttons:

- *Matching.* Compares every matching Compare To file in the target directory with the corresponding 1st File in the source directory.

- *Different.* Compares files that have different names.

- *Cancel.* Returns you to the PC Tools Desktop screen without performing a comparison.

6. Answer **OK** to the message

    `Confirm using Second Path as the Target.` *pathname*

    where *pathname* is the name of the target drive and directory.

If you choose the **M**atching command button in the File Compare dialog box, Desktop performs the compare operation on every pair of like-named files until all matching pairs of files have been compared.

When you choose the **D**ifferent command button, Desktop displays the name of the original file being compared. The program prompts you to enter the name of the file to compare in the target directory. Enter the name and extension, choose **OK**, and then choose Co**m**pare. Desktop proceeds with the compare operation. Continue this procedure until all the 1st files have been compared.

During the compare operation, Desktop first checks the size (in bytes) of both files and then compares the contents of the files byte by byte. When no discrepancies are found, Desktop displays the message `Files are identical`.

If the two files are of different size, however, your computer beeps and displays the message `Compare UNSUCCESSFUL, not the same size.` If the size is the same but a mismatch in file contents is found, your computer beeps and Desktop displays

    `Mismatch in sector` *nnnnnnnn* `at offset` *nnn*

where the *n*'s are replaced by numbers that indicate in the file the location of the discrepancy. As shown in figure 4.9, Desktop displays in the dialog box the differing values in ASCII and hexadecimal formats.

Make a note of the discrepancy and select the **OK** command button to continue the comparison. Repeat this procedure until Desktop displays the message `File compare finished`. If an error in the contents of a file is found, you can use the **H**ex Edit option (accessed by choosing Chan**g**e from the **F**ile menu) to make corrections (see the section "Using the Hex Editor" later in this chapter for more information).

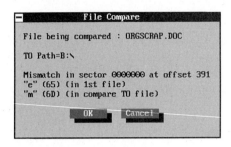

Fig. 4.9

Finding a
mismatch
during a file
comparison.

Verifying a File

A second way to check a file for possible discrepancies is to use the
Verify option (which you access by choosing Information from the File
menu). This option confirms that all sectors in the file can be read. If
you are sending files to someone and want to be absolutely sure that
the files are intact, verifying them is good practice. To determine
whether all sectors of the current file or one or more selected files are
readable, choose **Verify** from the **I**nformation menu. Desktop tries to
read all the sectors in each selected file.

After PC Tools Desktop successfully reads all sectors in a selected file,
the program displays the message

> `filename verifies OK!`

where *filename* is the name of the file Desktop has just verified. If no
errors are encountered, Desktop proceeds until all selected files are
verified.

Occasionally, from failure of the magnetic media or some other mishap,
some portion of a file may become unreadable. If, during execution of
the Verify option, Desktop cannot read a file sector, the program displays

> `filename has an ERROR in logical sector nnnnnnn. Using`
> `Edit option may enable you to correct errors.`

Three command buttons are also displayed:

■ *View/Edit.* Displays the contents of the file in hexadecimal code so
that you can use the hex editor to try to repair the file. Refer to
the section "Using the Hex Editor" later in this chapter for more
information.

■ *Verify.* Continues verifying the files.

■ *Cancel.* Stops the verification procedure.

Modifying Files

All commands discussed in the previous sections of this chapter make no changes to the files on which they operate. In contrast, you can use the commands described in this portion of the chapter to modify files or even erase files from the disk. The sections that follow discuss how to rename files; delete and undelete files; clear files; use the file editor and hex editor to modify files; and change file attributes, dates, and times.

Renaming Files

Next to copying files, the second most frequently used file-related function is probably renaming files. You may want to rename a file for many reasons. For example, you may want to use the current file name for another file, or perhaps you want to create a new name that better describes the contents of the current file. Whatever the reason, you can rename a file with the Rename option.

To rename the current file, follow these steps:

1. Choose Rename from the File menu. The File Rename dialog box appears (see fig. 4.10).

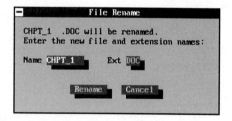

Fig. 4.10

The File Rename dialog box for a single file.

2. Type the new file name in the Name text box and the extension in the Ext text box.

3. With the cursor in the Ext text box, press Enter. Alternatively, choose the Rename command button. PC Tools Desktop renames the file.

Desktop enables you to rename files globally—all selected files at one time. You may need to change the file name extension for a group of files, for example. To globally rename files, follow these steps:

1. Select the files you want to rename.

2. Choose Rename from the File menu. Desktop displays the Global File Rename dialog box, which contains the two option buttons: Global and Single.

3. Choose Global and then OK. Desktop displays the File Rename dialog box, which contains two text boxes (Name and Ext) and two command buttons (Rename and Cancel).

4. Type the new file name and extension in the appropriate text boxes.

   Use the asterisk (*) wild-card character to take the place of multiple characters you don't want to change. Use the ? wild-card character to represent any single character in a particular position in the file name. Any other characters you type in either text box become a part of each new file name.

   To change the file names of the selected files—CHPT_1.DOC and CHPT_2.DOC to CHAPTER1.DOC and CHAPTER2.DOC, for example—type **CHAPTER?** in the Name text box and * in the Ext text box.

5. To execute the rename operation, choose the Rename command button.

Deleting Files

No disk has unlimited storage space, and nearly every file eventually becomes obsolete. PC Tools Desktop, therefore, provides a way for you to delete files: the File menu's Delete command.

When you want to delete the current file or one or more selected files, choose Delete from the File menu. Desktop displays the File Delete dialog box, shown in figure 4.11, which contains the message

    filename will be DELETED

where *filename* is the name of the first selected file. The dialog box also contains the following command buttons:

■ *Delete*. Deletes the file whose name is listed in the dialog box. If you are deleting a group of files, Desktop then proceeds to the next selected file.

■ *Next File*. Skips to the next selected file without deleting the file listed in the dialog box. (This option isn't displayed when you delete a single file.)

■ *Delete All.* Deletes all selected files. (Delete All is not displayed when you delete a single file.)

■ *Cancel.* Ends the operation without deleting the displayed file.

Fig. 4.11

The File Delete dialog box.

> **CAUTION:** Unlike the DOS DEL command, Desktop's Delete option enables you to delete files with any attribute, including read-only, system, or hidden files. Although you may find this capability useful, use it with care: system files are essential to proper system functioning.
>
> You can have Desktop check with you before deleting system files, and you can even exclude system files from appearing in the File window. From the **C**onfigure menu, choose **C**onfirmation to display the Confirmation Options dialog box; then choose Confirm on **S**ystem Files or **H**ide System Files.

After Desktop finishes deleting the specified files, the program removes the File Delete dialog box from the screen and returns to the Desktop screen.

Undeleting Files

Because of the way DOS deletes files, undeleting a file is relatively easy—but only if you do so promptly. When Desktop deletes a file, the program actually instructs DOS to delete the file. DOS, in turn, changes one character in the file name in the directory file so that the deleted file no longer is listed. As far as DOS is concerned, the file is gone, but DOS does not erase the modified file name from the directory and does not erase any data from the disk.

Eventually, as you add new files to the disk, DOS reallocates the disk space that had been assigned to the deleted file, causing new data to overwrite the old data. Soon the file and its data are permanently gone.

If you use Desktop's Undelete command before DOS has had a chance to overwrite a deleted file's data, however, Desktop can reverse the Delete operation easily.

In Desktop Version 8.0, the Undelete option is found on the Tools menu because it is actually a separate program. Refer to Chapter 10, "Recovering Damaged or Deleted Files," for a full discussion of the PC Tools Undelete program.

Using Wipe To Clear Files

In some cases, you may want to make sure that a file's data is obliterated. You may want to wipe sensitive electronic-mail files clear, for example, so that prying eyes can never read the files, even if some sort of undelete command is used.

To wipe the current file or a selected file or files clear of data, choose Change from the File menu. From the submenu, choose Wipe. Desktop starts the Wipe program and displays the Wiping dialog box (see fig. 4.12).

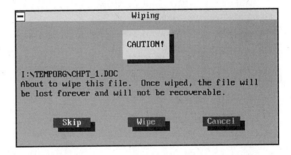

Fig. 4.12

The Wiping dialog box.

NOTE Wipe, like Undelete and FileFind, is a stand-alone program. Desktop starts Wipe when you select the Wipe option from the Change submenu. As an alternative to using Wipe from within Desktop, you can start Wipe from the DOS command line. Refer to Chapter 13, "Securing Your Data with PC Secure and Wipe," for information.

The Wiping dialog box displays the following caution:

```
filename
About to wipe this file. Once wiped, the file will be
lost forever and will not be recoverable.
```

where *filename* is the name of the first file selected in the File window. The Wiping dialog box also displays three command buttons: Skip, Wipe, and Cancel. To proceed with the wiping operation, choose **W**ipe. To skip the current selected file, choose **S**kip. To return to the PC Tools Desktop screen without wiping the selected file, choose **C**ancel.

If you choose Cancel, Wipe displays the Operation Stopped dialog box and asks Do you want to stop? Choose **OK** to stop the wipe operation or **C**ancel to return to the Wiping dialog box. If you choose **OK**, Wipe displays a summary screen indicating the files that were wiped (if any) and the files that were skipped. Choose **OK** again to return to the Desktop screen.

> **CAUTION:** You cannot undo a wipe operation. After Desktop overwrites the data on the disk, you cannot recover it.

After you choose the **W**ipe command button from the Wiping dialog box, Wipe briefly displays a dialog box which informs you that the selected file is being wiped from the disk. After the wiping operation is complete, Wipe returns to the Wiping dialog box if other files are selected; if all files have been wiped or skipped, Wipe displays the Wipe Summary screen. Choose **OK** to return to PC Tools Desktop. In Version 8.0, the file list is immediately updated after a file is wiped.

Using the File Editor

Chapter 16, "Using PC Tools Notepads," explains how to use the simple word processor that is a part of PC Tools Desktop Accessories. In that chapter, you learn how to use Notepads to edit Notepads and ASCII files. Often, however, you need to edit ASCII files while you are using Desktop. Desktop, therefore, provides a command that enables you to use a word processor-like feature known as the *file editor* to edit ASCII files.

By default, Version 8.0 uses Desktop's internal editor as its file editor. You can customize Desktop to use Notepads or another text editor of your choice.

When you want to edit from within Desktop an ASCII file such as a batch file, highlight the file in the File window and then choose Change from the **F**ile menu. From the submenu, choose **E**dit. Desktop displays the Edit File dialog box (see fig. 4.13).

Fig. 4.13

The Edit File
dialog box.

The Edit File dialog box asks whether you want to edit the file or create a new file. It also includes the following command buttons:

■ *Edit.* Displays the selected file in the File Editor screen so that you can edit the file (see fig. 4.14).

■ *Create.* Creates a new file and displays a blank screen. Desktop prompts you for a file name later, when you save the new file to disk.

■ *Cancel.* Returns to the Desktop screen without editing the listed file.

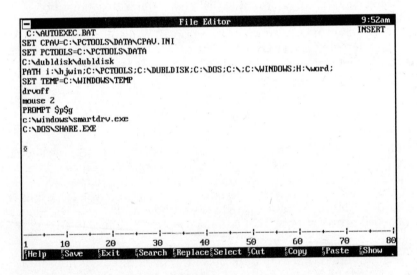

Fig. 4.14

The File Editor
screen.

The File Editor screen has a close box, which appears in the upper left corner of the window border; however, no Resize box or zoom feature is available because you cannot resize, zoom, or move this screen.

When you first display the File Editor screen, the file editor is in insert mode, denoted by the word INSERT in the upper right corner of the screen. New typing is inserted, pushing any text after it ahead. To re-place existing text with newly typed text, toggle on overtype mode by pressing the Ins key.

Use the mouse or the cursor-movement keys, listed in table 4.1, to move around the File Editor screen.

Table 4.1 Cursor-Movement Keys for the File Editor Screen

Key	Movement
↓	Moves down one line
↑	Moves up one line
→	Moves one character right
←	Moves one character left
Backspace	Erases one character to the left
Ctrl+→	Moves one word right
Ctrl+←	Moves one word left
Home *	Moves to left end of line containing cursor; press again to move to the top of the window
End **	Moves to right end of line containing cursor; press again to move to the bottom on the window
Ctrl+Home	Moves to beginning of file (line 1, column 1)
Ctrl+End	Moves to end of file
PgDn	Moves down one-half screen
PgUp	Moves up one-half screen
Enter	Inserts a carriage return and moves down one line

* If the cursor is at the beginning of the line, Home moves the cursor to the beginning of the first line in the window.

** When the cursor is already at the end of the line, End moves the cursor to the beginning of the last line in the window.

The file editor has a number of the features found in Notepads, which you can access through the commands listed in the File Editor screen's message bar. Table 4.2 lists these commands, which you can execute by using one of the following methods:

■ Click the command you want to execute (using the left or right mouse button).

■ Press the shortcut key for the command. The message bar and table 4.2 list the shortcut keys.

■ Press and hold down the Alt key to display a horizontal menu across the bottom of the screen; then press the letter highlighted in the command. To execute the **S**ave command, for example, press Alt+S.

After you finish editing the ASCII file, press F2 (Save) or Alt+S to save the file. Desktop saves the file to disk and displays a dialog box containing the message `File saved successfully`. Choose **OK** to return to the File Editor screen. You can continue editing or quit.

Table 4.2 Message-Bar Commands for the File Editor Screen

Key	Command	Function
F2	Save	Saves file as ASCII file
F3 or Esc	Exit	Exits the File Editor screen and returns to the Desktop screen
F4	Search	Searches for a string of up to 32 characters
F5	Replace	Searches for and replaces one character string with another character string
F6	Select	Selects a block of text
F7	Cut	Deletes selected text to paste buffer
F8	Copy	Copies selected text to paste buffer
F9	Paste	Inserts contents of paste buffer at cursor
F10	Show	Displays carriage return characters as highlighted left arrows (←). This command is a toggle.

To quit from the file, press F3 (Exit) or Alt+X. If you have not saved your changes, Desktop alerts you and gives you a chance to save the file. You then return to the Desktop screen.

Using the Hex Editor

In addition to using the file editor, you can edit data in hexadecimal (base 16) format by using a feature called the *hex editor*. You use this feature primarily to view or edit program files and other files not stored in ASCII character format or some other format that an applications program can edit. This section summarizes how to view and edit files in hex mode. The hex editor applications are beyond the scope of this book.

When you want to view or edit a file in hexadecimal format from within Desktop, highlight the file in the File window and choose Change from the File menu. Then choose Hex Edit from the submenu. The hex editor's File Edit screen appears (see fig. 4.15).

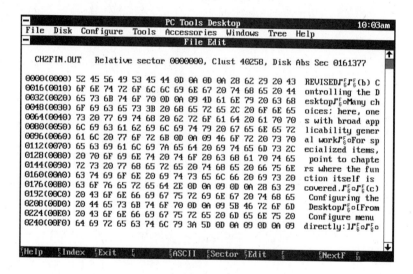

Fig. 4.15

The File Edit screen of the hex editor.

Viewing Files in the File Edit Screen

The hex editor File Edit screen overlays the Desktop window and includes a message bar and a vertical scroll bar. In the message bar, Desktop displays the available function key commands, listed in table 4.3. (You cannot use the horizontal menu bar, which is part of the underlying Desktop window.)

Key	Name	Function
F1	Help	Displays the context-sensitive Help facility
F2	Index	Displays the Help facility index
F3 or Esc	Exit	Cancels the current process or closes the dialog box
F5	ASCII	Switches to ASCII format (from Hex format)
F5	Hex	Switches to Hex format (from ASCII format)
F6	Sector	Goes to a particular relative sector
F7	Edit	Switches to the Sector Edit screen to edit the file (see the next section, "Editing Files on the Sector Edit Screen")
F9	NextF	Displays next selected file

Table 4.3 Function Key Commands for the Hex Editor File Edit Screen

The third line of the hex editor File Edit screen displays the name of the file, the relative sector number, the cluster number, and the absolute sector number.

A *sector* is a 512-byte segment of a file. The first sector on the disk is absolute sector 0000000, and the first sector in a file is relative sector 0000000; the second sector on the disk is absolute sector 0000001, and the second sector in a file is relative sector 0000001; and so on.

A *cluster* is the minimum block of storage space allocated by DOS. A cluster can consist of 512 to 8,096 bytes, depending on the type of disk and version of DOS. Hard disks typically are formatted so that every cluster is 2,048 bytes. In other words, the minimum space reserved for a file or a portion of a file is 2,048 bytes, even if the file doesn't need that much space. High-density floppy disks usually reserve 512 bytes per cluster.

The main portion of the File Edit screen is divided into three areas: offset, hexadecimal, and ASCII. The *offset area*, on the left side of the screen, lists the offset of the first byte displayed in the row. The *offset* is the number of bytes from the beginning of the current sector. The first number is a decimal value, and the number in parentheses is its hexa-decimal (base 16) equivalent. The number 0128(0080), for example, means that the first byte in the line is 128 bytes (hex 80) from the beginning of the currently displayed sector.

The middle area in the File Edit screen is the *hexadecimal area*, which consists of 16 columns of 2-digit hexadecimal values. Every 2-digit value represents 1 byte (8 bits) of data. The third area is the *ASCII area*. Every character displayed in the ASCII area corresponds directly to a particular byte in the same row of the hexadecimal column.

From the File Edit screen in figure 4.15, you can view but not change the contents of the file. You can press the PgDn and PgUp keys to move the cursor around screen by screen in the file. Press Home to move the cursor to the beginning of the file, and press End to move to the end of the file. You can use the F6 (Sector) command to move to a particular sector. When the sector of the file you want to edit is displayed, press F7 (Edit). PC Tools Desktop switches to the Sector Edit screen, which the following section discusses in more detail.

Editing Files on the Sector Edit Screen

The message bar in the Sector Edit screen, shown in figure 4.16, dis-plays a different set of function key commands. Table 4.4 lists these commands.

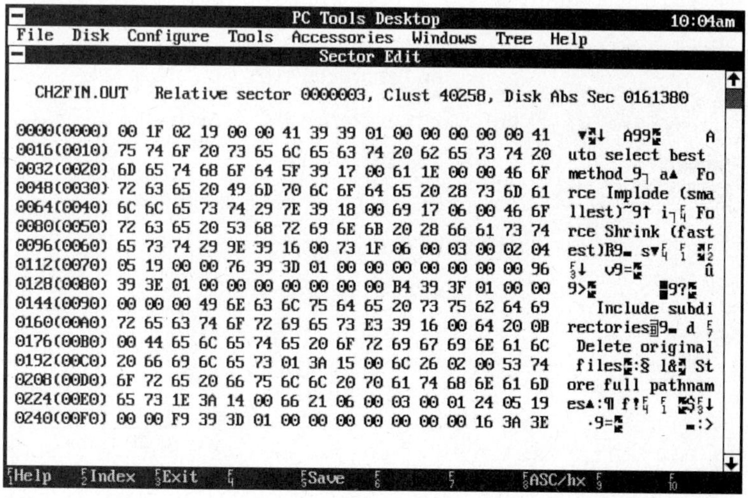

```
┌─────────────────────────────────────────────────────────────────┐
│ ▬                         PC Tools Desktop              10:04am   │
│ File  Disk  Configure  Tools  Accessories  Windows  Tree  Help    │
│ ▬                           Sector Edit                        ▲  │
│                                                                   │
│  CH2FIN.OUT    Relative sector 0000003, Clust 40258, Disk Abs Sec 0161380 │
│                                                                   │
│ 0000(0000) 00 1F 02 19 00 00 41 39 39 01 00 00 00 00 00 41  ▼▓↓ A99▓    A │
│ 0016(0010) 75 74 6F 20 73 65 6C 65 63 74 20 62 65 73 74 20  uto select best │
│ 0032(0020) 6D 65 74 68 6F 64 5F 39 17 00 61 1E 00 00 46 6F  method_9┐ a▲ Fo │
│ 0048(0030) 72 63 65 20 49 6D 70 6C 6F 64 65 20 28 73 6D 61  rce Implode (sma │
│ 0064(0040) 6C 6C 65 73 74 29 7E 39 18 00 69 17 06 00 46 6F  llest)~9t i┐▓ Fo │
│ 0080(0050) 72 63 65 20 53 68 72 69 6E 6B 20 28 66 61 73 74  rce Shrink (fast │
│ 0096(0060) 65 73 74 29 9E 39 16 00 73 1F 06 00 03 00 02 04  est)R9▄ sv▓ ▓ ▓▓ │
│ 0112(0070) 05 19 00 00 76 39 3D 01 00 00 00 00 00 00 00 96  ▓↓ v9=▓          û │
│ 0128(0080) 39 3E 01 00 00 00 00 00 00 00 B4 39 3F 01 00 00  9>▓          ▓9?▓ │
│ 0144(0090) 00 00 00 49 6E 63 6C 75 64 65 20 73 75 62 64 69     Include subdi │
│ 0160(00A0) 72 65 63 74 6F 72 69 65 73 E3 39 16 00 64 20 0B  rectories▓9▄ d ▓ │
│ 0176(00B0) 00 44 65 6C 65 74 65 20 6F 72 69 67 69 6E 61 6C   Delete original │
│ 0192(00C0) 20 66 69 6C 65 73 01 3A 15 00 6C 26 02 00 53 74  files▓:§ l&▓ St │
│ 0208(00D0) 6F 72 65 20 66 75 6C 6C 20 70 61 74 68 6E 61 6D  ore full pathnam │
│ 0224(00E0) 65 73 1E 3A 14 00 66 21 06 00 03 00 01 24 05 19  es▲:¶ f!▓ ▓ ▓§▓↓ │
│ 0240(00F0) 00 00 F9 39 3D 01 00 00 00 00 00 00 16 3A 3E     ·9=▓       ▬:> │
│                                                                ▼  │
│ F1Help  F2Index  F3Exit  F4    F5Save   F6    F7    F8ASC/hx F9    F10 │
└─────────────────────────────────────────────────────────────────┘
```

Fig. 4.16

The Sector Edit screen.

Table 4.4 Function Key Commands for the Sector Edit Screen

Key	Name	Function
F1	Help	Displays the context-sensitive Help facility
F2	Index	Displays the Help facility index
F3 or Esc	Exit	Returns to the File Edit screen (see the preceding section, "Viewing Files in the File Edit Screen")
F5	Save	Saves the file to disk
F8	ASC/hx	Switches between hexadecimal column and ASCII column

To move the cursor around the Sector Edit screen, you can use the cursor-movement keys listed in table 4.5 or the mouse and the scroll bar. Notice that these keys are similar to the ones available in the File Editor screen.

Table 4.5 Cursor-Movement Keys for the Sector Edit Screen

Key	Movement
↓	Moves down one line
↑	Moves up one line
→	Moves one character right
←	Moves one character left
Backspace	Moves one character to left
Home	Moves to left end of first line in the sector
End	Moves to right end of last line in the sector
PgDn	Moves to last half of the sector
PgUp	Moves to first half of the sector

Desktop enables you to edit a sector byte by byte in the Sector Edit screen. You can choose to edit a byte in the hexadecimal column or the ASCII column. When you first display the screen, the cursor is in the hex column. To switch to the ASCII column, press F8 (ASC/hx).

After you make changes, press F5 (Save) to save the sector to disk. Click the close box or press Esc or F3 (Exit) to return to the File Edit screen.

To edit a different sector, use PgDn or PgUp to target the sector you want and press F7 (Edit) to display the Sector Edit screen again. Save the changes and return to the File Edit screen. After you are finished, click the close box or press Esc or F3 (Exit) to return to the PC Tools Desktop screen.

Changing File Attributes, Date, and Time

In every directory file, DOS stores a list of all files contained in that directory. In this list, DOS stores several characteristics about each file, including file name, file attributes, and date and time the file was last modified.

This section describes how to use Desktop to modify the file attributes and the date and time. You can also change attributes and the file date by running the PC Tools utilities FileAttr and FileDate directly from DOS. These utilities are explained in the next section, "Changing File Attributes and Dates from DOS."

The file attributes are stored in a 1-byte value that specifies the following status indicators, which you can toggle on or off:

- The *hidden* attribute bit prevents the DOS DIR command from listing the file. (DIR displays a list of all files in the current directory.) The attribute does not hide files in the Desktop File window. The default value for this bit is off.

- The *system* attribute bit identifies special files used by DOS, such as the operating system files IO.SYS and MSDOS.SYS (or IBMBIO.COM and IBMDOS.COM). Like the hidden attribute bit, this bit also prevents the DOS DIR command—but not Desktop—from listing the file. By default, the system bit is off.

- When the *read only* attribute bit is on, the file can be read but not modified or erased. By default, this attribute bit is off.

- The *archive* bit indicates whether the file has been backed up (archived) since last being modified. The default value is on, meaning that the file has not been archived yet. When you use the DOS BACKUP command or the PC Tools program PC Backup to archive a file, this bit is turned off.

You can manually change the value of these attribute bits for the current file or for one or more selected files. From the **F**ile menu, choose Chan**ge**. From the submenu, choose **A**ttribute to display the File Attribute window, which lists the current file or all the selected files. Figure 4.17 shows the File Attribute window listing two files, CHPT_1.DOC and CHPT_2.DOC, currently selected in the B:\ drive.

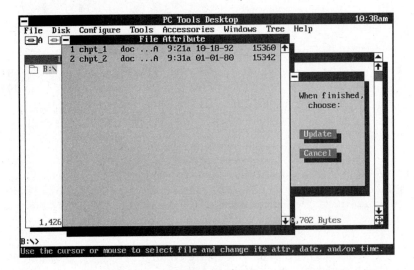

Fig. 4.17

The File Attribute window.

In the File Attribute window, Desktop lists the file names and extensions, followed by the attribute byte values. The attribute bits are represented as a series of dots (if the attribute is off) or letters (is the attribute is on), as follows:

Attribute Value	Meaning
H	Hidden bit on
S	System bit on
R	Read-only bit on
A	Archive bit on
.	Bit off

The attribute value ...A, for example, means that the first three attribute bits are off and the archive bit is on. This attribute byte value is the default. An attribute value of ..RA means that the file is read only and has not been archived since last being modified.

To change the value of an attribute bit, use the up- or down-arrow keys in the File Attribute window to move to the line that lists the file, and then type the letter that corresponds to the attribute bit you want to change. You also can click the appropriate letter or dot to toggle each attribute bit on and off. You may want to toggle the archive bit on, for example, to have a file backed up in the next backup session.

In the File Attribute window, you also can edit the date and time that DOS stores in the directory listing with a file. You may find this capability useful if you have created or modified files during a period when the system date was incorrect (after a battery failure, for example). Press the up- or down-arrow keys to move to the appropriate file and then use the right- and left-arrow keys to move to and between the date and time values. Type the new values you want to use.

After you make all necessary changes to the file attributes and the date and time, choose the Update command button. Alternatively, you can choose the Cancel command button, click the close box, or press F3 (Exit) or Esc when you want to cancel any changes you have made. You return to the PC Tools Desktop screen.

Changing File Attributes and Dates from DOS

You can quickly check or change a file attribute or change a file date from DOS with the FileAttr and FileDate utilities. The File Attr command is similar to the DOS ATTRIB command, but it spells out the attributes instead of showing their initials.

To check a file's attributes, type the following command at the DOS prompt and press Enter:

    FILEATTR *filename*

To check a group of files, you can use wild-card characters in the file name. To include subdirectories in the list, after the file name include the parameter **/S**.

To set one or more attributes for a file, at the DOS prompt enter **fileattr**, the file name, and one (or more) of the following switches:

Switch	Description
/HID+	Sets the hidden bit on
/SYS+	Sets the system bit on
/R+	Sets the read-only bit on
/A+	Sets the archive bit on

To remove an attribute, use a minus sign (-) rather than a plus sign after the parameter. You also can check or change attributes for a directory by using the /D switch.

To change a file's date or time, at the DOS prompt enter **filedate**, the file's name, and one or more of the following switch settings:

Switch	Description
/D*mm-dd-yy*	Sets the date to the specified month, day, and year specified in mm-dd-yy format
/T*hh:mm:ss*	Sets the time to the specified hour, minute, and (optionally) second specified in hh:mm:ss format

Omitting the parameters sets the date and time to the current system values. To change a group of files, you can use wild cards in the file name.

To list the files whose date or time you have changed, type the following command at the DOS prompt and press Enter:

    FILEDATE /L

For the FileAttr and FileDate utilities, you enter the command followed by **/?** to see the valid parameters. To see the file date-setting options, for example, at the DOS prompt type the following command and press Enter:

    FILEDATE /?

Encrypting and Decrypting Files

If you store sensitive files on your computer disks—files you want only authorized individuals to read—be aware that DOS doesn't provide adequate security against a persistent intruder. The only security feature offered by DOS is the hidden attribute, discussed in the preceding section. As you have learned, however, this attribute provides no security at all because programs such as PC Tools can list the names of all files on your disk, hidden or not. PC Tools, however, does provide an excellent security tool in the program PC Secure.

To access PC Secure from within PC Tools Desktop, choose Secure from the File menu. From the submenu choose Encrypt. PC Tools temporarily suspends PC Tools Desktop and starts PC Secure. To set the method of encryption, choose Secure Options from the Configure menu. Later, you can undo the encryption by selecting Decrypt from the Secure submenu.

NOTE   You must select a master key password before you use Encrypt. Refer to Chapter 13, "Securing Your Data with PC Secure and Wipe," for more about using PC Secure.

For Related Information

◀◀ "Using Your Own Text Editor," p. 69.

FROM HERE...

Printing

From time to time, you may need to print the contents of a disk file—most often, an ASCII file such as the README.TXT file distributed with PC Tools. Occasionally, however, you may want to print the contents of a file in hexadecimal code, like that displayed in the hex editor File Edit screen (see "Using the Hex Editor" earlier in this chapter). You sometimes may want a hard copy (printout) of a directory listing instead. The following sections describe how to use PC Tools Desktop to print ASCII files, how to "dump" file sectors in hexadecimal format, and how to print directory lists.

Printing Files

Desktop gives you substantial control over the printing of ASCII files. To print the current file or one or more selected files, choose Print from the File menu. From the submenu choose Print File. PC Tools Desktop displays the File Print dialog box (see fig. 4.18).

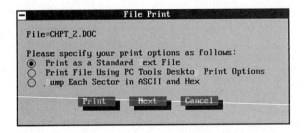

Fig. 4.18

The File Print
dialog box.

The File Print dialog box presents the following options:

- *Print as a Standard Text File.* Prints the contents of the ASCII file exactly as is, without adding any print options. Use this option when the file is already properly formatted (with margins, page breaks, page numbers, and so on).

- *Print File Using PC Tools Desktop Print Options.* Displays another dialog box that enables you to control print formatting.

- *Dump Each Sector in ASCII and Hex.* Prints the file sector by sector in hexadecimal (base 16) code and ASCII characters. Programmers and power users who want to use the hex editor to edit the sectors directly should find this option particularly useful.

After you choose the appropriate option, choose the **P**rint command button to proceed. If you choose the first or third option, Desktop immediately sends the file to the printer. If you choose Print File Using PC Tools Desktop Print Options, Desktop displays a second File Print dialog box (see fig. 4.19).

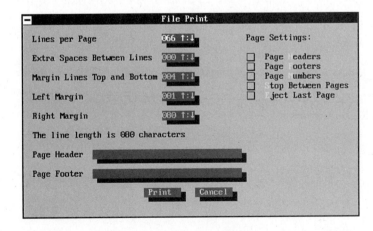

Fig. 4.19

The File Print
dialog box with
print formatting
options.

The second File Print dialog box lists the following options:

- *Lines per Page.* This option indicates the length of the paper in terms of lines. The default is 66, which is an 11-inch page with 6 single-spaced lines per vertical inch.

- *Extra Spaces Between Lines.* Type a number in this text box to indicate the number of blank lines, if any, you want PC Tools Desktop to add between printed lines. The default value is 0, which produces single-spaced lines (6 lines printed per vertical inch). Type **1** for double-space printing (3 lines per vertical inch).

- *Margin Lines Top and Bottom.* In this text box, specify the number of blank lines you want included at the top and bottom of every page. Headers and footers print in these margins. The default value is 4.

- *Left Margin.* Type a number in this text box to indicate the space at which you want PC Tools Desktop to start printing. The default value is 1, which means that printing starts at the first space on the line. To create a 1-inch left margin, for example, change this value to 10 (assuming that the printer by default prints at 10 characters per inch).

- *Right Margin.* In this text box, type a number to specify the last space on the line in which you want PC Tools Desktop to print. The default is 80, which is approximately one-half inch from the right margin (if you have not changed the left margin). With the left margin set at 10, change this value to 75, for example, to leave a 1-inch margin on the right side of 8 1/2-by-11-inch paper.

- *Page **H**eaders.* To print the same header at the top of every page in the printout, check the Page **H**eaders check box and type the header text in the text box. If you're printing several files, you can identify the printouts by entering the name of the file as a header.

- *Page Footers.* To create a footer, which prints specified text at the bottom of every page, check the Page **F**ooters check box. In the text box, type the text that you want PC Tools Desktop to include in the footer.

- *Page Numbers.* Select this check box to cause PC Tools Desktop to print page numbers at the bottom right of the page.

- *Stop Between Pages.* Select this check box when you are using cut-sheet paper and want PC Tools Desktop to pause the printer after every page so that you can feed another sheet of paper.

- *Eject Last Page.* Select this check box when you want Desktop to eject the last page of the printout.

After you make all necessary changes, choose the **Print** command button. Desktop displays the prompt Insert forms in printer. Again choose the **Print** command button. Desktop sends the file to the printer, using the print formatting characteristics you specified.

 If carriage returns were inserted at the end of every line in the ASCII file you are printing, you may not be able to change left or right margins without first editing the file (using the file editor or Desktop Accessories Notepads) and removing unneeded carriage returns. To see carriage returns in Notepads, choose **C**ontrol Character Display from the **C**ontrols menu.

You can suspend printing at any time by selecting the **C**ancel command button. Desktop displays the message You have suspended the print service. Choose **P**rint to continue or **C**ancel to exit.

NOTE The Print File option on the File menu's Print submenu sends the file only to LPT1, the first parallel printer port. Make sure that your system is configured to print to this port.

Printing Directories

When you want to print a file directory, select the target directory in the Tree window, choose Print from the **F**ile menu, and then choose Print **D**irectory from the submenu. Desktop prints a list that indicates the name of the directory and the following characteristics for every file in the directory:

> File name
>
> File size in bytes and clusters
>
> File date and time
>
> File attributes

The printout shows the total number of files listed, the number selected, the disk space occupied by the directory, and the bytes yet available for storage on the current disk.

Printing directories is an invaluable tool for documenting your system and for avoiding "mystery" floppy disks. You can print the directory and then store it with the floppy.

T I P

Chapter Summary

This chapter explains how to use PC Tools Desktop to perform many file-related operations. You first learned how to *select* or *make current* the file or files on which you want PC Tools Desktop to operate. Then you examined how to use Desktop's many file-related commands to look for file discrepancies, make changes to files, and print file contents. Chapter 5, "Locating and Viewing Files," examines Desktop's disk-related commands.

Locating and Viewing Files

Before you can perform an operation on a file, you must be able to find the file. The FileFind utility enables you to quickly locate a file anywhere on your computer's hard disk and even on the hard disks in a Novell network to which your computer is connected. You can access FileFind by selecting the **Locate** option on the **File** menu. The Desktop Search Files option enables you to search files for the occurrence of specific text.

After you locate a file, you must make sure that it is the file you really wanted to find. The PC Tools View utility enables you to instantly view files created by any one of more than 30 PC applications programs, without having to run the program itself. You can even view PC Paintbrush (PCX format) graphics files.

In this chapter, you learn how to search for a file by its contents, how to locate files by file name, and how to group files by association with a particular applications program. The chapter then describes how to use View to look at file contents running the application that created the file.

Locating Files with FileFind

Personal computers commonly have storage media that can hold millions of bytes of information in hundreds or even thousands of files. Ideally, you keep the files on your computer's hard disk, organized and cataloged by program and by subject matter. In reality, however, you may have many files with similar-looking file names scattered throughout your hard disk. Finding a certain file can sometimes be a daunting task. PC Tools Desktop can come to the rescue with the FileFind utility, available from the Desktop or from DOS.

With FileFind, you can quickly scan your computer's hard disk by using one of these approaches:

- Use FileFind to find in a certain directory or on the current disk all files that have a file name with a particular pattern, and use PC Tools Desktop to search these files for a character string.

- Use FileFind to find on the current disk or in a certain directory all files in a predefined *search group*—a group of files defined by a list of file-name specifications associated with a particular applications program. Use Desktop to search these files for a character string.

- Use the FileFind Filter option to find files matching your specifications (of attributes, size, dates, and so on).

- Use the Drives command to limit the search to specific directories, to search other drives on the system, and even to search multiple drives.

- Use Desktop's Search Files option to find all files listed in the current directory or in the current search group that contain a certain character string or a certain hexadecimal number (base 16—used by programmers).

The following sections describe how to use these methods to find files.

 NOTE   Refer to the section "Looking at Files with View" later in this chapter for a description of how to use the View window to see the contents of a file located with FileFind.

Starting FileFind

You can start the FileFind program in one of two ways: from the DOS command line and from within PC Tools Desktop. To start FileFind from

DOS, type **ff** at the DOS command line and press Enter. FileFind loads into memory and displays the FileFind window (see fig 5.1).

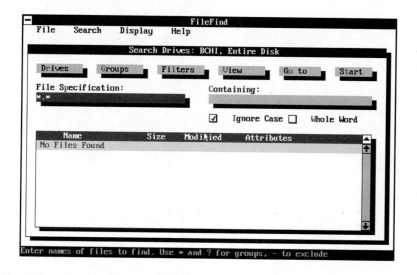

Fig. 5.1

The FileFind window.

To start FileFind from within PC Tools Desktop, press F7 (Locate) or select **F**ile from the horizontal menu bar to display the File menu, and choose the **L**ocate option. Desktop temporarily suspends its operation, and FileFind loads into memory. FileFind displays the FileFind Window.

Whether you start FileFind from DOS or from PC Tools Desktop, you can locate files on your computer's disks. The Desktop method, however, provides more flexibility. When you start FileFind from PC Tools Desktop and then exit the program, Desktop returns with the located files listed on-screen. You then can use all of Desktop's file-manipulation commands on the located files. However, when you exit FileFind after starting the program at the DOS command line, FileFind returns the cursor to the DOS command line.

The remainder of the discussion about FileFind assumes, unless otherwise stated, that you started FileFind from within Desktop by pressing F7 (Locate) or by selecting **L**ocate from the **F**ile menu.

The FileFind window has the same screen elements as a dialog box (see Chapter 1, "Navigating the Desktop," for a discussion of dialog boxes). The window contains six command buttons (Drives, Groups, Filters, View, Go To, and Start), two text boxes (File Specification and Containing), two check boxes (Ignore Case and Whole Word), and a list box (the matching-files list).

Locating Files by File Name

Many times you probably have an idea of the name of a file you want but are not exactly sure of the spelling, or you may have scattered files of a certain type in various subdirectories and now want to consolidate them in one place. PC Tools FileFind enables you to search the current disk or a specific directory to locate a group of files whose file names match given criteria. Such a group of files is called a *search group*.

FileFind enables you to define different search groups by specifying file names every time you search for a file. The program also enables you to create predefined search groups (discussed in the following section). You then can scan the contents of the files in the search group for a particular character string.

When you want to create a search group by file name, display the FileFind window. The cursor blinks in the File Specification text box. Type one or more file specifications in the text box, and separate each file specification from the previous one with a space. You also can use the DOS wild-card characters * and ?. If you include a directory name, you limit the search to that directory. You can even *exclude* files that meet a certain file specification by preceding the specification with a minus sign (–).

Suppose, for example, that you want to search your disk for the first chapter of your novel, but you cannot remember which directory contains the chapter, and you are not sure whether the file name is CHP1.DOC or CH01.DOC. You are certain, however, that the file is not in the \GRAPHICS directory; therefore, you type the following entry in the File Specification text box:

        CH?1.DOC -\GRAPHICS*.*

This entry tells FileFind to search all directories, except the GRAPHICS directory, on the current disk and to locate every file that has a name beginning with CH followed by any character, the number 1, and the extension DOC. (**Note:** Include a space before each directory specification or before the minus sign in front of the directory specification.)

To the right of the File Specification text box, FileFind displays the Containing text box. In the text box, you can type a search string, a character string of up to 32 characters. The search string narrows the search to files matching the name criteria and containing the specified text. Suppose, for example, that you recall that the first sentence of the chapter you are looking for is "It was the best of times, it was the worst of times." You can type **worst of times** in the Containing text box. (To locate all files matching the name criteria, leave the Containing box blank.)

Below the Containing text box are the following check boxes:

■ **Ignore Case.** Choose this option to select a file that contains the search string, regardless of whether the matching string matches the case (upper- or lowercase) of every character in the search string. This box is checked by default.

■ **Whole Word.** Select this option to ignore strings embedded in longer strings. For example, the search string *dog* matches *dogged*, *doggerel*, and *hang-dog* unless you specify Whole Word. Select Whole Word if you want to match only the word *dog*. By default, this box is not checked .

To initiate the search, press Enter, select the Start command button, or choose **S**earch from the horizontal menu bar. Desktop displays the Search menu; select Start. FileFind begins scanning the disk for the specified files and then searches the files for the character string.

As the search proceeds, the names of any matching files appear in the matching-files list. If you spot the file you're looking for, you can stop the search by pressing Esc. FileFind displays the Pausing Search dialog box with the following message:

```
Do you want to continue the search?
```

Choose the **C**ancel button to abandon the search, freezing the current matching-files list. Choose **OK** to resume the search.

When FileFind finishes searching the disk, the program displays a message box containing the following message:

```
Search complete

Return to DESKTOP?
```

Select **OK** to return to PC Tools Desktop, where you can use Desktop's file manipulation commands on the list of located files. Select **C**ancel to remain in FileFind, for example, to try different criteria if your search didn't reveal the expected files. Without exiting to Desktop, you also can perform basic file management tasks from FileFind's File menu, selecting files and using commands such as Delete, Rename, Copy, Move, Select All, Set Attributes, or Print a List (of files found). To return to Desktop, press Esc or F3 (Exit), or choose **Fi**le and then E**x**it.

When you exit FileFind and return to Desktop, the program displays a full-screen window called the Located Files window (see fig. 5.2). In this example, FileFind has found one file, the file CH01.DOC in the I:\WORDDOCS directory, that meets both the file-specification criteria and the character-string criteria.

T I P	If you started FileFind from DOS, you can exit and change directories at the same time, for example, to switch to the directory where files were located. In the matching-files list, highlight or select a file in the desired directory. Select the **Go** To command button, or choose **File** and then **Go** to Directory. You return to DOS, in the specified directory. (The Go To function is not available if you start FileFind from Desktop.)

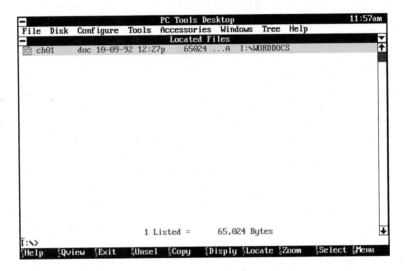

Fig. 5.2

The Located Files
window.

You can now use Desktop's File commands to proceed with the desired action on the found files. To return to the normal file list window, press Esc. The Located Files window closes, and the previous Desktop file list appears. If you selected files before exiting FileFind or from Desktop in the Located Files window, those files are still selected.

Press Esc or F3 (Exit) to return to the normal Desktop screen.

Locating Files by Using Predefined Search Groups

A second way to use FileFind to locate files on your hard disk is to use a predefined *search group*. Search groups are automatically defined when PC Tools does an application search, either at installation or from Desktop. Search groups are created for application programs installed in the

Desktop Menu window (refer to Chapter 3, "Using the Desktop as a
Program Manager," and Appendix A, "Installing and Configuring PC
Tools," for more information about that process). In addition, you can
define your own search groups, and you can modify previously defined
search groups.

From the Desktop screen, press F7 (Locate) or select File and then
Locate to display the FileFind windows. Select the Groups command
button (or select Groups from the Search menu) to display the Search
Groups dialog box (see fig. 5.3).

Fig. 5.3

The Search
Groups dialog
box.

The example in figure 5.3 shows search groups for PKZip, Zip, and Windows Write files, all created during installation. Install created a search
group for programs it added to Desktop's Menu window.

FileFind enables you to add, delete, and edit search groups. Select the
Edit command button from the Search Group dialog box; FileFind displays the Edit Search Groups dialog box (see fig. 5.4).

Fig. 5.4

The Edit Search
Groups dialog
box.

Adding a Search Group Entry

To create a new search group, display the Edit Search Groups dialog box; then select the **New** command button. FileFind places the cursor in an empty Group Name text box. In the Group Name text box, type the name you want to appear in the search group list. This name can be any descriptive text that helps you remember the focus of the search group.

Suppose, for example, that you want to add an entry for the word processing program Microsoft Word to the File Locate dialog box. You enter the following text in the Group Name text box and press Enter:

MS-Word documents

Next, in the File Specification text box, type a list of file specifications associated with the applications program. List a specific directory in this File Specification text box if you want FileFind to routinely search only that directory. You can skip (or not search for) a particular directory by typing a minus sign (–) to the left of the directory specification.

NOTE The information you enter in the File Specification text box is usually the same list you type in the corresponding File Associations text box in the Advanced Program Item Information dialog box when you create a program list item for this applications program. See Chapter 3, "Using the Desktop as a Program Manager," for more details.

MS-Word documents usually have the extension DOC, but documents in Rich Text Format (another format often used with Word) have the extension RTF. For these files, you type the following entry in the File Specification text box and then press Enter:

*.DOC *.RTF

Press Enter and select the **OK** command button. FileFind returns to the Search Groups dialog box, displaying the new entry in the list of search groups (see fig. 5.5).

Editing a Search Group Entry

You can edit a search group entry to change any aspect of its definition. You may want to add a new file specification to the MS-Word group, for example, if you have begun naming a certain category of file with an extension different from DOC or RTF.

Fig. 5.5

The Search
Groups dialog
box with the MS-
Word documents
search group
added.

To edit an entry, follow these steps:

1. In the Search Groups dialog box, choose **E**dit to display the Edit
    Search Group dialog box.

2. In the Search Group list box, scroll to highlight the entry you want
    to change. FileFind displays the search group's name and file
    specification in the Group Name and File Specification text boxes,
    respectively.

3. Use Tab or the mouse to move to the text box you want to edit
    and make the desired modifications.

4. Select **S**ave to accept the changes; then select **OK** to return to the
    Search Groups dialog box.

Deleting a Search Group Entry

When you want to delete a search group entry in the Search Group
dialog box, display the Edit Search Group dialog box and scroll the
highlighted bar in the Search Group list box to highlight the entry you
want to remove. FileFind displays the search group's name and file
specification in the Group Name and File Specification text boxes,
respectively. Select the **D**elete command button to delete the entry.
When you finish making deletions, select the **OK** command button to
return to the Search Groups dialog box.

Using a Search Group Entry

After you define a search group, using the group to locate files and then
search for a character string is simple. In fact, you can even use several
search groups together.

Suppose, for example, that you are looking for a cookie recipe you received several months ago from your good friend Mrs. Fields. You remember that you stored this file as an MS-Word word processing file that contains the word *cookie*. To find this file, follow these steps:

1. Starting in PC Tools Desktop, press F7 (Locate) or choose **F**ile and then **L**ocate to run FileFind.

2. From the FileFind window, select the **G**roups command button to display the Search Groups dialog box.

3. Use the mouse or the cursor-movement keys to select the appropriate search group entry—MS-Word documents, in this case.

   FileFind highlights the entry name in the Search These Groups list box.

4. Use the mouse or the cursor-movement keys to select the desired search group entries.

5. After you select the search groups you want, select the **OK** command button.

   FileFind returns to the FileFind window and, in the File Specification text box, enters the file specification for each search group.

6. Press Tab or use the mouse to move the highlighted bar to the Containing text box; then type the string for which you want FileFind to search. You can use as many as 32 characters. To search for the cookie recipe, for example, type **cookie**.

7. Check the appropriate check buttons and press Enter.

FileFind searches your hard disk for all files that meet the file specifications from the selected search group or groups, and then the program searches for files that contain the search string. Finally, FileFind indicates that the search is complete and asks whether you want to return to Desktop. Select **OK**, and FileFind returns you to Desktop and the Located Files screen, which displays a list of located files (see fig. 5.6). In this case, FileFind finds only one file that matches the file specifications and search string—COOKIE.DOC in the H:\WORD directory.

Adding Filters

In addition to searching for files by file name specifications and search groups, with FileFind you can narrow the scope of every search by using *search filters,* which enable you to search for files by file attributes, date, time, and file size. To use search filters, start FileFind and select the **F**ilters command button (or select **F**ilters from the **S**earch menu).

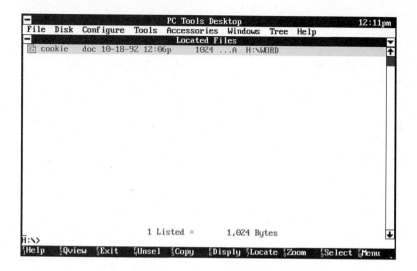

Fig. 5.6

Using a search group entry to find a specific file.

Search filters work somewhat differently on stand-alone and networked systems and use different dialog boxes. If you are running Desktop stand-alone, read the next section only. If you are on a network, read the next section for a description of basic search filters (size and modification date) and then go on to the section "Filters on a Network."

Filters on a Stand-alone System

On Desktop stand-alone, choosing Filters displays the Search Filters dialog box (see fig. 5.7).

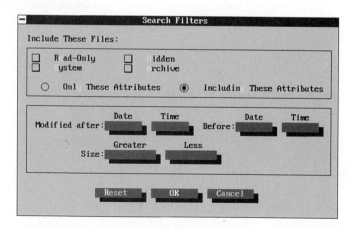

Fig. 5.7

The Search Filters dialog box.

The Search Filters dialog box contains the following check boxes:

- *Read-Only.* Select this option to search for read-only files.

- *System.* Select this option to search for files with system attributes.

- *Hidden.* Select this option to find hidden files.

- *Archive.* Select this option to search for files with the archive bit set.

As with all check boxes, the preceding attribute filters are independent. You can check none, one, two, three, or four of these boxes. Every time you check a box, you narrow the search to only files that have the checked attributes.

After you select attributes, choose one of these two option buttons:

- *Only These Attributes.* Select this option to limit files to those containing only the attributes you selected.

- *Including These Attributes.* Select this option to limit searches to files that contain *at least* the selected attributes.

The Search Filters dialog box contains the following text boxes, which you can leave blank or, if you want to narrow the search criteria, fill in:

- *Modified After/Before.* To indicate a span of time for which you want FileFind to search, type dates and times in these two pairs of text boxes. You specify a time when you want to select only files that have been created or last modified within the specified time period.

- *Size.* In the Greater and Less text boxes, type the upper and lower limits, in bytes, of the file sizes for which you want FileFind to look.

Filters on a Network

If your computer is connected to a local area network running the Novell Netware operating system, selecting the Filters command button from the FileFind window displays the Network Filters dialog box (see fig. 5.8). In addition to searching for size and modification date, as described in the previous section, the Network Filters dialog box enables you to search for file owner, last modifier, last accessed, last archived, and creation date.

On a Novell network, you can search for files that have one or more of the following file attributes: read-only, system, hidden, archive, execute-only, shareable, delete inhibit, hidden, index, rename inhibit, archive, transactional, and purge. To search for network file attributes, select the Edit **A**ttributes command button from the Network Filters dialog box. FileFind displays the Search Attributes dialog box (see fig. 5.9). Choose between the Only These Attributes option button and the Including These Attributes option button.

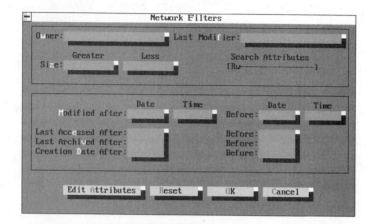

Fig. 5.8

The Network Filters dialog box.

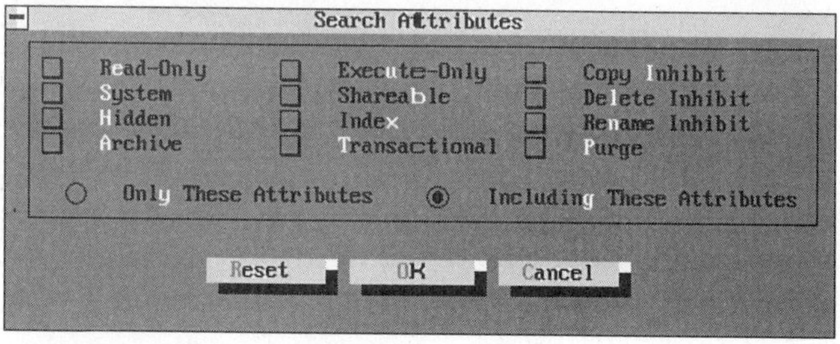

Fig. 5.9

The Search Attributes dialog box.

Using the Specified Filters

After you make the desired selections from the search filters, select the **O**K command buttons until FileFind displays the FileFind window, and choose Start to execute the search. FileFind limits its search to the files that meet the filter criteria you established.

Selecting Drives and Directories

By default, FileFind searches all directories on the current drive for files that match the specified criteria. The Drives command enables you to limit the search to specific directories, to search other drives on the system, and even to search multiple drives. This wide-ranging scope can be lifesaving if you have forgotten where you stored certain files. If your computer is connected to a Novell network, you can extend the search to network drives as well.

NOTE   If you are connected to another computer through DriveMap, the search can include those remote drives.

From the FileFind window, select the **D**rives command button (or select **S**elected Drives from the **S**earch menu). FileFind displays the Select Drives/Directory dialog box (see fig. 5.10).

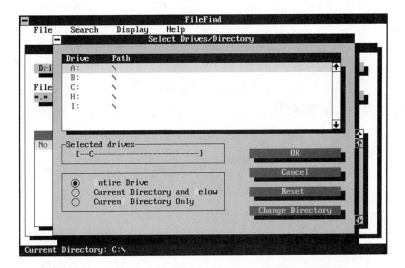

Fig. 5.10

The Select Drives/Directory dialog box.

The Select Drives/Directory dialog box contains a list box, three option buttons, and four command buttons. The list box lists the drives available on your system. The Selected Drives box, displayed just below the list box, shows a list of all drives selected for inclusion in the search. The Selected Drives box in figure 5.10, for example, indicates that drive C is currently the only selected drive. On a Novell network, the Select Drives/Directory dialog box lists network drives as well.

FileFind displays in high-intensity characters the drive letter and current path for each selected drive. To add drives to the search, click the mouse button on the drive letter in the list box or type the drive letter. FileFind adds the drive letter to the Selected drives box and displays this drive letter in the list box in high intensity.

The Select Drives/Directory dialog box lists the following option buttons:

■ *Entire Drive.* Select this option to search the entire disk drive for each drive selected. This option is the default.

■ *Current Directory and Below.* Select this option to search, in each selected drive, the current directory—the directory whose name appears under Path in the Selected Drives list box—and all its subdirectories (if any).

■ *Current Directory Only.* Select this option to search only the current directory in each selected drive.

 As FileFind searches, the DOS command line displays the directories being searched.

If you choose Current Directory and Below or Current Directory Only, the search applies to the currently selected directory (shown under Path) in each of the selected drives. You cannot change the path information in the Selected Drives list box by typing a new path; you must use the Change Directory command button.

To search a different directory, highlight in the Selected Drives list box the drive whose directory path you want to change. Select the Change **D**irectory command button. FileFind displays the Change Directory dialog box, with the current directory displayed. Type the new directory name and press Enter; then select the **OK** command button. FileFind returns to the FileFind window with the appropriate drive's current directory reset as specified.

Finding Duplicates

Unless you are lucky or have an exceptional memory, you probably have accidentally given the same name to two files on your disk or scattered different versions of the same file around your hard disk. DOS ordinarily prevents you from using a name more than once on the same directory but is perfectly satisfied with duplicate file names in different directories on a disk. When you use a file name more than once on a disk, however, you are likely to use the wrong version of a file in an operation. You can use FileFind to locate all occurrences of the duplicated file names on the selected disk or disks. Then you can use View (discussed later in this chapter) to take a quick look at the file contents.

To find duplicate files, you first display the FileFind window. Then you choose Find **D**uplicates from the **S**earch menu. FileFind displays the Duplicate Search Status box on the right side of the FileFind window.

The cursor rests in the File Specification text box. Type a file specification and press Enter. FileFind searches the selected drives and directories for duplicate files that meet the file specification.

T I P

Normally, the search considers any files with the same name and size to be duplicates; however, you can narrow the search to find duplicate copies of the same version of the file. Choose the Filters button to display the Duplicate Search Filters dialog box, and then choose Name, Size, **Date**. Alternatively, you can expand the search to find duplicate copies based on name alone by choosing **Name** in the dialog box.

As FileFind searches for files, the progress of the search appears in the Duplicate Search Status box. When the program finishes its search, FileFind displays a message indicating that the search is complete and the number of files found. Select **OK** to remove the message from the screen and to return to the FileFind Window.

In the list box that dominates the bottom half of the FileFind window, FileFind displays the file names of duplicate files in pairs (see fig. 5.11). Upon finding more than a single pair of duplicate file names, FileFind lists the file names in ascending order. You then can use the View File command on the File menu to determine the content of the duplicate files. You can use other commands from the File menu (Copy, Rename, Delete, Move, and Attributes on the Change submenu) to manipulate the files listed in the list box.

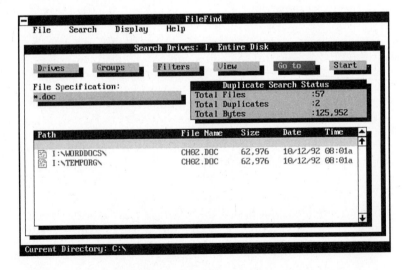

Fig. 5.11

The duplicate files found.

With the dual list display on, you can use the Compare Windows command from the Windows menu to compare file lists across directories or drives. Using Compare Windows, *nonmatching* files are selected. One useful application of Compare Windows is to make sure you have copied all the files from a hard disk subdirectory to a floppy.

T I P

For Related Information

◄◄ "Using Dialog Boxes," p. 42.

◄◄ "Adding and Editing Program Groups," p. 100.

◄◄ "Running Programs and Launching Files," p. 137.

FROM HERE...

Searching Files for Text

A third method of locating files involves using Desktop's Search Files option to search files listed in the current file list window or Located Files window. You can search for text or for a *hexadecimal number*, which is a base 16 number used primarily by programmers, by following these steps:

1. Make current the directory you want Desktop to search, or use FileFind to display a list of files in a Located Files window.

2. To limit the search to only some of the files in the current window, select those files. (Refer to Chapter 4, "Working on Files," for more information).

3. Select **F**ile and then Sear**c**h Files. FileFind displays the Text Search dialog box (see fig. 5.12).

   The Text Search dialog box displays a text box, five option buttons, and three command buttons.

4. In the text box, type the character string for which you want to search. You can use from 1 to 32 characters. Make sure that you type the string, referred to as the *search string*, exactly as you think it occurs in the target file. You don't have to be concerned, however, about whether characters are in upper- or lowercase. PC Tools Desktop ignores the case of letters when it searches.

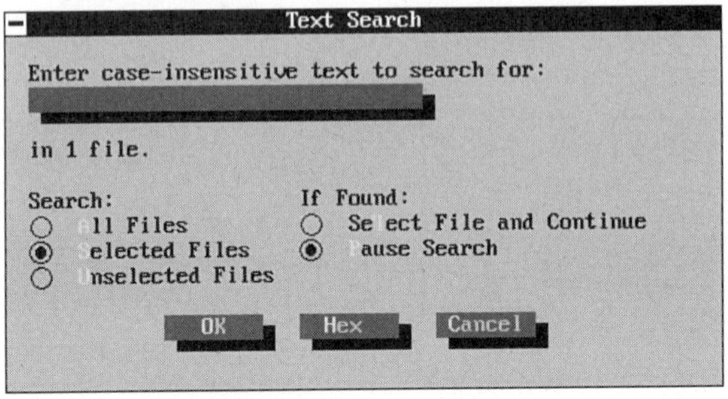

┌───┐
│ Text Search   │
│   │
│ Enter case-insensitive text to search for: │
│ ▓▓▓▓▓▓▓▓▓▓▓▓▓▓▓▓▓▓▓▓▓▓▓▓▓▓   │
│   │
│ in 1 file.   │
│   │
│ Search: If Found: │
│   ○ All Files   ○ Select File and Continue │
│   ◉ Selected Files   ◉ Pause Search   │
│   ○ Unselected Files   │
│   │
│   OK   Hex   Cancel   │
└───┘

Fig. 5.12

The Text Search
dialog box.

5. Press Tab to move the highlight to the Search option buttons.
   Select one of the following options:

   ◼ *All Files* searches all files in the current File List or Located
     Files window.

   ◼ *Selected Files* searches only selected files in the current
     window. This option is the default setting.

   ◼ *Unselected Files* searches in the current window only files
     that are not selected.

6. Press Tab to move the highlight to the If Found option buttons.
   Then select one of the options to specify the action you want
   Desktop to take when it finds a file that contains a string matching the search. The following list briefly describes the available
   options:

   ◼ *Select File and Continue* selects every file that contains the
     search string and then continues the search.

   ◼ *Pause Search* pauses Desktop when it finds a match. This
     option is the default setting.

7. Select the **OK** command button to start the search.

When Desktop finds a file that matches the search string, the resulting
action depends on which If Found option button you chose. If you selected the Select File and Continue button, Desktop selects each file
and continues the search. If you selected the Pause Search button,
Desktop displays the following message in the Text Search dialog box
when a match is found and changes to a different set of command
buttons:

    Found in file *filename*

The *filename* is the name of the file that contains the search argument.
The following lists the new command buttons available:

■ *Select* selects the file and continues the search. Desktop does not display this option if you chose the **S**elected Files option button in the Text Search dialog box (refer to fig. 5.12).

■ *Next File* continues the search in the next file (works only if you selected the **P**ause Search option in the Text Search dialog box).

■ *Edit* uses the hex editor to edit the file. (See Chapter 4, "Working on Files," for information about the hex editor.)

■ *Cancel* stops the search.

If no matches are found, the message in the Text Search dialog changes to the following:

```
The search string WAS NOT found.
```

For Related Information

◄◄ "Selecting and Deselecting Files," p. 134.

◄◄ "Using the Hex Editor," p. 157.

FROM HERE...

Looking at Files with View

The preceding sections in this chapter discussed how to find disk files that contain a particular text string that can be no longer than 32 characters. Often you need to see more than 32 characters of a file before you determine whether that file is the one you want. With the Quick View command, you can view files through the View window and an impressive array of *file viewers*, behind-the-scenes Desktop utilities that enable you to look at files without running the applications that created them. To look at a file, you do not need to choose a file viewer; if the file type is recognized, Desktop automatically selects the proper viewer. You can view the contents of any ASCII text file, any binary file, and files created by more than 30 different programs.

Displaying the View Window

Several methods are available for turning on the View window; the most common methods use Desktop's Windows menu and Quick View feature. You can also start View as a stand-alone program from the DOS command line. (At the DOS command line, type **view** and press Enter.) In addition, you can access the View window from within these PC Tools programs: Undelete, File Fix, FileFind, and CP Backup.

When you use the Windows menu method to display the View window in PC Tools Desktop, the View window fills only half the screen; if you use any of the other methods, the View window fills the entire screen. (The Windows menu method is described in Chapter 1, "Navigating the Desktop," and in Chapter 2, "Controlling the Desktop.") In all cases, the View window displays the contents of the current file—the file highlighted in the file list window, Located Files window, and so on.

 If one or more files are selected, the View window displays the first selected file, regardless of whether it is currently highlighted.

Use the View window when you want to scroll, in one part of the screen, through several files in the PC Tools Desktop file list window or in a Located Files window and, at the same time, want to see the contents of each file in another part of the screen. Because the Windows menu method displays the View Window in only half the screen, you can easily see the list of selected files and the contents of the files at the same time.

When Desktop displays the View window in the default horizontal orientation, the program shrinks the Tree window and File window until they fit in the upper half of the screen and then displays the View window in the lower half of the screen (see fig. 5.13). If Desktop is displaying a Located Files window when you turn on the View window, the Located Files window shrinks to fit in the upper half of the screen, and the View window becomes the lower half of the screen.

Alternatively, you can switch to the vertical orientation, which displays the View window as the right half of the screen, the Tree window in the upper-left quadrant, and the File window in the lower-left quadrant (see fig. 5.14). If you are viewing a Located Files window and View window combination when you switch to vertical orientation, the Located Files window becomes the left half of the screen, and the View window becomes the right half of the screen. To switch the view, choose Display Options from the **C**onfigure menu. From the Display Options submenu, choose Split **H**orizontal. The command is a toggle; to switch back to a horizontal orientation, choose the command again.

Sometimes you may want to see more data than fits in half the screen. In this situation, you can press F8 (Zoom) from the View window to zoom to a full screen. If the View window is not open yet, you can use the Quick View feature to display a full-screen view. Press F2 (QView) or select **Q**uick View from the **F**ile pull-down menu. If the Tree or File window is active, Desktop immediately opens a full-screen View window displaying the current file (see fig. 5.15).

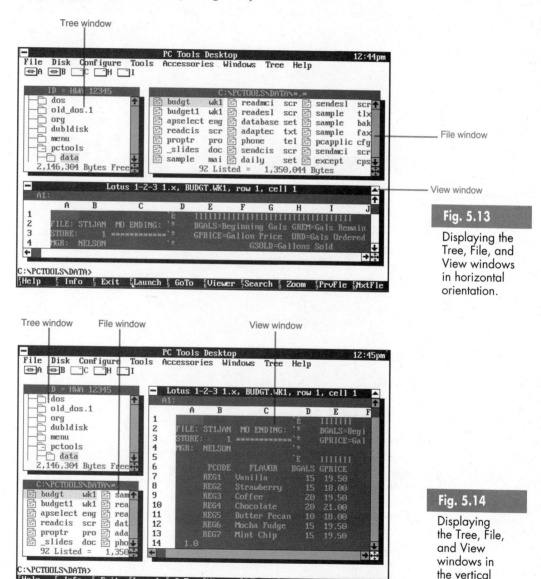

Fig. 5.13

Displaying the Tree, File, and View windows in horizontal orientation.

Fig. 5.14

Displaying the Tree, File, and View windows in the vertical orientation.

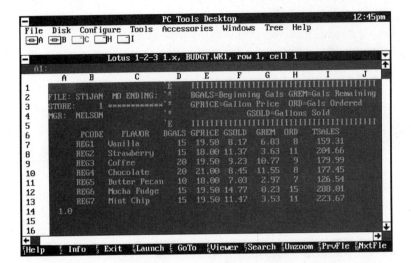

Fig. 5.15

The full-screen
View window
displaying the
current file.

If you are using PC Tools Desktop with windows hidden when you press F2 (QView), Desktop displays a dialog box containing the File To View text box. Type the directory and name of the file you want to view and press Enter. Desktop displays the file in a full-screen View window, similar to figure 5.15 but without the horizontal menu bar at the top. (Refer to Chapter 1, "Navigating the Desktop," for more information about hiding Desktop windows.)

Understanding the PC Tools Desktop Viewers

In most cases, the View window displays each file by using a viewer designed specifically to display files created by a particular PC-based applications program. PC Tools Desktop recognizes whether a file is associated with one of the recognized applications programs by examining the file's extension and contents. The viewers supplied with PC Tools Desktop enable you to view files created by any of the applications programs listed in the following:

Word Processors

    ASCII

    DCA Final Form

    DCA Revisable Form

Desktop Accessories Notepads

Display Write 3.0 through 6.0

Multimate 3.3

Microsoft Windows Write

Microsoft Word 5.0 and 5.5

Microsoft Works

Text

WordPerfect 4.2 through 5.1

WordStar 3.0 through 5.5

WordStar 2000

XyWrite

Spreadsheets

Lotus 1-2-3 1A, 2.0, and 3.0

Lotus Symphony 1, 2

Microsoft Works spreadsheet

Microsoft Excel

Mosaic Twin

Quattro

Quattro Pro

 VP Planner Plus is not listed, but these files will display with the Lotus viewer.

Database Managers

dBASE II, III, IV 1.0 through 1.2

Desktop Accessories database

Microsoft Works database

Paradox 3.0, 3.5

R:BASE 3.0

Miscellaneous

ARC

Binary

LHARC

PAK

PC Paintbrush (PCX format)

PC Secure

ZIP

ZOO

NOTE The archive viewers, such as the viewers for ZIP and ARC, display the archive file list. They do not allow viewing the archived files themselves.

By examining the file name extension and the contents of a file, PC Tools Desktop determines which viewer to use. In addition to program-specific viewers, PC Tools Desktop uses the binary viewer to display files that end in the extension EXE, COM, OBJ, BIN, or SYS. If no specific viewer is associated with the file's extension, Desktop uses the default viewer. When you install PC Tools Desktop, the default viewer is the Text Viewer, which displays a file as ASCII characters, regardless of whether the file actually contains ASCII characters.

T I P If you are viewing a PC Paintbrush graphic (or any graphic in PCX format), you can press F8 to toggle between full-screen graphic display and a text display. The text display is simply a summary of file statistics.

Moving around the View Window

Often, the information you need to see in the current file is located too deep in the file to be visible in the View window when you first display the file contents. To see the file, you must be able to move around within the View window itself. While the View window is the active window, you can use the mouse and the scroll bar that appears on the right side of the View window or the various cursor-movement keys to scroll to view any portion of the file.

The effects of the View window cursor-movement keys vary, depending on whether Desktop is displaying a spreadsheet file, a database file, or another type of file (text, word processing, PCX graphic, or binary). See table 5.1 for a description of the effects of the available cursor-movement keys.

Table 5.1 Cursor-Movement Keys for the View Window

Spreadsheet Files

Key	Effect
↓	Move down one cell
↑	Move up one cell
→	Move right one cell
←	Move left one cell
Ctrl+→	Scroll right one window
Ctrl+←	Scroll left one window
Home	Move to beginning of row
End	Move to end of row
PgDn	Scroll down one window
PgUp	Scroll up one window

Database Files

Key	Effect in Browse Mode	Effect in Record Mode
↓	Scroll down one line	Scroll down one field
↑	Scroll up one line	Scroll up one field
→	Scroll right one column	Scroll right one character
←	Scroll left one column	Scroll left one character
Home	Move to beginning of row	Move to beginning of record
End	Move to end of row	Move to end of record
PgDn	Scroll down one window	None
PgUp	Scroll up one window	None

Text, Word Processing, and Binary Files

Key	Effect
↓	Scroll down one line

continues

Table 5.1 Continued	
Text, Word Processing, and Binary Files	
Key	*Effect*
↑	Scroll up one line
Home	Move to first line in file
End	Move to last line in file
PgDn	Scroll down one window
PgUp	Scroll up one window

Understanding Viewer Function Key Commands

PC Tools Desktop provides a number of special function key commands and other keystroke commands in the View window. Table 5.2 lists all function key commands available in the View window.

The commands available when you are viewing a spreadsheet file are different from the commands that are available when you view a database or a word processing file. In a spreadsheet viewer, for example, you can use the F5 (GoTo) command to move to a particular cell. You can use the same function key command in a database viewer to move to a particular database record or to go to a particular line in a word processing file.

Key	Name	Viewer	Function
F1	Help	All	Displays the context-sensitive Help facility
F2	Info	All	Displays the name of the viewer and information about the file, including file name and date of last update.
		Spreadsheet	Lists number of rows and columns
		Database	Lists field names, field types, and field size

Table 5.2 Function Key Commands for the View Window

Key	Name	Viewer	Function
Shift+F2	Fields	Database only	Displays the Fields window, which lists the name, type, and length of every field in the file
Shift+F2	Cells	Spreadsheet only	Displays the Cells window, which lists the cell column letter (Name), cell type (Type), and cell width (Length)
F3 or Esc	Exit	All	Exits the current View window
Shift+F3	Wrap/ No Wrap	Text only	Turns on or off the feature that breaks lines to fit within the current window size
Shift+F3	Modes	PCX only	Displays a list of available video modes and shows which is selected
Shift+F3		1-2-3 Release 3 only	Displays a list of worksheets from which you can choose
F4	Launch	All	When View is started from Desktop, runs the applications program associated with the current file and loads the current file into the program (see Chapter 4)
F4	Files	All	When View is started from the DOS command line, displays the file list window on top of the viewer
Shift+F4	Tables	R:BASE only	Displays the R:BASE Tables dialog box showing number of rows and columns in every table in the database
F5	Goto	Spreadsheet	Goes to a specified cell
		Database	Goes to a specified record
		Word processing	Goes to a specified line and column
F6	Viewer	All	Displays the Viewers dialog box, from which you can check the current viewer and select from among the viewers supported by View

continues

Table 5.2 Continued

Key	Name	Viewer	Function
F7	Search	All	Performs character string search
Shift+F7	Again	All	Continues character string search
F8	Zoom or Unzoom	All	Displays View window display in full-screen size
		Paintbrush PCX	Toggles between graphics and text display
F9	PrvFle	All	Displays previous selected file or next file listed in file list window if no files are selected
Shift+F9	Record	Database only	Switches between browse (table) and record (form) modes
F10	NextFle	All	Displays next selected file or next file listed in file list window if no files are selected
Alt+ space bar	System Control	All	Displays the System Control menu

FROM HERE...

For Related Information

◄◄ "Understanding the PC Tools Desktop Windows," p. 33.

◄◄ "Moving, Resizing, Zooming, and Hiding the Windows," p. 36.

◄◄ "Displaying the View Window," p. 83.

◄◄ "Running Programs and Launching Files," p. 137.

Chapter Summary

In this chapter, you learned how to search for a file-by-file specification, how to group files by association with a particular applications program, and how to find files that contain specified text. You also learned how to apply filters to the search specification and how to add drives and directories to the search. This chapter also describes how to use View to see file contents.

Turn to Chapter 6, "Working on Disks," to learn how to use PC Tools Desktop and the Directory Maintenance program to work on your system's disks and directories.

Working on Disks

The capacity to pack hundreds—even thousands—of pages of information on a small, efficient, magnetic disk is one of the technological advancements that has helped fuel the PC explosion. Most personal computers use one or more magnetic disks to store software and data. This chapter explains many of PC Tools Desktop's disk- and directory-related functions, including the commands on PC Tools Desktop's pull-down Disk menu and the DM Directory Maintenance program. This chapter also discusses the disk-formatting program PC Format and the new Build Emergency Disk utility.

First, you learn how to prepare a disk for use. This chapter not only explains how to use PC Tools Desktop and PC Format to format disks, make system disks, prepare an emergency disk, and copy disks, but also describes how to use PC Tools Desktop to display information about the disk (the space available for storage, for example) and how to assign or change the disk volume label.

Next, you learn how to use PC Tools Desktop to scan a disk for data discrepancies. You examine how to compare the contents of two different disks and the files in two different directories. This chapter discusses how to scan the contents of a disk for a specific character string or hexadecimal value.

One of the keys to managing a computer's hard disk is appropriate use of directories. In this chapter's discussion of Desktop's Directory Maintenance functions, you learn how to add, rename, delete, move, and copy a directory, as well as how to modify the attribute byte of a directory file. You also learn how to use the stand-alone and highly visual DM program (available from the Disk menu) to work with network directories, or any fairly complex directory structure, at the tree level.

 Version 7.1's Park Disk Heads command is no longer available from the Disk menu, but the Park utility is still part of PC Tools. You can park disk heads before moving your computer by simply typing **park** at the DOS prompt and pressing Enter. This method is also available in Version 7.1. (The heads unpark when you press any key or turn the system off and then on again.)

Preparing a Disk

When you buy a box of computer disks, the disks usually are not ready for storing data. Although the manufacturer has tested the disks for magnetic integrity, the disks must be formatted by your computer's software before you can use them. (***Note:*** A relatively small percentage of disks intended for use in personal computers are sold already formatted; when disks are preformatted, the manufacturer states this fact clearly on the disk's label.) Depending on how you plan to use a disk, you may want to perform several other operations to prepare the disk for use. The sections that follow explain how to use PC Tools Desktop and PC Format to do the following:

- Format a disk
- Make a system disk
- Assign or change a disk's volume label
- Make a complete copy of another disk
- Display a report that includes such information as total disk space and total space available for storage

Formatting a Disk

A magnetic disk must be *formatted* before you can use it for storing data. Formatting, the function performed by the operating system (DOS) FORMAT command, divides the disk into sectors and creates a *boot* sector, a *file allocation table* (*FAT*) sector, and a *root directory* sector. (For more information about the different sectors created during the formatting process, see the section about viewing and editing disk contents later in this chapter.) Formatting also checks the disk for defects, marking defective areas (*bad sectors*) so that they are not used. In addition, the DOS FORMAT command displays a report that shows total storage space available on the disk, the number of bad sectors, the space used by system files, and the total remaining free storage space.

PC Tools provides a more user-friendly alternative to the DOS FORMAT command: the PC Format program. This section describes how to access and use the PC Format program to format floppy as well as hard disks.

PC Format is a replacement for the DOS FORMAT command. If you use this tool to format your disks, the Unformat utility program (see Chapter 11, "Recovering Damaged or Formatted Disks") can unformat a disk—even a floppy disk—you accidentally format. If you do not use PC Format, Unformat may not be capable of restoring an accidentally formatted floppy disk.

The DOS FORMAT programs prior to Version 5.0 format a floppy disk in such a way that the PC Tools program Unformat cannot restore any data that was on the disk. The FORMAT command included with DOS 5.0, however, is actually a PC Format version, licensed to Microsoft by Central Point Software. If a disk was formatted with DOS 5.0's FORMAT command, you should be able to recover an accidentally formatted disk, unless the disk was formatted with the destructive unconditional (/U) format option.

PC Format and versions of the DOS FORMAT command before DOS 5.0 differ significantly in the way they format a floppy disk. The old DOS FORMAT command is destructive when it formats a floppy disk. DOS FORMAT writes the hexadecimal value F6 to every sector in the disk and erases all existing data. PC Format, on the other hand, first determines whether the disk has been formatted previously. If so, PC Format clears the File Allocation Table (FAT) and the first character from every file name, but it does not erase any data (the program scans the entire disk, however, for bad sectors). PC Format saves the first letter of every file name to a safe place on the disk where Unformat can find it. If the disk has never been formatted, PC Format overwrites every track.

The pre-DOS 5.0 version of FORMAT and PC Format handle hard disk formatting in different ways. Most versions of DOS FORMAT do not overwrite data in formatting a hard disk, but they do erase the File Allocation Table (FAT), the root directory, and the boot record. (***Note:*** Compaq DOS Version 3.2 and earlier, AT&T DOS Version 3.1 and earlier, and some versions of DOS from Burroughs overwrite all data on the hard disk.) PC Format, however, deletes the FAT and the boot record but erases only the first character of every file name in the root directory; it saves every erased first character in a safe place on the disk where Unformat can find it.

To format a floppy disk, first display PC Tools Desktop. Select **Disk** from the horizontal menu bar to display the Disk pull-down menu, shown in figure 6.1, and then choose **Format**. PC Tools Desktop clears the screen and starts PC Format, displaying the PC Format screen and the Drive Selection dialog box (see fig. 6.2).

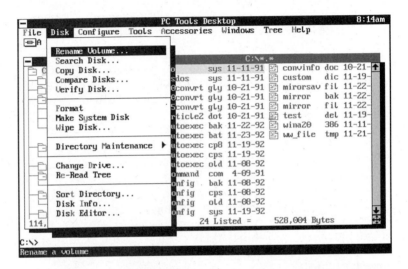

Fig. 6.1

PC Tools Desktop Disk menu.

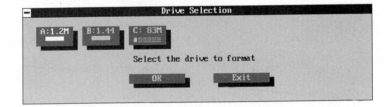

Fig. 6.2

PC Format's Drive Selection dialog box.

Alternatively, you can start PC Format from DOS. At the DOS command line, type the following command and press Enter (see the section, "Running PC Format from the DOS Command Line," for more about using PCFORMAT from the command line):

    PCFORMAT

PC Format loads and displays the PC Format screen and the Drive Selection dialog box.

Although you can run PC Format from the DOS command line, the easiest way to use PC Format is through PC Tools Desktop. Assuming that you have loaded PC Tools Desktop as a memory-resident program, you can even format a disk from within another DOS applications program.

The Drive Selection dialog box displays a rectangular icon for every disk drive in your computer. Each icon includes the drive letter and a number that indicates the disk's storage capacity. In figure 6.2, for example, the dialog box has disk drive icons for the following: 1.2M floppy disk drive A, 1.44M floppy disk drive B, and 83M hard disk drive.

Either click the drive letter or type the letter that corresponds to the drive you want to format and select the **OK** command button. PC Tools Desktop displays the Select Format Options dialog box (see fig. 6.3).

To double-check that you selected the desired drive, look at the dialog box title bar. It includes the name of the drive you are about to format.

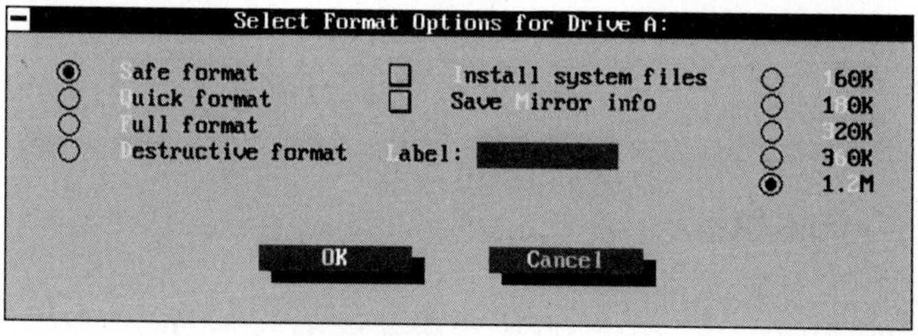

Fig. 6.3

The Select Format Options dialog box.

The Select Format Options dialog box displays the following option buttons:

■ *Safe Format.* Use this option, the default, to make PC Format format the disk in such a way that the Unformat program can recover the disk. The program scans the entire disk for bad sectors.

■ *Quick Format.* Select this option when you are formatting a disk that has been formatted previously. Quick Format is also a "safe" format because you can later use Unformat to recover data that was on the disk. Using this option is faster than the Safe format option, however, because the Quick Format option does not scan the disk for bad sectors.

■ *Full Format.* Use this option to rejuvenate a disk that might have marginal sector IDs. This option causes PC Format to read and store in memory the data from each track on the disk, format the track, rewrite the data, and then clear the root directory and file allocation table. Because the data is still intact, this option also is a safe format option.

■ *Destructive Format.* Employ this option for security purposes when you want to be positive that no one can recover any data from the disk after you complete the format operation. This option causes PC Format to overwrite all data on the disk.

The Select Format Options dialog box also contains the following check boxes:

■ *Install System Files.* Select this box when you want the disk to be *bootable*. A bootable disk, also called a *system disk*, contains a copy of three operating system files needed to *boot* (start up) your computer's operating system (DOS). Two of these files, which must be installed in the disk's first track (track 0), usually should be copied to the disk before any other file is added (these two files are IBMBIO.COM and IBMDOS.COM when you use IBM DOS, or IO.SYS and MSDOS.SYS when you use MS-DOS). Choose this option if you want the two hidden files and COMMAND.COM to be copied to the formatted disk. ***Note:*** The Make System Disk command on the Disk menu creates a system disk in a single step.

■ *Save Mirror Info.* Check this box when you have installed the PC Tools Mirror program and want to capture information about current files, in case you want to unformat the disk (see Chapter 11, "Recovering Damaged or Formatted Disks"). Using this option causes PC Format to take longer than it would otherwise but improves the chances of recovering all files on the disk if you later realize it was formatted by mistake.

When you format a 5 1/4-inch floppy disk in a high-density disk drive, PC Format lists five option buttons on the right side of the dialog box: 160K, 180K, 320K, 360K, and 1.2M. If you are formatting a disk in a double-density 5 1/4-inch drive, the fifth option is not listed. Similarly, the following options are available for a 3 1/2-inch high-density drive: 720K and 1.4M (PC Format displays a 2.8M option for drives capable of formatting disks to that capacity). When you are formatting a disk in a double-density 3 1/2-inch drive, 720K is the only option listed. Choose the option button that matches the disk you want to format.

NOTE Low-density disks formatted in a high-density drive can be used in the high-density drive but may not work reliably in a low-density drive. Also, do not try to format a high-density disk at a lower density, as you might try to do to move files to a computer with a low-density drive.

The Select Format Options dialog box includes one text box, the Label text box. Type an optional volume label in this text box. The label can contain up to 11 characters.

After you make the necessary selections from the option buttons and check boxes and fill in the label text box (if you want a volume label), select the **OK** command button to continue.

If PC Format finds any files on the disk, the programs shows you the files so that you can decide whether to go on. A dialog box lists any existing files and informs you that PC Format is ready to delete them. Select the **OK** button to proceed. (Select **C**ancel to start over with a different disk.) The program begins formatting the disk and displays the progress window (see fig. 6.4).

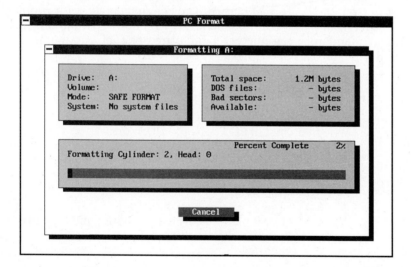

Fig. 6.4

The PC Format progress window showing the percentage of completed formatting.

As PC Tools Desktop formats the disk, the progress of the operation is shown as a growing horizontal bar. The progress window displays the drive letter, the format type, and whether system files will be copied to the formatted disk. When the formatting is finished, PC Format displays in the progress window the total space on the disk, the space available, and a disk volume serial number. Select **E**xit if you do not want to format another disk; select **OK** to return to the Select Format Options dialog box to format another disk. If you select OK and return to the Select Option dialog box, you can cancel from there as well.

NOTE The volume serial number is a sequential number assigned by PC Format and is unrelated to the volume label, if any, that you assign to the disk. DOS 4.01+ also adds a nonsequential serial number, meant as a "unique-as-possible" identifier for the disk.

Running PC Format from the DOS Command Line

As mentioned in the preceding section, you can access the PC Format screen and dialog boxes by typing **pcformat** at the DOS command line and pressing Enter. If you prefer, however, you can run PC Format entirely from the command line, without having to select options and buttons from the PC Format screen. The command syntax for running PC Format from the DOS command line is as follows (parameters in **bold** are mandatory; parameters in *italic* are optional; parameters in UPPERCASE must be spelled exactly as shown):

PCFORMAT d: */? /V /V:label /S /Q /P /TEST /VIDEO /1 /4 /8 / N:xx /T:yy /F:nnnn /R /F /DESTROY*

NOTE When you install PC Tools, the DOS Format command is renamed to FORMAT!.COM to remove it from active service. A batch file is created to run PC Format when you enter **format**. Consequently, you can type **pcformat** or **format** and get the same result.

Substitute the drive letter for **d**. This drive designation must be preceded by a space. To format a disk in drive A, for example, using the default parameters, type the following command and press Enter:

PCFORMAT A:

The follow paragraphs explain the use of the remaining parameters.

/? displays the help screen shown in figure 6.5.

/V enables you to add a volume label to the disk. As soon as PC Format finishes formatting the disk, it prompts you to enter a volume name. Type as many as 11 characters (including spaces) and press Enter.

```
PC Format V8.0 (c)1987-1992 Central Point Software, Inc.

   PCFORMAT [d:] [parameters...]

  d:     - Drive to format - must be included to format from the command line
General Parameters:
  /V     - Prompt for new volume label
  /V:label - Specify new volume label
  /S     - Include DOS system files - make it bootable
  /Q     - Quickly erase a previously formatted disk
  /P     - Print information on the screen to LPT1 (PRN)
  /TEST  - Simulate format without writing to disk
  /?     - Display this command-line help
  /VIDEO - Display command-line help for video/mouse parameters
Additional Parameters for Floppy Disks:
  /1     - Single-sided format
  /4     - Format 360K disk in 1.2MB drive
  /8     - 8 sectors per track
  /N:nn  - Specify number of sectors per track (nn = 8,9,15,18,36)
  /T:m   - Specify number of tracks (nn = 40,80)
  /F:nnnn - Specify disk size (nnnn = 160,180,320,360,720,1200,1440,2880)
  /R     - Read each track, reformat it, and rewrite data
  /F     - Like /R but also delete all files
  /DESTROY - Format and erase all data
C:\>
```

Fig. 6.5

The PC Format
help screen.

/V:label adds the volume label specified in the parameter *label*.

/S copies the system files to the newly formatted disk, creating a bootable disk.

/Q performs a quick format. Use this option when the disk already is formatted and you want PC Format to just erase the directory and FAT but not to do a surface scan.

/P prints all screen messages to the printer connected to LPT1 (the first printer port).

When */TEST* is added to any PC Format command, this parameter simulates formatting. Use this option when you are not sure what PC Format will do in response to a particular PC Format option. PC Format seems to execute the command, displaying all prompts and messages, but it does not actually format the disk. You can preview the format procedure before it takes effect, which is useful if you have any doubt that you selected the proper disk format.

/1 formats a disk as a single-sided media (floppy drive only).

/4 formats 5 1/4-inch double-density disks (360K or 180K) in a high-density 5 1/4-inch drive. Disks formatted in this manner may not be readable in a double-density drive (floppy drive only).

/8 formats 8 sectors per track rather than the standard 9 sectors per track. DOS versions before Version 2.0 read only 8 sectors per track (floppy drive only).

/N:s/T:t specifies the number of sectors per track (*s* = 8, 9, 15, 18, or 36) and number of tracks per side (*t* = 40 or 80)—floppy drive only. If you use this parameter, you must specify both *s* and *t*. This parameter is an alternative to the */F:nnnn* parameter.

The */F:nnnn* parameter specifies the type of media you want to format. The options for *nnnn* are (in kilobytes) 160, 180, 320, 360, 720, 1200, 1440, and 2880 (1440 kilobytes = 1.44M; 2880 kilobytes = 2.88M). This parameter is an alternative to the */N:s/T:t* parameters (floppy drive only). If you do not use any of these parameters, PC Format defaults to the largest capacity that the drive is capable of formatting. If your drive is a high-density 3 1/2-inch drive, for example, PC Format defaults to 1440.

The */R* parameter causes PC Format to recondition or clean up marginal-sector identifying marks while retaining the data (floppy drive only). This operation helps to ensure that DOS can read all sectors on the disk. PC Format reads each track, reformats the track, and then rewrites the data back to the track. The reconditioning requires more time to complete than a normal format. See Chapter 11, "Recovering Damaged or Formatted Disks," for a discussion about the similar Revitalize a Disk command in the DiskFix program.

The */F* parameter is the same as /R, but it erases also the File Allocation Table (floppy drive only). This parameter is equivalent to the Full Format option button on PC Format's Select Format Options dialog box.

Use the */DESTROY* parameter to overwrite the contents of the entire floppy disk. If you use this parameter to format a disk, you cannot recover the disk with Rebuild because all data is erased from the disk (floppy drive only). This parameter is equivalent to the Destructive Format option button on PC Format's Select Format Options dialog box.

Some of these parameters duplicate options available when you run PC Format from Desktop, and some (such as the */P* and */T* parameters) are unique. The capability to save Mirror information when formatting is not available from DOS.

When you execute a PC Format command from the command line, it informs you of the drive letter, disk type, and current parameters. The program tells you how many sectors, cylinders (tracks), and sides are going to be formatted. Figure 6.6, for example, shows PC Format using the /F parameter and formatting 15 sectors, 80 cylinders, and 2 sides. If this disk, a 1.2M disk, already contains data, PC Format tells you. To approve the format, type **yes** and press Enter. PC Format formats your disk and uses any parameters you have specified.

```
C:\>PCFORMAT A: /f
PC Tools disk formatter V8
(c)1987-1992 Central Point Software, Inc.

Will format drive A:  (physical # 00h, type= 1.2M 5.25-inch)
Using options - /F

Formatting 15 sectors, 80 cylinders, 2 sides.
Press Enter when ready...

Diskette may already contain data.

Are you SURE you want to do this?
If so, type in YES; anything else cancels.
? No
```

Fig. 6.6

Formatting a
1.2M disk.

Making a Disk Bootable

If you turn on your PC one day and the system fails to start, or *boot*, from the hard disk, you can still start your PC from the A drive—if you have a bootable disk, also called *a system disk* because, in addition to being formatted, this disk includes basic system information. As explained in the preceding two sections, PC Format enables you to copy the system files to a newly formatted disk by either checking the **I**nstall System Files check box in the Select Format Options dialog box or using the /S parameter from the command line.

PC Tools Desktop, however, provides a shortcut. When you want to format a disk and make it bootable, select Make S**y**stem Disk from the **D**isk menu. PC Tools Desktop starts PC Format with the /S parameter. Refer to the preceding sections for a full discussion of PC Format. After PC Format formats the specified disk and installs the requisite system files, the screen returns to PC Tools Desktop.

If your computer won't boot, a system floppy disk can get you started, but it won't be able to help you solve any serious disk problems, or recover any lost information. For full protection, create a PC Tools emergency disk. Instructions are provided in "Preparing an Emergency Disk" later in this chapter.

T I P

Renaming a Disk Volume Label

Every disk can have an optional *volume label* (a name that can contain from 1 to 11 characters, including spaces). Volume labels are particularly useful when you use many floppy disks. By using clear, descriptive volume labels, you can keep track of the information stored on your disks. To make a disk readily identifiable, write on the actual label attached to the floppy disk the name used as the volume label .

PC Tools Desktop gives you an opportunity to add a volume label when you format a disk. To later modify a volume label or to add a label to a disk that does not yet have a name, make current the disk drive that contains the disk you want to label and select **R**ename Volume from the **D**isk menu. PC Tools Desktop displays the Disk Rename dialog box. In this box, PC Tools Desktop displays the current volume label and a text box in which you enter the new label. Type the new name, and then select the **R**ename command button. If you decide not to change the name, select **C**ancel.

Copying a Disk

You often may need to make a complete copy of an entire floppy disk. For example, a good practice is to make a copy of every disk distributed in a new software package and then use the copies to install the software (subject to limitations stated in the licensing agreements). You can use PC Tools Desktop's disk **C**opy Disk command to make a complete copy of a DOS-formatted disk, including any system files and other hidden files. (If necessary, this command even formats the target disk as it copies.)

> **NOTE** Some disks distributed by software publishers are *copy protected*, which means that these disks have been coded during manufacturing so that they cannot be copied successfully with normal disk-copy programs. PC Tools Desktop's **C**opy Disk command does not make usable copies of such disks. Special utility programs are available, however, for making backup copies of copy-protected software. One such program is the popular Copy II PC from Central Point Software, the publisher of PC Tools.

Like the DOS DISKCOPY utility, PC Tools Desktop requires identical drive type and disk density for the source and target disks. Unless you have more than one drive of the same type, this means using the same drive for the source and target disk, which could require swapping disks several times. In Version 8.0, the source disk is read in one pass: no swapping is necessary. Also, you can make multiple copies of the same disk without rereading the source information.

> **CAUTION:** If you use as the target disk a disk that already contains data, the original data is overwritten and unrecoverable.

> Before you start copying a disk, place a tab over the original disk's write-protect notch (for 5 1/4-inch disks) or slide open the original disk's write-protect hole (for 3 1/2-inch disks). This practice protects against data loss if you accidentally try to copy the target disk to the original.

T I P

To use PC Tools Desktop to copy a disk, first place the source disk in one disk drive and the target disk in another (both drives must be the same type, and the disks must be the same density). If you have only one floppy disk drive, place the source disk in the drive. Make current the drive that holds the source disk and verify that it contains the files you want to copy. Select **Disk** to display the pull-down Disk menu, and then choose the **C**opy Disk option. PC Tools Desktop displays the Disk Copy dialog box (see fig. 6.7).

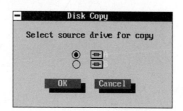

Fig. 6.7

The Disk Copy dialog box.

The Disk Copy dialog box lists the floppy drives installed in your computer. A message in the dialog box prompts you to select the source drive. Select the option button that corresponds to the drive that contains the source disk. Choose the **OK** command button.

> **NOTE** PC Tools Desktop lists both drive A and drive B even if only one floppy disk drive is installed. In that case, both drive letters refer to the same physical drive.

Next, PC Tools Desktop prompts you to select the target drive. Select the option button that corresponds to the drive that contains (or will contain) the target disk. PC Tools Desktop displays a second Disk Copy dialog box containing the message `Insert SOURCE diskette in drive d`, where *d* is the letter of the drive you selected to contain the source disk. To begin the copy procedure, select the **OK** command button.

> **NOTE**   The disk must be in DOS format and it must not be copy-protected.

As PC Tools Desktop performs the disk-copy procedure, the program displays the message `Disk Copy proceeding` and depicts progress as a series of letters displayed beneath track numbers. When PC Tools Desktop reads a track, R appears beneath the track number being read (see fig. 6.8). PC Tools Desktop reads the disk information and then prompts you to insert the target disk in the drive you selected. Place the target disk in the appropriate drive (switch disks if you are using one drive only) and again select the **OK** command button.

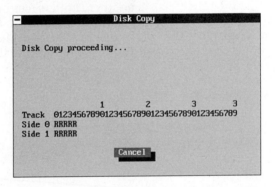

Fig. 6.8

Reading the source disk during the disk-copy procedure.

While writing data to the target disk, PC Tools Desktop indicates progress by changing each R first to F, then to W, and finally to a period (.). The F means that PC Tools Desktop is formatting the track; the W means that PC Tools Desktop is writing the track; the period means that the track has been copied successfully.

After the disk has been copied successfully, Desktop gives you the option of making another copy of the same disk. Select **OK** to make a duplicate; select **C**ancel to return to Desktop.

Obtaining Disk Information

After you format (and as you use) a disk, you may want to determine
the amount of space available for storing files. PC Tools Desktop's Disk
Info command provides this (and other) information.

To display disk information, make current the drive that holds the disk
in which you are interested, select **D**isk, and choose Disk **I**nfo. PC Tools
Desktop displays the Disk Information dialog box (see fig. 6.9).

```
┌─────────────────────────────────────────────┐
│ ■        Disk Information                     │
│                                               │
│  Volume Label HWA 12345    created on  6-17-91 at  1:29 │
│        83,793,920 bytes of total disk space.  │
│         1,456,128 bytes available on volume.  │
│        54,149,120 bytes in      7 hidden files. │
│        28,123,136 bytes in    855 user files.  │
│            65,536 bytes in     22 directories. │
│                 0 bytes in bad sectors.        │
│               512 bytes per sector.            │
│                 4 sectors per cluster.         │
│                34 sectors per track.           │
│            40,915 total clusters.              │
│           164,013 total sectors.               │
│             4,824 total tracks.                │
│                 5 sides.                       │
│               965 cylinders.                   │
│                                               │
│                  ▐  OK  ▌                      │
│                                               │
└─────────────────────────────────────────────┘
```

Fig. 6.9

The Disk Informa-
tion dialog box.

In addition to the volume label, the Disk Information dialog box lists
several facts about storage space, including the total amount of storage space (in bytes), the amount of storage space still available for use,
the amount of storage space occupied by hidden files, the amount of
space occupied by user files (nonsystem files), and the amount of
space occupied by directory files. This dialog box also reports several
characteristics of the disk. These characteristics include the number of
bad (unreadable) sectors, the number of bytes in a single sector, the
number of sectors per cluster; the number of sectors per track; the
total number of clusters; the total number of sectors; and the number
of tracks, sides, and cylinders. Although not of great interest for many
computer users, this information can be vital to the person who repairs
your computer if you encounter disk problems.

To return to the PC Tools Desktop screen, click the close box, select
the **O**K command button, or press Esc or F3 (Exit).

For Related Information

▶▶ "Revitalizing a Disk," p. 429.

FROM HERE...

Preparing an Emergency Disk

One of the most useful functions of Version 7.1 of PC Tools was its capability to create a recovery floppy disk to allow rebooting the computer and rebuilding the disk in the event of hard disk problems. The option to create this disk, however, was available only from the PC Tools Install program. Updating the disk, recommended after any change to system configuration, required re-running Install.

In Version 8.0, this option, now called the Build Emergency Disk command, is placed on the Desktop Tools menu. (You can use this command to update a recovery disk created with Version 7.1.) The emergency disk has three uses:

- You can use the emergency disk to start your system without automatically placing in memory all the usual device drivers and memory-resident programs (those listed in the hard disk's CONFIG.SYS and AUTOEXEC.BAT files). Some PC Tools programs, such as DiskFix and Compress, require that memory be cleared before they are run. By restarting from the emergency disk, you can be certain no miscellaneous programs are lurking in the background.

- You can use the emergency disk to boot the system if the hard disk boot sector has been altered by a virus or otherwise damaged.

- Because the emergency disk copies vital information about your system's CMOS and partition table, you can use this disk to recover from almost any hard disk disaster. With a toolkit of PC Tools recovery utilities, such as DiskFix and Undelete, you can work your way back from otherwise irreversible emergencies.

> **WARNING:** The emergency disk is specific to the system on which it was created. If you have more than one PC, do not try to use the same emergency disk on both. Make a separate disk *on* each one, *for* each one, and label each disk clearly.

For instructions on using the emergency disk, refer to Chapter 11, "Recovering Damaged or Formatted Disks."

Creating a New Emergency Disk

To create an emergency disk, insert a floppy disk (formatted or unformatted) in drive A. Choose **T**ools and then choose Build Emergency Disk. Alternatively, from DOS, type **edisk** and press Enter. After scanning your system for viruses and analyzing the system, the program displays the Build Emergency Disk Options dialog box (see fig. 6.10).

> **NOTE** When you create an emergency disk, you must use the boot drive, usually drive A. You also should use the highest-capacity disk compatible with the drive.

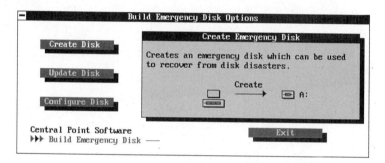

Fig. 6.10

The Build Emergency Disk Options dialog box.

You can let Edisk create the disk automatically using what it judges to be the optimum setup, as described in the following paragraph, or you can review the setup and make your own choices.

If you want to create the disk with the maximum amount of recovery information, choose **C**reate Disk. Edisk scans the floppy for viruses and then analyzes the format. If the disk contains existing files, you are given the option to choose another disk or overwrite the files. The program then copies the system information and recovery utilities to the disk. At a minimum, on a low-density 360K disk, these elements include the DiskFix program, special AUTOEXEC.BAT and CONFIG.SYS files, COMMAND.COM, the IO.SYS and MSDOS.SYS system files (or their IBM DOS counterparts), and the PARTNSAV.FIL that contains the all-important CMOS and partition data.

> If you have a low-density drive, create an emergency disk that will start your system and perform a basic disk repair; then create separate disks (using PC Config) containing other programs such as Undelete, Unformat, Memory Information (MI), and DiskEdit.
>
> **T I P**

To review and possibly change the utilities that will be installed, choose Configure Disk. The program displays the Configure Emergency Disk dialog box listing the options for your particular system (see fig. 6.11). The program's choices for the optimum setup are checked, and the total space required is shown next to the Media box. To remove a file from the list, highlight it and press Enter, or click the file: the check will be removed.

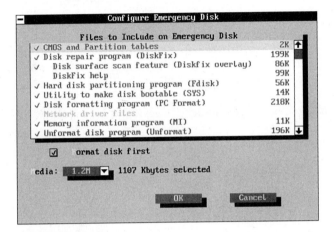

Fig. 6.11

The Configure
Emergency Disk
dialog box.

When you are satisfied with the choices, choose **OK**. Edisk copies the selected files to the disk.

After the emergency disk has been prepared, the program displays the message that the operation is complete and the disk should now be tested. See the section, "Testing the Disk," for details on this important step.

Updating after a Configuration Change

If you created an emergency disk when you installed PC Tools 8.0, or a recovery disk with Version 7.1, you can use the Build Emergency Disk command to update it. Updating is recommended when you have made a change to your system configuration, such as adding or changing a drive, partitioning the hard disk differently, or adding or removing a mouse, keyboard, or other input device.

Insert the current emergency disk in drive A and follow the steps described in the preceding section, "Creating a New Emergency Disk," to access the Build Emergency Disk Options dialog box. Choose **Update Disk**. The program determines what files must be recopied and updates the disk accordingly.

Testing the Disk

The emergency disk is useless if it doesn't work—something you do not want to discover during an emergency. Take a moment to check the disk immediately after you create it so that you can enjoy peace of mind rare among computer users.

To test the disk, insert it in drive A and close the drive door. Press Ctrl+Alt+Del to reboot the system. If the disk is intact, the computer boots from drive A, and the A prompt appears, with the message `Central Point Emergency Disk V8.0`. On the next line, the program displays the date and time the disk was created. Now, put a label on the disk, put a tab over the write-protect notch (on a 5-1/4 inch disk) or slide open the write-protect hole (on a 3-1/2 inch disk), and put the disk in a safe place. Finally, press Ctrl+Alt+Del to restart your computer.

If the system did *not* boot successfully, give it a second try. If the problem continues, make sure that you are using the proper media format for your disk drive; then run the Edisk program again (from DOS or Desktop).

Looking for Discrepancies after Copying

When copying electronic information, whether an entire disk or files within a directory, making sure that the operation was successful and complete is often essential. With the Compare Disk command, you can make sure that the media did not fail in copying a disk. With the Compare Windows command, you can make sure that you did not fail to select all the intended files—or the proper versions—to copy or move. Compare Windows checks file names, sizes, and dates; Compare Disk checks actual information on the disk, sector by sector. Finally, with the Verify command you can make sure that all sectors of a copied disk are readable.

Comparing the Contents of the Two Disks

Using PC Tools Desktop's Compare Disk command, you can compare the contents of two disks. The purpose of this command is to determine whether two disks are identical; this command is most useful for determining whether a disk-copy operation was successful.

To compare the contents of two disks, select Compare Disk from the Disk menu. PC Tools Desktop displays the Disk Compare dialog box. A message in the dialog box prompts you to select the source drive. Select the option button that corresponds to the drive which contains the source disk. Choose the OK command button.

Next, PC Tools Desktop prompts you to select the target drive. Select the option button that corresponds to the drive which contains (or will contain) the target disk. PC Tools Desktop displays a second Disk Compare dialog box containing the message Insert first diskette in drive d, where d is the letter of the drive you selected to contain the source disk. Select the OK command button.

As PC Tools Desktop performs the disk-compare procedure, the program displays the message Comparing disk in drive n to disk in drive m and depicts progress as a series of letters displayed beneath track numbers. When PC Tools Desktop reads a track from the original disk, R appears beneath the track number being read. PC Tools Desktop reads as many tracks as will fit in memory and then prompts Insert second diskette in d, where d is the target disk drive. Place the target disk in the second drive (switch disks when you use the same drive) and again select the OK command button.

While comparing the target disk's data to that of the original disk, PC Tools Desktop indicates progress by changing each R to a C and then to a period (.). The C means that PC Tools Desktop is comparing the track; a period means that the track has been compared successfully.

If the contents of both disks are identical, PC Tools Desktop displays the message Diskette compare complete. Select the Cancel command button to return to the PC Tools Desktop screen.

If PC Tools Desktop finds a discrepancy between the two disks, the following message appears:

Mismatch in logical sector nnnnnnn at offset nnn

"asc" (hex) in 1st disk, "asc" (hex) in 2nd disk

PC Tools Desktop replaces the ns in this message with numbers, asc with ASCII characters, and hex with hexadecimal numbers. Use this message to determine what is different between the two disks. You can use the Hex Edit File command (on the Change File submenu) to fix the error, or you can use the Copy Disk command to make a good copy of the original disk.

If you want to approve the compare-disk operation, select the OK command button. PC Tools Desktop marks (with the letter E) the track that contained the error. To return to the PC Tools Desktop screen without completing the comparison, select Cancel.

If a disk holds more data than can be stored in your computer's memory (RAM), PC Tools Desktop cannot compare the entire disk in one pass. You are prompted to swap disks as many times as necessary. Repeat this procedure until the disks have been compared completely.

Comparing the Contents of Two Directories

With the dual list display turned on, you can visually scan the file lists of two directories to determine whether they match (after copying files) or do not match (after moving files, for example). In Version 8.0, however, PC Tools Desktop provides a command that automatically scans for differences. This command is especially useful when you work with large directories.

To compare two directories or drives, follow these steps:

1. Select the first directory (or drive).

2. Choose **W**indows and then Dual **L**ist Display. PC Tools Desktop displays files for the selected directory in both File windows.

3. In one of the Tree windows, select the comparison directory or drive. Desktop displays those files in the associated File window.

4. From the **W**indows menu, choose **C**ompare Windows.

Desktop compares the two lists and selects all the files, in each directory, that are not matched in the other, as shown in figure 6.12. To match, files must be identical in name, size, and date last modified.

You then can make active the File window for the most current directory, and use the **F**ile menu **C**opy command to copy the selected files to the other directory.

Verifying a Disk

A second way to check a disk for possible discrepancies is to use the Verify Disk command, which confirms that all sectors in a DOS-formatted disk can be read. Verifying a disk is not quick (a few minutes for a typical floppy), so use this option if you suspect some problem, or the disk is so important you cannot afford any possible error.

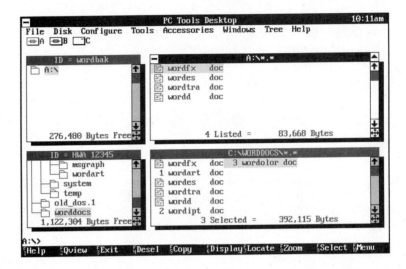

Fig. 6.12

Dual file lists
after comparing
windows.

The Verify Disk command operates on the current disk and drive, so before verifying, change drives if necessary. To ascertain whether all sectors of the current disk are readable, select **D**isk and choose **V**erify Disk. Desktop displays the Disk Verify dialog box containing the message Drive *d* is about to be verified, where *d* is the drive letter of the current disk drive. Select the **V**erify command button (or **C**ancel if you realize the wrong disk is selected). Desktop tries to read all the sectors on the disk.

If Desktop successfully reads all sectors on the disk, the program displays the message No errors found. Drive *d* has been Verified (*d* is the drive containing the disk being verified). Select the **C**ancel command button to return to the Desktop screen.

During the initial format procedure, unreadable sectors of the disk are marked as bad sectors and set aside so that they are never used for storing data. Occasionally, through failure of the magnetic media or some other mishap, an additional portion of a disk may become un-readable. If, during execution of the Verify command, Desktop cannot read a sector that has not been marked as a bad sector, the program displays the following message:

    Logical sector nnnnnn (Drive d) has an error

Desktop indicates whether the sector is in the DOS system area, in a file, or not allocated. If the sector is not allocated, you are given the option of marking the sector as bad. To do so, select the **M**ark Bad command button. If the sector is in use by a file or is part of a DOS system area, Desktop displays a message dialog box recommending that you run the PC Tools program DiskFix (described in Chapter 11, "Recovering Damaged or Formatted Disks") by using its **S**urface Scan command to move the data to a reliable part of the disk.

If Desktop can read all sectors on the disk, the program displays a message that no errors were found and that the drive is verified.

Searching a Disk

Chapter 5, "Locating and Viewing Files," explains how to search individual files for character strings. This section explains how to search all sectors in an entire disk for a character string or a hexadecimal (base 16) number.

If you believe that the data is somewhere on the disk but not contained in any file or if you have no idea in which files to look, use the **S**earch Disk command to find the data.

 NOTE   To view or change information at the disk level, you can use the Disk menu's Disk Editor option. Refer to Chapter 12, "Editing a Disk with DiskEdit," for details.

If you can narrow your search to particular files, use the File menu's Search Files command or Locate command rather than the Disk menu's Search Disk command. PC Tools Desktop can find the target character string more quickly. Refer to Chapter 5, "Locating and Viewing Files," for more information about searching specific groups of files for data by using the Search Files and Locate commands on the File menu, as well as by using the FileFind program.

PC Tools provides many data-protection features—such as Mirror, the Delete Tracker, the Data Sentry, and the Undelete program, for example—which together enhance the chances of recovering accidentally abandoned data. Make use of these utilities whenever possible to avoid the need to search an entire disk for specific data and to increase the likelihood of recovering a file that contains the target data.

Before you begin the search, make current the disk you want PC Tools Desktop to search. Then select **D**isk and choose **S**earch Disk. PC Tools Desktop displays the Disk Search dialog box. When you want PC Tools Desktop to search for normal (ASCII) text, type in the text box the *search string*—the character string (as much as 32 characters long, including spaces) for which you want PC Tools Desktop to search. The search for ASCII characters is not case sensitive.

If you want PC Tools Desktop to search for a hexadecimal (base 16) value, choose the **Hex** command button to display a wider Disk Search dialog box and type the hexadecimal search string. Type a string of as many as 64 hexadecimal digits. (PC Tools Desktop enables you to type only 0 through 9 and A through F, which are valid hexadecimal digits.) Each pair of hexadecimal digits constitutes 1 byte. As you enter a pair of hexadecimal digits, PC Tools Desktop displays in the next line of the dialog box any ASCII character equivalent to the hex value (but not every pair of digits translates into an ASCII character).

Most data files (and even many program files) contain at least some displayable ASCII text. Even though an entire file cannot be displayed as an ASCII file, it might contain a word or phrase stored on the disk as an ASCII character string. Whenever you search for data on a disk, try to think of an ASCII character string that can be found within the data; instruct PC Tools Desktop to search for that string. Ordinarily, only computer programmers and power users accustomed to doing their own programming are familiar enough with hexadecimal code to use it effectively for tracking lost data.

To begin the search, select the **OK** command button. PC Tools Desktop searches the disk for the search string and displays a message that it is searching for the search string (see fig. 6.13). You can stop the search at any time during the search operation by selecting the **C**ancel command button.

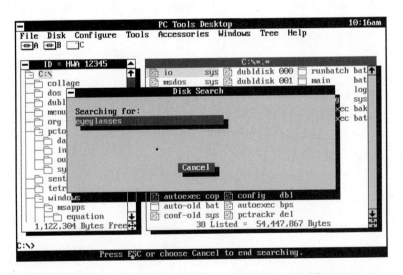

Fig. 6.13

Searching for an ASCII search string.

When PC Tools Desktop locates a match for the search string, the program displays the message Found. See options below. Select from among the following command buttons:

- *OK* okays the search for the next occurrence of the search string.

- *Name* displays a dialog box that contains the name of the file containing the search string. If the string is not contained in a file, PC Tools Desktop indicates whether the string is in the file allocation table (FAT), the boot sector, a directory entry, the root directory, or in an unallocated sector. Select **C**ancel to return to the Disk Search dialog box.

- *Edit* displays the Sector Edit screen. Refer to Chapter 4, "Working on Files," for information about using the Edit screen to edit disk data.

- *Cancel* cancels the search operation, as well as any changes you may have made in the Sector Editor screen.

If PC Tools Desktop does not find a match, the program displays this message:

    The search string was NOT found

The disk-search features of the new Undelete program are similar to the Search command discussed in this section; you can try to create a file from data abandoned in unallocated sectors. See Chapter 10, "Recovering Damaged or Deleted Files," for a discussion of the Undelete program.

For Related Information

◀◀ "Editing Files on the Sector Edit Screen," p. 159.

FROM HERE...

Using the Tree List Window

DOS enables you to organize a disk by using a hierarchical file structure. The first or top level of this structure is the *root directory*; the sublevels are *subdirectories* (or just *directories*). DOS enables you to create multiple levels in this structure—with subdirectories of subdirectories, like the branches of a tree. This treelike structure is depicted by the line diagram in PC Tools Desktop's Tree window. You can navigate this directory structure in PC Tools Desktop's Tree window and manage this directory structure with the Directory Maintenance commands or with the visual DM program.

This section describes how to use the Tree window. See the "Maintaining Directories in PC Tools Desktop" section later in this chapter for a full discussion about how to use the Directory Maintenance commands and the stand-alone DM Directory Maintenance Program.

Understanding the Tree List Window

When you first start PC Tools Desktop, the screen is divided into four areas, as shown in figure 6.14: the drive line (at the top of the screen), the DOS command line (at the bottom of the screen), and two larger areas—the Tree window (on the left) and the File window (on the right).

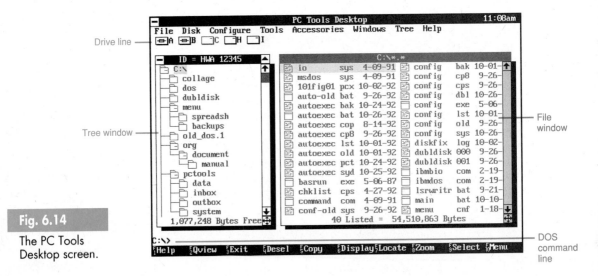

Fig. 6.14

The PC Tools Desktop screen.

The *drive line* indicates the current disk drive by highlighting one of the drive icons. Figure 6.14, for example, shows that C is the current disk drive.

The *Tree window* graphically depicts the directory structure of the disk in the current drive. The root directory of the current disk appears at the top of this window. Other directories are listed below the root icon and connected to it by a vertical line. The name of every directory is listed to the right of its icon. All directories—the root directory and any subdirectories—appear as folder-shaped icons.

At any time during a session with PC Tools Desktop, one directory name is highlighted. This directory is the *selected directory*. When you first start PC Tools Desktop, the directory that is current when you start the program is the selected directory (usually the root directory of the boot disk). The *File window* lists the file names of the files stored in the selected directory.

Selecting a Different Disk and Refreshing the Tree

To display the directory structure of a different disk, you must change drives. The easiest method is to select the icon for that disk in the drive line of the PC Tools Desktop window. Position the mouse pointer on the letter for the desired disk drive in the drive line, and press either mouse button. As an alternative, press Ctrl+*d*, substituting the disk drive letter for *d*. In Version 8, you also can change drives from the Disk menu; choose **Disk**, and then choose Change **Drive**. Desktop displays a drive selection box. Select the new drive and then choose **OK**.

Whichever method you use, PC Tools Desktop displays the message Reading system areas followed by the message Reading directories while it reads the list of directories and files on the destination disk. Then PC Tools Desktop displays the files and directories from the new disk in the PC Tools Desktop windows.

> After the first time a drive is read, you can speed up drive switching by turning off the automatic rereading of directories and files. See the section "Configuring the Tree List" for more information.

T I P

If you add or delete directories from DOS, PC Tools Desktop may not be aware that you altered the file structure or directory structure on the disk and, consequently, display an inaccurate list of files or directories. The tree list also may be out-of-date after you sort a directory (explained at the end of this chapter) or switch to a network drive. In addition, when you change disks in a floppy drive, the previous list no longer applies.

To make the program reread the directory tree, you can select **Disk** and then **Re**-Read Tree, or you can repeat the change drive operation described earlier, but this time select the current drive. PC Tools Desktop reads the list of directories and files on the current disk and displays an accurate file and directory list.

Navigating the Tree

Often you have to display the file names in a directory other than the currently selected directory. Use one of the following methods to select a different directory in the directory tree:

- Click the target directory name. If the tree list is too long to view in the Tree window, use the scroll bar on the right side of the Tree window to scroll to the target directory name. Then click the directory name.

- Press Tab or Shift+Tab repeatedly until you select the Tree window. Use the up- and down-arrow keys to scroll through the directories. As you scroll up or down, PC Tools Desktop displays in the File window the names of files found in every directory in the Tree window.

- Use the mouse or press the Tab key to make the Tree window the current window. Type the first letter of the directory name you want to be current. PC Tools Desktop opens the Speed Search dialog box, which displays in a text box the letter you typed. PC Tools Desktop moves the highlighted bar to the first directory name, in the tree list, that begins with the letter you typed. Type the second letters of the file name, and the third and fourth, and so on, until the highlighted bar rests on the name of the directory you want to use.

 NOTE   Be sure you are at the Tree window and not the DOS line when you try to access the Speed Search dialog box. If the Tree or File window is active, typing a character accesses the dialog box and moves the highlight to the first entry with that spelling; if you are at the DOS line, the Speed Search dialog box does not appear.

Collapsing and Expanding Branches

The DOS directory structure is treelike, with the root directory representing the trunk of a tree and all directories representing the tree's branches. PC Tools Desktop graphically represents—as an upside-down tree in its Tree window—this treelike nature of DOS's directory structure.

When you first start PC Tools Desktop, the program shows the DOS directory structure in multiple levels. Every first-level directory—a directory attached directly to the root—is depicted as a *branch* of the tree. Just as branches of a real tree can have offshoot branches, every DOS directory can contain certain offshoot directories. PC Tools Desktop indicates that a directory is an offshoot of another directory by indenting the name of the offshoot directory below the name of the parent directory. In the Tree window, an L-shaped line connects the icon from every parent directory to the icon of every offshoot directory. Figure 6.14, for example, shows the following directories as offshoots of drive C's root directory:

COLLAGE

DOS

DUBLDISK

MENU

OLD_DOS.1

ORG

PCTOOLS

The following four directories are shown as offshoots (or *subdirectories*) of the PCTOOLS directory:

DATA

INBOX

OUTBOX

SYSTEM

You can think of this list of directories as the PCTOOLS *branch* of the directory tree.

PC Tools Desktop indicates that a directory has subdirectories by placing a minus sign (–) in the directory icon. Figure 6.13 shows the minus sign in the directory icon for the root directory (C:\), as well as for the following directories:

MENU

ORG

PCTOOLS

If your computer's hard disk has a large storage capacity, you probably have many programs stored on the disk. The directory tree displayed by PC Tools Desktop is too long to fit on one screen. PC Tools Desktop provides a method of *collapsing* the tree so that you can navigate the entire directory structure more easily. PC Tools Desktop enables you to *collapse* any branch of the directory tree, including the entire root directory.

To collapse a directory, click the minus symbol in the directory icon, or do one of the following:

- Use the mouse or the cursor-movement keys to select the directory you want to collapse, and press the minus key.

- Use the mouse or cursor-movement keys to select the directory you want to collapse, and then choose Collapse from the Tree menu.

PC Tools Desktop removes the selected directory's branch from the Tree window and places a plus sign (+) in the selected directory's icon. Figure 6.15, for example, shows the result of collapsing the ORG branch.

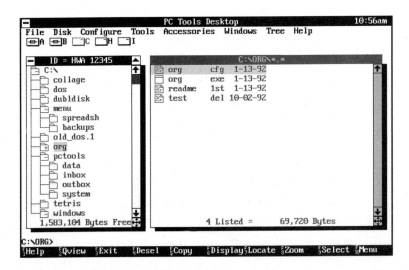

Fig. 6.15

The Tree window after collapsing the ORG branch.

T I P   You can customize Desktop so that when the tree list opens, only the first level of directories is shown. See the section "Configuring the Tree List" for information.

The opposite of collapsing is *expanding*. To *expand* one level of a collapsed directory branch, click the + in the directory icon, or do one of the following:

■ Use the mouse or the cursor-movement keys to select the directory you want to expand, and press the plus key.

■ Use the mouse or the cursor-movement keys to select the directory you want to expand, and then choose **E**xpand One Level from the **T**ree menu.

NOTE If you have worked with an outline processor, you may find manipulating the tree very similar.

On a large hard disk you may find it useful to divide the directory into several major divisions, each of which is subdivided further. You might divide your hard disk's directory, for example, into the following major divisions (directories):

PCTOOLS	WINDOWS
SPREADSH	UTILITY
DOS	DATABASE
WORDPROC	NET

To see the overall structure of your hard disk's directory, you can collapse the entire tree and then expand one level. First, to collapse the root directory, click the root directory's icon or select the root directory and press the minus key. PC Tools Desktop removes the entire tree from the Tree window and displays only C:\. Click the root directory's drive icon again or press the plus key. PC Tools Desktop expands the first level of the directory tree (see fig. 6.16).

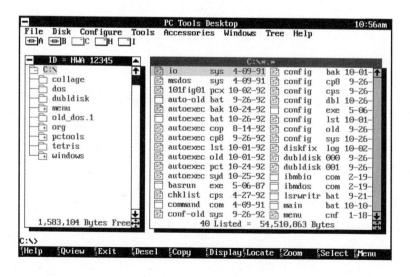

Fig. 6.16

The Tree window after collapsing the entire tree and expanding one level.

A directory tree similar to the one shown in figure 6.16, although neat and tidy, can result in files being pushed several levels out on a branch of the tree. When you collapse the entire tree and expand one level, you may get a better sense of the structure of the entire directory, but finding a particular offshoot directory or file may be a bit more tedious. PC Tools Desktop enables you to quickly and easily expand individual branches of the tree and the entire tree so that you can find the off-shoot directories and files for which you are looking.

When you want to expand a single branch, you can expand a single level of the branch, as described earlier in this section, or you can expand the entire branch in one step. To expand the entire branch, select the directory in the Tree window and do one of the following:

- ■ Press the * key.

- ■ Choose the Expand **B**ranch option from the **Tree** menu.

Figure 6.17, for example, shows the result of expanding a single level of the ORG directory tree branch. Figure 6.18 shows the result of expanding the entire branch.

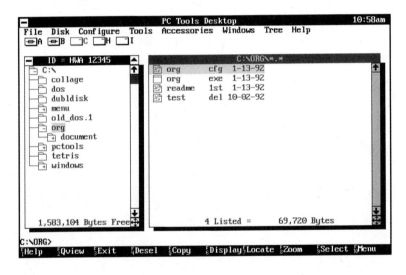

Fig. 6.17

Expanding one level of the ORG directory tree branch.

When you want to expand all levels of all branches in the tree, do one of the following:

- ■ Select the root directory in the Tree window, and press the * key.

- ■ Choose the Expand **A**ll option from the **Tree** menu.

PC Tools Desktop expands the entire tree in the Tree window (refer to fig. 6.14).

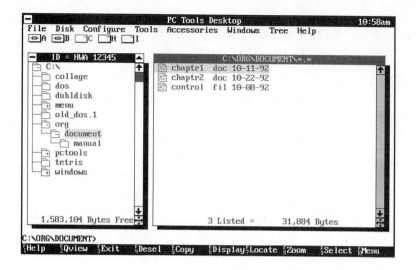

Fig. 6.18

Expanding the entire ORG directory tree branch.

Configuring the Tree List

After you work with the tree list, you may notice certain aspects you want to change. You might prefer the list to normally show only the first level of directories. If your disks contain many directories, you may grow impatient waiting for Desktop to re-read the tree each time you change drives, even if no information has changed. When you close Desktop, you may want to be returned to the directory you started from, rather than the directory that happened to be current when you exited. Finally, if you use drag and drop to copy or move files to different drives, you may prefer that the files are copied to the drive's root directory rather than the current directory.

You can change all these tree aspects from the Configure menu's Tree submenu. If you save the configuration when you exit Desktop, the changes will be used the next time you start the program.

To change tree list configuration, first choose **C**onfigure and then **T**ree to access the Tree submenu, shown in figure 6.19.

If you want the Tree window to routinely display only the first level of subdirectories, choose Startup **F**irst Level from the Tree submenu. The display changes the next time you start the program.

If you want to skip tree rereading so that the drive changing speeds up, choose **L**ocal Tree from the Tree submenu. Desktop uses the tree list file it created the last time the drive was accessed. *Note:* If you run Desktop after adding or deleting directories from DOS, you can use the **D**isk menu **R**e-Read Tree option to update the list.

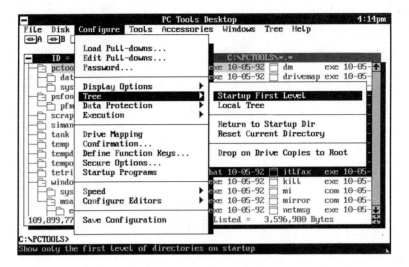

Fig. 6.19

The Tree
submenu.

To exit Desktop and return, each time, to the directory you were in
when you started the program, choose **R**eturn to Startup Directory
from the Tree submenu. To select a different directory to exit to (for
this time only), select the desired directory in the tree list; then choose
Reset **C**urrent Directory from the Tree submenu. Desktop displays the
greater than (>) sign next to the selected directory. (The Reset command applies only when Return to Startup is checked.)

Finally, to copy or move files to a drive's root directory when you use
drag and drop, choose **D**rop on Drive Copies to Root from the Tree
submenu.

Maintaining Directories in
PC Tools Desktop

Desktop provides two sets of tools for directory management, each
with its own advantages—and with somewhat confusing names. You
access each tool from the Disk menu. Using commands on the Directory Maintenance submenu, you can add, rename, delete, and move
directories, and change a directory's file attribute byte. You also can
move and copy directories bypassing menus entirely, by using drag
and drop. Using the DM Directory Maintenance program, you can perform these functions, a few disk functions (change the drive, rename
the volume), and view your access rights for a Novell network directory.

What determines which tool you should use? For many operations, the tool you use doesn't matter, but the guidelines discussed in the following paragraphs can help you decide.

For basic directory housekeeping (adding, deleting, and so on), using the commands on the Directory Maintenance submenu is faster. This submenu does not require that you run a separate program. In 8.0, this submenu includes a new Expunge Directory command that enables you to delete a directory without first emptying it—a facility previously available only from the DM program.

If you work with complex directory structures—where you cannot see the tree for the forest of files—using the DM program is preferable. The DM display is highly visual and focuses only on the tree and its structure. This display shows all levels of the tree at all times, but it expands the display to make the structure extremely clear. (If you want to see a file list, you must access a list window, which closes after you review it.) DM even includes a colorful bar graph to show comparative sizes of directories—often more meaningful than an absolute number. DM also provides a unique command to print the tree structure. (You can print a list of files in a directory by choosing Print from Desktop's File menu and then choosing Print Directory from the submenu that appears.)

> **NOTE** To maintain a directory on a network, you must use the DM program.
>
> The DM program is sometimes referred to as the "full" directory maintenance program, reflecting earlier versions of PC Tools where it included commands unavailable from Desktop's basic Directory Maintenance command set.

This section describes using the Directory Maintenance submenu. The DM Directory Maintenance program is explained in the next section, "Using the DM Directory Maintenance Program."

To access the Directory Maintenance submenu commands, select **D**isk, and then choose Directory **M**aintenance. PC Tools Desktop displays the Directory Maintenance submenu (see fig. 6.20).

Adding a Directory in PC Tools Desktop

To add a directory to a disk's file structure, display the Directory Maintenance submenu and select the **A**dd Directory option. PC Tools Desktop displays the Directory Add dialog box; the prompt `Select the directory to add to` asks you to indicate the directory to which you want PC Tools Desktop to add a subordinate directory.

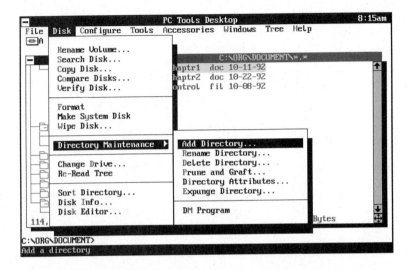

Fig. 6.20

The Directory
Maintenance
submenu.

To add a subordinate directory, in the Tree window, click the directory
to which you want to add another directory, or use the cursor-move-
ment keys to move the highlighted bar to the directory and then press
Enter. To add the directory at the root of drive C, for example, select
C:\ in the Tree window; to add a directory beneath C:\PCTOOLS, select
C:\PCTOOLS in the Tree window.

As soon as you indicate the directory to which PC Tools Desktop
should add the new directory, PC Tools Desktop prompts Enter the
new directory name. Type the name in the Name text box. Then select
the **OK** command button. PC Tools Desktop adds the new directory to
the disk's file structure and immediately displays the directory in the
Tree window, regardless whether the branch it is on is expanded or
not.

T I P   Although you *can* type an optional file name extension, don't. Some
applications programs may not recognize a directory name with a
file name extension.

Renaming a Directory in PC Tools Desktop

Occasionally, you may want to change the name of a directory. You may want to use the current name for another purpose, for example, or a program you are using may require a different directory name. You may just want to change the directory name so that it better describes the directory's contents. With PC Tools Desktop's Rename Directory function, you can easily rename a directory.

DOS does not provide a way to change a directory name. To change a directory name by using only DOS, you must create a new directory with the new name, copy all files from the original directory to the new directory, and then delete the old directory. PC Tools Desktop's Rename Directory function enables you to rename a directory in one step.

To rename a directory, first display the Directory Maintenance submenu and then select the **R**ename Directory option. PC Tools Desktop displays the Directory Rename dialog box, which prompts Select the directory to rename.

In the Tree window, click the directory you want to rename or press the cursor-movement keys to move the highlighted bar to the directory and then press Enter. As soon as you indicate which directory to rename, PC Tools Desktop prompts Enter the new directory name. Type the name in the Name text box. Then select the **O**K command button. PC Tools Desktop changes the directory name and immediately displays the directory in the Tree window.

Deleting a Directory in PC Tools Desktop

Directories, like disk files, can become obsolete or unneeded and can be removed. You can use the Delete Directory command to remove an empty directory, as in DOS, or the new Expunge Directory command to delete a directory, any subdirectories, and all files.

To delete a directory in the conventional way, the first step is to delete the files within the directory. (Refer to Chapter 4, "Working on Files," for instructions on deleting files.) When the directory is empty, display the Directory Maintenance submenu and select **D**elete Directory. PC Tools Desktop displays the Directory Delete dialog box, which prompts `Select the directory to delete`.

In the Tree window, click the directory you want to delete, or press the cursor-movement keys to move the highlighted bar to the directory and then press Enter. As soon as you indicate which directory to delete, PC Tools Desktop prompts `Confirm the deletion`. To delete the directory, select the **OK** command button; if you decide not to delete the directory, select the **Ex**it command button.

To delete a directory and all files, display the Directory Maintenance submenu and select **E**xpunge Directory. PC Tools Desktop displays the Directory Expunge dialog box, which prompts you to select the directory to delete.

In the Tree window, click the directory you want to delete, or press the cursor-movement keys to move the highlighted bar to the directory and then press Enter. Desktop displays a Caution dialog box reminding you that the directory, all its files, and all subdirectories will be deleted. To delete the directory, select the **OK** command button; if you decide not to delete the directory, select the **Ex**it command button.

Regardless of the delete command you use, the Desktop screen returns after PC Tools Desktop deletes the specified directory. If the File window is on, the program displays the contents of the directory that preceded the deleted directory.

Undeleting a Directory

Because of the way DOS deletes directory files, undeleting a directory file is relatively easy, but only if you do so promptly. You first must undelete the directory file, and then you can undelete files from the directory. When Directory Maintenance deletes or expunges a directory file, the program actually instructs DOS to delete the file. DOS no longer lists the directory in the file structure but does not erase any data from the disk. Eventually, as you add new files to the disk, DOS reallocates the disk space assigned to the deleted directory file, causing new data to overwrite the old. Soon the file and its data are gone permanently. If you use PC Tools Undelete program before DOS has had a chance to overwrite the data in a deleted directory file, however, you easily can reverse the delete command.

The Undelete feature which is a separate stand-alone program, is available from the Tools menu. See Chapter 10, "Recovering Damaged or Deleted Files," for a full discussion about this capability, including how to use the Undelete feature to undelete a directory.

Moving a Directory in PC Tools Desktop

Just as DOS provides no easy way to rename a directory, DOS also provides no easy way to move a directory full of files to a different position in the file structure. Suppose, for example, that after creating the directory C:\SPREADSH\FINANCE and adding a couple of files to it, you decide that you want this directory to be a directory in the C:\SPREADSH\LOTUS directory. (In other words, the new directory will be C:\SPREADSH\LOTUS\FINANCE.) To make the change by using DOS, you must go through a cumbersome series of steps:

1. Use the MD command to create a new directory (C:\SPREADSH\LOTUS\FINANCE).

2. Use the COPY command to copy all files from C:\SPREADSH\FINANCE to C:\SPREADSH\LOTUS\FINANCE.

3. Use the DEL command to delete all files from C:\SPREADSH\FINANCE.

4. Use the RD command to delete the C:\SPREADSH\FINANCE directory.

In contrast, you can use PC Tools Desktop's **Prune and Graft** command to achieve the same result. To move a directory and all its files to another location in the file structure, follow these simple steps:

1. Display the Disk Maintenance menu and select **Prune and Graft**. PC Tools Desktop displays the Directory Prune and Graft dialog box, which prompts Select the directory to prune.

2. In the Tree window, click the directory you want to move or press the cursor-movement keys to move the highlighted bar to the directory and then press Enter.

   As soon as you indicate which directory to move, PC Tools Desktop prompts Please confirm that the highlighted sub-directory is to be "pruned" (moved).

3. To continue with the move procedure, select the **OK** command button. To cancel the move, select **Exit**.

   In the Tree window, PC Tools Desktop displays a marker (>) to the left of the directory being moved. The program then displays the prompt Select where to "graft" (attach) the "pruned" (moved) sub-directory(s).

4. In the Tree window, use the mouse or the cursor-movement keys to select the directory's destination.

PC Tools Desktop displays the prompt `Please confirm that the grafting operation is to proceed.`

5. Select the **OK** command button.

PC Tools Desktop moves the directory and all its files to the new location.

Moving or Copying a Directory with Drag-and-Drop

With Version 8.0's enhanced drag-and-drop capability, you can use the mouse to move or copy a directory by simply dragging the directory to the new location in the Tree window. You also can drag-and-drop the directory to a drive icon. The move function duplicates the Prune and Graft command, but the copy function has no submenu counterpart. In earlier versions, you could copy directories only by using the DM program.

> **NOTE** Drag-and-drop only allows moving or copying to a directory visible in the Tree window; you cannot scroll the Tree window while you're dragging. If you have a long directory list and want to copy a directory to a directory that is not visible in the window, use the DM program's Copy command.

The steps to move or copy a directory are identical, except that you press the Ctrl key while pressing the mouse button if you want to move.

To copy a directory and all its files to a different location, point to the directory name in the Tree window, press the left mouse button to select it (do not release the button). As you drag, a *banner* (a small rectangular box) appears with the message `Can't Drop Here`. When you drag to another directory name or a drive icon, the banner changes to `Copy Directory`. When the banner is at the location where you want to copy the directory, release the button. A Copy message box appears briefly. Select **OK** to copy the directory. Desktop briefly displays a Current File box reporting the names of files in the directory as they (and it) are being copied.

To move a directory and all its files, follow the preceding steps, except this time press Ctrl as you press the left mouse button to select the directory. When the banner is next to a directory or drive icon, the message changes to read `Move Directory`. After you release the button, the Current File box reports the files being copied, and then Desktop displays a box reporting the files being deleted from the original location.

> Normally when you drop a directory on a drive, the directory is copied to the directory current on that drive. You can make sure that the directory is copied to the root directory. Refer to the earlier section "Configuring the Tree List."
>
> **T I P**

Modifying the Attribute Byte in PC Tools Desktop

PC Tools Desktop enables you to modify the attribute byte of a directory file in much the same way you modify the attribute byte of any file. (*Note:* You cannot use this option on a network.) First, display the Directory Maintenance submenu, and then select the Directory Attributes option. PC Tools Desktop displays the Modify Directory Attributes dialog box, which prompts Select the directory to modify.

In the Tree window, click the directory whose attribute byte you want to modify, or press the cursor-movement keys to move the highlighted bar to the directory and then press Enter. As soon as you indicate the directory, PC Tools Desktop displays the Modify Directory Attributes dialog box.

The Modify Directory Attributes dialog box lists four check boxes, one for every attribute status indicator—hidden, system, read only, and archive. Refer to Chapter 4, "Working on Files," for the meaning of each status indicator.

> **CAUTION:** Although the Directory Attributes command may seem convenient for protecting files, use this command sparingly. Never change the attributes of the root directory or of the directory that contains DOS files required to boot your computer. Other programs also may balk if a directory used by the program is set as Read Only.

After you make your selections from the dialog box, select the Update command button. PC Tools Desktop alters the directory file's attribute byte and returns to the PC Tools Desktop screen.

Using the DM Directory Maintenance Program

The DM Directory Maintenance program is a visual way to manage complex directory structures. You can use this program with network drives, unlike the Directory Maintenance submenu commands.

To access this program from within PC Tools Desktop, select Disk and then Directory Maintenance. From the Directory Maintenance submenu, choose DM Program. Alternatively, you can type **dm** at the DOS command line. PC Tools Desktop displays the Directory Maintenance screen (see fig. 6.21).

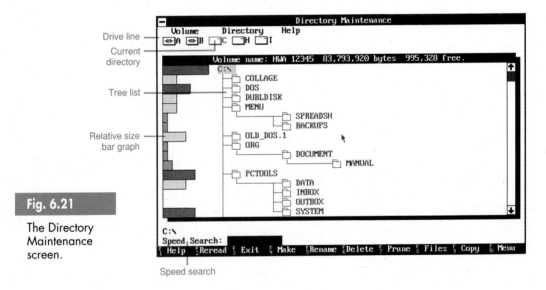

Drive line
Current directory
Tree list
Relative size bar graph

Fig. 6.21

The Directory Maintenance screen.

Speed search

When you first display the Directory Maintenance screen, the program displays a tree list similar to the one displayed in PC Tools Desktop's Tree window. As in PC Tools Desktop, a file-folder shaped icon represents every directory in the tree, and a highlighted bar rests on the icon that represents the current directory.

The display shows the tree fully expanded and does not include a file list. If you want to work with directories and files simultaneously, use PC Tools Desktop.

A drive line is located just below the horizontal menu bar. The name of the current directory is listed near the bottom of the screen below the tree list. Table 6.1 lists the function key commands that appear in the message bar of the Directory Maintenance screen. The sections that follow in this chapter describe how to use each function key command.

Moving the highlighted bar around the Directory Maintenance screen is similar to moving around PC Tools Desktop's Tree window, but the effect is slightly different. You can scroll through the list by using the mouse or the cursor-movement keys or you can use the speed-search technique. (Refer to the section "Navigating the Tree," earlier in this chapter for more information about moving around the screen.)

In contrast to PC Tools Desktop, moving the highlighted bar in the Directory Maintenance screen does not immediately change the current directory. To change the current directory, double-click the directory icon or highlight the icon and press Enter. Directory Maintenance changes the current directory, exits from the program, and returns to the screen from which you started Directory Maintenance.

Table 6.1 Directory Maintenance Function Key Commands

Key	Name	Function
F1	Help	Displays context-sensitive Help facility
F2	Reread	Rereads the tree list
F3	Exit	Exits from Directory Maintenance
F4	Make	Creates a new directory
F5	Rename	Renames selected directory
F6	Delete	Deletes directory (and its files)
F7	Prune/Graft	Moves selected directory and its files
F8	Files	Lists files contained in selected directory
F9	Copy	Copies selected directory
F10	Menu	Activates horizontal menu bar

The Directory Maintenance program is not the most efficient tool for changing the current directory. When you just want to change the current directory, use the CD (or CHDIR) command at the DOS command line or use PC Tools Desktop. Directory Maintenance is very efficient, however, when you want to make, rename, delete, or move a directory with clear visual feedback.

To display a list of the files contained in the highlighted directory, press F8 (Files), or select **D**irectory from the horizontal menu bar to display the Directory menu and then choose Show **F**iles. Directory Maintenance appears in a File window on the right side of the screen (see fig. 6.22). The window closes as soon as you click the mouse button or press F3 or Esc.

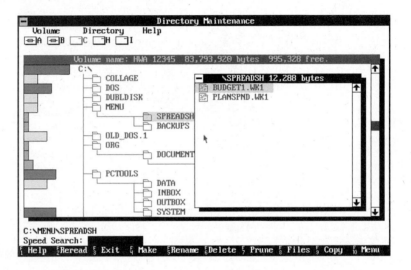

Fig. 6.22

The Directory Maintenance File window.

Sometimes you want to know how much storage space a directory branch occupies. To see that information in the Directory Maintenance screen, use the mouse or the cursor-movement keys to move the highlighted bar to the name of the directory. Then choose **B**ranch Size from the **D**irectory menu. The program displays the Branch Size dialog box, which indicates the following:

- *Total size of files* denotes the sum of all the sizes of the files contained in the branch.

- *Total allocated space* denotes the number of bytes of storage space allocated to the files in the branch.

- *Number of files and directories* denotes the number of files and directories contained in the branch.

The total size of the files in a branch usually does not equal the total allocated space for the same files. DOS allocates space in groups of bytes called *clusters*. The sizes of most files do not fall on an even cluster. The unused portion of an allocated cluster cannot be used by any other file.

To display the directory structure of a different disk, you can select the icon for that disk in the drive line of the Directory Maintenance screen. Use the mouse to position the mouse pointer on the letter for the desired disk drive in the drive line, and press either mouse button. As an alternative, press Ctrl+*d*, substituting the disk drive letter for *d*. Directory Maintenance displays the files and directories from the new disk.

Occasionally, Directory Maintenance may not be aware that you altered the file or directory structure on the disk and, consequently, displays an inaccurate list of files or directories. To force the program to reread the directory tree, do one of the following:

- Press F2 (Reread).
- Select **V**olume and select **R**eread Tree.
- Click the drive letter in the drive line.
- Press Ctrl+*d*, substituting the drive letter for *d*.

Directory Maintenance reads the list of directories and files on the current disk and displays an accurate file and directory list.

Changing the Tree Data Display in DM

When you first start Directory Maintenance, the program depicts the relative size of the various directories by displaying a series of bar graphs on the left side of the screen. The bar graph to the left of each particular directory name in the tree list represents the contents of the directory. By comparing the size of one bar to another, you can get a sense of which directory contains files that occupy the larger amount of disk storage space. The bar graphs in figure 6.22, for example, indicate that the files in the C:\PCTOOLS\SYSTEM directory occupy about the same amount of storage space as the files contained in the C:\PCTOOLS directory, and the INBOX and OUTBOX are empty. This "bird's-eye" view of your system's directory structure can be useful whenever you decide to rearrange files and directories on your hard disk.

Directory Maintenance provides several ways to depict directories in the Directory Maintenance screen. Select **V**olume from the horizontal menu bar to display the Volume menu, and choose **T**ree Data Display. The program displays the Tree Data Display dialog box. This dialog box presents the following option buttons:

■ *None* turns off the graph display.

■ *Bar Graph-Linear* displays relative-size bar graphs to the left of the tree. This option is the default.

■ *Bar Graph-Exponential* displays relative-size bar graphs on a logarithmic scale. Exponential display enables you to see relative size if some directories are much bigger than others, as may be the case if you use a disk compression program.

■ *Size* displays a number to the left of every directory icon in the tree. Each number represents the approximate number of bytes occupied by the files stored in the particular directory. DM uses the physical space the directory occupies, which may be slightly more than the sum of the file sizes. You can switch to this display when you want to check actual numbers.

■ *Creation Date* (Novell network drive only) displays to the left of every directory icon the date the directory was created.

■ *Owner* (Novell network drive only) displays to the left of every directory icon the network user ID of the user who created the directory.

■ *Rights* (Novell network drive only) displays to the left of every directory icon the network rights that you have to each directory. (See your network user's manual for an explanation of the rights listed.)

After you select an option button, choose the **OK** command button. DM returns to the Directory Maintenance screen.

Changing the Volume Label in DM

When you format a disk by using the DOS FORMAT command or PC Format, you can give the disk a *volume label*, which is an optional name for the disk. If you decide to use a volume label, the label should describe the contents, such as WP_DATA or MY_PAYROLL. Volume labels can be 11 characters long, including spaces.

You occasionally may decide to add or change a volume label after you format the disk. The DM Directory Maintenance program provides a command for this, as does Desktop's Disk menu.

To add or modify a volume label in DM, follow these steps:

1. Display the Directory Maintenance screen and select Volume to display the Volume pull-down menu; then choose the Rename Volume option.

Directory Maintenance displays the Rename volume dialog box, which displays the current volume label (if any) and prompts you to enter the new label.

2. Type the new volume label in the text box.

3. Choose the **OK** command button.

Adding a Directory in DM

The Directory Maintenance program enables you to add a new directory to the directory tree. To add a new directory to the tree, follow these steps:

1. Using the mouse or the cursor-movement keys, move the highlighted bar to the directory to which you want to add a subordinate directory.

2. Press F4 (Make). Alternatively, select **Directory** from the horizontal menu bar to display the Directory menu, and choose **Make Directory**.

   The program displays the Make Directory dialog box, which prompts you to enter the new directory name.

3. In the text box, type a name, up to 11 characters not including spaces—8 to the left of the decimal and 3 to the right.

4. Choose the **OK** command button.

Directory Maintenance adds the new directory to the disk's file structure and immediately displays the directory in the Tree window.

Although you can type an optional file name extension, not doing so is a better practice. Some applications programs may not recognize a directory name with a file name extension.

Renaming a Directory in DM

From time to time you may want to change the name of a directory. You may want to use the current name for another purpose, or a program you are using may require a different directory name. You may want to change just the directory name to better describe the directory's contents. With the Directory Maintenance **Rename** Directory function, you can easily rename a directory.

To rename a directory, use the cursor-movement keys or the mouse to highlight the directory name you want to change. Press F5 (Rename), or choose **D**irectory to display the Directory menu and then select the **R**ename Directory option. PC Tools Desktop displays the Rename Directory dialog box, which prompts you to Enter the new directory name.

In the Name text box, type the name. Then select the **OK** command button. Directory Maintenance changes the directory name and immediately displays the name in the tree list. The C:\MENU\BACKUPS directory in figure 6.22, for example, has been renamed C:\MENU\OLDFILES (see fig. 6.23).

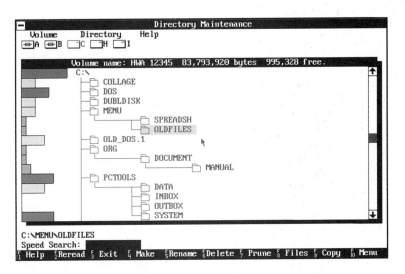

Fig. 6.23

Renaming a directory.

Deleting a Directory in DM

The DM delete function is the counterpart of Desktop's Directory Maintenance submenu's Expunge command; it deletes a directory and all its files and subdirectories. To delete a directory, use the mouse or the cursor-movement keys to highlight the directory name you want to delete. Press F6 (Delete), or choose **D**irectory to display the Directory menu and then select **D**elete Directory. The program displays a Caution dialog box reminding you that the directory, all its files, and all subdirectories will be deleted. To delete the directory, select the **OK** command button; if you decide not to delete the directory, select **C**ancel.

> **CAUTION:** When you choose the Delete Directory command, DM does not ask you to select the directory to delete. DM assumes that you made your choice by highlighting the desired directory name. (In contrast, the Directory Maintenance Delete and Expunge Directory commands require you to explicitly select a directory.) Be sure to have the correct directory highlighted when you use the Delete Directory command.

Copying a Directory Branch in DM

One of the more useful but least-used DOS commands is the XCOPY command. Among the many uses of XCOPY is to copy an entire directory and all its files and directories (offshoots) to another directory or drive. But XCOPY often is not employed for that purpose because the command is difficult to use because you must remember which of the eight possible switches to use to accomplish the task. When you use the DM Directory Maintenance program, however, copying a directory is easy.

To copy a directory, its files, and its subdirectories, display the Directory Maintenance screen and move the highlighted bar to the directory's file-folder shaped icon. Press F9 (Copy), or select **D**irectory and choose **C**opy Tree. The program makes a temporary (on-screen) copy of the directory name and its branch of the tree and then highlights this copy. The original directory and its branch are not affected. Figure 6.24, for example, shows a highlighted copy of the ORG directory.

Use the cursor-movement keys or the mouse to position the highlighted directory branch at the destination position you want. To place the copy on another disk, click the disk icon or press Ctrl+*d*, where *d* is the drive letter. Directory Maintenance displays the directory structure of the other disk with the highlighted tree superimposed.

After you position the highlighted branch, press Enter. The program displays a dialog box that asks you to confirm the copy operation. Select the **OK** command button. Directory Maintenance informs you as it performs the copy operation and warns you not to interrupt the process.

After Directory Maintenance copies a directory branch, the program does not automatically reread the directory tree. The new copy of the branch appears in its new location, but the tree list does not reflect the files contained in the branch. No bar graphs are displayed to the left of the directory names in the branch, for example. Press F2 (Reread) if you want the program to read the tree.

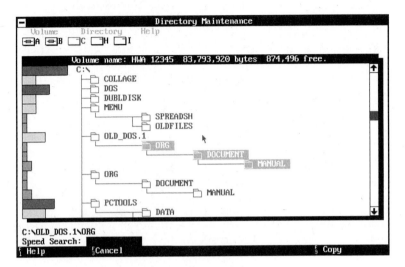

Fig. 6.24

Copying a
directory branch.

Moving a Directory Branch (Prune and Graft) in DM

The preceding section explains how to make a copy of a directory branch. Sometimes, however, you may want to move a directory full of files to a different position in the file structure.

Suppose that after creating the directory C:\MENU\SPREADSH and adding a couple of files to it, you decide that you want this directory to be an offshoot of the C:\PCTOOLS\DATA directory. (You want the new directory to be C:\PCTOOLS\DATA\SPREADSH.) To make the change by using DOS only, you would have to make a series of cumbersome steps:

1. Use the MD command to create a new directory (C:\PCTOOLS\DATA\SPREADSH).

2. Use the COPY command to copy all files from C:\MENU\SPREADSH to C:\PCTOOLS\DATA\SPREADSH.

3. Use the DEL command to delete all files from C:\MENU\SPREADSH.

4. Use the RD command to delete the C:\MENU\SPREADSH directory.

In contrast, you can use the Directory Maintenance program's Prune and **G**raft command to achieve the same result. To move a directory and all its files to another location in the file structure, follow these steps:

1. Highlight the directory name of the directory you want to move.

2. Press F7 (Prune), or display the **D**irectory menu and select Prune and **G**raft. The program highlights (in a different color) the directory and its entire branch, including all offshoots (subdirectories).

3. Use the mouse or the cursor-movement keys to move the highlighted directory branch up or down through the directory tree.

4. When the branch is in the desired position in the tree, press Enter or F7 (Graft). The program displays the Prune and Graft dialog box, which asks you to confirm the graft operation.

5. Select **O**K to finish the operation, or choose **C**ancel to abort the operation.

Figure 6.25 shows the Directory Maintenance screen after the SPREADSH directory has been moved to be an offshoot of the C:\PCTOOLS\DATA directory.

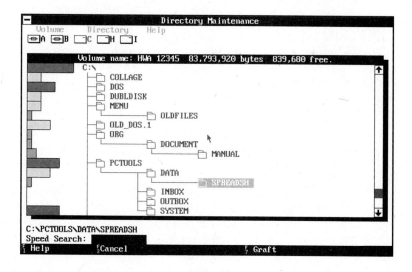

Printing the Tree

To review a tree structure off-line or document changes you have made, you can print the tree. Note that this differs from Desktop's Print

Directory command (in the Print submenu of the File menu) which prints the file list in a selected directory. Printing the tree allows focussing on the tree structure alone.

To print the tree, choose **Volume** and then **P**rint Tree. DM displays the Print Tree dialog box. By default, the tree prints with graphic characters depicting icons and bar graphs. If your printer does not support graphics, you can choose **N**on-graphics Chars. If you choose the **List** only option, a flat list of directories and subdirectories prints; otherwise, the list appears much as it does on-screen. Select **P**rint to print the tree.

T I P   On a graphics dot-matrix printer, printing graphic characters may be very slow. For faster printing, choose **N**on-graphics Chars; the resulting tree representation is still reasonably visual.

Modifying the Attribute Byte in DM

The Directory Maintenance program enables you to modify the attribute byte of a directory file in much the same way that you modify the attribute byte of any file. First display the Directory Maintenance screen and then highlight the name of the directory you want to modify. Select **D**irectory from the horizontal menu bar to display the Directory menu, and choose Modify **A**ttributes. PC Tools Desktop displays the Modify Attributes dialog box.

The Modify Attributes dialog box lists two check boxes: **H**idden and **S**ystem. Chapter 4, "Working on Files," discusses the attributes in this dialog box in detail.

> **CAUTION:** Although the Modify Attributes command might seem convenient for protecting files, use this command sparingly. Never change the attributes of the root directory or the directory that contains DOS files required to boot your computer.

After you make your selections from the dialog box, select the **OK** command button. The program alters the directory file's attribute byte and returns to the Directory Maintenance screen.

Displaying Network Rights in DM

When your computer is connected to a Novell network (and you are logged on to the network), the Directory Maintenance program enables you to list the effective rights you have to a particular directory on a network file server. *Effective rights* are the trustee rights you have been granted by the network administrator, limited by any maximum-rights mask placed on a particular directory. Use the mouse or the cursor-movement keys to highlight the name of the directory in which you are interested. Display the **D**irectory menu and select **N**etwork Rights. The program displays the Effective Rights dialog box, similar to the one in figure 6.26. The dialog box lists a different set of rights if you are connected to a Novell 286 server.

Fig. 6.26

The Network Effective Rights dialog box (Novell 386).

On a Novell 386 network, the Effective Rights dialog box indicates whether you have *read, write, create, erase, modify, file scan, access control,* or *supervisor* rights to the directory. The dialog box lists the following rights on a Novell 286 system: *read, write, open, create, delete, search, modify,* or *parental.* Refer to your network's documentation for a description of these rights. A check mark indicates that the specified right is turned on. An o indicates that the specified network right is turned off.

The Effective Rights dialog box is for information only. The Directory Maintenance program does not provide a way to change or alter your network rights to the specified directory. If you want additional network rights for a particular directory, contact your work-group manager or network administrator.

Exiting from the Directory Maintenance Program

After you make changes or adjustments to the directory structure of your computer's disks, you are ready to return to PC Tools Desktop or to DOS, depending on how you started the program. To exit from Directory Maintenance, return to the Directory Maintenance screen and do one of the following:

- Press Enter.

- Press Esc.

- Press F3 (Exit).

- Click the program close box.

Directory Maintenance unloads from memory and returns to the screen from which the Directory Maintenance program was started.

FROM HERE...

For Related Information

◄◄ "Changing File Attributes, Date, and Time," p. 161.

Sorting a Directory

The operating system stores files to disk in the order that data is added, not in order by file name or date. Often, being able to see a file in PC Tools Desktop's File window would be easier if the file names were in some discernible order. At other times, you might want to see which files in a directory were added or changed most recently. Seeing the files listed in reverse order by date and time would be more convenient. By using the Sort Directory command on PC Tools Desktop's Disk menu, you can easily accomplish such directory sorts.

The Sort Directory feature differs from the F6 (Display) command (which displays the Display Options dialog box) discussed in Chapter 2, "Controlling the Desktop." The F6 (Display) command enables you to sort a directory, but the new sorted order is shown on-screen and is not saved to disk. By contrast, the Sort Directory command on PC Tools Desktop's Disk menu enables you to store the directory to disk in the new order. If you use the DOS DIR command, the file list will be sorted.

NOTE With DOS 5, you can sort with the DIR command by adding the sort parameter /O and a letter for the type of sort (N for Name and D for Date, for example). This sorting, however, is temporary, as it is when you use Desktop's File Display Options. The next time you use DIR without the parameter, the list is unsorted.

To sort a directory, select **Disk** and then select **Sort** Directory. PC Tools Desktop displays the Directory Sort dialog box (see fig. 6.27).

Fig. 6.27

The Directory Sort dialog box.

From the first group of option buttons, choose the file characteristic by which you want to sort the files—by name, extension, size, date and time, or selection order. From the second group of option buttons, choose ascending (the default) or descending order for the sort. Use the mouse or press the highlighted number to choose one option from each group. Then select the **Sort** command button.

T I P

Sorting by selection order provides a way to rearrange files in any order you like. Simply select the files in the new order before choosing the Sort command.

PC Tools Desktop sorts the file names in the new order but before displaying the names presents a second Directory Sort dialog box. From this dialog box, choose from the following four options:

- *View* displays the file names listed in the new sorted order but does not make the new sequence permanent. In the message bar, PC Tools Desktop displays the following message:

```
Press any key or the mouse to return to the sort
options
```

When you click the mouse button or press a key, PC Tools Desktop returns to the second Directory Sort dialog box.

■ *Update* displays the file names in the new order and saves this new sequence to disk. PC Tools Desktop then displays the file names in this order every time you view the File window or use the DOS DIR command.

■ *Resort* returns to the previous dialog box so that you can choose a different sort order.

■ *Cancel* returns to the PC Tools Desktop screen. Pressing Esc or F3 (Exit) does the same thing. File names are sorted in the new order but only until you change the active directory. When you return to this directory, the file names are listed in the original order.

NOTE   System files in a directory are always listed first, no matter what sort order is applied.

Chapter Summary

This chapter covers many of PC Tools Desktop's disk-related functions and explains how to use the commands on PC Tools Desktop's Disk menu, as well as how to use the visual DM Directory Maintenance program. You learned about preparing a disk for use: formatting, making system disks, copying disks, making an emergency disk, and displaying certain information about a disk. The chapter also describes how to assign or change the disk volume label.

In addition, this chapter explains how to use PC Tools Desktop to scan a disk for data discrepancies and how to scan the contents of a disk for a specific character string or hexadecimal value. You learned how to use Desktop's Directory Maintenance commands as well as the separate DM program to add, rename, delete, and move a directory. You also learned how to modify the attribute byte of a directory file. Finally, this chapter examines how to use PC Tools Desktop to sort a directory.

Now that you are familiar with the capabilities of the PC Tools Desktop Disk menu and the DM Directory Maintenance program, turn to Chapter 7, "Protecting Your Data with Central Point Backup," to learn about protecting your data by doing routine backups.

Using the System Utilities

PART

II

OUTLINE

Protecting Your Data with Central
   Point Backup

Speeding Up Your Hard Disk with
   Compress

Obtaining System Information

Protecting Your Data with Central Point Backup

This chapter is the first of Part II, "Using the System Utilities." In this chapter's description of using Central Point Backup, you learn how to quickly make backup copies of the data stored in your computer's nonremovable disks. Part III, "Using the Recovery and Security Utilities," describes how to use several PC Tools stand-alone programs, including Central Point Backup, Compress, and System Information (SI).

Your computer's hard disk contains millions of bytes of data—programs and data files—that provide a service to your computer (operating system software, for example) or provide a service to you (application and utility software). These bytes of data represent the single most significant investment of money, time, and effort into your computer system. Losing that investment—if your data were to become lost or damaged—would be devastating to most computer users. But Central Point Backup gives you the perfect tool to help avoid that kind of loss or damage.

This chapter first explains how to start Central Point Backup, how to set up a default configuration, and how to decide whether you want to back up the entire hard disk or just selected files or directories. You then learn how to perform the backup operation and how to compare the backup files to the original files on the hard disk.

The chapter also explains how to restore, from backup disks or tapes, an entire disk or tape—or only selected directories and files—to your hard drive. The last sections of the chapter explain how to change the program's configuration and how to create and use setup files.

Starting Central Point Backup

The standard way to start Central Point Backup (CP Backup) is to type the following command at the DOS command line:

> CPBACKUP *d*:

For the letter *d*, substitute the drive letter of the disk drive for which you want to make a backup, called the *backup-from setting*, or the *source drive*. If you omit the disk designator, CP Backup assumes the backup-from setting is your current drive. You also can use several special parameters, or *switches*, with the CP Backup command. You can type **cpbackup /?** at the DOS command line to see a list of the available parameter options and their meanings. See this chapter's "Using CP Backup Command Line Parameters" section for a list of available command line switches.

Alternatively, you can select CP Backup from within PC Tools Desktop by selecting the **T**ools option from the top horizontal menu and then selecting CP **B**ackup.

 If you used INSTALL to install PC Tools, CP Backup is one of the options listed on the program list menus. Refer to Chapter 3, "Using the Desktop As a Program Manager," for a description of how to start a program from the program list.

CAUTION: Unload all memory-resident (TSR) programs from your computer's memory before you perform a backup operation with CP Backup; otherwise, you may have insufficient memory resources to load and run CP Backup. If you must leave any memory-resident program loaded while running CP Backup, do not hot-key into those programs while a backup operation is in progress. You run the risk of damaging a file in use by CP Backup, which may result in an error condition. If you have installed a fax card in your computer, unload its drivers from memory or disable the card before beginning any backup procedure.

Answering Initial Configuration Questions

When you start CP Backup for the first time, the program reads the directory tree on your hard disk and then displays the Welcome screen (see fig. 7.1).

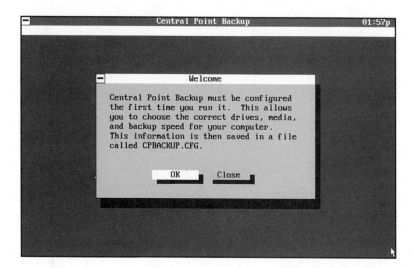

Fig. 7.1

The CP Backup Welcome screen.

You must answer several questions about your computer system's hardware configuration. (You can reconfigure your hardware setup later if needed.) To access the first set of configuration questions, choose the **OK** command button. Next, CP Backup displays the message `Testing Hardware. Please wait` and then displays the Choose Tape Type dialog box (see fig. 7.2).

If you have no tape drive installed in your computer, choose the **No Tape** box and press Enter. If you do have a tape drive installed, select either **QIC** 40/80-FDC or **SCSI**, which is new to Version 8.0, and press Enter. CP Backup displays the Automatic Search dialog box, in which you can either configure your tape drive or let CP Backup search your hardware for a tape drive and configure the drive for you (see fig. 7.3).

NOTE   Be sure no tape cartridge is inserted in your tape drive prior to selecting Search. CP Backup needs to be able to read the hardware and determine the *actual* capacity of the drive rather than the capacity of the inserted cartridge.

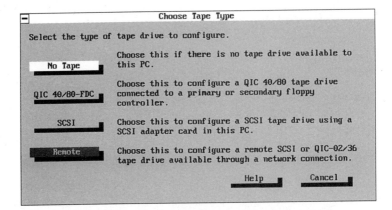

Fig. 7.2

The Choose
Tape Type
dialog box.

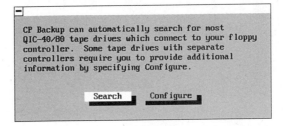

Fig. 7.3

The Automatic
Search dialog
box.

CP Backup analyzes your system configuration to determine what disk
drives are installed and then displays the Define Equipment dialog box,
similar to the one shown in figure 7.4.

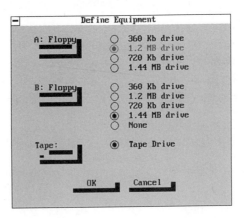

Fig. 7.4

The Define
Equipment dialog
box.

Based on its analysis of your hardware, CP Backup has already selected an option from each group of option buttons. If these selections are correct, choose the **OK** command button at the bottom of the dialog box. If one or more of the buttons is not correct, select the correct option and then choose **OK**.

 NOTE CP Backup lists four drive types in each group of option buttons, but only one is appropriate for each of the drives installed in your computer. If you have a 720K drive, for example, do not choose the 1.44 MB drive option.

Next, CP Backup displays the Choose Drive & Media dialog box, similar to the one shown in figure 7.5. Select the disk or tape drive and type of disk or tape (media) you plan to use routinely for making backups. Although you can change this choice later, for now select the drive and media you expect to use most often.

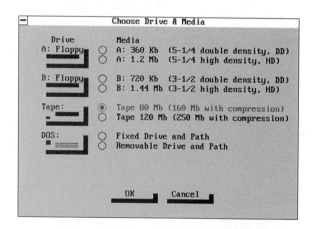

Fig. 7.5

The Choose Drive & Media dialog box.

In addition to the floppy and tape drives compatible with CP Backup, the Choose Drive & Media dialog box lists the following two option buttons:

■ *Fixed Drive and Path.* Select this option button when you plan to back up your disk routinely to another hard disk, another hard disk partition, a DOS-compatible tape drive, or a floppy disk drive other than A or B. When you choose **OK**, CP Backup displays a dialog box into which you must type the DOS drive and path for the disk or tape you plan to use.

■ *Removable Drive and Path.* Select this option if you plan to normally back up your hard disk to a Bernoulli box or other mass storage device that has removable media.

When your system has two floppy drives of the same type and size, CP Backup lists another pair of options:

■ *One Drive Backup.* Select this option when you want to always back up to a single floppy drive.

■ *Two Drive Backup.* Choose this option when you want to use both floppy drives to back up to. The program alternates between drives during the backup process. The entire process is faster because the program doesn't have to wait for you to replace a disk.

After making a selection in the Choose Drive & Media dialog box, choose the **OK** command button. CP Backup displays the Backup Confidence Test dialog box (see fig. 7.6). The Confidence Test is a simulated backup operation that determines the fastest speed at which your system can reliably back up data to a backup disk or tape.

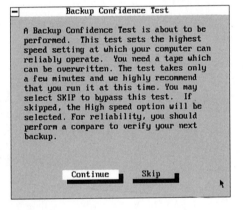

Fig. 7.6

The Backup
Confidence Test
dialog box.

Place a new disk or tape (or a disk or tape containing files you know can be overwritten) into the floppy disk or tape drive you specified in the previous dialog box and choose Continue to run the confidence test.

Because the test erases any data on the disk or tape you use in this step, CP Backup displays a warning similar to that shown in figure 7.7. Choose **OK** to continue with the test.

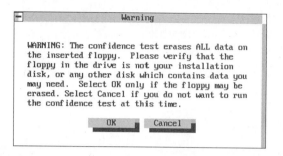

Fig. 7.7

The Confidence
Test Warning
dialog box.

As CP Backup performs the confidence test, it displays a dialog box similar to the one shown in figure 7.8. The dialog box contains information about the current backup simulation in process, including the drive being backed up, the number of files remaining, and a scale showing the percentage of completion.

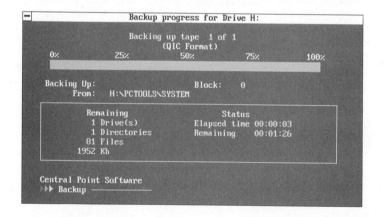

Fig. 7.8

The Confidence
Test Progress
dialog box.

CP Backup uses the highest transfer speed available to back up several files from your hard disk for the confidence test and then confirms that the files were accurately copied by performing a comparison test of the files that were backed up. If no errors are detected during the test, CP Backup displays the window shown in figure 7.9.

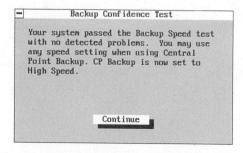

Fig. 7.9

The window that
appears if no
errors are found.

When the confidence test is complete, CP Backup writes the new configuration data to the file CPBACKUP.CFG (the default configuration file) in your \PCTOOLS\DATA directory, rereads the directories on your hard disk, and finally displays the Express Backup window shown in figure 7.10.

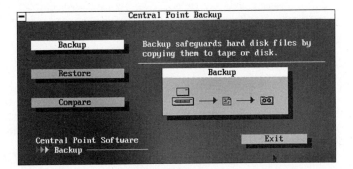

Fig. 7.10

The Express
Backup window.

The next time you start CP Backup, the program reads data from the configuration file CPBACKUP.CFG and immediately displays the Express Backup window. You do not have to answer the questions asked during the initial CP Backup session again.

Examining the Express Backup Window

When you start CP Backup for the first time, the program is in *Express mode*. From the Express Backup window, select **B**ackup to display the Backup window similar to the one shown in figure 7.11.

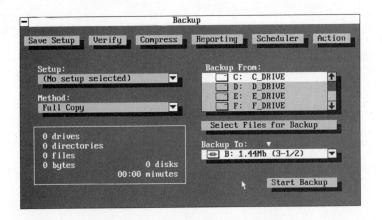

Fig. 7.11

A second Express
Backup window.

The Express Backup window is the control center from which you can quickly back up your entire hard disk. Express mode is optional, however, and the specific menus, buttons, and lists available depend on the current *user level*.

By default, CP Backup uses Express mode and the Advanced user level. If you prefer to take more direct control over your backup operations, CP Backup enables you to turn off Express mode. Conversely, you can reduce the number of options in the Express Backup window by selecting the Beginner or the Intermediate user level. Refer to the section "Changing the User Level" later in this chapter for a discussion of how to turn off Express mode and change the user level.

Like all PC Tools screens, as well as the earlier versions of CP Backup, the Express Backup window has a horizontal menu bar at the top and a message bar at the bottom. What makes this window different from earlier versions of the program are the many command buttons and drop-down list boxes that appear on-screen (refer to fig. 7.11). The Express Backup window contains the following command buttons:

- *Save Setup* displays the Save Current Settings dialog box (available in the Advanced and Intermediate user levels only). See the section "Creating a Setup File" later in this chapter for more information on this option.

- *Verify* displays the Verify Options dialog box (available in the Advanced user level only). See the section "Verifying Data" later in this chapter for more information about verifying data.

- *Compress* displays the Compress Options dialog box (available in the Advanced user level only). See the section "Compressing Backup Files" later in this chapter for more information.

- *Reporting* displays the Report Options dialog box. See the section "Creating a Backup Report" later in this chapter for more information.

- *Scheduler* displays the Schedule Backups dialog box (available in the Advanced and Intermediate user levels only). See the "Scheduling Backups" section later in this chapter for more information.

- *Action* returns to the Express Backup window (refer to fig. 7.10).

In the Beginner and Intermediate user levels, some of these command buttons are displayed on-screen but are *grayed out* because they are inaccessible at those particular user levels. These command buttons provide shortcuts to operations that can also be performed through the menu system. Selecting the Compress command button, for example, has the same effect as selecting **O**ptions on the horizontal menu bar and then choosing the **C**ompress option.

The Express Backup window also displays four drop-down list boxes: Setup, Method, Backup From, and Backup To (see fig. 7.11). Each drop-down list box is identified with a downward-pointing arrowhead or with both upward- and downward-pointing arrows along the right edge. These drop-down list boxes provide an easy way to change your current backup settings and are offered as alternatives to changing the settings through menu options and dialog boxes. Each drop-down list box displays the current value of a particular CP Backup setting. To access the drop-down list, use one of the following methods:

- Click the drop-down list box that displays the setting you want to change.

- Press the letter highlighted in the name of the drop-down list box.

- Press the Tab key until the box is highlighted and then press Enter.

For each of these selection methods, a list of choices drops down. To make a selection from this list, click the option or use your cursor-movement keys to move the highlighted bar to the desired option, and then press Enter. To close the list without making a change, press Esc or click the list box again.

To select a different backup method, for example, select the **Method** drop-down list box. CP Backup displays a list of choices (see fig. 7.12). Select the new method you want the program to use. (See the "Changing the Backup Method" section later in this chapter for more information.) This procedure is equivalent to selecting **O**ptions, choosing **B**ackup Method, and selecting an option button from the Backup Method dialog box.

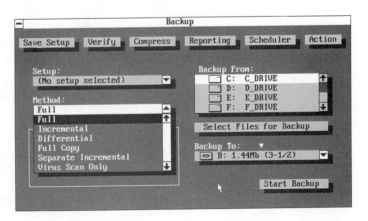

Fig. 7.12

The Backup Method drop-down list.

In addition to the command buttons and the drop-down list boxes, the Express Backup window displays the Backup From list box on the right side of the screen. The Backup From list box lists the hard drives available on your system, with the current backup-from setting highlighted. Figures 7.11 and 7.12, for example, show the backup-from setting as drive C.

Performing a Full Backup from the Express Backup Window

Making a backup copy of all the files on your hard disk is easy from the Express Backup window. Follow these steps to perform a full backup:

1. From the Backup From list box, select the drive or drives you want to back up by clicking each drive name once or moving the highlighted bar to each drive name in the Backup From list box and then pressing the space bar. CP Backup displays the message that it is reading the drive's directories and asks you to wait.

   After the program reads the directories, CP Backup lists information about the drives and your selected backup operation in the lower left corner of the screen. CP Backup lists the number of drives to be backed up, the total number of directories, the total number of files, the storage space currently occupied by the files you want to back up, the number of disks that may be needed for the backup operation, and an estimate of time for the procedure.

T I P

CP Backup displays an estimate of the number of disks or tape cartridges required for a complete backup. You will probably need fewer disks than this number because CP Backup compresses data (increasing backup speed and reducing disk space) while performing the backup, causing the files to occupy less storage space.

CP Backup can back up the files in even less space if you select the **C**ompress option from the **O**ptions menu and then select Minimize **S**pace-Maximum. When you use this method, however, you may sacrifice backup speed. Refer to the section "Setting Backup Options" later in this chapter for more about the Options menu.

---

2. Select the **S**tart Backup command button. CP Backup displays the Name Backup Set dialog box (see fig. 7.13).

Fig. 7.13

The Name
Backup Set
dialog box.

```
┌─────────────────────────────────────────────┐
│ ─            Name Backup Set                  │
│  Description: ┌──────────────────────────┐█  │
│              └──────────────────────────┘   │
│  Password:    ┌──────────┐█                  │
│              └──────────┘                    │
│                  ┌──────┐     ┌────────┐      │
│                  │  OK  │█    │ Cancel │█     │
│                  └──────┘     └────────┘      │
└─────────────────────────────────────────────┘
```

3. Type as many as 30 characters in the Description text box and press Enter.

   You might, for example, type the following description for a backup performed October 17, 1992:

   WP BACKUP 10-17-92

4. For additional security, you can type a password (as many as eight characters) in the Password text box and then press Enter, or you can leave the Password text box blank and select **OK** to continue.

   > **WARNING:** Do *not* forget to write down your backup passwords. Without the password, you cannot restore any data or files from your backup sets.

5. Select the **OK** command button. CP Backup begins the backup operation and displays the Backup Progress window (see fig. 7.14).

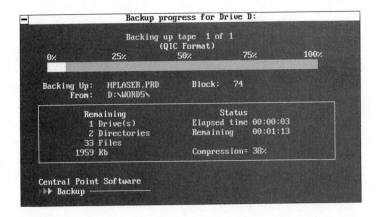

Fig. 7.14

The Backup
Progress window.

CP Backup instructs you to insert disk number 1 (or a tape cartridge if you are using a tape drive) into the backup device.

6. Place a disk (or tape) into the proper drive listed in the Backup To drop-down list box. Disks do not have to be formatted; if you are backing up to a tape drive, however, use a formatted tape to save time.

> **NOTE** The floppy drive light normally comes on and stays on throughout the backup procedure.

If you insert a disk that has been formatted by DOS or by PC Tools' PCFORMAT program and which appears to contain data, CP Backup displays a warning asking if you want to overwrite the disk or replace the disk. Similarly, if the disk contains data from a previous backup, CP Backup asks you to confirm the backup procedure.

After CP Backup fills a disk or tape, it prompts you to insert another disk or tape.

7. Label a new disk or tape with the number indicated on the screen and the current date. Remove the current disk or tape from the drive and insert the new one. CP Backup continues with the backup.

CP Backup continuously displays status information in the Backup Progress window (refer to fig. 7.14), including the file and directory names of the files currently being backed up, the elapsed time, the approximate time remaining, the percentage of completion (as a thermometer-style bar graph), and the number of directories, files, and bytes of files remaining. This box also shows the percentage of data that CP Backup has been able to compress during the backup and the disk or tape track currently being written to.

When CP Backup finishes backing up, the program displays the following message:

    Writing directory information. Please wait.

The program then writes the *history file* to the last backup disk or to the end of the tape cartridge. This history file stores information about the backup procedure, including a list of the files backed up and the disk or tape upon which each file is stored.

Finally, CP Backup displays the Backup Complete dialog box (see fig. 7.15). This dialog box indicates the number of directories backed up, the total number of files, the total kilobytes of storage used, the number of disks used, the total backup time, the backup speed (in kilobytes per minute), and the total compression. Choose **OK** to return to the Express Backup window.

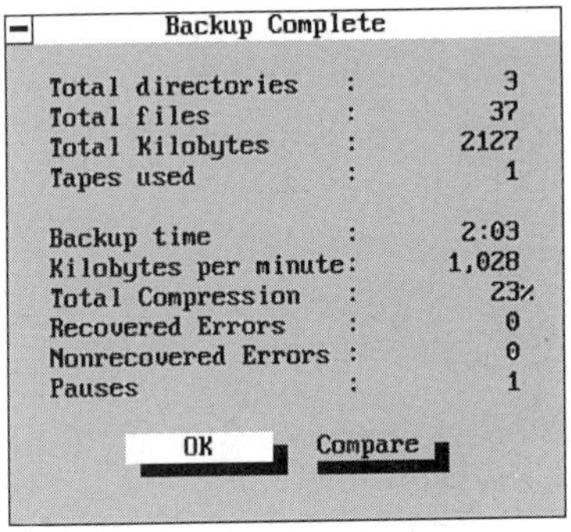

```
┌─────────────────────────────────┐
│ ─        Backup Complete         │
├─────────────────────────────────┤
│  Total directories   :       3   │
│  Total files         :      37   │
│  Total Kilobytes     :    2127   │
│  Tapes used          :       1   │
│                                  │
│  Backup time         :    2:03   │
│  Kilobytes per minute:   1,028   │
│  Total Compression   :     23%   │
│  Recovered Errors    :       0   │
│  Nonrecovered Errors :       0   │
│  Pauses              :       1   │
│                                  │
│     ┌──────┐    ┌─────────┐      │
│     │  OK  │    │ Compare │      │
│     └──────┘    └─────────┘      │
└─────────────────────────────────┘
```

Fig. 7.15

The Backup Complete dialog box.

T I P To ensure that CP Backup has made an accurate copy of your data, choose the Compare command button in the Backup Complete dialog box immediately after backing up. Refer to the section "Comparing and Restoring Data," later in this chapter, for more information about this option.

Performing a Selective Backup

As an alternative to Express mode, CP Backup enables you to display the normal CP Backup window, which resembles more closely the screens in previous versions of the program. To turn off Express mode, select Configure from the horizontal menu bar and choose Express Interface so that the check mark is removed. Alternatively, highlight Express Interface with your cursor control keys, and then press Enter. CP Backup reads the hard disk's directories and displays the CP Backup window (see fig. 7.16).

The CP Backup window, which closely resembles the PC Tools Desktop screen, has a Directory Tree window on the left side, a File window on the right, a horizontal menu bar at the top, and a message bar at the bottom. The message bar often displays a list of function key commands. Table 7.1 lists the function key commands and other keystroke commands available in CP Backup.

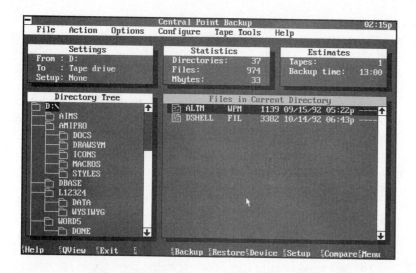

Fig. 7.16

The CP Backup
window.

Table 7.1 Using Keystroke Commands in CP Backup

Key	Name	Function
F1	Help	Displays context-sensitive Help facility
F2	QView	Displays contents of current file
F3	Exit	Exits from CP Backup
F4	NxtDriv	Displays tree list and file list for the next drive during multiple drive backup
F5	Backup	Starts backup
F6	Restore	Starts restore operation
F7	Device	Chooses drive and media
F8	Setup	Defines equipment
F9	Compare	Starts comparison
F10 or Alt	Menu	Activates horizontal menu bar
Enter	Select	Selects and deselects directories and files
Esc	Cancel	Cancels the current process
Tab or Shift+Tab	Tree/Files	Moves between windows

Each of the two windows in the CP Backup window has a title bar. The title of the active window is highlighted. Although both windows have vertical scroll bars, you can neither move nor resize these windows.

Just below the horizontal menu bar, the Settings box lists the *backup-from setting*, the drive that contains the source files you want to back up; the *backup drive and media*—the drive to which CP Backup backs up the selected files; and the name of the *current setup file*—a file that maintains a list of backup options.

The Statistics box lists the number of directories selected, the number of selected files, and the total storage space occupied by the selected files (in kilobytes). The Estimates box lists the number of disks or tapes required to back up the selected files and the time, in minutes and seconds, CP Backup estimates will be needed to perform the backup.

Even though CP Backup has many options, the default configuration is more than adequate for creating a reliable backup. This section focuses on how to back up an entire hard disk, specific directories, or specific files using a minimum of effort and the default configuration. As you become more familiar with CP Backup, turn to "Setting Backup Options" later in this chapter. In that section, you learn how to perform incremental backups to back up only files that have changed since the last backup operation and how to add such features as file compression.

T   I   P

Although CP Backup is intended to provide insurance against accidental loss of files on your hard disk, it also provides a handy method of copying a directory structure and many files from one computer to another. For example, you may want to set up all computers in an office with exactly the same software, installed in precisely the same manner. Although you can install the software on each system individually, an easier method is to install the software on one computer, use CP Backup to create a backup copy, and then restore the backup on each of the other systems in the office. (*Note:* This scenario assumes that your company owns the necessary number of software licenses.)

Specifying the Drive To Back Up

When you start CP Backup the first time, you set up a default backup-from setting—the disk you usually want to backup. On most computer systems, the default backup-from setting is drive C. (If you want to back up all files and all subdirectories from the default entry, skip to the "Starting the Backup" section later in this chapter.)

You may not always want to back up the default backup-from setting, however. Perhaps you have two hard disk drives, C and D, installed in your system, or perhaps your computer's hard disk is partitioned into two *logical drives* (a single physical drive is configured so that DOS treats it as two drives). In situations like these, you normally need to perform a separate backup operation for each hard disk or a single backup operation for all hard disks.

You can use one of two methods to choose a different backup-from setting. For the first method, move the highlighted bar to the Backup From list in the Express Backup window. Then highlight the drive you want CP Backup to back up and press the space bar to select that drive. Repeat for each disk drive you want to include in the backup operation.

For the second method, use the Backup from Directory dialog box shown in figure 7.17. You can access this dialog box by selecting **Act**-ion to display the Action menu and then selecting Backup **F**rom (see fig. 7.18).

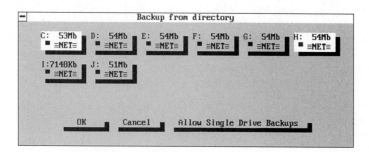

Fig. 7.17

The Backup from Directory dialog box.

In the Backup from Directory dialog box, click each drive icon for each drive you want to add to the backup operation. (Alternatively, use the cursor-movement keys to highlight the drive icons and then press Enter.) When C is selected and you want to add drive F, for example, click the icon for drive F. After you select the drives you want to back up, choose the **OK** command button to return to the CP Backup window.

When you select multiple hard drives, the From line in the Settings box lists the current drive followed in parentheses by the letter names of any other drives you selected. If you select drive C and drive F as the drives to back up, for example, the From line in the Settings box displays C: (F).

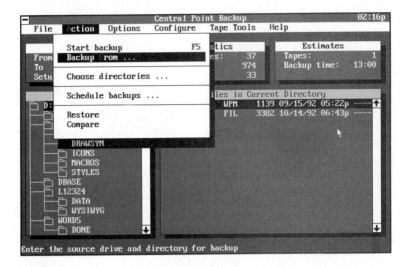

Fig. 7.18

The Action menu.

Choosing Specific Directories

Although you should always have a complete backup of all the files on your hard disk, on some occasions you may need to back up specific directories and files separately. By default, CP Backup backs up all directories on the designated hard disk or disks. If you want to back up only some of the directories and files, you must deselect all files and then select only those files you want to back up.

If you are backing up multiple hard disks, you must select the disk before you can specify the directories you want CP Backup to copy. To select the disk, do one of the following:

■ Display the Express Backup window. Move the highlighted bar to the Backup From list. Highlight the target drive and then press Enter. CP Backup displays a window with the Directory Tree window on the left and the Files in Current Directory window on the right.

■ Display the CP Backup window and press F4 (NxtDriv) repeatedly until the desired disk is current.

To indicate specific directories to be backed up, do one of the following:

■ Display the Express Backup window and the Directory Tree and Files in Current Directory windows. Press Tab until the Directory Tree window is the current window.

■ Display the CP Backup window and press Tab until the Directory Tree window is the current window. Alternatively, you can select **Ch**oose Directories from the **A**ction menu.

Initially (and by default), all the directory names listed in the Directory Tree window appear in high-intensity video or in a different color on color monitors. These directories are selected for backup. At least one directory name is also highlighted in inverse video, depending on the default setup file you selected.

Files from the highlighted directory—the *current* directory—are listed in the Files in Current Directory window on the right side of the CP Backup window.

Before you can select one or more specific directories, you must first deselect all the directories that CP Backup has preselected. Use the mouse or the cursor-movement keys listed in table 7.2 to move the highlight in the Directory Tree window to the root directory. Then press the mouse button or press Enter. CP Backup deselects all directories and displays the directory names in normal-intensity video.

Table 7.2 Using Cursor-Movement Keys in CP Backup

Key	Cursor Movement
↓	Down one file or subdirectory name
↑	Up one file or subdirectory name
→	Right one column in Files window
←	Left one column in Files window
Home	To first file or subdirectory in window
End	To last file or subdirectory in window
PgDn	To last file or subdirectory in column
PgUp	To first file or subdirectory in column

When you want to back up an entire directory (all its files and sub-directories), click the directory name or use the cursor-movement keys to move the highlight to that directory name in the Directory Tree window and then press Enter. CP Backup selects the directory and all its contents, again displaying in high-intensity video the selected directory and the file names listed in the Files window.

T I P   By default, selecting a directory selects all subdirectories, too. CP Backup enables you to change a setting on the Options menu, however, so that subdirectories are not selected automatically. Refer to this chapter's "Setting Backup Options" section for more information.

Selecting Files

Sometimes you may want to back up only specific files. After deselecting all directories, use the cursor-movement keys to move the highlight in the Directory Tree window to the name of the directory containing the files you want to back up. Do not press Enter, an action that selects all files in the directory. Instead, press Tab to make the Files in Current Directory window active. Then select every file you want CP Backup to copy. Either click the file name or press the cursor-movement keys to highlight the file name and then press Enter.

You also can use the mouse to quickly select multiple files listed one after the other in the Files window. Move the mouse pointer to the first file you want to select, hold down the right mouse button, press and hold down the left mouse button, and move the mouse pointer down the list to select each of the files. When all the appropriate files are selected, release both mouse buttons.

When you want to scroll quickly through the entire directory and select files as you scroll, hold the right mouse button, press and hold the left mouse button, and move the mouse pointer to the lower edge of the window border. CP Backup scrolls the window and selects files until you release a mouse button. Hold the mouse buttons until all appropriate files are selected.

Starting the Backup

After you select the disks and files you want CP Backup to back up, you are ready to start the backup procedure. To do so, use one of the following procedures:

- Display the Express Backup window; then select the Start Backup command.

- Display the CP Backup window; then press F5 (Backup) or choose **S**tart Backup from the **A**ction menu.

CP Backup displays the Name Backup Set dialog box (refer to fig. 7.13). Type as many as 30 characters in the Description text box and then press Enter. You might type the following description for your backup, for example:

WP DATA BACKUP 10-17-92

This *backup set name* helps remind you later that the backup contains WP data files from WP subdirectories. The description also reminds you that the backup of the files was completed October 17, 1992.

> Ideally, you should use a description that clearly identifies the backup in the Name Backup Set dialog box, distinguishing each backup set from others. If you use the exact description you used for another backup, CP Backup does not warn you.
>
> One good practice that reduces the likelihood of duplication is to include the current date as a part of the description.

T I P

CP Backup enables you to password-protect your backup. To prevent anyone from restoring the backup files to a hard disk without authorization, type a password (up to eight characters long) in the Password text box in the Name Backup Set dialog box.

> **WARNING:** Do *not* forget to write down your backup passwords. Without the password, you cannot restore any data or files from your backup sets.

After typing the description (and optional password), choose the **OK** command button to proceed with the backup. CP Backup instructs you to insert disk number 1 (or a tape cartridge if you are using a tape drive) into the backup drive. If you insert a disk formatted by DOS or by PC Tools' PCFORMAT program, CP Backup warns you that the disk contains data. Similarly, if the disk contains data from a previous backup, CP Backup prompts you to confirm the backup procedure. Choose **OK** to continue.

After CP Backup fills a disk (assuming that you are backing up to disk rather than to tape), the program prompts you to insert another disk. Label a new disk with the number indicated and the current date. Remove the current backup disk and insert the new disk. CP Backup continues with the backup.

CP Backup continuously displays status information in the Backup Progress box, which replaces the Statistics and Estimates boxes on-screen, including the time that has elapsed, the percentage of completion, and the number of disks remaining. This box also indicates the percentage of data CP Backup has been able to compress during the backup and the disk or tape track currently being written to.

T I P When you are backing up files from more than one hard disk in one operation, CP Backup still treats each hard disk separately. Be careful to label backup disks with the name of the source hard disk. After backing up all selected files from the first hard disk, the program writes the directory to the backup disk and then prompts you to insert disk 1. Do not be confused by this prompt. Write "disk 1 for drive *d*" on the new disk's label, where *d* is the source drive; then insert the disk into the backup device. CP Backup then starts placing the files from the second hard disk on the disk in the backup device.

When CP Backup finishes backing up a disk, the program displays a dialog box containing the message `Writing directory information. Please wait`. The program then writes a history file to the last backup disk. The history file stores information about the backup procedure, including a list of the files backed up and the disk on which each file is stored.

After CP Backup backs up all selected files from all selected disks and directories, it displays the Backup Complete dialog box (refer to fig. 7.15). Choose **OK** to return to the CP Backup window.

Comparing and Restoring Data

Performing a backup operation is much like buying insurance. You hope you never have to use it, but if disaster strikes, you have a way to recover from your loss. The sections that follow describe how to restore a backup to your hard disk or disks.

The purpose of CP Backup is to ensure that you don't lose data because of hardware failure or accidental erasure of your hard disk data. But how can you be sure that the data is backed up properly before it is too late to do anything about it?

CP Backup answers this question with the *compare* operation. By using this operation, you can ensure that the backup produced by CP Backup is valid, or you can use this operation just to see how many files have been changed since the last backup.

Selecting a Backup Set and Destination

The first step in a compare or restore operation is to choose which backup set you want to compare or restore. You can use one of two procedures. With the first method, you display the Express Backup window and choose the Compare or Restore command button, as appropriate. CP Backup displays the Express Compare window, as shown in figure 7.19, or the Express Restore window. Select the History drop-down list box. CP Backup displays a list of backup sets similar to the one shown in figure 7.19.

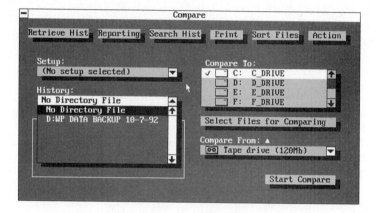

Fig. 7.19

The Express Compare window with History drop-down list.

Using the second method, you display the CP Backup window and select Action to display the Action menu. Then select Choose Directories. CP Backup displays the Choose Directory dialog box (see fig. 7.20).

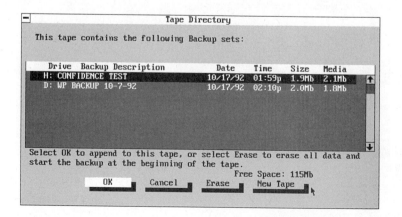

Fig. 7.20

The Choose Directory dialog box.

The screen displays a list of backup sets (history files), one for each backup operation you performed using CP Backup. (This list does not appear if you have turned off the Save History option. Instead, CP Backup prompts you to insert the last disk of the backup set. Refer to the section "Setting Backup Options" for more information.) Use the cursor-movement keys or the mouse to select the name of the backup set you want to compare or restore. If you are using the Choose Directory dialog box, select the **OK** command button to return to the CP Backup window.

T I P

Although CP Backup enables you to back up several hard disks in a single operation, the program creates a separate set of disks and, consequently, a separate backup set (history file) for each hard disk. Each backup set is listed individually in the History drop-down list or Choose Directory dialog box, shown in figures 7.19 and 7.20, respectively.

After you select the backup set from the Choose Directory dialog box, CP Backup displays the backup set's directory from the backup history file. Figure 7.21, for example, shows the directory from drive D for the WP BACKUP 10-17-92 backup set. This history file is saved on the hard disk as part of the backup procedure unless you turned off the Save History option on the **O**ptions menu.

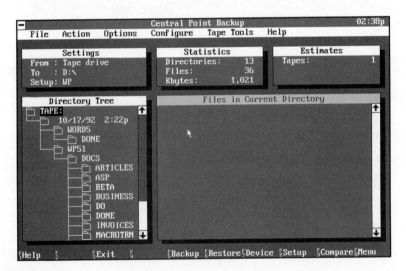

Fig. 7.21

The sample backup set directory.

NOTE If you are using Express mode, CP Backup displays the backup set's directory but does not display the horizontal menu bar or the Settings, Statistics, and Estimates boxes. Press F10 (GoBack) or Esc to return to the Express Compare or Express Restore window.

In addition to selecting the backup set you want to compare to or restore from, you also must select the *destination disk*—the disk that contains the files you want CP Backup to compare to, or the disk to which you want to restore the backup. Use one of the following procedures:

■ If you are using Express mode, CP Backup automatically selects the files' original source disk as the destination disk. If the files originated on drive C, for example, Express chooses drive C as the destination for the compare or restore operation. You can use the mouse or the cursor-movement keys to select a different entry in the Compare To or Restore To list box.

■ If you are using the CP Backup window, select Compare To in the Action dialog box, and then select the desired destination disk for the compare or restore operation.

After you select a backup set and specify a destination disk, you are ready to begin a compare operation or a restore operation.

Starting the Compare Operation

To compare the backup set to the original files on disk, use one of the following procedures (multiple disk backups must be compared one disk at a time):

■ From the Express Compare window, select Start Compare.

■ From the CP Backup window, press F9 (Compare) or select Action and Start Compare. (If Start Compare is not the first option on the Action menu, select Compare and then choose Start Compare.)

At the prompt, insert the first disk of the set you want to compare. CP Backup begins comparing this backup set with the original files on the hard disk. When you are comparing disks (rather than tapes), the program prompts you to replace disk 1 with disk 2 and to continue with this procedure until all disks have been compared.

As CP Backup finishes comparing each file, the program displays one of the following symbols to the left of the file name in the Files window:

Symbol	Meaning
=	The backup file is identical to the original file on the hard disk.
<	The backup file is older and has different contents than the corresponding file on the hard disk. You have modified this file since last performing the backup.
>	The backup file is newer, and the contents of the files do not match.
s	The file sizes of the backup file and the original file are the same, but the date and time differ.
x	The date and time of the files match, but the contents do not.
-	The backup file is missing from the original hard disk.

When CP Backup finishes the compare operation, the program displays a dialog box that reports the total number of disks used and the total number of directories, files, and bytes compared (see fig. 7.22).

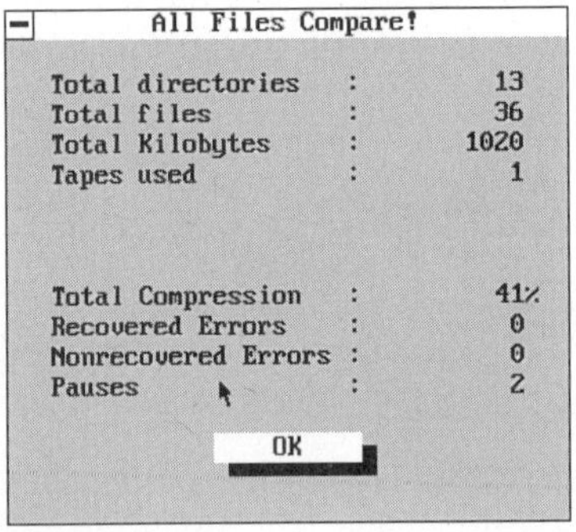

Fig. 7.22

The compare operation window report.

When no errors are found during the compare operation, this dialog box is titled All Files Compare! (refer to fig. 7.22). When one or more files on the backup media is different in some way from their corresponding original files, the dialog box is entitled Files Did Not Compare. The dialog box then lists the number of files missing, files that are older, files that are newer, files with different times or dates, and the number of backup files whose contents did not match the contents of the corresponding files on the hard disk. Select the **OK** command button to return to the CP Backup or Express Backup window.

Performing a Restore Operation

Before you can perform a restore operation, both DOS and CP Backup must be installed on your hard disk. If you have lost all the files on the hard disk and want to use CP Backup to restore those files, follow the instructions in your DOS manual to install the operating system (DOS), and then follow the instructions in Appendix A, "Installing and Configuring PC Tools," to install CP Backup. You are then ready to proceed with the restore operation.

> **NOTE** CP Backup writes data to a backup tape in one of two formats: either a QIC-compatible format or in a proprietary format that can be read only by CP Backup. The proprietary format provides higher speed, greater compression levels, and better error recovery than the QIC-compatible format. This design means, though, that CP Backup can only read tapes that are QIC-compatible in a format it can recognize or in its own proprietary format. Refer to the *PC Tools for DOS* manual for specific information about supported and unsupported tape drives.

Although you may occasionally need to restore a complete hard disk, you are more likely to want to separately restore one or more specific directories or files. By default, CP Backup restores all directories and files listed in the backup set's directory. To restore only some of the directories or files from the backup media—a *partial restore*—you must first deselect all files and then select only the files you want restored.

The procedure is the same as selecting specific directories or files for backing up. Refer to the sections "Choosing Specific Directories" and "Selecting Files" for more details. After you choose the backup set and destination disk and select the appropriate directories and files, use one of the following procedures to begin the restore operation (multiple disk backups must be restored one disk at a time):

■ From the Express Restore window, select **S**tart Restore.

■ From the CP Backup window, press F6 (Restore) or select **A**ction and then **S**tart Restore. (If Start Restore is not the first option on the Action menu, select **R**estore and then **S**tart Restore.)

At the prompt, insert the first disk or tape of the set you want to restore. CP Backup begins copying the files from the backup set to the destination hard disk.

CP Backup first compares the list of files in the backup directory with the list of files in the hard disk directory. If a duplicate is found, CP Backup displays the Overwrite Warning dialog box (see fig. 7.23).

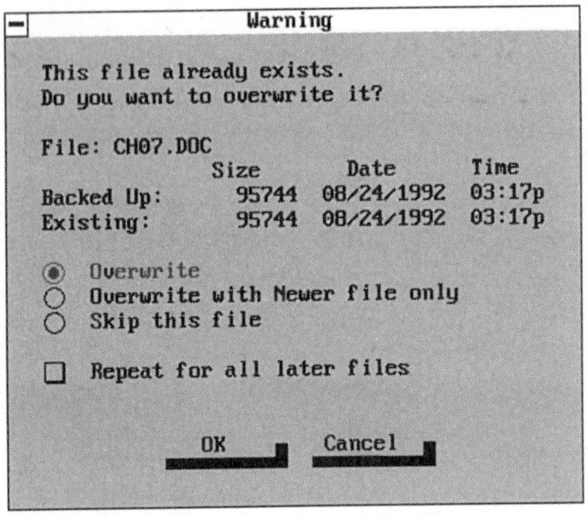

```
┌─────────────────────────────────────────────────┐
│ ─                    Warning                      │
├───────────────────────────────────────────────────┤
│  This file already exists.                        │
│  Do you want to overwrite it?                     │
│                                                   │
│  File: CH07.DOC                                   │
│                   Size      Date       Time       │
│  Backed Up:       95744   08/24/1992   03:17p      │
│  Existing:        95744   08/24/1992   03:17p      │
│                                                   │
│  ⊙  Overwrite                                     │
│  ○  Overwrite with Newer file only                │
│  ○  Skip this file                                │
│                                                   │
│  ☐  Repeat for all later files                    │
│                                                   │
│              ▆ OK ▆      ▆ Cancel ▆               │
└───────────────────────────────────────────────────┘
```

Fig. 7.23

The Overwrite
Warning dialog
box.

The Overwrite Warning dialog box warns you that the backup file already exists on the hard disk. In response to the question Do you want to overwrite it?, choose one of the following option buttons:

- ■ *Overwrite.* Choose this option to overwrite the file on the hard disk with the corresponding file on the backup disk. This option is the default.

- ■ *Overwrite with Newer file only.* Choose this option to overwrite a file on the hard disk only if the corresponding backup file is newer.

- ■ *Skip this file.* Choose this option to skip this backup file without writing anything to the hard disk.

In addition to the three option buttons, CP Backup presents a Repeat for All Later Files check box. Select this check box to process any further overwrite warnings in the same manner as this one. You may, for example, indicate that CP Backup should skip this file. If you also check the Repeat for All Later Files check box, CP Backup skips (but does not restore) all files that already exist on the hard disk.

After you make your selections from the Overwrite Warning dialog box, choose the **OK** command button. CP Backup first prompts you to insert the first disk or tape from the backup set you want to restore. If the set contains multiple disks, replace disk 1 with disk 2 when you are prompted and continue with this procedure until all disks have been restored. CP Backup then displays the Restore Completed message box, indicating the total number of directories, files, kilobytes, and disks used in the restore operation. Choose **OK** to return to the Express Restore window or the CP Backup window.

Reconfiguring CP Backup

By answering the questions that CP Backup asks when you first start the program, you provide the minimum configuration information necessary to perform a backup. CP Backup stores this information in CPBACKUP.CFG, which maintains a list of all the following CP Backup parameters (each of which is discussed in this chapter):

- Attribute exclusions
- Backup method
- Backup schedule
- Backup speed
- Color selections
- Current drive and directory
- Date range selections
- Default backup device
- Equipment list
- Include and exclude files
- Overwrite warning setting
- Reporting setting
- Subdirectory inclusions
- User level

You can change any of these settings, which are stored in the default configuration file. From the Configure menu, you can change any of the information provided at the initial start-up and also user level and screen colors. From the Options menu, you can change the other settings stored in the configuration file. This section describes the Configure menu. See "Setting Backup Options" later in this chapter for information about changing the other settings.

When you want to change the equipment list, backup device, backup speed, user level, screen colors, or backup schedule, select **C**onfigure to display the Configure menu (see fig. 7.24).

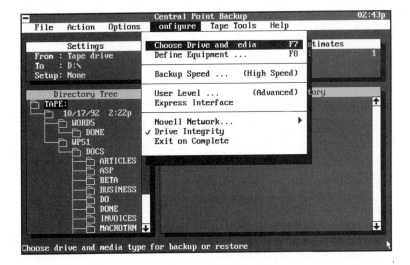

Fig. 7.24

The Configure menu.

> **T I P**   As an alternative to changing the default configuration, CP Backup enables you to create and use additional configuration files. These *setup files* contain the same group of settings as the default configuration file but can be customized and loaded selectively for special purposes. See the "Saving the Setup" section for more information about how to create setup files.

Changing the Backup Device

If you add a new floppy disk drive to your system and want to use this new drive to make backups, you must reconfigure CP Backup. Either press F8 (Setup) or choose **C**onfigure and then Define **E**quipment. First, a dialog box asks whether your system has a tape drive. Respond **Y**es or **N**o, as appropriate. CP Backup then displays the Define Equipment dialog box. Follow the procedure described earlier in this chapter in the section "Answering Initial Configuration Questions" to add the drive to the configuration as the default destination drive and media.

If you have not installed a new drive but want to select a different drive or media as the default backup device, press F7 (Device) or choose **C**onfigure and then Choose Drive & **M**edia. CP Backup displays the Choose Drive & Media dialog box. Follow the steps described in the "Answering the Initial Configuration Questions" section to specify the drive and media you want to use as the default backup device.

Changing the Backup Speed

One of the reasons for using a program such as CP Backup rather than DOS when you back up your hard disk is the program's relative speed. By default, CP Backup uses the DMA (Direct Memory Access) controller in your computer to enable your computer to read data from the hard disk and simultaneously write data to the backup device. This process works when the backup device is a floppy disk drive or a tape drive. The result is significantly reduced backup time.

Some computers do not have a DMA controller, however, or for some reason are incompatible with CP Backup's fastest speed. The program, therefore, provides a method for selecting a slower speed. To change the speed, choose **C**onfigure and then **B**ackup Speed. CP Backup displays the Backup Speed dialog box (see fig. 7.25).

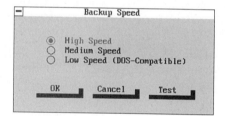

Fig. 7.25

The Backup
Speed dialog
box.

The Backup Speed dialog box lists the following option buttons:

■ *High Speed.* This option, which is the default, causes CP Backup to use the DMA controller. You can use this option only with floppy disks or tape backup.

■ *Medium Speed.* Use this option only after determining that you either cannot use High Speed or your PC lacks a DMA controller. Like High Speed, this option can be used only with floppy disks or tape backup.

■ *Low Speed.* Use this DOS-compatible option only when the other two options are not available. You must use the low speed when you back up to another hard disk, across a network, or to any other DOS device. (This option is only available for floppy disk drives.)

After you select a new speed, you can accept the change by choosing the **OK** command button, or you can perform a confidence test to determine whether CP Backup can perform a successful backup operation at the new speed.

To initiate the confidence test, select the **Test** command button. CP Backup displays the Backup Confidence Test dialog box. Select **Con**tinue to continue with the test. Refer to "Answering the Initial Configuration Questions" earlier in this chapter for more information about this speed test.

Changing the User Level

Just as PC Tools enables you to select from three *user levels*, so does CP Backup. The three levels are Beginner, Intermediate, and Advanced (the default). The distinction among the three user levels lies in the number and complexity of the available CP Backup options. The menu selections available on the Files, Action, and Configure menus are the same for all user levels, but the choices on the Options menu differ among user levels. The section "Setting Backup Options" describes the options available at each level and provides more information about customizing CP Backup for your specific requirements.

When you want to change the user level, select **Configure** and then **User Level**. CP Backup displays the User Level dialog box (see fig. 7.26). Select the appropriate user-level option button, and then select **OK** to return to the Configure menu.

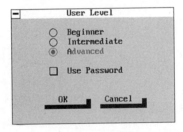

Fig. 7.26

The User Level dialog box.

In addition to the three option buttons, the User Level dialog box enables you to toggle the **Use Password** option on or off.

After making your selections from the User Level dialog box, choose the **OK** command button. The program reads the hard disk's directories and displays the CP Backup window or the Express Backup window, depending on the configuration you saved.

Saving the Configuration Changes

After you change one of these configuration settings, CP Backup returns to the Configure menu. The configuration change is effective immediately, but only for the current CP Backup session. This process enables you, for example, to change the backup device for a single backup operation and leave the default setting unchanged. To make this new setting a part of the default configuration so that CP Backup uses it the next time you run the program, however, you can select the Save as **D**efault option from the **F**ile menu.

Scheduling Backups

Even though CP Backup does a good job of reducing the amount of time needed to back up your computer's hard disk, each backup session still can be lengthy, especially if you have a large hard disk. CP Backup provides two ways for you to schedule CP Backup to run unattended, at predetermined times, to back up your hard disk to a tape drive or to another hard disk:

■ The Desktop Appointment Scheduler (CPSCHED)

■ The Central Point Backup Scheduler

 You cannot use these schedulers to make unattended back ups to floppy disks, although they work fine for tape and hard disk-to-hard disk backups.

To use CP Backup's Scheduler feature, you must run the memory-resident program CPSCHED (Central Point Scheduler) before running CP Backup. As explained in Appendix A, "Installing and Configuring PC Tools," during the installation process you can have the PC Tools' installation program add to your computer's AUTOEXEC.BAT file a command that loads CPSCHED as a memory-resident program every time you turn on your computer. (If you did not choose to have Install add CPSCHED to AUTOEXEC.BAT, you must exit from CP BACKUP and type **cpsched** to start CPSCHED.) Alternatively, you can run CPSCHED from PC Tools Desktop if you originally launched CP Backup from Desktop.

A message appears on-screen indicating that Central Point's Scheduler program is loaded. After CPSCHED is memory-resident, run CP Backup; then choose **A**ction to display the Action menu and select Sche**d**ule Backups. CP Backup displays the window shown in figure 7.27.

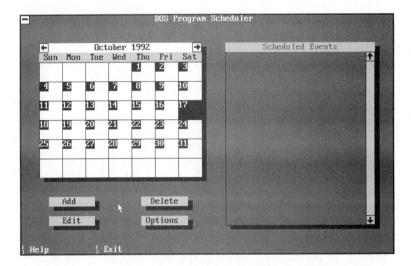

Fig. 7.27

The DOS
Program
Scheduler
window.

The DOS Program Scheduler window displays a monthly calendar on
the left side of the screen and a list of scheduled events, if any, on the
right side of the screen. The window has four command buttons at the
bottom—Add, Edit, Delete, and Options, explained in the following:

- *Add* adds a blank scheduler entry. You can have as many as 10
  different scheduler entries stored in the Scheduler entry list at
  any one time. You may, for example, want a daily entry that performs an incremental backup operation each evening and a
  weekly entry that performs a full backup once a week.

- *Edit* enables you to modify the highlighted and previously saved
  scheduler entry.

- *Delete* deletes the highlighted entry.

- *Options* provides days and event options allowing you to customize your individual scheduled events in the Scheduler Options
  dialog box (see fig. 7.28). The Scheduler entry list is saved in the
  file CPBACKUP.TM.

After you add one or more entries to the schedule list, these menu options appear in the DOS Program Scheduler window that appears when
you select Schedule Backup from the Configure menu.

To schedule backups, select Add. The Schedule or Edit an Event dialog
box shown in figure 7.29 appears, with the current date and time already filled in. The defaults for Setup Files, Frequency, and Events are
also filled in and can easily be changed by selecting the lines and then
pressing Enter to display choices available for each option.

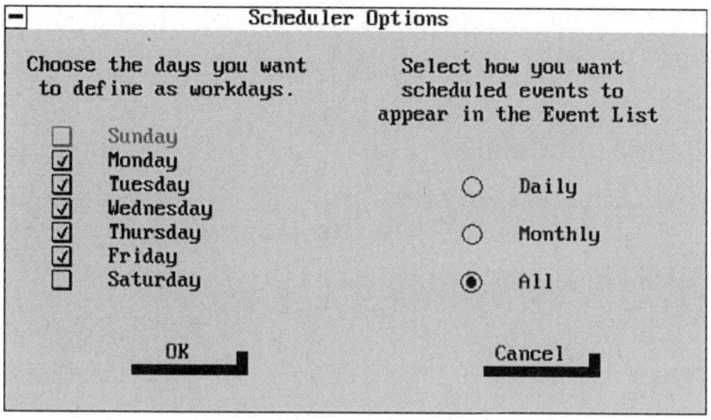

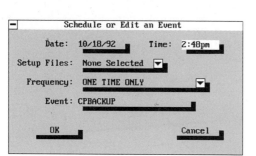

Fig. 7.28

The Scheduler Options dialog box.

Fig. 7.29

The Schedule or Edit an Event dialog box.

To add a setup named DAILY to make an incremental backup at midnight on Monday through Thursday, select **A**dd to schedule an event. The Schedule or Edit an Event dialog box appears, with the current date and time in the Date and Time box already filled in. To use a setup named DAILY, for example, to make an incremental backup at midnight on Monday through Thursday, follow these steps:

1. In the Schedule or Edit an Event dialog box, type **1200a** in the Time text box and press Enter.

2. In the Setup Files box, press Enter to display the Setup File Name drop-down box, highlight DAILY, and press Enter.

3. Press Tab to move to the Frequency box, press Enter to display the drop-down box, highlight WORKDAYS ONLY, and press Enter.

   Notice that CP Backup automatically changes the Event to read CPBACKUP DAILY.

4. Press Enter twice to return to the Program Scheduler window.

To change this new DAILY scheduled event to perform only on Monday through Thursday, follow these steps:

1. Select **O**ptions from the DOS Program Scheduler window. The Schedule Options dialog box appears (refer to fig. 7.28).

2. Press Tab until you reach the Friday check box and then press Enter to remove the check mark.

3. Press Tab until you reach the **OK** box and press Enter to return to the Program Scheduler window.

At the end of every workday, make sure that the target tape drive or hard disk is prepared to receive a backup. Leave your computer running (with CPSCHED memory-resident). At the appointed time, Scheduler runs CP Backup and creates a backup named Unattended Backup.

T I P   Start with a new tape for every weekly full backup, and add each daily incremental backup to the preceding weekly full backup tape. If you use this procedure, no data is ever overwritten.

FROM HERE...

For Related Information

◄◄ "Scheduling Programs with the Scheduler," p. 125.

Setting Backup Options

CP Backup's default configuration is more than adequate to perform most of your backup needs. As you become more familiar with the program, however, you might become curious about the extent to which you can customize its features.

When you decide to customize a CP Backup option, choose **O**ptions to display the Options menu. Table 7.3 lists the menu options at each of the three user levels: Beginner, Intermediate, and Advanced. All options are available at the default Advanced User level.

CP Backup indicates the status of each option in one of two ways:

■ When an option has more than two possible settings, CP Backup displays the current setting in parentheses to the right of the option name in the Options menu. Figure 7.30, for example, indicates that the Backup Method is set at Incremental.

■ When an option has only two possible values, on or off, CP Backup shows which option is active by displaying a check mark to the left of the option name in the menu. The absence of a check mark means that the option is off. Figure 7.30, for example, indicates that Error Correction is on and Format Always is off.

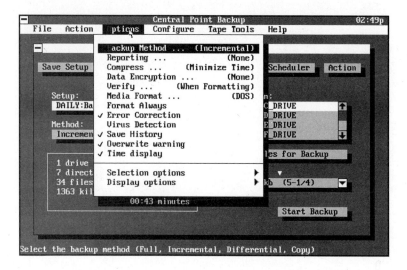

Fig. 7.30

The Backup Method set to Incremental.

The last two options on the menu, **S**election Options and **D**isplay Options, display submenus.

Table 7.3 Using the Options Menu

Advanced level	Intermediate level	Beginner level
Backup Method	Backup Method	Reporting
Reporting	Reporting	
Compress	Overwrite Warning	
Verify	Selection Options	
Media Format	Display Options	
Format Always		
Error Correction		
Virus Detection		
Save History		
Overwrite Warning		
Time Display		
Selection Options		
Display Options		

Regardless of the user level you choose, CP Backup starts (by default) with the option settings listed in table 7.4.

Table 7.4 The Default CP Backup Option Settings

Option	Default setting
Backup Method	Full
Reporting	None
Compress	Minimize Time
Data Encryption	None
Verify	When Formatting
Media Format	DOS
Format Always	Off
Error Correction	On
Virus Detection	Off
Save History	On
Overwrite Warning	On
Time Display	On
Manual Subdirectory Inclusion	On
Include/Exclude Files	On
Attribute Exclusion	Off
Date Range Selection	Off
Sort Options	Name (submenu)
Long Format	On (submenu)

This combination of option settings provides the easiest, safest, and most secure backup method. For this reason, when you are using the Beginner user level, you cannot modify these settings. When you use the Intermediate level, CP Backup enables you to turn off all options except Save History, Time Display, and Error Correction. At the Advanced level, you can make any changes you choose. The sections that follow describe when and how to change each of these options.

Setting Procedural Options

The first group of options listed on the Options menu control the procedure that CP Backup (not Express Backup) follows in completing a backup. These options include Backup Method, Reporting, Compress, Data Encryption, Verify, Media Format, Format Always, Error Correction, Virus Detection, Save History, Overwrite Warning, and Time Display.

Changing the Backup Method

Use the **B**ackup Method option to change the backup method. When you select this option, CP Backup displays the Backup Method dialog box, which contains the following option buttons (note that the options appear differently depending on the mode—Standard or Express—you enabled):

- *Full*, which is the default for floppy drive and DOS device backups, makes a complete backup of all selected files on the hard disk and resets the archive bit for backed-up files.

- *Full/Append to Tape* performs a full backup and adds it to the tape immediately following the previous backup, without overwriting the previous backup. (CP Backup lists this option, which is the default for tape backups only if you are using a tape backup system.)

- *Full Copy* makes a complete backup of all selected files on the hard disk but does not reset the archive bit on backed-up files.

- *Full/Erase Tape* performs a full backup, starting at the beginning of the tape and overwriting any previous backup you may have copied to the same tape. CP Backup lists this option only if you are using a tape backup system.

- *Differential* backs up all selected files that have changed or been added since the last full backup to separate media. Because this method does not reset the archive bit, it should not be mixed with either incremental method. Reuse the same media for all differential backups until the next full backup. Restore the last full backup first; then restore differential backups.

- *Separate Incremental* backs up to separate media all selected files that have changed or been added since the last full or separate incremental backup. Do not mix with either the incremental method or the differential method. This method resets the archive bit. Restore the full backup set first; then restore each separate incremental backup set in the order created.

■ *Incremental* backs up all selected files that have changed or been added since the last full or incremental backup to the end of the last backup tape or disk.

■ *Virus Scan Only* scans the hard disk for viruses before starting the backup operation.

After selecting an option, select **OK** to return to the Options menu.

T I P   The *archive bit* is one bit in the attribute byte that DOS and CP Backup use to determine whether a file has been added or changed since the last backup (see Chapter 4, "Working on Files"). When you place a new file on the disk or make a change to an existing file, DOS sets the archive bit. Backup programs, such as CP Backup, then normally reset this archive bit on every file that is backed up. Consequently, incremental backup operations can use the archive bit to identify files that need to be backed up.

Creating a Backup Report

Use the **R**eporting option from the Options menu to send a report to the printer or to a disk file at the completion of the backup operation. When you select this option, CP Backup displays the Report Options dialog box. Select **N**one to choose no reporting (the default); Report to **P**rinter to send the report to the printer; or Report to **F**ile to send the report to a file.

When you use Report to **F**ile, CP Backup names the file, using the format *xyymmdda*.RPT, where *x* is the backup drive letter; *yy* is the year; *mm* is the month; *dd* is the current date; *a* indicates 1 for the first backup of the day, 2 for the second backup, and so on; and RPT is the file name extension.

After selecting one of the options in the Report Options dialog box, choose **OK** to accept the change and return to the Options menu, or select **C**ancel to return to the Options menu without accepting any changes.

The backup report includes a great deal of information about the backup, including date, time, backup method, drive, media type, backup type, backup from, backup to, date range, include and exclude criteria, total directories, total files, disks used, total bytes, and a list of all files, showing the location of each file within the set of backup disks.

NOTE You can generate the same report later by choosing the **P**rint command button in the Choose Directory dialog box. Refer to the section "Comparing and Restoring Data" earlier in this chapter for more information.

Compressing Backup Files

Select **C**ompress from the **O**ptions menu when you want CP Backup to use the minimum amount of space on the backup media. When you select this option, CP Backup displays the Compress Options dialog box, which provides the following choices:

- *None* turns off compression.

- *Minimize Time* uses compression only to the extent that the backup time is not increased. This option, the default, results in more compression on computers with faster processors and hard disks (such as the IBM/PC AT and compatibles or PCs based on the Intel 80386 or 80486 processors) than on computers with slower processors (such as the IBM/PC XT and compatibles).

- *Minimize Space-Moderate* uses compression to create a backup on fewer disks than an uncompressed backup. This method is significantly faster than Minimize Space-Maximum.

- *Minimize Space-Maximum* uses compression to the fullest extent necessary to create a backup on the smallest number of disks (or least amount of tape) possible. Compression varies from 10 to 60 percent, depending on the types of files being compressed.

After selecting an option, select the **OK** command button to return to the Options menu.

Verifying Data

Verification of a backup tape (also called certification) involves checking the tape formatting for accuracy and blocking out bad sectors. This process is particularly important when you use unformatted backup tapes because tapes are more prone to have bad sectors that the verification process locates and locks out. (Central Point Software recommends that you buy preformatted tapes to save the considerable time—one to three hours—necessary to format a tape.)

The Verify option on the Options menu enables you to choose when CP Backup verifies that the data written to the backup media is readable.

When you select **Verify**, CP Backup displays the following options:

- *None.* CP Backup doesn't verify the backup media. This option saves time but is not as safe as the other options.

- *When Formatting.* CP Backup verifies any disk or certifies any tape formatted during backup. By default, CP Backup formats only disks or tapes that are not already formatted; consequently, it verifies a particular disk or tape only the first time you use it. This option, the default, usually provides adequate testing to certify that the media will provide trouble-free storage as a backup disk.

- *Always.* CP Backup verifies data readability on every backup disk or tape. Use this option for maximum protection. When you are using a backup tape, this option rewinds the tape at the completion of the backup and compares the contents of the original files to those on the backup tape.

After selecting an option, choose **OK** to return to the Options menu.

Selecting Media Format

The Media Format option enables you to choose whether CP Backup formats disks or tapes using a special proprietary formatting process or the more widely used formatting standards. When you choose this option, CP Backup displays the Media Format dialog box, which contains two pairs of option buttons. The first pair of option buttons deal with disk formatting:

- *CPS Floppy Format* uses a proprietary formatting process that squeezes an additional track on each disk. If you select this option, backups require fewer disks; however, you cannot use DOS to display a directory of any backup disk.

- *DOS Standard Format* formats disks in the standard format recognized by DOS. This setting is the default for disks.

The second pair of option buttons affect how CP Backup formats tapes:

- *CPS Tape Format* formats backup tapes in such a manner that you can pause and restart the backup process and that data is compressed. This formatting method is the default for tapes.

- *QIC-Compatible Format* formats tapes to the published QIC standard so that you can use the backup tape with other backup programs.

After selecting an option, choose **OK** to return to the Options menu.

Formatting Backup Media

Check the Format Always option on the **O**ptions menu to have CP Backup format every backup medium, regardless of whether it is formatted already. With this option set, tape backups take considerably longer than they do without formatting. By default, this option is turned off.

Correcting Errors

Check the **E**rror Correction option from the **O**ptions menu (this option is on by default) if you want CP Backup to store additional correction information on the backup disk. This procedure enables CP Backup to correct, during a restore operation, many errors that might result from damage to a backup disk or tape. Because tape media is more prone to errors, leave this option checked (on) when you are backing up to tape. Using this option, however, does increase backup time.

Virus Detection

When you activate the Vir**u**s Detection option (off by default), CP Backup scans the entire hard disk for known *software viruses* (destructive programs that attach themselves to other programs and files for the purpose of disrupting or destroying data).

When you start a backup operation, the program scans the entire disk for viruses before beginning the backup operation. You can perform only a Virus Scan by selecting **V**irus Scan Only as the Backup Method. Refer to the section "Changing the Backup Method," earlier in this chapter, for more about that option. If CP Backup locates a virus, the program displays a dialog box that contains the following choices:

■ *Continue* continues without marking or excluding the infected file (the file to which the virus is attached).

■ *Rename* marks the infected file by changing the file name extension to V*nn* where *nn* is a number between 00 and 99, assigned by CP Backup.

■ *Cancel* stops the backup procedure.

Saving a Copy of the Backup History File

Check the Save **H**istory option (the default setting is on) to save to the hard disk a copy of the backup history file routinely stored with every backup set. (The backup copy is saved on the last backup disk when you are backing up to disk.) This history file includes the following information about a backup set: backup set name, date, time, backup method, drive, media type, backup type, backup from, backup to, date range, include and exclude criteria, total directories, total files, disks used, total bytes, and a list of all files, showing the location of each file within the set of backup disks.

Protecting Duplicate Files

Check the **Overwrite Warning** option (the default is on) when you want CP Backup to warn you when the restore operation is about to over-write a file that exists on the hard disk. Refer to the section "Performing a Restore Operation" earlier in this chapter for a discussion about the Overwrite Warning dialog box.

Timing the Backup

The **Time Display** option, which is on by default, causes CP Backup to display elapsed time in the backup status bar during the backup process. The timer tick that controls this time display might cause problems in some networks or on certain PC compatibles. If you are experiencing problems during backup, try toggling off this option.

Setting Selection Options

The second group of options on the CP Backup Options menu determines which files are backed up. This group consists of the options that appear on the Selection options submenu, which you access by choosing **Selection** options on the **Options** menu. The options, explained in the following sections, include Manual Subdirectory Inclusion, Include/Exclude Files, Attribute Exclusions, and Date Range Selection options.

Including Subdirectories

Check the Manual **Su**bdirectory Inclusion option (the default) when, in addition to selecting or deselecting a directory, you want to select or deselect all subdirectories within that directory. With this option turned on, for example, CP Backup deselects all directories and files on the hard disk drive C when you deselect the drive C root directory (C:\). With this option turned off, the same action deselects only the files stored at the root level of the hard disk. All previously selected subdirectories and files remain selected.

Selections made before you change the Manual Subdirectory Inclusion option are not affected by this option. For example, you can select the root directory C:\ while this option is on, and CP Backup selects all files on the hard disk. If you then turn off the Manual Subdirectory Inclusion option, all files remain selected. You then can deselect the root directory, and CP Backup deselects only the files stored at the root level. All other files on the hard disk remain selected.

Including Files

Select the Include/Exclude Files option to change the default *selection list*, a list of selection criteria that determines which files are selected automatically for backup. CP Backup displays the Include/Exclude Files dialog box, shown in figure 7.31.

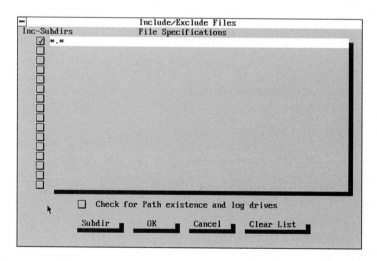

Fig. 7.31

The Include/ Exclude Files dialog box.

The initial selection list contains one selection criterion, *.*, which includes any file name and file name extension. When this criterion is listed, all files on the hard disk or directory (specified by the Backup From setting) are selected. You can type as many as 16 criteria in this list, each one on a separate line, and use both DOS wild cards (* and ?). To exclude certain files, precede a criterion with a minus sign (-).

To select all 1-2-3 spreadsheet files, for example, type the criteria
*.WK? in the Include/Exclude Files dialog box. (You can select Clear
List to erase all criteria from the list to start over.) Choose the **OK** command button, and CP Backup processes the criteria from top to bottom,
displaying the message `Reprocessing selection list. Please`
`wait`. The program then selects only files meeting the criteria (files
with file name extensions beginning with the letters *WK*, for example)
and returns to the Options menu.

Think of the selection list as a shortcut method of selecting or deselecting files. As soon as you choose **OK** at the Include/Exclude Files dialog
box, CP Backup processes the selection or deselection criteria in the
selection list, just as though you had manually selected or deselected
the file names in the Files window. You can still manually select or deselect additional directories or files if necessary. Keep in mind also that
changes to the Manual **S**ubdirectory Inclusion option affect only subsequent changes to the **I**nclude/Exclude Files selection list. That is,
changing the Manual **S**ubdirectory Inclusion setting does not automatically reprocess the selection list for subsequent CP Backup operations
unless you select Save as **D**efault from the **F**ile menu.

Excluding Files by Attribute

Select **A**ttribute Exclusions to exclude the files that have certain attribute bits set. (See Chapter 10, "Recovering Damaged or Deleted
Files," for more information about file attributes.) When you select this
option, CP Backup displays the following list of check boxes:

- *Exclude **H**idden Files* excludes files in which the hidden bit in the
  attribute byte is turned on. System files and copy-protection files
  often are hidden. Because these types of files normally must be
  placed on the hard disk by a special installation program rather
  than a restore operation, you usually have no need to include
  hidden files in the backup. The default setting for this box is unchecked.

- *Exclude **S**ystem Files* excludes files in which the system attribute
  bit is turned on. Because system files, such as IO.SYS or
  MSDOS.SYS (IBMBIO.COM and IBMDOS.COM on IBM systems),
  must be installed during formatting or with the use of SYS.COM,
  they usually do not need to be included in a backup. The default
  setting for this box is unchecked.

- *Exclude **R**ead-Only Files* excludes files in which the read-only
  attribute bit is turned on. The default setting for this box is unchecked.

After you make necessary selections in this list of check boxes, choose the **OK** command button. After displaying the message `Reprocessing selection list. Please wait`, CP Backup then returns to the Selection Options submenu. A check mark appears to the left of the Attribute Exclusions option whenever you check one or more attribute-exclusion check boxes. In contrast to the Manual Subdirectory Inclusion option, changing an Attribute Exclusions setting reprocesses the Include/Exclude Files selection list.

Including Files by Date

Use the Selection Options submenu choice of Date Range Selection in conjunction with the Include/Exclude Files option to limit the backed-up files to those created or last changed within a given range of dates. When you select **D**ate Range Selection, CP Backup displays the Date Range Selection dialog box in figure 7.32.

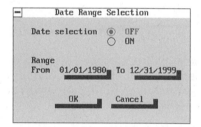

Fig. 7.32

The Date Range Selection dialog box.

To turn on this feature, select the On option and type beginning and end dates in the From and To text boxes, respectively. Then choose **OK**. CP Backup displays the message `Reprocessing selection list. Please wait` and then returns to the Selection Options submenu. A check mark appears to the left of the Date Range Selection option whenever the On option has been selected. This option is effective only when the Include/Exclude Files option also is on. Like the Attribute Exclusions option, Date Range Selection causes CP Backup to reprocess the Include/Exclude Files selection list.

Setting Display Options

Each option in the final group on the CP Backup Options menu—the options on the Display options submenu—determines how files are listed in the directory tree. When you choose **D**isplay Options from the **O**ptions menu, CP Backup displays the Display options submenu, which includes both the Sort **O**ptions and **L**ong Format options.

Choosing Sort Options

By default, CP Backup lists files in order by file name. If you want files listed in some other order, select Sort **O**ptions from the Display Options submenu. The program displays the Sort Options dialog box, which lists these choices:

- ■ *Unsorted* does not sort file names.

- ■ *By Name*, the default setting, sorts files by name.

- ■ *By Extension* sorts by file name extension only.

- ■ *By Date* sorts by file date.

- ■ *By Size* sorts by file name.

The Sort Options dialog box also displays a Sort Descending check box. Choose this check box if you want the file names sorted in reverse order (from Z to A rather than from A to Z).

Changing the Display Format

By default, the CP Backup directory tree displays file names, file extension, file size, date and time last modified, and file attributes. This display format is called *long format*. CP Backup gives you the option of displaying only file names so that more files can be listed at one time.

To turn off the long file name format, display the **O**ptions menu and choose **D**isplay options. CP Backup displays the Display options submenu. Select **L**ong Format to toggle off the long-format display. The program removes the check mark from the screen.

Saving the Setup

After you change any backup options, CP Backup enables you to save your changes as the new default configuration. Choose **F**ile and then select Save as **D**efault from the menu. CP Backup saves the current option settings in the file CPBACKUP.CFG, the default configuration file. Press Esc to return to the CP Backup or Express Backup window.

Creating a Setup File

As an alternative to changing the default configuration, you can create and use additional configuration files called *setup files*. A setup file contains the same setting categories as the default configuration file but can be customized and loaded selectively for special purposes.

To create a setup file from your current option settings, display the Files menu and select Save Setup As. CP Backup displays the Save Setup File dialog box. In the Setup File Name text box, CP Backup displays the file name None by default. You can type a name as long as eight characters.

Make the setup name descriptive. For example, you might use one setup to do daily incremental backups Monday through Thursday and another setup to do a full backup on Friday evening. First, set the Backup Method to Incremental and save that setup under the name DAILY. Then change the Backup Method to Full and save the setup again, but this time use the name WEEKLY. CP Backup saves both files to disk with the extension SET.

Select the Save File Selections check box in the Save Current Settings dialog box to save the list of files you have manually selected.

Using a Setup File

Each time you start CP Backup, it reads the file CPBACKUP.CFG to determine the default configuration and then immediately displays the CP Backup window. But you can use a named setup file rather than the default configuration file.

To load a named setup file at start-up, type the following command at the DOS prompt and then press Enter:

CPBACKUP *setup name*

Replace *setup name* with the file name of the setup file you want CP Backup to load. To load CP Backup and use the settings stored in the setup file WEEKLY.SET, for example, type

CPBACKUP WEEKLY.SET

and press Enter. CP Backup starts and uses the options and settings stored in WEEKLY.SET for the configuration settings.

Another option is to load a setup file after you start CP Backup. Display the File menu and select Load Setup. CP Backup displays the Load Setup File dialog box, which shows a list of available setup files. (If no setup files exist, CP Backup displays an appropriate warning.) Choose the setup file you want to load, and then choose OK to load the file.

Using Tape Tools

Central Point Backup offers new capabilities for tape drive users. With the Tape Tools option available on either the Express Backup or CP Backup window, you can select from these options:

- *Directory* enables you to display the backup sets contained on the tape cartridge you inserted.

- *Information* provides information about how much space is free on the tape cartridge, the tape name (if any), the date the tape was formatted, and what program formatted the tape.

- *Quick Erase* erases the tape catalog so that CP Backup will see the tape as unused. When the catalog on the tape has been erased, data on the tape cannot be recovered.

- *Secure Erase* completely removes all data from the tape cartridge by writing over all the data on the tape. Depending on the amount of data on the tape and the tape's capacity, this process can take from a few minutes to several hours.

- *Format* enables you to format the tape cartridge in QIC or Central Point's proprietary format, depending on your current setup. Format is not applicable to SCSI tape cartridges.

- *Retension* runs the tape fast-forward to the end and then rewinds it to reset the proper tension for the media. Proper tension is essential to maintaining your tape cartridges.

Using CP Backup Command Line Parameters

The standard way to start CP Backup is to type the following command at the DOS command line:

CPBACKUP *d*:

You can also use several special parameters, or switches, with the CP Backup command. Table 7.5 lists the command line switches available. The syntax is shown in the following:

CPBACKUP *[d:] [setname] [filespec...] [parameters...]*

Table 7.5 CP Backup Command Line Switches

Parameter	Meaning
/?	Display this command-line help
d:	Drive to back up
setname	Name of setup file without a file extension
filespec	Files to back up (* wild card accepted)
/R	Automatically start restore mode
/SAVE	Save history to hard disk
/NOSAVE	Don't save history to hard disk
/ECC	Use error correction
/NOECC	Don't use error correction
/SF	Use standard formatting
/NONSF	Use nonstandard formatting
/MTASK	Protect against files changing in multitasking modes
/VIDEO	Display command-line help for video/mouse parameters

File Selection Parameters	Meaning
/FULL	Full backup; mark as backed up
/INC	Incremental backup (append to full)
/SEP	Separate incremental backup
/COPY	Full backup; don't mark as backed up
/FULLERASE	Full backup; ERASE TAPE before backup
/DIF	Differential backup
/DATE=mmddyy-mmddyy	Specify dates of files to back up
/EXATTR=HSR	Exclude (H)idden, (S)ystem, (R)ead-only

Hardware Parameters	Meaning
/DRIVE=TAPE or /DRIVE=d:n	Specify drive and media (that is, B:1440)
/ADDR=base-i-d	Specify I/O addresses for tape drive where base=hex base address, i=IRQ, d=DMA channel

continues

Table 7.5 Continued

Hardware Parameters	Meaning
/RATE=*rate*	Set data rate (*rate*=1MB, 500KB or 250KB) (***Note:*** controller must support rate)
/NO	Don't use overlapped I/O
/DOB	Use Deluxe Option Board for format

Chapter Summary

This chapter describes how to start Central Point Backup (CP Backup), how to establish a default configuration, and how to indicate whether you want to back up the entire hard disk or just selected files or directories. In this chapter, you learned how to perform the backup operation, compare the backup files to the original files on the hard disk, restore an entire disk, and restore files selectively from backup media to your working disk. The last sections of the chapter explain how to change the program's configuration file and how to create and use setup files.

Turn to Chapter 8, "Speeding Up Your Hard Disk with Compress," to learn how to use Compress to speed up your hard disk.

Speeding Up Your Hard Disk with Compress

Applications today are data intensive, more so than they have been in the past. With data-intensive operations comes *file fragmentation*, which occurs when files you access most become spread out in chunks and pieces around your disk drive's physical sectors. When your files are fragmented, the overall speed and efficiency of your computer system decreases.

When all the sectors of a file are stored in one location on the disk and all the directories are at the beginning of the disk, your hard disk operates most efficiently. After you use a disk for a while, adding, changing, and deleting files, DOS cannot allocate a single, contiguous block of space to every file. When DOS places added and changed files in several places on your hard disk, retrieving the file takes more time because the file is not *contiguous* (that is, in one piece). PC Tools Compress can unfragment noncontiguous files on a disk and move all these files to the beginning of the disk.

T I P   Compress can use *upper memory*, the region of memory between 640K and 1M, which enables you to compress more files than previous versions were able to compress. See table 8.4 at the end of this chapter for command line options you can use to enable or disable upper memory options.

Having your files reside on your disks in a contiguous form improves your chances of recovering a file that was deleted when you were not running Delete Protection. (See Chapter 10, "Recovering Damaged or Deleted Files," for information about recovering deleted files.)

This chapter explains how to use Compress from inside PC Tools Desktop and from the DOS command line. You learn how to analyze a disk to determine whether you need to use Compress to rearrange the disk. You also learn how to customize Compress by choosing different compression techniques, selecting a particular order in which you want files arranged, or printing a report. Finally, this chapter explains how a typical compress operation is run.

> **WARNING:** Compress is not designed for use on network file servers, networked drives, mapped drives, or OS/2 volumes. In addition, Compress does not run under Windows, DesqView, or other multitasking systems. Attempting to use Compress in any of these environments may result in data loss.

FROM HERE...

For Related Information

▶▶ "Using Undelete To Recover Deleted Files," p. 383.

Checking for File Fragmentation with FileCheck

FileCheck can be run as a stand-alone program from the DOS command line. (File Check cannot be run through a menu from PC Tools Desktop.) Before running Compress, use FileCheck to check for fragmentation levels, lost clusters, cross-linked files, and FAT (File Allocation

Table) errors. You also can configure FileCheck to run from within a batch file (such as your AUTOEXEC.BAT file) to check for and report fragmentation levels, cross-linked files, lost clusters, and FAT mismatches.

FileCheck checks your current disk drive or a drive you specify for errors and reports to you the number of archive files found, the number of fragmented files found, the total fragments, and the percentage of total disk fragmentation.

To run FileCheck, type the following command line at the DOS prompt and press Enter:

FILECHK *d*: /ARC /BATCH /LIST /P /Q /?

In the preceding line, the command FILECHK activates the main file-checking program, and the parameters (the italicized options following the command) perform different functions, explained in the following list:

Option	Description
d:	Tells FileCheck which drive to analyze; if no drive is indicated, FileCheck uses the current drive
/ARC	Shows the total percentage of archive files instead of the amount of fragmentation
/BATCH	Displays information about running FileCheck from within a batch file instead of from the command line
/LIST	Displays a list of fragmented files for the specified or current drive and the total number of fragments found
/P	Pauses each full screen so you can review its report
/Q	Turns on Quiet mode and turns the screen display off, which is useful for batch file use
/?	Displays quick on-line help on how to use parameters with FileCheck

Using FileCheck from within batch files enables you to report on-screen or to a file the level of fragmentation on your system, the percentage of that fragmentation, or other problems you should be aware of. Refer to the PC Tools reference manual for examples of using FileCheck within batch files and for more information about FileCheck.

For Related Information

▶▶ "Checking for Problems with FileCheck," p. 419.

Starting Compress

To display the Compress main program window, select D**i**sk Optimization from the **T**ools menu in the PC Tools Desktop program or type **compress** on the DOS command line and press Enter. Compress loads and displays the Compress window and the Compress Recommendation dialog box (see fig. 8.1).

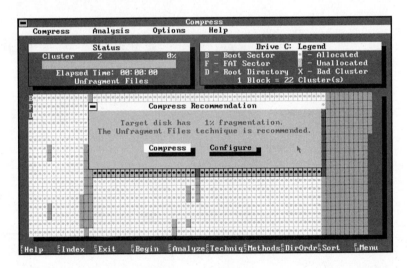

Fig. 8.1

The Compress main window and the Compress Recommendation dialog box.

The Compress Recommendation dialog box shows the percentage of fragmentation on a hard disk. In figure 8.1, for example, the hard disk is one percent fragmented. Select **C**ompress to begin the compress operation; choose the C**o**nfigure command button to display the **O**ptions menu; or press Esc or F3 (Exit) to remove the dialog box and display the Compress window.

The Compress window displays four options in the horizontal menu bar: Compress, Analysis, Options, and Help. This window also shows function-key commands in the message bar. These functions keys are listed in table 8.1.

Table 8.1 Keystroke Commands Available in Compress

Key	Name	Function
F1	Help	Displays Help facility
F2	Index	Displays Help facility index
F3	Exit	Cancels current process or exits from Compress (same as Esc)
F4	Begin	Begins compress operation
F5	Analyze	Analyzes disk directory organization
F6	Techniq	Displays Choose Compression technique dialog box
F7	Methods	Displays Choose Ordering Method dialog box
F8	DirOrdr	Selects Directory Ordering dialog box
F9	Sort	Displays Choose Sort Method dialog box
F10 or Alt	Menu	Activates horizontal menu bar
Esc	Cancel	Cancels current process or application (same as F3)
Ctrl+*d*	Switch	Switches current drive to *d*

The Status box appears in the upper left corner of the screen. This area of the screen displays information about the status of a compression operation. While the program is unfragmenting a disk, the Status box indicates the current cluster, the percentage complete, the time elapsed since you started compressing the disk, and the number of unfragmented files.

Compress displays the Legend box in the upper right corner of the screen. This box lists the cluster allocation and surface-analysis codes, explained in table 8.2. The title line of this box indicates the current drive (drive C in figure 8.1). The *current drive* is the drive that was current when you started Compress.

To switch active drives, select **C**ompress to display the Compress menu and then select the **C**hoose Drive command. When the Drive Selection dialog box appears, choose the drive icon that represents the disk you want to compress. Click the selected drive or press the letter of the target drive. Choose the **OK** command button to select the drive and return to the Compress window.

You can activate a particular disk immediately by adding the disk drive designator to the start-up command. To start Compress and activate drive A, for example, type **compress a:** and press Enter.

The central portion of the Compress window, the *drive map*, depicts the cluster allocation of your disk. Compress uses codes listed in the Legend box to show whether a cluster contains the boot sector, the FAT, or the root directory; whether a cluster is allocated to a file or is unallocated; and whether a cluster is marked bad. Table 8.2 describes these codes and other codes used with the **S**urface Analysis command, which you access from a pull-down menu.

Table 8.2 Cluster-Allocation and Surface-Analysis Codes

Code	Meaning
B	Boot sector
F	FAT sector
D	Root directory
X	Bad cluster
•	Allocated to a file
(Shaded)	Unallocated cluster
*	Unreadable cluster

With shortcut commands and menu options from the Compress window or with parameters added to the start-up command at the DOS command line, you can perform the following functions:

■ Analyze a file or disk for file fragmentation to determine whether running Compress will improve disk access speed.

■ Analyze the surface of a disk for bad or marginal sectors.

■ Rearrange the files on a hard disk so that every file is placed contiguously on the disk.

■ Move directories to the beginning of the hard disk for faster access.

■ Sort your disk's directories in a particular order.

NOTE   Despite its name, Compress does not reduce the amount of space that files occupy on your disk. Another PC Tools program, PC Secure, provides that service. (See Chapter 13, "Securing Your Data with PC Secure and Wipe," for more information.)

CAUTION: Compress clears the delete tracking file (PCTRACKR.FIL) created by the Data Monitor utility and renders deleted files that existed on the disk prior to running Compress completely inaccessible.

To undelete a file you accidentally erased, do so before running Compress.

T I P

 NOTE The compress operation does not affect any file that has a hidden or system bit set in the attribute byte. Copy-protected software that depends on a hidden file should continue to operate normally after a compress operation.

Analyzing Your Disk

You do not need to compress files every day, particularly because the procedure is relatively time-consuming. Use Compress only when the files on your disk are sufficiently fragmented to slow disk performance.

The Compress program provides several commands for analyzing and evaluating fragmentation on your disk. One of the commands helps you locate and mark marginal sectors on your disks so that DOS no longer uses them.

Analyzing Disk Allocation

To perform a quick disk-allocation analysis, press F5 (Analyze) or select **A**nalysis and then **D**isk Statistics to display the Disk Statistics dialog box (see fig. 8.2).

Compress reads your disk's two file allocation table (FAT) copies to determine whether they match. If the copies match, Compress displays the message `File Allocation Tables match`. The program also lists the following disk statistics:

■ *Allocated clusters*. The disk space currently allocated to files.

■ *Unallocated clusters.* The number of clusters not allocated to any files.

■ *Total bad clusters.* The total number of clusters already marked and recognized by DOS as unreadable.

■ *Total file chains.* The total number of files and directories.

■ *Fragmented file chains.* The number of file chains with noncontiguous fragments on the disk.

■ *Percent file-fragmentation factor.* The number of fragmented files as a percentage of all files on the disk.

■ *Non-contiguous free-space areas.* The number of separate portions of the disk not allocated and not located as a single block at the end of the disk.

■ *Cross-linked file chains.* The number of file chains that appear to have been allocated the same space as another file on the disk.

■ *Unattached file clusters.* The number of clusters marked in the FAT as being used but not allocated to any particular file chain.

■ *Bad clusters within file chains.* The number of unreadable clusters contained within file chains.

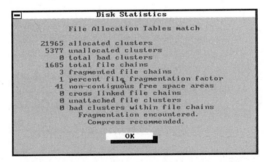

Fig. 8.2

The Disk Statistics dialog box.

T I P   If any of the last three statistics—cross-linked file chains, unattached file clusters, or bad clusters within file chains—has a value listed greater than 0, Compress displays a warning instructing you to use DiskFix to correct the error before continuing with Compress. See Chapter 11, "Recovering Damaged or Formatted Disks," for more information about using DiskFix.

When your disk contains fragmented files, Compress displays the following message under the statistics in the dialog box:

```
Fragmentation Encountered
  Compress Recommended
```

If Compress does not find fragmented files, it displays the following message:

```
    Fragmentation NOT Encountered
Evaluate with File Fragmentation Analysis option
```

Use these recommendations and the listed statistics to determine when to compress files. In figure 8.2, for example, drive C has 3 fragmented file chains from a total of 1,685 total file chains. The program recommends running the compress operation.

When you finish reviewing the Disk Statistics dialog box, select the **OK** command button to return to the Compress window. Even when this command does not recommend compression, the **File Fragmentation Analysis** command, discussed in the following section, may still recommend the operation.

Analyzing a File

Although undesirable, file fragmentation can be tolerable if you seldom use the fragmented files. With the **File Fragmentation Analysis** command, you can determine which files are fragmented. Select **Analysis** and then **File Fragmentation Analysis** to reach the File Fragmentation Analysis dialog box (see fig. 8.3).

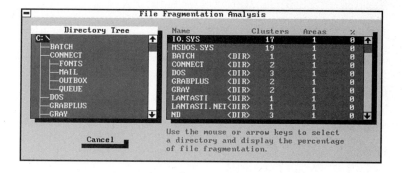

Fig. 8.3

The File Fragmentation Analysis dialog box.

The File Fragmentation Analysis dialog box contains two list boxes: the Directory Tree and the File List. The Directory Tree list box lists the directory structure of the disk you plan to compress. The File List box groups in columns the following information:

- *Name.* The name of a file, directory (denoted by <DIR>), or volume (denoted by <VOL>).

- *Clusters.* The number of clusters occupied by the file or directory file.

- *Areas.* The number of fragments into which the file chain is divided. Any number greater than 1 indicates that the file is fragmented.

- *%.* The percentage of the file contents not located in the first cluster in the file.

To move through the directory tree or the file list, use the scroll bar or the cursor-movement keys listed in table 8.3. Note which files and directory files are fragmented. Press Esc or F3 (Exit) to return to the Compress window. You also can exit by pointing to and clicking the close box in the upper left corner of the dialog box.

Table 8.3 File Allocation Analysis Cursor-Movement Keys

Key	Move cursor
↓	Down one line
↑	Up one line
Home	To the top of the directory
End	To the bottom of the directory
PgDn	Down one screen
PgUp	Up one screen

When the only fragmented files are ones you rarely use, you may decide to postpone running Compress. If files you frequently use are fragmented, however, compress the disk to improve disk performance. (You cannot unfragment a single file or a single directory with Compress.)

NOTE You can use the PC Tools Desktop File Map command to see the relative location on the disk of each segment. See the discussion of File Map in Chapter 9, "Obtaining System Information."

Showing Files in a Map Block

On a hard disk drive, each block shown on the Compress window's drive map represents more than one cluster on the disk. The number of clusters represented by a block appears in the Legend box. In figure 8.1, for example, every block in the drive map represents 22 clusters. The larger the hard disk, the more clusters represented by one block. Compress provides a way to see which files and clusters are included in a particular block and to determine whether these files or clusters are fragmented.

From the Compress window, select **A**nalysis from the horizontal menu bar and then choose the **S**how Files in Each Map Block option. The cursor blinks in the upper left corner of the drive map. Use your cursor-movement keys to move the cursor over the block you want to examine and press Enter. As Compress analyzes the block, the following message appears:

```
Processing Map Block Entries to
determine fragmentation
```

Compress then displays the Files in This Map Block dialog box (see fig. 8.4), which lists the cluster number, the file name, and the fragmentation status (Fragmented, Optimized, or Not in Use).

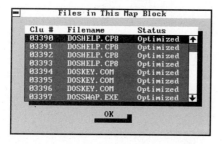

Fig. 8.4

The Files in This Map Block dialog box.

For Related Information

▸▸ "Mapping a File," p. 360.

▸▸ "Using DiskFix," p. 422.

FROM HERE...

Using Compress Options

With Compress, you can choose from six compression techniques and four ordering options. After you make your selections, Compress enables you to perform an additional analysis of the disk's current directory organization to determine whether you should continue with the compress operation.

Selecting the Compression Technique

To select a compression technique, press F6 (Techniq) or select **O**ptions to display the Options menu and choose **C**ompression Technique (see fig. 8.5). Compress displays the Choose Compression Technique dialog box (see fig. 8.6).

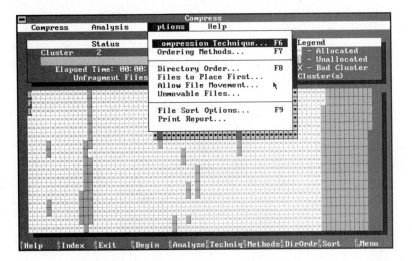

Fig. 8.5

The Options menu.

The Choose Compression Technique dialog box contains the following option buttons:

- *Optimize **D**irectories* moves directory files to the beginning of the disk for faster access but does not unfragment files. Use this option after you add or remove directories.

- *Optimize Free Space* moves all currently allocated clusters to the beginning of the disk, which has the effect of moving all free space to the end of the disk. Use this option immediately before you copy large files to the hard disk to ensure that the files are not fragmented.

```
┌─────────────────────────────────────────────────────────┐
│ ■        Choose Compression Technique                     │
├─────────────────────────────────────────────────────────┤
│  ○   Optimize Directories    Choose this when you add/delete
│                              subdirectories.
│
│  ○   Optimize Free Space     Choose this if you need to copy
│                              large files to your disk.
│
│  ◉   Unfragment Files        Choose this frequently for a
│                              quick optimization.
│
│  ○   Full Optimization       Choose this monthly to completely
│                              optimize your disk.
│
│  ○   Full Opt. w/Clear       Same as above but will clear
│                              unused space for security.
│
│  ○   File Sort               Sorting only, no compression.
│
│           ▄ OK ▄          ▄ Cancel ▄
└─────────────────────────────────────────────────────────┘
```

Fig. 8.6

The Choose Compression Technique dialog box.

■ *Unfragment Only*, the default option, rearranges files so that no file is fragmented; however, this option does not move all files to the beginning of the hard disk. As a result, unallocated sectors are still spread around the disk. Because DOS might have trouble finding a single block of unallocated clusters large enough for every new file you create, your disk soon may be badly fragmented again. This technique must be used frequently to be effective.

■ *Full Optimization* unfragments all files and moves them to the beginning of the disk. When the operation is complete, all free space (unallocated clusters) is in one block at the end of the disk. As you create new files, DOS adds them as single blocks in the free space. This technique takes longer than the other techniques but has a more lasting effect on optimizing disk performance.

■ *The Full Opt. w/Clear* technique is like the Full Compression technique, but this option also erases all data in unallocated sectors and clears any old directories (directories deleted from the drive or directory but still physically present on the disk).

> **NOTE** The Full Opt. w/Clear technique does not erase deleted files protected by the Delete Sentry. Refer to Chapter 10, "Recovering Damaged or Deleted Files" for more about the Delete Sentry.

■ *File Sort* sorts the files on the disk in the order specified in the Choose Sort Method dialog box (discussed in the "Sorting Directories" section later in this chapter) but does not unfragment or move files to the beginning of the disk.

To run the compress operation directly from the DOS command line or from within a batch file, use the following parameters with the command for starting Compress to select a compression technique:

Parameter	Compression technique
d:	Drive to be compressed
/CD	Optimize **D**irectories
/CS	Op**t**imize Free Space
/CU	**U**nfragment Only
/CF	**F**ull Optimization
/CC	Full Opt. w/**Cl**ear

To compress drive C in Full Optimization with Clear, for example, type the following command at the DOS prompt and then press Enter:

COMPRESS C: /CC

T I P When you exit Compress for the first time, it prompts you to save the configuration. Select the **S**ave option before exiting to speed up Compress the next time you run it.

Choosing an Ordering Method Option

The order of directories and files on your disk can affect how quickly your disk accesses them. In addition to using Compress to unfragment files and consolidate free space, you can use Compress to reorder the directories and files on your disk.

Press F7 (Methods) or select **O**ptions and then **O**rdering Methods. Compress displays the Choose Ordering Method dialog box (see fig. 8.7).

Compress lists the following four option buttons in this dialog box:

■ *Standard*, the default option, places all directory files at the beginning of the hard disk followed by files in any order. This option usually yields the fastest compress operation. Using the F8 (DirOrdr) command, you can specify the order in which directories are placed on the disk (discussed later in this section).

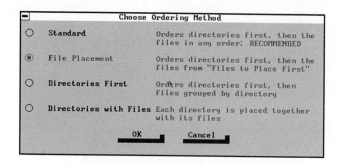

Fig. 8.7

The Choose
Ordering Method
dialog box.

■ *File Placement* places directories first, followed by the files specified in the Files to Place First dialog box (discussed later in this
section). By default, this option places all executable program
files at the front of the disk.

■ *Directories First* places all directory files at the beginning of the
disk and then groups all files by directory. This order results in
the fastest disk-access speed because it groups files likely to be
used together.

■ *Directories with Files* places every directory file immediately before the files it contains. Use this option if you routinely create
and delete directories of files rather than individual files.

After you select an ordering option, Compress returns to the Compress
window.

To run the compress operation directly from the DOS command line or
from within a batch file, add the following parameters to the start-up
command to select ordering options:

Parameter	Ordering option
/OS	Standard
/OF	File Placement
/OO	Directories First
/OD	Directories with Files

To optimize drive C by using directories-with-files ordering, for example, type the following command at the DOS prompt and then press
Enter:

COMPRESS C: /OD

Specifying Directory Order

Regardless of which ordering method you choose, you can specify the order in which Compress arranges directory files. From the Compress window, press F8 (DirOrdr) or select **O**ptions and then **D**irectory Order. Compress displays the Directory Ordering dialog box (see fig. 8.8).

The Directory Tree list box lists the directory structure for the current disk drive. The Path list box lists the directories that Compress will place first in the optimized directory. To add a directory to the Path list box, highlight the directory's name in the Directory Tree list and press Enter or select the **A**dd command button.

To delete a directory from the Path list box, press Tab to move to the Path list, highlight the directory name you want to remove from the list, and select the **D**elete command button. To move a directory name in the Path list box, tab to the Path list, highlight the name, select **M**ove, use the arrow keys to position the directory name in the desired position in the list, and select **O**K. When you are satisfied with the directory order, choose **O**K.

The Directory Ordering dialog box shown in figure 8.8, for example, shows how Compress organizes the directory files on drive C during the optimization process, placing them in the order shown.

Placing Files First

If you chose the File Placement option as the ordering method, you may want to specify the categories of files that should be placed first on the disk.

From the Compress window's horizontal menu bar, select **O**ptions to display the Options menu and choose **F**iles to Place First. Compress displays the Files to Place First dialog box (see fig. 8.9).

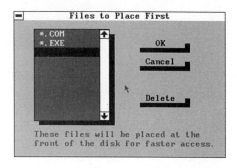

Fig. 8.9

The Files to Place
First dialog box.

By default, Compress lists the following file specifications in the Files to Place First list box:

> *.COM

> *.EXE

These file specifications represent executable files. To delete a file specification, highlight the specification and choose the **D**elete command button. To add a different specification, such as *.BAT, move the highlight to a blank line in the list box and type the new specification. Choose **O**K when you are satisfied with the new list. During the optimization process, Compress places the files you specified at the front of the disk.

Specifying Unmovable Files

Some files on your computer are hidden from the DOS directory (DIR) command. The two system files IBMBIO.COM and IBMDOS.COM (for IBM DOS users) or IO.SYS and MSDOS.SYS (for MS-DOS users), for example, are required to boot your computer but are not listed by the DIR command (they are listed by PC Tools) and are ignored by other DOS commands such as COPY and DEL. However, some applications software will not start unless their own hidden files placed on the disk during installation can be located.

When you optimize your disk using Compress, the program is careful not to move any hidden files. Compress will not make any changes that can cause your copy-protected software to operate incorrectly after compression.

If you find you need to make some of your hidden files *unmovable*, display the **O**ptions menu and select **U**nmovable Files. Compress displays the Unmovable Files dialog box (see fig. 8.10). The dialog box contains a list box that indicates the files Compress will not move (in addition to the hidden files).

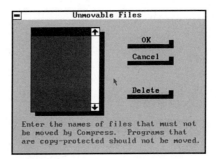

Fig. 8.10

The Unmovable
Files dialog box.

For every file you want to add to the list box, type in the list box the
name of the file Compress should not move, and then press Enter.
Choose the **OK** command button to accept the list of unmovable files
and return to the Compress window.

Sorting Directories

Compress enables you to sort directories by date and time, file name,
file extension, or file size. This option is an alternative to the PC Tools
Desktop **D**irectory Sort command. (See Chapter 6, "Working on Disks,"
for more information.)

To sort the files in every directory in a particular order, press F9 (Sort)
or select File **S**ort Options from the **O**ptions menu. Compress displays
the Choose Sort Method dialog box (see fig. 8.11).

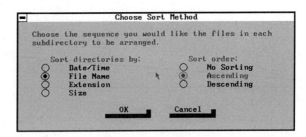

Fig. 8.11

The Choose Sort
Method dialog
box.

The Choose Sort Method dialog box contains two groups of option
buttons. The first group, Sort Directories By, contains these choices:

■ *Date/Time* sorts files in order by date and time.

■ *File Name* sorts files in order by file name.

■ *Extension* sorts files in order by file name extension.

■ *Size* sorts files in order by file size.

By default, none of these sort options is selected. If you want Compress to sort directories and files in a particular order as it optimizes the disk, choose a characteristic from the preceding group.

The second group of option buttons, Sort Order, includes these options:

- *No Sorting*, the default, does not sort files at all.

- *Ascending* sorts files in ascending order (from A to Z or from 0 to 9).

- *Descending* sorts files in descending order (from Z to A or from 9 to 0).

After you select one of the sort options in the first group of option buttons, Compress automatically selects **A**scending in the second group. Select **D**escending to reverse the order. Choose the **N**o Sorting option (the default) if you do not want files sorted in any particular order.

Compress sorts the files in the new order the next time you run a compress operation.

To run the compress operation directly from the DOS command line or from within a batch file, use the following parameters to select sorting options:

Parameter	Sorting options
/SF	Sort by file name
/ST	Sort by file date and time
/SE	Sort by file extension
/SS	Sort by file size
/SA	Ascending sort
/SD	Descending sort

To unfragment drive C and sort files by name, for example, type the following command at the DOS prompt and press Enter:

    COMPRESS C: /SF

Printing a Report

Having a record of your compress operations can come in handy at times. You can print a report listing the time required to run the compress operation and the options selected, as well as the number of allocated, unallocated, and bad clusters on the disk when you ran Compress.

To print a report at the conclusion of the compress operation, display the **O**ptions menu and select **P**rint Report. Compress displays three command buttons: Printer, Disk, and Cancel. Select **P**rinter to send the report to the first printer port (LPT1). Choose **D**isk to send the report to the file COMPRESS.RPT. Select **C**ancel to prevent Compress from generating a report to a printer or file.

T   I   P
To print or save a report to disk, make sure that you select the **P**rint Report option before you run the compress operation.

FROM HERE...

For Related Information

◀◀ "Sorting a Directory," p. 254.

▶▶ "Using Undelete To Recover Deleted Files," p. 383.

▶▶ "Purging Delete Sentry Files," p. 401.

Running Compress

After you choose a compression technique and order, you are ready to start Compress. Press F4 (Begin) or display the **C**ompress menu and select **B**egin Compress. Compress displays a warning that all memory-resident programs, except PC Tools programs, should be unloaded from memory. This warning states also that any disk activity must be suspended while the compress operation is continuing. Finally, this warning recommends that you back up the disk before running Compress.

T   I   P
Turn off any fax board installed in your computer so that it receives no calls during the compress operation.

After you heed all the warnings, select **OK** to continue with the compress operation. Compress displays the following message:

```
SORTING DIRECTORIES and PREPARING for DISK OPTIMIZATION
```

Compress then displays the Disk Compression window and begins rearranging files.

Compress shows the progress of the operation in several ways. When the program reads a cluster in a directory or file, the screen displays the letter *R* at the position of the cluster. When the program writes the clusters to their new location, the letter *W* is displayed at the position of each cluster. Compress lists the elapsed time, percentage complete, and the number of the cluster being moved.

When the compress operation is completed, Compress prints a report, if you requested one, and displays a message indicating that you can run Mirror. Select the **Mirror** command button to save a copy of the newly revised FAT, root directory, and boot sector to the file MIRROR.FIL. Taking this action ensures that Unformat can recover from an accidental formatting of the disk. (See Chapter 11, "Recovering Damaged or Formatted Disks.")

Press Esc or F3 (Exit) or select **Exit** Compress. You also can click the close box in the upper left corner of the screen. Compress displays a warning message urging you to reboot your computer before taking any other action. Compress then returns to the DOS command line or the PC Tools Desktop, depending on how you invoked the program. Reboot your computer immediately by choosing the **Reboot** command button or by pressing Ctrl+Alt+Del.

After you reboot your computer, you can return to the Compress window to see the newly compressed disk organization. Figure 8.12, for example, shows the result of running the compress operation on hard disk C. Compare this screen with the screen in figure 8.1. You will notice that all files are contiguous because all clusters have been rearranged by Compress.

Command Line Options

Compress provides command line parameters for Compression options, Ordering Methods options, and Sort options, which were described earlier. Compress provides two additional sets of command line options, detailed in table 8.4.

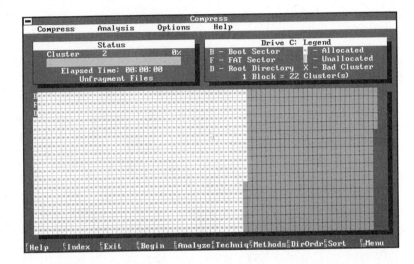

Fig. 8.12

The newly compressed hard disk C map.

Table 8.4 Additional Command Line Options

Option	Description
/SKIPUMB	Disables the use of the 384K upper memory between 640K and 1M
/SKIPEMS	Disables the use of expanded memory
/SKIPALL	Disables all upper memory blocks (both the 384K region above 640K, expanded, and extended memory)
/NM	Suppresses MIRROR following a Compress operation
/?	Displays command-line help for Compress options

Chapter Summary

This chapter explains how to use the PC Tools program Compress. You learned first how to analyze the disk to determine whether you need to use Compress to rearrange files on the disk. Then you learned how to customize Compress, choosing different compression techniques, sorting orders, or report possibilities.

Turn to Chapter 9, "Obtaining System Information," to learn how to obtain helpful technical information about your computer system.

Obtaining System Information

This chapter, which concludes Part II, "Using the System Utilities," covers several commands that provide information about the system as well as about the System Information (SI) and the Memory Information (MI) programs. This chapter teaches you how to obtain information about your system, covering the following components and peripherals in your computer:

System Type	Operating System	Video Adapter
I/O Ports	Keyboard	Mouse
CMOS Information	Device Drivers	Software Interrupts
Hardware Interrupts	Disk Drive Summary	Disk Details
Network Performance	Memory Statistics	Extended Memory
Expanded Memory	CPU Speed	Disk Speed
Overall Speed		

Knowing the configuration of your hardware and software is important if you want to successfully install and use peripherals such as printers, modems, scanners, and so on. Understanding how your system is configured is also important when you install software such as memory managers, keyboard drivers, and communications software.

Without detailed information to help you diagnose and correct problems related to hardware and software use, you will not be able to properly use the hardware or software you installed. PC Tools' System Information program (and its accompanying Memory Information program) provides you with the information you need to diagnose and correct any installation and configuration problems you may encounter.

Displaying General System Information

System Information (SI) is accessible from inside PC Tools Desktop by selecting the **Tools** menu and then selecting System Information. You also can run System Information as a stand-alone program from the DOS prompt by typing **si** and pressing Enter.

Whether you run SI from the DOS command line (DOS prompt) or from inside PC Tools Desktop, SI performs a quick examination of your system for the information it needs to display in the initial System Information window (see fig. 9.1).

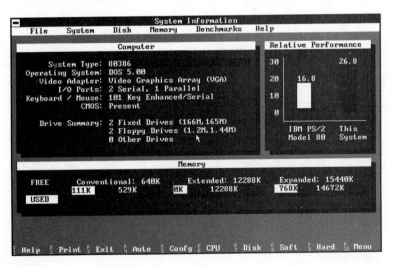

Fig. 9.1

The System Information (SI) window.

As in all other PC Tools programs, the top line in the System Information window is a horizontal menu bar. The bottom line of the window contains the list of available function key commands, listed in table 9.1.

Table 9.1 The SI Function Key Commands

Key	Name	Function
F1	Help	Displays the context-sensitive Help facility
F2	Print	Prints an SI report
F3	Exit	Cancels the current process
F4	Auto	Displays AUTOEXEC.BAT
F5	Confg	Displays CONFIG.SYS
F6	CPU	Runs benchmark tests on your system's CPU
F7	Disk	Runs benchmark tests on your hard disk
F8	Soft	Lists software interrupts
F9	Hard	Lists hardware interrupts
F10 or Alt	Menu	Activates the horizontal menu bar
Alt+space bar	Control	Displays the system control menu

The SI window initially displays three panels of summary information about your computer. The first panel, titled Computer, lists the following information:

- *System Type* indicates the main CPU chip (8088, 80286, 80386, or 80486). The example figure shows 80386.

- *Operating System* lists the current operating-system software and version number. Figure 9.1, for example, indicates that the computer's operating system is DOS 5.0.

- *Video Adapter* denotes the type of video adapter installed in the system (CGA, EGA, VGA, or Mono). The screen in figure 9.1 indicates that the computer contains a Video Graphics Array (VGA) video adapter.

- *I/O Ports* indicates the number of serial and parallel ports.

■ *Keyboard / Mouse* lists whether your system has an enhanced or standard keyboard and whether your mouse is serial, bus, PS/2, Inport, or Hewlett-Packard.

■ *Network* indicates that you are connected to a Novell network. This line is not displayed if you have not logged in to the network.

■ *CMOS* indicates whether your computer has a CMOS (Complementary Metal-Oxide Semiconductor).

■ *Drive Summary* lists the number and size of fixed disk drives, floppy disk drives, and other types of drives (such as network drives).

Every row in the Computer panel is also, in effect, a command button. To select a row, click the row or press the highlighted letter. Every command duplicates the effect of an option on one of the pull-down menus and is covered later in the chapter.

The second panel in the System Information window is titled Relative Performance. This panel reflects, as a bar graph, the speed of your computer system's CPU compared to that of a named computer of a different brand. The numbers shown are indexed based on the speed of a standard IBM PC XT (4.77 MHz). The example in figure 9.1 indicates that the clock speed of the current computer is 26.8 times faster than an IBM PC XT. The Relative Performance panel does not contain any command buttons or other elements that you can select.

The Memory panel, the third panel in the System Information window, shows both graphically and numerically the amount of conventional, extended, and expanded memory free and in use in your computer. Every item in this panel is a command button (Conventional, Extended, and Expanded).

The sections that follow describe how to display more detailed information about every item listed in the main System Information window.

System Type

The System Type line in the SI dialog box lists the main CPU chip; however, the program can display more detailed information about the system type. Select System Type in the Computer panel or select System from the horizontal menu bar and choose System Type. SI displays the General Information window (see fig. 9.2).

The General Information window lists the following information:

■ *CPU Type* displays the type of CPU (8088, 80286, 80386, or 80486).

■ *Co-Processor* indicates whether a math coprocessor is installed on your computer's motherboard.

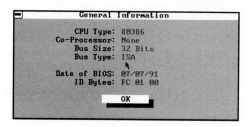

Fig. 9.2

The General
Information
window.

■ *Bus Size* indicates the number of bits of data that are transferred together between the CPU chip and the computer's memory. This number can be 8, 16, or 32.

■ *Bus Type* indicates whether the computer's data bus uses the industry standard architecture (ISA), extended ISA (EISA), or Micro-Channel Architecture (MCA).

■ *Date of BIOS* displays the date electronically "stamped" on your system's basic input-output system (BIOS) chip. This date indicates the last time the BIOS firmware was updated, which helps you determine whether to replace the BIOS chips.

■ *ID Bytes* displays a hexadecimal number that uniquely identifies the brand of computer.

To return to the System Information window, press Esc or Enter.

Operating System

The Operating System line in the System Information window lists your computer's operating system. To display more detailed information about the operating system, select **O**perating System in the Computer panel or select **S**ystem from the horizontal menu bar and choose **O**perating System. SI displays the Operating System Information dialog box (see fig. 9.3).

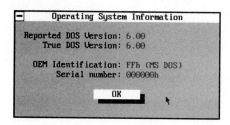

Fig. 9.3

The Operating
System Informa-
tion dialog box.

This dialog box lists the following information:

- *Reported DOS Version* indicates what version of the operating system is being reported to the SI program.

- *True DOS Version* reports the actual version of the operating system that SI has determined is running on your computer. This number might differ from the version indicated in the Reported DOS Version line.

- *OEM Identification* reports the manufacturer of the operating system. For most manufacturers, SI lists MS-DOS.

- *Serial Number* indicates the serial number, if any, of the operating-system software. Most PC operating-system software does not have a serial number.

Click the close box, select the **OK** command button, press F3 (Exit), or press Esc to return to the main System Information window. You can also use any of the function key commands listed at the bottom of the screen.

Video Adapter

The Video Adapter line in the System Information window lists the type of video controller in your computer. To display more detailed information about the video adapter, select **V**ideo Adapter in the Computer panel or select **S**ystem from the horizontal menu bar and choose **V**ideo Adapter. SI displays the Video Information dialog box, shown in figure 9.4.

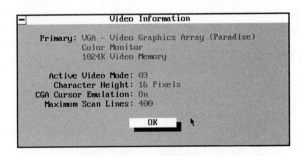

This dialog box lists the following information:

- *Primary* reports the type of video board, including whether the board is connected to a color or monochrome monitor. This line lists the amount of video memory installed on the video board.

- *Active Video Mode* indicates the video mode in use by the adapter. The modes available depend on the type of adapter. For example, SI normally sets a VGA adapter to video mode 03.

■ *Character Height* lists the height of every character in pixels. Most PC screens use 16-pixel-high characters.

■ *Maximum Scan Lines* indicates the height of the display in scan lines. This number depends on the type of video board as well as the current screen mode. On a VGA board, for example, SI (and other PC Tools programs) normally use video mode 3, which uses 400 lines. Using 16-pixel-high characters, 25 lines of text can be displayed on-screen at one time.

Click the close box, select the **OK** command button, or press F3 (Exit) or Esc to return to the main System Information window. You can also use any of the function key commands listed at the bottom of the screen.

I/O Ports

The I/O Ports line in the System Information window lists the number of serial and parallel ports installed in your computer. To display more detailed information about the input and output ports installed in your system, select I/O Ports in the Computer panel or choose **S**ystem from the horizontal menu bar and then choose I/O **P**orts. SI displays the I/O Port Information window (see fig. 9.5). This dialog box lists information in three columns: Label, I/O Base Address, and UART.

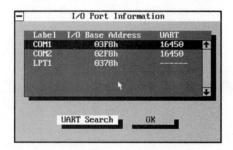

Fig. 9.5

The I/O Port Information window.

When you first display the I/O Port Information window, only the first two columns contain information. The Label column indicates whether a port is a serial (COM1, COM2, and so on) or parallel (LPT1, LPT2, and so on) port. The I/O Base Address column indicates the memory address to which program control is passed when a program calls the interrupt for the specified port. For a list of the current hardware interrupts, see the Hardware Interrupt Information dialog box in the section "Hardware Interrupts" later in this chapter.

Every serial port includes, in its circuitry, a special chip known as a *UART* (Universal Asynchronous Receiver/Transmitter). Occasionally, you may need to know which type of UART chip your computer has. Display the I/O Port Information window and select the **U**ART Search command button. SI searches the hardware and lists UART chips in the UART column.

NOTE   You may have to reboot your computer after using the **U**ART Search feature in order to use your computer's mouse.

Click the close box, select the **O**K command button, or press F3 (Exit) or Esc to return to the main System Information window. You can also use any of the function key commands listed at the bottom of the screen.

Keyboard/Mouse

The Keyboard/Mouse line in the System Information window indicates whether your computer has a standard or enhanced keyboard and whether the mouse interface type is serial, bus, PS/2, Inport, or Hewlett-Packard.

To display more detailed information about the keyboard and mouse, select **K**eyboard/Mouse in the Computer panel, or select **S**ystem from the horizontal menu bar and choose **K**eyboard/Mouse. SI displays the Keyboard/Mouse Information window (see fig. 9.6).

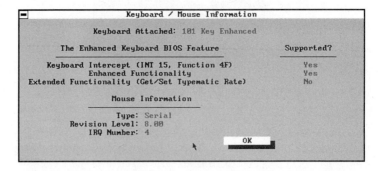

Fig. 9.6

The Keyboard/Mouse Information window.

The Keyboard/Mouse Information window lists the following information:

- *Keyboard Attached* indicates the number of keys on the keyboard and the keyboard type: standard or enhanced.

- *Enhanced Keyboard BIOS Feature* lists the enhanced keyboard features supported by your computer: keyboard intercept, enhanced functionality, and extended functionality.

■ *Mouse Information* displays the mouse type: serial, bus, PS/2, Inport, or Hewlett-Packard. The window also lists the version number of the mouse driver loaded into memory (usually the mouse driver is loaded through CONFIG.SYS or AUTOEXEC.BAT), using the revision numbering scheme employed by Microsoft.

In addition, the dialog box lists the IRQ (interrupt request line) used by the mouse. Use this information to diagnose problems you may have with your computer's mouse. See the Hardware Interrupt Information dialog box in the later section "Hardware Interrupts" to determine to which port the mouse is attached.

Click the close box, select the **OK** command button, press F3 (Exit), or press Esc to return to the main System Information window. You can also use any of the function key commands listed at the bottom of the screen.

CMOS Information

The CMOS line in the System Information window indicates whether a CMOS (Complementary Metal-Oxide Semiconductor) is present in your computer. IBM PC-AT and PS/2 computers and compatibles store certain configuration information in a battery-powered CMOS device. If your computer contains a CMOS device, you can display a list of the information contained in the device by selecting **C**MOS in the Computer panel. Alternatively, select **S**ystem from the horizontal menu bar and choose **C**MOS Information. SI displays the CMOS Information window (see fig. 9.7).

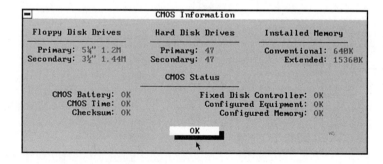

The CMOS Information window.

The CMOS Information window provides the following information:

■ *Floppy Disk Drives* lists the primary and secondary floppy disk drives, including disk size and storage capacity.

■ *Hard Disk Drives* lists the primary and secondary hard disk drives, including disk type.

- *Installed Memory* lists the amounts of installed conventional memory (less than 640K) and extended memory (more than 1024K).

- *CMOS Status* indicates whether the CMOS battery is charged sufficiently to maintain the information stored there. The dialog box also indicates whether the information stored in the CMOS regarding time, checksum, fixed disk controller, equipment configuration, and memory configuration seems to be accurate.

Click the close box, select the **OK** command button, press F3 (Exit), or press Esc to return to the main System Information window. You can also use any of the function key commands listed at the bottom of the screen.

T I P   Occasionally, the battery that maintains the information in the CMOS no longer maintains a charge. As a result, your computer might display an error message when you turn it on. The computer message may state that the amount of memory installed does not match the CMOS configuration or that the hard disk is not recognized. To restore the CMOS after a battery failure, you can run the Setup program that comes with your computer (and which is sometimes stored in ROM) or use the PC Tools Emergency disk, which was created when you installed PC Tools.

Network Information

The Network line in the System Information window lists Novell when your computer is connected to a Novell Netware local area network (LAN). This line is not displayed if you are not logged in to such a network. To display more detailed information about the operating system, select Network in the Computer panel or select **S**ystem from the horizontal menu bar and choose Network. SI displays the Network Information dialog box (see fig. 9.8). The information displayed in this dialog box is of most interest to network administrators.

The Network Information dialog box contains a list box, which displays these columns:

- *Server Name* indicates the name of the Novell server to which your computer is attached.

- *Netware Version* indicates the NetWare version number. The screen in figure 9.8, for example, indicates that the network server is running Novell NetWare Version 3.11.

■ *Total Users* lists the number of network users logged in to the network.

■ *Current User* indicates your network user name (the name you used when you logged in to the network).

■ *Login Time* denotes the time you logged in to the network, at the beginning of the current session on the network.

■ *Login Date* indicates the date you logged in to the network.

■ *Connection* indicates your connection number on the network, a number assigned automatically by the network when you log in.

This list box displays a separate row for every server on your network.

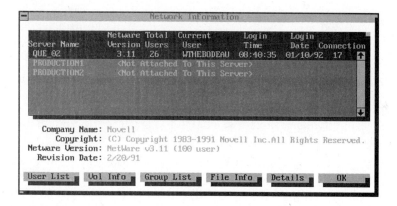

Fig. 9.8

The Network Information dialog box.

The Network Information dialog box lists, below the list box, the network software manufacturer, copyright information, the NetWare version, and the NetWare revision date for the server highlighted in the list box.

You can gather a variety of other information about the network through the Network Information dialog box. Use the mouse or cursor-movement keys to move the highlighted bar, in the list box, to the network you want to learn more about. Select one of these command buttons:

■ *User List* displays the Network User List dialog box, shown in figure 9.9, which displays a list box of the users logged in to the network. This list box indicates the log-in time, log-in date, connect number, network number, and node address for every user attached to the selected server. From the Network User List dialog box, you can send a message to one or more network users and list the disk space being used by a selected user.

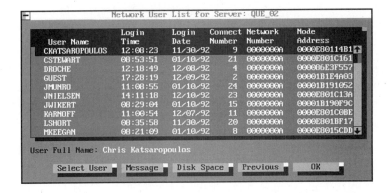

Fig. 9.9

The Network
User List dialog
box.

You must have at least console-operator rights to view another user's disk space. Select the **P**revious command button to return to the preceding dialog box, or select **OK** to return to the System Information window.

■ *Vol Info* displays a list of volume names for the selected network server, including total blocks used, blocks free, bytes used, and bytes free. Select the **P**revious command button to return to the preceding dialog box, or select **OK** to return to the System Information window.

■ *Group List* displays the Network Group List dialog box, shown in figure 9.10, which lists all groups defined on the network. To see a list of users from the selected group who are logged in to the network, select the group and choose the **O**nline Members command button. SI displays the Network User List dialog box.

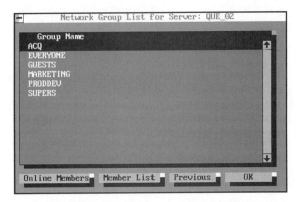

Fig. 9.10

The Network
Group List dialog
box.

To see a list of all network users in a particular group, select the group and choose the M**e**mber List command button. SI displays the Network User List dialog box. If a user is logged in, the dialog box indicates log-in time and date, connect number, network number, and node address. Otherwise, the dialog box indicates that the user is not on-line. Select the **Previous** command button to return to the preceding dialog box, or select **OK** to return to the System Information window.

■ *File Info*, which is only available for NetWare 286 users, displays a dialog box that lists the number of open files, maximum number of files that can be opened, largest number of files that have been opened, total files opened, total file-read requests, and total file-write requests. Select the **Previous** command button to return to the preceding dialog box, or select **OK** to return to the System Information window.

■ *Details* displays the Network Detailed Information dialog box (see fig. 9.11). This dialog box lists information about the network software, including manufacturer's name, version, copyright, revision date, network serial number, server name, number of connections supported, number of connections in use, peak number of connections used, SFT level, TTS level, number of volumes supported, and the versions of various network loadable modules (NLMs).

After you finish viewing information about the network, select the **OK** command button, press F3 (Exit), or press Esc to return to the main System Information window. You can press also any of the function key commands listed at the bottom of the screen.

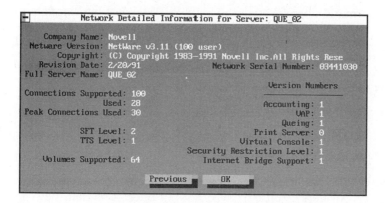

Fig. 9.11

The Network Detailed Information dialog box.

Software Interrupts

Your computer's central processing unit (CPU) and operating system provide certain *services*, such as sending the screen contents to the printer port (print screen), on the occurrence of a set condition. A program can alert the system that such a service is required by sending a special signal called an *interrupt*—so named because it can interrupt any ongoing task that the operating system is performing. Application software (such as a device driver or memory-resident program) frequently redirects an interrupt to perform some other action when the designated signal is received. The program that takes control of an interrupt is the *owner* of the interrupt.

Sometimes, to diagnose software conflicts, you must determine which currently running program owns a particular interrupt. From the System Information window, press F8 (Soft), or choose Software Interrupts from the **System** menu. SI displays the Software Interrupt Information dialog box (see fig. 9.12).

```
┌─┬─────────── Software Interrupt Information ──────────────┐
│─│                                                          │
│  │  #    Address    Interrupt Name              Owner       │
│  │ 00  4B14:00E7  Division by zero           SI.EXE      ▲ │
│  │ 01  0070:06F4  Single Step                SYSTEM        │
│  │ 02  0659:0016  NMI / Parity Check         Stacks        │
│  │ 03  0070:06F4  Breakpoint                 SYSTEM        │
│  │ 04  0070:06F4  Overflow (INTO)            SYSTEM        │
│  │ 05  07D3:042C  Print Screen               SAVEPCT       │
│  │ 06  F000:EB43  Invalid opcode (2/3/486)   BIOS          │
│  │ 07  F000:EAEB  Coprocessor emulation (2/3/486)  BIOS    │
│  │ 08  07D3:0543  Timer-tick Hardware Interrupt  SAVEPCT   │
│  │ 09  0659:0045  Keyboard Hardware Interrupt  Stacks      │
│  │ 0A  0659:0057  Cascaded Interrupt Controller  Stacks    │
│  │ 0B  0659:006F  Asynchronous adapter       Stacks        │
│  │ 0C  0401:02CC  Asynchronous adapter       MOUSE       ▼ │
└──┴──────────────────────────────────────────────────────┘
```

Fig. 9.12

The Software Interrupt Information dialog box.

The information displayed in the Software Interrupt Information dialog box is of interest primarily to programmers and power users. Use the mouse or press the cursor-movement keys to scroll the list. This dialog box lists the interrupt number, the hexadecimal address in memory where the interrupt service routine begins, the interrupt name, and the owner of the interrupt.

NOTE   *Software interrupts* are routines built in to an application program. PC Tools Desktop program, for example, installs its own software interrupt for the Scheduler accessory in order to perform tasks you schedule to run in the background. Hardware interrupts are used by fax boards, mouse drivers, printers, and other peripherals so that they can work properly with the operating system.

When you finish examining the Software Interrupt Information dialog box, select **OK** to return to the System Information window.

Hardware Interrupts

Some interrupts are caused by the system's hardware rather than by software. A signal coming in one of the system's serial ports, for example, causes an interrupt to be sent to the CPU. Such a *hardware interrupt* is called an *IRQ* (*interrupt request* line). As with software interrupts, applications programs often are designed to intercept a hardware interrupt and cause the CPU to process instructions at a particular address in the computer's memory.

To see a list of hardware interrupts, as well as any programs that own the interrupts, display the System Information window and press F9 (Hard), or select **S**ystem from the horizontal menu and then choose **H**ardware Interrupts from the System menu. SI displays the Hardware Interrupt Information dialog box (see fig. 9.13).

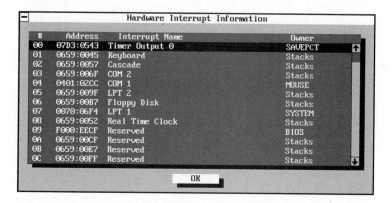

Fig. 9.13

The Hardware Interrupt Information dialog box.

The information displayed in the Hardware Interrupt Information dialog box is of interest primarily to programmers and power users. Use the mouse or cursor-movement keys to scroll the list. This dialog box lists the interrupt number, the hexadecimal address in memory where the interrupt service routine begins, the interrupt name, and the owner of the interrupt.

When you are finished examining the Hardware Interrupt Information dialog box, select **OK** to return to the System Information window.

Displaying Disk Drive Information

The Drive Summary line in the System Information window lists your computer's disk drives, indicating the number and size of drives. To display more detailed information about the drives, select Drive Summary from the System Information window or select **Disk** from the horizontal menu bar and choose **Drive** Summary from the Disk menu. SI displays the Logical Drive Information dialog box, which contains a list box that shows the drive name, drive capacity, and current default directory for every drive (see fig. 9.14).

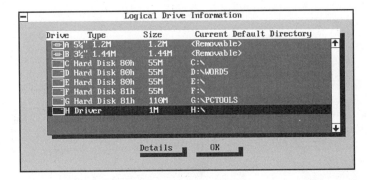

Fig. 9.14

The Logical Drive Information dialog box.

To display more information, select the Details command button from the Logical Drive Information dialog box or select **D**isk from the horizontal menu bar and choose **D**isk Details. SI displays the Logical Drive Detailed Information dialog box.

The Logical Drive Detailed Information dialog box displays a list of drive icons inside a list box on the right side of the screen. Select the disk for which you want to display detailed information and select Details. The dialog box displays the following data about the selected disk drive:

Logical drive letter

Physical drive number

Disk size and number of bytes available

Total number of clusters on the disk

Bytes per cluster and sectors per cluster

Media descriptor

File allocation table (FAT) type and number of FATs

FAT starting sector and total number of sectors occupied by the FAT

Root starting sector and total number of sectors in the root

Starting data sector and total number of sectors in the data area of the disk

Select the **P**revious command button to return to the preceding dialog box, or select **OK** to return to the System Information window.

To display physical details about the selected drive, select the **P**hysical Details command button from the Logical Drive Detailed Information dialog box. SI displays the Physical Drive Detailed Information dialog box (see fig. 9.15), which lists the following items:

Hexadecimal physical-drive identifier

Physical drive size

Number of drive sides (heads)

Number of tracks (or cylinders)

Number of sectors per track

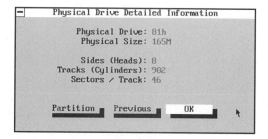

The Physical Drive Detailed Information dialog box.

Select the **P**revious command button to return to the Logical Drive Detailed Information dialog box, or select **OK** to return to the System Information window.

When you are analyzing a hard disk, you can also look at the hard disk partition. From the Physical Drive Detailed Information dialog box, choose the **Pa**rtition command button. The program displays the Partition Table Information dialog box (see fig. 9.16).

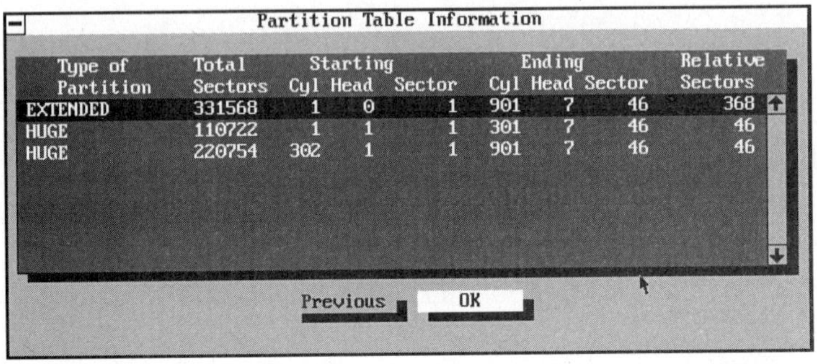

Fig. 9.16

The Partition Table Information dialog box.

For every partition, this dialog box displays these items:

Type of partition

Total number of sectors allocated to the partition

Starting cylinder, head, and sector

Ending cylinder, head, and sector

The Partition Table Information box displays the relative sectors. Select the **P**revious command button to return to the Physical Drive Detailed Information dialog box, or select **OK** to return to the System Information window.

Displaying Memory Information

The bottom portion of the System Information window displays the Memory panel. This panel lists, using graphics and numbers, the amount of free and used conventional memory, extended memory, and expanded memory. The following list briefly defines the types of memory.

■ *Conventional memory* is the portion of RAM (random-access memory) from 0 to 640K.

■ *Extended memory* is the portion of RAM above 1M (1,024K).

■ *Expanded memory* meets a published specification known as the Lotus-Intel-Microsoft Expanded Memory Specification (LIM EMS or just EMS).

All PCs have some conventional memory, but not all PCs have extended or expanded memory. Your computer can have any combination of expanded and extended memory; for instance, you may have extended memory and no expanded memory, expanded memory and no extended memory, both types of memory, or neither. SI enables you to display more detailed information about how DOS has allocated every type of memory that may be present in your computer system.

Conventional Memory

To determine how the operating system has allocated conventional memory, select Conventional from the System Information window or select Memory from the horizontal menu bar and choose Conventional. SI displays the Conventional Memory Information dialog box (see fig. 9.17).

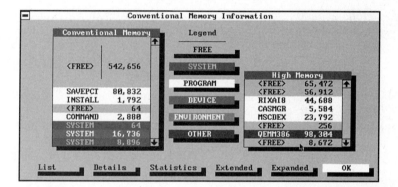

Fig. 9.17

The Conventional Memory Information dialog box.

By default, the Conventional Memory Information dialog box graphically displays a summary of how DOS has allocated conventional memory and *high memory*—the area of RAM between 640K and 1,024K.

 The high memory area is also referred to as *reserved memory* and sometimes as *upper memory block* memory (UMB memory).

On the left side of the dialog box, the Conventional Memory list box shows the amount of memory allocated to drivers and programs resident in memory as well as to the system (DOS). Areas of memory not allocated to a program or driver are marked as <FREE>.

The High Memory list box shows how the high memory area is allocated to programs, devices, and the system. A legend, displayed between the two list boxes, assigns specific screen colors to programs, devices, and the system.

NOTE If no UMB provider (such as DOS 5's EMM386.EXE) is running, the Conventional Memory Information dialog box does not display the High Memory Area list box.

SI enables you to display listings that give you more specific information about memory allocation. To see a list of the memory addresses for every allocated block of memory, select the **L**ist command button from the Conventional Memory Information dialog box. SI displays the Conventional Memory List dialog box. Select **G**raph to return to the preceding dialog box, or select the **O**K command button to return to the System Information window.

From the Conventional Memory Information dialog box (refer to fig. 9.15) or the Conventional Memory List dialog box, you can display further information about conventional and high memory by selecting one of the following command buttons:

- *Details* expands the listings to show explicitly which portions of memory are allocated to specific device drivers, as well as the portions of RAM reserved as environments for COMMAND.COM and applications programs. Select the Summary command button to return to the default listings.

- *Statistics* displays the Conventional Memory Statistics dialog box. With regard to conventional memory, this dialog box lists these statistics: total conventional memory, free conventional memory, and largest free block of memory. The dialog box also indicates the current memory-allocation strategy for conventional memory.

With regard to high memory (reserved or UMB memory—assuming that a UMB provider is in operation), the Conventional Memory Statistics dialog box indicates the total number of bytes free and the largest block of high memory free. Select the **P**revious command button to return to the preceding dialog box, or select **O**K to return to the System Information window.

Extended Memory

To determine how the operating system has allocated extended memory, select E**x**tended from the System Information window or select **M**emory from the horizontal menu bar and choose E**x**tended. SI displays the Extended Memory Information dialog box (see fig. 9.18).

One of two types of extended memory may be present in your system: *plain* extended memory (referred to by SI as *BIOS data*), and XMS memory (referred to by SI as *XMS data*). All extended memory is BIOS extended memory, unless an extended memory manager (which complies with the Extended Memory Specification) is loaded in memory. An extended memory manager changes plain extended memory to XMS memory.

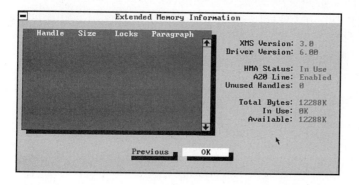

Fig. 9.18

The Extended
Memory Informa-
tion dialog box.

The Extended Memory Information dialog box displays an XMS Data
column on the left side of the dialog box and a BIOS Data column on the
right side. The XMS Data column lists the version of the XMS driver (if
any), the number of bytes of XMS memory available, and whether the
HMA (high memory area—the first 64K of memory above 1,024K) is in
use.

Expanded Memory

To determine how the operating system has allocated expanded
memory, select Expanded from the System Information window, or
select Memory from the horizontal menu bar and choose Expanded
from the Memory menu. SI displays the Expanded Memory Information
dialog box (see fig. 9.19).

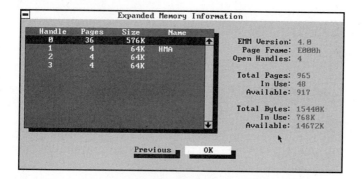

Fig. 9.19

The Expanded
Memory Informa-
tion dialog box.

The Expanded Memory Information dialog box displays a list box that
includes a row for every program to which expanded memory has been
allocated. For every program, the dialog box lists the EMS handle, the
number of EMS pages, the number of bytes allocated, and the program
name.

To the right of the list box, the Expanded Memory Information dialog box lists the following information:

EMS version number

EMS page frame

Number of open EMS handles

Total number of 16K EMS pages

Number of pages in use

EMS pages available

The Expanded Memory Information dialog box also lists the total number of bytes of conventional memory installed, the total number of bytes of conventional memory in use, and the number of bytes of conventional RAM available.

Select the **Pr**evious command button to return to the Expanded Memory Information dialog box, or select **OK** to return to the System Information window.

Device Drivers

The Device Drivers Information dialog box, which you access by choosing **D**evice Drives from the **M**emory menu, displays a list box that includes a line for every device driver loaded into memory. For every device driver, the dialog box lists the name of the driver, how much memory has been allocated by the driver, and the device driver version.

Running Benchmarks

Occasionally, you may want to know how well your computer performs relative to other similarly equipped computers. When you first display the System Information window, the program depicts the relative overall performance of your computer in the Relative Performance panel. This graph is based, however, on the CPU's clock speed, not on its actual performance.

To give you a more accurate picture of how your computer stacks up to other similar computers, SI offers a series of benchmark tests that measure the actual performance of your computer's CPU and disk drives. Using SI, you can also check the performance of any Novell NetWare local area network to which your computer is attached.

CPU Speed Test

To test the performance of your computer's CPU, press F6 (CPU) or select **B**enchmarks from the horizontal menu bar and choose **C**PU Speed Test. SI executes a group of machine instructions designed to test the chip's processing speed. SI then displays the Relative CPU Performance Index dialog box (see fig. 9.20).

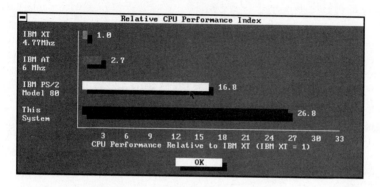

Fig. 9.20

The Relative CPU Performance Index dialog box.

The Relative CPU Performance Index dialog box shows a horizontal bar graph that depicts the speed of your computer indexed against the speed of an IBM PC XT and compared to the speed of an IBM PC AT and one other computer.

Click the close box, press Esc or F3 (Exit), or select the **OK** command button to return to the System Information window.

Disk Speed Test

To test the performance of the hard disk or disks installed in your computer, press F7 (Disk) or select **B**enchmarks from the horizontal menu bar and choose **D**isk Speed Test. SI checks your hardware configuration. If you have more than one hard disk, the program asks you to choose a hard disk for testing. SI executes a number of read-write tests designed to test the disk's speed. SI then displays the Relative Disk Performance Index dialog box.

The Relative Disk Performance Index dialog box shows a horizontal bar graph that depicts the speed of your computer's disk indexed against the speed of a standard-issue hard disk in an IBM PC XT and compared to the speed of a typical hard disk installed in one other computer.

Below the graph, SI lists the numeric results of the disk-performance test including BIOS-seek overhead time, track-to-track time, average seek time, and data transfer rate.

Click the close box, press Esc or F3 (Exit), or select the **OK** command button to return to the System Information window.

Overall Speed Test

Perhaps the best way to estimate your computer's computing power is to consider both CPU performance and hard disk performance together. SI, therefore, enables you to benchmark your computer's overall performance by using a test that takes into account both CPU speed and disk speed.

To test the overall performance of your computer, select **Benchmarks** from the horizontal menu bar and choose **O**verall Performance. SI performs both CPU tests and hard disk tests and then displays the Relative Overall Performance Index dialog box (see fig. 9.21).

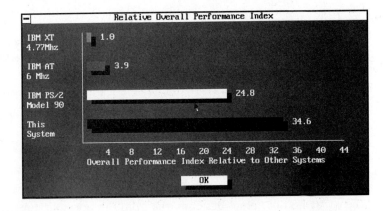

Fig. 9.21

The Relative Overall Performance Index dialog box.

NOTE   If SI has already executed a hard disk test during this SI session, the program does not run the test again.

The Relative Overall Performance Index dialog box shows a horizontal bar graph that displays the overall speed of your computer, indexed against the speed of a standard IBM PC XT and compared to the speed of an IBM PC AT and one other computer.

Network Performance

In addition to testing the performance of your computer's CPU and disks, SI enables you to gauge the performance of the input/output of any Novell NetWare local area network to which your computer is attached.

To test the network's I/O, select **B**enchmarks from the horizontal menu bar and choose **N**etwork Performance. SI displays the Choose Network Drive dialog box, which contains a list of network drives from which you can choose. Highlight the drive you want to test, and choose the **S**elect command button. SI performs both read and write tests to check access times and then displays the Relative Network Performance Index dialog box.

> To perform this test, you must have network read-and-write privileges to the current directory on the network volume you are testing.
>
> **T I P**

The Relative Network Performance Index dialog box shows a horizontal bar graph that reflects in kilobytes per second read access time, write access time, and overall access time (the average of the other two times). Performing this test under differing network traffic conditions results in differing access times.

This network performance test is an excellent tool to test the effect on network performance of a program that makes heavy use of network resources.

Displaying System Files

As you are installing new software, optimizing the performance of your computer, or diagnosing a hardware or software problem, it is often necessary to take a quick look at your system's AUTOEXEC.BAT and CONFIG.SYS files. SI provides an easy way to display these files.

To view your computer's AUTOEXEC.BAT file, display the System Information window and then choose **F**ile to display the File menu. Choose View **A**UTOEXEC.BAT. SI displays the file in a scrollable window.

Similarly, to view CONFIG.SYS, display the System Information window, and then choose **F**ile to display the File menu. Choose View **C**ONFIG.SYS. SI displays the file in a scrollable window.

Click the close box, press F3 (Exit) or Esc, or select the **OK** command button to return to the System Information window.

Printing an SI Report

In addition to displaying technical information about your computer, SI can send the information to your printer. To print a report, press F2 (Print), or select **F**ile from the horizontal menu bar and choose **P**rint Report. SI displays the Reporting Options dialog box. The Reporting Options dialog box in figure 9.22 shows the check boxes for print report options.

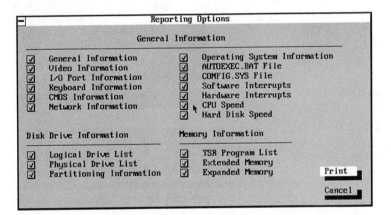

Fig. 9.22

The Reporting Options dialog box.

Every check box represents information you can display in a dialog box. Select from among this list and choose the **P**rint command button. SI displays the Printing Options dialog box.

The Printing Options dialog box lists five options: LPT1, LPT2, COM1, COM2, and Disk File. Select the printer port (**L**PT1 or LPT2) or serial port (**C**OM1 or COM2) to which your printer is connected. Choose the **P**rint command button, and SI prints the report.

To send the report to a file instead of a printer, select **D**isk File in the Printing Options dialog box. Then select **P**rint. SI creates a file named SI.RPT, which contains the contents of the report. SI normally stores this file in the \PCTOOLS\DATA directory.

System Information Command Line Options

The following shows the command line options available for SI.COM:

SI [/MEM] [/RPT] [/DEMO] [/NOVID] [/VIDEO] [/?]

If you want to run SI directly from the DOS command line or from within a batch file, use the following parameters to select information reporting options:

Parameter	Description
/MEM	Displays the Conventional Memory Information dialog box
/RPT	Prints a full system information report to the file SI.RPT
/DEMO	Demonstrates several of the more important SI dialog boxes automatically
/NOVID	Disables extended video controller checking
/?	Displays command-line help
/VIDEO	Displays command-line help for mouse and video options

If you want SI to display the conventional memory dialog box, for example, type the following command at the DOS prompt and press Enter:

SI /MEM

Mapping Files, Disks, and Memory

Even though PC Tools includes the separate System Information (SI) program, you may find useful several reports displayed by PC Tools Desktop. The sections that follow describe how to use options on the PC Tools Desktop Tools menu to map the contents of a file, a disk, or memory.

Mapping a File

The contiguity of the sectors that make up a file directly affects the speed at which a disk drive reads a particular file. When all clusters of a file are stored together in one location on the disk, the drive operates most efficiently. But, after you use the disk for a while, deleting, changing, and adding more files, DOS is unable to allocate space to each file as a contiguous block. Files become *fragmented*, or noncontiguous, and disk drive performance suffers.

To determine whether a file is fragmented, mark current the file you want to map, choose **M**aps from the **T**ools menu, and select **F**ile Map. PC Tools displays the File Mapping dialog box which shows a diagram of the file's cluster locations (see fig. 9.23).

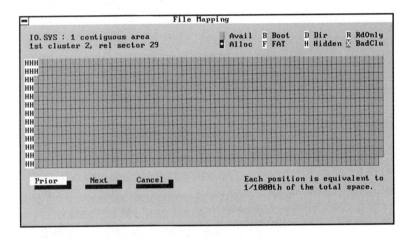

Fig. 9.23

A file map
of IO.SYS in
drive A.

SI uses the codes listed near the top of the screen to inform you whether the file is hidden or read only. These codes are also listed in table 9.2. In the lower left corner of the window, SI displays these command buttons:

- *Prior* maps the previous file in the directory.

- *Next* maps the next file in the directory.

- *Cancel* returns you to the PC Tools Desktop.

Table 9.2 File and Disk Mapping Cluster-Allocation Codes

Code	Meaning
(Shaded)	Available (not allocated)
B	Boot record sector
F	File-allocation sectors
D	Directory
•	Allocated to a file
H	Hidden file
R	Read-only file
X	Bad cluster

Figure 9.23 shows a map of the hidden system file IO.SYS. Because this file is the first file to be copied to the disk, the file is not fragmented. All clusters are contained in one contiguous area on the disk (indicated by a message at the top of the screen).

> When you notice that many files on a disk are fragmented, use the Compress program to unfragment the disk. Compress is the subject of Chapter 8, "Speeding Up Your Hard Disk with Compress."
>
> **T I P**

Mapping a Disk

In addition to file mapping, PC Tools provides disk mapping. To display a disk map, select **M**aps from the **T**ools menu; then choose Disk **M**ap to display the Disk Mapping dialog box (see fig. 9.24).

The Disk Mapping dialog box, which resembles the File Mapping dialog box, depicts the disk graphically; however, rather than show the clusters of only one file, the Disk Mapping dialog box shows all allocated clusters on the disk. Again, this information is useful in determining whether the disk should be unfragmented with Compress.

PC Tools uses the cluster allocation codes listed on-screen and in table 9.2 to denote the location of the boot record, the file allocation table, directories, hidden files, read-only files, bad clusters, and allocated clusters. Figure 9.24 shows a map of a bootable floppy disk in drive A. All files are near the beginning of the disk.

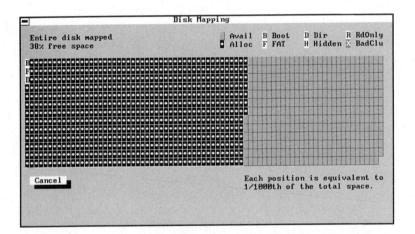

Fig. 9.24

The Disk Map-
ping dialog box.

Contrast the map of drive A (refer to fig. 9.24) with the disk map in figure 9.25, which shows the file allocation for drive C (a hard disk). As
you add files to the disk, DOS fills in these areas, contributing to more
severe file fragmentation.

Fig. 9.25

A drive C Disk
Map dialog box.

The Disk **M**ap command provides a quick bird's-eye view of how sectors are allocated on the disk. This look can be generally helpful in sug-
gesting when to unfragment a disk. The Compress program, discussed
in Chapter 8, "Speeding Up Your Hard Disk With Compress," can do a
more thorough analysis of file fragmentation.

Mapping Memory

With all the powerful memory-resident programs available for use on personal computers (including several PC Tools programs), you often have several programs loaded into memory at the same time. PC Tools provides a command on the Tools menu under Maps and a separate program for "mapping" memory to determine which programs control different portions of RAM. Memory mapping is useful primarily to programmers and power users.

When you want to display a memory map, select Tools to display the menu, and then select Maps and then Memory Map. PC Tools starts SI, which displays SI's Conventional Memory Information dialog box. Refer to the "Conventional Memory" section earlier in this chapter.

Using MI.COM

You can generate a memory map report directly from the DOS command line with a separate program, MI.COM, distributed with PC Tools, as well as from the Tools Menu (choose Maps from the Tools menu; then choose Memory Info from the Maps submenu). With MI.COM, you can review a memory map without first having to load PC Tools into memory.

To use MI.COM, type this command at the DOS prompt:

    MI /A /E /F /N /O /Q /V /?

With this command, MI initiates the program. The letters in italics represent optional parameters the report displays to the screen. When you type **mi** by itself and press Enter, MI lists only memory blocks that contain programs in the on-screen report.

You can use the parameters alone or with other parameters. You can, optionally, create and assign parameters to an environment variable named MI*OPT. MI automatically uses parameters found in MI*OPT. The parameters have the following effects:

Parameter	Result
/A	Shows all memory blocks.
/C	Shows all conventional memory, ignoring extended and expanded memory.
/D	Shows the device driver list.
/E	Ignores the MI*OPT environment variable.

Parameter	Result
/F	Filters unprintable characters in generating the report so that you can redirect the report to a printer.
/H	Lists your EMS and XMS handles.
/N	Disables the screen with a screen-pause feature, causing the program to display the entire report in a continuous stream. Ordinarily, MI pauses the display of the report when the screen is full so that you must press a key to display the next page.
/O	Displays an optional report that does not list device drivers.
/Q	Displays an abbreviated report (*quick summary*) that lists only the total conventional memory, largest executable program, amount of extended memory, and amount of expanded memory.
/V	Lists blocks occupied by programs as well as by system *vectors* (also called *interrupts*) that are being intercepted or "hooked" by memory-resident programs.
/?	Displays the list of available parameters with their meanings.

FROM HERE...

For Related Information

◄◄ "Using Compress Options," p. 322.

◄◄ "Running Compress," p. 330.

Chapter Summary

This chapter, the last in Part II, covers PC Tools commands that provide information about the system, the System Information (SI) program, and the memory information program, MI. You have learned how to obtain information about the system, including system type, video adapter, I/O ports, keyboard, mouse, CMOS information, network information, software interrupts, hardware interrupts, disk drive summary, disk details, memory, statistics, extended memory, expanded memory, CPU speed, disk speed, overall speed, and network performance.

You are now ready to turn to Part III, "Using the Recovery and Security Utilities."

Using the Recovery and Security Utilities

PART

III

OUTLINE

Recovering Damaged or Deleted Files

Recovering Damaged or Formatted Disks

Editing a Disk with DiskEdit

Securing Your Data with PC Secure and Wipe

Protecting Your System with CP Anti-Virus

Recovering Damaged or Deleted Files

Nothing is more frustrating than attempting to fire up an important spreadsheet or database file, only to be greeted by a message that the file contains invalid or corrupted data and cannot be loaded. Perhaps you had a power failure while you were last saving the file, or maybe one of the sectors that contain the file has become defective. You often can repair the file effectively and recover the data with FileFix. The FileFix utility in PC Tools 8 repairs many more file types— files created with popular database, spreadsheet, and word processing software, for example—than before. For a complete list of programs, see table 10.1. This chapter describes how to use FileFix.

Perhaps as exasperating as trying to load a damaged file, and certainly more common, is realizing that you accidentally deleted an important file from your disk. PC Tools 8 also has a special data-recovery utility, Undelete, for recovering accidentally deleted files. Undelete is explained at the end of this chapter.

Table 10.1 File Types that FileFix Can Repair

Databases	Extension
dBASE (all), FoxBase, FoxPro, and Clipper	.DBF
Paradox	.DB
R:BASE	.RBF

NOTE Paradox and R:BASE are new to Version 8.0.

Spreadsheets	Extension
Excel	.XLS
Lotus 1-2-3 Release 1.*x*	.WKS
Lotus 1-2-3 Release 2.*x*	.WK1
Lotus 1-2-3 Release 3.*x*, Lotus 1-2-3 for Windows Release 1.*x*	.WK3
Quattro Pro	.WQ1
Symphony Release 1.0	.WRK
Symphony Release 1.1 or later	.WR1

NOTE Excel and Quattro Pro are new to Version 8.0.

Word Processing	Extension
WordPerfect	.DOC

NOTE WordPerfect files do not automatically end with the DOC extension. To fix a WordPerfect file, you must either type the name in the file name text box or change the filter to *.*, which enables you to see all files in the directory. Renaming the file is not a good idea because you don't want to write to disk until you are confident of the fix.

Choosing the Right Utility

PC Tools comes with a variety of utilities that enable you to recover from many different errors. The following list explains procedures you may take when confronted by different errors:

- Determine whether an error you receive is a disk error or a file error. If DOS cannot copy a file, for example, the system area of the disk may be damaged. You must use DiskFix to repair the disk. See Chapter 11, "Recovering Damaged or Formatted Disks," for directions on using DiskFix. If, after the disk is repaired, you find that files are damaged, try repairing the files with FileFix.

- If you cannot boot from your hard disk, use your emergency disk to boot your computer. Then use DiskFix to repair the disk errors. If file damage has occurred, repair the file by using FileFix.

- Before you take the time to repair a file, determine whether you have a recent back-up copy of the file. Don't spend time repairing a file when you can spend less time restoring the file. Always use a *copy* of the backed up file, not the original backup.

- If you accidentally delete a file, use Undelete right away to undelete that file. If you continue writing information to the disk, you run the chance of overwriting the contents of the deleted file. The Undelete utility is explained at the end of this chapter.

Using FileFix

The FileFix program enables you to easily recover damaged database, spreadsheet, and document files. Most programs encode their data files so that you can retrieve the information in the file only if the program can read the file. Even though you can use the DOS TYPE command and view some of the information from a dBASE IV database file, for example, you must use dBASE IV to retrieve and manipulate the data in a meaningful way. The data in the damaged database file, then, will be difficult to use unless you can repair the damaged file so that the program that created the file can read it. The FileFix utility in PC Tools 8 is intended to make this chore an easy one.

To start FileFix from the DOS command line, type the following command and press Enter:

FILEFIX

FileFix loads and displays the File Repair window (see fig. 10.1).

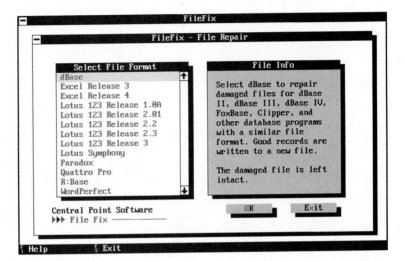

Fig. 10.1

The File Repair
window.

The Select File Format list box on the left side of the File Repair window shows the file types you can repair. As you use the arrow keys to move the cursor to the file format you want to use, additional information appears in the File Info box on the right.

Selecting Files To Repair

You can select one of many file formats, including WordPerfect, Lotus 1-2-3, dBASE IV, and Paradox. Use the up- and down-arrow keys to move the highlight bar to the desired file type, and then press Enter. The Select File To Fix dialog box appears (see fig. 10.2).

In the Filename text box, FileFix displays the default file-selection criterion. Because dBASE IV was the file format selected, the default is *.DBF. The asterisk (*) is a wild card character that stands for any combination of one to eight characters. The asterisk is followed by the default file name extension for type of file you are repairing, which is DBF in this example. FileFix looks through the current DOS directory and displays every file name with that extension. Because the list box has room to show only eight entries at a time, you usually must scroll through the list box to see the complete list.

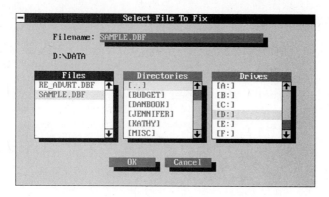

Fig. 10.2

The Select File To
Fix dialog box.

FileFix lists the names of other directories in the Directories list box and other disk drives in the Drives list box. Every directory is denoted by its name enclosed in square brackets. Every disk drive is denoted by a letter enclosed in square brackets. At the top of the Directories list box is the designation [. .], which represents the parent to the current directory.

If the file you want to fix is not in the current directory, use the mouse or the cursor-movement keys to select a different directory in the Directories list box. To change drives, select another drive in the Drives list box and press Enter. Use the Tab key or mouse to move from list box to list box. When the correct drive and directory have been set, select the file you want to repair from the Files list box and press Enter. Alternatively, double-click the file.

You have learned the basics of selecting files to fix. The sections that follow describe how to use FileFix to repair database, spreadsheet, and document files.

Repairing Database Files

FileFix can repair database files created with R:BASE, Paradox, dBASE, Clipper, FoxBase, and FoxPro. All database files have a file header. Header information consists of the record structure: field name, field length, and field type (character, date, or numeric). Paradox databases also have indexing information in the header. When the header is damaged, even undamaged data is unreadable. FileFix can copy the header from an undamaged file with the same structure or create a new header. This repair is much easier if you have a hard copy of the file before it was damaged. As you repair the header, you may need to re-type the field names, types, and lengths.

Repairing R:BASE Files

R:BASE requires three files for a single database: the data dictionary file, the data file, and the index file. When FileFix repairs an R:BASE file, it repairs all three separate files. If you want to repair an R:BASE file, choose R:BASE from the File Repair window (refer to fig. 10.1). FileFix displays a Select File To Fix dialog box similar to the one shown in figure 10.2. Select the name of the R:BASE file you want to repair and choose the **OK** command button. For complete details about using the Select File To Fix dialog box, refer to the section "Selecting Files To Repair" in this chapter.

The RBase Repair Options dialog box appears (see fig. 10.3). This dialog box displays the name of the original file and the name assigned to the repair file. The destination file is in the same directory as the original file and has the name FIXED1.RBF. Save the repair file to a diskette or another hard disk drive to prevent accidentally overwriting the file you are attempting to repair.

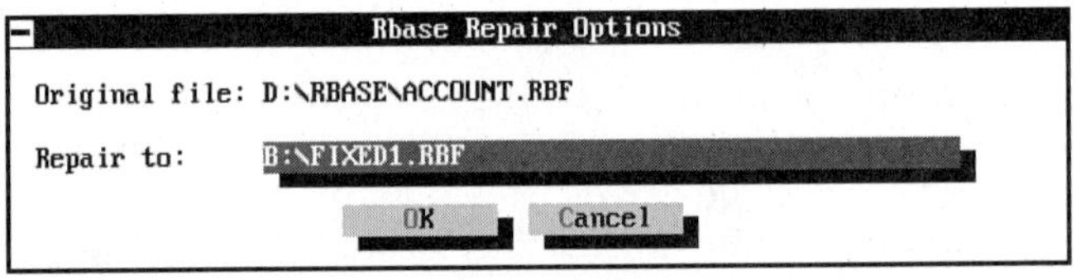

Fig. 10.3

The RBase Repair Options dialog box.

```
┌─────────────────────────────────────────────────┐
│ ─           Rbase Repair Options                 │
│                                                   │
│  Original file: D:\RBASE\ACCOUNT.RBF              │
│                                                   │
│  Repair to:     B:\FIXED1.RBF                     │
│                                                   │
│               ┌──────────┐   ┌──────────┐         │
│               │    OK    │   │  Cancel  │         │
│               └──────────┘   └──────────┘         │
└─────────────────────────────────────────────────┘
```

T I P   If your file repair is botched and you have written the repair file to the same drive, you may have overwritten some of your data. By writing the repair file to a different drive, you eliminate that risk. You can then try to repair the file by using another method or another program.

You do not need to configure any special repair options, so repairing R:BASE files is simple. When you are satisfied with the name and destination for the repair file, choose **OK**. FileFix repairs the file and returns to the main FileFix menu. You can then repair another file or exit FileFix.

After you repair a damaged database, immediately make a copy of the file; then use the PC Tools Rename or DOS RENAME command to give the file the proper extension. Load the database back into the application to make sure that the repaired file works. If the file doesn't work, you may need to try the file repair option again. Don't delete a damaged file until you have loaded the repaired file and made sure that you have recovered as much data as possible.

Repairing Paradox Files

If you want to repair a Paradox file, choose Paradox from the File Repair window. The program displays a Select File to Fix dialog box similar to the one shown in figure 10.2. Select the name of the Paradox file you want to repair and choose **OK**. After you select the Paradox file to repair, the Paradox Repair Options dialog box appears (see fig. 10.4).

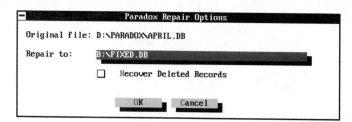

Fig. 10.4

The Paradox Repair Options dialog box.

The Paradox Repair Options dialog box displays the name of the original file and the name assigned to the destination file. The destination file is in the same directory as the original file and is called FIXED.DB. Change the drive to another disk drive, however, so that you don't accidentally write over the data you are trying to recover.

Only one option is available for repairing Paradox files: Recover Deleted Records. When you mark the **R**ecover Deleted Records check box, FileFix restores all records in the file array no matter what the header says exists. If you do not select Recover Deleted Records, FileFix restores only the number of records specified in the header even if other, recoverable records are on the disk.

 Records deleted during an Edit session are not recoverable; however, records globally deleted with a Delete operator in a query form are recoverable with Filefix.

After you decide whether you want to use the Recover Deleted Records option and you are satisfied with the file name and destination for the file, choose **OK**.

> **NOTE**
>
> If you have already repaired a file and you did not specify an alternate directory for the repair destination, you are warned that FIXED.DB already exists. Choose **C**ancel if you haven't deleted the damaged file and renamed FIXED. DB to the original file name after recovering a file. Otherwise, choose **O**verwrite.

After choosing OK, a progress report appears telling you how many records were recovered. You can view the repaired file by choosing **OK** in the View dialog box. After you view the file, the Report Options dialog box gives you the option to send a report to the printer or a file. If you send the report to a file, the file is written in the current directory under the name *FILENAME*.RPT, where *filename* is the name of the original file.

Repairing dBASE Files

In addition to repairing scrambled dBASE headers, FileFix can reunite "zapped" records with the header. This repair is most complete if you use FileFix to unzap the records immediately after you use the dBASE ZAP command. If you want FileFix to repair a damaged dBASE file, choose dBASE from the File Repair window. The program displays a Select File to Fix dialog box similar to the one shown in figure 10.2. Select the name of the dBASE file you want to repair and choose **OK**. FileFix displays the dBASE Repair Options dialog box (see fig. 10.5).

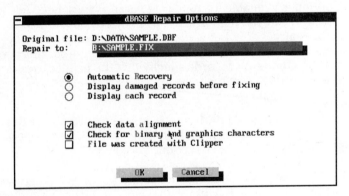

```
┌──────────────── dBASE Repair Options ─────────────────┐
│                                                        │
│  Original file: D:\DATA\SAMPLE.DBF                     │
│  Repair to:    ▓B:\SAMPLE.FIX▓▓▓▓▓▓▓▓▓▓▓▓▓▓▓▓▓▓▓▓▓▓▓▓  │
│                                                        │
│                                                        │
│          ◉   Automatic Recovery                        │
│          ○   Display damaged records before fixing     │
│          ○   Display each record                       │
│                                                        │
│                                                        │
│          ☑   Check data alignment                      │
│          ☑   Check for binary and graphics characters  │
│          ☐   File was created with Clipper             │
│                                                        │
│                 ▓ OK ▓      Cancel                      │
│                                                        │
└────────────────────────────────────────────────────────┘
```

Fig. 10.5

The dBASE Repair Options dialog box.

The dBASE Repair Options dialog box displays near the top of the dialog box the name of the original file and the name assigned to the destination file. The destination file is in the same directory as the original file and has the same name, but with the extension FIX. Change the drive to another disk drive, however, so that you don't accidentally write over the data you are trying to recover.

The following three option buttons are listed in the dBASE Repair Options dialog box:

- *Automatic **R**ecovery* attempts to recover the file without the need for further input on your part. Always try this option first.

- *Display **D**amaged Records Before Fixing* displays every damaged record so that you can attempt to correct any problem manually. Try this option only after Automatic Recovery fails.

- *Display **E**ach Record* shows every record so that you can decide which ones are defective and how to repair them. Use this option only if the other options are not effective.

The dBASE Repair Options dialog box also displays three check boxes:

- *Check Data **A**lignment.* FileFix looks at and fixes data alignment. This box is checked by default, and you should leave it on.

- *Check for **B**inary and Graphiçs Characters.* Checking this option replaces any graphics or nonprintable characters with blanks. This option is checked by default. Clear the check from this box if the file intentionally contains graphics characters.

- ***F**ile Was Created with Clipper.* Choosing this option compensates for the formatting characteristics that are unique to files created with the database program Clipper (from Nantucket Software).

After choosing one of the option buttons and any of the check boxes, choose **OK**.

If you chose Display Damaged Records Before Fixing or Display Each Record, the following additional options become available, as shown in figure 10.6:

- *Accept* adds the record to the file.

- *Reject* discards the record.

- *Mode* enables you to switch from looking at records one at a time to letting FileFix repair the remainder of the file automatically.

- *Cancel* discards the repairs and returns you to the File Repair window.

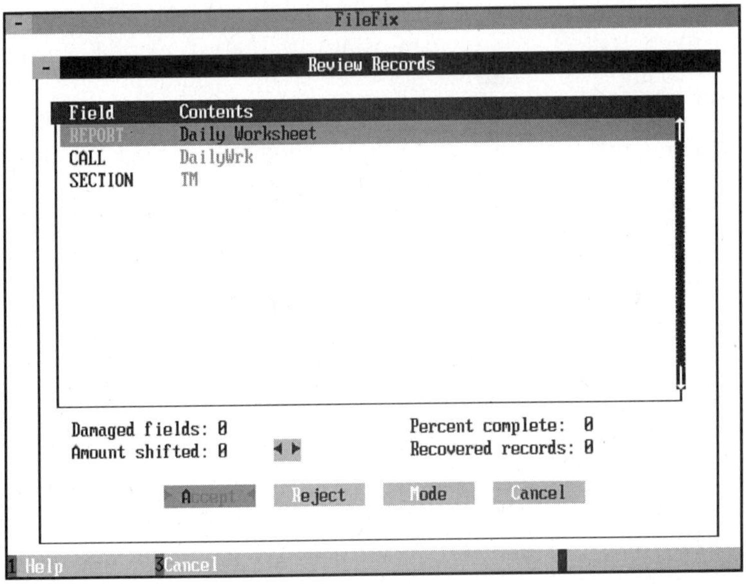

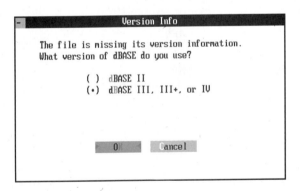

Fig. 10.6

The Review
Records screen.

Repairing dBASE File Headers

FileFix begins the repair process by checking the file's header for defective bookkeeping information. If the program finds any error in the file header, the Version Info dialog box, shown in figure 10.7, appears.

Fig. 10.7

The Version Info
dialog box.

Choose the dBASE version and select **OK**. The File Header Damaged or Missing dialog box appears (see fig 10.8). Select **OK**.

The Structure Options dialog box, which gives you the following repair options, appears (see fig. 10.9):

- *Edit the Existing Structure.* You type in field names, types, and lengths.

- *Import the Correct Header from Another dBASE File.* You copy the header information from another file with the same structure.

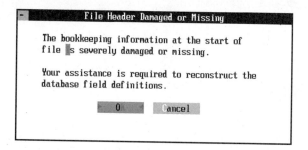

Fig. 10.8

The File Header Damaged or Missing dialog box.

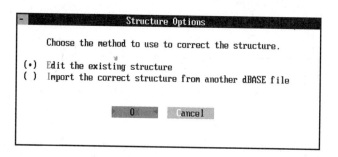

Fig. 10.9

The Structure Options dialog box.

Choose the appropriate option and select **OK**. If you chose the Import the correct structure from another dBASE file, the Select Header to Import dialog box, which resembles the Select File to Fix dialog box, appears. Choose files in this dialog box the same way you choose files in the Select File to Fix dialog box. The Imported Header OK dialog box appears. Choose **OK** to continue with the recovery process. Choose **R**eview to check the imported structure.

If you choose Edit the existing structure, you must locate the first character in the file. Place the first character of the file at the beginning of dialog box and choose **OK**. After you specify the first characters of the first record, choose the **S**earch button to display the Search dialog box.

You can search the data forward or backward from the cursor location by choosing the appropriate option box. Next you type the text you want to find in the text box. To find text that matches the capitalization exactly, choose the Case Sensitive check box; then choose **OK** to start the search. If the search text is found, the Edit Record Structure dialog box reappears with the text highlighted. If the text is not found, you must manually search the database. After the data is aligned, choose **OK**. The Edit Record Structure dialog box appears (see fig. 10.10).

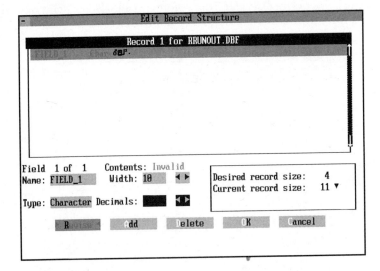

The Edit Record Structure dialog box.

Position the cursor next to any field you want to edit and choose the **R**evise button. Choose **A**dd to insert new fields. Choose **D**elete to remove a field. Choose **OK** when you are finished with your changes.

After you correct the file's header information, select **OK**. FileFix attempts to recover all records, using the corrected database structure. If you instructed the program to display a damaged record before making a correction, FileFix displays each proposed correction to a damaged record one at a time. Select **A**ccept to confirm the change, or choose **R**eject to skip the record. Choose the **M**ode command button to select a different repair option, or select **C**ancel to end the repair procedure.

If FileFix detects that the dBASE file has been zapped, the program asks whether you want to unzap the file. Choose **OK**, and FileFix attempts to recover the zapped records. After FileFix recovers all records, the program gives you an opportunity to view the corrected file and to send a report of the corrections to your printer or to a file.

After FileFix repairs the file and prints the report, it returns to the File Repair menu. Choose E**x**it to return to DOS. Use the View program or dBASE to confirm that you can load the repaired version of the file (the file with the FIX extension).

If the repaired file doesn't load, try to repair the file again by using a different repair option. Don't discard the damaged file until you are certain that the fixed version of the file is usable.

Repairing Spreadsheet Files

As with databases, spreadsheet files come in several types—Lotus 1-2-3, Excel, Quattro Pro file types, for example. FileFix recovers and repairs invalid cell entries, invalid version numbers, damaged formula cells, and damage to the header of a file.

Spreadsheet files have records with format information and records with data. Information stored in the format records includes global settings and column widths. The spreadsheet application expects the format information in a certain order. If the information is out of order, or if the spreadsheet is damaged, the spreadsheet does not load correctly or completely. FileFix can recover this information.

If you want FileFix to repair a damaged spreadsheet file created with Quattro Pro, Excel, Lotus 1-2-3, or Symphony, use the arrow keys to select the name from the Select File Format list box in the main FileFix window (refer to fig. 10.1). As you use the arrow keys to move the cursor to the file format you want to use, additional information is displayed in the File Info box. Select the file format that corresponds to the file you want to fix and press Enter.

FileFix displays a File Load dialog box that lists available spreadsheet files. From the Select File to Fix dialog box, select the file you want to repair and choose **OK**. FileFix displays the Spreadsheet Repair Options dialog box (see fig. 10.11).

```
┌─────────────────────────────────────────────────────┐
│ -           Spreadsheet Repair Options               │
├─────────────────────────────────────────────────────┤
│                                                       │
│  Original file: C:\EXCEL\BUDGET.XLS                   │
│                                                       │
│  Repair to:     D:\EXCEL\BUDGET.FIX                   │
│                                                       │
│                                                       │
│          [J]  Use Cell Content in Analysis            │
│          [ ]  Allow Add-In Cell Types                 │
│                                                       │
│              OK         Cancel                        │
│                                                       │
└─────────────────────────────────────────────────────┘
```

Fig. 10.11

The Spreadsheet Repair Options dialog box.

The name of the original file appears near the top of the Spreadsheet Repair Options dialog box. The program suggests a file name for the destination file in the Repair To text box. The suggested file name is in the same directory as the original file and has the same name, but with the extension FIX. Change the drive to another disk drive, however, so that you don't accidentally write over the data you are trying to recover.

Two option buttons are listed in the Spreadsheet Repair Options dialog box. The first option is **U**se Cell Content in Analysis. Selecting this option analyzes the linkage between cells but does not look at the contents of each cell. Selecting the other option, **A**llow Add-In Cell Types, ignores cells that do not match the selected application's cell format. If you have information stored in your spreadsheet from any other application, choose this option.

Choose **OK** in the dialog box to proceed with the file repair. The Repairing File dialog box appears. FileFix repairs as much of the file's data as possible. The program depicts repair progress as a growing horizontal bar graph. When the graph reaches 100 percent, choose **OK** to display the next screen.

After FileFix recovers all records, the program gives you an opportunity to view the corrected file and to send a report of the corrections to your printer or a file. After FileFix repairs the file and prints the report, it returns to the File Repair dialog box. Choose E**x**it to return to DOS.

After you repair a damaged spreadsheet, immediately make a copy of the file. Then use the PC Tools Rename or DOS RENAME command to give the file the proper extension. Load the spreadsheet back into the application to make sure that the repaired file works. If it doesn't work, change the options in the Spreadsheet Repair Options dialog box and try again. Don't delete a damaged file until you have loaded the repaired file and made sure that you have recovered as much data as possible.

Repairing WordPerfect Files

FileFix can repair most types of damage to WordPerfect text files. WordPerfect files contain three main sections: a file prefix, text that appears on-screen, and control codes that format the text appearance. WordPerfect files also may have graphics and information from other types of applications.

 NOTE FileFix can only reliably recover the text portion of your file. If the file includes figures imported from some other application, you must reinsert this material after the file is repaired.

To repair a WordPerfect file, choose WordPerfect from the File Repair dialog box. The program displays the Select File to Fix dialog box. Select the name of the file you want to repair. The WordPerfect Repair Options dialog box appears (see fig. 10.12).

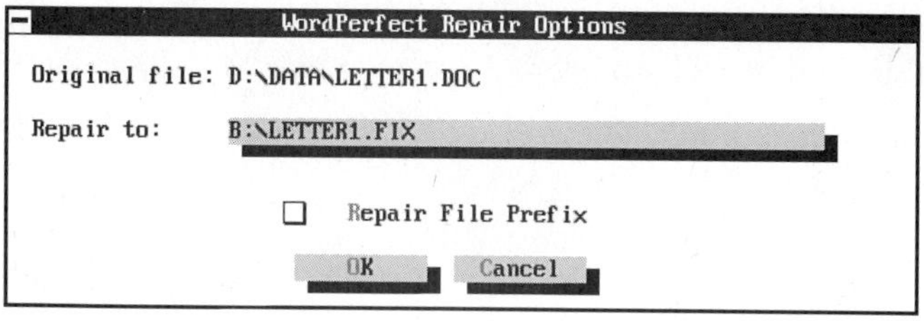

```
┌─────────────────────────────────────────────────────────┐
│ [-]              WordPerfect Repair Options               │
│                                                           │
│  Original file: D:\DATA\LETTER1.DOC                       │
│                                                           │
│  Repair to:     B:\LETTER1.FIX                            │
│                                                           │
│              ☐   Repair File Prefix                       │
│                   OK        Cancel                        │
└─────────────────────────────────────────────────────────┘
```

Fig. 10.12

The WordPerfect Repair Options dialog box.

The dialog box displays the name of the original file and the name assigned to the destination file. The destination file is in the same directory as the original file and has the same file name as the original file,
but with the extension FIX. Change the drive to another disk drive, however, so that you don't accidentally write over the data you are trying
to recover.

When you repair WordPerfect files, only one option is available: **R**epair
File Prefix. When you use this option, FileFix builds a new prefix for the
file. Because you lose all formatting information, such as fonts and special formatting, in the process of building prefix information, first try
repairing the file with this option turned off. If the file cannot be recovered with this option turned off, turn it on and repair the prefix. After
the prefix is repaired, run the file through the WordPerfect repair option again with this option turned off to repair the body of the file.

Choose **OK** to proceed with the file repair. FileFix repairs as much of
the file's data as possible. Rename the repaired file and load it back
into WordPerfect to test whether the file is usable. If the file isn't usable, try to repair the file's prefix.

If the prefix is missing or damaged, you need to check the **R**epair File
Prefix box in the WordPerfect Repair Options dialog box. Choose **OK**.
The WordPerfect Prefix Options dialog box appears (see fig. 10.13).

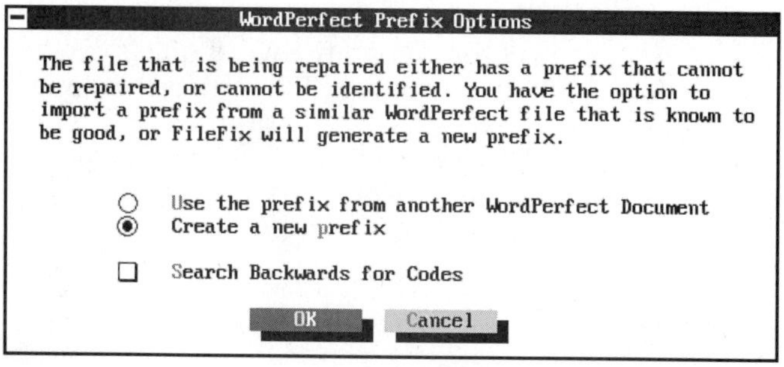

```
┌─────────────────────────────────────────────────────────┐
│ [-]              WordPerfect Prefix Options               │
│                                                           │
│  The file that is being repaired either has a prefix that cannot │
│  be repaired, or cannot be identified. You have the option to    │
│  import a prefix from a similar WordPerfect file that is known to │
│  be good, or FileFix will generate a new prefix.                 │
│                                                           │
│        ○   Use the prefix from another WordPerfect Document │
│        ◉   Create a new prefix                            │
│                                                           │
│        ☐   Search Backwards for Codes                     │
│                   OK        Cancel                        │
└─────────────────────────────────────────────────────────┘
```

Fig. 10.13

The WordPerfect Prefix Options dialog box.

The WordPerfect Prefix Options dialog box contains the following three
options for repairing a prefix:

- *Use the Prefix from another WordPerfect Document.* This option enables you to copy a prefix from a similar WordPerfect file.

- *Create a new prefix.* This option enables you to re-create the prefix for the file manually.

- *Search Backwards for Codes.* This option enables you to search for control codes that belong in the file but not in the prefix. You can select this option in combination with either of the other two options.

Choose the Use the Prefix from another WordPerfect Document or Create a new prefix option; then choose **OK** to proceed with the prefix repair. The Adjust Starting Position dialog box appears (see fig. 10.14).

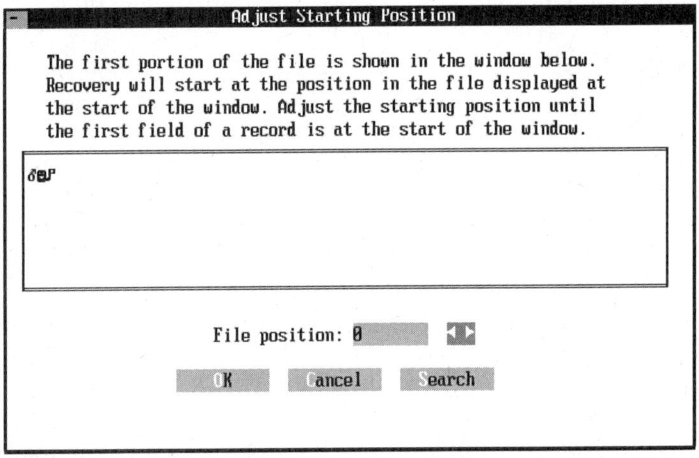

Fig. 10.14

The Adjust Starting Position dialog box.

If you choose Create a new **p**refix, you also may need to align the text to the starting point in the file. Move the text by pressing the arrow keys or clicking the arrowheads. If you know the first word in the file, use the Search command button to find the word quickly. When the text is aligned, choose **OK**. The Repairing File dialog box appears; choose **OK** to repair the file. When the repair is finished, PC Tools asks whether you want to view the file. Choose **OK** to see the file, or choose **C**ancel to return to the File Repair dialog box.

Quitting FileFix

When you are finished recovering damaged files, press Esc or F3 (Exit), and then choose **OK**. FileFix closes the FileFix screen and returns to DOS.

Using Undelete To Recover Deleted Files

Because of the way DOS deletes files, undeleting a file is relatively easy, but only if you do so soon after the file is deleted. When PC Shell deletes a file, the program instructs DOS to delete the file. DOS in turn changes one character in the file name in the directory file so that the target file no longer is listed. As far as DOS is concerned, the file is gone, but DOS does not erase the modified file name from the directory and does not erase any data from the disk. Eventually, as you add new files to the disk, DOS reallocates the disk space that had been assigned to the deleted file, causing new data to overwrite the old data. Soon the file and its data are permanently gone. If you use the Undelete program in PC Tools 8 before DOS overwrites a deleted file's data, however, you can easily recover the deleted file.

 NOTE When you discover that you accidentally deleted a file or directory, immediately try to recover it. The longer you wait, the less the chance that Undelete can recover the file completely.

Your chances of undeleting files improve if you use a file-protection method. The following is a quick overview of the features of some of the common delete-protection programs:

- *Delete Sentry.* Files are copied to a hidden directory and can be restored in perfect condition.

- *Delete Tracker.* Cluster addresses of deleted files are recorded. The file data is left on the disk, but DOS marks the file's clusters as available. Files protected by Delete Tracker can be undeleted in excellent condition as long as no new data has been recorded over any of the file's clusters. Delete Tracker protection was called Mirror Delete Tracking in earlier versions of PC Tools.

- *DOS.* Files are undeleted based on the information stored in the File Allocation Table (FAT). Data may be lost if the disk hasn't been compressed recently, because DOS doesn't keep track of all the file's clusters. If you have a Mirror file, choose Use **M**irror File from the **O**ptions menu. Undelete uses the Mirror's copy of the File Allocation Table to find all the file's clusters.

- *Netware 386.* This method must be set up by the system administrator, and the user must have CREATE rights to the directory to retrieve the file, using Undelete. Files can be recovered in perfect condition because they remain on the drive until purged or the space is needed by another file.

■ *Del/Watch.* Files protected by this DR DOS file-protection method can be undeleted in perfect condition.

Delete Tracker and Data Sentry are configured by using a program called Data Monitor. Add Data Monitor to your computer's AUTOEXEC.BAT file so that the program loads every time you boot your computer. Refer to Appendix A, "Installing and Configuring PC Tools," for more information about loading and configuring the Data Monitor.

Starting Undelete

To start Undelete from the DOS command line, type the following command and press Enter:

UNDEL

The program loads and displays the Undelete screen (see fig. 10.15).

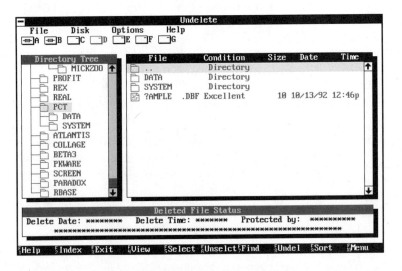

Fig. 10.15

The Undelete screen.

The Undelete screen is similar in appearance to the PC Shell screen. A Directory Tree window appears on the left side of the screen, and a File window appears on the right. As you probably expect, a horizontal menu bar appears at the top of the screen, a message bar appears at the bottom, and a drive line appears just below the horizontal menu bar. Table 10.2 lists all the function key commands available in Undelete.

Table 10.2 Keystroke Commands Available in Undelete

Key	Name	Function
F1	Help	Displays context-sensitive Help facility
F2	Index	Displays the Help facility index
F3	Exit	Cancels the current process or application (same as Esc)
F4	View	Uses the View program to display the contents of the highlighted file
F5	Select	Displays the Select by Name dialog box you use to specify files you want the program to undelete
F6	Unselect	Displays the Unselect by Name dialog box you use to specify files you want the program to unselect
F7	Find/ Tree	Switches between the Find Deleted Files dialog box, which enables you to search all deleted files for those that match a given file specification and contain a certain character string, and the directory tree display of the file list
F8	Undel	Undeletes all selected files
F9	Sort	Displays the Sort By dialog box, which enables you to sort files by name, extension, size, date, directory, and condition
F10 or Alt	Menu	Activates the horizontal menu bar
Esc	Cancel	Cancels the current process or application (same as F3)
Alt+space bar	Window Control	Displays the Window Control dialog box

By default, Undelete lists files in the File window in order by file name. Occasionally, seeing the deleted files in some other order can be more helpful. Select Options from the horizontal menu bar to display the Options menu, and then choose Sort By. Undelete displays the Sort by dialog box, shown in figure 10.16, which lists the following option buttons:

■ *Name* sorts the file list by file name. This option is the default sort order.

■ *Extension* sorts the file list by file name extension.

■ *Size* sorts the file list by file size.

■ *Deleted Date and Time* sorts the file list by the date and time the files were deleted.

■ *Modified Date and Time* sorts the file list by the date and time the files were last modified.

■ *Directory* sorts files by directory. This option is available only when Undelete is displaying the expanded file list. Undelete uses the expanded file list to display the names of deleted files on network drives and files that have been located by using the Find Deleted Files option on the File menu. Refer to the "Finding Deleted Files" section that follows.

■ *Condition* sorts the file list by the condition of the files (see the section "Undeleting Files" in this chapter).

```
┌─────────────────────────────────────┐
│ -            Sort by                 │
│           Sort files by:             │
│      (•)  Name                       │
│      ( )  Extension                  │
│      ( )  Size                       │
│      ( )  Deleted Date and Time      │
│      ( )  Modified Date and Time     │
│      ( )  Directory                  │
│      ( )  Condition                  │
│                                      │
│            OK      Cancel            │
│                                      │
└─────────────────────────────────────┘
```

Fig. 10.16

The Sort by
dialog box.

After you select an option, choose **OK**. Undelete returns to the Undelete screen and displays file names in the File window, sorted in the order you specified.

Often you may not be certain about the contents of a file listed in the File window of the Undelete screen. Undelete enables you to view the file's contents, even before you undelete the file. Use the mouse or cursor-movement keys to highlight the file you want to view, and then press F4 (View) or select **F**ile from the horizontal menu bar and choose **V**iew File from the File menu. Undelete displays the highlighted file by using PC Tools' viewers.

Finding Deleted Files

The first step toward recovering a deleted file is to determine which directory contained the file. Sometimes you realize immediately that you deleted the wrong file and you know precisely the directory that contained the file when you deleted it. On other occasions, however, you may no longer remember which directory contained the file you want to recover.

NOTE If you removed the directory that contained the deleted file, you must undelete the directory before you can undelete the file. The procedure for undeleting a directory is the same as that for undeleting a file. A deleted directory is identified in the File window by the annotation <dir> in the Size column.

When you know the name of the directory that contains the file you want to undelete, use the mouse or the Tab key to make the Directory Tree window current, and then use the mouse or the cursor-movement keys to highlight the name of the directory that contains the deleted file. The name of the file you want to recover appears in the File window on the right side of the screen.

When you do not know the directory that contains the accidentally deleted file, you can take advantage of one of Undelete's many methods for finding a deleted file. You can search the disk by file name, by search groups, by file contents, and by data type. Undelete even enables you to search for data in the unallocated sectors of the disk.

Finding Files by File Name

To search by file name, press F7 (Find) or select File on the horizontal menu bar to display the File menu, and then choose the Find Deleted Files option. Undelete displays the Find Deleted Files dialog box (see fig. 10.17).

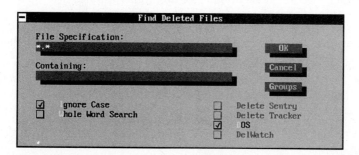

Fig. 10.17

Finding deleted files by file name.

The cursor blinks in the File Specification text box. Type one or more file specifications in the text box and separate the file specification with a space. You can use the DOS wild card characters * and ?. If you include a directory name, you limit the search to that directory. You also can exclude files that meet a certain file specification by preceding the specification with a minus sign (-).

Suppose that you want to search your disk for your family-budget spreadsheet, but you cannot remember which directory the budget was in and are not sure whether the file name was BUDGET.WKS, BUDGET.WK1, or BUDGT.WKS. Type the following in the File Specification text box:

BUDG*.WK?

You can speed up the search by specifying a directory not to be searched by placing a minus sign before the directory name. If, for example, you don't want to search the DOS or Paradox directories, you would type the following in the File Specifications dialog box:

BUDG*.WK? -\DOS*.* -\DATABASE\PDOX4*.*

Below the File Specification text box, Undelete displays the Containing text box. In the text box, type a character string of as many as 32 characters that can be found in the file. These characters represent the *search string*, the string for which you want Undelete to search. Suppose, for example, that you recall that the title at the top of the spreadsheet is *Family Spreadsheet*. You can type **family** in the Containing text box.

Below the Containing text box are six check boxes, which enable you to customize your search. These boxes are explained in the following list:

- *Ignore Case.* Choose this check box when you want Undelete to select a file that contains the search string regardless of whether the matching string matches the case (upper- or lowercase) of every character in the search string. The default value for this box is checked.

- *Whole Word Search.* Choose this check box to ignore strings contained within longer strings. For example, if *it* is the string for which you are searching, checking this option only finds *it*. The search ignores these characters within words such as w*it*h, h*it*, and so on. A string must match exactly the search string to be considered a match. The default value for this box is not checked.

- *Delete Sentry.* Choose this check box to instruct Undelete to search for files protected by the Delete Sentry delete-protection method. This check box is not available (and is grayed out) if you have not been using the Data Monitor's Delete Sentry feature.

- *Delete Tracker.* Choose this check box to cause Undelete to search for files protected by the Delete Tracker delete-protection method. This check box is not available (and is grayed out) if you have not been using the Data Monitor's Delete Tracker feature.

- *DOS.* Choose this check box to search for deleted files that have been protected by neither of the Data Monitor's two available methods (Delete Sentry and Delete Tracker).

- *DelWatch.* Choose this check box to cause Undelete to search for files protected by the DelWatch delete-protection method. This check box is not available (and is grayed out) if you have not been using DelWatch.

To initiate the search, choose **OK**. Undelete begins scanning the disk for the specified files and then searches the files for the character string. To cancel the search, press Esc and then press F7 (Tree) to return to the full Undelete window, with Directory Tree and File windows displayed.

When Undelete finishes searching the disk, the program displays the File window (see fig. 10.18). In this example, Undelete has found one file that meets both the file-specification criteria and the character-string criteria: the file BUDGT.WK1 in the directory C:\SPREADSH\LOTUS\FIN.

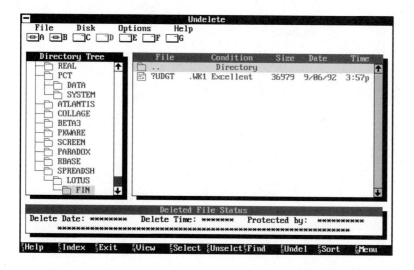

Fig. 10.18

A deleted file found by using file name search.

Finding Files by Using Predefined Search Groups

A second way of using Undelete to locate files on your hard disk is to use a predefined *search group*. The search group is predefined both by Install during installation and by you. When you install PC Tools 8, its installation program—Install—defines a search group for every application program installed in the PC Shell program list menus (refer to Chapter 3, "Using the Desktop as a Program Manager," and Appendix A, "Installing and Configuring PC Tools," for more information about that process).

From the Undelete screen, either press F7 (Find) or select **F**ile and then select **F**ind Deleted Files to display the Find Deleted Files dialog box. Select the **G**roups command button to display the Search These Groups dialog box (see fig. 10.19).

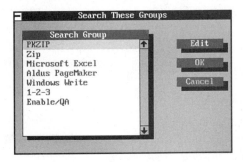

Fig. 10.19

The Search These Groups dialog box.

Notice that the example in figure 10.19 shows search groups for PKZip, Zip, Microsoft Excel, Aldus PageMaker, Windows Write, 1-2-3, and Enable/QA files. Every search group except the Enable/QA files group was created during installation by the Install program. Refer to Chapter 5, "Locating and Viewing Files," for information about adding and modifying a search group.

Use the mouse or the cursor-movement keys to highlight the appropriate search group entry for every search group you want to use for this particular search. To complete the selection, press the space bar or click the entry. Undelete highlights every entry you select in the Search These Groups list box. After you select all desired search groups, choose **OK**. Undelete returns to the Find Deleted Files dialog box and enters in the File Specification text box the file specification for every selected search group.

Press Tab or use the mouse to move the highlighted bar to the Containing text box in the Find Deleted Files dialog box. Type the string for which you want Undelete to search. You can use as many as 32 characters. To search for the family-budget spreadsheet, for example, follow these steps:

1. Select the Groups button in the Find Deleted Files dialog box. The Search These Groups dialog box appears (refer to fig. 10.19).

2. Select the 1-2-3 files search group in the Search These Groups dialog box and choose **OK**. The Search These Groups dialog box closes, and you return to the Find Deleted Files dialog box. The wild card *.WKS has been added to the File Specification text box.

3. Type **family** in the Containing text box of the Find Deleted Files dialog box, activate the appropriate check boxes, and then choose **OK**.

Undelete begins searching your hard disk for all files from the selected search groups that meet the file specifications, and then the program displays a list of located files (refer to fig. 10.18). In this case, Undelete finds only one file that has *.WK1 or *.WKS extension and the string family inside the file: BUDGT.WK1 in the C:\SPREADSH\LOTUS\FIN directory.

Scanning Free Clusters for Deleted Files

When you are unable to locate a particular file by using any of the methods described in the preceding sections, the file still may be located on the disk, in unallocated disk clusters called *free clusters*. You may need to find more than one free cluster in order to find the entire file. Undelete enables you to locate deleted files in free clusters in three ways. Select the Disk option on the horizontal menu bar to display the Disk menu, which contains the option you use to find the free clusters for a file (see fig. 10.20).

Choose one of the following menu options:

■ *Scan for Data Types* displays the Scan for Data Types dialog box, from which you choose 1-2-3 and Symphony data, dBASE data, or Normal text. Choose **OK**, and Undelete scans the entire disk looking for data that meets the selected data format.

■ *Scan for Contents* displays the Scan for Contents dialog box. Type a character string for which you want the program to search and then choose **OK**. Undelete scans the disk for free clusters that contain the specified character string.

Fig. 10.20

Three menu
options you can
use to scan for
deleted files.

■ *Scan for Lost Deleted Files* displays the Scan for Lost Files dialog
box. Select Delete Sentry, Delete Tracker, and DOS check boxes,
as appropriate, to indicate the type of delete protection you have
been using. Choose **OK**. Undelete scans the disk for clusters that
were protected by the specified delete-protection method but that
are no longer allocated to any file. Undelete first scans the Delete
Sentry file, if it exists, then the Delete Tracking file, and finally, all
free clusters. Undelete assigns a unique name to every cluster it
finds and lists the file in the Find in the Located Files list box.

You can limit the scan procedure to a specific set of clusters on the
disk by choosing the **Set Scan Range** option on the **D**isk menu. Specify a
starting cluster and an ending cluster, and then choose **OK**. By default,
the scan range includes all free clusters.

After you choose your scanning option and select **OK**, the scan begins.
When the scan is finished, the results are displayed on-screen (see
fig. 10.21). To view the contents of a file, highlight the file; then open
the **F**ile menu and choose View File. The contents appear in a window
at the bottom of the screen (see fig. 10.22). When you find a file you
want to undelete, open the **F**ile menu and choose Undelete; choose
Undelete **T**o if you want to save the file to another drive.

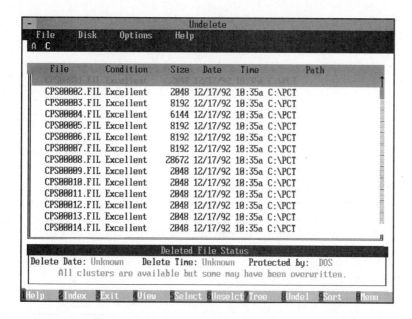

Fig. 10.21

The results of
the scan.

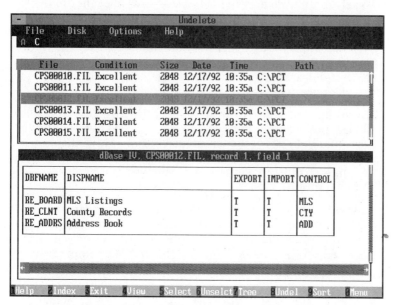

Fig. 10.22

The file contents.

Selecting Files To Undelete

After you locate the directory that contains the file you want to undelete, the next step is to select the file or files for recovery. Use the arrow keys or the mouse and the scroll bar to scroll the Directory Tree window until you see the name of the directory that contains the files you want to select. Position the mouse pointer on this directory name and press the left button. Alternatively, highlight the directory with the arrow keys and press Enter. The files for that directory appear in the File window.

Press Tab or click the File window to make the File window the current window. Use the mouse and the scroll bar or the arrow keys to scroll the File window. When the file you want is highlighted, click with the left button or press Enter. You can choose additional files by highlighting them and clicking the left mouse button. To use the keyboard to choose files, use the arrow keys to position the highlight, and then press Enter.

Use one of these procedures to select multiple files:

■ To select multiple files not listed one after the other in the File window, move the mouse pointer to the first file you want to select and click the left mouse button. Repeat this procedure for each file you want to select with the mouse. To select multiple files from the keyboard, use the arrow keys to highlight the file name and press Enter; repeat this procedure until all of the files you want are selected.

■ To scroll down quickly through the entire directory and select all files, press and hold down the right mouse button, and then press and hold down the left mouse button. Move the mouse pointer into the lower edge or right edge of the window border. Undelete scrolls the window, marking files, until you release a mouse button.

■ To scroll up quickly through the entire directory and select files, press and hold down the right mouse button, press and hold down the left mouse button, and move the mouse pointer to the upper edge or left edge of the window border. Undelete scrolls the window, marking files, until you release a mouse button.

■ To select files by name in the current directory, press F5 (Select) or select Options from the horizontal menu bar to display the Options menu and choose the Select by Name option. When Undelete displays the Select by Name dialog box, type a file name in the File Specification text box. Choose OK. Undelete selects in the current directory all files that match the file specification.

■ To select files by using the keyboard, display the Undelete screen, press Tab to make the Directory Tree window the active window, and press the cursor-movement keys to move the highlighted bar to the directory that contains the files you want to select. Press the Tab key to activate the File window. Press the cursor-movement keys to move the highlighted bar to the file you want to select or make current. Press Enter to select the file and to move the highlight to the next file.

Repeat the same procedure to *unselect* a file. To unselect all selected multiple files in one step, press F6 (Unselect) or select **O**ptions from the horizontal menu bar to display the Options menu and choose the **U**nselect by Name option. When Undelete displays the Unselect by Name dialog box, type a file specification in the File Specification text box. Choose **OK**. Undelete unselects all selected files in the current directory that match the file specification. To use the mouse to unselect all selected files, just click any directory name in the Directory Tree window, except the name of the current directory.

Undeleting Files

After you locate and select the file or files you want to recover, you are ready to attempt to undelete the file. In the File window, Undelete lists information about the file, including file name and the date and time the file was last modified. More significantly, Undelete lists in the Condition column of the File window a prognosis of recovery. The following prognoses are possible:

■ *Perfect* denotes that the deleted file is protected by the Delete Sentry. A copy of the file is stored in the hidden \SENTRY directory. Chances of recovery are 100 percent.

■ *Excellent* means that the file is protected by the Delete Tracker or by DOS. Chances of recovery are high. All clusters are available, but some data in the file may have been overwritten.

■ *Good* indicates that one or more of the file's clusters are in use by another file and some of the file's data may be overwritten.

■ *Poor* denotes that the first cluster in the file is not available. The only way to recover this data is through the Advanced Undelete option on the File menu (discussed later in this chapter).

■ *Destroyed* indicates that all clusters of the file are in use by other files, which means that the file's data probably has been overwritten. Recovering some of the data may be possible, but only through the Advanced Undelete option.

■ *None* means that you have used the Scan feature to locate data, and the program has created this file from a previously deleted cluster.

■ *Existing* indicates that the file is not deleted. Undelete lists existing files when you toggle on the Show Existing Files option on the Options menu.

■ *Lost File* means that the deleted file no longer is assigned to a directory, probably because the directory is also deleted.

■ *Recovered* denotes that the file has been undeleted during the current session.

■ *Purged* indicates that the file has been purged from the Delete Sentry directory during the current session.

In addition to displaying information about the deleted files in the File window, Undelete enables you to display information about the selected file in a dialog box. Select **F**ile, and then choose File **I**nfo from the File menu. Undelete displays the File Information dialog box, which lists the following information about the selected file:

File name

File size

Directory path

Date the file was last modified

Date the file was deleted

First cluster

File condition

Delete-protection method

The File Information dialog box also indicates whether any clusters in the file have already been reallocated. Choose **OK** to return to the Undelete screen.

Using the Automatic Method

When the condition of a file is Perfect, Excellent, or Good, you can use the *automatic method* of recovering files. Press F8 (Undel), or select **F**ile to display the File menu, and then select **U**ndelete. For every file for which Undelete is successful, the program displays `Recovered` in the Condition column.

If you are not using the Delete Tracker or Data Sentry to protect against accidental file deletion, and if the condition of a file is Excellent or Good, you still can use the automatic method of undeletion. Undelete displays the Enter First Character dialog box (see fig. 10.23). A message in this dialog box indicates that the original first letter of the file name was destroyed by DOS when you deleted the file. Undelete displays a question mark character in place of the missing first character. To recover the files, you must type a new letter in place of the question mark (?). After you type a letter, choose **OK**. The program returns to the Undelete screen and displays the word Recovered in the condition column.

Using the Manual Method

When the file you want to recover is listed in Poor or Destroyed condition, you cannot use the automatic method to undelete the file. You still can attempt to undelete the file, however, by using the *manual undelete method.*

To access the manual-undelete method, follow the steps to find and select the files you want to recover (described earlier in this chapter). Select **F**ile from the horizontal menu bar to display the File menu, and then choose **A**dvanced Undelete to display the Advanced Undelete submenu. Select the **M**anual Undelete option on the submenu.

If you were not using either Delete Sentry or Delete Tracker at the time the file in question was deleted, Undelete displays the Enter First Character dialog box (refer to fig. 10.23). Supply the first character in the file name and choose **OK**.

Undelete next displays the Manual Undelete dialog box (see fig. 10.24). This dialog box lists in its upper left quadrant the file name, the current file size (this value grows as you build the file), file date, file time, and next available cluster. The dialog box also contains a List of Added Clusters list box, which indicates the file's starting cluster, the number of clusters needed to match the original FAT entry, and the number of clusters you have added so far in the manual-undelete session.

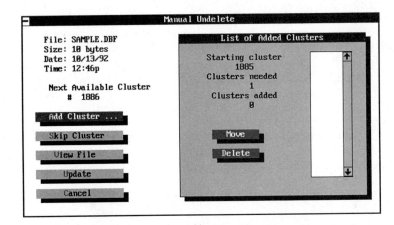

Fig. 10.24

The Manual
Undelete dialog
box.

The Manual Undelete dialog box lists the following command buttons:

- **Add Cluster** displays the Cluster Options dialog box, shown in figure 10.25, which enables you to add, view, and scan clusters for a specific character string. Through the Cluster Options dialog box, you automatically add to the file the same number of clusters as were listed originally in the FAT for this file; or you can add clusters manually according to the contents you find in every successive cluster. Every time you add a cluster, Undelete adds the cluster to the file in memory and moves to the next cluster.

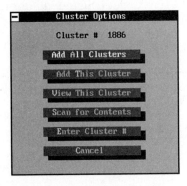

Fig. 10.25

The Cluster
Options dialog
box.

- **Skip Cluster** skips the current cluster and moves to the next cluster, without adding the current cluster to the file.

- **View File** displays the contents of the clusters that you have added to the file so far.

- *Update* saves to disk all the clusters added to the file in memory and updates the FAT. Undelete returns to the Undelete screen and displays Recovered in the Condition column for the manually undeleted file.

- *Cancel* ends the attempt to undelete a file.

- *Move* enables you to move a cluster in the cluster box after you have added the cluster.

- *Delete* enables you to delete a cluster from the cluster list.

After you manually undelete a file, you may discover that a portion of the file is still missing. Undelete, therefore, enables you to add clusters to an existing file. Select the existing file in the File window, and select the **A**ppend to Existing File option on the **A**dvanced Undelete submenu (which you access through the File menu). Undelete displays the Append To a File dialog box, which is virtually identical to the Manual Undelete dialog box discussed earlier (refer to fig. 10.24). Use the options listed in this dialog box to add the missing clusters to the existing file, and then choose **U**pdate. Undelete appends the newly added clusters to the end of the existing file and returns to the Undelete screen.

 NOTE If the file to which you want to add clusters is not listed in the File window, choose the **Sh**ow Existing Files command on the **O**ptions menu to list the names of all existing files.

Using the Create-File Method

Sometimes a file does not show up on the list of deleted files displayed by Undelete. When this situation occurs and you believe the data may still be on the disk, you can make a last-ditch effort to find the lost data by using the *create-file method.*

The create-file method is feasible only when the contents of the file can be identified easily. Most often, only ASCII text files can be recovered successfully with this method. But because many PC-based word processing programs store text mostly as displayable ASCII characters, the create-file method may be worth the effort. This method enables you to recover the file contents, but you may not be able to recover the file header, which contains the formatting information. After you create a new document, you can read the document back into the word processor and format it.

First, make current the drive and directory that you believe contain the missing file. Then open the **F**ile menu and select **A**dvance Undelete to display the Advanced Undelete submenu; select **C**reate a File. Undelete displays a dialog box containing the message Enter the name of the file you wish to create. Type the name and extension in the text box and choose **OK**. Undelete displays the Create a File dialog box, which also is nearly identical in appearance to the Manual Undelete dialog box (refer to fig. 10.24). Refer to the "Using the Manual Method" section earlier in this chapter for a discussion of this dialog box.

Undeleting a Directory

If you use your computer daily, you probably attempt to periodically "tidy up" your computer's hard disk by deleting unneeded files and then removing unused directories. This practice, although necessary to provide room for new programs and files, can sometimes result in accidental deletion of a file you still need. Before you can restore a deleted file that was contained in a directory you removed, you first must restore the directory.

> **NOTE** These procedures are used for accidents only. Do not allow recovery methods to take the place of a proper backup.

Undeleting a directory is nearly the same as undeleting a file. Depending on the method of deletion protection you are using (Delete Tracker, Delete Sentry, or none), you may have to provide the first letter of the directory's name. Use the mouse or the cursor-movement keys to make current the directory that contained the deleted subdirectory. Use the cursor-movement keys or the mouse to highlight the File window entry for the directory you want to recover. (*Note:* You can identify directory entries by the value <dir> in the Condition column.) Press F8 (Undel) or display the File menu and select Undelete. If you are prompted, type the first letter of the directory name, and then choose **OK**. Undelete recovers the directory and adds the name to the directory tree.

After you have recovered the deleted directory, you can proceed to recover deleted files from that directory.

Undeleting Files on a Network

You can undelete files on network drives, provided that the files were protected by either Delete Sentry or Novell NetWare 386 and that you have CREATE rights to the directory where the deleted file is located. The deleted files are shown in an expanded files list. Network directories that are hidden will not appear unless you change the hidden attribute. If you are using Delete Sentry, you see only those files deleted using your current user name. If you are using Novell NetWare 386, you see all deleted files. Undelete works only if one of these delete-protection methods was used.

The following commands are not available if you are undeleting files on a network drive:

Tree & File List Advanced Undelete (File menu)

All commands (Disk menu)

Show Existing Files Use Mirror File (Options menu)

Purging Delete Sentry Files

By keeping a copy of deleted files, the Delete Sentry does a great job of protecting you against inadvertent deletion of files. Depending on how you configure this utility (see Appendix A, "Installing and Configuring PC Tools"), Delete Sentry keeps deleted files for a set number of days (the default is seven days) or until the available disk space is full. (By default, the Delete Sentry directory is limited to 20 percent of the disk's storage capacity.) After the specified number of days has elapsed or when the reserved disk space is full, the oldest files are *purged*—permanently erased.

At times, however, you may need to purge some of the files in the Delete Sentry to make room for more files or, for security reasons, to permanently erase certain files in the Delete Sentry directory. The Undelete program provides the capability to purge Delete Sentry files.

Use the methods described earlier in this chapter for finding and selecting the files you want to purge from the Delete Sentry directory. After you select the files, choose the File option on the Undelete screen's horizontal menu bar and select Purge Delete Sentry File. Undelete displays the Purge File dialog box, which displays this warning:

```
         Warning!

   Files purged from Delete Sentry may
   no longer be recoverable.

   Choose Purge to purge selected file.
   Choose Purge All to purge all files
   currently protected by Delete Sentry
   on this drive.
```

Choose **P**urge to purge the Delete Sentry files you have selected on the Undelete screen, or choose Purge **A**ll to permanently erase all files that are protected.

Quitting Undelete

When you finish recovering deleted files, press Esc or F3 (Exit) and choose **O**K; alternatively, choose the **F**ile option on the Undelete window's horizontal menu bar to display the File menu, and then select E**x**it. Undelete closes the Undelete screen and returns to DOS.

FROM HERE...

For Related Information

◄◄ "Adding a Search Group Entry," p. 178.

◄◄ "Editing a Search Group Entry," p. 178.

Chapter Summary

This chapter describes how to recover damaged and deleted files. You learn how to use FileFix to recover damaged files and how to repair dBASE files, 1-2-3, Symphony, and other files. This chapter also explains how to use Undelete to recover deleted files. You learned how to find deleted files by file name, by predefined search group, and by scanning free clusters for deleted files. You also learned how to select files for recovery, as well as how to use the automatic method, the manual method, and the create-file method to undelete files. Finally, you learned how to undelete a directory and how to purge a Delete Sentry entry.

Now that you understand how to recover damaged or accidentally deleted files, look at Chapter 11, "Recovering Damaged or Formatted Disks," for information about how to recover usable data from damaged disks and from accidentally formatted disks.

Recovering Damaged or Formatted Disks

The PC Tools utility programs Mirror, PC Format, Unformat, FileCheck, and DiskFix are potentially the most important power tools in the PC Tools 8.0 toolbox. Working as a team, Mirror, PC Format (discussed in Chapter 6, "Working on Disks"), and Unformat enable you to recover data accidentally erased by the DOS FORMAT or RECOVER command. FileCheck enables you to spot potential problems by searching for lost file fragments; with the easy-to-use DiskFix utility, you can recover damaged hard disk partition and boot-sector information, restore "forgotten" CMOS setup data, and solve many other disk-related problems.

This chapter begins by explaining how to run Mirror daily to make a safe copy of your hard disk's file allocation table (FAT) and root directory. The chapter also explains how to use Mirror to make a copy of a hard disk's partition table and boot sector as well as your computer's CMOS setup and how to use an emergency disk. Next you learn how to use Unformat to recover data lost because you accidentally formatted a disk. Then you see how to use the FileCheck program to check for lost file fragments caused by the unformat process. The final section of the chapter shows you how to use DiskFix to restore partition, boot-sector, and CMOS data and how to solve other types of disk-related problems.

> **NOTE**   The Rebuild command no longer exists. Use the Diskfix command with the /Rebuild parameter instead.

Using Mirror

The PC Tools program Mirror has a twofold purpose: Mirror can help you recover an accidentally formatted hard disk, and it can save a copy of every hard drive's partition table, CMOS data, and boot-sector data to a floppy disk for safekeeping. The sections that follow describe both uses of Mirror.

> **NOTE**   Both the version of Mirror distributed in PC Tools Version 6 and a similar version of the program included with MS-DOS 5.0 are used to initiate *delete tracking*, a memory-resident utility that keeps a log of deleted files for the purpose of facilitating the recovery of an accidentally deleted file. The Mirror program included with PC Tools 8.0 does not handle delete tracking, however, because that job is done by PC Tools 8.0's new Delete Tracker program. See Appendix A, "Installing and Configuring PC Tools," for a discussion of installing and configuring Delete Tracker with the Data Monitor program. In addition to tracking deleted files, Data Monitor handles directory-locking, write-protecting, and screen-blanking duties.

The syntax of the Mirror start-up command is as follows (parameters in *italics* are optional):

> MIRROR *d1: d2: ... dn: /1 /PARTN /NOCMOS /?*

The MIRROR /? command displays a short help screen giving brief descriptions of available parameters (see fig. 11.1).

```
C:>mirror/?

Records information about one or more disks.

MIRROR [drive:[ ...]][/1][/Tdrive[-entries][...]]

MIRROR [/U]

MIRROR [/PARTN]

drive:    Specifies the drive for which you want to save information.

/1        Saves only the lastest disk information (does not back up previous information)

/Tdrive   Loads the deletion-tracking program for the specified drive.

-entries  Specifies the maximum number of entries in the deletion-tracking file.

/U        Unloads the deletion-tracking program.

/PARTN    Saves hard disk partition to a floppy diskette.

MIRROR, UNDELETE, and UNFORMAT copyright  1987-1991 Central Point Software, Inc.

C:>
```

The Mirror help screen.

Each parameter is covered in more detail in one of the following sections.

Saving System Information to the Mirror-Image File

You can use Mirror to make a copy of your hard disk's file allocation table (FAT) and root directory. Mirror saves this information to disk in a file named MIRROR.FIL, called the *mirror-image file*. Armed with the data stored in MIRROR.FIL, the companion program Unformat can recover an accidentally formatted hard disk.

NOTE   Some versions of FORMAT *are* destructive—notably COMPAQ's MS-DOS Version 3.2 and earlier, AT&T's MS-DOS Version 3.1 and earlier, and some versions of MS-DOS supplied by Burroughs. These versions of FORMAT erase not only the FAT, root directory, and boot record, but also all data on the hard disk. These commands erase the mirror-image file created by Mirror along with all other files on the hard disk. Afterward, Unformat is unable to recover (unformat) the hard disk. Unformat can unformat an accidentally formatted disk with the PC Tools program PC Format. By default, therefore, the PC Tools installation program renames any FORMAT command to FORMAT! and replaces the command with the PC Tools program PCFORMAT.COM.

When you format a hard disk in most versions of DOS, using the FOR-MAT command does not destroy existing data. Rather, the FORMAT command clears the FAT and the root directory, leaving all data intact. Thus, if you have used the Mirror program to save to the mirror-image file an extra copy of the FAT and the root directory, Unformat can recover from an accidental use of FORMAT by restoring that copy of the FAT and root directory.

T I P   All versions of DOS FORMAT before DOS 5 are destructive when you format a floppy disk. Unformat can recover a floppy disk only if you were using PC Format or DOS 5's FORMAT when you accidentally formatted the disk.

Run Mirror to save your hard disk's FAT and root directory at least every time you turn on the computer. The easiest way to do so is to run the program from the AUTOEXEC.BAT file. During the installation of PC Tools, you are presented with an option to run Mirror every time you turn on the computer. Choose this option to install Mirror in your AUTOEXEC.BAT file. Refer to Appendix A, "Installing and Configuring PC Tools," for a discussion of Install and the AUTOEXEC.BAT file.

By default, Install adds a command to the AUTOEXEC.BAT file that causes Mirror to save the FAT and root directory of the boot disk to the MIRROR.FIL file. If you have more than one hard disk or have partitioned your hard disk into more than one logical drive, you have to edit the AUTOEXEC.BAT file to specify which additional drives Mirror should process.

In the Mirror start-up command, *d:* denotes the drive you want Mirror to process. If you don't specify a drive, Mirror processes the current drive. The following command causes Mirror to save drive C's FAT and root directory:

MIRROR C:

To save drive D's FAT and root directory as well as those for drive C, type this command and then press Enter:

MIRROR C: D:

Mirror places a separate copy of MIRROR.FIL on every drive. Mirror saves drive C's FAT and root directory in C:\MIRROR.FIL and drive D's FAT and root directory in D:\MIRROR.FIL. You can specify as many drives as you want.

The parameter /1 in the start-up command enables you to turn off the default feature that normally causes Mirror to keep two copies of MIRROR.FIL. By default, when you run Mirror, it renames the most recent copy of MIRROR.FIL to MIRROR.BAK and overwrites the previous copy of MIRROR.BAK. Unless you are running severely short on disk space, do not use the /1 parameter to circumvent this backup process. The earlier copy of MIRROR.FIL, stored as MIRROR.BAK, provides additional assurance that you can restore the hard disk after an accidental erasure. Having two Mirror files enables you to recover your disk if Mirror is run after the hard disk is formatted or if some other disaster occurs. If MIRROR is run after the hard disk is formatted, the MIRROR.FIL file would contain garbage, and you would need the earlier version of the file, MIRROR.BAK, to reclaim your data.

> If you accidentally format a hard disk, do not run Mirror again before using Unformat to recover the deleted files. Refer to the "Using Unformat" section of this chapter for more information.
>
> **T I P**

Saving the Partition Table, CMOS Data, and Boot Sector

As a part of the initial setup of your computer, the DOS program FDISK was used to create one or more partitions on every hard disk in your system. A *partition* is a section of a hard disk set aside for use as a unit. You must have at least one DOS partition on your computer, but you can have more than one. You can have one or more partitions set up for use with another operating system, such as UNIX. DOS stores partition information in a file called the *partition table*. If the partition table is damaged, DOS cannot locate any files on the disk.

IBM PC AT computers, IBM PS/2 computers, and compatibles store information about the computer's hardware configuration—hard disk type and size, video adapter type, memory configuration, and so on—in a battery-powered device called a CMOS (Complementary Metal-Oxide Semiconductor) device. Occasionally, your computer may "forget" the contents of the CMOS—perhaps because of a weak or dead battery.

The second purpose of Mirror, therefore, is to save a copy of the partition table, the boot sector, and the CMOS data to a floppy disk for safekeeping. If your computer does not boot or indicates an error or inconsistency in the CMOS setup, you can use the disk created by Mirror to recover the partition table, boot disk, or CMOS data as needed. The DiskFix program then can restore the CMOS, boot sector, and hard disk partition in case one or more of these essential elements of your computer system are somehow lost or damaged.

NOTE Mirror can save standard DOS partition tables only. Some hard disk manufacturers distribute special start-up programs with large hard disks that create nonstandard partitions. The programs Disk Manager (from On-Track) and SpeedStor (from Storage Dimensions) are examples of programs that create partition information Mirror cannot save to a floppy.

To save the partition, boot-sector, and CMOS information to a floppy disk, type this command at the DOS command line and press Enter:

MIRROR /PARTN

If you decide that you don't want the program to save the CMOS data, add the switch /NOCMOS.

When you execute this command, Mirror displays these messages:

```
Mirror V8 1987-1992 Central Point Software, Inc.

Disk Partition Table saver.

The partition information from your hard drive(s) has
been read.

Next, the file PARTNSAV.FIL will be written to a floppy
disk. Please insert a formatted diskette and enter the
name of the diskette drive.

What drive? A
```

Place a formatted disk, preferably your Emergency Disk, in a floppy disk drive, type the letter that denotes the floppy drive, and press Enter. (For drive A, just press Enter.) Mirror saves to the floppy disk, in a file named PARTNSAV.FIL, the partition table, boot-sector information, and CMOS information. Put this disk in a safe place so that the data is available if the hard disk partition table, boot sector, or CMOS information is lost or damaged. Refer to the "Using DiskFix" section in this chapter for instructions on how to restore this information.

You must repeat this MIRROR /PARTN routine whenever you use FDISK to change your hard disk's partition information or make a change to the CMOS setup (because you have added memory to your computer, for example).

For Related Information

◄◄ "Formatting a Disk," p. 202.

FROM HERE...

Using the Emergency Disk

During the PC Tools 8.0 installation process, the installation program gives you the opportunity to create an Emergency Disk (see Chapter 6, "Working on Disks"). Assuming that you have created an Emergency Disk, you can make use of the disk in several ways. Using the Emergency Disk, you can conveniently boot your computer from a floppy disk when your hard disk fails to operate properly or when you simply want to start the computer without loading all the device drivers and memory-resident programs that normally are loaded by the CONFIG.SYS and AUTOEXEC.BAT files.

Most significantly, however, the Emergency Disk enables you to rebuild your hard disk's boot sector and partition table. If either area of a disk is corrupted or damaged to the extent that the operating system no longer can read its contents, you lose the use of the hard disk. If you have handy the Emergency Disk (or another disk that contains the file PARTNSAV.FIL created by the Mirror command), you probably can recover the lost information and regain access to the data on the hard disk.

> If you didn't create an Emergency Disk during installation, you still can. Turn to Chapter 6, "Working on Disks," for instructions.
>
> **T I P**

The Emergency Disk created by Install contains the files listed in table 11.1.

Table 11.1 Contents of the Emergency Disk

File	Description
ADVICE.HLP	Contains on-line troubleshooting information that is displayed when you choose the Advice option on the DiskFix Main Menu screen.
AUTOEXEC.BAT	Not a copy of the AUTOEXEC.BAT file from your hard disk, the Emergency Disk version contains only these lines:

continues

Table 11.1 Continued

File	Description
| | ```
@echo off
echo
echo
echo Central Point Emergency
  Disk V8.0
echo
echo This disk was created
  10/01/92 at 6:04a
echo
echo on
prompt $P$G
``` |
| COMMAND.COM | The DOS command interpreter. |
| CONFIG.SYS | Not a copy of the configuration file from your hard disk, the CONFIG.SYS file stored on the Emergency Disk contains only these two lines:<br><br>```
files=35
buffers=35
``` |
CPAV.EXE, CPAV.HLP	Central Point's Anti-Virus program and the help file for it. The Anti-Virus program is explained in Chapter 14, "Protecting Your System with CP Anti-Virus."
CPSCOLOR.DAT	Contains global configuration settings for PC Tools programs.
CPSHELP.OVL	The engine for all on-line help.
CPSMAIN.FNT	Contains the screen font used to display information in many of these utilities.
CPSMM.BIN	Enables specific PC Tools programs to access expanded memory.
DE.EXE, DE.HLP	DiskEdit files that enable you to view and edit the data on your disk at the cluster and byte level. See Chapter 12, "Editing a Disk with DiskEdit," for complete instructions.
DISKFIX.EXE, DISKFIX.OV1, DISKFIX.OV2, DISKFIX.OV3, DISKFIX.HLP	The PC Tools 8.0 DiskFix program, which is discussed later in this chapter, and the overlays and help needed to make the program work.

File	Description
FDISK.EXE	Contains DOS's Fixed Disk Setup program, which you can use to create a partition or change the active partition. See your DOS manual for a complete explanation.
IO.SYS, MSDOS.SYS (or IBMBIO.COM, IBMDOS.COM)	The DOS hidden system files.
LIBPCTOO.DLO	Contains information needed by several PC Tools utilities.
MI.COM	A Memory Info file that displays a summary of how your memory is being used. See Chapter 9, "Obtaining System Information," for complete details.
PARTNSAV.FIL	Created by Mirror to contain a copy of the hard disk's partition table and boot sector, as well as a copy of the computer's CMOS contents.
PCFORMAT.EXE	The PC Format engine. PC Shell accesses this program.
SYS.COM	Contains the DOS program that can install the DOS system files and command interpreter on a disk to make the disk bootable.
UNDEL.EXE, UNDEL.HLP	The PC Tools 8.0 program that enables you to recover accidentally deleted files on a disk and the help file for this program. Undelete is discussed in Chapter 10, "Recovering Damaged or Deleted Files."
UNFORMAT.EXE	The PC Tools 8.0 program that enables you to recover accidentally formatted files from a disk. Unformat is discussed in the next section of this chapter.
VIRULIST.CPS	Contains virus information that is used by Central Point's Anti-Virus program. See Chapter 14, "Protecting Your System with CP Anti-Virus," for more details on keeping this virus list up-to-date.

When you want to boot from a floppy disk, either because your hard disk is not functioning or because you want to boot without loading drivers and memory-resident programs, place the Emergency Disk in floppy drive A and *boot* your computer (turn the computer power on or, if the power already is on, press Ctrl+Alt+Del). Your computer and DOS run through the normal start-up procedures.

After you boot the computer with the Emergency Disk, you can use any program on the disk to attempt to remedy the problem that exists. See the discussions in this chapter on using Unformat and DiskFix. Consult your DOS manual for assistance in using SYS to transfer DOS system files.

Using Unformat

Sooner or later it happens to virtually every PC user. You accidentally format a disk. PC Tools Unformat is your best hope for undoing the damage.

Ideally, you will never need to use the Unformat program. Because it completely rebuilds your hard disk's FAT, root directory, and boot record, use Unformat only as a last resort. If you accidentally delete a file, use the Undelete program to recover it. To recover from a crashed hard disk, scrambled file, or physical damage to the disk, use DiskFix (covered later in this chapter). If you accidentally format an entire disk, however, you must use Unformat to recover the data that was on the disk. The degree of success you have in completely recovering all files depends partly on whether and how recently you ran Mirror. It also depends on which program you used when you accidentally formatted the disk.

> **CAUTION:** If the disk you accidentally formatted contains PC Tools and Unformat, you must use a copy of Unformat on another disk. *Do not install PC Tools on the problem hard disk* because the PC Tools files overwrite files you want to recover. Do not copy or save files of any kind to the reformatted hard disk. If you must reboot the computer, use a bootable floppy disk. *Do not install DOS on the formatted hard disk before using Unformat after an accidental format.*

Recovering from an Accidental Format by Using the Mirror-Image File

Suppose that you have just accidentally formatted a disk (or inadvertently used the DOS RECOVER command). Now is the time to use Unformat. If you formatted the disk with PC Format (or DOS 5.0's

FORMAT) or have been routinely running Mirror on the disk, Unformat can use the information stored in the file MIRROR.FIL to restore the FAT, root directory, and boot record to the state they were in when MIRROR.FIL was created.

> **CAUTION:** Do not reboot from an accidentally formatted hard disk. If you must reboot the computer, do so only from a floppy disk, such as the Emergency Disk created during PC Tools 8.0 installation. Do not copy any files to the hard disk. Run Unformat from the floppy disk instead to restore the hard disk's files.

To use the Unformat command to unformat an accidentally formatted disk on which you have recently run Mirror or a disk that was format-ted with PC Format (or DOS 5.0's FORMAT), insert your Emergency disk, type the following command at the DOS command line, and press Enter:

UNFORMAT *d*:

Substitute the drive designation for *d* in this command. Unformat loads itself into memory and first displays the Drive Selection dialog box (see fig. 11.2). The drive you specified in the start-up command should be selected already. If so, press Enter. Otherwise, select the drive you want to unformat and choose **OK**.

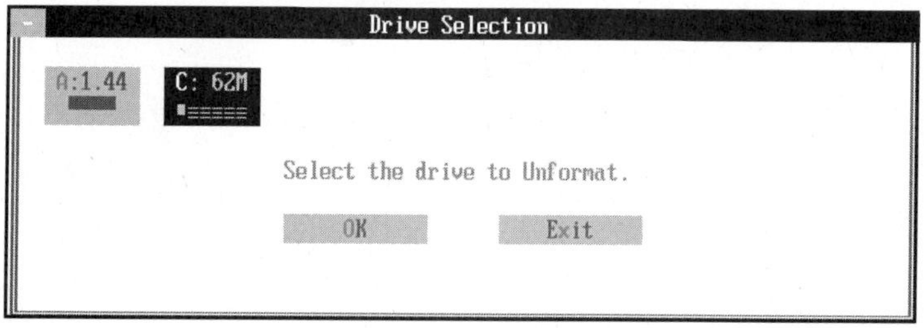

Fig. 11.2

The Drive Selection dialog box.

Next, Unformat displays the Mirror Used? dialog box, which asks whether you used Mirror to make a copy of the system area for the selected drive (see fig. 11.3). If you have been using Mirror or if you formatted the disk with either PC Format or DOS 5.0's FORMAT (or if you don't know), choose the **Y**es command button. (If you have not used Mirror, choose the **N**o command button and refer to the following section, "Recovering from an Accidental Format without Using the Mirror-Image File," for further instructions.)

Fig. 11.3

The Mirror Used?
dialog box.

After you indicate that you used Mirror, Unformat examines the target disk's current directory. If Unformat discovers that you added files to the disk since you formatted the disk, the program displays the Files Found on Drive C: dialog box, which lists the added files (see fig. 11.4). The dialog box informs you that the program will purge the listed files. If this result is not what you intend, choose the **C**ancel command button, use the DOS Copy command to copy the existing files to another disk, and start the Unformat operation again. Otherwise, to continue with the Unformat operation, choose **OK**.

Fig. 11.4

The Files Found
on Drive C:
dialog box.

Next, Unformat searches the disk for mirror-image files and displays the Unformat screen (see fig. 11.5).

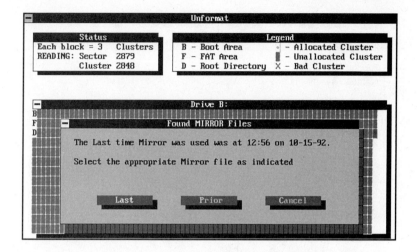

Fig. 11.5

The Unformat
screen.

Choose one of the following command buttons from the bottom of the dialog box:

- *Last* tells Unformat to use the most recent copy of the mirror-image file—MIRROR.FIL—to restore the files on the target disk.

- *Prior* tells Unformat to use the previous copy of the mirror-image file—MIRROR.BAK—to restore the files on the target disk. (Remember that Unformat maintains a backup copy of the MIRROR.FIL file, stored on disk as MIRROR.BAK, which is the file created the previous time you ran Mirror.) Use this option if you have inadvertently run Mirror since you accidentally formatted the hard disk (because MIRROR.FIL contains the newly formatted system area rather than the system area as it existed before the format).

- *Cancel* returns you to DOS without restoring the target disk.

As it restores the files on the target disk, Unformat indicates its progress in a growing horizontal bar near the top of the screen (see fig. 11.6). Finally, Unformat displays the Unformatting dialog box, as shown in figure 11.7, indicating that unformatting is complete. Choose **E**xit to return to the DOS command line. Then reboot your computer and use the **R**epair a Disk option of DiskFix to make sure that the file allocation tables are error-free (see "Repairing a Disk" later in this chapter).

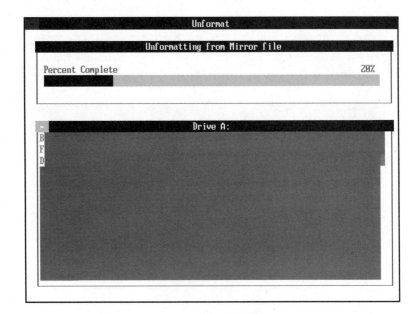

Fig. 11.6

Unformat indicating its progress with a horizontal bar.

Fig. 11.7

The Unformatting dialog box.

Recovering from an Accidental Format without Using the Mirror-Image File

For versions of DOS before DOS 5, the Unformat program still may be able to recover most of the otherwise lost data (for hard disks only), even if you have not used Mirror before accidentally using the DOS FORMAT command. This process takes more time, however. Unformat can recover an accidentally formatted floppy disk only if you were using PC Format or DOS 5 when you accidentally formatted this disk.

Keep in mind that because the DOS FORMAT command in DOS 4.01 and earlier versions deletes the root directory, Unformat cannot recover any root-level files and must rename all root-level subdirectories. To attempt to unformat an accidentally formatted hard disk on which you have not run Mirror, type this command at the DOS command line and press Enter:

    UNFORMAT *d*:

Replace *d*: with the drive designator of the accidentally formatted hard disk.

Next, Unformat displays a dialog box that asks whether you used Mirror to make a copy of the system area for the selected drive. Choose the **N**o command button to indicate that you have not used Mirror on the disk you want to recover.

If Unformat discovers that you added files to the disk since you format-ted the disk, the program displays a dialog box listing the added files and informing you that the program will purge the listed files. If this result is not what you intend, choose the **C**ancel command button, copy the existing files to another disk, and start the Unformat operation again. Otherwise, to continue with the Unformat operation, choose **OK**.

Unformat begins searching the disk for files, and displays this message:

    `Analyzing disk for lost files and directories`

Unformat graphically depicts the search in a screen similar to the one shown in figure 11.8.

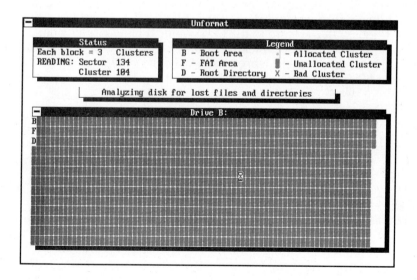

Fig. 11.8

Searching the disk for lost files and directories.

After Unformat completes its search of the hard disk data, the program displays a warning:

```
Warning! The next phase of the operation writes to
disk.
Are you SURE you want to continue?
```

To proceed with the Unformat operation, choose **OK**. Unformat then begins checking for file fragmentation. If you have not used a program such as the PC Tools program Compress to unfragment the files on your hard disk, many files on the disk are undoubtedly stored in several different sections of the hard disk (refer to Chapter 8, "Speeding Up Your Hard Disk with Compress"). When Unformat locates such a fragmented file, the program has no way to find the next segment of the file, so you are offered these choices:

- *Delete* marks the next fragmented file as deleted and continues to search. After the Unformat operation is complete, you may be able to use the Undelete command to recover the file.

- *Delete All* deletes all fragmented files. After the Unformat operation is complete, you may be able to use the Undelete command to recover these files.

- *Truncate* recovers the first block of contiguous data in the next fragmented file and then continues to search.

- *Truncate All* recovers the first block of contiguous data in every fragmented file on the disk.

After you make a choice, Unformat proceeds to recover files on the disk. When Unformat is finished, it tells you the number of files recovered. Choose **OK** to return to the DOS command line. At this point, most files that were not truncated or deleted by the procedures discussed in the preceding list are intact. Use the Undelete program to recover files deleted by Unformat.

NOTE Unformat may include in a file data that doesn't belong to that file. This situation can happen when the file was fragmented into two blocks of data that at some point were separated on the disk by data from another file. The other file was deleted later, leaving an unallocated space. This space could appear to Unformat to be a part of the file. The only way to discover this type of error is to use the file (run the program or display the file contents).

For Related Information

◀◀ "Starting Compress," p. 314.

◀◀ "Using Compress Options," p. 322.

FROM HERE...

Checking for Problems with FileCheck

FileCheck diagnoses potential disk problems in a complementary fashion to the DOS CHKDSK command. FileCheck looks for disk fragmentation, lost clusters, cross-linked files, file allocation table errors, and the percentage of files that need to be backed up. You can use FileCheck periodically to examine the "health" of your disk, or you can set up the program in batch files to alert you to potential problems, such as file fragmentation exceeding five percent. (If you set up FileCheck in this manner, for example, it then reminds you to run Compress.)

To start FileCheck, type this command at the DOS command line and press Enter:

FILECHK *d*:

Replace *d*: with the drive designator of the drive you want to check. FileCheck then scans the disk. Messages flash on-screen, and then a report similar to the following appears:

```
File Check 1992 Central Point Software, Inc.

76 files found with the Archive bit set.
8 files found with fragmentation.
18 total fragments found on the disk.
4 percent of total disk fragmentation.

File Check Complete!
```

FileCheck has a number of command-line options that enable you to pinpoint the information you want. You can use these options in any combination as long as you start each one with a slash. These command-line options are described in table 11.2.

Table 11.2 Using FileCheck's Options

Option	Description
/ARC	Changes the last line of the report to show the percentage of files that need to be backed up.
/BATCH	Gives a list of FileCheck return codes and a sample batch file showing how to use these codes to start up other PC Tools utilities.
/LIST	Shows the names of files that are fragmented and the number of fragments per file.
/P	Pauses the display after the screen has filled. Handy for using with /LIST if you have a large fragmented hard disk.
/Q	Switches to quiet mode, which does not print anything to the screen. You may want to use this option if you are running FileCheck from a batch file.
/?	Displays on-screen help for options.

If instead of learning the percentage of file fragmentation, for example, you want to know the percentage of files that have their archive bit on and, therefore, need to be backed up, type this command and press Enter:

FILECHK *d*: /ARC

The report resembles the following:

```
File Check 1992 Central Point Software, Inc.

76 files found with the Archive bit set.
8 files found with fragmentation.
18 total fragments found on the disk.
85 percent of total files have their Archive bit set.

File Check Complete!
```

To see the names of files that have fragments and, therefore, need to be compressed, type this command:

FILECHK *d*: /LIST /P

The report resembles the following:

```
File Check 1992 Central Point Software, Inc.

NEWS2   .STY    2 fragments
BALLOON .PFN    2 fragments
BALLOON .CAR    2 fragments
```

```
BIPLANE .CAR      3 fragments
NEW2    .STY      2 fragments
NOVX    .DOC      3 fragments
SERGEANT.ARM      2 fragments
4MORE   .DOC      2 fragments

76 files found with the Archive bit set.
8 files found with fragmentation.
18 total fragments found on the disk.
4 percent of total disk fragmentation.

File Check Complete!
```

You can create a FileCheck batch file to use as part of your file maintenance program. In this batch file, you can tell FileCheck to check the status of your disk and to run the Compress utility if the percentage of fragmented files is above a certain number; to run DiskFix if cross-linked files, lost clusters, or mismatched file allocation table entries are found; and to run CP Backup if the percentage of unarchived files is above a certain amount.

As FileCheck runs, it emits DOS error-level return codes that are kept internally by DOS's COMMAND.COM. These codes are not shown on-screen but are available to batch programs. Therefore, if FileCheck finds a problem, the FileCheck batch file can take action to correct it. Table 11.3 provides a list of the error codes and their meanings.

Table 11.3 Error Codes Produced by FileCheck

Error Code	Meaning
0	No fragmentation, errors, or archived files (if you specified the /ARC option)
1-100	A percentage of the number of fragmented files or, if you specified the /ARC option, the percentage of files with the archive bit on
101	Cross-linked files found
102	Lost cluster found
103	Mismatched file allocation tables

The following is a simple example of a FileCheck batch file:

```
c:\pctools\FILECHK C:
if errorlevel 101 goto run_diskfix
c: \pctools\FILECHK C:
if errorlevel 102 goto run_diskfix
```

```
c: \pctools\FILECHK C:
if errorlevel 103 goto run_diskfix
c: \pctools\FILECHK C:
if errorlevel 10 goto run_compress
goto endit
:run_diskfix
c:\pctools\diskfix
goto endit
:run_compress
c:\pctools\compress
:endit
```

Using DiskFix

DiskFix is a deceptively easy program to use—deceptive because its ease of use belies its power. You can use this program to fix a multitude of hard and floppy disk problems. If you are having trouble with your hard disk or your computer will not start, put your Emergency Disk in drive A and then restart your computer. You may also want to use your Emergency Disk to start your computer if you have disk-caching software or memory-resident programs other than those from Central Point because these memory-resident programs may attempt to access the disk during the repair operation and confuse the process.

To start DiskFix, type this command at the DOS command line and press Enter:

DISKFIX *d*:

Replace *d* with the drive designator of the drive you want to fix. DiskFix first displays its logo screen. This screen includes a warning that, before running DiskFix, you must unload all disk-caching programs and other memory-resident programs that might access the disk, except for PC-Cache and other PC Tools programs. Choose OK to proceed. Choose Cancel to exit DiskFix if you need to unload memory-resident programs.

DiskFix begins its process by running an equipment check, comparing the BIOS, CMOS (for PC AT and PS/2 computers and compatibles), partition table, and boot sector to the data in the mirror file. If an apparent discrepancy is found, DiskFix displays a description of the problem, a list of symptoms, and a suggestion for correcting the problem. DiskFix then displays the DiskFix Main Menu screen (see fig. 11.9).

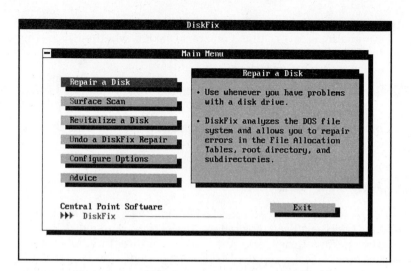

Fig. 11.9

The DiskFix Main
Menu screen.

The Main Menu lists the following options on the left side of the screen and a description of the option on the right side of the screen. As you highlight these options, the description changes.

■ *Repair a Disk.* This option checks six different characteristics of a selected disk in an effort to uncover error conditions. You normally use this option when you have encountered severe problems or error messages involving one of your disks.

■ *Surface Scan.* This option causes DiskFix to attempt to read every cluster on the disk and to mark and set aside any cluster that cannot be read. Use this option when DOS displays the Sector not found message while attempting to read a hard disk. Use the option periodically on any disk to avoid future loss of data because of failure of the disk media.

■ *Revitalize a Disk.* This option causes DiskFix to clean up marginal-sector identifying marks on a floppy disk while retaining any data that might be on the disk. Use this option when DOS displays the Sector not found message while attempting to read a floppy disk.

> **NOTE** Do not use Revitalize a Disk to correct errors or retrieve data unless you have already tried to use Surface Scan.

■ *Undo a DiskFix Repair.* This option reverses any changes made by the DiskFix Repair a Disk option. This option is effective only if you choose to save the DiskFix undo information during the DiskFix operation.

- *Configure Options.* This option determines which tests are run automatically every time you start DiskFix, whether DiskFix uses the BIOS surface-scan option, and whether DiskFix uses standard or custom error messages.

- *Advice.* This option displays extensive cross-referenced advice on common disk- and file-related problems.

Each of the Main Menu options is discussed in the sections that follow.

Repairing a Disk

The Repair a Disk option on the DiskFix Main Menu can help you solve problems such as a hard disk failure, inability to read a disk, lost or damaged subdirectories, or a scrambled root directory. After you choose **R**epair a Disk from the DiskFix Main Menu, the program displays the Drive Selection dialog box containing a list of available drives. This dialog box also prompts you to select the drive to analyze and repair (see fig. 11.10). After selecting the appropriate drive, choose **OK**.

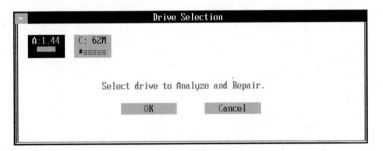

Fig. 11.10

The Drive Selection dialog box.

DiskFix then displays the Repair Drive window, which lists the following tests that are to be executed by DiskFix:

- *Boot Sector* tests the integrity of the DOS boot sector (or boot record), which contains information needed by DOS. DiskFix checks for damage to this section of the disk.

- *FAT Integrity* checks to make sure that both copies of the FAT are readable.

- *FAT Comparison* compares the two copies of the FAT to ensure that they are identical. If DiskFix discovers an error in one copy of the FAT, the program copies the readable copy on top of the corrupted copy. DiskFix compares any found mirror-image file with the FAT files. If a discrepancy is found between the two FATs, DiskFix asks whether you want to use the mirror-image file to update the FAT.

■ *Media Descriptors* determines whether the media descriptor bytes (which identify the disk drive type) for each disk drive are stored correctly in both copies of the FAT. DiskFix determines whether the media descriptor stored in the FAT matches the drive being analyzed.

■ *FAT Data Analysis* ensures that neither FAT contains invalid entries.

■ *Directory Structure* scans all directory files on the disk for invalid entries or file-allocation errors such as invalid file names, file size, and FAT allocation. If DiskFix finds duplicate file names, it assigns a new name to the second file. When the repair is complete, the name of the original file and the name DiskFix assigned to the duplicate are included in the report.

■ *Cross-linked Files* searches for files to which DOS has allocated the same disk space; these files are called *cross-linked files*. If any cross-linked files are found, DiskFix attempts to determine to which file the sectors in question should be allocated. DiskFix automatically fixes cross-linked files, a process that can take several minutes.

■ *Lost Clusters* looks for disk clusters that are marked in the FAT as allocated to some file but in fact are not assigned to any particular file. If DiskFix finds lost clusters, the program asks whether you want to save or delete the clusters. If you choose **S**ave, DiskFix stores every chain of clusters as a separate file, using the names PCT00000.FIX, PCT00001.FIX, PCT00002.FIX, and so on. DiskFix saves lost directories as LOST0000.SUB, LOST0001.SUB, and so on. Choose **D**elete rather than Save if you want to delete the lost clusters.

As DiskFix executes each test in this list, the program depicts its progress in a growing horizontal bar graph near the bottom of the screen. A sentence or two explaining the test in progress appears in the box to the right of the test list box. When a test is completed, DiskFix places a check mark to the left of the test name (see fig. 11.11). If DiskFix finds no errors in a test, the program displays OK to the right of the test name. If DiskFix finds an error during a test and is going to make a repair, the program first prompts you to confirm the repair.

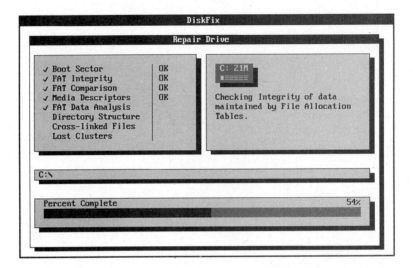

The Repair Drive window while a disk is being repaired.

The first time the program is ready to make a repair, DiskFix asks whether you want to save a copy of all pertinent information in case you want to "undo" the changes the program makes. Instruct the program to create this undo file and to save the file on a floppy disk other than the disk being repaired. The Undo a DiskFix Repair command on the DiskFix Main Menu works only if you previously instructed DiskFix to save this data before any repair was made.

When DiskFix finishes all the tests, choose OK to generate a report of the results. Then choose whether to send the report to a printer or to a disk file (the default file name is DISKFIX.RPT). Choose Skip to skip the report. DiskFix returns to the Main Menu screen.

Scanning the Disk Surface

The DiskFix Surface Scan option attempts to locate and correct bad sectors on a disk. Use this option when DOS displays the Sector not found message while attempting to read a hard disk. Use the option periodically on any disk to avoid future loss of data due to failure of the disk media.

When you choose Surface Scan from the DiskFix Main Menu, the program displays a list of available drives. Select the drive you want DiskFix to analyze, and choose OK. DiskFix displays the message Reading System Areas and then displays the Pattern Testing Options dialog box (see fig. 11.12).

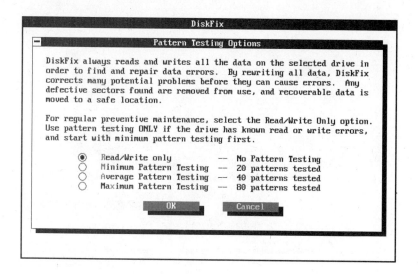

┌───┐
│   DiskFix   │
│ ┌───┐│
│ │─   Pattern Testing Options   ││
│ │   ││
│ │ DiskFix always reads and writes all the data on the selected drive in ││
│ │ order to find and repair data errors. By rewriting all data, DiskFix ││
│ │ corrects many potential problems before they can cause errors. Any ││
│ │ defective sectors found are removed from use, and recoverable data is ││
│ │ moved to a safe location.   ││
│ │   ││
│ │ For regular preventive maintenance, select the Read/Write Only option. ││
│ │ Use pattern testing ONLY if the drive has known read or write errors, ││
│ │ and start with minimum pattern testing first.   ││
│ │   ││
│ │   ⦿ Read/Write only   -- No Pattern Testing ││
│ │   ○ Minimum Pattern Testing -- 20 patterns tested ││
│ │   ○ Average Pattern Testing -- 40 patterns tested ││
│ │   ○ Maximum Pattern Testing -- 80 patterns tested ││
│ │   ││
│ │   OK   Cancel   ││
│ └───┘│
└───┘

Fig. 11.12

The Pattern
Testing Options
dialog box.

The Pattern Testing Options dialog box prompts you to choose one of the following options:

- *Read/Write Only* reads and writes all data on the disk, removing any defective sectors and moving data to safe readable sectors. This test realigns the data with the disk drive heads. This option is the default pattern-testing option. Use this test weekly to avoid future problems in reading and writing data to the disk.

- *Minimum Pattern Testing* reads and writes 20 test patterns to detect flaws in the disk that would not be detected by the standard read/write test. Use this option whenever your computer is reporting read/write errors.

- *Average Pattern Testing* reads and writes 40 test patterns. This option performs a more thorough test than the Minimum Pattern Testing option but is twice as fast as the Maximum Pattern Testing method.

- *Maximum Pattern Testing* reads and writes 80 test patterns, providing the most assurance of disk drive integrity.

> **CAUTION:** Do not use Maximum Pattern Testing on RLL drives; the drive configuration is not compatible and may result in data loss.

After you choose a pattern-testing option, choose **OK** to proceed with the surface scan. DiskFix then displays the Surface Scan drive map (see fig. 11.13).

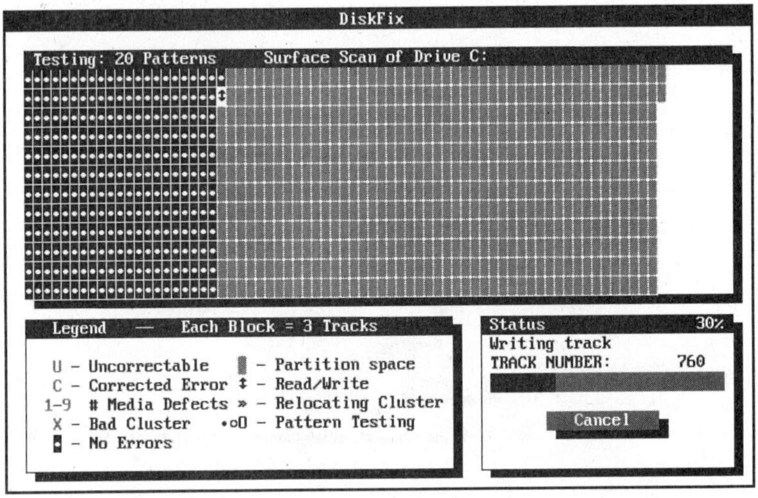

Fig. 11.13

The Surface Scan
drive map.

This screen is similar in appearance to the Disk Mapping dialog box displayed by PC Shell when you execute the **M**aps command from the **T**ools menu, and then choose **D**isk Map from the submenu.

As DiskFix scans the disk, the program depicts its progress as a growing horizontal bar graph in the Status panel in the lower right corner of the DiskFix window. The codes displayed in the Legend panel help you interpret the drive map and let you know whether the scanned sectors have no errors, are uncorrectable, are corrected, have media defects, or are bad clusters. Table 11.4 describes these codes briefly.

Table 11.4 Disk Mapping Sector-Allocation Codes

Code	Meaning
(shaded)	Partition space
•	No errors
↕	Block currently being read
»	Relocating cluster
U	Uncorrectable data error
C	Corrected data error
1-9	The number of media defects in an unused sector
X	Bad cluster

When DiskFix completes its surface scan, the program displays the message

        Do you want a log report of the results?

If you want a report that indicates any errors that were found, choose **OK**. DiskFix then gives you a choice between sending the report to the printer or to a file (the default file name is DISKFIX.LOG). If you don't want to print a report, choose the **S**kip command button. DiskFix returns to the Main Menu.

Revitalizing a Disk

Use the Revitalize a Disk option when DOS reports the Sector not found message while reading a disk, and you are not able to repair the disk with either the **R**epair a Disk or **S**urface Scan option. The revitalize operation performs a series of tests on your system and then does a low-level, nondestructive format of the disk.

> **CAUTION:** Do not use the Revitalize a Disk option if you are also using Stacker or SuperStor. Drives using these programs are actually files containing drive information. If you perform a low-level format, you may destroy that drive information.

To begin the process, display the DiskFix Main Menu and choose Revitalize a Disk. The Drive Selection dialog box appears. Select a drive to analyze and repair from the Drive Selection dialog box. DiskFix begins by testing these system facilities for integrity:

- *Partition Mapping* determines whether the DOS partition is valid.
- *System RAM* checks the memory (RAM) necessary to perform the entire test.
- *Disk Controller* makes sure that the disk controller works.
- *Controller RAM* checks the integrity of the controller's on-board RAM.
- *Timer System* verifies that the computer's timing chip is working properly.
- *Active Caching* ensures that no hardware or software cache is active. DiskFix automatically turns off PC-Cache.

When DiskFix finishes these tests, the program displays the message System integrity testing finished. If the program finds any errors, it recommends the action you should take before continuing with the test. If no errors were found, choose **OK** to continue with the disk-revitalization process.

When testing a floppy disk, the program next displays the Revitalize a Disk disk map and begins immediately to revitalize the disk. DiskFix reads every track of data, formats the track, and rewrites the data. The result is the same as the Surface Scan operation, but with formatting added.

If DiskFix is testing a hard disk, the program performs an analysis of the disk drive's timing characteristics. For hard disks, the program checks the time required to move a disk head from one track to the next track on the disk, the time to move a head from the first track on the disk to the last track, and the average time required to move the head from one track to another. When the test is complete, a message appears. Choose **OK** to continue with the tests.

After executing the Timing Characteristics test, DiskFix performs a Physical Parameters test (hard disks only). In this test, the program checks these characteristics:

- *Drive RPM.* The revolutions per minute of the hard disk's platters.

- *Intersector Angle.* The physical angle of an individual sector on the hard disk.

- *Bits per Track.* The number of bits contained in each track.

- *Data Encoding Type.* The method the hard disk controller uses to encode data on the disk (MFM, RLL, or ERLL).

 NOTE This process takes several hours or more, depending on the size of the hard disk and the speed of your computer. Run the test at the end of the day to allow plenty of time to complete the process.

- *Hard Disk BIOS.* The memory address of the controller firmware.

- *Current Interleave.* The current interleave ratio.

- *Track Transfer Rev.* The number of platter revolutions required to read or write one track of data.

- *Maximum Data Rate.* The maximum number of bits per second that the drive can read or write.

Choose **OK** to continue. DiskFix then analyzes the disk drive's interleave ratio and determines whether changing the ratio would increase performance. The program tests the data transfer rate at eight different interleave ratios and then reports the results. If a change in interleave would be beneficial and if your disk drive permits you to change the interleave ratio, DiskFix gives you the opportunity to select the optimum value.

Choose **OK** again to continue. Assuming that your hard disk is a type that can be formatted at a low level, DiskFix displays the Pattern Testing Options dialog box, similar to the one discussed earlier in this chapter (refer to fig. 11.12). Choose no-pattern, minimum-pattern, average-pattern, or maximum-pattern testing. If you are merely attempting to improve the disk's performance and have not been experiencing read/write errors, use the no-pattern testing option. The greater number of read/write errors you have encountered, the greater the number of patterns you should instruct DiskFix to use. Choose **OK** to begin the nondestructive low-level formatting.

DiskFix displays the Revitalize a Disk drive map, which has a similar appearance to the Surface Scan drive map. DiskFix then begins reading sectors, rewriting the sector address markers on the drive, resetting the interleave (if applicable), writing pattern tests (if selected), and, finally, writing the original data back to the disk.

As DiskFix revitalizes the disk, the program depicts its progress as a growing horizontal bar graph in the Status panel, located in the lower right corner of the window. DiskFix displays in the Legend panel the codes listed in table 11.4 to let you know whether the sectors have no errors, are uncorrectable, are corrected, have media defects, or are bad clusters.

Finally, when DiskFix completes its disk revitalization, the program displays the following message:

    Do you want a log report of the results?

If you want a report, choose **OK**. DiskFix gives you a choice between sending the report to the printer or to a file (the default file name is DISKFIX.LOG). If you don't want to print a report, choose the **S**kip command button. DiskFix returns to the Main Menu.

Configuring DiskFix

DiskFix Version 8.0 gives you the power to customize the way the program operates to a certain degree. From the Main Menu, choose **Config**ure Options. DiskFix displays the Configure DiskFix dialog box, which offers these options:

- *Test **P**artition Information* causes DiskFix to test hard disk partition information and the boot sector before displaying the initial DiskFix Main Menu. (This box is checked by default.)

- *Check **B**oot Sector for Viruses* causes DiskFix to test the boot sector for known computer *viruses* (destructive programs that might be hidden in software) as a part of the initial DiskFix testing. (This box is checked by default.)

- *Look for Mirror File* causes DiskFix to check for a mirror-image file on the disk and, if one is found, to compare the file with the disk's FAT files. This procedure provides the highest level of data protection. (This box is checked by default.)

- *Use BIOS **S**urface Scan* causes DiskFix to use a method of scanning the disk that is most likely to recover lost data. Do not use this option if your computer uses a hardware cache, a translating controller (ESDI, SCSI, and IDE), or a special device driver (such as Disk Manager). PC Tools can usually detect when a system is incompatible and automatically deselects this option. If you have problems when this option is selected, uncheck it.

- *Use Custom **E**rror Messages* replaces all DiskFix error messages with a message you specify and disables any repairs made by the Repair a Disk option. Check this box when you plan to permit relatively inexperienced users to run DiskFix as a diagnostics tool, but you do not want them to effect any repairs. Choose the Edit Custom Message command button to display the Edit Custom Error Message dialog box. Type your message and choose **OK**.

- *Enable Manual **F**ix* allows you to use DiskEdit to fix errors yourself. Leave this option unchecked if you want PC Tools to repair the errors automatically.

Choose the check boxes you want DiskFix to use, and then choose **OK**. DiskFix returns to the Main Menu.

Exiting DiskFix

When you complete the analysis and repair of the disk with which you were having problems, choose the Exit command button from the DiskFix Main Menu screen. DiskFix returns to DOS.

Using DiskFix from the DOS Command Line

PC Tools 8 enables you to select many of DiskFix's options from the DOS command line, which means that you can run a specific test without using the Main Menu. Command-line options also enable you to run the program's tests from a batch file. You can choose any of the items that follow. If two items are in the square brackets together, you can choose only one of the pair.

The complete syntax of the DiskFix command is as follows:

> DISKFIX [*d*:] [/TEST or /SCAN] [/RO:*path\filename*]
> [/RA:*path\filename*] [/HCACHE] [/HCARD] [/CMOS] [/LIST] [/?]
> [/VIDEO] [/REBUILD]/

For *d*, substitute the drive you want DiskFix to test. The default is the current drive.

/TEST causes DiskFix to run the Repair a Disk command without making repairs.

Use the /RO parameter with the /SCAN or /TEST parameter. The result of the scan or test is written to the path and file name you specify with *path\filename* (the default file name is DISKFIX.RPT).

Use the /RA parameter with the /SCAN or /TEST parameter. The result is added to the end of the file you specified with the path\filename.

/SCAN causes DiskFix to run the Surface Scan command.

Use the /HCACHE parameter only if you have a HardCache card installed. Use /HCARD only if you have a HardCard card installed.

Use /CMOS to restore the CMOS information stored on your Emergency Disk. DiskFix checks the validity of the CMOS data before writing it to your system. Make sure that you keep your Emergency Disk up-to-date. See the "Using Mirror" section earlier in this chapter for instructions on how to save CMOS data to your Emergency Disk.

/LIST displays partition table data stored on the disk.

The /REBUILD parameter replaces the REBUILD command in earlier PC Tools versions. Use /REBUILD to transfer the partition table information from your Emergency Disk back to your hard disk. DiskFix checks the validity of the information before writing it to your hard disk, so make sure that you keep your Emergency Disk up-to-date. See the "Using Mirror" section earlier in this chapter for instructions on how to save partition data to your Emergency Disk.

Use the /? parameter to see command-line help for the DiskFix parameters.

The /VIDEO parameter shows command-line help for different types of screens and mouse options.

Chapter Summary

This chapter teaches you how to use the features that may very likely be the most important tools in the PC Tools 8.0 toolbox. The chapter discusses how to run the Mirror program daily to make a safe copy of your hard disk's file allocation table (FAT) and root directory, and explains how to use Mirror to make a disk copy of a hard disk's partition table and boot sector as well as your computer's CMOS setup. You also learned how to use Unformat to recover data lost because you accidentally formatted a disk and how to use FileCheck to search the disk for file fragments. Finally, the chapter explains how to use DiskFix to restore partition, boot-sector, and CMOS data and recover from other types of disk-related problems.

Now that you have learned how to protect and repair your disks by using Mirror, Unformat, and DiskFix, turn to Chapter 12 to learn how to edit a disk by using DiskEdit.

Editing a Disk with DiskEdit

DiskEdit is new to the Central Point suite of utilities and is a natural follow-up to the existing FileFix utility covered in Chapter 10, "Recovering Damaged or Deleted Files," and the DiskFix utility covered in Chapter 11, "Recovering Damaged or Formatted Disks." When both FileFix and DiskFix cannot recover your damaged files and disks, DiskEdit gives you one more opportunity for recovery: low-level editing of damaged files and disks.

This chapter discusses how to start, configure, and use DiskEdit. In this chapter, you learn how to use DiskEdit to obtain more information about your system, including how to display the file allocation and partition tables and how to view the boot-sector cluster information for logical and physical disks. You also learn how to choose a different editor to view data, files, directories, and other important information about your system, as well as how to work with objects (files, directories, partition tables, and so on) within DiskEdit windows.

> **CAUTION:** DiskEdit is not designed for the novice computer user. The program's ability to change boot-sector information, file allocation table (FAT) or partition table information, and the master boot record are powerful enough to cause serious damage to your system if you are unfamiliar and unknowing.
>
> Although built-in safeguards have been provided, you can seriously damage your files and your disks or render your hard disk completely unbootable if you're not familiar with the low-level editing capabilities DiskFix provides.
>
> If you are at all in doubt about what you are doing or how the program works, do not use DiskEdit. Instead, seek the advice of competent technical support.

Starting and Configuring DiskEdit

DiskEdit is a powerful—and potentially dangerous—utility that can help you recover lost files and damaged partition tables and boot-sector records and solve other disk problems. With DiskEdit, you can change file cluster information, disk partition locations, and critical boot information for your computer, bypassing DOS functions to access your hardware, if necessary.

To start DiskEdit, choose **D**isk from the PC Tools Desktop menu. From the Disk menu shown in figure 12.1, choose Dis**k** Editor to invoke DiskEdit.

If you're not running PC Tools Desktop, you can run the DiskEdit program by typing **de** at the DOS command line and pressing Enter. For more information on the command line, see the section titled "Exploring Command-Line Options" later in this chapter.

After you invoke DiskEdit, the message `Building Tree Structures:` appears. When DiskEdit has completed reading in the information about your current drive and building information about your hard disk tree structure for the currently selected drive, the program displays a screen, similar to the one shown in figure 12.2. The message box informs you that you are in *Read Only mode*. DiskEdit starts in Read Only mode (a mode where only reading the disks is enabled and all writing to the disk is disabled) for your safety when you begin using the utility for the first time. As described later in the chapter, you can change from Read Only mode through the Tools menu.

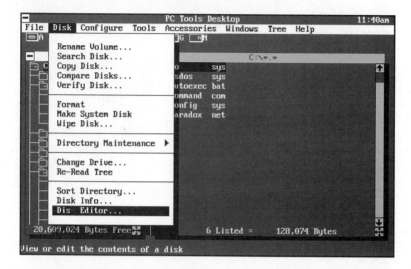

Fig. 12.1

PC Tools Desktop's Disk menu.

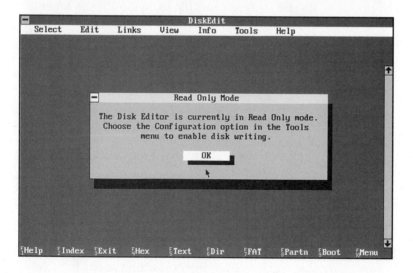

Fig. 12.2

The Read Only Mode message box in the DiskEdit screen.

Press Enter or choose **OK** to confirm the initial Read Only Mode configuration. DiskEdit displays its Main Menu, similar to that shown in figure 12.3.

```
┌─────────────────────────────── DiskEdit ────────────────────────────────┐
│ Select    Edit    Links    View    Info    Tools    Help                 │
├─ C:\ ─────────────────────────────────────────────────── Offset 0 ──────┤
│ Sector 215                                                      Hex 0     │
│ NAME    EXT    SIZE     DATE      TIME    CLU#   ARC R/O SYS HID DIR VOL   │
│ IO     .SYS   33430  4/09/91   05:00a      2        R/O Sys Hid        ▲  │
│ MSDOS  .SYS   37394  4/09/91   05:00a     19        R/O Sys Hid           │
│ BATCH  .          0  9/01/92   04:33p   1095                    Dir       │
│ CONNECT.          0  9/01/92   04:33p     76                    Dir       │
│ DOS    .          0  9/01/92   04:34p   6042                    Dir       │
│ GRABPLUS.         0  9/16/92   06:59p  11857                    Dir       │
│ GRAY   .          0 10/14/92   10:44p    140                    Dir       │
│ LANTASTI.         0  9/28/92   12:15p   1092                    Dir       │
│ LANTASTI.NET      0  9/28/92   12:16p   2614                    Dir       │
│ ND     .          0  9/01/92   04:35p     71                    Dir       │
│ OFFICE .          0  9/01/92   04:38p   9709                    Dir       │
│ QEMM   .          0  9/01/92   04:40p  11935                    Dir       │
│ QUICKEN.          0  9/01/92   04:40p  11923                    Dir       │
│ SK2    .          0  9/01/92   04:41p   6626                    Dir       │
│ TAPE   .          0  9/01/92   04:21p     62                    Dir       │
│ UU     .          0  9/06/92   03:27p  10128                    Dir       │
│ XTALK4 .          0 10/01/92   10:17p   2470                    Dir       │
│ AUTOEXEC.BAT    855 10/21/92   11:39a     75    Arc                      │
│ COMMAND .COM  47845  4/09/91   05:00a     38                           ▼  │
│ Help  Index  Exit  Hex  Text  Dir  FAT  Partn  Boot  Menu                │
└──────────────────────────────────────────────────────────────────────────┘
```

Fig. 12.3

The DiskEdit
Main Menu.

The top line in the DiskEdit Main Menu is a horizontal menu bar similar to the one that appears in all other PC Tools programs. The menu selections are described in the following paragraphs:

- *Select* enables you to select specific DiskEdit objects for editing or viewing.

- *Edit* enables you to mark and fill blocks inside objects; copy to or paste from the Clipboard; change the date, time, and file attributes of an object; write or discard changes; and in most cases, undo changes you have made.

> **NOTE** If you have not accessed the Tools Configuration command and changed the initial setup to disable the default Read Only status, the Edit command is grayed out and inaccessible.

- *Links* provides shortcut keys enabling you to switch quickly between objects, such as first viewing a file and then changing to a directory display.

- *View* changes the current view mode from one method or one area to another, such as from Hex to Text mode, or from viewing the directory to viewing the partition table.

- *Info* gives you information about the currently selected object. This menu also gives you the option to map the object you are currently viewing.

■ *Tools* provides a variety of services to DiskEdit. You can search for text in Hex or Text mode, write and print objects, synchronize the file allocation tables (if this option is not already set up as the default), use the built-in Hex calculator to convert from decimal to hexadecimal notation, view an ASCII table, and change the configuration of DiskEdit.

■ *Help* provides on-line, context-sensitive help for the currently selected option.

The bottom line of the Main Menu contains the list of available function key commands. These function key commands are listed and described briefly in table 12.1.

Table 12.1 DiskEdit Function Key Commands

Key	Name	Function
F1	Help	Displays context-sensitive Help
F2	Index	Shows the Help index
F3	Exit	Cancels the current process
F4	Hex	Switches to Hex Editor viewing mode
F5	Text	Switches to Text Editor viewing mode
F6	Dir	Selects a directory to view
F7	FAT	Selects the FAT Editor
F8	Partn	Selects the Partition Table Editor
F9	Boot	Selects the Boot Record Editor
F10 or Alt	Menu	Activates the horizontal menu bar
Alt+space bar	Control	Activates the Control menu

NOTE The F8 (Partn) function key may not be included in the list of function key commands at the bottom of the screen if you are viewing a logical or extended DOS drive rather than the physical boot drive (usually C). The display of available function key commands is usually dependent on the type of hard drive installed in your computer.

Using the DiskEdit Editors

Objects are edited within DiskEdit with specific editors for each of the types of objects available to view, change, or modify. *Objects* include files, directories, partition tables, file allocation tables (FATs), and boot records. *Editors* are included for directories, files, the file allocation tables (FATs), partition tables, boot records, and hex and text editing and viewing. DiskEdit initially configures itself in Auto View mode, meaning it intelligently selects the appropriate editor for the type of object you have chosen to view.

You can disable Auto View by choosing Configuration from the Tools menu. In the Configuration Changes dialog box that appears, shown in figure 12.4, choose Auto View to turn off the Auto View option.

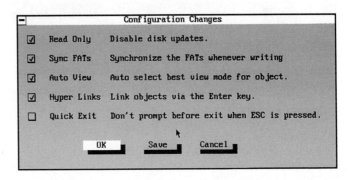

Fig. 12.4

DiskEdit's
Configuration
Changes
dialog box.

Changing the current editor for an object, if you have enabled Auto View mode, is as easy as opening the Select menu and choosing an object—Drive, Directory, and so on—from the list (see fig. 12.5). You also can use the function-key commands listed on the bottom of the screen to change the current view of a selected object.

Using the Directory Editor

When you choose Directory from the Select menu (refer to fig. 12.5), DiskEdit displays a dialog box showing all the directories for the current drive. Select a specific directory to view and press Enter to complete the selection action.

After you select a directory to view, you can move vertically through the list of files and directory names that appears on the left side of your screen by using your cursor-movement keys, by pressing PgUp and PgDn to move a screen at a time, or by using the mouse and the scroll bar on the right of your screen.

A directory is represented as a file name with no extension on the left side of the screen, a size of 0 in the SIZE column, and the word *Dir* in the DIR column (located near the right side of the screen). Figure 12.6, for example, shows the \BATCH directory on C drive as the currently selected directory, as indicated in the top line of the screen.

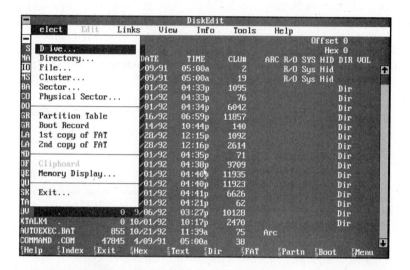

Fig. 12.5

DiskEdit's Select menu.

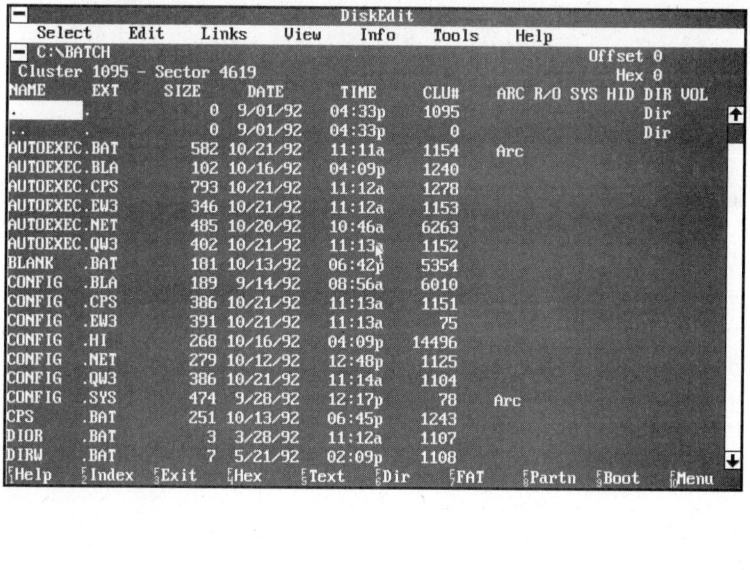

Fig. 12.6

Viewing the \BATCH directory on drive C.

T I P Pressing Enter takes you immediately to the appropriate editor for the currently highlighted file or directory name in the list.

Figure 12.7 shows the file AUTOEXEC.BLA in Hex mode as the currently selected file. The currently selected file name, as well as the cluster and sector number of the selected file's location on the drive, appear in the upper left corner of the screen. In figure 12.7, DiskEdit also shows you in the upper right corner of the screen the current position of your cursor (the position is represented by both Offset and Hex values).

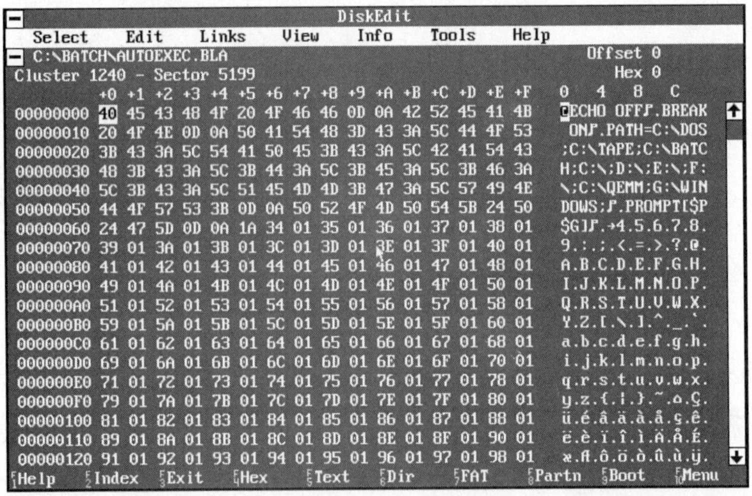

Fig. 12.7

Viewing a file in Hex mode.

To view a different file, use your cursor-movement keys or your mouse to highlight a file name, and press Enter to automatically view the file with the correct editor.

In the remainder of the screen, DiskEdit shows you in hexadecimal, decimal, and ASCII the contents of the file you selected. Figure 12.7, for example, shows the AUTOEXEC.BAT file. Pressing F5 (Text) while you are viewing a file in Hex mode will change the view to Text mode (see fig. 12.8).

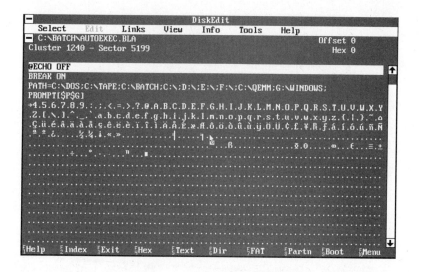

Fig. 12.8

Viewing a file in
Text mode.

> Pressing Esc at this point does not return you to the previously
> selected viewing mode. Instead, DiskEdit prompts you to choose
> OK to quit or Cancel to stay in the program. To return to the pre-
> viously selected viewing mode, choose **D**irectory from the **S**elect
> menu, select the directory from which you originated, and then
> press Enter to complete the operation.

T I P

You can map the currently selected file to see its location on the current drive. Highlight a file or directory on the display and press Enter,
choose **I**nfo from the horizontal menu bar, and then choose **M**ap of
Object. As shown in figure 12.9, DiskEdit shows you a graphical representation of your current drive, with a colored or shaded *F* marking the
file's location to indicate its position relative to other files on the disk.

To return to the Directory Editor display screen, choose **O**K or press
Enter.

With the Directory Editor, not only can you view entries shown on the
display, but you also can make changes to entries if you have disabled
Read Only mode. You can change a file or directory's name, size, date
and time, and the system attributes simply by typing over the information in the current highlight bar.

Pressing Tab moves you between the columns of information, and as
mentioned previously, pressing Enter invokes the appropriate editor
based on the highlighted field of information.

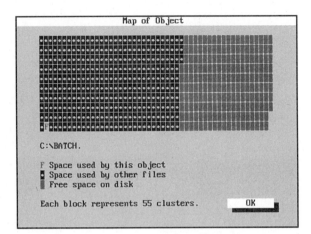

Fig. 12.9

Viewing a map of a file in the Map of Object window.

Using the File Allocation Table Editor

Most disks have at least one copy of the file allocation table (FAT) and a second copy that DOS creates on your disk as a backup copy just in case the first FAT becomes damaged. When you choose the 1st Copy of FAT or the 2nd Copy of FAT command from the Select menu, DiskEdit takes you immediately to the first sector and cluster of the selected file allocation table for the currently selected drive, as shown in figure 12.10.

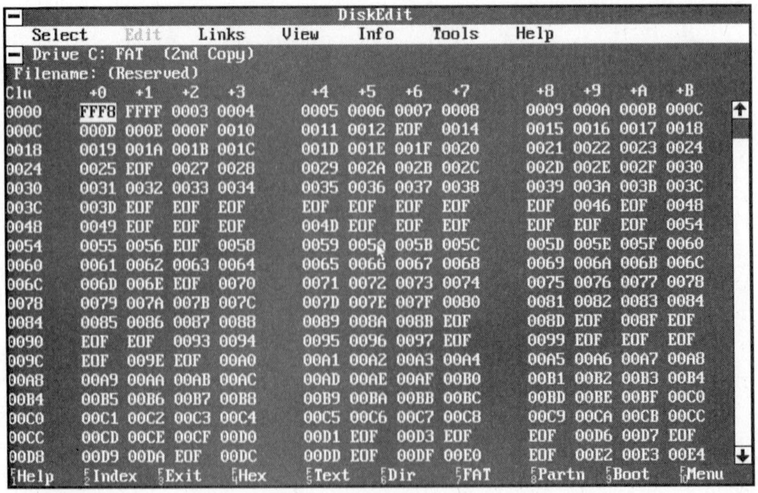

Fig. 12.10

The 2nd Copy of FAT display.

Each set of four digits represents part of a *cluster chain* in the FAT you are viewing. Each of the cluster chains displayed is an editable field (so long as you have disabled Read Only mode in the Configuration Changes dialog box).

In the upper left corner below the horizontal menu bar, DiskEdit shows you the current drive (C: in figure 12.10), the copy of the FAT you are viewing (2nd Copy in figure 12.10), and a file name, (if you had one selected before you chose 1st Copy of FAT or 2nd Copy of FAT from the Select menu). In figure 12.10, for example, the screen shows (Reserved) as the file name.

Pressing Tab or the cursor-movement keys changes the file name displayed. As the file name changes, the cluster chain display changes to show you the full cluster chain of the file in a shade or color different from the rest of the screen. You also can see your cursor's position within the cluster chain containing the file.

Highlighting a specific cluster chain and pressing Enter (selecting the chain) invokes the appropriate editor to show you, normally, in hex and text formats, the file you selected (refer to figures 12.9 and 12.10 for examples of this type of display).

NOTE The Configuration submenu, which you access by choosing **C**onfiguration from the **T**ools menu, lists the option Resync FATs. Technically, if you want both file allocation tables to match as you make changes to files and directory entries with DiskEdit, leave this option selected. You have no reason to disable the Resync FATs option.

Using the Partition Table Editor

The larger your hard disk, the more chances there are that you partitioned, or *logically divided*, the drive into partitions, such as C, D, and E, where C is the boot drive, and D and E are the logical partitions. These partitions are also referred to as *extended partitions*. When a hard disk is partitioned, DOS creates a *partition table*, a definition (to DOS) of the logical division of sectors and clusters on your hard disk.

In most cases, losing a partition table renders the data on your disk drive completely inaccessible. Certainly, you could repartition and reformat your drive and then restore your backup disks or tapes by using Central Point Backup after booting from your Emergency Disk. But what about those files that were changed or created between the end of the last backup and the time the partition table was lost?

> **CAUTION:** Make a backup of the partition table before proceeding to a file or to another disk or drive so that if you make a mistake, you can restore the original partition table.
>
> To back up your partition table, choose Partition **T**able from the **S**elect menu. Then open the **T**ools menu and choose **W**rite Object. Choose **C**urrent Object, choose To a File, and press Enter. Finally, type in a directory and file name to which you want to write the copy. Choose **O**K.

If you have lost important data by losing a partition table on your hard disk, the Partition Table Editor may be able to help you recover the partition data and, more importantly, the data you lost. But try using DiskFix (see Chapter 11, "Recovering Damaged or Formatted Disks," for information) before running DiskEdit to see whether your partition table can be recovered.

Each partition on your hard disk has a partition table. To open the partition table for the C drive, follow these steps:

1. Choose D**r**ive from the **S**elect menu, and then choose the drive you want to view.

2. From the **S**elect menu, choose Partition **T**able to open the Partition Table window, an example of which is shown in figure 12.11.

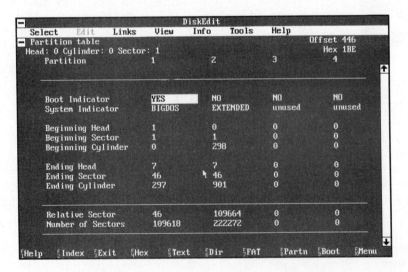

Fig. 12.11

The Partition Table window.

Each available partition on the single physical drive's partition table is displayed. The Partition Table Editor displays the physical characteristics of the current drive (cylinders, heads, and sectors per track) in addition to information about the size of the file allocation tables, types of partitions (DOS, extended, non-DOS), and starting and ending sector numbers of the partition currently selected.

Using the Boot Record Editor

The Boot Record Editor is two editors in one. Not only can the Boot Record Editor load the proper boot record to your hard disk (with the two required system files necessary to make a disk bootable), but it can also provide DOS with specific information about the hard disk's physical characteristics.

> **CAUTION:** Make a backup of the boot record before proceeding to a file or to another disk or drive so that if you make a mistake, you can restore the original boot record information.
>
> Be careful about editing information in the boot record. You easily can type in a wrong number, which could cross-link a cluster chain and possibly damage files permanently.

To view the boot record of drive C, for example, follow these steps:

1. Select the drive you want to view by choosing **D**rive from the **S**elect menu and selecting a drive.

2. From the **S**elect menu, choose **B**oot Record. DiskEdit displays a screen of information in two-column format similar to that shown in figure 12.12.

The boot record contains a great deal of information significant to DOS in terms of how DOS recognizes and works with your hard disk. The Boot Record window, for example, provides information about the DOS version installed on the hard disk, the number of sectors and bytes per cluster and per sector, the total number of sectors on the hard disk, and the volume label.

Depending on the version of DOS you are currently using, the last four items listed in figure 12.12 may or may not appear in the Boot Record window.

T I P

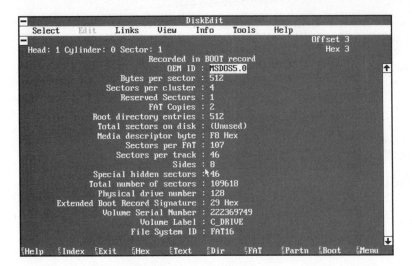

Fig. 12.12

The Boot Record
window.

As with the other editor functions built into DiskEdit, you can change
the information displayed in the left column of the Boot Record window
by simply typing new information over the original information. (Again,
you must have first disabled Read Only mode in the **Tools** **C**onfiguration menu.)

Pressing Enter with any of the items listed in the Boot Record window
highlighted immediately invokes the proper editor or view screen for
more detailed information about the highlighted item.

Using the Hex Editor

The default editor for DiskEdit is the Hex Editor, which you can open
directly by choosing **H**ex from the **V**iew menu or by pressing F4 (Hex).
The Hex Editor window appears, as shown in figure 12.13.

A typical Hex Editor window displays both ASCII and hex values. The
cluster number is represented on the extreme left, the hex codes in the
center, and the ASCII characters (some high ASCII characters are
remapped to not display extended ASCII codes) on the extreme right of
the window. At the top of the window, the Hex Editor displays the current file name, the cluster and sector numbers of that file, and the offset and hex numbers indicating the current position of the cursor.

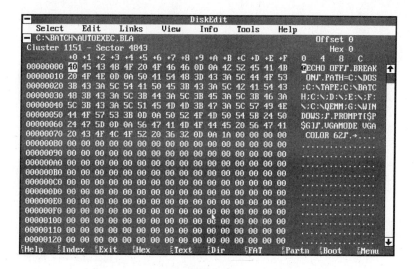

Fig. 12.13

The Hex Editor
window.

Displaying and Mapping Objects

DiskEdit can quickly display objects if you know what information you want displayed and how you want that information to appear. You can display file names, directory names, drive characteristics, file allocation and partition tables, and any other information about your hard disks by choosing the appropriate option from the horizontal menu bar or by pressing the appropriate function key.

If you prefer, you also can split the screen horizontally and display, for example, a specific file name in the upper window and the hex representation of that file in the lower window. When one window is active, the other is inactive, although any changes you make are reflected in both windows. Figure 12.14 shows an example of a split screen.

T   I   P

If your monitor can display more than the normal 24 lines per screen, use the PC Tools /43 or /50 configuration parameter to increase the number of lines per window you want to display when loading DiskEdit. Refer to Appendix A, "Installing and Configuring PC Tools," for more information on command line parameters.

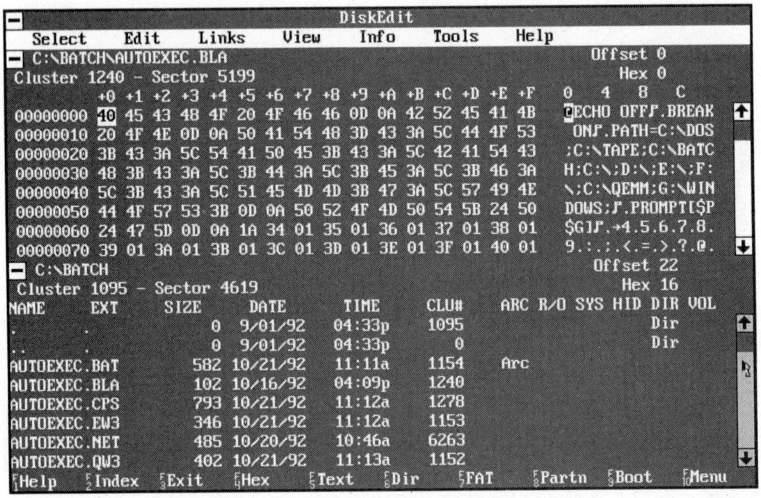

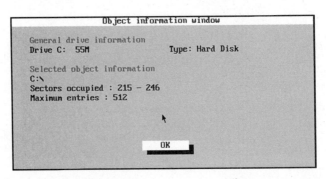

Fig. 12.14

Two windows displayed in a split screen.

Normally, you use the split screen feature when you want to conform two files without having to switch back and forth between the two. Or you might use the split screen feature to manually edit a FAT so that both copies are the same, for example.

To use the split screen feature, choose View from the horizontal menu, and then choose Split Screen. To restore the screen to its original full-screen view, choose View and then choose Split Screen again to deselect the option. You also can click the control buttons in the top left corner of the window to switch from full to split screen, or you can simply press Ins to split the screen and Del to restore the screen to its normal size.

If you want to display basic object information about a currently highlighted entry on your screen, choose Info from the horizontal menu, highlight Object Information, and press Enter to see an Object Information dialog box similar to the one shown in figure 12.15.

Fig. 12.15

The Object Information dialog box.

When you map an object, the Object Information dialog box provides general drive information for the current drive, the type of drive (floppy or hard disk, for example), and information about the currently selected object (file, directory, and so on). This dialog box also tells you the attribute, date, and time status or settings for the file, as well as the starting cluster location and the file's size on the current drive.

Similarly, you can map objects—files, directories, clusters, or sectors—by choosing Info from the horizontal menu bar and then selecting the appropriate Map option you want to perform.

NOTE You cannot map partition tables and boot records.

To map the current object, first be sure you have selected the object (usually by pressing Enter on the object in the Editor window), and then choose **M**ap of Object from the **I**nfo menu to see a map of the current object. Figure 12.16 shows an example of a mapped object.

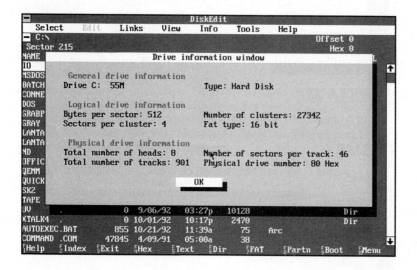

Fig. 12.16

The Drive Information Window.

Marking, Copying, and Pasting Objects

When you are ready to make changes, or to copy and paste information, to and from files or other disks for review or backup purposes, you need to enable the Mark, Copy, and Paste features in the Tools menu under **C**onfiguration. You enable these features by disabling Read Only mode.

T I P Take advantage of the Search and Repeat Search commands on the Tools menu. If you know the information you want to locate, copy, and paste to another area on the disk, the Search and Repeat Search features can find them much more quickly than you can search for them manually.

To mark data to be copied from one disk to another, first use the mouse or the cursor-movement keys to select the data you want to copy, and then choose **M**ark Block from the **E**dit menu. Choose the **C**opy to Clipboard command to copy the marked data to the Clipboard buffer.

NOTE The Clipboard holds a limited amount of data—about two pages. If the data you are trying to copy takes up more room than that, use the **W**rite or the **P**rint option in the **T**ools menu and then choose File as the print destination, specifying the path and file name to which you want to print.

To paste data from the Clipboard to another file or location, choose **P**aste from Clipboard from the **E**dit menu, position the cursor where you want to place the Clipboard text, and press Enter to complete the paste operation. If you make a mistake, you can reopen the **E**dit menu and then choose **U**ndo to undo the paste.

The next section provides more detail about making changes to your files and disks.

FROM HERE...

For Related Information

▶▶ "Copying and Pasting Text," p. 600.

▶▶ "Editing Text in the Clipboard," p. 609.

▶▶ "Printing from the Clipboard," p. 611.

Repairing Disks and Data with DiskEdit

DiskEdit picks up where FileFix and DiskFix leave off. The major advantage to DiskEdit is that it can access portions of your hard disks that even DOS cannot access, giving you another opportunity to recover damaged partitions and files you might otherwise not be able to recover.

 NOTE DiskEdit cannot recover every file and partition that becomes damaged by virtue of the DOS environment in which it runs.

DiskEdit can help you locate and retrieve data from damaged disks that you otherwise could not retrieve. To retrieve data from bad disks, you can use DiskEdit to try to recover the file manually. Follow this step-by-step procedure to find and recover a single damaged file from a floppy disk (you use the same procedure to recover files on a hard disk):

1. From the **T**ools menu, choose **C**onfiguration. In the Configuration Changes dialog box, choose **A**uto View to disable the Auto View mode (refer to fig. 12.4).

2. From the **S**elect menu, choose **D**rive; then select the drive containing the damaged file. Be sure you select the drive as a logical (rather than physical) drive.

3. From the **S**elect menu again, select the name of the directory where the damaged file resides. If you locate the file's name in the display, press PrintScrn to print the current screen to your printer so that you have a printed record of the file's size, as well as the starting cluster number from the CLU# field. Write step 3 on this printout so that you can identify it later.

4. If you cannot locate the file's name in the display, choose **C**luster from the **S**elect menu and read in all the clusters from the directory. Then choose **S**earch from the **T**ools menu, type the file's name in the dialog box, and choose OK to have DiskEdit search for the file name in the data read in from all the clusters.

T I P   If the file name you are searching for has fewer than eight characters
as the first part of the file name, be sure to use spaces to fill out
the full eight characters. Then type the extension *without the period
between the file name and the extension.* For example, type
MYFILE••DOC. (The dots represent spaces.)

5. If you can find the file name in the directory list, open Select Directory from the **View** menu to display the directory. Hotprint this
screen as well (and write step 5 on the printout) to have a record
of the starting cluster number and the file size of the directory
and file you are trying to recover. Proceed to step 6.

If you see nothing but garbled data on-screen, choose **R**epeat
Search from the **T**ools menu and return to step 4 to continue
searching for more data.

If you didn't find the file name in the directory list, choose **S**earch
from the **T**ools menu and type in a phrase or word that was in the
beginning of the damaged file. (See figure 12.17 for an example of
a Search dialog box and figure 12.18 for an example of a search
result.)

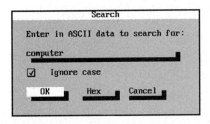

Fig. 12.17

The Search
dialog box.

When DiskEdit stops with the first match in your search, press
Enter to view the data the program found. If the data is part of
your file, hotprint the screen so you will have a printed record of
the cluster number.

If you know that this file contains more data, proceed to step 6. If
the file has no more data, skip to step 10.

6. Access the **I**nfo menu and choose **D**rive Info to take a look at the
drive information for that logical drive.

Calculate the number of bytes per cluster by multiplying the bytes
per sector by the sectors per cluster, and then compare the result
with the number on the hotprint you marked in step 5. If the result
is larger, you have found the entire file and can move on to step 8.
If the result is smaller, go to step 7.

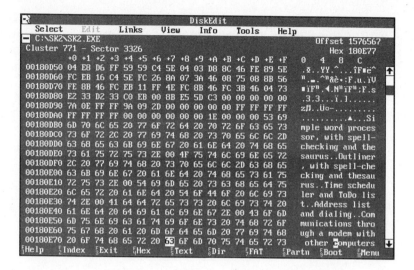

Fig. 12.18

A search result
window.

7. If the file you found is smaller than the result you calculated in step 6, determine how many clusters were in the original file, as closely as possible. To do so, divide the file size by the cluster size and round up. If the file you searched for had 20,480 bytes, for example, and the cluster size shown in your hotprint from step 5 is 2048, the file would take up exactly 10 clusters.

8. From the **S**elect menu, choose **1**st Copy of FAT and fill in the file's first, or starting, cluster number (from the step 5 printout). Select the entry, and then try to walk through the entire cluster chain until you get to the entry that reads EOF.

   Now, compare the number of cluster chains you have walked through with the result you wrote down in step 6. If the results match, go on to step 9.

9. From the **S**elect menu, choose **C**luster to read in every cluster chain that you walked through in step 8. You need to type in the first cluster number from step 3 and then type in the last cluster number on the disk from the printout you created in step 3.

   Press F4 (Hex) to view the data in the clusters you selected, and write down the cluster numbers that look as if they belong in the file for which you're searching.

10. Choose **C**luster from the **S**elect menu. Then type in the first cluster number from step 3 as the starting cluster range.

    Choose **W**rite Object from the **T**ools menu to display the Write Object dialog box, shown in figure 12.19. Then choose the **F**ile option and type a new path and file name. Use a drive other than the drive from which you are recovering the file. Repeat this step until all the clusters you want to save to the new file have been saved.

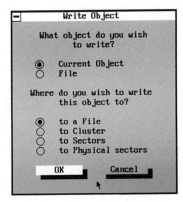

Fig. 12.19

The Write Object
dialog box.

T I P   Be sure to select **A**ppend from the Write Object dialog box on the second and succeeding write operations so that you add data to the file you created instead of overwriting your new file.

For Related Information

FROM HERE...
◀◀ "Using FileFix," p. 369.

◀◀ "Using DiskFix," p. 422.

Displaying Memory Information

Displaying information about programs and device drivers currently loaded into memory can be extremely helpful in debugging device or program conflicts, but DiskEdit does not enable you to make any changes to this information because of the possibility of corruption. You can use the Mark, Copy, and Paste features discussed in this chapter's section "Marking, Copying, and Pasting Objects" to copy groups of clusters containing data and write those groups to a file on another disk. Consult your PC Tools manual for additional information about this feature.

Exploring Command-Line Options

DiskEdit provides several command-line options you can use to start the program from the DOS command line. The complete syntax of the various parameters is shown in the following:

```
DE /drive /filename /P /W /VIDEO /?
```

These parameters are described in table 12.2.

Table 12.2 DiskEdit's Command-Line Options

Option	Description
/drive	Specifies the logical drive on which to start
/filename	Specifies a specific file name as a DiskEdit File Object
/P	Bypasses DOS and goes to direct physical access of the disk
/W	Disables Read Only mode when invoking the program
/VIDEO	Shows the range of video options you can use to control how options appear on-screen
/?	Shows command-line help options

Chapter Summary

In this chapter, you learned about the low-level capabilities of a powerful tool, DiskEdit. Note that FileFix and DiskFix are the utilities you should use *before* resorting to DiskEdit. Also keep in mind that none of these utilities are able to recover from *every* damaged, deleted, or destroyed file, partition, boot sector, or related problem.

Now turn to Chapter 13, "Securing Your Data with PC Secure and Wipe," to learn how to secure your data.

Securing Your Data with PC Secure and Wipe

One of the nagging weaknesses of the personal computer is its lack of security features. Other than a keyboard lock, introduced in the IBM PC AT, users are left to their own devices to protect programs and data from unauthorized access. This chapter introduces you to the PC Tools 8 answer to the data-security question—PC Secure and Wipe.

PC Secure is a sophisticated encryption and decryption program capable of *encrypting* (scrambling) any DOS file to protect it from prying eyes. PC Secure uses the DES (Data Encryption Standard) encryption algorithm, which meets stringent federal government standards. (The encryption/decryption feature is available only in PC Tools 8 packages shipped to the United States. In non-U.S. versions, only file compression and expansion are available.) When you use the program to encrypt a file, you assign a password or key to the file. Without the key, no one (including you) can convert the file back to a readable form. This high-security utility is indispensable when your nonremovable hard disk contains sensitive data and your computer is accessible to other users not authorized to view the sensitive data.

This chapter begins by explaining how to start PC Secure and then describes how to select encryption options such as full DES encryption, quick encryption, and file compression. You learn how to assign keys, hide encrypted files, make files read-only, delete original files, toggle Expert mode, and save PC Secure settings you normally want to use. Finally, the chapter explains how to run the encryption and decryption operations from the PC Secure menus or directly from the DOS command line.

PC Secure can encrypt data files, files on networks, and program files. However, you should not encrypt some files:

- **Do not encrypt PC SECURE itself or important operating system files, such as COMMAND.COM.** Encrypted program files do not run; they must be decrypted first. You can control access to sensitive applications, such as payroll, by encrypting the program and giving the password to authorized users only.

- **Do not encrypt copy-protected files.** Some copy-protection schemes rely on checking information at a certain location on the disk. When you encrypt and decrypt a file, the contents at any particular location are not likely to be the way they were before the encryption process.

Starting PC Secure

You can operate PC Secure through typical PC Tools shortcut key commands and pull-down menus. Alternatively, you can execute PC Secure commands directly from the DOS command line by adding special parameters to the start-up command. To learn how to run PC Secure in command mode, see the section "Encrypting and Decrypting Files from the DOS Command Line" later in this chapter. If you prefer to use the PC Secure menus, start the PC Secure program by typing the following command at the DOS command line and then pressing Enter:

PCSECURE

If you choose to use INSTALL to install applications in the PC Shell program-list menus, you can start PC Secure by displaying the Security Tools submenu of the PC Tools menu and selecting PC Secure. Refer to Appendix A, "Installing and Configuring PC Tools," for a discussion of INSTALL.

The first time you start PC Secure, the program displays a message explaining that you must install a master-key password before you can encrypt or decrypt files. Select the **OK** command button to continue. PC Secure then prompts you to enter the password. A message at the bottom of the screen reads Please enter the password. The password, or *master key*, can unlock all files encrypted with your copy of PC Secure, except files encrypted when Expert mode is toggled on.

Entering the Master Key

PC Secure gives you the option of typing an alphanumeric key containing from 5 to 32 characters or a 16-digit hexadecimal key. If you prefer to use an alphanumeric key, begin typing at the Please enter the password prompt. If you make a mistake when you enter your password the second time, the error message The keys are not equal appears. Press Enter to remove the message. The program then returns to the Master Key dialog box where you can start over. Keep in mind that PC Secure distinguishes between upper- and lowercase letters typed in an alphanumeric key. The key *Big Apple*, for example, is different from *BIG APPLE*.

NOTE Choose your master key with care because if you want to change the master key, you must reinstall PC Secure (see Appendix A, "Installing and Configuring PC Tools").

Your PC Secure master key is like the master key to a hotel. Even though every encrypted file can have its own distinct key, the master key can decrypt every file created with your copy of PC Secure (except files encrypted with Expert mode toggled on). Do not use a master key that is easy to guess. Poor choices for a master key are your Social Security number, your spouse's name, birthdays, and so on. The best master key is a random one—a string of letters and numbers that are in no particular order and have no meaning. This type of key is hard to remember, so write it down and store the written copy of the key in a secure place.

T I P

As you type each alphanumeric character in your password, PC Secure displays an asterisk (*) rather than the character you type. This security precaution prevents anyone from learning your key by watching over your shoulder. After typing the master key, press Enter. To make sure that you did not make an error while typing the key, PC Secure blanks the text box and again displays the same messages prompting you to enter the master key. Type the same password again and press Enter.

Because a 16-digit number is virtually impossible to guess, using a hexadecimal key increases the security level. If you prefer to use a hexadecimal key, press F9 at the `Please enter the password` prompt. PC Secure shortens the text box to 16 characters and shortens the prompt to `Please enter the hex key`. The program displays this prompt in the status line:

```
Enter 16 Hex characters for the Key. F9 for text key
```

Type 16 digits, using the numerals 0 through 9, the uppercase or lowercase letters *A* through *F*. In contrast to the way PC Secure handles alphanumeric keys, the hexadecimal password entry screen is not sensitive to the case of hexadecimal letters A through F. The key 01a1f098d620ca33 is the same as the key 01A1F098D620CA33. PC Secure displays the hexadecimal numeral as you type it, and you do not have to type the key a second time for verification.

After you type your key (whether hexadecimal or alphanumeric) and press Enter, PC Secure responds with the message `Now installing master key in PCSECURE.EXE` and then displays the PC Secure screen with the File pull-down menu displayed (see fig. 13.1).

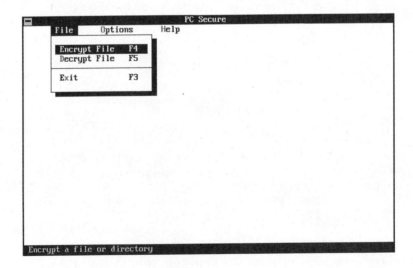

The PC Secure screen.

NOTE Several times during a PC Secure session, you may need to type a key (a password). The key is always required the first time you encrypt a file in a session. In addition, you may have to type the key every time you encrypt or decrypt a file. For all these key inputs, you use the same procedures you used to type the master key.

Examining the PC Secure Screen and Its Functions

In all sessions after your first PC Secure session, the program displays the PC Secure screen, skipping the prompt for the master key and the logo screen. The PC Secure screen is similar in appearance to other PC Tools screens. As you can see in figure 13.1, the File, Options, and Help menus are displayed in the horizontal menu bar at the top of the screen. Unlike other PC Tools programs, PC Secure does not require you to press Alt or F10 to select an option from the PC Secure horizontal menu bar. You just select the first letter of any of these menus to display a pull-down menu. Then, to choose one of the menu options, press the letter highlighted in the option name. (To select a command button from a dialog box, however, you still have to press the Alt key while you press the highlighted letter.)

As mentioned earlier, when you initially open the PC Secure screen, the File menu is open. Press Esc to close the menu. The PC Secure screen displays function-key commands in the message bar. These function-key commands and other keystroke commands available in PC Secure are described in table 13.1.

Table 13.1 Keystroke Commands Available in PC Secure

Key	Name	Function
F1	Help	Displays the context-sensitive Help facility
F2	Index	Displays the Help facility index
F3	Exit	Cancels the current process and exits from PC Secure.
F4	Encrypt	Begins the encryption operation
F5	Decrypt	Begins the decryption operation
Esc	Cancel	Cancels the current process or exits from PC Secure

The shortcut keys for commands and menu options accessible through the PC Secure screen enable you to perform the following functions:

- Encrypt (scramble) one or more files, by using the DES encryption method

- Encrypt one or more files, using a quicker but less secure subset of the DES encryption method

- Decrypt (unscramble) one or more files

- Compress one or more files so that they occupy less storage space on the hard disk

Other options, available only from the pull-down menus, enable you to hide files, create read-only files, and toggle on Expert mode, which disables the master key. The sections that follow explain when and how to use these functions.

Selecting Options

Before you begin the encryption procedure, you can check to make sure that the PC Secure options are set to your preferences. Select **Op**tions from the PC Secure menu to display the Options pull-down menu (see fig. 13.2). A check mark next to an option indicates that the option is turned on.

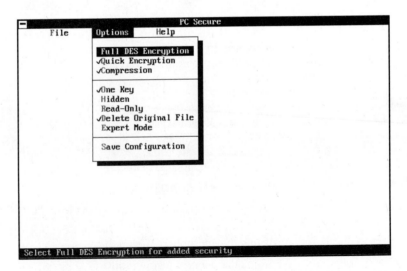

Fig. 13.2

The PC Secure Options menu.

Choosing the Type of Encryption

When you want the highest degree of security or must comply with federal or other regulatory guidelines that require DES encryption, select the Full DES Encryption option from the PC Secure Options menu. This option uses the DES algorithm to create an encrypted version of the target file. Files encrypted in this manner are "bullet proof." Even if your file fell into the hands of a group of computer science grad students with access to a Cray computer, your file would remain secure. Selecting the option a second time toggles off DES encryption.

By default, PC Secure uses a quicker, but less secure, variation of the DES algorithm, referred to as *Quick Encryption*. Notice that when you first display the Options menu, a check mark appears beside the Quick Encryption option. This option is a mutually exclusive alternative to the Full DES Encryption option; selecting one turns off the other.

For example, you may share a PC with a colleague but want to maintain a degree of privacy with regard to some of the files you create on the system. The quick-encryption algorithm is sufficient for maintaining privacy. By contrast, imagine that you are using your computer to create a multimillion-dollar contract bid and want to work on one of the files at home. To provide the maximum level of security, use DES encryption before copying the file to a floppy disk.

 If you toggle off both Full DES Encryption and Quick Encryption, PC Secure does not encrypt the target file at all.

Compressing Files

In addition to encrypting files, PC Secure can compress files so that they occupy less disk space. This feature is particularly useful when you want to fit as many files as possible on a floppy disk. The PC Tools distribution disks, for example, contain some files compressed by PC Secure. Probably the most common use of file-compression programs, however, is to prepare a file to be transmitted by modem over a telephone line. Because compressed files are smaller, they take less time to send, saving not only time but also long-distance tolls.

 Send encrypted files over the phone only if both the sender and receiver use the same version of PC Tools; otherwise, the receiver will not be able to decrypt the files.

T I P   Despite the similar-sounding terminology, the **C**ompression option does not achieve the same result as the PC Tools Compress program. Refer to Chapter 8, "Speeding Up Your Hard Disk with Compress," for a full discussion of using Compress to optimize the performance of your hard disk.

By default, the **C**ompression option is turned on. Sometimes, however, encrypting a file with this option turned on can result in a larger file. This problem occurs when a file already has been compressed by PC Secure or another compression program, such as ARC or PKZip. When you are going to encrypt a file that is already compressed, select **C**ompression from the **O**ptions menu to toggle off this feature. You may also want to avoid using compression if you plan to use a modem to send the file over a noisy phone line because the compression adds just another level of possible errors during the decryption phase.

Using One Key Per Session

Every time PC Secure encrypts or decrypts a file, you must provide a key (a password). When the One Key option on the Options menu is turned on, however, PC Secure prompts you for a key only the first time you run the encryption procedure during a PC Secure session. The program assumes that you want to use the same key for subsequent encryptions and decryptions. The program asks for a key again only when you decrypt a file that the initial key cannot unlock. To turn on this option, display the **O**ptions menu and choose **O**ne Key. PC Secure adds a check mark to the left of the One Key option in the Options menu.

Occasionally you may want to encrypt several files, each with a different key. For example, you might be preparing a spreadsheet for every employee, showing the employee's yearly salary, deductions, and benefits to date. You want to use PC Secure to encrypt and compress every spreadsheet but do not want to use the same key for every employee's file. If you want PC Secure to prompt you for a separate key for every file, display the **O**ptions menu and choose **O**ne Key to turn off the option.

Taking Additional Precautions

Encrypting a file provides substantial security, but PC Secure provides four options—Hidden, Read-Only, Delete Original File, and Expert

Mode—that enable you to increase the level of security. The first two options help protect the encrypted file from being erased accidentally. The last two options help ensure that even persons with relatively free access to your computer cannot decrypt an encrypted file.

One way to reduce the likelihood that someone will erase a file is to hide it. If you want PC Secure to hide an encrypted file, choose **O**ptions, and then select **H**idden from the Options menu. (By default, this option is off.) When you run the encryption operation, PC Secure turns on the hide bit in the encrypted file's attribute byte. (See Chapter 10, "Recovering Damaged or Deleted Files," for more about the file attribute byte.) You still can use PC Tools Desktop to list and delete the file, but the DOS DIR and DEL (or ERASE) commands ignore the file.

An even better way to prevent someone from accidentally erasing a file is to turn on its read-only attribute bit so that the file can be read but not modified or erased. To make a file read-only, select **R**ead-Only from the **O**ptions menu. Then, when you run the encryption operation, PC Secure turns on the read-only bit in the encrypted file's attribute byte. You still can use PC Tools Desktop to list and delete the file, but the DOS DEL (or ERASE) command responds with the message Access denied.

You still can use PC Secure to decrypt a file that is hidden or read-only (PC-Secure warns you when a file is read-only). The decryption operation turns off the hide and read-only attribute bits.

T I P

By default, PC Secure takes one precaution that probably seems obvious. In addition to making an encrypted copy of the original file, the program deletes the original file. PC Secure deletes the original only after successfully making an encrypted copy and then renames the copy to the original file name. Therefore, in order for PC Secure to encrypt a file, your disk must have enough room for both the original file and the encrypted copy.

Occasionally, you may want to have an encrypted copy for transmittal to someone else but keep the original copy for daily use. Suppose, for example, that you are working on a sales-projection spreadsheet that you want to send by modem to your head office. You want to encrypt and compress the copy to be sent and keep an unencrypted copy on which to do further work. To prevent PC Secure from deleting the original, select **D**elete Original File from the **O**ptions menu to turn off the deletion feature. Then PC Secure makes the encrypted copy of the file and gives the copy the same file name as the original but with the file name extension SEC. The original file remains unaltered.

The next option on the Options menu, Expert Mode, provides the tightest security by disabling the master key. By default, this option is off. If you select Expert Mode from the Options menu to turn on Expert mode, you can decrypt an encrypted file only when you provide the key specifically assigned to the file. Your master key does not work.

Saving the PC Secure Configuration

When you make changes to the PC Secure options, the changes are effective only for the current session of PC Secure. To make any changes to the default settings, display the Options menu and select Save Configuration. PC Secure saves the new settings to the file PCSECURE.CFG in the \PCTOOLS\DATA directory.

Encrypting Files

After you select the appropriate encryption options, press Esc to return to the PC Secure screen. You are ready to encrypt a file or directory. Either press F4 (Encrypt) or select File and then Encrypt File. The program displays the File Selection dialog box, similar to the one shown in figure 13.3.

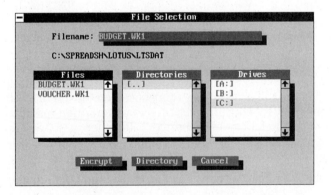

Fig. 13.3

The File Selection dialog box.

The File Selection dialog box contains the Filename text box, three list boxes, and three command buttons. The Files list box, the first list box on the left side of the screen, shows a list of files contained in the current directory. PC Secure highlights the first file listed and displays that file name in the Filename text box. Use the mouse and scroll bar or the cursor-movement keys to move up and down through the list and highlight different files. PC Secure displays only six file names at a time.

By scrolling up and down in the list, you can display the name of any file stored in the directory.

In the Directories list box, the program lists directories. The Drives list box lists drives. To move to another disk or directory, click either the directory name in the Directories list box or the disk name in the Drives list box, or highlight the name and press Enter.

Selecting Individual Files

When the list box contains the name of the file you want to encrypt, click the file name or highlight the file and choose the **E**ncrypt command button. Suppose, for example, that you are in the C:\ directory in the File Selection dialog box, but you want to encrypt the 1-2-3 spreadsheet file BUDGET.WK1, located in the C:\SPREADSH\LOTUS\LTSDAT directory. First, highlight [SPREADSH] in the Directories list box and then press Enter. Then highlight [LOTUS] and press Enter. Finally, highlight [LTSDAT] and press Enter. The Files list box displays the names of files contained in the directory C:\SPREADSH\LOTUS\LTSDAT (refer to fig. 13.3). Move the highlighted bar to the Files list box and highlight the file you want to encrypt.

An alternative to highlighting the file name in the list box is selecting the file you want to encrypt by typing the path and file name in the Filename text box. Then choose the **E**ncrypt command button.

After you select a file and choose Encrypt, PC Secure displays the Password dialog box, which contains a text box and the prompt `Please enter the password` (see fig. 13.4). Type the password (key) you want to use and then press Enter. (Refer to the section "Entering the Master Key" earlier in this chapter for a reminder on typing a password.) If you type an alphanumeric key, PC Secure prompts you to enter the password again for verification. Type the key again and press Enter. PC Secure then begins encrypting the file.

Fig. 13.4

The Password dialog box.

If the One Key command is turned on (the default), PC Secure does not display the Key Input dialog box on subsequent encryption or decryption procedures during the current PC Secure session. Rather, PC Secure uses the same key you specified the first time you encrypted a file during the session.

T I P

As PC Secure encrypts the file, the Progress dialog box is displayed. This dialog box uses a growing horizontal bar graph to depict the progress of the file-encryption process. The screen displays an ongoing tally of the total bytes read, the total bytes in the file, and the total bytes written to the encrypted file (see fig. 13.5). Finally, with the encryption finished, PC Secure displays the number of bytes read, the number of bytes written, and the message *** Completed ***. (If the program compressed the file, the number of bytes written is less than the number of bytes read.) Choose the **OK** command button to return to the PC Secure screen.

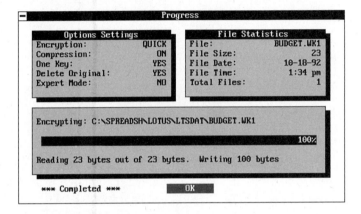

Fig. 13.5

The Progress dialog box.

When you want to compress two files with the same file name but different extensions—ACCOUNTS.DBF and ACCOUNT.TXT, for example—and have compressed the first file, the message This file already exists appears when you try to encrypt the second file. When the first file is encrypted, the DBF extension is changed to SEC so the file is renamed ACCOUNTS.SEC. PC Secure tries to give this same name to the second file as well. If you see the message This file already exists, choose **C**ancel and rename the second file or move the encrypted file to a different directory.

Selecting Entire Directories

Sometimes all the files in a directory are related to the same project, particularly in database applications. In such circumstances, you may prefer to encrypt all the files in the directory at one time rather than encrypt every file individually.

When you want to encrypt an entire directory, highlight the name of the directory in the Directories list box of the File Selection dialog box (refer to fig. 13.3). Choose the **Directory** command button. To encrypt the C:\SPREADSH\LOTUS\LTSDAT directory, for example, highlight [LTSDAT] in the list box and choose the **Directory** command button. The complete directory path name appears below the Filename text box (see fig. 13.6).

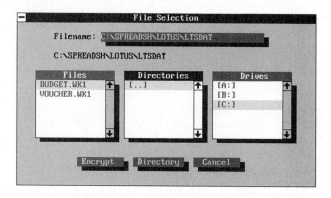

Fig. 13.6

Selecting the directory [LTSDAT].

When you choose **Directory**, PC Secure displays the prompt This will affect more than one file. OK to proceed? To encrypt all the files in the highlighted directory, choose **OK**. If you want to encrypt all files in all subdirectories of the highlighted directory, select the **I**nclude All Subdirectories check box before choosing **OK**.

As soon as you choose **OK**, PC Secure displays the Key Input dialog box, which contains a text box and the prompt Please enter the password. Type the key you want to use and then press Enter. (Refer to the section "Entering the Master Key" earlier in this chapter for a reminder on typing a password.) If you type an alphanumeric key, PC Secure prompts you to enter the password again for verification. Type the key again and press Enter. PC Secure then begins encrypting the directory.

While PC Secure encrypts each file in the directory, the Progress dialog box is displayed. When the program has encrypted all the appropriate files, it indicates the number of files processed, the total number of bytes read, and the number of bytes written, and then displays the message ***Completed***. Choose the **OK** command button in the Progress dialog box to return to the PC Secure screen.

Even when you encrypt an entire directory at one time, you still can decrypt every file individually if you prefer, or you can decrypt all files in the directory as a unit.

T I P

Decrypting Encrypted Files and Directories

Ultimately, any encrypted file or directory must be decrypted (unscrambled) before you can use it. When you want to decrypt a file or directory, press F5 (Decrypt), or select File and then Decrypt File. PC Secure displays the File Selection dialog box. To select the file or directory for decryption, use the same procedure you used to select the file or directory for encryption (refer to the "Encrypting Files" section earlier in this chapter).

After you select a file to decrypt, choose the Decrypt command button, or highlight the file and press Enter. If you have selected a directory rather than an individual file, choose the Directory command button. After you select a file or directory, PC Secure displays the Password dialog box containing a text box and the prompt Please enter the password. Type the key used to encrypt the file or directory and press Enter. (Refer to the "Entering the Master Key" section earlier in this chapter for a reminder on typing a password.) If the file was not encrypted with PC Secure, the program displays the message This is not a PC Secure file. Otherwise, PC Secure decrypts the file.

During decryption, you may see messages informing you of a problem. If the message says The keys are not equal, for example, you made a mistake when you typed the password. Choose the OK command button and try again. If you are trying to decrypt a file back to the original directory that contains a file with the same name, you may see the message The original file has not been changed since it was encrypted. Choose OK to overwrite it. If you see the message The original file has been changed, choose Cancel and rename or move the original file before decrypting the file to that directory.

T I P   You can use PC Secure Version 8.0 to decrypt files encrypted with Versions 6.0 and earlier, but you cannot use earlier versions of PC Tools to decrypt a file encrypted with PC Secure Version 8.0.

NOTE   If you are going to transfer an encrypted file over the phone, both parties must have the same version of PC Secure, and you need to use a communications package that supports an error-checking binary file protocol, such as XModem. You also need some way to set the key. Never transmit the unencrypted key over a phone line. Use a scrambled phone line or a trusted courier.

Exiting from PC Secure

When you are ready to exit from PC Secure, press Esc (Exit) or F3 (Exit). PC Secure displays a small Close PC Secure dialog box containing the message This will close PC Secure. Choose the **OK** command button to confirm that you want to close the program. Choose **C**ancel to return to the PC Secure screen. If you changed the PC Secure configuration in any way and want to save the changes, select the **S**ave Configuration check box.

For Related Information

◀◀ "Starting Compress," p. 314.

◀◀ "Using Compress Options," p. 322.

◀◀ "Using FileFix," p. 369.

FROM HERE...

Encrypting and Decrypting Files from the DOS Command Line

If you want to run the encryption operation directly from the DOS command line or from within a batch file, use the following syntax:

PCSECURE /C /F /Q /G /Kxxxxx /M /P /S /? /VIDEO /D filespec

The /D decryption parameter decrypts the specified files. The available encryption parameters and their meanings are listed in table 13.2.

Table 13.2 PC Secure's Available Encryption Parameters

Encryption Parameter	Function
/C	Turns off compression.
/F	Uses full DES encryption (16 rounds).
/Q	Provides quick DES encryption (two rounds). This option is available in the U.S. version only.

continues

Table 13.2 Continued

Encryption Parameter	Function
/G	Deletes original and overwrites the place on the disk where the file was with zeros; meets U.S. Government (Department of Defense) standards.
/Kxxxxxx	Uses the characters *xxxxx* typed in after the /K as the password (where *xxxxxx* stands for your password characters). If you press Space Bar or Enter after the K, the password is not valid.
/M	Enables you to encrypt a file multiple times. You must decrypt the file the same number of times entering the keys in reverse order.
/P	Enables you to encrypt a file with a password that your master key will not be able to decrypt.
/S	Indicates Silent mode, which you use in batch files so that no messages appear on the screen during encryption or decryption except to report errors.
/? or /H	Shows command-line help.
/VIDEO	Shows command-line help for video and mouse options.

To encrypt the file BUDGT.WK164 by using the quick-encryption method and the key RUBY_SLIPPERS, for example, type the following command at the DOS command line and press Enter:

    PCSECURE /Q /KRUBY_SLIPPERS BUDGT.WK1

The following command decrypts the same file:

    PCSECURE /D /KRUBY_SLIPPERS BUDGT.WK1

CAUTION: If you encrypt a file from the DOS command line, PC Secure does not automatically apply your master key to the file; therefore, you cannot use your master key to decrypt the file.

Using Wipe To Clear a File or Disk

In some cases, you may want to verify that a file's data is obliterated. You may, for example, want to wipe clear your sensitive electronic-mail files so that prying eyes can never read any data from the file, even if the would-be snoop uses some type of undelete command. Use PC Tools' Wipe program, which is capable of permanently erasing an entire disk of data.

When you want to clear a single file, multiple files, or a disk, start the Wipe program. You can start Wipe from the DOS command line by typing **wipe** (using upper- or lowercase) and pressing Enter.

You also can start Wipe from within PC Tools Desktop. To erase a selected file or files permanently, select Change File from the **F**ile menu. From the Change File submenu select the **W**ipe File option. Refer to Chapter 4, "Working on Files," for a discussion about using Wipe from PC Shell in this manner.

If you chose to use INSTALL to install applications in the PC Tools Desktop program-list menus, you can start Wipe by opening the **D**isk menu and selecting **W**ipe Disk. Refer to Appendix A, "Installing and Configuring PC Tools," for a discussion about INSTALL and to Chapter 3, "Using the Desktop as a Program Manager," for complete coverage of PC Shell's program-list menus.

When you start Wipe from the DOS command line, Wipe loads and displays the Wipe Main Menu screen (see fig. 13.7).

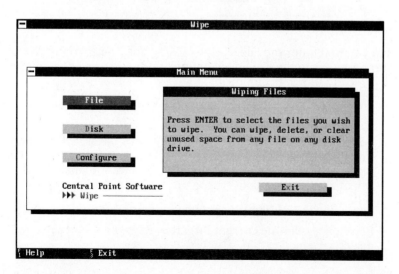

Fig. 13.7

The Wipe Main Menu screen.

The Main Menu screen displays the following three command buttons:

- *File* clears specified files from the disk.

- *Disk* clears an entire disk or, optionally, only the unused portions of the disk.

- *Configure* sets the wipe options, which determine what character Wipe uses to overwrite wiped files or disks and the number of times the overwrite procedure is repeated.

The sections that follow discuss these commands.

Wiping Files

When you want to clear one or more files from a disk, start Wipe and select File from the Wipe Main Menu screen (refer to fig. 13.7). The program displays the File Options dialog box (see fig. 13.8).

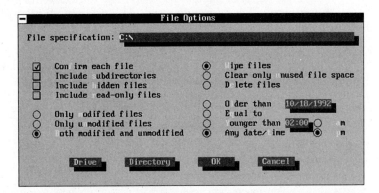

Fig. 13.8

The File Options dialog box.

When you first enter the File Options dialog box, the current drive directory appears in the File Specification text box. To select a different disk drive, do one of the following:

- Backspace over the disk letter in the File specification and type a new specification.

- Select the **D**rive command button. Wipe displays the Drive Selection dialog box. Type the drive letter or use the mouse or cursor-movement keys to highlight the drive you want to make current. Select the **OK** command button.

To select a different directory, do one of the following:

- Backspace over the current directory name and type a new directory specification.

■ Select the Directory command button. Wipe displays a dialog box that lists any subdirectories of the current directory (see fig. 13.9). To move up a level in the directory tree, select the directory marked by two dots (..). To move to a subdirectory, select the subdirectory's name from the dialog box. After you choose the directory, select the **OK** command button.

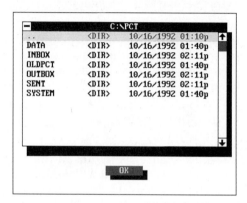

Fig. 13.9

Selecting
a different
directory.

To specify which file or files you want to erase, type a file specification in the text box. You can use any valid DOS file specification, including the two wild-card characters * and ?.

After you specify a file specification that identifies the drive, directory, and files you want Wipe to erase, you can select from the options discussed in the remainder of this section.

The File Options dialog box displays the following check boxes (refer to fig. 13.8):

■ *Confirm Each File* requests confirmation before Wipe erases each file. This box is checked by default.

■ *Include Subdirectories* erases files in subdirectories of the current directory that match the file specification.

■ *Include Hidden Files* erases hidden files that match the file specification.

■ *Include Read-only Files* erases read-only files that match the file specification.

The File Options dialog box lists three groups of option buttons. The first group of options determines whether Wipe uses the archive bit to determine to erase a file. This group includes the following options:

- *Only Modified Files* erases only files that have the archive bit set and that meet the file specification.

- *Only Unmodified Files* erases only files that do not have the archive bit set and that match the file specification.

- *Both Modified and Unmodified* erases all files that match the file specification (this setting is the default).

The second set of option buttons determine whether the program permanently erases the specified files, erases data remaining in unused portions of the clusters allocated to the specified files, or deletes the specified files in such a manner that they can be recovered. The following list includes these options:

- *Wipe Files* permanently erases specified files by overwriting the files with a set pattern of data. You cannot recover files erased in this fashion.

- *Clear Only Unused File Space* overwrites the unused portions of the clusters assigned to the specified files. Use this option to ensure that data from previously deleted files does not remain in portions of clusters not being used by the specified files.

> **NOTE** DOS allocates disk space to files in clusters, rather than byte-by-byte. DOS typically allocates four 512-byte sectors per cluster. A file that occupies 577 bytes, for example, is allocated an entire cluster, which is 2,048 bytes. Of these 2,048 bytes, only 577 bytes contain data from the file. The remaining 1,471 bytes are allocated to the file but are not used to store data. Data from a previously deleted file may still reside in this unused space.

- *Delete Files* deletes files by using the same method as the DOS and PC Shell delete commands. You can use Undelete to recover files deleted in this manner. If you want to delete all of the files on a disk, type *.* in the File Specification text box. Make sure the Include Subdirectories box has been checked.

The last group of option buttons enables you to limit the files that are erased according to the date the files were last modified. The following options are in this group:

- *Older Than* erases every file that matches the file specification and that has a file date and time the same as or earlier than the date and time specified in the two text boxes that appear to the right of this group of option buttons.

- *Equal To* erases every file that matches the file specification and that has a file date and time the same as the date and time specified in the text boxes that appear to the right of this group of option buttons.

- *Younger Than* erases every file that matches the file specification and that has a file date and time the same as or later than the date and time specified in the two text boxes that appear to the right of this group of option buttons.

- *Any Date/Time* erases all files that match the file specification, without regard to the file dates and times. This option is the default.

After you have chosen from among the available check boxes and option buttons, select the **OK** command button to proceed with the operation.

Wiping Disks

To wipe all data from an entire disk, choose the **D**isk command button from the Wipe Main Menu screen. Wipe displays the Disk Options dialog box (see fig. 13.10).

Fig. 13.10

The Disk Options dialog box.

By default, Wipe lists your first floppy disk drive as the drive that contains the disk you want to erase. The example in figure 13.10 lists drive A. To erase a different disk, select the Change **D**rive command button. Wipe displays the Drive Selection dialog box. Type the drive letter or use the mouse or cursor-movement keys to highlight the drive you want to choose. Select the **OK** command button. Wipe returns to the Disk Options dialog box.

The Disk Options dialog box displays these option buttons:

- *Wipe Disk* permanently erases the contents of the entire disk by overwriting a set pattern of data to every sector on the disk.

■ *Clear Only Unused Disk Space* permanently erases the contents of all unused space on the disk, including unused portions of allocated clusters.

After you choose from these options, select the **OK** command button to proceed with the operation. Wipe displays a caution message to remind you that the program is about to wipe the specified disk (or clear the unused area). Select **W**ipe (or **C**lear) to complete the process.

As Wipe wipes or clears the disk, the program displays the Percent Completed dialog box, which indicates the operation's progress.

Configuring Wipe

By default, Wipe permanently erases data by overwriting all target bytes with the hexadecimal value 00 (decimal 0). The program writes this value once to every byte you specified. For an additional measure of security, Wipe enables you to change the characters written to the disk and to increase the number of times Wipe overwrites the data. You can configure the program to comply with Department of Defense (DOD) requirements for erasing sensitive information.

To change Wipe's configuration, display the Wipe Main Menu screen and select the **C**onfigure command button. Wipe displays the Configuration Options dialog box (see fig. 13.11).

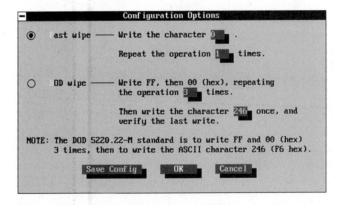

To change the value that Wipe writes over bytes being erased, select the **F**ast Wipe option button and use the mouse or cursor-movement keys to highlight the Write the Character text box. Type the ASCII decimal value of the character you want Wipe to use. In the Repeat the Operation text box, type a number that indicates the number of times you want Wipe to overwrite the bytes being erased.

When you want or need to comply with Department of Defense requirements for erasing sensitive data from a disk, select the **D**OD Wipe option button. The next time you use Wipe to erase a file or disk, the program writes FF (hexadecimal) and then 00 (hexadecimal) to every byte, and then repeats the same procedure two more times.

For Related Information

◀◀ "Changing an Item's Position or Program Group," p. 117.

◀◀ "Using Wipe To Clear Files," p. 152.

▶▶ "Running Install," p. 911.

FROM HERE...

Wiping Files from the DOS Command Line

You can wipe selected files or all the files from a disk from the DOS command line by using the following the parameters:

WIPE d: /DISK /GOVT /QUIET /REP:n /UNUSED /VALUE:n /VIDEO /?

Rather than wiping a complete disk, you can wipe files by using the following parameters:

WIPE d: filespec /DELETE /GOVT/HIDDEN /READONLY /MODIFIED /NOCONFIRM /QUIET /REP:n /SUB /UNMODIFIED /UNUSED / VALUE:n /VIDEO /?

Table 13.3 lists the parameters from the syntax lines above and their meanings.

Table 13.3 Available Wipe Parameters

Parameter	Meaning
d:	Substitute the name of the drive you want to wipe or from which you want to wipe files.
/DISK	Wipes all of the files from the entire disk. When you use the /DISK parameter, you cannot use the following parameters: *filespec*, /DELETE, /HIDDEN, /MODIFIED, /NOCONFIRM, /READONLY, /SUB, or /UNMODIFIED.

continues

Table 13.3 Continued

Parameter	Meaning
/DELETE	This parameter is analogous to the DOS DELETE command. Files that are removed from the disk with the /DELETE command can be recovered with the Undelete utility. When you use the /DELETE parameter, you cannot use the following parameters: /DISK, /GOVT, /REP, or /VALUE.
filespec	Substitute the name of the file or files to be wiped from the disk. You can use either full names or the wildcards * and ? to include a group of files. When you use the *filespec* parameter, you cannot use the /DISK parameter.
/READONLY	Use the /READONLY parameter to wipe all the read-only files from the subdirectory. You also can use the /READONLY parameter with the /DELETE parameter to delete all read-only files in the specified directory. When you use the /READONLY parameter, you cannot use the /DISK parameter.
/GOVT	Follows the U.S. Department of Defense standards for wiping a disk. When you use the /GOVT parameter, you cannot use the /DELETE parameter.
/HIDDEN	Wipes all the hidden files from the subdirectory. You also can use the /HIDDEN parameter with the /DELETE parameter to delete all hidden files in the specified directory. When you use the /HIDDEN parameter, you cannot use the /DISK parameter.
/MODIFIED	Wipes all the files that have been modified since the last backup from the subdirectory. You can also use the /MODIFIED parameter with the /DELETE parameter to delete all files modified since the last backup in the specified subdirectory. When you use the /MODIFIED parameter, you cannot use the /DISK or the /UNMODIFIED parameter.
/NOCONFIRM	Wipes or deletes files without requiring confirmation for each file. When you use the /NOCONFIRM parameter, you cannot use the /DISK parameter.
/QUIET	Displays only status information, no prompts.
/READONLY	Wipes all the read-only files from the subdirectory. You can also use the /READONLY parameter with the /DELETE parameter to delete all read-only files in the specified directory. When you use the /READONLY parameter, you cannot use the /DISK parameter.

Parameter	Meaning
REP:*n*	Repeats the wiping process *n* times. The default is 1. When you use the /REP parameter, you cannot use the /DELETE parameter.
/SUB	Wipes all the files from the subdirectory. You can also use the /SUB parameter with the /DELETE parameter to delete all files in the specified subdirectory. When you use the /SUB parameter, you cannot use the /DISK parameter.
/UNMODIFIED	Wipes all the files that have not been modified since the last backup from the subdirectory. You can also use the /UNMODIFIED parameter with the /DELETE parameter to delete all files that have not been modified since the last backup in the specified subdirectory. When you use the /UNMODIFIED parameter, you cannot use the /DISK or the /MODIFIED parameter.
/UNUSED	Wipes only the unused space on the disk. When you use the /UNUSED parameter, you cannot use the /DISK parameter.
/VALUE:*n*	This parameter is the character to be written over data during a wipe. Use the character's ASCII number in place of *n*. The default is 0. When you use the /VALUE parameter, you cannot use the /DELETE parameter.
/VIDEO	Displays command line help for the video and mouse options.
/?	Displays command line help.

To Wipe all the files from a disk using two repetitions to meet the DOD standards and using the NOCONFIRM parameter, for example, type the following statement:

WIPE C: /GOVT /REP2 /NOCONFIRM

To wipe only the unused part of the disk, type the following statement:

WIPE C: /UNUSED

To only delete all the files in the budget directory and any subdirectories, type the following statement:

WIPE C:\Budget /DELETE /SUB

When you use the /SUB parameter, Wipe deletes the files from the specified directory and all the subdirectories; however, the subdirectories remain. You have to use the DOS RD (Remove Directory) command to remove the directories.

Chapter Summary

This chapter explains how to use PC Secure. You learned how to start the program, enter password keys, and select the type of encryption. You learned also how to choose other options, such as hiding encrypted files, making files read-only, deleting the original files, using Expert mode, and saving your PC Secure settings. The chapter also discusses how to run the encryption and decryption operations. Finally, this chapter teaches you how to use Wipe to erase the contents of files and disks.

Protecting Your System with CP Anti-Virus

Computer viruses are programs that attach to program files and become active when you use the program. Many types of viruses exist. Some viruses locate themselves in your computer's memory; other viruses attach themselves to the boot-sector or partition table; still other viruses attach themselves to your executable files.

Some viruses can be destructive. These viruses, for example, can damage the files with which they come in contact, delete all the files on your hard disk at a certain day and time, or damage the partition table of your hard disk. Other viruses, although not destructive, can be annoying. These viruses, for example, can issue random sounds or send off-color messages to the screen.

The chances that a computer virus may attack your computer are increasing, especially if you work in an office with multiple PCs connected to local area networks or PCs that communicate over modem lines. Often, downloading files from bulletin boards introduces viruses into computers. Because files are uploaded to bulletin boards every day, someone can easily load a file that infects the memory of the host machine. Afterward, everyone who calls may unknowingly download an infected file. Most reputable BBS's use virus protection software and scan files as they are uploaded to prevent contamination. To be safe, scan all files before you copy them to your hard disk.

You must take steps to protect the precious data on your computer. Using Central Point Anti-Virus daily is a good start. This chapter discusses how to use Central Point Anti-Virus to detect and remove viruses from your system, how to immunize your system against future attacks, and how to keep your virus definitions up-to-date. You also learn how to use the Express Menu and the full menus.

In addition, you learn how to defend your computer from viruses by installing into memory either VSAFE or VWatch (two programs that watch for viruses attempting to enter your System). You learn how to use BootSafe to protect the partition table and boot sector on your computer. Finally, you learn about other steps you can take as preventive measures, such as creating a rescue disk, configuring scheduler to do a daily anti-virus check, and immunizing files.

Scanning with Express

To start Central Point Anti-Virus Express, type the following command on the command line and press Enter:

    CPAV /E

You can use Central Point Anti-Virus in two ways. You can use the full menus or you can use the simpler Central Point Anti-Virus Express menu. If you are unfamiliar with virus software, you may want to begin with the Express menu.

When you start the program, the Express Menu appears (see fig. 14.1). The Express Menu enables you to do the basics: you can detect and clean viruses, select a new drive, and switch to full menus. The Express Menu displays function-key commands in the message bar. The function-key commands and other keystroke commands available for the Express Menu are shown table 14.1.

Using the shortcut keys for commands and menu options accessible through the Express Menu, you can perform these functions:

■ *Detect* enables you to search the memory and currently selected disk for viruses. If Detect finds a virus, select *Detect & Clean* to remove the virus from your disk.

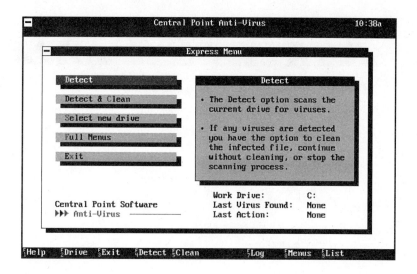

Fig. 14.1

The Express
Menu.

NOTE You may want to copy the infected file to a disk as a precaution. If the file repair is not successful, you can call Central Point and update your virus definitions and try the repair again. Be sure to label the disk as infected.

- *Detect & Clean* scans the memory and the selected disk. If a virus is found, it cleans the disk, removing the virus automatically, and updates the Last Action taken information on the lower right corner of the screen.

- *Select New Drive* enables you to change the drive you want to scan. The current drive is displayed in the lower right corner of the screen.

- *Full Menus* switches you to the full menu version of Central Point Anti-Virus.

- *Exit* closes Central Point Anti-Virus.

Table 14.1 Keystroke Commands Available in Central Point Anti-Virus

Key	Name	Function
F1	Help	Displays the context-sensitive Help facility
F2	Drive	Enables you to change to a different drive

continues

Table 14.1 Continued

Key	Name	Function
F3	Exit	Cancels the scan and exits from the Express Menu
F4	Detect	Begins scanning memory and files
F5	Clean	Begins scanning of memory and the selected disk and cleans any found viruses off the disk
F7	Log	Displays the current activity log
F8	Menus	Switches to full menus
F9	List	Displays the virus list
Esc	Pauses	Pauses or cancels the current process or exits from Central Point Anti-Virus.

Searching for Viruses

To check a disk to see whether it contains a virus, choose **D**etect or press F4 (Detect). The Scanning Memory for Viruses appears with a progress bar showing the percentage of memory that has been scanned (see fig. 14.2). When the memory scan is complete, the box leaves the screen, and the scan of the disk begins. Two progress bars appear in the Detect information box (see fig. 14.3). These bars give you an idea of how many files are yet to be scanned in the directory and how many directories remain to be scanned.

Fig. 14.2

The Scanning Memory for Viruses dialog box.

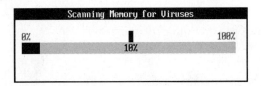

NOTE Memory is only scanned the first time you do a scan, not for additional scans.

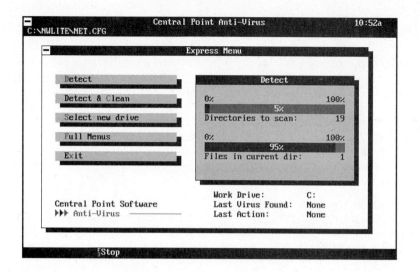

Fig. 14.3

The Express Menu while a scan is in progress.

Scanning your disk the first time takes longer than later scans because a special file called CHKLIST.CPS is created in each directory. The next time you scan will be faster because the files are already in place.

When the scan finishes, a summary of the scan appears in the Viruses Detected and Cleaned dialog box (see fig. 14.4). This summary shows which disks were checked, how many COM and EXE files were checked, and how many files of another type were checked. It also shows the total number of files that were checked, whether any files were infected, and whether any files were cleaned. Choose **OK** after viewing this information. If any viruses were found, see the following section, "Running Detect and Clean."

```
┌─────────────────── Viruses Detected and Cleaned ─────────────────┐
│                                                                  │
│                    Checked        Infected        Cleaned        │
│                                                                  │
│   Hard disks    :     1              0               0           │
│   Floppy disks  :     0              0               0           │
│   Total disks   :     1              0               0           │
│                                                                  │
│   COM Files     :    48              0               0           │
│   EXE Files     :   121              0               0           │
│   Other Files   :   428              0               0           │
│   Total Files   :   597              0               0           │
│                                                                  │
│   Scan Time     :  00:04:36                                      │
│                                                      ┌────────┐  │
│                                                      │   OK   │  │
│                                                      └────────┘  │
└──────────────────────────────────────────────────────────────────┘
```

Fig. 14.4

The Viruses Detected and Cleaned dialog box.

Running Detect and Clean

If your programs are not working properly or if your computer is not behaving as it normally does, you may have a virus. You may have no "symptoms" and still have a virus. Regular scans can spot viruses early. If you suspect your computer has a virus, shut the computer off and restart it with the Emergency Disk you created during the installation process. The Emergency Disk has a virus-free copy of Central Point Anti-Virus on it, as well as other useful utilities for repairing disks. For information about how to create a write-protected emergency disk, see Chapter 6, "Working on Disks."

If you do not have an Emergency Disk, start your system from a write-protected floppy disk with a copy of the system files that match those currently installed on your computer. Then start Central Point Anti-Virus by typing the following command at the DOS prompt and pressing Enter:

    CPAV /E

Choose Detect & Clean from the Express Menu or press F5 (Clean). A dialog box containing the message Scanning memory for viruses and a progress bar showing the percentage of memory that has been scanned appears. When the memory scan is complete, the box disappears, and the scan of the disk begins. Two progress bars appear in the Detect information box (refer to fig. 14.2). These bars give you an idea of how many files are yet to be scanned in the directory and how many directories remain to be scanned.

As each file is scanned, its name appears briefly in the path line in the upper left corner of the screen. The program doesn't stop if it finds a virus. Viruses are cleaned automatically as they are detected. If a virus is found, the virus name and the fact that it is being cleaned appears in the information window. This same information is also stored in the Viruses Detected and Cleaned summary and in the Activity Log. You can pause the scan at any time by pressing Esc; to stop the scan completely, press F3 (Exit).

Changing Drives

To search for viruses on a different drive, choose Select New Drive from the Express Menu or press F2 (Drive). Drive icons appear at the top of the screen, starting on the left side (see fig. 14.5). Choose the icon that represents the drive you want and press Enter. When you change to a different drive, the Reading Disk information box appears. After a few moments, the box clears and you can begin scanning the new disk. The new drive letter follows the words Work Drive under the information box.

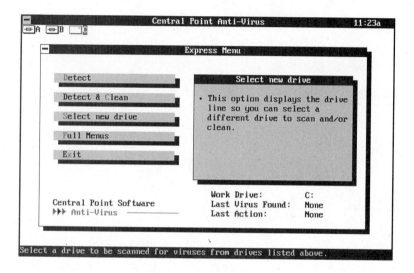

Fig. 14.5

The current drive designated in the Work Drive section.

Switching to Full Menus

To take advantage of the full functionality of Central Point Anti-Virus, you can switch to the full menus by choosing Full Menus from the Express Menu or pressing F8 (Menus). A feature-by-feature explanation of the full menus begins with the section "Starting Central Point Anti-Virus Using Full Menus."

Exiting from the Express Menu

To exit from the Express Menu, choose Exit or press F3 (Exit). The Close Central Point Anti-Virus dialog box appears (see fig. 14.6). If you have made any changes to the configuration of the program, make sure the Save Configuration box is checked, and then choose OK. Central Point Anti-Virus closes and returns to the DOS prompt.

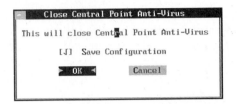

Fig. 14.6

The Close
Central Point
Anti-Virus dialog
box.

FROM HERE...

For Related Information

◀◀ "Preparing an Emergency Disk," p. 216.

Starting Central Point Anti-Virus Using Full Menus

To protect your files from viruses, follow these four guidelines:

- Immunize your files and create checklist files and checksums. These precautions describe how the files look on the disk without a virus present.

- Keep your virus list up-to-date by calling Central Point regularly.

- Install VSAFE or VWATCH in your AUTOEXEC.BAT file to detect viruses.

- Scan your disks regularly.

If this is the first time you are starting Central Point Anti-Virus, the Express Menu may appear instead of the main menu. If it does, press F8 (Menus) to see the full menus (see fig. 14.7). The top third of the main Central Point Anti-Virus window contains a horizontal menu bar, a drive line, and panels containing file information, virus information, and last action information. The Directory Tree and Files in Current Directory panels take the majority of space in the Window. A message bar, which shows the shortcut keys for the important operations in the Anti-Virus program, appears across the bottom of the screen.

The following lists and describes the contents of the main window:

- The *horizontal menu bar* contains the Scan, Options, Configure, and Help menus. To open any of the menus, press the first letter in the menu name.

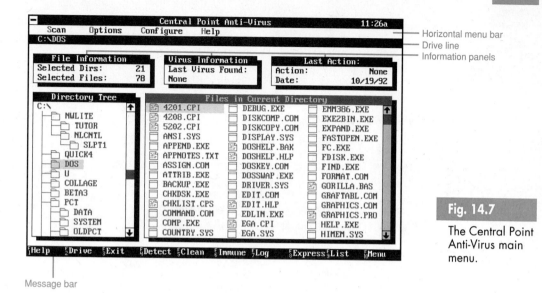

Horizontal menu bar
Drive line
Information panels

Fig. 14.7

The Central Point Anti-Virus main menu.

Message bar

■ The *drive line* appears below the menus. The names of each of the files being scanned flash across the drive line. When scanning is not taking place, the drive line shows the path name of the currently selected directory.

■ The *File Information panel* shows the number of selected directories and files. Selected files and directories appear in boldface in the Directory Tree and Files in Current Directory panels.

■ The *Virus Information panel* shows the name of any virus found during the last scan in this session. Most of the time, this box says None.

■ The *Last Action panel* tells you the last action that you took—Detect, Clean, Immunize, and so on. At the start of each session, this panel says None.

■ The *Directory Tree panel* shows a graphical representation of the directory structure of the working disk. To scan a single directory, select the directory in this window before choosing Detect or Clean from the Scan menu.

■ The *Files in Current Directory panel* shows the names of the files in the currently selected directory. This panel automatically updates as you move the highlight bar in the Directory Tree panel. You can select a single file or a group of files in this directory before you choose Detect or Clean from the Scan menu.

■ The *message bar* shows the shortcut keys for the important operations in the Anti-Virus program. Messages also appear in this space: for example, if you open the Scan menu, the Detect command is highlighted. The message in the message bar says `Scans selected files for viruses`. Check the message bar from time to time for useful messages.

Table 14.2 shows a brief explanation of the shortcut keys in the message bar.

Table 14.2 Shortcut Keys in the Central Point Anti-Virus Message Bar

Key	Name	Function
F1	Help	Displays the context-sensitive Help facility.
F2	Drive	Enables you to change to a different drive.
F3	Exit	Cancels the scan and exits from the Central Point Anti-Virus Menu.
F4	Detect	Begins scanning memory and files.
F5	Clean	Begins scanning the memory and the selected disk and cleans any found viruses off the disk.
F6	Immune	Immunizes the selected files.
F7	Log	Displays the current activity log.
F8	Express	Switches to the Express Menu.
F9	List	Displays the virus list.
F10	Menu	Moves the cursor to the menu bar.
Esc	Pauses	Pauses or cancels the current process or exits from PC Secure.

Choosing a File, Disk, or Directory To Scan

When you use the long menus, you can scan the entire disk, or you can selectively scan a directory or a file. Choosing what you want to scan before you start scanning can save time.

■ *Changing Drives.* Each time you start Central Point Anti-Virus, your *working disk* is the disk in which the Anti-Virus program is located. To choose another disk to scan, open the **C**onfigure menu and choose Change Work **D**rive. Alternatively, press F2 (Drive). Drive icons appear in the drive line (see fig. 14.8).

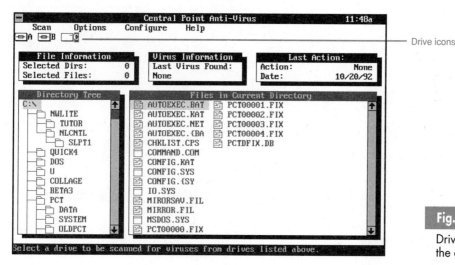

Drive icons

Fig. 14.8

Drive icons in the drive line.

Choose the icon that represents the drive you want and press Enter. When you change to a different drive, the Reading Disk information box appears. After a few moments, the box clears, and you can begin scanning the new disk. The new drive letter appears in the drive line, and the Directory Tree and Files in Current Directory panels are updated to show the contents of the new drive.

■ *Choosing a Directory.* When Central Point Anti-Virus starts, it selects all files in all directories. To scan only one directory, activate the Directory Tree panel by clicking it. Alternatively, press Tab until the title bar is highlighted. Then click the first entry in the tree or press the space bar; in the File Information panel, a zero appears after Selected Dirs and Selected Files. Highlight the directory you want to scan by clicking the directory or by pressing the space bar. When you choose a directory, all files in the directory and any subdirectories are selected as well.

■ *Choosing a File.* If you want to scan only a file or group of files and all files are selected, make the Directory Tree panel the active panel by clicking it or by pressing Tab until the title bar is highlighted. Then click the first entry in the tree or press the space bar; in the File Information panel, a zero appears after Selected

Dirs and Selected Files. In the Files in Current Directory panel, highlight the file you want to scan by clicking the file name or by highlighting the file name with the arrow keys and pressing the space bar.

You can now perform any command; you can detect, clean, or immunize the currently selected disk, drive, or files.

Searching for Viruses Using the Long Menus

To check a disk for a virus, open the **S**can menu and choose **D**etect, or press F4 (Detect). A dialog box containing the message Scanning memory for viruses appears, and a progress bar showing the percentage of memory that has been scanned appears.

When the memory scan is complete, the dialog box leaves the screen, and the scan of the disk begins. The scan starts with the files in the root directory; the highlight bar moves down each row of files names as the files are scanned. When all the files in a directory are scanned, the highlight bar moves down in the directory tree and the files in the new directory are scanned. The name of each file scanned flashes through the drive line.

Scanning your disk the first time takes longer than later scans will, because a special file called CHKLIST.CPS is created in each directory. The next time you scan will be faster because the files are already in place.

When the scan is finished, a summary of the scan appears in the Viruses Detected and Cleaned dialog box (refer to fig 14.4). This summary shows which disks were checked, how many COM and EXE files were checked, and how many files of another type were checked. This dialog box also shows the total number of files that were checked and whether any files were infected or cleaned. Choose **OK** after viewing this information. If any viruses were found, see the following section, "Cleaning Viruses."

Cleaning Viruses

If you suspect that your computer has a virus, shut your computer off and restart it with the Emergency Disk you created during the installation process. The Emergency Disk has a virus-free copy of Central Point

Anti-Virus on it, as well as other utilities useful for repairing disks. For information about how to create an Emergency Disk, see Chapter 6, "Working on Disks."

If you do not have an Emergency Disk, start your system from a write-protected floppy disk with a copy of the system files that match those currently installed on your computer. Then start Central Point Anti-Virus by typing the following command at the DOS prompt and pressing Enter:

    CPAV

Open the **S**can menu and choose **C**lean or press F5 (Clean). A dialog box containing the message Scanning memory for viruses appears, with a progress bar showing the percentage of memory that has been scanned. When the memory scan is complete, the box leaves the screen, and the scan of the disk begins. You see the same scanning process as described in the earlier section "Searching for Viruses Using the Long Menus."

When a virus is found, the computer beeps; the virus name and information appears in the Virus Found dialog box (see fig. 14.9). (This information is also stored in the Viruses Detected and Cleaned summary and in the Activity Log.) Choose **C**lean to remove the virus. Choose **C**ontinue to continue the scan without removing the virus. Choose **S**top to end the scan. Choose **D**elete to remove the infected file instead of cleaning it. You can pause the scan at any time by pressing Esc; to stop the scan completely, press F3 (Exit).

Fig. 14.9

The Virus Found dialog box.

NOTE Some people prefer making a copy of the file before cleaning it in case the virus damage cannot be reversed. Mark the disk "infected," and store it separately so that you don't use this infected disk by mistake. Others prefer to delete infected files and reinstall fresh files from the write-protected program disk. This method ensures the virus is gone and the program will function correctly in the future.

Immunizing Your Files

Another way that Central Point Anti-Virus can help keep your files virus-free is by immunizing them. *Immunizing* files adds less than 1K to the file and does not cause the file to occupy any additional space in memory. If a virus attempts to change an immunized file, it can set off an alert similar to the following:

```
Central Point Anti-Virus   1992 CPS

Self Integrity Check warning - File was changed!

Choose an option:

[R]      Self Reconstruction

[C]      Continue Execution

[E]      Exit to DOS

Press R, C, or E:
```

When you see this message, press R for Self Reconstruction. Then start Central Point Anti-Virus and scan the entire disk.

When you are ready to immunize the files, select the disk, directories, or files from which you want to immunize; see the earlier section "Choosing a File, Disk, or Directory To Scan" for an explanation of selection techniques. Open the **S**can menu and choose **I**mmunization or press F6 (Immune). The highlight bar moves across each file as immunization is added, and the name of each file appears on the drive line. To pause the immunization process, press Esc or F3 (Exit).

 NOTE If Immunize is grayed on the Scan menu, open the **O**ptions menu and choose Set **O**ptions. Uncheck the Detection Only option. See "Setting Options" later in this chapter for a complete explanation of all options.

When the immunization process is finished, a dialog box with statistics of how many and what type of disks and files were immunized appears. These statistics are saved in the activity log so that you can consult them later. Choose **OK** to clear the dialog box from the screen and return to the main window.

Removing Immunization

Because each immunization file uses about 1K of space, you may want to remove an immunization from your files if you are short on disk space. Or you may find a file acting a little strangely. In this case, remove the immunization and add the file to the Immunization Exceptions List as described in the next section.

To remove immunization, select the disk, directories, or files from which you want to remove the immunization. (See the earlier section "Choosing a File, Disk, or Directory To Scan" for an explanation of selection techniques.) Open the **S**can menu and choose **R**emove Immunization. As immunization is removed from the files, the highlight bar moves across each file, and the name of each file appears on the drive line. You can pause the immunization removal process by pressing Esc or F3 (Exit).

 NOTE   If Remove Immunization is grayed on the Scan menu, open the **O**ptions menu and choose Set **O**ptions. Uncheck the Detection Onl**y** option. See "Setting Options" later in this chapter for a complete explanation of all options.

After you remove the immunization from all selected files, the Files DisImmunized dialog box appears, containing statistics of how many and what type of disks and files had their immunization removed. These statistics are saved in the activity log so that you can consult them later. Choose **OK** to clear the dialog box from the screen and return to the main window.

Setting Immunization Exceptions

Sometimes a program that has been immunized does not function correctly. If that is the case, you can return the file to normal by removing the immunization. In addition, Central Point Anti-Virus automatically adds the following files to the Immunization Exceptions box if these files are found during a scan:

- EXE files with overlays or debugging information at the end of the file
- EXE files with a corrupted header
- EXE and COM files smaller than 14 bytes (excluding the header)
- COM files larger than 63K
- Files with their own self-checking system
- Windows or OS/2 files

To add a file to the Immunization Exceptions list, follow these steps:

1. Open the Configure menu and select Immunization Exceptions. The Immunization Exceptions dialog box appears (see fig. 14.10).

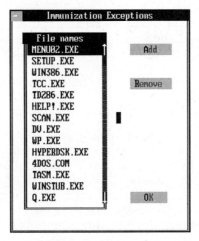

Fig. 14.10

The Immunization Exceptions dialog box.

2. Choose Add. The Add to Exception List dialog box appears (see fig. 14.11).

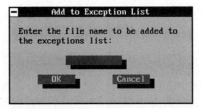

Fig. 14.11

The Add to Exception List dialog box.

3. In the text box, type the file name and choose OK. You are returned to the Immunization Exceptions dialog box.

4. Choose OK again to close the Immunization Exceptions dialog box and return to the main menu.

You can remove a file from the list at any time by opening the Configure menu and selecting Immunization Exceptions. The Immunization Exceptions dialog box appears (refer to fig. 14.11). Highlight the file and choose Remove. Choose OK to close the Immunization Exceptions dialog box and return to the main menu.

Setting Options

You can set several options that affect scanning. You also can limit the actions that someone using the program can take. If you share a computer or if you are a system administrator, you can customize Central Point Anti-Virus's options and protect the options with a password. To change options, open the Options menu and choose Set Options. The Options Settings dialog box appears (see fig. 14.12). Choose any options you want to change, and then choose OK.

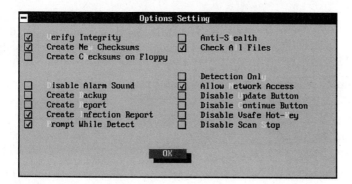

Fig. 14.12

The Options Settings dialog box.

The following list explains each option in the Options Settings dialog box.

- *Verify Integrity*. When on, this option compares the current checksums of executable and system files to what those options were the last time a scan was run. If a difference is found, a Verify Error Warning appears on-screen each time an error is found in a file. When this option is on, you can also turn on the Anti-Stealth option. If a Verify Error is found, Central Point Anti-Virus launches a special error-checking routine to perform a low-level search for a *stealth virus*, which uses different ways of evading detection.

   If you turn Verify Integrity off, the Anti-Stealth option is also turned off. For the highest level of virus protection, leave both the Anti-Stealth and Verify Integrity options turned on.

- *Anti-Stealth*. This option works with Verify Integrity; if you turn this option on, Verify Integrity is also turned on. This option causes a low-level check for stealth viruses when a verify error is found. For the greatest protection from stealth viruses, turn this option and Verify Integrity on.

■ *Create New Checksums.* This option makes a file named CHKLIST.CPS for each directory during scanning. The file keeps statistics—size, attributes, date, time, and checksum, for example—about the executable files in the directory. A *checksum* is a mathematically created value that uniquely identifies the file. After a checksum is created for each file, future scans compare the current checksum to the original. If a difference exists, the file may be infected.

■ *Create Checksum on Floppy.* This option does for floppy disks the same thing that Create New Checksums does for directories.

■ *Check All Files.* This option causes data files and executable files to be checked for viruses. When this option is off, only files with the following extensions will be scanned: APP, BIN, CMD, COM, DLL, DRV, FON, ICO, OV? OVL, OVR, OVY, PGM, PRG, SYS, and 386.

■ **Disable Alarm Sound.** This option prevents an alarm from sounding when a warning message appears.

■ *Create Backup.* This option creates a backup of the file before Central Point Anti-Virus attempts to clean the file and renames the extension VIR so that the file cannot be executed accidentally.

■ *Create Report.* This option makes an ASCII report file called Central Point Anti-Virus.RPT in the root directory of the selected drive after any action is taken. If the disk is write-protected, an error message appears. If you want the report, you must remove the write protection. The report contains the following information:

```
          Central Point Anti-Virus

          Virus search report for the date: 10/15/92,
Time 09:15:32.

          Virus Dark Avenger was found in the file:

          C:\SPREADSH\BIGSHEET.XLS

          Total boot sector viruses  FOUND    :    0

          Total boot sector viruses  REMOVED :    0

          Total Files  CHECKED             :   982

     Total File viruses      FOUND        :    1

          Total File viruses  REMOVED      :    1

          END OF REPORT
```

■ *Create Infection Report.* This option makes a \REPORTS directory under the directory where Central Point Anti-Virus is located. A report is created each time you use Anti-Virus, and each report has a numbered extension, starting with 000. If the program is run from a network drive, the activity report shows the user name of the person who ran the program where the drive ID and volume name normally appear.

■ *Prompt While Detect.* This option displays the Virus Found dialog box if a virus is found during a scan. The Virus Found dialog box gives you the option to clean the virus or to continue. If this option is disabled, viruses are cleaned automatically.

■ *Detection Only.* When you choose this option, you cannot use the following options: Clean, Immunize, Remove Immunization, and Delete Checklist Files.

■ *Enable Network Access.* This option enables you to scan a network drive from your desktop machine.

■ *Disable Update Button.* This option prevents you from updating a checksum if a verify error is found and a Verify dialog box appears. If you have VSafe installed and a VSafe Warning box appears saying that an executable file has changed, the Update button is disabled.

■ *Disable Continue Button.* This option prevents you from continuing the scan if a Virus Found dialog box appears. You must clean the file, delete the file, or stop the scan. By turning this option off, you also turn off the continue button in all VSafe alert dialog boxes.

■ *Disable VSafe Hot-Key.* This option prevents you from using the VSafe control menu with its hotkey, ensuring that users do not bypass the use of VSafe.

■ *Disable Scan.* This option prevents you from interrupting a scan by pressing the F3 Stop key.

Using Checklist Files and Checksums

Because new viruses that change the contents of your disk in new and unpredictable ways are being unleashed every day, Central Point Anti-Virus needs a benchmark to show how the uninfected disk looks. One way to create a benchmark is to create a checksum for each file. A checksum is created automatically the first time a directory is scanned, as long as you have left the Create New Checksums option set in the Options Setting dialog box.

A *checksum* is a mathematically created value that uniquely identifies the file. After a checksum is created for each file, future scans compare the current checksum to the original. During scanning, Central Point Anti-Virus stores checksums for each directory as part of a file named CHKLIST.CPS. The file keeps statistics—such as size, attributes, date, time, and checksum, for example—about the executable files in the directory. If a difference exists between the current file and the checksum, the file may be infected. You might want to remove the checksum file from the directory, however, for two reasons.

First, if you are tight on disk space and need the additional space to store some important data, you may want to forgo this virus protection measure. Second, if you just bought an upgrade for one of your software packages, the new program files have new checksum values, causing you to set off Verify Warning Error messages unnecessarily. In this case, remove the checksum from the directories used by this program and then rescan the directories with the Create New Checksums option on. Also remove immunization from the affected directories and immunize those directories again so that you do not get error messages about infected files. (See the section "Immunizing Your Files" earlier in this chapter for specific instructions.)

To remove the Checksums, select the directory or directories from which you want to remove the Checksums, as described in the section "Choosing a File, Disk, or Directory To Scan." Open the **S**can menu and choose Delete Checklist **F**iles. The Delete Checklist Files dialog box appears. Choose **D**elete.

Setting Exceptions for Checksums

Some people like to tinker with their AUTOEXEC.BAT and CONFIG.SYS files, yet constantly rescanning these directories to keep the checksums up-to-date can be very time-consuming. The alternative is to list these and other frequently changing files in the Verification Exceptions list. The list can be password-protected and can contain up to 3,000 entries.

To add a file to the list, follow these steps:

1. Open the **C**onfigure menu and select **V**erification Exceptions. The Verification Exceptions dialog box appears.

2. Choose **A**dd. The Add to Exception List box appears (see fig. 14.13).

3. Type in the file name and choose **OK**. You return to the Verification Exceptions dialog box.

Fig. 14.13

The Add to
Exception List
dialog box.

4. Choose **OK** again to close the Verification Exceptions dialog box and return to the main menu. To implement the new exceptions, reboot your system.

To remove a file from the list at any time, open the **C**onfigure menu and select **V**erification Exceptions. The Verification Exceptions dialog box appears. Highlight the file and choose **R**emove. Then choose **OK** again to close the Verification Exceptions dialog box and return to the main menu.

Scheduling Automatic Detection and Cleaning

PC Tools Scheduler can run Central Point Anti-Virus Detect or Clean automatically and unattended. You can set it up to check drives on your computer or network drives. To be completely automatic, your computer must be on and the scheduler program CPSCHED must be included in your computer's AUTOEXEC.BAT file. This chapter shows the basics about using the scheduler. For complete details, see Chapter 3, "Using the Desktop as a Program Manager."

If you happen to be using your computer at the scheduled scanning time, a message telling you the scheduler is about to run appears. You then have 15 seconds to exit the program in which you are working, or you can stop the scheduler.

You can also start the scheduler from the DOS prompt by typing the following command and pressing Enter.

    CPSCHED

You can remove the scheduler from memory. At the DOS prompt, type the following command and press Enter.

    CPSCHED /U

To schedule a scan, follow these steps:

1. Open the **C**onfigure menu and choose **S**chedule Anti-Virus Scanning. The DOS Program Scheduler 8.0 window appears (see fig. 14.14).

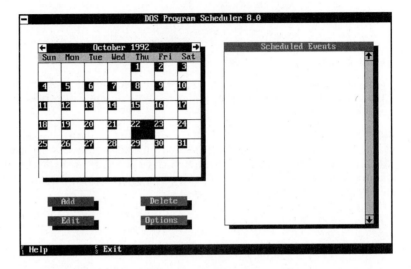

2. On the Calendar, select the day you want the scan to run and choose **A**dd. The Schedule or Edit an Event dialog box appears (see fig. 14.15).

3. Fill in the date, time, and frequency.

4. Type **Central Point Anti-Virus** and any additional parameters in the event name dialog box. (See the section "Using Command Line Options with Anti-Virus" later in this chapter for command line parameters you can use with Central Point Anti-Virus.)

5. Choose **O**K to save the information.

6. Press F3 when you are finished. The Close dialog box appears. Make sure the Save Changes in Schedule option is checked.

> **NOTE** If you have a password, you must remove the password; otherwise, Central Point Anti-Virus cannot start.

To edit scheduled information, follow these steps:

1. Open the **C**onfigure menu and choose **S**chedule Anti-Virus Scanning. The DOS Program Scheduler 8.0 window appears (refer to fig. 14.14).

2. On the Calendar, select the day you want to change the scan and choose **E**dit. The Schedule or Edit an Event dialog box appears (refer to fig. 14.15).

3. Change the date, time, frequency, or parameters.

4. Choose **OK** to save the information.

5. Press F3 (Exit). The Close dialog box appears.

6. Make sure the Save Changes in Schedule option is checked.

To delete a scan from the schedule, open the **C**onfigure menu and choose **S**chedule Anti-Virus Scanning. On the calendar section of the DOS Program Scheduler 8.0 dialog box, select the day from which you want to delete the scan, and choose **D**elete. Press F3 (Exit) to exit the scheduler. The Close dialog box appears. Make sure the Save Changes in Schedule option is checked.

Using the Activity Log and Infection Reports

Every time you scan, clean, immunize, or remove immunization from a file, an entry is added to the activity log. The activity log is stored as a file called ACTIVITY.CPS in the directory with your PC Tools. The log holds 200 entries. When filled, the older entries are deleted from the end and the newer entries are added to the top. If a virus was found, the log entry appears in a contrasting color.

To view the Activity Log, follow these steps:

1. Open the **S**can menu and choose Activity Log; then from the **A**ctivity Log submenu, choose **S**how. The Activity Log dialog box appears.

2. Highlight an entry where a virus was found.

3. To see the Infection Report, select **I**nfo. The Infection Report dialog box appears (see fig. 14.16).

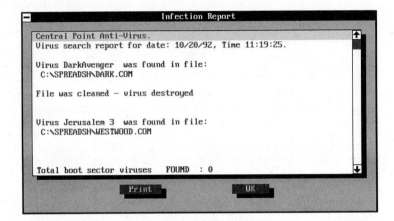

Central Point Anti-Virus.
Virus search report for date: 10/20/92, Time 11:19:25.

Virus DarkAvenger was found in file:
 C:\SPREADSH\DARK.COM

File was cleaned - virus destroyed

Virus Jerusalem 3 was found in file:
 C:\SPREADSH\WESTWOOD.COM

Total boot sector viruses   FOUND : 0

Fig. 14.16

The Infection Report dialog box.

4. To print the Infection report, choose **P**rint.

5. Choose **OK** to return to the Activity Log dialog box.

NOTE   The Activity Report shows NET and the user name of the person who ran the program.

To print a copy of the log, open the **S**can menu and choose Activity Log; then select **P**rint from the Activity Log dialog box. Alternatively, press F7.

To clear all entries from the Activity Log, open the **S**can menu and choose Activity Log; then choose **C**lear from the submenu. A confirmation dialog box appears. Choose **OK** to delete the log file.

Using the Virus List

The Virus List dialog box shows the names of all the viruses Central Point Anti-Virus can detect (see fig. 14.17). The Virus list shows the common name of the virus, the type of virus, and its size. To view the Virus list, open the **S**can menu and choose **V**irus List; then choose **S**how from the Virus List submenu. Alternatively, press F9 (List). The Virus List dialog box appears. You can print the Virus list by choosing the **P**rint command button.

To get specific information about a virus, select the name of the virus in which you are interested and press Tab. Then choose **I**nfo. The Virus Characteristics list box appears. Choose **OK** when you are finished viewing the Virus Characteristics dialog box.

When you are finished viewing the virus list, choose **OK**.

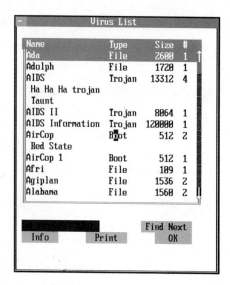

Name	Type	Size	#
Ada	File	2600	1
Adolph	File	1720	1
AIDS	Trojan	13312	4
Ha Ha Ha trojan			
Taunt			
AIDS II	Trojan	8064	1
AIDS Information	Trojan	120000	1
AirCop	Boot	512	2
Red State			
AirCop 1	Boot	512	1
Afri	File	109	1
Agiplan	File	1536	2
Alabama	File	1560	2

Info   Print   Find Next   OK

Fig. 14.17

The Virus List
dialog box.

Updating the Virus List

As new viruses are discovered, Central Point creates signature files to
define the virus. If you keep your virus signatures up-to-date, you improve your chances of detecting a virus before it does damage.

You can get updated virus signatures by phone or by mail. To get virus
signatures by phone, call the Central Point BBS or CompuServe. To get
virus signatures by mail, contact Central Point technical support and
tell them you want to subscribe to the Continuous Anti-Virus Protection (CAP) Service. Members of this service receive disks quarterly.

When you receive the update, you also receive information on how to
decompress the compressed files and copy these files to your PC Tools
directory. The next time you start Central Point AntiVirus, the new
virus signatures are loaded.

Sending Network Notification Messages

If your computer is part of a Novell network, you can notify the system
administrator when a virus is found on your machine. To set up a notification message, follow these steps:

1. Open the Configure menu and choose Send Network Messages To.
   If you have a password, the password dialog box appears. Type in
   your password and choose OK.

   The Network Messages dialog box appears (see fig. 14.18).

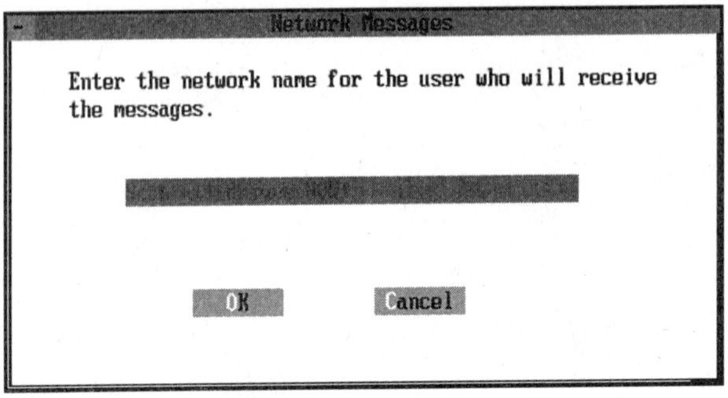

Fig. 14.18

The Network
Messages dialog
box.

2. Type in the user name of the person who should be notified if a virus infection is present.

3. Choose **OK**.

If a virus is found on your system, a message appears on the screen of the person you named and on the system console.

Changing Alert Messages

When a virus is found, you can create a supplemental message, such as "Insert Emergency Disk in A and Reboot," to appear along with the regular CPAV Alert Message. This message will be issued by both the Anti-Virus program and VSafe.

To create your own message, open the **C**onfigure menu and choose Change **A**lert Message. If you have a password, the password dialog box appears. Type in your password and choose **OK**. The Customized Message box appears. Enter your message and choose **OK**.

Setting Passwords

You can set a password to protect certain functions in Central Point Anti-Virus; for example, to change from the Express Menu to the Full Menu, you can make entering a password mandatory. After a password has been activated, you must use it every time you want to change any of the following:

- Alert Messages
- Immunization Exceptions
- Options in the Set Options dialog box
- Send Network Messages
- Verification Exceptions

NOTE Central Point Anti-Virus cannot be password-protected and run automatically from the scheduler.

To create or change a password, follow these steps:

1. Open the **C**onfigure menu and choose Change **P**assword. The Change Password dialog box appears (see fig. 14.19).

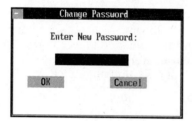

Fig. 14.19

The Change Password dialog box.

2. Enter the existing password, if one exists, or type in a new one and choose **OK**.

3. Enter the new password again for verification and choose **OK**.

To remove a password altogether, follow these steps:

1. Open the **C**onfigure menu and choose Change **P**assword. The change Password dialog box appears.

2. Enter the existing password and choose **OK**.

3. When the prompt changes to Enter New Password, choose **OK**.

4. Choose **OK** again to close the New Password dialog box.

Exiting from Central Point Anti-Virus

To Exit from the Central Point Anti-Virus, choose E**x**it from the **S**can menu or press F3 (Exit). The Close Central Point Anti-Virus dialog box appears. If you made any changes to the configuration of the program, make sure the **S**ave Configuration box is checked. Then choose **OK**.

FROM HERE...

For Related Information

◄◄ "Scheduling Programs with the Scheduler," p. 125.

Using Command Line Options with Anti-Virus

You can use any of the following parameters when you start Central Point Anti-Virus from the command line or in the Scheduler or in a batch file. All of the parameters, shown in the following, can be used together except for /S and /C; you must pick /S or/C, not both:

CPAV *d:* *pathname* *filename* [/S or /C] /A /E /F /I /L /N /P /R /? /VIDEO

These parameters are defined in table 14.3.

Table 14.3 Central Point Anti-Virus Parameters

Parameter	Meaning
/S	Scans the specified disk or files for viruses. Cannot be used with the /C parameter.
/C	Scans and cleans the specified disk.
/A	Scans all hard disks associated with your computer, including network drives. Does not scan A or B, which are typically floppy disk drives.
/E	Starts Central Point Anti-Virus using the Express Menus.
/F	Prevents names of files scanned from being displayed on-screen. This parameter can only be used with /N or /P.
/I	Scans, cleans, and immunizes specified disk and files. Immunization cannot be removed from the command line. Do not use this command with the /P or /N option.

Parameter	Meaning
/L	Scans only local hard drives.
/N	Sends interface information to the Central Point Anti-VIRUS.TXT file, if one exists.
/P	Starts Central Point Anti-Virus using the command-line interface instead of the long menus or Express Menus.
/R	Starts Central Point Anti-Virus with the Create Report option on.
/?	Shows command-line help.
/VIDEO	Shows command-line help for video and mouse options.

Defending against Viruses

PC Tools offers a choice between two memory-resident programs that act as sentries to prevent viruses from infecting your program files.

Use *VSafe* for maximum, continuous protection. VSafe checks files for known viruses before it starts them; it also checks to make sure their checksums have not changed (for more information about checksums see "Using Checklist Files and Checksums" earlier in this chapter). VSafe has eight configurable options and protects your system from both known and unknown viruses.

Use *VWatch* if you have memory constraints. VWatch checks files for known viruses before a program is started or a disk is accessed. If a virus is found, a warning appears on-screen, and all disk activity is halted, giving you have the opportunity to start Central Point Anti-Virus and clean the disk of viruses. VWatch, which has no configurable options that you have to worry about, protects you only against known viruses.

The amount of conventional memory you need depends on whether expanded or extended memory is available, as explained in table 14.4. For example, if you are using VSafe and you have expanded memory available, VSafe only uses 7K of your conventional memory. If you have no expanded memory, then VSafe uses 44K of your conventional memory.

Table 14.4 Conventional Memory Requirements

If VSafe is Using	Conventional Memory Required
Expanded memory	7K
Extended memory	23K
Conventional memory only	44K

If VWatch is Using	Conventional Memory Required
Expanded memory	2K
Extended memory	7K
Conventional memory only	28K
Disk swapping	9K

You only need VWatch or VSafe on your system, so choose the one that best suits your needs.

Installing VSafe or VWatch

You can install VSafe and VWatch from the DOS prompt, or you can place them in your AUTOEXEC.BAT file (for information about adding them to your AUTOEXEC.BAT, see Appendix A, "Installing and Configuring PC Tools").

To install VSafe from the DOS prompt, type **vsafe** or **vwatch** and press Enter. The VSafe or the VWatch logo appears.

Configuring VSafe for Your Current Session

After you install VSAFE, you can access any of its eight configurable options from the command line or through the TSR manager when Windows is running. No matter which way you make the changes, those changes are in effect only until you shut your computer off or reboot. To make permanent changes to the configuration of VSAFE, you must make the changes through the installation program or by editing your AUTOEXEC.BAT file. For help with configuring VSafe, see Appendix A, "Installing and Configuring PC Tools."

To configure VSafe from the command prompt, press the VSafe hotkey
Alt+V. The VSafe Warning Options menu appears (see fig. 14.20). To
change any of the settings, press the number associated with the option. When you finish making changes, press Esc to exit.

```
The VSafe Warning Options Menu

Option      Description                  Default

/1          HD low-level format warning  On

/2          Resident warning             Off

/3          General write protects       Off

/4          Check executable files       On

/5          Boot sector viruses          On

/6          Protect HD boot sector       On

/7          Protect FD boot sector       Off

/8          Protect executable files     Off
```

Fig. 14.20

The VSafe
Warning Options
Menu

To configure VSafe from the TSR manager, open the TSR manager and
double-click the minimized icon on the Desktop or double-click the TSR
Manager icon in the Central Point program group. Then click the VSafe
icon. The VSafe options appear. See table 14.5 for an explanation of
each option.

Table 14.5 VSafe Options

Option	Actions When Selected	Default
HD Low-Level Format	Issues a warning when a command is given to low-level format your disk and destroy all the data.	On
Resident Programs	Issues a warning if a program attempts to use regular DOS methods to terminate and stay resident in the memory. Many programs do this intentionally, including PC Tools Shell. This warning does not necessarily mean that a virus is present.	Off

continues

Table 14.5 Continued

Option	Actions When Selected	Default
General Write Protect	Makes writing anything to the hard disk impossible. You may want to use this option to run a program that you suspect has a virus. Choose Continue to allow the program to continue functioning.	Off
Check Executable	Any time an executable file starts to run, even if only to print or copy information, VSafe checks the file for a virus before allowing it to start. If you turn this option off, VWatch still checks the files each time the file is executed, but not if it is just being opened by DOS or copying or printing.	On
Boot Sector Viruses	Checks all disks for boot sector viruses.	On
Protect HD Boot Sector	A warning message appears on-screen if any program attempts to write to the hard disk's boot sector.	On
Protect Floppy Boot Sector	A warning message appears on-screen if any program attempts write to the floppy disk's boot sector.	Off
Protect Executable Files	A message appears if any attempt is made to modify an executable file.	Off

Using Command Line Options with VSafe

You can load VSafe Configuration options into memory from the command line and specify the parameter number followed by a plus sign to turn the option on or a minus sign to turn the option off. (Do not insert a space between the option and the plus or minus sign.) You can have a space between option groups if you want. For example, to start VSafe with all options on, type the following:

VSAFE /2+/3+/7+/8+

You can add any of the additional parameters listed in table 14.6.

Table 14.6 Additional VSafe Parameters

Option	Description
/Az	Enables you to set a new hotkey using Alt and any letter.
/C z	Enables you to set a new hotkey using Ctrl and any letter.
/D	Disables the creation of checksums, which are stored in each directory as CHKLIST.CPS files.
/U	Removes VSafe from memory.
/N	Allows access to any network drives that are loaded after VSafe has loaded.
/NE	Prevents VSafe from loading into expanded memory.
/NX	Prevents VSafe from loading into extended memory.
/?	Displays the help screen for VSafe.

To assign Ctrl+S as the hotkey for VSafe and to make sure that VSafe does not load into expanded memory, type the following at the command line:

VSAFE /C S /NE

You can also combine configuration parameters with any of the above parameters. To load VSafe to protect executable files and change the hotkey to Alt+H, for example, type the following at the command line:

VSAFE /8+ /AH /NE

These changes apply only until you reboot your computer. To make the configuration changes permanent, use these parameters in the AUTOEXEC.BAT file.

Using Command Line Options with VWatch

You can load VWatch into memory with any of the following parameters, using this syntax:

VWATCH /x

The VWatch parameters are listed in table 14.7.

Table 14.7 VWatch Parameters

Option	Description
/D	Permits disk swapping to keep the conventional memory requirements to a minimum.
/NE	Prevents VWatch from loading into expanded memory.
/NX	Prevents VWatch from loading into extended memory.
/U	Removes VWatch from memory if it was loaded either through AUTOEXEC.BAT or from the command line.

To load VWatch without allowing it to use expanded memory, type the following command at the command line:

VWATCH /NE

To unload VWatch from memory, type the following command at the command line:

VWATCH /U

Unloading VWatch from Memory

To remove VWatch from memory, make sure that you remove any terminate and stay resident (TSR) programs that were installed after VWatch was installed. Before you attempt to unload VWatch, remove these TSRs in reverse order of their original installation order; otherwise, your system might hang. When you are ready to remove VWatch, type **vwatch /u** at the DOS prompt. After you type the command, the message VWatch successfully installed appears.

Unloading VSafe from Memory

If you ever need to remove VSafe from memory, make sure that you remove any terminate and stay resident (TSR) programs installed after VSafe's installation. Before you attempt to unload VSafe, remove these TSRs in reverse order of their original installation; otherwise, your system might hang. When you are ready to remove VSafe, type the following command at the DOS prompt:

VSAFE /U

Using BootSafe

BootSafe is a program that checks your boot sector and partition table for viruses every time the computer is restarted. You can add BootSafe to your AUTOEXEC.BAT file. BootSafe can also save your partition table and CMOS information to your Emergency Disk. DOS stores partition information in a file called the *partition table*. If the partition table is damaged, DOS cannot locate any files on the disk. See Chapter 11, "Recovering Damaged or Formatted Disks," for an explanation of boot sectors and partition tables.

IBM PC AT computers, IBM PS/2 computers, and compatibles store information about the computer's hardware configuration—hard disk type and size, video adapter type, memory configuration, and so on—in a battery-powered device called a CMOS (Complementary Metal-Oxide Semiconductor) device. Occasionally, perhaps because of a weak or dead battery, your computer may "forget" the contents of the CMOS.

The second purpose of BootSafe, therefore, is to save a copy of the partition table, the boot sector, and CMOS data to a floppy disk for safekeeping. If your computer does not boot or indicates an error or inconsistency in the CMOS setup, you can use the disk created by BootSafe to recover the partition table, boot disk, or CMOS data, as needed.

 BootSafe is only effective on conventional hard disks; it does not work on network drives. You can, however, use Central Point Anti-Virus to scan network drives.

Saving Your Partition Table with BootSafe

When you are ready to start BootSafe and save your partition table, put your Emergency disk in the A drive, type the following command on the command line, and press Enter.

BOOTSAFE C: /M

NOTE   To save the partition table of a different disk, substitute that drive letter for the letter C.

A dialog box containing the message `Save partition table to drive A:? [Y] Yes [N] No` appears. Choose **Yes** to save the partition table image to drive A. Press Enter to confirm that a disk is in drive A. If you saved the partition table from drive C, BootSafe creates a file called CBOOT.CPS. Repeat this process for each hard disk you have. Label this disk and save it in a safe place.

You must update this disk if you upgrade to a different version of DOS or if you add a disk-compression utility such as Stacker by Stac Electronics or DR DOS 6.

Using BootSafe To Search for Partition Table Viruses

To use BootSafe to search for partition table viruses, type the following command at the DOS prompt and press Enter:

BOOTSAFE C:

You can check multiple drives by listing them one after the other on the command line and pressing Enter. For example, to search for partition tables on drives C, D, and E, type the following:

BOOTSAFE C: D: E:

Using BootSafe To Restore a Partition Table

If your partition table or boot sector has been damaged by a virus, restore it from your Emergency Disk by typing the following command at the DOS prompt:

    A:BOOTSAFE C: /R

This command restores the partition table image on the disk in drive A to the C drive. To restore the partition table to another disk, substitute that drive letter designation in place of C. A dialog box appears to confirm that you want to restore the partition table to the disk. Choose **Yes**.

> **CAUTION:** Do not restore a partition table created on a different computer or on a different hard drive to any location other than the original computer or disk from which the partition table image was taken. Restoring a partition created on another computer may make the computer unable to boot.

Using Command Line Options with BootSafe

You can run BootSafe from the command line using the following syntax and parameters:

    BOOTSAFE d: /x

These parameters are listed in table 14.8.

Table 14.8 BootSafe Command Line Options

Option	Description
/A	Exits from the program without prompting. This option only works with the /T option. These options work well in a batch file.
/M	Saves partition table and boot sector information to the A drive.

continues

Table 14.8 Continued	
Option	Description
/R	Restores partition table and boot sector information from the disk in the A drive.
/T*x*	Issues a reminder to do a scan once every *x* number of days. Replace *x* with any number; the default is 7.
/?	Displays the command line help screen for BootSafe.

If you want BootSafe to check the partition tables of disks C, D, and E, type the following command at the command line:

BOOTSAFE C: D: E:

To create a partition table and boot sector images of disks D and E on disk A, type the following command at the command line:

BOOTSAFE D: E; /M

To restore the partition table or boot sector information back to drive C, type the following command:

BOOTSAFE C: /R

Chapter Summary

In this chapter, you learned about viruses and how to protect your computer from them. You learned how to use Central Point's Anti-Virus to scan your disk at regular intervals and create checksums and immunize your files to create data to show how an uninfected disk looks so that, in the event that your files become infected, you can restore the files to their original condition. You learned how to update your virus signatures regularly and upgrade your copy of Central Point Anti-Virus any time an upgrade is offered.

You also learned how to install VSafe or VWatch, memory-resident programs that continually monitor your disk for viruses; how to create an emergency disk; how to use BootSafe to save a copy of the partition table, boot sector, and CMOS data for each hard disk to your Emergency Disk; and how to update these files weekly and every time you upgrade your operating system software or change the disk's partitions.

This chapter concludes Part III, "Using the Recovery and Security Utilities." The next chapter, "Navigating the Desktop Accessories," introduces you to PC Tools Accessories programs.

Using the Desktop Manager

PART

IV

OUTLINE

Navigating the Desktop Accessories

Using PC Tools Notepads

Using PC Tools Clipboard

Using the Outliner

Using PC Tools Databases

Managing Your Appointment
  Schedule

Automating Your PC Using PC Tools
  Macros

Using the Calculators

Navigating the Desktop Accessories

This chapter introduces you to PC Tools Desktop Accessories, one of the programs that make up PC Tools Version 8.0. Desktop contains a number of modules that help you perform tasks common to virtually all businesses. You can think of Accessories as your business toolbox.

Accessories provides a variety of capabilities usually found only in integrated applications, such as Symphony, Enable, or Microsoft Works. Desktop Accessories includes the following:

- *Notepads* is a basic word processor.

- *Outlines* is an outline processor.

- *Databases* is a simple database-management system.

- *Appointment Scheduler* is a personal time-management module.

- *Telecommunications* is a module that enables you to use telephone lines to connect your computer to other computers. The module enables you to send and receive facsimile (fax) transmissions through your computer or a computer on a local area network (LAN). See Part V, "Communicating by Modem, Fax, or Local Area Network," for details on this option.

- *Macro Editor* is a keystroke recorder for automating repetitive tasks.

- *Clipboard* is an electronic clipboard that enables you to copy information from one application to another.

- *Calculators* is a module that consists of four electronic calculators.

- *Utilities* is a group of functions that control Desktop parameters.

This chapter gets you started with PC Tools by explaining how to get around the Accessories. You learn how to use and respond to the menus, prompts, and messages that Desktop Accessories displays on your computer screen, often called the *user interface*. Although this chapter focuses on learning how to understand and navigate the PC Tools Desktop user interface, you can apply many of the skills and concepts you learn here to the other programs, such as PC Shell and CP Backup, that comprise PC Tools.

In this chapter, you learn how to select options from menus by using the keyboard or a mouse. You also learn how to open one or multiple Desktop windows; change window colors; move, resize, and zoom windows; switch between open windows; and close windows. In addition, you learn how to respond to the several types of dialog boxes—screen prompts and messages—that appear on-screen. Finally, you learn how to activate the Accessories' built-in, on-line help facility when you cannot remember how to use a particular Desktop feature.

Activating PC Tools Desktop Accessories

The discussions in this chapter and throughout the book assume that you used Install to install PC Tools on a hard disk in the DOS directory C:\PCTOOLS. Instructions are provided for using the keyboard and a Microsoft-compatible mouse (if one is attached to your computer) to access commands.

You can install Desktop Accessories as a *terminate-and-stay-resident* (TSR) program, meaning that a portion of a program is loaded into memory but remains inactive. You can activate the program by using a specific hot-key combination. When you exit a TSR program, the program terminates itself and passes control back to COMMAND.COM, but the portion first loaded into memory remains. This portion of the TSR is not written over by the next program that you run. You can reactivate the TSR while another program is running by pressing the hot-key combination. See Appendix A, "Installing and Configuring PC Tools," for more information.

Installing PC Tools Desktop Accessories as a terminate-and-stay-resident program offers several advantages, in addition to the most obvious advantage of immediate accessibility:

- You can use the Clipboard to cut and copy data from one DOS application and paste it into another DOS application.

- The Clipboard cut and paste capabilities are available when you use PC Tools Desktop to launch DOS applications.

- You can run Accessories macros and access the Calculator, Autodial, or addresses stored in Databases while a DOS application is active.

- You can set alarms in the Appointment Scheduler so that Accessories will interrupt another DOS application to announce the appointment.

Running Desktop Accessories as a standard application also has its advantages:

- If you run Windows regularly and want to access Desktop Accessories, Accessories can only be run as a standard application.

- Many DOS applications require a large amount of conventional memory to operate. Desktop Accessories occupies 32K of conventional memory when resident but not active, limiting the amount of memory available for other applications.

- More conventional memory is available for DOS applications when these applications are run within Windows. To run a DOS application in Windows 386-Enhanced mode, Windows creates a block of conventional memory (usually about 640K) called a *virtual machine*. Each virtual machine is kept separate and protected by the design of the 386 hardware. Every TSR and device driver loaded before Windows is run consumes memory in every virtual machine. This is true even though you cannot access Desktop Accessories as a TSR within Windows.

- When Desktop Accessories is memory-resident and you run a DOS application in Windows, the virtual machine created for the DOS application has the same amount of conventional memory that was available at the DOS prompt but consumes up to 640K of memory resources. This price in unavailable conventional memory is paid even though you cannot access Desktop Accessories as a TSR within Windows.

If you decide to run Desktop Accessories as a TSR included in your AUTOEXEC.BAT file, Install configures everything for you. If you decide to start Desktop Accessories yourself, use one of the following command lines:

DESKTOP	Use this line to run as a standard application.
DESKTOP /R	Use this line to run as a TSR.

When run memory-resident, Desktop Accessories temporarily suspends the application you are running and takes a snapshot of the contents of the *random-access memory* (RAM). Accessories uses this RAM image to restore the contents of memory when you hot key back into the DOS applications program. The program then writes this RAM image to any expanded memory (compatible with Lotus, Intel, Microsoft-LIM) that your system may have. Accessories writes to a disk file any portion of the RAM image that will not fit in expanded memory (the entire RAM image writes to disk when your system has no expanded memory). Finally, Accessories loads into memory the Desktop program file and the Desktop Accessories main menu selection, which you can open by clicking it or pressing Enter (see fig. 15.1).

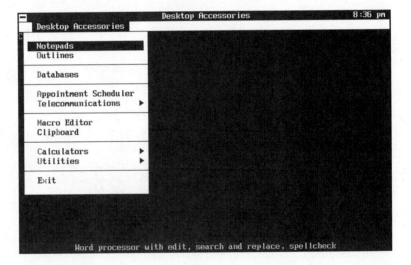

The Desktop Accessories main menu.

This menu lists nine desktop modules and the Exit command. Desktop displays the mouse pointer in the center of the screen. The first menu option, Notepads, is highlighted by a reverse video menu-selection bar. When you choose the Exit option, you leave Desktop and return to the screen that appeared when you activated the Desktop program.

For Related Information

◄◄ "Starting PC Tools Desktop," p. 24.

FROM HERE...

Opening an Application Window

To select one of the applications listed on the Desktop Accessories main menu, move the mouse pointer to an option and click the mouse button (or press the key that corresponds to the highlighted letter in the name of the menu option you want to select). You also can use the arrow keys to move the selection bar to the option you want, and then press Enter. For more information about selecting from menus, see the following section, "Using Desktop Accessories Menus."

When you select Notepads, Outlines, Databases, Appointment Scheduler, or Macro Editor, you are prompted for a file name. After you specify a file name, Desktop displays the appropriate Desktop application in an application window. Figure 15.2 shows the window that appears when you load the Notepads file README.TXT—a file distributed with PC Tools. See the section "Understanding Desktop Accessories Windows" later in this chapter for a full discussion of how to customize the color, position, size, and shape of Accessories application windows.

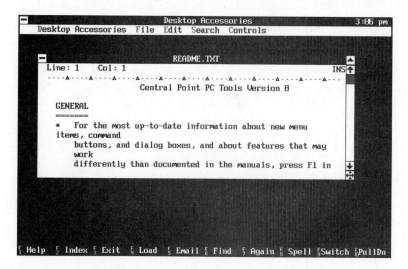

Fig. 15.2

A Notepads window containing the file README.TXT.

When you select Clip**b**oard, Accessories displays the application screen in a window. When you select **C**alculators, **T**elecommunications, or **U**tilities, Accessories displays another menu listing several options. After you make a selection from this second menu, Accessories displays the application screen.

Every Desktop Accessories application has a screen design that best suits its purpose. Although the screens in the Accessories are not identical, they do share a number of common features. These features are labeled in figure 15.3, which shows a Notepads window.

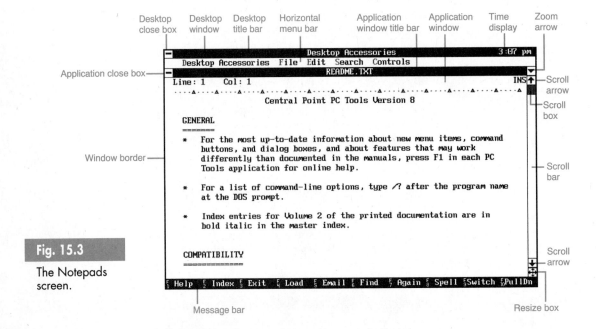

Fig. 15.3

The Notepads screen.

Using Desktop Accessories Menus

You can initiate virtually every desktop operation in PC Tools Desktop Accessories by choosing options from a series of menus. These Accessories menus fall into two categories: the horizontal menu bar and pull-down menus.

Using the Horizontal Menu Bar

The top line of every Accessories application window is called the *horizontal menu bar*. A listing of all available menu options for that application appears here. The right end of the horizontal menu bar is called the *time display*. Accessories displays the current system time at this position.

You can select an option from the horizontal menu bar in one of three ways:

- Move the mouse pointer to an option and click (press and release) the left or right button.

- Press the F10 key or the Alt key to activate the horizontal menu bar. Accessories places a highlighted menu selection bar on the first menu option in the list and highlights one letter in each of the other menu options. Press the key that corresponds to the highlighted letter in the name of the menu option you want to select. To select **E**dit from the menu in figure 15.3, for example, press F10 (Menu) and then E or press Alt+E.

- Press F10 or Alt, use the right- or left-arrow key to move the highlighted menu selection bar to your choice, and press Enter. This method is sometimes called the *point-and-shoot* method.

Although the point-and-shoot method requires the greatest number of keystrokes (and, therefore, takes more time), there is an advantage to using this menu-selection procedure, especially when you are learning the program. As you move the highlighted bar to various menu options, Accessories displays, in the *message bar* (the bottom line of the screen), a message that describes the highlighted option. When **D**esktop Accessories is highlighted, for example, the message bar reads

```
Shows main menu and allows running another Desktop
Accessories application
```

If you press the right-arrow key to highlight **F**ile, this message appears in the message bar:

```
Load, save, print, autosave, or exit without saving
```

When you are not sure which option to select, you can read the screen messages displayed in the message bar to make an educated guess.

Using Pull-down Menus

When you select an option from the horizontal menu bar, Desktop displays a *pull-down menu*, which contains options below the horizontal menu bar. If you select **E**dit, for example, Desktop displays the Edit pull-down menu (see fig. 15.4).

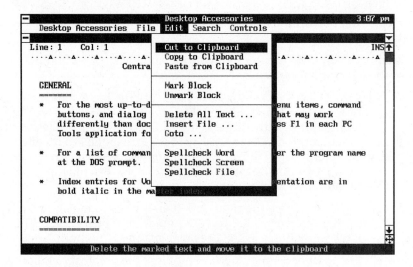

Fig. 15.4

The Edit pull-down menu.

You can select an option on a pull-down menu by clicking the option or by using the up- and down-arrow keys to highlight the option and then pressing Enter.

Using Shortcut Commands

When you display a Desktop Accessories window, the message bar contains a list of shortcut commands available in the particular Accessories application. (These commands are called *function keys* in the Desktop Accessories Help facility.) In a Notepads window, for example, the message bar contains this list of shortcut commands:

```
F1 Help F2 Index F3 Exit F4 Load F5 Email F6 Find
F7 Again F8 Spell F9 Switch F10 PullDn
```

To execute a shortcut command, press the corresponding function key or use the mouse to click the shortcut command in the message bar. To spell-check a file by using the menu method, for example, you press F10

(Menu), select Edit, and then select Spellcheck File. Using the shortcut command, however, you press only F8 (Spell), saving two keystrokes.

Seven shortcut commands (five of which are listed in the message bar) are available in all Desktop applications. These commands are listed in table 15.1. Their use is explained throughout this chapter. The shortcut commands specific to each Desktop application are listed and explained fully in the chapter that discusses the respective application.

Table 15.1 Desktop Keystroke Commands Available in All Desktop Applications

Key	Name	Function
F1	Help	Displays context-sensitive Help facility
F2	Index	Displays Help facility index
F3 or Esc	Exit	Exits from current process or application
F9 or Ctrl+Esc	Switch	Switches active window
F10 or Alt	PullDn	Activates horizontal menu bar
Alt+space bar	System Control	Displays System Control window

NOTE This book recommends using keystroke commands (including application-specific shortcut commands) where available. So that you can learn the keystroke commands quickly, this book lists the name of the command (as it appears in the message bar or in table 15.1) in parentheses immediately after the keystroke itself. When the book indicates that you should press F4 (Load), for example, press the F4 key or use the mouse to click this command in the message bar. When the book instructs you to press F10 (Menu) or Alt (Menu), you can press or click F10 or press the Alt key.

For Related Information

◄◄ "Using PC Tools Desktop Menus," p. 27.

FROM HERE...

Understanding Desktop Accessories Windows

When Desktop Accessories is initiated, the Accessories window, which contains a close box and title bar, appears (refer to fig. 15.3). The lines between the Desktop Accessories title bar and message bar are available for use by Accessories applications. Every application can control some or all of this area of the screen. The portion of the screen controlled by an application is called an *application window* and is surrounded by a *window border*. The window border is more than just cosmetic trimming. The border has several functional components:

- *Application title bar.* The first line of an applications window, this title bar displays the document's file name. You also use the application title bar to move the application window.

- *Close box.* The top left corner of the applications title bar contains a small box containing a minus sign. You can double-click this box with the mouse to close the application window. Alternatively, you can press Alt+space bar to access the Control menu, which enables you to move, size, and close the box by using the keyboard. Refer to the "Closing a Window" section for more information.

- *Resize box.* At the bottom right corner of the window border is a small four-way arrow icon. Not all Desktop applications windows display this box; however, when this box is present, you can use the mouse to resize the window by *dragging* the resize to a different location. Refer to the section "Resizing a Window," later in this chapter for more information.

- *Zoom arrow.* At the top right corner of the window border, Desktop displays an upward-pointing triangle—the zoom arrow. You can click this symbol to expand the window to full-screen size; the symbol becomes a downward-pointing triangle. This feature acts as a toggle switch. When you click the symbol while the window is full size, Desktop returns the window to its previous size.

- *Scroll bar.* You use the scroll bar to scroll the document backward and forward on-screen. Simply use the mouse to drag the scroll box up or down the scroll bar.

Accessories enables you to open as many as 15 application windows at one time, but only one window is *active*. The active window is denoted by a bright (or colored) title bar, and all other windows have dimmed (grayed-out or black) title bars. Figures 15.3 and 15.4 both show a single active Notepad window; figure 15.5 shows two Notepad windows—one containing the README.TXT file, the other containing the SAMPLE.TXT file. The SAMPLE.TXT window is the active window, indicated by the bright title bar. Refer to the "Using Multiple Windows" section later in this chapter for a discussion of how to open and use more than one application window at a time.

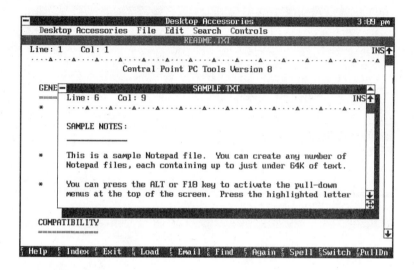

Fig. 15.5

Two Notepads windows.

Accessories initially displays an application window using default settings for window colors, position, and size. You can customize these settings. Version 8.0 enables you to take advantage of EGA and VGA display systems by displaying 43 or 50 lines of text at one time. The paragraphs that follow describe how to make these adjustments. See Appendix A, "Installing and Configuring PC Tools," for more information about this option.

Changing Window Colors

Although PC Tools Desktop Accessories makes good use of color in its screens, you may decide that you want different color combinations. Accessories enables you to select your own color scheme for application windows. You can change the colors that Accessories uses in menus and dialog boxes. See Appendix A, "Installing and Configuring PC Tools," for information about how to customize the colors of these items.

When you want to modify the colors of a single application window, click the close box or press Alt+space bar to activate the System Control menu. The System Control menu for Notepads is shown in figure 15.6.

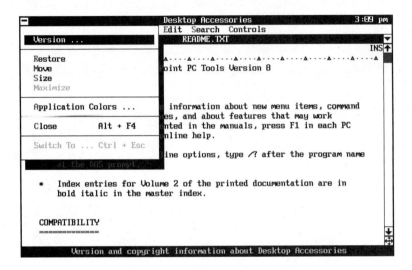

Fig. 15.6

The System Control menu in a Notepads window.

From the System Control menu, select **A**pplication Colors. Desktop Accessories displays a Change Colors dialog box, as shown in figure 15.7.

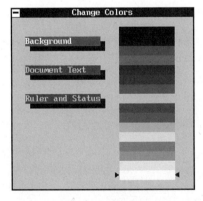

Fig. 15.7

The Change Colors dialog box.

You can change the color of three areas in the window display: the background, document text, and top two lines in every window—the ruler and status lines. These areas are listed on the left side of the dialog box (refer to fig. 15.7). On the right side of the dialog box, Accessories lists the available colors.

To select a different color, first select the area you want to change by clicking the area name or pressing the Tab and Shift+Tab keys to highlight the area name. Then select a color option by clicking the option with the mouse; alternatively, you can highlight the option by pressing the arrow keys. Repeat these two steps for every area in which you want to alter the screen color.

Suppose, for example, that you want to change the document text color (often called the *foreground* color) in a Notepads window from high-intensity white to black. Display the Change Colors dialog box and select *Document Text*. To make the change, click the black color bar or press the arrow keys to select it. Accessories changes the color of all document text to black. Press Esc (Exit) or F3 (Exit) to close the dialog box. As you select different colors, the change is previewed for you in the application window visible in the background. Press Esc (Exit) or F3 (Exit) to close the dialog box.

The new colors affect only the on-screen document. You can use the **S**ave Setup option from the **C**ontrols menu option to save these color selections for the active application. The colors available in the Change Colors dialog box can be varied in PC Config, as described in Appendix A, "Installing and Configuring PC Tools."

Moving, Resizing, and Maximizing Windows

By default, the window border of a Notepads, Outline, or Macro Editor window begins in the seventh line and fifth column of the screen. Figure 15.8 shows a Notepads window containing the new file SAMPLE2.TXT to which text can now be added. The window border encloses room for nine lines, each containing as many as 64 characters, to be displayed on-screen at one time (not counting the two lines occupied by the status line and tab ruler at the top of the window).

Databases windows begin in the third line and sixth column of the screen and provide space for 17 lines by 60 characters. A Clipboard window normally begins in the fifth line and fifth column of the screen. The default size of the Clipboard is 12 lines by 67 characters. Accessories enables you, however, to change the position and size of any application window. The discussions that follow explain how to make these changes.

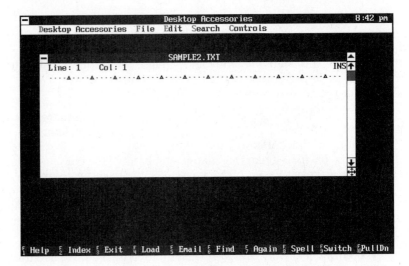

Fig. 15.8

A new Notepads
window with
default size and
screen position.

Moving an Application Window

Accessories enables you to easily move an application window within
the limits of the 23-line-by-80-column work area on your screen. When
several application windows are open, you often must move one window to see a portion of the window behind it. You can move a window
by using your mouse or the arrow keys on the keyboard.

To move a window by using the mouse, position the mouse pointer in
the application title bar. Be careful not to touch the close box in the
upper left corner. Press and hold down the left or right mouse button.

Move the mouse in the direction you want to move the window. Accessories moves the window along with the pointer—a process called
dragging the window. Drag the window to the on-screen position you
want and release the mouse button. Figure 15.9 shows the same
Notepads window shown in figure 15.8 moved to the upper left corner
of the screen.

You also can move an application window by using the menus. Click
the close box or press Alt+space bar to display the System Control
menu; then select **M**ove. Desktop displays a box prompting you to use
the cursor-movement keys to adjust the location of the window. Use
the arrow keys (↑, ↓, ←, and →) to move the window to the screen location you want, and then press Enter or Esc to accept the new location.

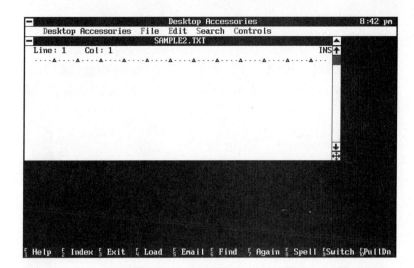

Fig. 15.9

A Notepads window moved to the upper left corner of the screen.

Resizing a Window

You typically resize windows so that you can see several windows at one time or so that you can see the DOS application from which you hot keyed into Desktop. Whenever you want to change the size or shape of an application window, the easiest method is to use the mouse. Move the mouse pointer to the Resize box at the bottom right corner of the window. Press and hold down the left or right mouse button.

To make the window larger, drag the Resize box down and to the right side of the screen. The upper left corner of the window remains stationary. You can make the window smaller by dragging the Resize box up and to the left. When the window is the size you want, release the mouse button. Figure 15.10 depicts the same Notepads window shown in figure 15.9 resized to double the window length.

> To increase the range available for resizing, use the **M**ove command from the System Control menu or the mouse to move the application window to the upper left corner of the screen (refer to fig. 15.9).

T I P

As an alternative to using the mouse, Accessories enables you to resize an application window by using only the keyboard. Select **S**ize from the System Control menu. Desktop displays a dialog box that instructs you to use the cursor-movement keys to adjust the size of the window.

Press the arrow keys (↑, ↓, ←, and →) to move the Resize box until the window is the size you want, and press Enter or Esc.

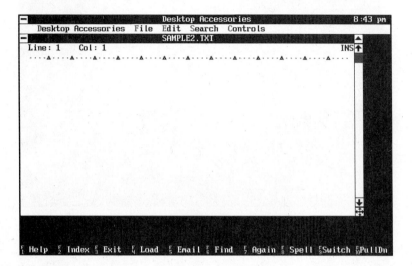

Fig. 15.10

A resized Notepads window.

Maximizing a Window

You may want the window to fill the entire 23 lines between the horizontal menu bar and the message bar so that more information is displayed at one time. Accessories enables you to easily maximize the window to full size in Notepads, Outlines, Databases, Macro Editor, and Clipboard.

The easiest way to maximize the window to full size is to use the mouse. Move the mouse pointer to the zoom arrow in the upper right corner of the window border, and click the right or left mouse button. Accessories zooms the window to full-screen size.

You also can use the menus to maximize a window to full size. Select **M**aximize from the System Control menu. Desktop expands the size of the window until it fills the space between the horizontal menu bar and the message bar. Figure 15.11 shows the Notepads window in figure 15.10 zoomed to full size.

Later, you may decide to return the window to its previous size and position. Click the zoom arrow or select **R**estore from the System Control menu. Accessories reduces the window to the its size and position before you zoomed it to full size.

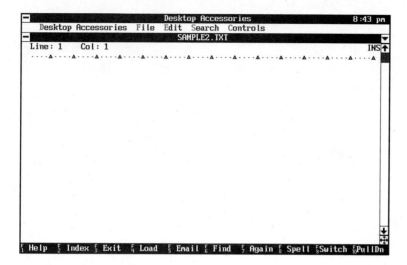

Fig. 15.11

The Notepads window shown in figure 15.10 maximized to full size.

Saving the Setup

Every change to an application window's color, size, or position normally affects only the file in which you are currently working. The next time you load this file, the program displays the application window using the color, size, and position you last·selected for that file. When you create a new file, however, default settings for window color, size, and position determine the appearance of the new application window. You can change these default settings.

To customize color, size, and position settings for a Desktop Accessories application, you first must display a file in an application window and then make your changes to color, size, and window position. For example, you might want all Notepads windows to be full-screen size with black background and green document text. Therefore, display a Notepads window, maximize the window to full size, and change the colors to green on black.

After you adjust window color, size, and position for the current file, you are ready to save the setup and make the settings for this file the new default settings. Select Controls from the horizontal menu bar to display the Controls pull-down menu (see fig. 15.12). Then select Save Setup. Accessories saves the window color, size, and position settings for the active file as the new default settings. The next time you display a window in the same application, Accessories uses the new default settings to determine window color, size, and position. Files created before you changed the default settings retain their original configuration, however.

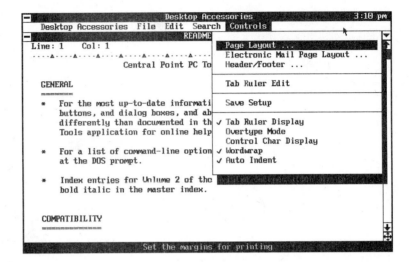

Fig. 15.12

The Controls
pull-down menu.

NOTE Desktop Accessories saves the new settings for window color, size, and position. These window settings apply only to the single Desktop application that is current when you execute the command. The **S**ave Setup command, however, saves printing and formatting settings such as page margins, page headers, page footers, word wrap, and tab ruler settings. Unlike the window settings, however, the **S**ave Setup command applies printing and formatting default settings to several applications. Whenever you select **S**ave Setup from the Controls menu in a Notepad, Outline, Macro Editor, or Database window, Desktop makes the current printing and formatting settings the new default settings for all four applications. See Chapter 16, "Using PC Tools Notepads," for more information about customizing default printing and formatting options.

Scrolling through a File

Files created by the various Desktop Accessories applications are often too large to be displayed entirely in a single application window. Although a Notepads file can contain approximately 60,000 characters, a Notepads window expanded to full size can display no more than 18 lines, each line containing as many as 76 characters (considerably fewer characters than can be contained in a Notepads file). Therefore, Desktop enables you to move an application window around in a file so that you can display any portion of the file. This process is called *scrolling* the window through a file. Refer to the remaining chapters in Part IV for specific discussions about scrolling application windows.

Closing a Window

When you are finished working in an application window, you often want to remove the window from the screen. To remove a file, you close the file. As with moving and resizing a window, you can close an application window by using a mouse or the keyboard.

To use the mouse to close an application window, click the close box in the upper left corner of the window border. Accessories closes the window. If no other window is open, Accessories returns to the Desktop Accessories main menu; otherwise, Desktop displays another application window.

You can close the active application window by pressing Esc (Exit) or F3 (Exit).

When you close a window by using any method described in this section, Accessories routinely saves any changes you made to the file. Whenever Accessories saves the contents of a file, it saves the window size, position, and color. See the other chapters in Part IV for more information about how to save a file.

T I P

CAUTION: If you retrieve a Notepads file and then cut information from it, closing the window saves the version of the file without the cut information. See Chapter 16, "Using PC Tools Notepads," for information on how to quit from a Notepads window without saving changes.

For Related Information

◀◀ "Understanding the PC Tools Desktop Windows," p. 33.

▶▶ "Saving the Setup," p. 596.

▶▶ "Setting Screen Colors," p. 921.

Using Multiple Windows

PC Tools Desktop Accessories enables you to open as many as 15 application windows at one time. These windows can be all one type or several different types. Suppose, for example, that you're using the Accessories Financial Calculator to compute the rate of return on an investment you're evaluating. In the middle of your computations, you receive a telephone call from a client you have been trying to contact for weeks. As you take the call, you quickly access your client database and find the client's record. You want to refresh your memory about the date and quantity of the customer's last order.

During the conversation, the client asks you to drop by at your earliest convenience. Consequently, you fire up your Accessories Appointment Scheduler and inform him that you are free Thursday at 9 A.M. As you hang up the telephone, you display a Notepads window and type a note to the client to confirm your conversation and the appointment. At this point, you have four windows open: a Financial Calculator window, a Databases window, an Appointment Scheduler window, and a Notepads window.

This section examines how to open and switch among multiple windows.

Opening Another Window

When one application window is already open, you must display the main menu to open another window. Select **D**esktop Accessories from the horizontal menu bar to access the main menu (see fig. 15.13). Select an option from this menu to open another application window.

To open a database window, for example, select **D**atabases from the main menu. Figure 15.14 shows an active Databases window overlapping an inactive Notepads window.

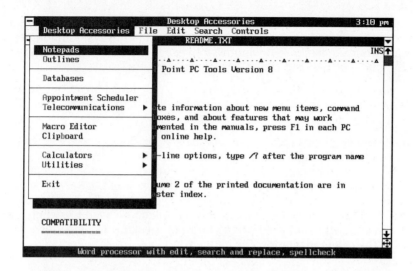

Fig. 15.13

The Desktop
main menu.

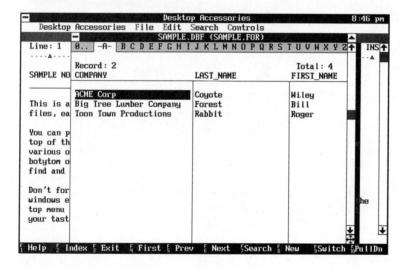

Fig. 15.14

An active Data-
bases window
overlapping an
inactive Note-
pads window.

Switching among Windows

Even though Accessories enables you to open multiple windows (as
many as 15 at one time), only one window is active at any time. The
active window contains the cursor and has a bright (or colored) title
bar. When the windows overlap one another, the active window is always the one on top.

When several windows are open, you may want to switch to a different window. Desktop Accessories provides at least two ways—sometimes three—to make a different window active: a menu method, a shortcut command method, and sometimes a mouse method.

To use the menu method, activate the System Control menu by clicking the close box or by pressing Alt+space bar and then selecting Switch To from the menu.

To use the keyboard method, press Ctrl+Esc or F9 (Switch). When only two windows are open, the other window becomes active. If three or more windows are open, Desktop Accessories displays the Change Active Window dialog box (see fig. 15.15). Either press the arrow keys to select the window you want and press Enter, press the number or letter that corresponds to the window to which you want to switch, or use the mouse to click the option you want. Desktop Accessories makes the selected window the active window.

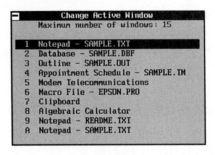

Fig. 15.15

The Change
Active Window
dialog box.

Sometimes, you can use the mouse to switch to a different active window. Occasionally, Desktop application windows overlap in such a way that portions of inactive windows are still visible. Using the mouse, click a displayed portion of the inactive window to switch to that window.

T   I   P   When you use the Desktop Accessories main menu to open several windows of the same application, each new window opens directly over the previous window. In order to use the mouse to make a window active, a portion of the window must be visible. So that part of the window remains visible when you open the next window, move each window as it is opened.

For Related Information

◄◄ "Moving between Windows," p. 35.

FROM HERE...

Using Dialog Boxes

As you work with Desktop Accessories applications, the program routinely displays messages and prompts in shaded or colored boxes called *dialog boxes*. These dialog boxes fall into three categories: message dialog boxes, command dialog boxes, and help dialog boxes. The first two types, message dialog boxes and command dialog boxes, are described in this section. Refer to the following section, "Getting Help from Desktop Accessories," for information about how to display and use help dialog boxes.

A *message box* provides a caution or instruction about what is happening or about to happen. Typically, a message box offers only two buttons: one button to confirm an operation you have initiated and a second button to cancel your choice. An example of a message box is the warning box.

A command dialog box, on the other hand, provides an array of options you use to instruct the program how to process an operation. You can specify color changes for various parts of the screen; select drives, directories, and files to load; and set up all the details necessary for a print job and other complex tasks. An example of a command dialog box is the Change Colors dialog box (refer to fig. 15.7).

For Related Information

◄◄ "Using Dialog Boxes," p. 42.

FROM HERE...

Getting Help from Desktop Accessories

As you learn to use PC Tools Desktop Accessories, you may occasionally forget what options are available to you in a particular application window, or you may not know how to perform a certain task. To help you in these situations, Accessories provides a convenient, on-line, context-sensitive Help facility that is available at the touch of a key.

The first shortcut command listed in the message bar is F1 (Help), which means that you can access an on-line Help facility by pressing the F1 key. In the Accessories window and any application window, you can press F1 (Help) to immediately access pertinent on-screen documentation in a *help screen*.

Every help dialog box accessed through the F1 (Help) key contains a description of the current operation. The help is sometimes several screens long. You can move between pages (screens) by pressing the PgUp and PgDn keys or the up- and down-arrow keys, or by using your mouse and the vertical scroll bar. You can press Home to move to the beginning of the help screen or End to move to the end. Several function-key help options, listed in the following table, are available:

Key	Name	Function
F4	Topics	Provides a list of help topics available
F5	Go Back	Moves back through the previously viewed topics
F6	Print	Prints a copy of the current help topic
F7	Previous	Moves to previous topic in the list
F8	Next	Moves to next topic in the list
F9	Manuals	Accesses a list of on-line help manuals

To return to the application screen, select the Cancel command button, click the close box, or press Esc (Exit) or F3 (Exit).

Suppose, for example, that you are working in an Outlines window and want a general description of the window's available features. While the Outlines window is active, press F1 (Help). Accessories opens the Outlines help dialog box on top of the Outlines window. Figure 15.16 shows the first screen of information available for display in the Notepads/Outlines help dialog box.

On most screens, several key words or phrases are displayed in a very light color. The first of these key words is highlighted. These words or phrases are linked directly to help screens that provide additional information about that command or element. Use the Tab key to move the highlight bar from phrase to phrase; to see the help screen linked to that word or phrase, press Enter. If you are using the mouse, you can move to the linked help screen by clicking the desired word or phrase, even if it isn't highlighted.

In addition to the general help screens, Desktop provides a help index that lists all the available help screens—not only the help screens of the applications in which you are working. Some of the help screens provide more specific information about application functions. To access the help index, press F2 (Index) from any application screen. Accessories then displays the Help Index dialog box, shown in figure 15.17.

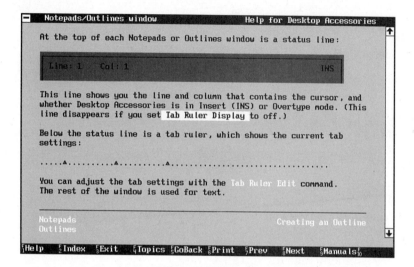

Fig. 15.16

The first Notepads/ Outlines help dialog box.

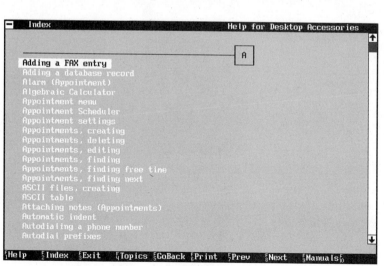

Fig. 15.17

The Help Index dialog box.

After Desktop Accessories displays the Help Index dialog box, use the PgUp and PgDn keys, the up- and down-arrow keys, or the vertical scroll bar to scroll the contents of the dialog box until you see a help-screen topic listed that interests you. Click the topic or highlight the topic with the highlighted bar and press Enter. Accessories displays the selected help dialog box.

For Related Information

FROM HERE...   ◀◀ "Getting Help from PC Tools Desktop," p. 48.

Using Desktop Accessories Utilities

Utilities, one of the applications listed on the Desktop Accessories main menu, is a miscellaneous collection of tools that, with one exception, can affect all the other Accessories applications. When you select **Utilities** from the Desktop **A**ccessories menu, Accessories displays the Utilities submenu (see fig. 15.18).

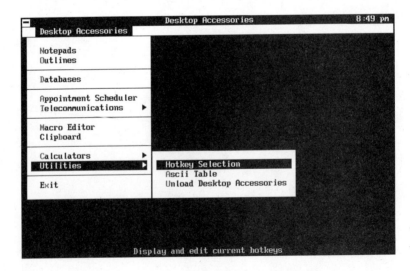

Fig. 15.18

The Utilities submenu.

The options on the Utilities submenu enable you to perform the following tasks:

■ Select a different keystroke combination for activating Desktop Clipboard Paste, Clipboard Copy, and Screen Autodial.

■ Display a table of ASCII characters.

■ Remove Desktop from your computer's memory.

This section describes how to use each utility.

Selecting Hotkeys

The keystroke combination that activates a memory-resident program, such as Desktop Accessories, is called a *hotkey*. As explained at the beginning of this chapter, the discussions in this and subsequent chapters assume that PC Tools Desktop Accessories has been loaded into memory as a terminate-and-stay-resident (TSR) or memory-resident program. While Accessories is resident in memory but not active, it uses only a small portion of your computer's memory, and you can run other DOS programs. Press the hot-key keystroke combination or activate the program. (This is true except with Microsoft Windows. If you are using Windows, open Accessories as a standard application.)

Similarly, a number of other Accessories functions can be executed from within other DOS programs by means of a hotkey. In addition to Desktop itself, these Desktop features include Clipboard Paste, Clipboard Copy, and Autodial. The default hotkeys for these Accessories memory-resident functions are listed in table 15.2.

Table 15.2 Default Desktop Hotkeys	
Hotkey	**Function**
Ctrl+space bar	Activates Desktop
Ctrl+Ins	Clipboard Paste
Ctrl+Del	Clipboard Copy
Ctrl+O	Screen Autodial

Occasionally, one of the hotkeys in table 15.2 might be the same as a keystroke used by another program that you plan to run while Accessories is resident in memory. Or a hotkey might be used by another memory-resident program that you want to run concurrently with Accessories. To avoid these situations, Accessories provides a way for you to reassign one or more of these hotkeys, if necessary.

To make a change to one of the Accessories hotkeys, first select **Utilities** from the **D**esktop Accessories main menu. Accessories displays the Utilities submenu (refer to fig. 15.18). Select **H**otkey Selection to access the Hotkey dialog box.

After Desktop displays the Hotkey dialog box, use the up- or down-arrow key to highlight one of the following choices:

- *Hotkey*. Select this option to reassign the hotkey that activates PC Tools Desktop Accessories.

- *Clipboard Paste*. Select this option to reassign the keystroke combination that performs the Clipboard paste operation (see Chapter 16, "Using PC Tools Notepads," for more information).

- *Clipboard Copy*. Select this option to reassign the keystroke combination that performs the Clipboard copy operation (see Chapter 16, "Using PC Tools Notepads," for more information).

- *Screen Autodial*. Select this option to reassign the keystroke combination that activates the Autodialer for the purpose of dialing a telephone number that appears on your screen (see Chapter 23, "Using PC Tools Telecommunications," for more information).

After you select one of these options, press the keystroke combination that you want to use as the new hotkey. Accessories displays the new hot-key keystroke combination in the Hotkey dialog box.

Suppose, for example, that the word processor program you normally use already employs the keystroke combination Ctrl+O. This keystroke is the default hotkey for Autodial and should be reassigned. You decide to assign the keystroke combination Ctrl+D as the new Autodial hotkey. Select **H**otkey Selection from the Utilities submenu, highlight Screen Autodial in the Hotkey dialog box, and then press Ctrl+D.

When you have made all the desired changes to the hotkeys, close the dialog box by clicking the close box or by pressing Esc (Exit) or F3 (Exit). Accessories saves the changes. You can begin using the newly assigned hotkeys immediately.

Displaying the ASCII Table

When you are typing at your keyboard, every character sent to your computer's display adapter is represented in *ASCII* (American Standard Code for Information Interchange). The display adapter translates every coded character into the shape you see on-screen. The IBM version of ASCII used by the personal computer can represent 256 different characters. At various times when you work with a computer and with software, you may find that you need to know the hexadecimal (base 16) or decimal (base 10) ASCII code for a particular character. Accessories provides a complete ASCII (IBM extended ASCII character set) table.

For example, many applications programs enable you to send special control codes to your printer. These codes are sent in Ascii code, and you usually have to provide either the decimal or hexadecimal code for every character you want the application to send to the printer.

To display the Accessories ASCII table, first select **U**tilities from the **D**esktop Accessories main menu, and then select **A**scii Table from the submenu. Accessories displays the ASCII table shown in figure 15.19. If your screen does not look like the figure, press Home to get to the beginning of the table.

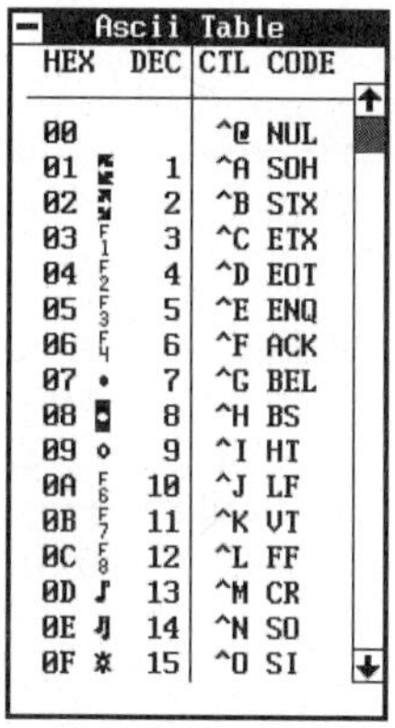

Fig. 15.19

The Ascii Table (dialog box).

The ASCII table lists all 256 ASCII characters in the IBM extended ASCII character set on nine screens (or pages). You can move among screens by using the PgUp and PgDn keys, the up- and down-arrow keys, or your mouse and the scroll bar. You can move directly to the screen that contains a particular character by typing that character on the keyboard. To move to the ASCII table screen that contains the codes for the character *z*, for example, type **z**. Accessories immediately displays the fifth screen of the table.

The first two screens of the table depict the codes for 16 ASCII characters and are a total of five columns wide.

The first column is headed by the label HEX, which means that the numbers in this column are *hexadecimal* (base 16) numbers, a notation often used by programmers. Every HEX number corresponds to the ASCII character listed in the same row and second column of the table. Programmers can use certain programming languages to send the appropriate HEX number to the screen or to another output device, to display a given character.

The second column of characters has no heading. This column contains the ASCII characters that correspond to the HEX number and DEC number in the same row of the table.

The third column in the table is headed DEC. This column contains the *decimal* (base 10) numbers that correspond to the ASCII characters listed in the same row and second column of the table. Many programming languages and PC programs enable you to send ASCII characters to output devices by using the DEC number code.

The fourth column is headed CTL. This heading means that the column contains Ctrl+key combinations. Every entry in this column starts with the caret (^) character, which represents the Ctrl key. The caret is followed by a keyboard character. The *Ctrl+key combination* code means that holding Ctrl and pressing the character that follows the caret is equivalent to sending to an output device the ASCII character listed in the table's fifth column. To display the character that appears in the fifth row of the ASCII table (HEX 04, DEC 4), for example, press Ctrl+D.

The fifth column, headed CODE, contains the ASCII character code potentially generated by the Ctrl+key combination listed in the fourth column. Pressing Ctrl+M (listed as ^M in the fourth column), for example, sends the carriage return (listed as CR in the fifth column) to an output device. These codes generally are used only by programmers and "power users" for application development because the results can be unpredictable. Most PC programs use at least some of the Ctrl+key combination keystrokes listed in the CTL column for purposes other than generating ASCII characters.

Screens 3 through 9 of the ASCII table depict the codes for 32 ASCII characters each and are a total of six columns wide. The first and fourth columns are headed HEX and contain hexadecimal codes. The third and sixth columns, headed DEC, contain decimal codes. Every entry in the second and fifth columns lists the displayable ASCII character that corresponds to the HEX and DEC codes listed in the columns to the left and right of the entry, respectively.

When you are finished looking at the ASCII table, click the close box or press Esc (Exit) or F3 (Exit) to return to the application screen (or to the Accessories main menu, depending on where you started).

Unloading Desktop Accessories

When Desktop Accessories is running as a terminate-and-stay-resident (TSR) or memory-resident program, the last feature included on the Utility menu enables you to remove Accessories from your computer's memory to free up the memory for use by other programs. To perform this task, display the Utility menu and select Unload Desktop Accessories. Before Desktop unloads from memory, the program displays a dialog box containing a warning (see fig. 15.20).

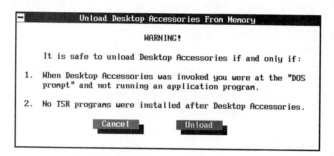

Fig. 15.20

The warning that appears when you unload Accessories from memory.

Before you attempt to unload Accessories from your computer's memory, make sure that the following conditions exist:

- You activated Accessories with the hotkey from the DOS prompt rather than from within another DOS program.

- No other terminate-and-stay-resident (TSR) program is loaded in memory after Accessories.

Both of these criteria can be boiled down into one rule: Programs must be unloaded from memory opposite the order in which they were loaded into memory.

Before you can attempt to unload Accessories, Accessories must be the last program loaded into memory. If some other program was loaded into memory after Accessories, you must remove this other program from memory before you can remove Desktop Accessories.

If you are sure that both criteria described in the preceding paragraphs are met, select the Unload command button in the dialog box. Accessories unloads itself from memory.

> **CAUTION:** If you select this command without ensuring that Accessories was activated with the hotkey from the DOS prompt and that no other terminate-and-stay-resident (TSR) program was loaded in memory after Accessories, the computer might *freeze up*, requiring you to reboot (restart) it.

When you want to unload Accessories from memory, you can use an alternative to the Unload Desktop Accessories command on the Utility menu. Assuming that no other terminate-and-stay-resident (TSR) program is loaded in memory after Desktop, type **kill** at the DOS prompt and press Enter. Accessories removes itself from memory. Regardless of the method you use to unload Accessories, the following message appears when Accessories is successfully unloaded:

```
DESKTOP ACCESSORIES HAVE BEEN REMOVED FROM MEMORY.
```

This command also removes PC Tools Desktop from memory (refer to Part I of the book, "Using the Desktop," for more information about PC Tools Desktop).

Returning to DOS

When you are finished using Desktop Accessories, you can easily return to the screen that was displayed when you activated Accessories. Accessories provides two alternative methods: use the hotkey to go directly to DOS, or close all application windows and exit from Desktop to DOS.

Even with Desktop Accessories application windows open, you can return to the DOS screen by pressing the Accessories hotkey. The default hotkey is Ctrl+space bar. Press Ctrl+space bar to return to the screen that was displayed when you activated Accessories. (If you used the **Hotkey Selection** option on the **Utilities** menu to assign a different hotkey, press the new hotkey instead). Desktop Accessories returns to the DOS screen.

Later, you can reactivate Desktop Accessories by pressing the hotkey again. Accessories loads all the application windows that were open when you returned to DOS.

When you don't expect to use any open Accessories application windows again, you can close each window by pressing Esc (Exit) or F3 (Exit) for each window or by clicking each window's close box. Accessories returns to the Desktop Accessories main menu. Select Exit or press Esc (Exit) or F3 (Exit), and Accessories returns to the screen from which you activated Desktop. The next time you activate Accessories, the program displays the Desktop Accessories main menu, with no application windows open.

> When you use the hotkey to return to DOS or a DOS program from which you hot keyed into Desktop Accessories, Accessories saves the current Desktop configuration. Even if you reboot (restart) your computer before reactivating Accessories, the program loads all the Accessories application windows that were open when you pressed the hotkey to return to DOS.

T I P

Chapter Summary

This chapter introduces PC Tools Desktop Accessories, one of the programs making up PC Tools Version 8.0. You learned how to get around the Accessories user interface. The chapter describes how to select options from screen menus by using the keyboard or a mouse; how to open and work with Accessories windows (including how to change window colors and how to move, resize, and zoom windows); how to use dialog boxes; and how to activate Accessories' on-line help facility. The chapter describes how to use Desktop utilities to control Accessories parameters, such as hotkeys, to display the ASCII table, and to unload Desktop from memory.

Turn to Chapter 16, "Using PC Tools Notepads," to begin learning how to use Desktop's convenient pop-up word processor.

Using PC Tools Notepads

Now that you know your way around Desktop Accessories, you are ready to start learning about the application modules. This chapter describes Notepads, the Desktop Accessories word processor.

Word processing continues to be the most popular way to use personal computers. In most offices, microcomputer-based word processing programs have pushed the dedicated word processor into virtual extinction. The Notepads application is a small but surprisingly capable PC-based word processor. Notepads is just one of many tools available in PC Tools Desktop Accessories, but Notepads provides many features normally associated with full-featured word processing programs, such as page headers and footers, a find-and-replace function, and a spelling checker. With Notepads, you can create files as long as approximately 60,000 characters, or from 14 to 17 pages, depending on whether you print at 10 or 12 cpi (characters per inch).

Unlike feature-rich word processing programs such as WordPerfect, Notepads always is available at the touch of the Accessories hotkey (Ctrl+space bar) regardless of the applications program you might be using.

This chapter explains how to create files and describes how to edit a file and use wordwrap, auto indent, the Accessories Clipboard, and the spelling checker. This chapter also explains using Notepads find-and-replace capabilities, saving the contents of a Notepads window to a disk file, and printing the file.

You can apply much of what you learn in this chapter to two other Desktop applications: Outlines (discussed in Chapter 18, "Using the Outliner") and Macro Editor (discussed in Chapter 21, "Automating Your PC Using PC Tools Macros"), which are built around the word processing interface in Notepads. In other applications, you use Notepads to attach brief notes to appointments, explained in Chapter 20, "Managing Your Appointment Schedule," or create form files to use with databases, explained in Chapter 19, "Using PC Tools Databases."

Opening a Notepads Window

To open a Notepads window, select **Desktop Accessories** from the horizontal menu bar and then select **Notepads**. Accessories displays the File Load dialog box (see fig. 16.1).

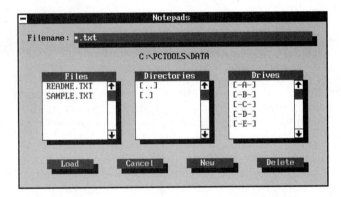

Fig. 16.1

Using the File Load dialog box to open a Notepads window.

NOTE Do not be confused by the name of the File Load dialog box. The proper name is the File Load dialog box, even though the title bar at the top of the dialog box displays only the name of the active application. When you select the Notepads, Outlines, Databases, Appointment Scheduler, or Macro Editor from the Desktop Accessories main menu, Accessories displays this dialog box, in which you must either select a file to load or create a new file. This dialog box also appears when you select Load from the File pull-down menu of each application's horizontal menu bar.

In the Filename text box, Accessories displays the default file-selection criterion. The asterisk (*) is a wild-card character that stands for any combination of one to eight characters. The default file name extension, TXT, follows the asterisk. The dialog box also contains three list boxes: Files, Directories, and Drives. Because the list boxes have room to show only eight entries at a time, you usually must scroll to see the complete list.

Desktop looks through the current directory and displays every file name with the extension TXT. In figure 16.1, for example, the file names README.TXT and SAMPLE.TXT appear in the list box.

The remaining two list boxes display the disk drives and directories in which you can store files. Use these list boxes to locate the file with which you want to work. A letter enclosed in brackets denotes each disk drive in the Drives list box. The first five entries in this list denote your computer's logical disk drives. Each directory is denoted by its DOS name.

T I P

The Drives list box can list disk drives that are not physically present, such as drives D and E. If you try to use a disk drive that doesn't physically exist or isn't installed properly, Accessories displays the message ERROR- Invalid path or path not found. Your computer may have one hard disk divided into two or more logical partitions, and each partition may have its own drive letter. Treat each partition as a separate disk drive.

At the top of the Directories list box is the designation [..], which stands for the *parent directory*. The parent directory contains the current directory. In figure 16.1, the current directory is C:\PCTOOLS\DATA, and the parent directory is C:\PCTOOLS in the root directory of drive C.

In the Directories list box, Accessories shows any directories you created in the default directory. If you create within the PCTOOLS\DATA directory a directory named NOTEPADS, for example, Accessories includes [NOTEPADS] in the list box.

The File Load dialog box can be configured to always display a specific drive and directory. You can also set up a different file name extension to use for your Notepads files, as explained in the following sections.

Assigning a Default File Name Extension

When you first install PC Tools 8, the default file name extension for Notepads files is TXT. If you already use this extension to designate text files, you may not want to use TXT for your Notepads files.

To change the default file name extension, you simply display the File Load dialog box and type *.ext* in the text box, where *ext* stands for the new extension you want to use. To use NPF (for "Notepad File") as the new default file name extension, for example, follow these steps:

1. Choose **Notepads** from the **Desktop Accessories** menu to access the File Load dialog box.

2. In the Filename text box, type ***.npf**; then press Enter.

3. Press Esc or F3 (Exit), or click the close box to close the File Load dialog box.

Accessories now uses NPF as the default file name extension for Notepads files. If you select a file rather than closing the box, Accessories continues to use the previous extension as the default extension.

When you name Notepads files, decide on the file name extension you want to use and then use that extension consistently to distinguish Notepads files from other types of files in the data directory. (This book uses TXT as the default file name extension for Notepads files.)

Assigning a Default Directory

When you first install PC Tools, the default directory for all Accessories applications can be C:\PCTOOLS or C:\PCTOOLS\DATA, depending on how you responded to the installation questions (see Appendix A, "Installing and Configuring PC Tools"). You can define a different default directory for each application, however, to better manage the files created by the various modules.

If the directory you want to use as the default data directory does not already exist, you must create the directory as explained in Chapter 6, "Working on Disks." Then choose **Notepads** from the **Desktop Accessories** menu to access the File Load dialog box. In the Filename text box, type the name of the new directory, including the complete DOS path; then press Enter. Accessories changes the default data directory to the directory you specified and lists files from this new data directory in the list box. This directory is now the default directory for Notepads.

You may want to store all Notepad files in the subdirectory C:\PCTOOLS\NOTEPADS, for example. Create this subdirectory, display the File Load dialog box, type the following in the text box, and then press Enter:

C:\PCTOOLS\NOTEPADS

Accessories moves the highlighted bar into the list box and changes the default directory to C:\PCTOOLS\NOTEPADS. The remainder of this chapter assumes that C:\PCTOOLS\NOTEPADS is the default directory for Notepads.

T I P

Assigning a new default data directory for Notepads does not affect where Accessories stores files created by applications other than Notepads. To assign a different default data directory to each Accessories application, you follow a similar procedure. If you assign a different directory to each application, Accessories still stores temporary files created during its operation in the initial default directory C:\PCTOOLS or C:\PCTOOLS\DATA.

Creating a Notepads File

After you settle on a standard file name extension and a default directory for Notepads files, you are ready to use the Notepads application. To create a Notepads file, display the File Load dialog box. In the Filename text box, type the name of the new file. When you begin to type, the new file name replaces any other entries in the text box.

You can type from one to eight characters for the file name, using letters, numbers, or any of these characters:

~ ! @ # % ^ & ( ) - _ { } '

Do not leave spaces in a file name. You can type a file name extension, but adding the extension defeats the purpose of the default—ensuring that all Notepad files have the same extension.

NOTE When you choose File on the horizontal menu bar to load or create a Notepads file while another Notepads file is active, the new Notepad file replaces the active Notepad. Refer to Chapter 15, "Navigating the Desktop Accessories," for instructions on how to have several Notepads files open simultaneously.

Suppose that you want to type a quick confirmation letter to a customer. Because the customer is from ABC Auto Parts, Inc., and today is June 14, you decide to name the file ABC-0614. To create this file, display the File Load dialog box and type **abc-0614** in the text box.

Select the **N**ew command button. Accessories displays a Notepads window (see fig. 16.2). Because you did not specify a file name extension, Accessories adds the default extension established previously. In this example, Accessories adds the extension TXT.

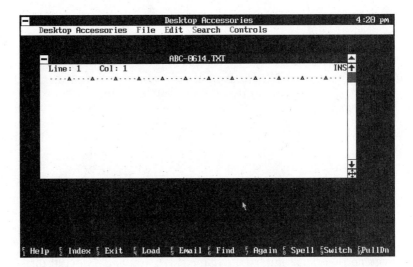

Fig. 16.2

The new Notepads window for the Notepads file ABC-0614.TXT.

T I P   If you type the new file name in the text box and press Enter rather than choose New, Accessories assumes that you intend to load an existing file by that name. Because the file does not yet exist, Accessories displays the message `File not found. Create a new file instead?` Select the **O**K command button to display a Notepads window for the new file.

Because you usually want Accessories to create the Notepads file in the default directory, you do not type a DOS path as part of the file name. To store a Notepads file in a different directory, include in the file name the complete DOS path specification. You may want to use Notepads to create a DOS batch file to start the program KillerAp, for example. To name the file KA.BAT and to store the file with your other batch files in the DOS directory named C:\BAT, choose **N**otepads from the **D**esktop

Accessories menu and type the following path and file name in the Filename text box:

C:\BAT\KA.BAT

Select the **New** command button. Accessories displays a new Notepads window for the file KA.BAT, and you can begin to type the lines of the batch file.

NOTE DOS batch files work only if they are stored on the disk in ASCII format rather than in PCTOOLS Desktop Accessories format. Refer to the section "Saving a Notepads File" later in this chapter for information about saving a file in ASCII format.

Loading an Existing Notepad

You may need to edit an existing Notepads file. To load an existing file, select **N**otepads from the **D**esktop Accessories menu to display the File Load dialog box. If you are already working in a Notepads window, you can use the shortcut command F4 (Load) to display the File Load dialog box.

NOTE Be sure to save the current document before loading a new one. Any changes not saved will be lost. See the section "Saving a Notepads File" later in this chapter for more infor- mation.

You can use one of the following procedures to load an existing file:

■ Type the file name in the Filename text box. If the file name does not use the default file name extension, type the extension. If the file is not located in the default directory, enter the complete DOS path. Press Enter or choose the **L**oad command button.

■ Press Tab to move the highlighted bar to the appropriate list box; press the arrow keys (or the scroll bar on the right side of the box) to scroll to the desired file, drive, or directory; then press Enter or choose the **L**oad command button.

■ Use the scroll bars on the right side of the list boxes to display the file, drive, or directory, and then double-click the file name.

You can edit an ASCII file with the Notepads application. Follow the same procedure described in this section for loading a Notepads file. When Accessories tries to load the ASCII file, the program recognizes that the file is in ASCII format and makes the appropriate internal adjustments to load and display the file. Accessories also automatically stores the file in ASCII format. Refer to the section "Saving a Notepads File" later in this chapter for more information about saving files in ASCII format.

For Related Information

◀◀ "Using Multiple Windows," p. 544.

FROM HERE...

Examining the Notepads Window

The screens in all Desktop Accessories applications are similar because they are built from a standard set of building blocks. Chapter 15, "Navigating the Desktop Accessories," discusses the standard Accessories elements, such as the application title bar, the horizontal menu bar, the window border, the close box, and the scroll bars. This section examines the aspects of the Notepads window that distinguish this window from other application windows.

NOTE   This discussion also applies to Outlines and Macro Editor windows, which are based on the Notepads interface.

The Notepads horizontal menu bar contains the menus Desktop Accessories, File, Edit, Search, and Controls. The message bar lists shortcut commands (refer to fig. 16.2). These and other keystroke commands available in Notepads are listed in table 16.1. Most of these commands are discussed later in this chapter.

The Notepads window is the area of the screen between the horizontal menu bar and the message bar. Figure 16.3 shows a letter displayed in a Notepads window.

Table 16.1 Keystroke Commands Available in Notepads

Key	Name	Function
F1	Help	Displays the context-sensitive Help facility
F2	Index	Displays the Help facility index
F3	Exit	Cancels the current process or application
F4	Load	Loads a different Notepad file into the window
F5	Email	Sends the current Notepad document as an electronic-mail message
F6	Find	Activates the find-and-replace feature
F7	Again	Repeats the last find operation
F8	Spell	Checks the spelling in the entire file
F9 or Ctrl+Esc	Switch	Switches between active windows
F10	PullDn	Activates the horizontal menu bar (same as Alt)
Alt	Menu	Activates the horizontal menu bar (same as F10)
Esc	Cancel	Cancels the current process or application (same as F3)
Alt+space bar	System Control	Displays the System Control pull-down menu

You can change the size and position of application windows on-screen (see Chapter 15, "Navigating the Desktop Accessories," for more information). Figures 16.3 and 16.4, for example, display the same letter. Figure 16.3 is the initial default window size, which shows only 9 lines by 64 characters at a time; figure 16.4, however, uses the full screen.

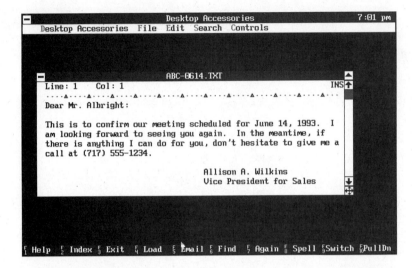

Fig. 16.3

A letter displayed
in a Notepads
window.

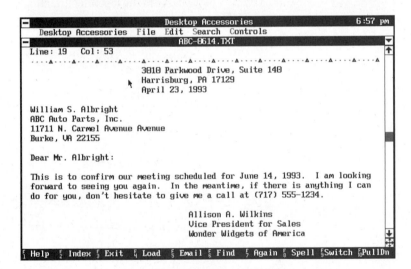

Fig. 16.4

A letter displayed
in a full-screen
Notepads
window.

The first line of a Notepads window—the status line—displays these
three pieces of information:

■ The Line number denotes the vertical position of the cursor in
the file. When the cursor is at the top of the file, the line number
is 1.

■ The Col (column) number represents the horizontal position of the cursor in the file. Every time you move the cursor one space to the right, the column number increases by one. Every time you move the cursor one space to the left, the column number decreases by one.

■ The mode indicator at the right end of the status line indicates whether Notepads is in insert mode (INS) or in overtype mode. (In overtype mode, this area is blank.) Insert and overtype modes are explained in "Inserting and Deleting Characters," later in this chapter.

In each Notepads window, Desktop displays the tab ruler. This line is made up of dots and triangles. The triangles show where tab stops are set. Refer to "Using the Tab Ruler" later in this chapter for more information on tab stops.

On the left side of every Notepads window, Accessories leaves a blank column two spaces wide (sometimes referred to as the *selection bar*). To select a line of text for a block copy or move operation, use the left mouse button to click this space at the immediate left of the target line. Accessories highlights the entire line of text. If you want to deselect the line of text, click the selection bar, using the right mouse button.

Entering Text

When you have a Notepads window displayed as the current application window, you are ready to type the document. Type the text as you would on a typewriter. You can type any of the characters on your computer's keyboard—including letters, numbers, and special characters. Desktop enables you to type other ASCII (American Standard Code for Information Interchange) characters by using Ctrl+key combinations. Refer to Chapter 15 "Navigating the Desktop Accessories," for information on how to use the Desktop utilities to access a list of the control codes you can use to type ASCII characters.

To display ASCII characters, hold down the Alt key and press the corresponding DEC (decimal) code for the character you want to display (as listed in the ASCII table in Chapter 15, "Navigating the Desktop Accessories"). This procedure enables you to use, for example, the ASCII box-drawing characters to create organizational charts.

When you are typing text, you can use the Tab key. Every time you press Tab, Accessories moves the cursor to the next tab stop denoted by the triangles in the tab ruler line near the top of the screen. See "Using the Tab Ruler" later in this chapter for more information.

Understanding Wordwrap

Don't worry about typing past the right margin in a Notepads window. By default, Accessories moves words that do not fit on the line to the next line. This feature, called *wordwrap*, is common in word processors. Accessories wraps words to the next line beginning with the 76th character in a default-sized window. When you want the text formatted in paragraphs, press Enter at the end of a paragraph to create a new paragraph.

Desktop Accessories formats any text to fit within the current window border (refer to Chapter 15, "Navigating the Desktop Accessories"). The Notepads window in figure 16.3, for example, is narrower than the window in figure 16.4, but both display the full body of the same letter. You may have to scroll vertically to read the entire document, but using the wordwrap feature—even in a narrow window—means that you do not have to scroll horizontally.

To create or edit a document that must be wider than the maximum width of a Notepads window, turn off the wordwrap feature. If, for example, you try to type a yearly sales report with wordwrap on, the screen looks scrambled (see fig. 16.5).

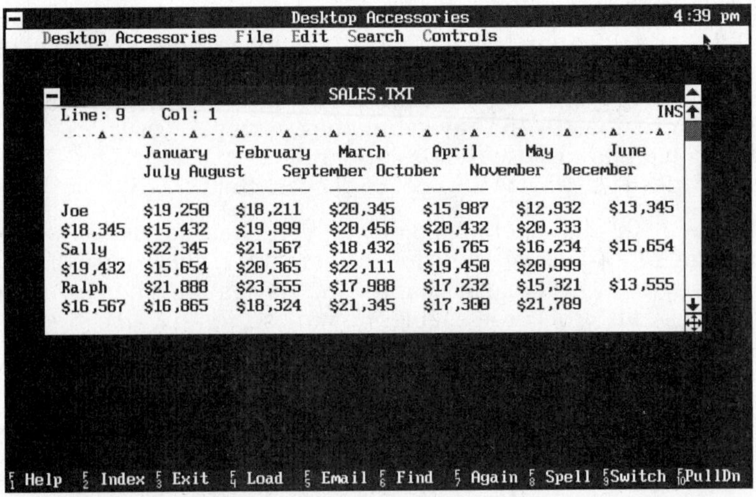

Fig. 16.5

An annual sales report with wordwrap on.

You can tell wordwrap is enabled by selecting the Controls pull-down menu (see fig. 16.6). If you see a check mark next to the Wordwrap option, this feature is active. From the Controls menu, choose **Wordwrap** to toggle off the feature.

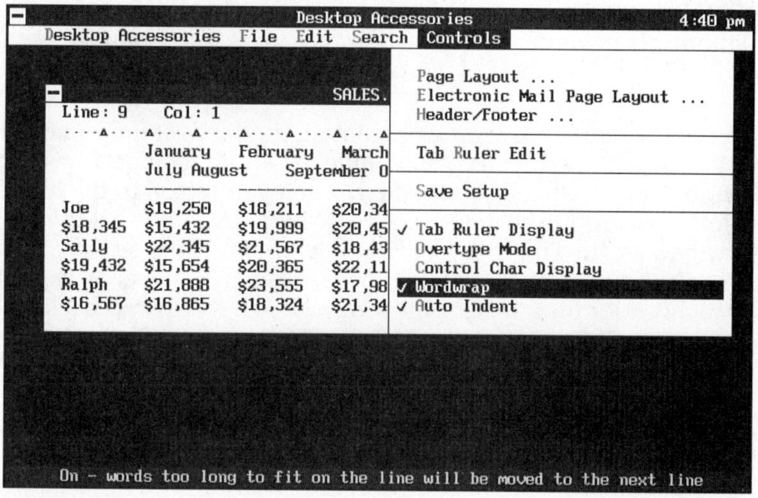

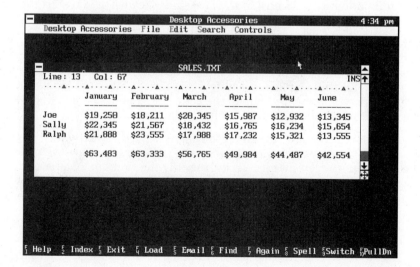

Fig. 16.6

The Wordwrap option in the Controls pull-down menu.

Compare figure 16.7 to figure 16.5. With wordwrap turned off, you can type all the necessary columns for the sales report, although not all the columns fit on-screen. Accessories doesn't wrap words back to the left side of the window border.

Fig. 16.7

The sales report with Wordwrap off.

T I P   The way the text wraps in the Notepads window has no relation to the way the printed text will appear. The margins you set determine the print layout. To have text in the Notepads window display the way it will print, size the window so that its edges are at the print margins. For details on setting margins, see "Setting the Page Layout" later in this chapter.

You can reactivate Wordwrap by repeating the same steps you used to toggle off the feature. If you close the file or switch to another window, wordwrap is automatically reactivated when you return to the file. In order for wordwrap to remain inactive even though you switch between windows, turn off the wordwrap feature and choose **S**ave Setup from the **C**ontrols menu. Wordwrap will remain inactive in all Notepads windows, even for future sessions until you turn wordwrap back on and choose **S**ave Setup again.

Using Auto Indent

When Notepads wordwrap feature wraps a word to the next line, the first character in the word is placed below the first character in the line above, even if that character is not in the first character column. When you press Enter, Accessories moves the cursor down one line and positions it beneath the first character of the preceding line. This feature is *auto indent*, which is active by default. If you start typing in column 1, you auto indent to column 1 in the next line; likewise, if you start typing in column 17, you auto indent to column 17.

Suppose, for example, that you are typing a letter. You type the first line of the return address beginning at column 35 of line 18. When you press Enter at the end of the first line, Accessories moves the cursor to column 35 for the next line, creating a temporary, indented left margin. If you start typing the first line of the customer's address in column 1, the cursor returns to column 1 in the next line.

You can deactivate auto indent in the same way you deactivate wordwrap. When you toggle off auto indent, Accessories always returns the cursor to the left margin. To indent only the first line of a paragraph, for example, toggle off auto indent. A check mark to the left of Auto Indent on the Controls menu indicates that the feature is active. To deactivate auto indent, choose **A**uto Indent to toggle off the feature. Auto indent remains off for this file until you reactivate the feature. As with wordwrap, if you close the file or switch between windows, auto indent is automatically reactivated when you return to the original file.

Displaying Control Characters

As you type in a Notepads window, Accessories displays letters, numbers, and other keyboard characters. When you press the space bar, Tab, or Enter, however, Accessories moves the cursor accordingly but displays nothing. Instead, the program stores a control character in the file.

When you are editing a file, you sometimes need to know where control characters are located. Every time you press the Tab key, for example, Desktop inserts a tab control character at the cursor and moves the cursor to the next tab stop. The default tab ruler sets tab stops five spaces apart so that every time you press Tab, Accessories moves the cursor five spaces. If you delete the tab character, Accessories moves the cursor and any text to the right of the cursor five spaces to the left.

Although tabs and spaces are invisible on-screen, the effect of deleting these characters isn't the same. If you use the space bar to move five spaces, for example, you must press the key five times. If you press the Backspace key to erase one of these blank characters, Accessories moves the cursor and any text to the right of the cursor only one space to the left. This discrepancy sometimes can lead to confusion. One way to avoid or alleviate confusion is to display the control characters.

To display control characters, choose Control Char Display from the Controls pull-down menu. Desktop returns the display to the Notepads window and the original text, but the control characters appear, as shown in table 16.2. Figure 16.8 shows a letter with control characters displayed. To toggle off the control characters, execute the same steps you used to turn on the display of these characters.

Table 16.2 Control Characters

Key	Control Character
Space bar	·
Tab	→
Enter	↵

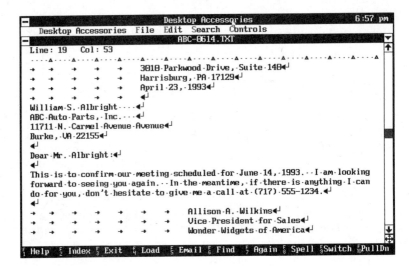

Fig. 16.8

A letter with
control charac-
ters displayed.

Moving around the Notepad

When you want to make a change in a Notepad, you first must move the
cursor to where the text needs to be edited. Accessories provides several ways to move the cursor in a Notepads window, as listed in table
16.3.

Table 16.3 Notepads Movement Keys

Key	Movement
↓	Moves down one line
↑	Moves up one line
→	Moves one character to the right
←	Moves one character to the left
Backspace	Erases character to the left
Ctrl+→	Moves to beginning of word to the right
Ctrl+←	Moves to space following the preceding word
Home	Moves to left end of the line containing the cursor
End	Moves right to the end of the line containing the cursor
Home, Home	Moves to upper left corner of screen

Key	Movement
End, End	Moves to end of the text visible in the window
Ctrl+Home	Moves to beginning of the file (line 1, column 1)
Ctrl+End	Moves to end of the file
PgDn	Moves down one screen
PgUp	Moves up one screen
Ctrl+PgDn	Scrolls the window down one line
Ctrl+PgUp	Scrolls the window up one line
Enter	Moves down one line below the first character on the left when Notepads is in overtype mode

You can use the mouse to move the cursor around the window. Use the left or right mouse button to click the position in which you want the cursor. You also can use the mouse and scroll bars to move the cursor quickly around the file. To scroll up or down, drag the scroll box on the vertical scroll bar on the Notepads window.

Accessories also provides a menu command to move the cursor directly to a specific line. Choose **G**oto from the **E**dit menu. Desktop displays the Go To dialog box (see fig. 16.9). To move the cursor to a particular line, type the number of the line in the Line Number text box and then choose OK. Desktop moves the cursor to the target line in the file. You also can choose **C**ancel to abort the command without moving the cursor.

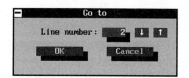

Fig. 16.9

The Go To dialog box.

Inserting and Deleting Text

When the cursor is located where you want to make a change, you must be able to insert and delete text as necessary. The following sections describe how to insert and delete characters and entire documents.

Inserting and Deleting Characters

The first time you load a Notepads window, Desktop is in *insert mode* (indicated by INS at the top right of the screen). As you type, Accessories displays the character at the cursor's position and pushes existing characters one space to the right.

If you want to replace the text already on-screen, you can type over existing characters in overtype mode. When you type a character in overtype mode, Accessories displays the character at the cursor's position, replacing any character already displayed at that position. To switch from insert mode to overtype mode, press the Ins key. Accessories removes INS from the top right of the screen. Pressing Ins again returns the program to insert mode.

T I P You can toggle between insert and overtype modes by using the menu bar. From the Controls menu, choose the Overtype Mode option. Desktop places a check mark to the left of the Overtype Mode option.

To delete a character, position the cursor on the character you want to delete and then press Del. Every time you press Del, Accessories deletes one character. The wordwrap feature, if active, adjusts the line length.

Inserting a File

One of the great conveniences of Desktop is the ease with which you can incorporate previously finished work into a new file. Suppose, for example, that you have saved a narrative resume in a file named RESUME.TXT, and you want to send this narrative to different businesses. You type the recipient's address and a salutation. After an opening paragraph describing the purpose of the letter, you want to include your prepared narrative.

To insert the entire contents of the RESUME.TXT file, place the cursor where you want the inserted text to begin. From the Edit menu, choose Insert File. Desktop displays the File Load dialog box. In the Filename text box, type the name of the file containing the text you want inserted—for this example, RESUME.TXT. Accessories inserts into the Notepads window the entire contents of the file, beginning at the cursor. Now you can add a closing paragraph and a signature block to finish the letter.

Deleting All Text in a Notepads Window

Accessories enables you to erase all the text in the Notepads window in one step. To delete the entire contents of a Notepads window, choose **D**elete All Text from the **E**dit menu. Desktop displays this message:

```
Warning: Please confirm that you want to erase the
document
```

Choose **OK** to confirm the deletion or **C**ancel if you don't want to delete the window's contents.

Choosing the **D**elete All Text command from the **E**dit menu deletes the document from the screen but not from the file stored on the disk. (For information on deleting entire files from disk, see "Deleting a Notepads File" later in this chapter.) If you delete the document from the screen and then realize that you made a mistake, you can recover the deleted text. Do not save the Notepads window or open another Notepads window; otherwise, Accessories saves the blank notepad to the disk file, overwriting the text you want to recover and preventing you from undoing the deletion.

When you realize that you made a mistake, choose Insert File from the **E**dit menu. Accessories displays the File Load dialog box. Type the name of the file containing the text you just erased from the screen or select the file name from the list box. Accessories inserts the contents of the file into the Notepads window. Make sure that you perform this task, however, before Accessories executes an Autosave operation. (See "Toggling Autosave" later in this chapter for information on that feature.)

Alternatively, you can abandon the current file immediately by choosing E**x**it without Saving from the **F**ile pull-down menu. Accessories closes the Notepads window without saving the changes you have made (or without changes since the last Autosave operation).

Copying and Moving Text

Occasionally, you may want to move or copy text when you are working in a Notepads window. To delete more than just a few characters and less than the entire file from the window, or to move or copy a portion of the text, you can use the cut-and-paste or the copy-and-paste features, accessed from the Desktop Accessories main menu.

Although similar, the copy and cut commands have one major difference. When you copy text, the original text remains intact, and a copy of the text appears in the new location. When you cut text, on the other hand, the original text is removed from the original location and moved to the new location.

When you cut or copy a block of text from a Notepads window, Accessories temporarily stores the block to the Clipboard. If you accidentally cut a block of text, you can retrieve the text from the Clipboard. Cutting or copying text to the Clipboard replaces previous Clipboard contents. The following sections explain how to use the basic cut and paste capabilities while working in a Notepads window.

> **NOTE** In PC Tools, the Clipboard is more than just a storage area for cut or copied text. The Clipboard, which enables you to move text blocks within a Notepads file and between windows, is a separate Accessories application that you use in conjunction with other Accessories applications. The Clipboard can hold as much as 4K of data (approximately 80 to 90 lines of text) and acts as a staging area or *buffer*. For more information regarding the Clipboard, see Chapter 17, "Using PC Tools Clipboard."

Marking a Text Block

The first step toward cutting, copying, or moving a text block is to highlight or mark the block. Accessories provides a number of ways to mark a text block:

- Position the mouse pointer at one end of the text block, press the left mouse button, and drag the highlight to the other end of the text block. If the text block extends beyond the current window, scroll the screen by moving the mouse pointer into the top or bottom window border while you continue to hold the left mouse button.

- Position the cursor at one end of the text block. Hold down the Shift key and press the cursor-movement keys to move the cursor to the other end of the block.

- Position the cursor at one end of the text block. Select **M**ark Block from the **E**dit menu. Press the cursor-movement keys to position the cursor at the other end of the text block.

These methods highlight the characters and blank spaces from the location where you began the marking to the location where you ended the marking.

Suppose, for example, that you are typing a letter to a customer to confirm an appointment for June 14, 1992. You want to copy the first two sentences from one letter to a new letter. Using one of the three methods described, you mark from the beginning of the first sentence to the period at the end of the second sentence (see fig. 16.10).

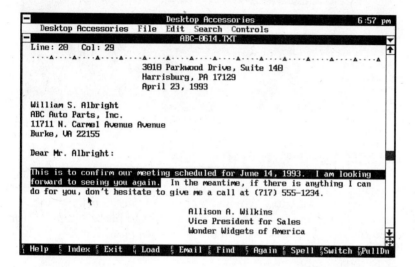

Fig. 16.10

Marking a
sentence.

NOTE Sometimes in a Notepads window, you may want to copy only a columnar portion of the text, such as the February column of figures from the annual sales report (refer to fig. 16.7). If you use one of the three standard methods of marking text, Accessories marks portions of all the columns, which is not what you intended (see fig. 16.11). Accessories provides another method of marking text suitable for copying a column of text. See Chapter 17, "Using the Clipboard" for a description of this method of copying text.

You can quickly deselect marked text by pressing any key, clicking either mouse button, or choosing **U**nmark Block from the **E**dit menu. To turn off marking while you are using the **M**ark Block menu option, press Esc (Exit) or F3 (Exit), or select **U**nmark Block from the **E**dit menu.

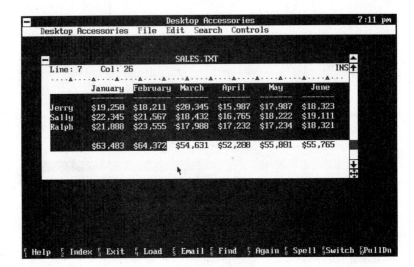

Fig. 16.11

An incorrectly marked sales report.

Cutting and Copying Text

When you want to delete or move marked text, you must cut the block from the original location. When you cut text from its original location, the text is moved to the Clipboard. If you want to place a copy of the marked block in another location in the file or in another Notepads file without removing the marked text from the original location, copy the block to the Clipboard.

To cut a marked block to the Clipboard, press Shift+Del or choose Cut to Clipboard from the Edit menu. Accessories removes the marked text from the Notepads window and places the text in the Clipboard.

If you want to copy marked text to the Clipboard, choose Copy to Clipboard from the Edit menu. Accessories places a copy of the marked text in the Clipboard but does not remove the text from its original location.

To copy to the Clipboard the highlighted sentences in the file ABC-0614.TXT (refer to fig. 16.11) so that you can include the sentences in another document, choose Copy to Clipboard from the Edit menu. To move these sentences to the end of the letter, however, you must cut the highlighted text to the Clipboard. Press Shift+Del or choose Cut to Clipboard from the Edit menu.

As mentioned earlier, the Clipboard can hold about 80 to 90 lines of text. If you try to cut or copy more text than fits in the Clipboard, Accessories displays this message:

```
Block will not fit in clipboard. Cut off to fit?
```

To continue with the cut or copy operation, select the **OK** command button. Desktop completes the operation but truncates (cuts off) the text that exceeds the Clipboard capacity. You can select **C**ancel to return to the Notepads screen without completing the operation. Cut or copy the text in a series of operations by marking smaller blocks of text each time.

Pasting Text

After you cut or copy the text to the Clipboard, you are ready to place, or *paste*, the Clipboard's contents into the target file. When you want to paste text into a Notepads file, move the cursor to the destination point. The intended destination can be within the same Notepads file that contained the original text or within a different window. When the cursor is located properly, press Shift+Ins or choose **P**aste to Clipboard from the **E**dit menu. Accessories copies the contents of the Clipboard into the target location, beginning at the cursor's position.

> **NOTE** To prevent overwriting existing text with pasted text, make sure that the destination Notepads window is in insert mode.

For Related Information

▶▶ "Copying and Pasting Text," p. 600.

FROM HERE...

Using Spellcheck

A few years ago, a program that could locate and correct misspelled words within a document was a luxury. Now, virtually all full-featured word processors include a spelling checker. Most general-purpose desktop-management programs do not have a spelling utility. PC Tools continues to go well beyond what you expect, however, and provides a capable spelling feature—*Spellcheck*—that you can use to correct spelling in a Notepads file.

Accessories offers three Spellcheck options on the Edit menu:

■ *Spellcheck **Word**.* Choose this option to check the spelling of one word.

■ *Spellcheck **Screen**.* Choose this option to check the spelling of all words in the current screen.

■ *Spellcheck **File**.* Choose this option to check the spelling of all the words in the file.

To check the spelling of all words in the file, you also can use the shortcut command F8 (Spell).

When Desktop begins the Spellcheck operation, the program displays in the window's title bar the message Spell checking in progress. Please wait. If Desktop finds a word not in its dictionary, the program highlights the suspect word and displays the Word Misspelled dialog box (see fig. 16.12).

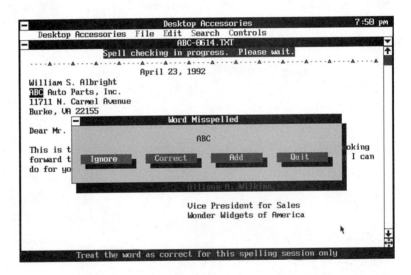

Fig. 16.12

The Word Misspelled dialog box.

In the Word Misspelled dialog box, Desktop displays the word that may be misspelled. In figure 16.12, for example, Accessories indicates that *ABC* is misspelled because Accessories cannot find *ABC* in its dictionary. Choose one of the four command buttons in the Word Misspelled dialog box:

■ *Ignore.* Choose this command button when the highlighted word is spelled correctly and you do not want to add the word to the dictionary.

■ *Correct.* Choose this command button when the word is misspelled and you want Desktop to display a list of possible correct
spellings. Desktop displays the Word Correction dialog box,
shown in figure 16.13, which contains a text box, a list box, and
two command buttons. The text box contains the misspelled
word, and the list box shows a list of possible spellings. To make
a correction, select the correct spelling from the list box. Alternatively, type the correct spelling in the text box, and then choose
Accept or press Enter twice. You can choose **C**ancel or press F3
(Exit) or Esc (Exit) to return to the Word Misspelled dialog box
without making a correction.

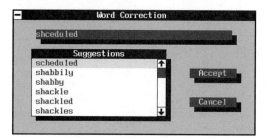

Fig. 16.13

The Word Cor-
rection dialog
box.

■ *Add.* Choose this button when the word is spelled correctly and
you want to add the word to the program dictionary. After the
word is added to the dictionary, Accessories no longer stops on
the word.

> **CAUTION:** Make sure that the highlighted word is spelled
> correctly before you add the word to the dictionary. Acces-
> sories provides no method for removing a word added to its
> dictionary. To remove the word, you must install PC Tools
> again and start with a "clean" dictionary.

■ *Quit.* Choose this command button to terminate the Spellcheck
operation without correcting the highlighted word. To quit from
Spellcheck, you also can press F3 (Exit) or Esc (Exit), or click the
close box in the upper left corner of the Word Correction dialog
box.

After you make a selection from the Word Correction dialog box, Accessories continues with Spellcheck. When the spelling check is complete,
the message is removed from the status line, and the cursor returns to
the normal Notepads display.

Searching a Notepads File

As you work in a Notepads file, you may want to find the occurrence of a particular word or phrase in a document. In an office memo, for example, you may want to find the section that discusses vacation days. (You can search for the word *vacation*.) You may want to replace a word or phrase you have used throughout a document with another word or phrase. If you discover that Ms. Smith's name is actually Ms. Smythe, for example, you can search for and replace all occurrences of *Smith*. Notepads' Search feature enables you to easily perform the search-and-replace tasks, as explained in the following sections.

Finding Text

When you want to find a certain text string in a file displayed in a Notepads window, choose **F**ind from the **S**earch menu. Accessories displays the Find dialog box.

In the text box, type the character string (which can consist of as many as 44 characters) for which you want Accessories to search. To look for a character string that exactly matches the case (upper- or lowercase), select the Case Sensitive check box. When this option is enabled, *Orange* does not match *orange*. When the Case Sensitive check box is empty, Accessories ignores the case of all characters.

By default, Accessories searches for all character strings, whether the string is an entire word or part of a word. If you search for *and*, for example, Accessories finds *and*, *hand*, *command*, and any other instances of this string. To search for just the word, select the Whole Words Only check box.

After you fill in the Search For text box and make the appropriate selections, choose the **F**ind command button to execute the search. Accessories searches from the cursor to the end of the file. If Accessories finds a match, the program places the cursor at the first character of the word (or phrase) that matches the search string. Choose **F**ind Again from the **S**earch menu or Press F7 (Again) to search for the next occurrence of the search string. When Accessories reaches the end of the file without finding another occurrence of the search string, you hear a beep.

> The search string you enter remains active until you close Desktop
> Accessories. When you finish searching a file and want to search for
> the string in another file, for example, you can open the file and then
> press F7 (Again) to find the first occurrence in the new file.
>
> **T I P**

Finding and Replacing Text

In addition to finding a particular character string in a Notepads file,
Accessories enables you to find and then replace a search string with
another character string. You can activate this feature in two ways:
press F6 (Find) or choose **R**eplace from the **S**earch menu. Desktop displays the Find and Replace dialog box (see fig. 16.14).

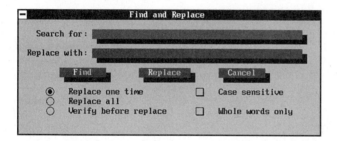

Fig. 16.14

The Find and
Replace dialog
box.

NOTE Despite its label, F6 (Find) actually opens the Find and Replace dialog box. You can access the Find command only by
choosing **F**ind from **S**earch menu bar. Then you can use F7
to find the next occurrence.

The Find and Replace dialog box contains two text boxes: Search For
and Replace With. In the Search For text box, type the text you want to
find. In the Replace With text box, type the character string with which
you want to replace the search string.

The Find and Replace dialog box also contains these three option
buttons:

■ *Replace One Time.* Choose this option when you want Desktop to
replace only the next occurrence of the search string and stop.

■ *Replace All.* Choose this option when you want Desktop to replace all occurrences of the search string.

■ *Verify before Replace.* Choose this option if you want Desktop to find the next occurrence of the search string and then ask for confirmation before replacing the string. During the search-and-replace operation, Desktop stops at every occurrence and displays this prompt in the message bar:

```
ENTER: make change ESC: abort SPACE: skip
```

Press Enter to perform the replacement, Esc to end the search-and-replace operation, or the space bar to skip to the next occurrence of the search string without performing a replacement this time.

Like the Find dialog box, the Find and Replace dialog box also contains the Case Sensitive and Whole Words Only check boxes. Refer to the section "Finding Text" for a description of these options.

After you fill in the text boxes and choose the appropriate options, choose one of these command buttons:

■ *Find.* Choose this option to find the next occurrence of the search string without replacing the entry with the replace string. The effect of this command button is the same as using the Find dialog box.

■ *Replace.* Choose this option if you want the program to find the search string and perform the specified search-and-replace operation, as indicated by the option button that you selected.

■ *Cancel.* Choose this option to cancel the search-and-replace operation.

Desktop continues to display the Find and Replace dialog box until the program finds no more occurrences of the search string or until you press Esc (Cancel).

Using the Tab Ruler

By default, Accessories displays the *tab ruler* line as the second line from the top of a Notepads window. The ruler appears as a line of dots and triangles. The triangles represent tab stops. Every time you press the Tab key, Accessories moves the cursor one tab stop to the right.

To remove the ruler from the screen, choose **T**ab Ruler Display from the **C**ontrols menu. (Accessories displays a check mark next to the option when the ruler is on-screen.) Accessories removes the ruler from the screen, providing an additional line in the Notepads window.

By default, Accessories places tab stops every five spaces. You can insert, delete, or change the position of the tab stops, however, as discussed in this section.

Accessories stores a control character in the file every time you press Tab, but does not display the character unless you choose **C**ontrol Char Display from the **C**ontrols menu (refer to "Displaying Control Characters" earlier in this chapter). When control characters are displayed, a → represents a tab character.

> Until you become comfortable with Notepads, you may want to display the tab ruler and toggle on the control characters so that you can see the effects of pressing the Tab key.

T I P

Typically, you use tabs to indent paragraphs and align text in columns. Suppose that you use Notepads to type a departmental phone list. You type a column of names and a column of phone numbers. Figure 16.15 shows the Notepads file with control characters displayed.

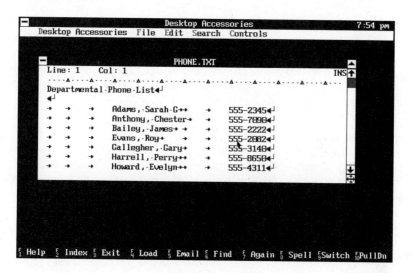

Fig. 16.15

Using tab stops to type a phone list in columns.

You may want to adjust the alignment of a tab stop, add a tab stop, or delete one or more tab stops. To edit the tab ruler line, choose Tab **R**uler Edit from the **C**ontrols menu. Accessories displays `Editing tab ruler` in the status line, and the cursor appears in the tab ruler.

Use the keys listed in table 16.4 to move the cursor along the tab ruler line to the position where you want to add, change, or delete a tab stop. Press Del to delete a tab stop or press Ins to set a new tab stop. While the cursor is in the tab ruler line, you can set evenly spaced tab stops by typing an integer from 3 to 29, representing the number of spaces you want between tab stops. After you finish adding, deleting, or realigning tab stops, press Esc (Exit) to accept the changes to the tab ruler line and return to normal editing.

Table 16.4 Tab Ruler Line Movement Keys

Key	Movement
→	One space to the right
←	One space to the left
Tab	One tab stop to the right
Shift+Tab	One tab stop to the left
Home	To the left end of the ruler
End	To the right end of the ruler

You may decide that you want to insert five more spaces between the name and phone number columns in the file PHONE.TXT. To move the phone numbers to the right, choose Tab **R**uler Edit from the **C**ontrols menu. Move the cursor to the tab stop between the name and phone number columns. Press Del. Press Esc, and Accessories moves the phone number list one tab stop—five spaces—to the right.

Any changes to the tab ruler are effective only in the current file but are saved with the file. The next time you use the file, the tab ruler displays the changes you made. Refer to the "Saving the Setup" section later in this chapter for details on how to make the changes permanent for all new Notepads files.

NOTE   As with many other features of Notepads, the tab stops you set are in effect for the entire file. If you plan on more than one table in your document or want to have a table and indented paragraphs, be sure to distribute tab stops so that they cover all your needs.

You do not have to display the tab-control characters to edit the tab ruler, but doing so may be a good practice. With the tab characters visible, you can see the effect of tab stops and determine more easily whether, and in what manner, you want to modify the tab ruler.

T I P

Printing a Notepads File

As you have seen, Accessories sets document margins according to the width of the window. If you change the window width, Accessories reformats the text to fit within the new borders. For printing a Notepads file, however, Accessories enables you to set specific left and right margins that do not vary with the size of the window. You also can set a number of other printing parameters, such as top and bottom margins, page size, lines per inch, and starting page number. You can assign headers and footers for text to be printed at the top and bottom of each page.

To add emphasis to some portion of the text, you may want to underline, italicize, or boldface the text, for example, or you may want to take advantage of your dot-matrix printer's capacity to print in near-letter quality. See Chapter 21, "Automating Your PC Using PC Tools Macros," for a discussion of how to use macros to insert the special printer-control commands necessary to turn on these printing attributes.

T I P

Setting the Page Layout

Accessories enables you to set most print parameters in the Page Layout dialog box. Before you print a file, check to see whether these settings are set properly for your document. Choose **P**age Layout from the **C**ontrols menu. Accessories displays the Page Layout dialog box (see fig. 16.16).

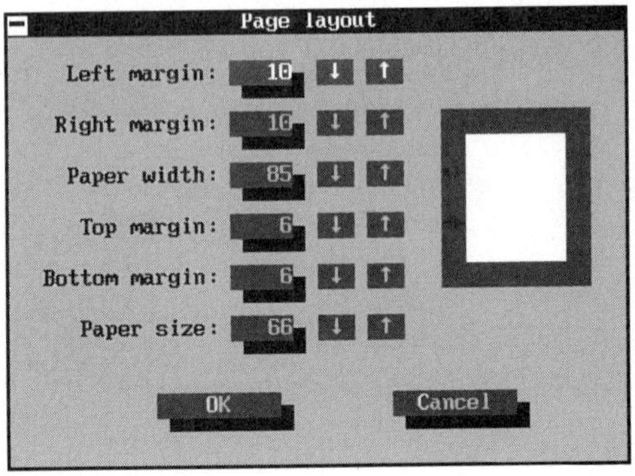

Fig. 16.16

The Page Layout dialog box.

The Page Layout dialog box contains six text boxes. You can type a new value or click the indicated arrows to increase or decrease the value. The text boxes contain the following settings:

- The *Left Margin* value determines the number of spaces from the left side of the paper at which Accessories begins printing (assuming that the left edge of the paper is aligned with the 0 on your printer's paper guide). The default is 10.

- The *Right Margin* setting determines the number of spaces from the right edge of the paper at which Accessories stops printing. The default is 10.

- The *Paper Width* value sets the total number of columns for printing on each piece of paper, including margins. The default width is 85 spaces, assuming that you are using 8 1/2-by-11-inch paper and a horizontal spacing of 10 cpi (character per inch).

T   I   P

Horizontal spacing is controlled by the type size printing commands you insert with macros, as described in Chapter 21, "Automating Your PC Using PC Tools Macros." Depending on your printer, your options are probably 10 and 12 cpi (characters per inch) and condensed print. If you change type size in the middle of a document, the margins for that area change proportionally.

- The *Top Margin* setting determines the number of lines Accessories ejects at the top of each page before beginning to print. The default value is 6. (Headers are printed within the top margin.)

- The *Bottom Margin* setting determines the number of lines Accessories leaves blank at the bottom of each page. The default value is 6. (Footers are printed in the bottom margin.)

■ The *Paper Size* value indicates the total number of lines available for printing on each piece of paper, including margins. The default length is 66 lines, assuming 8 1/2-by-11-inch paper and a vertical spacing of 6 lines per inch.

NOTE Each of these settings affects only how the printed document looks.

The right side of the dialog box shows a diagram of the page layout. This diagram serves as a reference as you change the layout parameters.

After you make any necessary adjustments, confirm the new settings by choosing **OK**. To cancel changes and return to the preceding page layout settings, choose **Cancel**. Any changes to page layout affect only the current file and are saved with the document. Refer to the section "Saving the Setup" later in this chapter to learn how to make the changes permanent for all new Notepads files.

Creating a Header or Footer

You may want to use a *header* (information recurring at the top of every page of a document) or a *footer* (information recurring at the bottom of every page) to label the pages of your document. For example, you may want to include the document title and page number at the top of every page. Headers and footers appear in top and bottom margins of a page, respectively.

To create a header or footer (or both), choose **Header/Footer** from the **C**ontrols menu. The Page Header & Footer dialog box appears (see fig. 16.17). In the Header text box, type the header text. In the Footer text box, type the footer text. Both boxes provide space for as many as 50 characters per line. Desktop then centers, within the defined left and right margins, the header text and the footer text.

Fig. 16.17

The Page Header & Footer dialog box.

By default, Accessories places the pound symbol (#) in the Footer text box. This special code causes Accessories to print the page number, centered at the bottom of each page. If you don't want to print page numbers, delete this symbol from the footer text box. To print page numbers in the header rather than in the footer, type the pound symbol in the Header text box and delete the symbol from the Footer text box. You also can accompany the page number with text.

After you finish typing the header or footer for your Notepads file, choose **OK** to accept the entry or **Cancel** to abandon any entries. Any header or footer you create appears only on the printed copy of the document; these elements do not appear on-screen.

Any changes to header and footer settings affect only the current file but are saved with the file. See the section "Saving the Setup" later in this chapter for details on how to make the changes permanent for all new Notepads files.

Printing the File

In most cases, the ultimate goal of creating a Notepads file is to print a document. Other times, however, you may need to send output to a file on disk—a *print file*—and then print the document directly from the print file. Accessories enables you to do either.

T I P See Chapter 21, "Automating Your PC Using PC Tools Macros," for information on how to send the appropriate control commands to your printer to set such printer parameters as font, type size, and printing mode.

After you type your document and adjust the print settings (margins, header, footer, and so on), you are ready to print the document. Choose **P**rint from the **F**ile menu. Accessories displays the Print dialog box (see fig. 16.18).

The Print dialog box contains six option buttons: LPT1, LPT2, LPT3, COM1, COM2, and Disk File. To send the Notepads output to your printer, determine the port to which your printer is connected and choose the appropriate option button (LPT1, LPT2, or LPT3 for parallel printers; COM1 or COM2 for serial printers). To create a disk file that you can use to send output to a printer, choose the Disk File option.

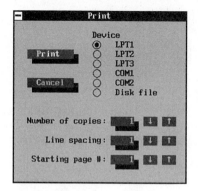

Fig. 16.18

The Print dialog box.

The Print dialog box also contains the following text boxes:

■ *Number of Copies.* By default, Accessories prints only one copy of each document. To print multiple copies of a document, type the number of copies in the text box.

■ *Line Spacing.* This setting determines the spacing between lines of text. By default, Desktop uses single spacing (as indicated by the 1 in the Line Spacing text box). If you want Accessories to leave one blank line between lines of text—double spacing— change the number to 2; for triple spacing (two blank lines between lines of text), change the entry to 3; and so on.

■ *Starting Page #.* If you have inserted a pound symbol in the header or footer (described in the preceding section), this option determines the number that Accessories uses as the page number on the first printed page. All subsequent pages are numbered in ascending numerical order.

To begin sending output to the printer or file, choose the **Print** command button. Desktop prints the document as many times as indicated in the Number of Copies text box. (If you decide not to begin printing after all, choose **Cancel** from the Print dialog box.) While Accessories prints the file or creates the disk file, the program displays this message:

```
Now printing. Press escape to cancel.
```

You can interrupt the printing by pressing the Esc key. Printing may not stop right away, however, because part of the document is probably in the print buffer.

When printing to a file, Desktop creates a file with the same name as the active Notepads file but uses the extension PRT. You can print this ASCII text file later by using a copy command (the DOS COPY command or the PC Tools Desktop **C**opy File command) or a print command (DOS PRINT or the PC Tools Desktop **P**rint File command). If you use Copy, copy the file to the device named PRN.

Suppose, for example, that you printed the Notepads file ABC-0614.TXT to a file. Accessories creates the print file named ABC-0614.PRT. To print this file, you can type the following DOS command:

COPY ABC-0614.PRT PRN

T I P To preview your print job, print to disk before sending output to a printer. Because the print file is an ASCII file, you can use Notepads to view the file. You have the opportunity to *dry run* the document to see how page margins, line spacing, headers, and footers look in the final product without wasting paper.

Deleting a Notepads File

PC Tools 8 can delete a notepad by using the File Load dialog box. Choose **N**otepads from the **D**esktop Accessories main menu to display the File Load dialog box. If you are working in a Notepads window and want to use the File Load dialog box to delete another Notepads file, you can use the shortcut command F4 (Load) to display the File Load dialog box.

When the File Load dialog box is displayed, you can use one of these two procedures to delete a file:

■ Type the file name in the text box. If the file name does not have the default extension, you must type the extension in the text box. If the file is not located in the default directory, include the complete DOS path in the text box. Then choose the **D**elete command button.

■ Use the scroll bar on the right side of the list boxes to scroll until you can see the file name you want, click the file name, and then choose **D**elete.

With either method, Accessories deletes the file from disk. You then can reuse the file name for a new file.

Saving a Notepads File

When you press Esc or F3 (Exit), click the close box, choose E**x**it from the **D**esktop menu, or open another Accessories application window, Accessories saves to disk any changes you made to the Notepads file since the file was last saved. Even if you don't close the window or open another window, the Accessories Autosave feature protects your changes by periodically saving the file to disk. Occasionally, you may want to save the files manually, as discussed in the following sections.

Choosing the File Format and Making a Backup

When you create a file using Notepads, the program usually saves the file in the default Desktop format. If you load an ASCII file into a Notepads window, however, Accessories saves the file as an ASCII text file. You may want to convert a Desktop-formatted file to an ASCII file or vice versa. The Accessories Save File to Disk dialog box, which you access by choosing **S**ave from the **F**ile menu, enables you to accomplish this conversion (see fig. 16.19). You can have Accessories keep the previous version of the file as a backup copy.

Fig. 16.19

The Save File to Disk dialog box.

To convert a file from Desktop format to ASCII or from ASCII to Desktop, choose the appropriate option button. By default, Accessories saves files in ASCII format, unless the file is a Desktop file when you load it.

By default, Desktop keeps the most recent version of a Notepads file as a backup copy. Desktop uses the same file name as the active Notepads file but adds the extension BAK. To toggle off this feature, remove the check mark from the Make Backup File check box.

After you select the proper format and decide whether you want a backup copy of the most recent version, choose **S**ave to save the file to disk.

NOTE If you save a file in ASCII format, the file no longer contains the formatting characteristics—tabs, margins, headers, footers, and so on.

Toggling Autosave

By default, Accessories saves the active Notepads file every five minutes, whether or not you make any changes. You can change this time interval or turn off the Autosave feature through the Automatic File Save dialog box, which you can access by choosing **A**utosave from the **F**ile menu.

To change the time interval between automatic saves, type a different number in the text box or click the arrows to increase or decrease the value, and then choose **OK**. The default is 5 minutes. To turn off the Autosave feature, choose Off and then **OK**. Choose **C**ancel to remove the dialog box without changing the Autosave feature.

Saving the Setup

Any change you make to an application window's color, size, or position or to any option on the Controls menu affects only the file in which you are working (the file displayed in the active window). As explained in Chapter 15, "Navigating the Desktop Accessories," however, you can establish a separate set of default settings for Notepads window color, size, and position by using the **S**ave Setup command from the **C**ontrols menu.

The Save Setup command saves the settings for page layout, headers and footers, tab ruler, insert and overtype mode, control-character display, wordwrap, and auto indent. The Save Setup command applies the changes to the Controls menu default settings to Outlines, Macro Editor, and Databases, as well as to Notepads.

Exiting Notepads

After you edit or print a Notepads file, you usually want to close the window to return to another application window or to another DOS application. Closing a Notepads window is as effortless as saving a Notepads file.

To exit a Notepads window, press Esc or F3 (Exit), or click the application close box. Accessories saves any changes and closes the window.

You may decide that you don't want the last changes you made saved to disk. To keep the preceding version of the file and to exit from a notepad without saving, choose Exit Without Saving from the File menu. Accessories closes the window but does not save the file to disk. If the Autosave feature is on, however, Accessories already may have saved the changes to disk.

 You also can use the Exit option on the Desktop menu to close a Notepads window, but this option saves any changes and then closes *all* open Desktop application windows.

Chapter Summary

This chapter explains how to use Desktop's built-in word processor, Notepads. The chapter describes how to open a Notepads window to create or edit a file and how to edit a Notepads file by using editing features such as wordwrap, auto indent, the Clipboard, and the spelling checker. This chapter also explains the search-and-replace capabilities of Notepads, how to save the contents of a Notepads window to a disk file, and how to print the Notepads file.

Much of what you learned in this chapter also applies to two other Desktop applications: Outlines and the Macro Editor. Both applications are built around the word processing interface in Notepads. Now that you are familiar with Notepads basic capabilities, turn to Chapter 17, "Using PC Tools Clipboard."

Using PC Tools Clipboard

I n ever-increasing numbers, computer users are installing some version of a DOS shell program that enables them to load several programs into memory simultaneously, to switch between the active programs as necessary, and to move data between programs to facilitate the creation of complex documents. PC Tools can be counted among those applications, known today as *desktop platforms* or *desktop environments*. PC Tools, however, has the additional advantage of including the most powerful disk utilities available.

Setting up PC Tools Desktop as your platform for running other applications is the focus of the discussion in Chapter 3, "Using the Desktop as a Program Manager." Give special attention to the discussion of the new Task Switcher application, also discussed in Chapter 3. With PC Tools Desktop and the Task Switcher properly configured, you need only the ability to cut and paste between applications to complete your desktop. This is the job of the Desktop Accessories Clipboard.

In this chapter, you learn how to copy text from DOS and Desktop Accessories applications into the Clipboard and how to paste this text into another application by using the hot-key method or the Clipboard menu commands. You learn how to edit text in the Clipboard and how to print text directly from the Clipboard. Finally, you learn how to set up the paste operation to suit the specific applications you use.

Understanding the Clipboard

When you use the cut-and-paste capabilities of various PC Tools applications, the text being moved passes through the Clipboard, which occupies a relatively small area of your computer's memory (RAM). The Clipboard acts as a staging area or *buffer* for up to 4K of data (approximately 80 to 90 lines of text). By using the Clipboard, you can delete, copy, and move a block of text within a Desktop Accessories file and between Accessories application windows. When Desktop Accessories is resident in memory, Clipboard enables you to copy text between other DOS programs, such as from a 1-2-3 spreadsheet to a WordPerfect document. Copying and pasting text from the Clipboard is explained in the section "Copying and Pasting Text."

When you cut or copy text from an application, the text is placed in the Clipboard. By opening the Clipboard application window, you can edit the contents before pasting the text into another application. Many of the Notepads editing commands, such as Search and Replace, are included on the Clipboard horizontal menu bar.

You may want to print the text immediately. If you want to print a portion of a Notepads or Outlines file, you must copy the desired portion to another window. With the Clipboard, however, you don't need to paste the Clipboard text into another Notepads or Outlines window to print it; you can print it directly from the Clipboard. If printing the text is your only purpose, you can then close the Clipboard window and proceed with other tasks. The next time you cut or copy any text, the new text overwrites the previous contents of the Clipboard.

Cutting and pasting text while working in a Notepads or Outlines window is explained in Chapter 16, "Using PC Tools Notepads." The next sections describe how to use the Clipboard to cut and paste between DOS and Accessories applications.

Copying and Pasting Text

Desktop enables you to copy a rectangle of text between any DOS character-based applications. You can create a travel-expense voucher in Lotus 1-2-3, for example, and then copy the voucher to a letter you are writing in WordPerfect 5.1. As long as Accessories is resident in memory, you can copy and paste text between DOS applications without having to open the Clipboard or activate Desktop Accessories.

You can use the Clipboard to copy text while you use Accessories or any DOS program that you loaded into memory after Accessories.

NOTE Although you can copy ASCII text or graphics characters to the Clipboard if you copy graphics screens such as those created by presentation-graphics programs or by programs that run in Graphics mode, inappropriate ASCII characters are substituted for the graphics.

Copying Text to the Clipboard

To copy a text block from one DOS application to another, you first must copy the text to the Clipboard. Position the document in the DOS or Accessories application so that all the text you want to copy is visible on-screen. (If the text you want to copy does not fit on one screen, perform more than one copy-and-paste operation; remember, however, to paste the first block of material before you copy the next block.) Next, press the hot-key combination Ctrl+Del to activate the Clipboard copy feature. Accessories places a rectangular cursor in the center of the screen of the DOS application.

NOTE If Ctrl+Del conflicts with a keystroke command from the DOS application, choose **U**tilities from the **D**esktop Accessories main menu, and then choose the **H**otkey Selection option from the Utilities submenu to assign a different hotkey to the copy function. See Chapter 15, "Navigating the Desktop Accessories" for more information.

The Accessories hot-key copy procedure copies a rectangular text block from the screen. You can mark this area by using one of the following methods:

■ Use the mouse to position the rectangular cursor at one of the corners of the text block you want to copy to the Clipboard. Press and hold either mouse button and drag the cursor to the opposite corner of the block. When all the text you want to copy is marked, release the mouse button.

■ Use the arrow keys to position the cursor at one of the corners of the text block you want to copy; press Enter. Then use the arrow keys to move the cursor to the opposite corner of the block. When all the text you want copied is marked, press Enter.

Accessories copies the marked text to the Clipboard, removes the highlighting, and returns control of the screen to the DOS application.

Suppose, for example, that you entered your travel expenses in a 1-2-3 spreadsheet (see fig. 17.1), and you now want to copy these figures into a WordPerfect file. First, display the 1-2-3 spreadsheet. Next, press Ctrl+Del, the Accessories copy hotkey, to activate the copy procedure. Use one of the two methods described in the preceding paragraph to mark the voucher data and copy the text to the Clipboard. Desktop copies the spreadsheet data to the Clipboard and returns control of the screen to 1-2-3.

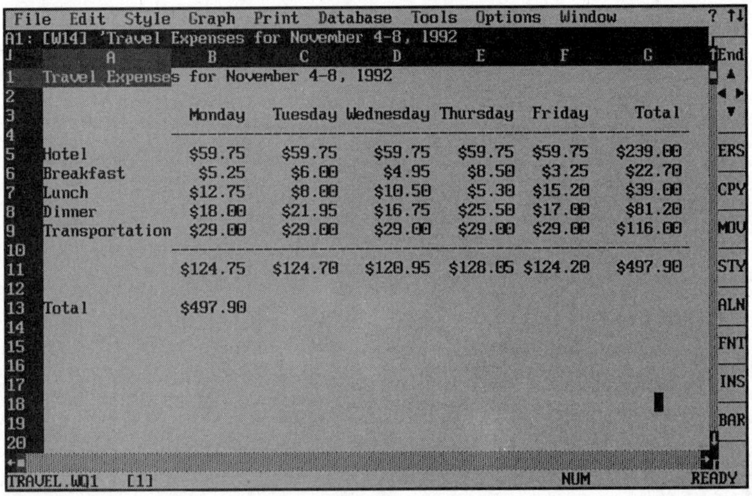

Fig. 17.1

A travel voucher as a 1-2-3 spreadsheet.

Occasionally, opening the Accessories Clipboard from within an application and using the commands on the Clipboard horizontal menu bar to copy text may be more convenient. To do so, follow these steps:

1. With the application active, press the Accessories hotkey, Ctrl+space bar, to access Desktop Accessories.

2. Open the Clipboard by choosing Clipboard from the Desktop Accessories main menu.

3. To copy text from the underlying application, choose Copy to Clipboard from the Copy/Paste menu. Accessories returns to the active application and places a rectangular cursor in the middle of the screen.

4. Using the arrow keys or the mouse, mark a block of text. After you finish marking the text, Accessories returns to the Clipboard, and the marked text appears in the Clipboard window.

The Clipboard now contains a copy of the travel-voucher information. In the Clipboard, you can edit data you copy from a DOS application. The next section describes how to display the Clipboard window so you can work with the copied text.

Pasting Text from the Clipboard

After you copy text into the Clipboard, the hot-key paste feature enables you to paste the text into any DOS application that accepts input by following these steps:

1. Activate the DOS program—for example, WordPerfect—and display the file in which you want Accessories to copy text. (If you launched the original program from the DOS prompt, you need to close that program first.)

2. Position the cursor where you want the Clipboard's contents to be inserted and press Ctrl+Ins. Figure 17.2 shows the spreadsheet data copied into a WordPerfect word processing file.

```
Travel Expenses for November 4-8, 1992

                Monday    Tuesday Wednesday Thursday  Friday     Total
               --------------------------------------------------------
Hotel           $59.75    $59.75    $59.75   $59.75   $59.75    $239.00
Breakfast        $5.25     $6.00     $4.95    $8.50    $3.25     $22.70
Lunch           $12.75     $8.00    $10.50    $5.30   $15.20     $39.00
Dinner          $18.00    $21.95    $16.75   $25.50   $17.00     $81.20
Transportation  $29.00    $29.00    $29.00   $29.00   $29.00    $116.00
               --------------------------------------------------------
               $124.75   $124.70   $120.95  $128.05 $124.20    $497.90

Total          $497.90




                                          Doc 1 Pg 1 Ln 1.17" Pos 1"
```

Fig. 17.2

The travel-expense voucher data copied into a WordPerfect screen.

You can use the hot-key copy-and-paste features to copy text within or between Accessories windows. Because only a rectangular block can be copied, this method is useful when you want to copy a column of data. You can use this method, for example, to copy to the Clipboard the February figures from the annual sales report. Figure 17.3 shows the February column successfully highlighted, using the hot-key method.

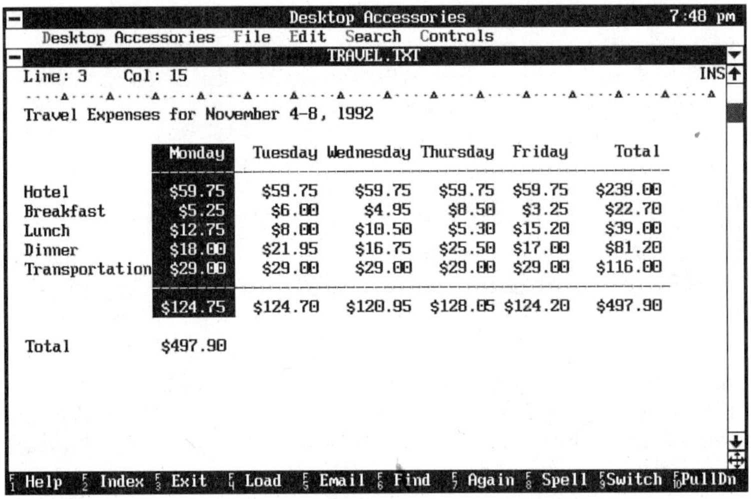

```
┌─┬──────────────────────────────────────────────────────────────────┬──┐
│■│                    Desktop Accessories                    7:48 pm │  │
├─┴────────────────────────────────────────────────────────────────────┤
│  Desktop Accessories  File  Edit  Search  Controls                     │
├─┬──────────────────────────────────────────────────────────────────┬─┤
│■│                          TRAVEL.TXT                               │▼│
├─┴──────────────────────────────────────────────────────────────────┴─┤
│ Line: 3    Col: 15                                              INS │▲│
│ ····▲····▲····▲····▲····▲····▲····▲····▲····▲····▲····▲····▲····▲··▲ │ │
│ Travel Expenses for November 4-8, 1992                             │ │
│                                                                    │ │
│                    ┌────────┐                                      │ │
│                    │Monday  │ Tuesday Wednesday Thursday Friday   Total  │ │
│ Hotel              │ $59.75 │ $59.75  $59.75    $59.75   $59.75  $239.00 │ │
│ Breakfast          │  $5.25 │  $6.00   $4.95     $8.50    $3.25   $22.70 │ │
│ Lunch              │ $12.75 │  $8.00  $10.50     $5.30   $15.20   $39.00 │ │
│ Dinner             │ $18.00 │ $21.95  $16.75    $25.50   $17.00   $81.20 │ │
│ Transportation     │ $29.00 │ $29.00  $29.00    $29.00   $29.00  $116.00 │ │
│                    │        │                                      │ │
│                    │$124.75 │$124.70 $120.95 $128.05 $124.20 $497.90 │ │
│                    └────────┘                                      │ │
│ Total               $497.90                                        │▼│
│                                                                    │↕│
├────────────────────────────────────────────────────────────────┤↓│
│ ▼Help ▼Index ▼Exit ▼Load ▼Email ▼Find ▼Again ▼Spell ▼Switch ▼PullDn  │
└──────────────────────────────────────────────────────────────────────┘
```

Fig. 17.3

The February sales figures selected using the hot-key method.

After you paste text, the original text remains in the Clipboard, available to be pasted again. This feature makes creating a document with multiple copies of the same text on a single page easy. You can, for example, design camp registration forms for a youth summer program and place three copies of the form on a single 8 1/2 by 11 inch page.

To use the Clipboard menu commands to paste text, you first must launch the application in which you want to paste the contents of the Clipboard and place the cursor where the text is to appear. Then activate Accessories and open the Clipboard by choosing Clip**b**oard from the **D**esktop Accessories main menu.

To paste the contents of the Clipboard, choose **P**aste from Clipboard from the **C**opy/Paste menu. Accessories returns to the application that was previously active and the contents of the Clipboard are entered on the screen one letter at a time.

Take advantage of text already in the Clipboard when you need to paste the same text into several files during a job. After you copy a name and address from a database to the Clipboard, for example, you can paste the address into a letter, into another file to print an envelope, and finally into a multi-page, multi-column, alphabetized membership list.

It does not matter what text is in the destination file when you paste text from the Clipboard to the file. You can paste a paragraph into the middle of a lengthy report. You can paste the body of a letter into an empty file and then add the recipient's address to the beginning and a signature block to the end. If you set up a database file to group the names and addresses of your correspondents—as shown in figure 17.4, for example—you can copy an address from the database to the letter you are writing (see fig 17.5).

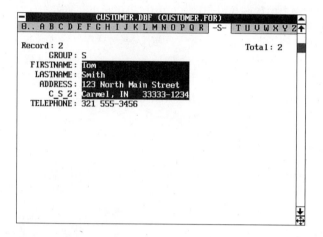

Fig. 17.4

An address marked for copying to the Clipboard.

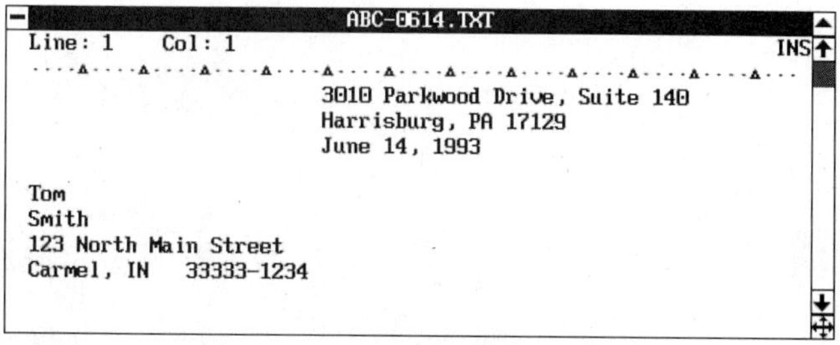

Fig. 17.5

The marked address pasted into a letter.

NOTE To prevent overwriting existing text with pasted text, make sure that the destination application is in insert mode.

As you can see in figure 17.5, a minor bit of editing must be done in the Clipboard to place Tom and Smith on the same line. The next section discusses how to edit text in the Clipboard.

NOTE Remember that you can copy ASCII graphics characters with the Clipboard. Some DOS applications use ASCII graphics characters to draw their screens. The Accessories Databases application, for example, uses lines between fields when the data is displayed in edit mode. If you copy several columns of data, the lines separating the columns are also copied.

Depending on the text and application with which you are working, you can use one method to cut or copy and another method to paste text. Keep in mind these few rules to guide your work:

- When copying or pasting in DOS applications, you must use the hotkeys (Ctrl+Del and Ctrl+Ins) to copy and paste text.

- If you have already selected text in Desktop Accessories, use Shift+Del to copy the text.

- To mark a rectangle or column of text in Desktop Accessories, use Ctrl+Del.

- When you paste text in a Desktop Accessories application window, you can use Shift+Ins and Ctrl+Ins interchangeably.

For Related Information

FROM HERE... ◄◄ "Selecting Hotkeys," p. 551.

Opening the Clipboard Window

To view the contents of the Clipboard from within another PC Tools or a DOS application, you first activate Desktop Accessories by using the Accessories hotkey, Ctrl+space bar. Next, select Clip**b**oard from the **D**esktop Accessories main menu. Figure 17.6 shows the Clipboard and the expense-voucher data copied from the 1-2-3 spreadsheet.

Unlike most other Accessories applications, you cannot open multiple Clipboard windows. Only one Clipboard exists, and it contains your most recently copied text. The next text you copy replaces the present Clipboard contents, even if you have not yet pasted the material to a new location.

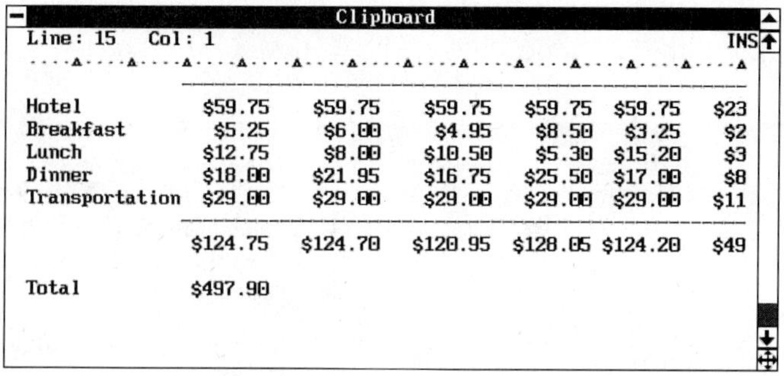

```
┌─────────────────────────────────────────────────────────┐▲
│─               Clipboard                                  │▲
│ Line: 15   Col: 1                                      INS│↑
│ ····▲····▲····▲····▲····▲····▲····▲····▲····▲····▲····▲    │
│ ─────────────────────────────────────────────────────────│
│ Hotel          $59.75   $59.75   $59.75   $59.75  $59.75  $23│
│ Breakfast       $5.25    $6.00    $4.95    $8.50   $3.25   $2│
│ Lunch          $12.75    $8.00   $10.50    $5.30  $15.20   $3│
│ Dinner         $18.00   $21.95   $16.75   $25.50  $17.00   $8│
│ Transportation $29.00   $29.00   $29.00   $29.00  $29.00  $11│
│                                                           │
│                $124.75  $124.70  $120.95 $128.05 $124.20  $49│
│                                                           │
│ Total          $497.90                                    │
│                                                          ▼│
│                                                          ⊞│
└─────────────────────────────────────────────────────────┘
```

Fig. 17.6

The spreadsheet data in the Clipboard window.

The Clipboard window has its own horizontal menu bar containing an abbreviated version of the commands available in a Notepads window. Table 17.1 lists the contents of the horizontal menu bar and the commands contained in each pull-down menu.

Table 17.1 Clipboard Menu Commands

Menu Item	Commands
File	Print
Copy/Paste	Paste from Clipboard
	Copy to Clipboard
	Set Playback Delay
Edit	Erase Block
	Mark Block
	Unmark block
	Delete All Text
	Insert File
	Goto
Search	Find
	Find Again
	Replace

With the exception of Set Playback Delay, all of the commands available in the Clipboard have their counterpart in the Accessories Notepads application. Refer to Chapter 16, "Using PC Tools Notepads" for detailed explanations of each of these commands.

The message bar at the bottom of the screen displays the keystroke commands, listed in table 17.2.

Table 17.2 Keystroke Commands Available in Clipboard

Key	Name	Function
F1	Help	Displays the context-sensitive Help facility
F2	Index	Displays the Help facility index
F3	Exit	Cancels the current process or application (same as Esc)
F6	Find	Activates the Find and Replace feature
F9 or Ctrl+Esc	Switch	Switches the active window
F10	PullDn	Activates the horizontal menu bar (same as Alt)
Alt	Menu	Activates the horizontal menu bar (same as F10)
Esc	Cancel	Cancels the current process or application (same as F3)
Alt+space bar	System Control	Displays the System Control pull-down menu

The keystrokes listed in table 17.2 access the same operations as their counterparts in the Accessories Notepads application. F6 (Find), for example, opens the Find and Replace dialog box, which you also can access by selecting **R**eplace from the **S**earch menu located on the horizontal menu bar.

Additional keystroke commands, which you can use in other Accessories and DOS applications to access the unique capabilities of the Clipboard, are also available. Table 17.3 lists these keystroke commands.

Table 17.3 Clipboard Keystroke Commands Available in Other Applications

Key	Function
Shift+arrow key	Marks a block of text in the direction of the arrow key
Shift+Del	Cuts the marked block of text to the Clipboard
Shift+Ins	Inserts the contents of the Clipboard at the cursor's location
Ctrl+Del	Marks and copies a rectangle of text from any DOS application to the Clipboard. Ctrl+Del is the copy hotkey.
Ctrl+Ins	Inserts the contents of the Clipboard at the cursor in any DOS application. Ctrl+Ins is the paste hotkey.

For Related Information

◄◄ "Copying and Moving Text," p. 577.

◄◄ "Searching a Notepads File," p. 584.

FROM HERE...

Editing Text in the Clipboard

One important convenience of the cut-and-paste facility is that Accessories enables you to edit the contents of the Clipboard. While working in the Clipboard, you can print the contents of the Clipboard, mark and delete a text block, delete all text, insert an entire file, move the cursor to a specific line in the file, find specified text, and find and replace text.

Before you can edit the Clipboard contents, however, you must open the Clipboard window. From the **D**esktop Accessories main menu, choose Clip**b**oard. On top of any active application windows, Accessories displays the Clipboard window containing any text you copied or cut to the Clipboard.

Suppose, for example, that you copied to the Clipboard the highlighted sentences in figure 17.7. You want to edit your work, however, before copying the text to the letter you are typing to another customer. Choose Clip**b**oard from the **D**esktop Accessories main menu. Accessories displays the Clipboard application window with the text you just copied (see fig. 17.8).

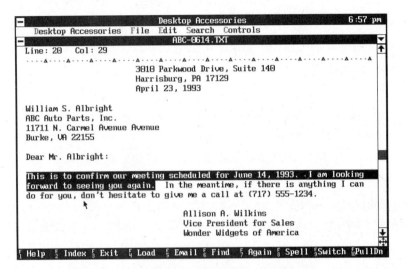

Fig. 17.7

Text marked for copying to the Clipboard.

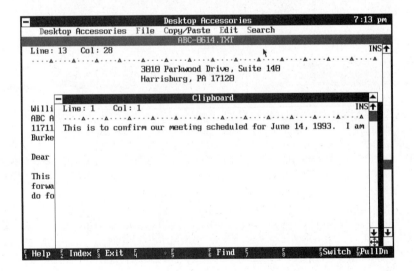

Fig. 17.8

The Clipboard window displaying the text marked in figure 17.7.

NOTE The Accessories Notepads wordwrap feature is not available in the Clipboard. The second sentence in figure 17.7 extends beyond the border of the Clipboard window.

While the Clipboard window is the active window, you can move, resize, and maximize this window like any other Accessories application window. Refer to Chapter 15, "Navigating the Desktop Accessories" for information on configuring windows. You can make any necessary modifications to the text by using the editing features discussed in Chapter 16, "Using PC Tools Notepads." For example, you may want to change the meeting date before copying the text to another letter.

Using the commands available on the horizontal menu bar, you can search and replace text, mark and unmark blocks of text, insert files, and delete all text if you no longer need it. If you decide you want to save the edited text, you must paste the text into a Notepads window or another application and use that application's Save feature.

For Related Information

◀◀ "Moving, Resizing, and Maximizing Windows," p. 537.

FROM HERE...

Printing from the Clipboard

After you copy text or other ASCII characters to the Clipboard, you may want to print the Clipboard contents. To do so, choose **P**rint from the **F**ile menu. The Print dialog box shown in figure 17.9 appears.

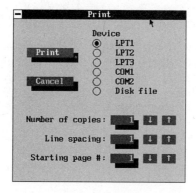

Fig. 17.9

The Print dialog box.

The Print dialog box contains six option buttons: LPT1, LPT2, LPT3, COM1, COM2, and Disk File. To send the Clipboard contents to your printer, determine the port to which your printer is connected and select the appropriate option button (LPT1, LPT2, or LPT3 for parallel printers; COM1 or COM2 for serial printers). To create a disk file that can be used for sending output to a printer, select the Disk File option button.

The Print dialog box contains three text boxes:

- *Number of Copies.* To print multiple copies of the Clipboard contents, type the number of copies in the text box.

- *Line Spacing.* Indicate by entering a number whether you want the text to be single spaced (1), double spaced (2) or triple spaced (3).

- *Starting Page #.* If the amount of text in the Clipboard exceeds the amount that will fit on a single page, indicate here the page number you want on the first printed page. Otherwise, Accessories starts with 1.

When you are ready to print, select the **P**rint command button. Desktop prints the document as many times as indicated in the Number of Copies text box. You can interrupt the printing by pressing the Esc key. If you decide not to begin printing, choose **C**ancel from the dialog box.

For Related Information

◀◀ "Printing a Notepads File," p. 589.

Setting Playback Delay

When you try to paste from the Clipboard to certain DOS applications, such as Microsoft Word, some characters might not appear because the characters are being inserted too quickly for the application to process. If this problem occurs, access Accessories and display the Clipboard window. Then choose **S**et Playback Delay from the **C**opy/Paste menu to display the Macro/Clipboard Playback Delay dialog box shown in figure 17.10.

Fig. 17.10

The Macro/
Clipboard
Playback Delay
dialog box.

To slow down the playback of the Clipboard text, type a number in the
Delay text box. The delay—measured in eighteenths (1/18) of a second—is the time that Accessories waits between characters when sending text from the Clipboard to an application. The default entry in the
text box is 0 for a default delay of 1/18 second. If you type *1* in the text
block, Accessories waits 2/18 second. Start with a small delay number
and test a Clipboard hot-key paste operation to determine whether the
delay should be longer.

You must remove or change the delay time to meet the requirements of
the next application with which you want to work. The delay time appropriate for Microsoft Word may differ from the delay time required
for another program. WordPerfect, for example, requires no delay time.

Using the Clipboard

No single best way to run the Clipboard exists. Running Desktop Accessories as a memory resident application is the easiest way to familiarize
yourself with its capabilities. Any time you are using a DOS application
and realize you want to copy and paste data, the Clipboard hotkey procedure is ready for you.

Some users find they use the Clipboard often enough that the process
of closing the application from which you copy data, opening another
application, and then loading a destination file is too cumbersome.
Using a task switching program to hot key from one application to another is the obvious solution. Refer to Chapter 3, "Using the Desktop as
a Program Manager" for information about the PC Tools Task Switcher
program.

You may decide that the programs you want to access with the Task
Switcher require too much typing and tinkering as part of your daily
startup procedure. PC Tools Desktop enables you to set up your preferred configuration of available programs. The well-known PC Tools
disk utility programs, as well as your favorite DOS applications, can be
installed in program group windows, making it possible for you to
launch them with a single keystroke or the click of a mouse button.

The Task Switcher can then be run to allow you to switch easily between WordPerfect and Lotus 1-2-3 as you try the practice examples given in this chapter. Again, refer to Chapter 3, "Using the Desktop as a Program Manager" for more information.

Although you must refer to the manuals for the best way to set up the Task Switcher, PC Tools Desktop, and the Clipboard so that they work together, as a rule of thumb load Desktop Accessories first. Accessories only works with applications that are loaded after you load Accessories.

FROM HERE...

For Related Information

◄◄ "Using the Task Switcher," p. 120.

Chapter Summary

This chapter explains how to use the Accessories Clipboard to copy marked text and then paste the text between DOS applications and the various Desktop Accessories applications. The chapter describes how to open the Clipboard, edit the contents of the Clipboard window, print the contents of the Clipboard, and configure a delay time for applications that require it. The chapter describes the ways you can set up the Desktop Accessories Clipboard as part of the overall configuration of your computer.

Turn to Chapter 18, "Using the Outliner" to learn how to use the Desktop Accessories Outlines application to make organizing your thoughts easier.

Using the Outliner

The Outlines module of PC Tools Desktop Accessories is a rudimentary outlining program that enables you to quickly and easily organize ideas into a coherent outline. This chapter begins with instructions for opening an Outlines window and then describes the elements that distinguish Outlines from Notepads—headlines and outline levels. Next, expanding and collapsing the outline is discussed. The chapter ends with instructions for saving and printing an outline.

Because Outlines is built on the Notepads word processor, familiarize yourself with the contents of Chapter 16, "Using PC Tools Notepads," before you proceed through this chapter.

Opening an Outline Window

As with Notepads, the first steps in using Outlines are opening an application window and loading a file. To open an Outlines window, select **O**utlines from the **D**esktop Accessories main menu. Desktop Accessories displays the File Load dialog box.

When you first install PC Tools, Desktop Accessories uses OUT as the default file name extension for Outline files. As with Notepads, however, you can assign a different file name extension (or a different DOS path). To change the default extensions (or DOS path), refer to Chapter 16, "Using PC Tools Notepads," for information on the File Load dialog box.

To create a new outline, type the outline file name in the text box and select **N**ew. To edit an outline, type the file name, press the arrow keys to highlight the file name, or click the file name with the mouse; then select **L**oad. To delete an outline, select the file name you want to delete and choose **D**elete.

Outlines windows are nearly identical to Notepads windows, with the addition of a Headlines command on the horizontal menu bar and a corresponding Headlines pull-down menu. You can use the same shortcut commands in Outlines that you use in Notepads. These commands are reproduced in table 18.1 for your convenience.

Table 18.1 Keystroke Commands Available in Outlines

Key	Name	Function
F1	Help	Displays context-sensitive Help facility
F2	Index	Displays the Help facility index
F3	Exit	Cancels the current process or application (same as Esc)
F4	Load	Loads another Notepads window
F5	Email	Sends the current Notepads document as an electronic-mail message
F6	Find	Activates the Find and Replace feature
F7	Again	Repeats the last find operation
F8	Spell	Checks the spelling in the entire file
F9 or Ctrl+Esc	Switch	Switches the active window
F10	PullDn	Activates the horizontal menu bar (same as Alt)
Alt	PullDn	Activates the horizontal menu bar (same as F10)
Esc	Cancel	Cancels the current process or application (same as F3)
Alt+space bar	System Control	Displays the System Control pull-down menu

For Related Information

◄◄ "Examining the Notepads Window," p. 566.

FROM HERE...

Editing an Outline

Because Outlines is a specialized version of the Accessories' Notepads application, you can load Notepads files into Outlines or vice versa. Notepads editing features work as usual in Outlines, with three exceptions:

■ In Outlines, press the Tab key to assign lower outline levels rather than to indent text. Use spaces to indent text when you don't want to assign the text to the next level.

■ Use the Backspace key to return to a higher outline level if the cursor is positioned at the beginning of a line. Within a line of text, Backspace erases to the left, as usual.

■ Because each line is a separate element of the outline, the Notepads word-wrap feature is not available.

These subtle differences from Notepads are necessary to assist you in creating operational outlines.

Creating Headlines

Each line or row in an Outline file is called a *headline*. You assign each headline a particular level in the outline. All lines that begin at the left margin are called *main headlines* or *level 1 headlines*. Use main headlines to label the broadest categories in your outline. Lines indented to the first tab stop are called *level 2 headlines*; *level 3 headlines* begin at the second tab stop; and so on.

Suppose, for example, that you're outlining a book about PC Tools. After loading a new file named BOOK.OUT into Outlines, you decide to divide the subject matter into six major parts: "Using the Desktop," "Using the System Utilities," "Using the Recovery and Security Utilities," "Using the Windows Utilities," "Using the Desktop Accessories," and "Communicating by Modem, Fax, or Local Area Network." These titles become the main or level 1 headlines for the book outline. Begin writing the outline by typing each headline on a separate line, starting at the left margin.

In this example, chapter titles for the book are the level 2 headlines. When you are entering the chapter titles, start each title on a new line and press Tab once before typing. If you press Tab too many times, press Backspace to delete the extra tabs. Figure 18.1 shows the book outline with the level 2 headlines added.

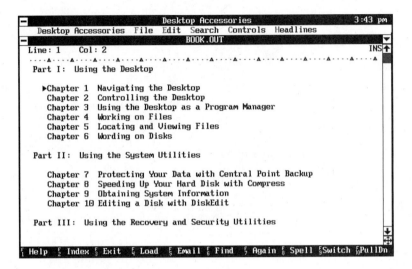

Fig. 18.1

Typing the
outline.

Complete the book outline by dividing the chapters into sections using level 3 headlines and by breaking the sections into subsections with level 4 or level 5 headlines. Press Tab twice before typing the level 3 headlines; press Tab three times before typing level 4 headlines; and so on.

Promoting and Demoting Headlines

So far, using Outlines is the same as entering an outline in Notepads. With the special capabilities of Outlines, however, you can promote and demote headlines—change their levels in the outline. By inserting or deleting tabs, you can demote or promote a single headline. You must use the **P**romote and **D**emote commands on the **H**eadlines menu, however, to promote or demote a headline and all the subheadings between the current headline and the next headline at the same level.

T I P

To see more easily what you're doing when you promote or demote headlines, turn on the display of control characters. The tab characters then appear as right arrows (→).

To promote the current headline and all the headlines below it, position the cursor anywhere in a current headline. Select **H**eadlines to display the Headlines pull-down menu (see fig. 18.2), and select **Pro**mote. Accessories moves the current headline and all subheadings below the current headline one level to the left.

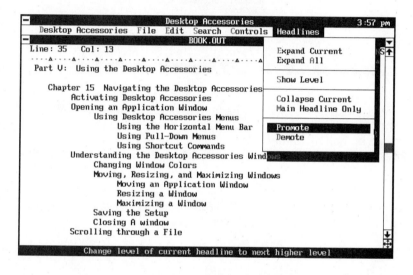

Fig. 18.2

The Headlines pull-down menu.

In the outline in figure 18.2, suppose that you decide to change the headline "Using the Desktop Accessories Menus" (third headline under the Chapter 15 headline) from level 4 to level 3—to promote it. Then the three headlines below "Using Desktop Accessories Menus" should be promoted from level 5 to level 4.

Position the cursor in the "Using Desktop Accessories Menus" headline. Select **H**eadlines to display the Headlines menu, and then select **Pro**mote. Accessories moves the current headline and the three subheadings one level to the left (see fig. 18.3).

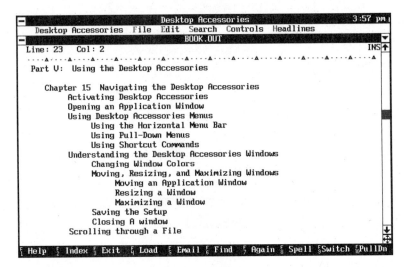

Fig. 18.3

Promoting
headlines.

Demoting headlines is the opposite of promoting headlines. With the
Demote command on the **H**eadlines menu, you can demote the current
headline and all headlines below it in one step. Follow the steps described for promoting a headline but select **D**emote rather than **Pro**-
mote from the menu.

Occasionally, you may prefer to insert a tab manually. If you are indeci-
sive about the level of a single headline, you do not want to move other
headlines unintentionally while you decide.

Collapsing and Expanding Headlines

Outlines' capacity to collapse and expand outline sections best distinguishes it from Notepads. Collapsing an outline hides some of its headlines, and expanding it uncovers collapsed (hidden) headlines.

Collapsing Headlines

Collapsing outlines serves several purposes. Sometimes, you may lose
track of where a particular section fits in an outline that has many levels. At other times, you may want to print a condensed version of an
outline.

Using Outlines, you can collapse any number of levels of the outline one at a time or as a group. Accessories places a triangular pointer to the left of the headline below which lower-level headlines are hidden (see fig. 18.4).

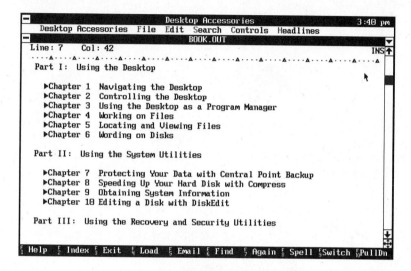

Fig. 18.4

Using Show Level to hide headlines below level 2.

Three commands are available on the Headlines pull-down menu for collapsing headlines: Show Level, which you use to hide all headlines at an outline level; Collapse Current, which you use to hide the current outline level; and Main Headline Only, which you use to hide only the main headline level. These commands are explained in more detail in the following:

- **Show Level.** Choose option to hide all headlines that are at an outline level lower than the current headline. To display only the main and level 2 headlines, for example, place the cursor in any level 2 headline and choose **S**how Level from the **H**eadlines pull-down menu. Accessories hides all headlines below level 2 (refer to fig. 18.4).

- **Collapse Current.** Choose this option to hide only the headlines below the current headline. Hidden headlines include those below the cursor and above the next headline at the level of the current headline. Using this command, you can selectively collapse headlines and leave some expanded for your viewing.

- **Main Headline Only.** Choose this command to hide all headlines except the main (level 1) headlines, regardless of cursor placement. You can accomplish the same effect by choosing **S**how Level while the cursor is at a main-level headline.

T I P   Be sure you expand your outline before you add more text. If you decide to add text to an outline while parts of the outline are collapsed, hidden text following the location of the cursor is pushed ahead of the text you insert. The text is not lost, but you will have to cut the text and paste it to its proper location.

Expanding Headlines

Desktop Accessories provides two commands on the Headlines pull-down menu to enable you to expand hidden headlines: Expand Current and Expand All. Select the Expand All option from the Headlines menu to expand every headline in the outline.

Select the Expand Current option to expand all subheadings up to the next headline at the same level. Suppose, for example, that you routinely work with the BOOK.OUT file with all headlines below level 2 collapsed, but you decide to make some changes to Chapter 19's outline. To expand only the Chapter 19 outline, place the cursor in the line with the Chapter 19 headline, display the Headlines pull-down menu, and choose Expand Current. Accessories expands only the headlines below the current headline and removes the pointer that was displayed to the left of the headline (see fig. 18.5).

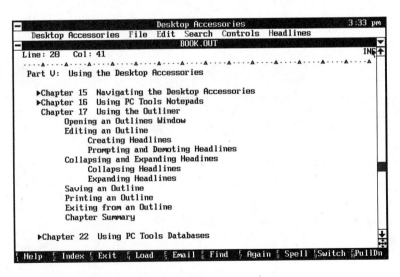

Fig. 18.5

Expanding headlines below the current headline.

Saving an Outline

Saving an Outlines file is similar to saving a Notepads file and is practically foolproof. Every time you exit from an Outlines file, Accessories automatically saves the file to disk. You can exit from an Outlines file without saving the file, however, by selecting Exit Without Saving from the File menu. See Chapter 16, "Using PC Tools Notepads," for more information about saving files.

If you save the Outlines file while headlines are collapsed, the headlines remain collapsed the next time you load the file in an Outlines window. The collapsed headlines are not gone; they are only hidden. Indeed, if you load the file into Notepads, all headlines are displayed.

Printing an Outline

Printing an Outlines file is essentially the same as printing a Notepads file, but collapsed headlines are not printed. If you do not want to print an entire outline, but you need only the higher-level headlines, collapse the unneeded headlines first. Then choose Print from the File menu to print the remaining headlines. (Refer to Chapter 16, "Using PC Tools Notepads," for more information.)

Exiting from an Outline

When you finish working with an Outline file, you usually want to close the window to return to another application window or DOS application. Closing an Outline window is identical to closing a Notepad window.

To close an Outline window, press Esc (Exit) or F3 (Exit) or click the close box. Desktop saves any changes you made and closes the window.

Chapter Summary

This chapter explains how to use Desktop Accessories' Outlines application, beginning with a brief description of opening an Outlines window. Because many Outlines features have parallels in Notepads, this chapter emphasizes features unique to Outlines: headlines, levels, collapsing, and expanding. The chapter closes with instructions for saving, printing, and exiting an outline.

To learn how to use Accessories' surprisingly powerful list manager, Databases, turn to Chapter 19, "Using PC Tools Databases."

Using PC Tools Databases

You can use Databases to keep track of information you usually store on cards or in notebooks. Databases is a business tool for managing large amounts of important information, such as a client list, while you continue working in another program. By pressing the Desktop Accessories hot key, you have access to a database program, even while you run your favorite spreadsheet program, word processor program, or other PC-based application. Accessories database program is compatible with database files already created by other popular dBase programs. You may be typing a letter in your word processing program, for example, and need a client's address. Just hot-key into Accessories and use Databases to display your client list.

In this chapter, you learn how to define and modify the structure of a database file; add, edit, and sort data; and search a database file for specific data. You also learn how to create custom forms for use in entering, displaying, and printing information in a database file. The last portion of the chapter explains how to transfer data between database files. You will find that, by using the Accessories database program, your computer can become an invaluable tool in helping you manage the current information explosion.

Understanding Database Fundamentals

You have constructed or used databases all your life. Whenever you organize information for later access, you create a database. Telephone books, card catalogs, recipe cards, customer files, and mailing lists are common databases. Computer databases operate on the same principle but store the data electronically.

All data in an Accessories database file is stored in individual records, each made up of a set number of fields. You might use Accessories to keep an address and telephone list, for example. Every row in the list is a record in the file. Every record contains the same number of fields: name, address, and phone number, for example.

Accessories database files are compatible with files created by the dBase family of programs. The dBase-compatible disk files, called *database files*, have the default file name extension DBF (used also in dBase).

For every database file (DBF), Databases maintains two ancillary disk files: a record file (REC) and a form file (FOR). Desktop automatically creates and maintains the record file, which contains housekeeping information such as the order for sorting information. The form file is an Accessories Notepads file for controlling how database records are displayed on-screen and printed. Accessories automatically creates one form file for every database, but you can use Notepads to create as many customized form files as you need.

 NOTE   Only the database files (DBF) are compatible with dBase. Record files (REC) and form files (FOR) are unique to Accessories and cannot be used with dBase. In addition, because Accessories does not support dBase memo fields, these fields are ignored when dBase files are used with Accessories. Further, Accessories character-type fields contain a maximum of 70 characters, yet dBase character fields can be as large as 254 characters. Accessories excludes data in a character field beyond the first 70 characters.

Creating a New Database: Defining the Database Structure

A database structure is defined by a series of fields. Every field in your database file should contain a single piece of information. For example, you typically define separate fields for first name, middle initial, and last name. If you assign one field for the entire name, you cannot alphabetize the last names or use only first names in the salutation of a letter.

The more fields you define for a particular database file, the longer it takes to sort or search for data, and the more disk space the file requires. When you decide which fields to include in a database file, follow two simple guidelines:

■ Collect all the information necessary for the output you want to generate (mailing lists, phone lists, and form letters, for example).

■ Do not collect any information that you will never need for output.

Desktop enables you to define a database file with as many as 128 fields per record and as many as 10,000 records in the entire file. Any single record can have as many as 4,000 characters.

Opening an Accessories Databases window is like opening a Notepads or an Outlines window. First, display the **D**esktop Accessories main menu, and then select **D**atabases. Accessories displays the File Load dialog box from which you can create a new database file or load or delete an existing database file (see fig. 19.1).

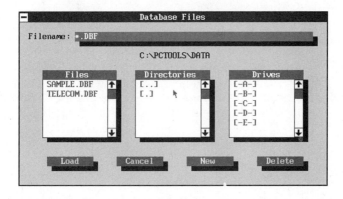

Fig. 19.1

The Databases File Load dialog box.

NOTE When you install PC Tools, Desktop Accessories uses DBF as the default file name extension for database files. As with Notepads, Accessories enables you to assign another default directory, but default file name extensions cannot be changed. For instructions about changing a default directory, see Chapter 16, "Using PC Tools Notepads."

To create a new database file, display the Databases File Load dialog box, and then type a file name in the Filename text box. Suppose, for example, that you want to create a telephone and address list—an on-screen Rolodex—in a database file named CUSTOMER.DBF. In the File Load dialog box, type **customer** and press Enter. The file name can be from one to eight characters long and can contain letters, numbers, or any of these characters:

> ~ ! @ # $ % ^ &—_ { }

Do not leave spaces in a file name, and do not type a file name extension. Accessories automatically adds the extension DBF. After you type the file name, select the **N**ew command button or press Enter to approve the creation of a new file. Accessories displays the Field Editor dialog box (see fig. 19.2).

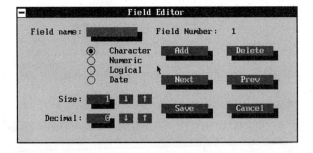

Fig. 19.2

The Field Editor dialog box.

When you create a new database, you first design the database structure by assigning a name to each field, specifying the type and length of each field, and specifying the number of decimal places, if appropriate. Fields are defined one at a time in the Field Editor dialog box.

Naming a Field

When the Field Editor dialog box is opened, Accessories places the cursor in the Field Name text box. Type the field name for the first field and press Enter. For the example database, CUSTOMER.DBF, type **staff** and press Enter. (Notice that Accessories later converts any lowercase letters in the field name to uppercase letters after it is added to the database.) In this example, customers are assigned to one of the three sales agents whose monthly sales results were displayed in Chapter 16, "Using PC Tools Notepads." Each sales agent has a letter—*J* for Jerry, *S* for Sally, and *R* for Ralph. The letter is entered on the record of their customers. This field can be used to divide the database by salesperson.

Field names can contain as many as 10 characters, including letters, numbers, ASCII graphics characters, and the underscore character (_). If you leave a blank in a field name, Accessories replaces it with an underscore character. You might decide to define the following fields:

STAFF	ADDRESS
COMPANY	CITY
LAST_NAME	ST
FIRST_NAME	ZIPCODE
MIDDLE_INI	CREDIT_LIM
TELEPHONE	CONTACTED
FAX_NUMBER	COMMENTS

Define telephone number fields before you define any other character field that might contain three or more consecutive numeric digits. This practice ensures that the Autodialer feature, discussed in Chapter 23, "Using PC Tools Telecommunications," dials the telephone number in the PHONE field rather than a number in some other field in the record.

Selecting Field Type, Field Size, and Decimals

After you type the name, Desktop moves the cursor down to the Field Type option buttons. These option buttons determine the kind of data that can be entered into the field:

- *Character field.* Choose this field type when you expect the data to consist of letters, numbers, special symbols (#, $, *, and &), ASCII graphics symbols, and the underscore character (_). Unless you have a specific reason for selecting another field type, choose the Character field type.

- *Numeric field.* With this field type, you can enter only numbers (+, -, and . are considered numeric characters). Use this field type only if you expect to perform computations on the field values. The default value for a numeric field (during data entry) is 0.

> **NOTE** Even though Desktop does not perform computations in reports from a database file, you can use the database file with dBase, which does permit computations in reports.

- *Logical field.* Use this field type when you want to enter a single character in the field that indicates true-yes or false-no. During data entry, press *T*, *t*, *Y*, or *y* to give a field a value of true (or yes). When the value of the field is false (or no), press *F*, *f*, *N*, or *n*. The default value for a logical field (during data entry) is F.

- *Date field.* Use the Date field type for storing date values, such as birthdays, in a field. Dates are entered in month, day, year (MM/DD/YY) format but are stored in a YYYYMMDD format for indexing purposes.

In the example, because the first field in CUSTOMER—the STAFF field—will contain a single letter (J, S, or R), select the **C**haracter option button.

After you select an option button to select a field type, Accessories moves the cursor to the Size text box. Enter a number to indicate the maximum length of the field. Table 19.1 lists the maximum allowable field sizes for every field type.

Table 19.1 Maximum Allowable Field Sizes

Field type	Maximum allowable field size	Default value
Character	70	1
Numeric	19, including +, -, and . (decimal point)	1 (0 decimal places)
Logical	1	1 (assigned automatically)
Date	8	8 (assigned automatically)

For example, because the STAFF field in the CUSTOMER.DBF file needs a length of only 1, enter that number in the Size text box and press Enter. (Because 1 is the default value in the Size text box, you can just press Enter.) If you enter a number larger than the maximum, Accessories substitutes the maximum allowable size. Mouse users do not have to press Enter; just point at the next "box" you want, and click with the left button.

After you press Enter at the Size text box, Accessories moves the cursor to the Decimal text box, which applies only to numeric fields. Accessories operates in a fixed-decimal-place mode. When you are defining a numeric field that contains data with digits to the right of the decimal point, type the number of decimal places in the Decimal text box. All values in this field are then given the number of decimal places you specify. A numeric field the size of 5 with two decimal places, for example, can hold 99.99 as the highest value or -9.99 as the lowest value.

After you specify a field name, field type, size, and decimal values, Accessories moves the cursor to the Add command button. Review your entries. Use Tab to move forward or Shift+Tab to move back through the available options. When the selections are correct, select **A**dd. Accessories saves the field definition to memory, resets the values in the Field Editor dialog box, and advances the field number displayed.

Repeat the field definition procedure for every field in the database, and assign to each field a field name, field type, size, and number of decimal places (numeric fields only).

To complete the definition of the CUSTOMER.DBF file, for example, you might define the remaining fields as follows:

Field Number	Field Name	Field Type	Field Size
2	COMPANY	Character	25
3	LAST_NAME	Character	20
4	FIRST_NAME	Character	15
5	MIDDLE_INI	Character	2
6	TELEPHONE	Character	12
7	FAX_NUMBER	Character	12
8	ADDRESS	Character	20
9	CITY	Character	15
10	ST	Character	2
11	ZIPCODE	Character	9
12	CREDIT_LIM	Numeric	7
13	CONTACTED	Date	8
14	COMMENTS	Character	50

Saving or Abandoning the Database Structure

After all fields are defined, select the **S**ave command button in the Field Editor dialog box. Accessories saves the database structure to disk and then displays the new database file in a Databases window as a table of columns (see fig. 19.3). Every field in the database is depicted as a separate column, headed by the field name. Every record in the database is a separate row in the table.

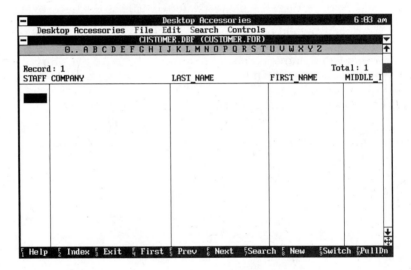

This tabular view of the database is called *Browse mode*, in which a Databases window can display as many as 18 records at a time, one record per row. Because all fields may not fit horizontally on one screen width, however, Accessories enables you to scroll the screen right and left. Press Tab to move the cursor one column to the right. Press Shift+Tab to move the cursor one column to the left.

When the Databases window appears, you can add data to the database. The record indicators, directly above the field listing at the extreme left and right, indicate that the cursor is on the first field in the first record.

At any time while you are defining a database structure and before you select the **S**ave command button in the Field Editor dialog box, you can discard the entire structure by selecting the **C**ancel command button or by pressing Esc (Exit) or F3 (Exit).

> **CAUTION:** Be careful not to press Esc (Exit) or F3 (Exit) acciden-
> tally while you are defining the database structure. Either key-
> stroke causes Desktop to abandon the database structure you are
> defining. This situation contrasts sharply with the operation of
> these keystrokes in Notepads, Outlines, or Macro Editor, in which
> they cause Desktop to save any changes you might have made to
> a file.

Toggling between Browse and Edit Modes

When Accessories saves the database structure to disk, the program
creates a default form that is used as a template to display the database one record at a time in a Databases window. This default form is a
notepad file you can edit by using the Notepads application. Accessories assigns this file the same name as the database file and adds the
file name extension FOR.

To view this default form, display the database in *Edit mode* by toggling
off Browse mode. Select **F**ile from the horizontal menu bar, and then
select **B**rowse to remove the check mark beside that option. Accessories switches the screen to Edit mode in which the field names are
listed down the left side of the screen, one name per line, rather than
across the top of the screen. Figure 19.4 depicts CUSTOMER.DBF in Edit
mode by using the default form CUSTOMER.FOR.

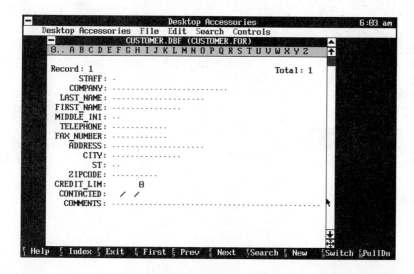

Fig. 19.4

A Databases
window in Edit
mode, containing
the database
CUSTOMER.DBF
and using the
default form,
CUSTOMER.FOR.

Modifying a Field Definition

As long as you display the Field Editor dialog box and until you save the database structure with the Save command button, you can return easily to any field you have already defined and change its definition. Select either the **N**ext or **P**rev button until the field definition you want is displayed. Press Tab until the entry you want to change is displayed, and make the change. You can delete a field definition by selecting the **D**elete command button while the field definition is displayed in the Field Editor dialog box.

Adding Records

When Desktop displays a Databases window in Browse mode, a highlighted bar rests in the first row (record) and first column (field) in the table. The record and field that contain this highlighted bar are called the *current record* and *current field*, respectively. If you have not yet added data to the database, all fields in the record contain only default values. Character fields are empty, logical fields contain the value F, numeric fields contain the number 0, and date fields display two slash marks (//).

T I P   You can change the field order easily by rearranging the fields in the form file, a procedure described later in this chapter, in the section "Using Form Files."

To enter data in the records, you must be in Modify mode. Select **M**odify Data from the **F**ile menu, and then press the cursor-movement keys listed in table 19.2 to move the highlight bar and cursor to the field in which you want to add data. You also can use the scroll bar (as in Notepads) to move through records in a larger database. Position the mouse pointer on the desired field and click the right or left button.

After you position the cursor in a field, type an acceptable entry according to the field type, as indicated in table 19.3. You can press the arrow keys, Home key, and End key to move the cursor within the field, as explained in table 19.2.

Table 19.2 Browse Mode Cursor-Movement Keys

Key	Cursor movement
→	One character to the right within current field; to next field from last character in current field
←	One character to the left within current field; to previous field from first character in current field
↑	Up to previous record
↓	Down to next record
Backspace	Erases character or space to the left
Tab	Accepts entry and moves to next field
Shift+Tab	To previous field
Enter	Accepts entry and moves to next field
Ctrl+→	One word to the right
Ctrl+←	One word to the left
Home	To beginning of record
Home, Home	To beginning of window
Home, Home, Home	To beginning of file
End	To end of current record
End, End	To end of window
End, End, End	To end of file
Ctrl+Home	To left end of first field of first record in database file
Ctrl+End	To left end of first field of last record in database
PgUp	Same column, up the number of rows (records) that can be displayed simultaneously in Databases window
PgDn	Same column, down the number of rows (records) that can be displayed simultaneously in Databases window
Ctrl+PgUp	Up one row while scrolling Databases window up one line

Table 19.3 Acceptable Entries for Desktop Accessories Databases

Field Type	Acceptable Characters
Character	Any character including letters (from A to Z), numbers (from 0 to 9), special symbols (!, @, #, and so on), ASCII graphics characters (entered by holding down the Alt key while typing the decimal number of the character), and the underscore character (_). Default value is a blank space. Be sure not to type more characters than will fit within the defined field size.
Numeric	Numbers (from 0 to 9), a minus sign (-), a plus sign (+), and a decimal point (.) if the field is defined as having one or more decimal positions. The default value is 0 and includes defined decimal places (for example, 0.00 for two decimal places).
Logical	Press *T*, *t*, *Y*, or *y* for true-yes; press *F*, *f*, *N*, or *n* for false-no; default value is F.
Date	Numbers (from 0 to 9) and the slash mark (/); use the format MM/DD/YY where MM is the two-digit designation for the month, DD is the day, and YY is the year.

Because data entry is often easier if the entire record can be seen, Accessories enables you to view database records one at a time in Edit mode. To toggle off Browse mode and switch to Edit mode, choose **F**ile and select **B**rowse to remove the check mark by it.

In Edit mode, Desktop initially displays every record one at a time, using the default form file (FOR) as a template. The default form lists every field on a separate line in the order of its definition in the database structure. Figure 19.4, for example, depicts the first record in a new database file, CUSTOMER.DBF, in Edit mode by using the default form file.

Down the left side of the window, the default form displays each field name, followed by a colon and space for data. If you have not yet added data to the database, all fields contain only default values. Character fields are filled with dots, indicating the total field size; logical fields contain the value F; numeric fields contain the number 0; and date fields display two slash marks (//).

When Accessories displays a Databases window in Edit mode, a blinking cursor is in the first field. The field and record that contain the blinking cursor are the current field and current record. Press the cursor-movement keys listed in table 19.4 or click the field. Acceptable entries in Edit mode are the same as in Browse mode (refer to table 19.3).

Table 19.4 Edit Mode Databases Cursor-Movement Keys

Key	Cursor movement
→	One character to the right within the current field
←	One character to the left within the current field
↑	Up one line
↓	Down one line if you are not on the last field
Backspace	Erases preceding character or space (does not erase field names)
Tab	To next field
Shift+Tab	To previous field
Enter	Accepts entry and moves to next field
Ctrl+→	One word to the right
Ctrl+←	One word to the left (actually to the blank space following the word to the left)
Home	To beginning of field
Home, Home	To beginning of current record window when Browse mode is enabled
End	To end of field
End, End	To beginning of last line in current record window
Ctrl+Home	To beginning of current record window
Ctrl+End	To beginning of last line in current record window
PgUp	Scroll up one window within current record
PgDn	Scroll down one window within current record
Ctrl+PgUp	Up one row while scrolling the Databases window up one line (the cursor appears to remain stationary)
Ctrl+PgDn	Down one row while scrolling the window up one line

When you are finished adding or editing data, press Esc (Exit) or F3 (Exit) to close the database window. If you are editing a field, press Tab or Enter to accept the change before pressing Esc (Exit). Accessories returns to the Desktop Accessories main menu or to the Accessories application window from which you opened the database window. Accessories remembers whether you were using Browse mode or Edit mode and uses the same mode the next time you display the database file.

Correcting Mistakes and Editing Records

You easily can correct typographical errors with the Backspace and Delete keys or by typing the new entry directly over the error. The Databases default is *overtype mode*, in which Accessories replaces any existing character at the cursor as you type. From time to time, you may want to insert one or more characters or spaces between existing characters. Press the Ins key, and Accessories displays INS in the top center of the Databases window to denote *Insert mode*. In Insert mode, whenever you type a character or press the space bar, Accessories pushes any existing character at the cursor one space to the right.

T I P   The easiest way to correct a numeric value is to delete the entire original value and then type the new value.

In addition to correcting errors, from time to time you have to update the information stored in your database files. In Accessories, editing data is as easy as entering data. To edit data in an Accessories Databases file, you first must display the file in a Databases window (see the section "Loading an Existing Databases File" later in this chapter for information about displaying the correct file). With the database file on-screen, move the highlight bar to the record and field you want to change. Select **M**odify Data from the **F**ile menu. You can change data by deleting and replacing or by using the overtype and insert modes. Use the cursor movement keys listed in table 19.2 or 19.4, depending on whether you are in Edit or Browse mode.

Saving or Abandoning a Field Entry

After you finish typing a value in a field, press Enter or Tab to accept the new entry and move to the next field. As soon as you accept the entry, Accessories saves the entry to the current record on disk.

Occasionally, you may decide—before you have accepted the new data—to abandon the entry. Before executing a save option, you can cancel all data entered in the field by pressing Esc (Exit) or F3 (Exit).

Desktop Accessories Databases displays records in every database file in order by the value contained in one of the fields in the file. This field, the *sort field*, by default is the first field defined in the database structure (field number 1). Accessories displays in alphanumeric order (numbers first in ascending order [from 0 to 9] and then letters in ascending order [from A to Z]) according to the values in this first field. In the CUSTOMER.DBF example, the default sort field is the STAFF field.

In Browse mode, as soon as you type an entry in the current sort field and accept it, Accessories moves the entire record to the appropriate position in the file, according to the sort field. You can continue to enter data in the record, but it is no longer Record 1 in the file. This result can be somewhat disconcerting because the record seems to jump from the top of the table into the midst of the existing records. In Edit mode, a new record displays Record: 1 in the upper left corner of the window. After you type an entry in the current sort field and accept it, the number changes to reflect the current position of the record in sorted order.

Exiting from or Displaying a New Record for Data Entry

When you finish entering data in the current record, you can exit from the Databases window or continue adding records. To exit, press Esc (Exit) or F3 (Exit). If you have a mouse, click the application control box in the upper left corner of the application window. Accessories returns to either the Desktop Accessories main menu or the Desktop application window that was active when you opened the database.

To begin adding data to another record, select **A**dd New Record from the **E**dit pull-down menu or press F8 (New). Accessories adds a new, empty record to the beginning of the database as record number 1, bumping all other records down one record number. For example, figure 19.5 shows the CUSTOMER.DBF file in Browse mode after the F8 (New) shortcut command has been executed.

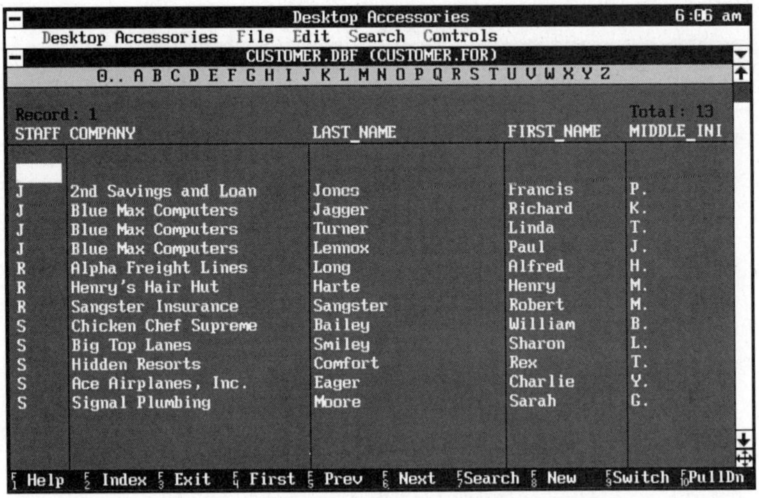

Fig. 19.5

Adding a new
record to the
CUSTOMER.DBF
database file.

Table 19.5 describes the keystroke commands available in Accessories Databases.

Table 19.5 Keystroke Commands Available in Databases

Key	Name	Function
F1	Help	Displays context-sensitive Help facility
F2	Index	Displays the Help facility index
F3	Exit	Cancels current process or application (same as Esc)
F4	First	Once—moves cursor to first field in record 1; twice—moves cursor to first field in last record
F5	Prev	Browse mode: moves cursor to same field in previous record (same as ↑) Edit mode: moves cursor to first field in previous record

Key	Name	Function
F6	Next	Browse mode: moves cursor to same field in next record (same as $\downarrow$) Edit mode: moves cursor to first field in next record
F7	Search	Displays Search Sort Field dialog box
F8	New	Displays a new record and positions cursor in its first field
F9 or Ctrl+Esc	Switch	Switches active window
F10 or Alt	Menu	Activates horizontal menu bar
Esc	Cancel	Cancels current process or application (same as F3)
Alt+ space bar	System Control	Displays System Control pull-down menu
Ins	Insert	Toggles between overtype mode and insert mode
Del	Delete	Deletes character or space at cursor

Loading an Existing Database File

To display, manipulate, add, or print information, you must load the database file. Also, you may want to use Accessories to load and use a database file created by dBase or a dBase-compatible program.

To load an existing database file, access the Desktop Accessories main menu and select **D**atabases to display the File Load dialog box (refer to fig. 19.1). Accessories displays the search criterion .DBF in the Filename text box. To load a particular file, use one of these methods:

■ Type the file name in the text box. If the file is not located in the default directory, include the complete DOS path in the text box. Press Enter or select the Load command button.

■ Press Tab to move the highlighted bar to the appropriate list box. Press the arrow keys (or use the scroll bar on the right side of the list box) to scroll to the file name, drive, or directory you want; then press Enter or select the Load command button.

■ Use the mouse and the scroll bar on the right side of the appropriate list box to reach the database file name (or path) you want and double-click the file name.

Modifying a Database Structure

Desktop Accessories Databases enables you to add or delete fields and also to change field names, field types, field sizes, and numbers of decimal places without redefining the database. When you want to modify a database's structure, first display the file in a Databases window in either Edit mode or Browse mode; be sure that the option **M**odify Data in the **F**ile menu is selected. Choose **E**dit and select **E**dit Fields from the Edit menu, shown in figure 19.6. Desktop displays the Field Editor dialog box on top of the Databases window. Figure 19.7 shows the Field Editor dialog box displayed for modifying the structure of the database file CUSTOMER.DBF.

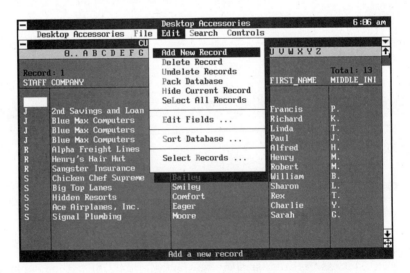

Fig. 19.6

The Databases Edit pull-down menu.

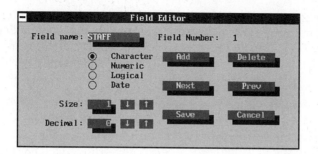

Fig. 19.7

The Field Editor dialog box for modifying the structure of an existing database file.

Adding or Deleting a Field Definition

When you add a field to a database structure, you must add it as the last field in the structure. After Accessories displays the Field Editor dialog box, select the **Next** command button until Accessories displays an empty Field Name text box. Type the name of the new field and press Enter. Continue by defining the field type and size. To save the field definition, select the **Add** command button. Select the **Save** command button to save the structure to disk and display the modified database in the current Databases window. In Browse mode, the new field becomes the rightmost field in the table. In Edit mode, the new field appears at the end of the form file.

To delete a field, display the Field Editor dialog box and select **Next** until you reach the field to be deleted. Then select the **Delete** command button and select **Save** to save the revised structure to disk. Accessories removes the deleted field from the database, as well as from the form file, and returns to the current Databases window.

Modifying a Field Definition

To modify a field definition, first display the definition in the Field Editor dialog box by pressing the **Next** button.

You may decide, for example, that you want to lengthen the field size of the CUSTOMER.DBF file's FIRST_NAME field from 15 to 22. To make this change, display this field and then move the highlighted bar to the appropriate field attribute and type **22**. Finally, select the **Add** command button to save the modified field definition to memory and select **Save** to save the structure to disk and return to the Databases window.

You can change field types; however, you should keep in mind these two restrictions: First, because character fields may include letters that would be unacceptable as logical, date, or numeric data, you cannot change this field type. Second, other field types can only be changed to character fields.

> **CAUTION:** You can increase field size without affecting data, but if you reduce the field size, Accessories truncates the data until it fits within the new field size. Accessories truncates character fields from right to left and numeric fields from left to right. The length of date and logical fields cannot be changed, for obvious reasons.

> **CAUTION:** When you modify field names, a new default form (FOR) file is created and the old one is replaced. If you edited the old default form, your changes are lost. You must manually change the modified field names in all custom form files you previously created.

Purging Records from the Database

Records that you display in a Databases window are active. Desktop provides two ways to make a record inactive so that it is not displayed in either Browse or Edit mode: delete or hide the record. Either procedure prevents the record from being printed. The program must be in Modify mode to perform either of these tasks. Be sure that the Modify Data option in the File menu is active before trying any of these operations.

When you *delete* a record, you prepare it for permanent removal from the file. (You remove files permanently by using the Pack Database command, discussed later in this chapter.) Generally, you delete records that are unnecessary or obsolete. *Hiding* a record, on the other hand, is used for temporarily removing a record so that it is not included in the display or report (printout).

Desktop Accessories Databases is designed so that at least one record must be displayed at all times. The program, therefore, discourages you from deleting or hiding all records at one time. If you execute a command that will result in all records being removed from the set of active records, Accessories displays a message dialog box with the warning: Do you want to hide (delete) the last record? Normally, you select the Cancel command button to return to the Databases window, and Accessories leaves at least one record displayed. Even if you select the OK command button, however, Accessories does not permit you to hide or delete the last record immediately. Instead, it displays the No Viewable Records dialog box (see fig. 19.8).

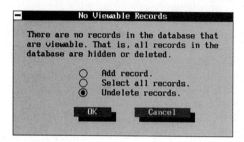

Fig. 19.8

The No Viewable Records dialog box.

Select the Add Record option button to display a blank record for the purpose of entering new data. Choose the Select All Records option button to redisplay all hidden records, or select the Undelete Records option button to redisplay all deleted records. Then select the OK command button. Accessories returns to the Databases window and displays the records you indicated.

If, however, you really do want to hide or delete all records, choose the Cancel command button in the No Viewable Records dialog box. Accessories then completely removes the database from the screen, closes the Databases window, and returns to either the Desktop Accessories main menu or another open application window. The next time you attempt to open this database file, Accessories again displays the No Viewable Records dialog box to enable you to unhide hidden records, undelete deleted records, or add a new record.

Deleting and Undeleting Records

Desktop Accessories enables you to delete records one at a time. Remember that deleting a record does not permanently remove the record from the database. Rather, a deleted record becomes inactive and is not displayed when the database is loaded into a Databases window and is not printed in a report. The record remains in the database until you execute the Pack Database command.

To delete an active record, use the cursor-movement keys or mouse to position the cursor in any field of the record, and then select **E**dit from the horizontal menu bar. Choose **D**elete Record from the Edit menu, and Accessories immediately removes the current record from the display. In Browse mode, the deleted row disappears and all rows below the cursor scroll up one line. In Edit mode, the deleted record is replaced on-screen by the next record in the database.

Because you may occasionally delete a record in error, Accessories enables you to undelete records (even in a later Databases session). You cannot, however, undelete records individually. To undelete an erroneously deleted record, undelete all currently deleted records before deleting the appropriate records individually.

To undelete all deleted records, select **E**dit, and then choose Undelete Records from the Edit menu. Accessories undeletes all currently deleted records that remain in the database. (All deleted records are removed from the database by the **P**ack Database command.) Accessories returns to the Databases window and displays all the active records including the newly undeleted records.

Packing a Database

Generally, you delete a record that you do not expect to need again. Because Accessories does not display deleted records, you may forget that these records are stored in the database file (DBF) on the disk. After several weeks or months of adding and deleting records, you may notice that the database file has grown rather large. Deleted records use valuable disk space. What's more, Databases limits you to 10,000 records per database, including deleted and hidden records. If your database approaches this limit, you may have to remove deleted records to allow room for more active records.

When you are sure that you no longer need the currently deleted records, you can permanently remove them from the database by using the **P**ack Database command. Select **E**dit and choose **P**ack Database from the Edit menu. Accessories displays a message dialog box (see fig. 19.9).

Because the pack operation is permanent, Accessories gives you the opportunity to cancel the command. To execute the pack operation, select the **O**K command button.

When the operation is completed, Accessories returns to the Databases window. Deleted records are no longer stored in the database file and cannot be restored with the Undelete feature.

Fig. 19.9

The warning for
packing the
database.

During the pack operation, Accessories creates a new copy of the database file that no longer includes the deleted records. The program does not, however, actually delete the original copy of the file. Instead, Accessories renames the original database file by changing the file name extension from DBF to DBU and then creating a new version of the database without the deleted records. The new file has the extension DBF. Therefore, you still can recover deleted records, but only if you act promptly.

Before adding, editing, deleting, or (again) packing any more records, use PC Tools Desktop (or DOS) to rename the current DBF file to some other file name. Then rename the DBU file (created by the erroneous pack operation) with the extension DBF. After erroneously packing the CUSTOMER database, for example, you can rename CUSTOMER.DBF to CUSTOMER.OLD (or any other name not currently used in the working directory) and rename CUSTOMER.DBU to CUSTOMER.DBF. After renaming the files, redisplay the database file and execute the Undelete Records command to return the erroneously deleted records to the active set of records. After you are certain that all records are displayed properly, you can use PC Tools Desktop or DOS to delete the extra copy of the database file (ROLODBF.OLD in the example).

> If your disk has insufficient space for two copies of the database file, Accessories displays an error message. Use PC Tools Desktop (or DOS) to erase enough files from the disk to provide room for a second copy of the database file.

T I P

Hiding and Selecting Records

When Accessories hides a record, the program neither displays the record in a Databases window nor prints the record in a report. In contrast to deleted records, hidden records are not removed permanently from the database by the Pack Database command. Choose Hide rather than Delete when you don't want to use certain records temporarily. This procedure avoids the potential danger of accidentally, yet permanently, erasing a deleted record by running Pack.

To hide a record, first position the cursor in any field of the record to be hidden (in either Browse mode or Edit mode). Activate the **E**dit menu and select **H**ide Current Record. In Browse mode, the hidden row disappears, and all rows below the cursor scroll up one line. In Edit mode, the hidden record is replaced on-screen by the next record in the database.

The opposite of hiding records in an Accessories database is selecting records. Accessories provides two commands on the **E**dit menu for selecting records for display. When you want to display one or more hidden records, use the Se**L**ect All Records command. When you want to display only a subset of the records in the database and hide all other records, use the Select **R**ecords command. For example, you may want to display or print from the CUSTOMER.DBF database a list of only your suppliers. From the **E**dit menu, choose Select **R**ecords. Accessories displays the Select Records dialog box (see fig. 19.10).

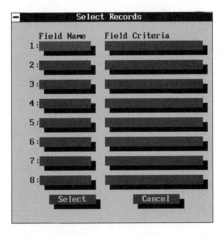

Fig. 19.10

The Select Records dialog box.

On the left side of the Select Records dialog box, Accessories displays eight Field Name text boxes. To the right of every Field Name text box is a corresponding Field Criteria text box. You use the Field Criteria text boxes to specify which records you want Accessories to display.

All the entries in the Field Name and Field Criteria text boxes are referred to collectively as the *selection criteria*.

Specifying Selection Criteria

You can specify selection criteria for character fields, numeric fields, logical fields, and date fields. To specify the selection criteria, type as many as eight field names from the database in the Field Name text boxes, and type a value in each corresponding Field Criteria text box. After you enter the criteria you want, choose the **S**elect command button. Accessories displays all active records containing the values you typed in the Field Criteria text boxes. All records that don't meet the selection criteria are hidden.

> Hidden records are not selected by the Select **R**ecords command, even if the record meets the selection criteria. So that you do not overlook a hidden record, execute the Se**L**ect All Records command before using the Select **R**ecords command.
>
> **T I P**

When you specify a selection criterion, you can indicate an exact match for the target field value. To display only Sally's records from your CUSTOMER.DBF database (Group S), for example, type **STAFF** in the first Field Name text box and type **S** in the first Field Criteria text box. Choose the **S**elect command button, and Accessories displays only records that meet the criteria—only records whose STAFF field contains the letter *S*. Accessories hides all other records.

You do not always have to specify an exact match in the selection criteria. You can type only the first few characters of the field value on which the selection should be based. When you specify in a Field Criteria text box a character or group of characters, usually called a *character string*, Accessories selects all records containing a value that at least begins with the character string.

To display all the records in the CUSTOMER.DBF file in which the CITY field is OCALA, for example, type **CITY** in the first Field Name text box and type **OCA** in the Field Criteria text box. Choose **S**elect, and Accessories displays all the records in which the CITY field value begins with the letters *OCA*. (The Accessories Search command is not case sensitive.)

Desktop Accessories permits use of a wild card character in a record-selection criterion. Type the question mark (?) to represent any character in a particular position in the character string. Perhaps, for example, you want to select all records from CUSTOMER.DBF with a credit limit of at least $10,000 but less than $20,000. Type **CREDIT.LIM** in the Field Name text box and **1?000** in the Field Criteria text box. Choose **S**elect to display the group of records.

Accessories enables you to specify a range of values as well. You can specify the lower limit, upper limit, or both limits of the range. To specify the upper and lower limit, type a character string (numbers, letters, or both) followed by two periods (..) and another character string. To specify only the lower limit of the range, type the character string followed by two periods (..). Indicate the upper limit only by preceding the character string with two periods (..).

This feature is most useful with numeric fields. To list records of individuals in the CUSTOMER.DBF file whose age is between 35 and 45, for example, type **AGE** in a Field Name text box and **35..45** in the corresponding Field Criteria text box. Choose **S**elect, and Accessories displays the specified records. For example, 35.. in the AGE field matches all ages 35 or older. Conversely, ..35 matches ages 35 or younger.

T I P   To specify ranges for dates, Accessories requires that you use the format YYYYMMDD.

For Related Information

◄◄ "Modifying Files," p. 149.

Deleting a Database File

In addition to deleting records, you may occasionally want to delete an entire database—when the data contained in the database is obsolete, for example. Accessories enables you to delete an existing database file from the Databases File Load dialog box, which you select from the Desktop Accessories main menu. To delete a database file, select the file and then select the **D**elete command button.

Accessories deletes the database file (DBF) and then returns the highlighted bar to the Filename text box.

CAUTION: Even though Accessories deletes the database (DBF) file, the program does not delete the associated record (REC) and form (FOR) files. Use PC Tools Desktop or DOS to delete these two files before creating another database with the same name.

For Related Information

◄◄ "Modifying Files," p. 149.

FROM HERE...

Sorting a Database

Accessories displays database records in alphanumeric (A-B-C or 1-2-3)
order by the values contained in one of the fields in the file. The field
that determines the order in which Accessories displays records is the
sort field. By default, Accessories uses the first field defined in the database structure as the sort field. As depicted in figure 19.11, Accessories
normally displays the CUSTOMER.DBF database file in order by the
values in the STAFF field. Staff J is first, followed by staff R, and then
staff S.

```
┌─────────────────────────────────────────────────────────────────┐
│ ▬           Desktop Accessories                        6:12 am    │
│    Desktop Accessories  File  Edit  Search  Controls              │
│ ▬              CUSTOMER.DBF (CUSTOMER.FOR)                      ▼  │
│        0.. A B C D E F G H I J K L M N O P Q R S T U V W X Y Z  ↑  │
│                                                                   │
│ Record: 1                                          Total: 13      │
│ STAFF COMPANY              LAST_NAME         FIRST_NAME MIDDLE_INI │
│                                                                   │
│ ┌───────┐                                                         │
│ J │       │ 2nd Savings and Loan  Jones        Francis     P.     │
│ J   Blue Max Computers   Jagger       Richard     K.              │
│ J   Blue Max Computers   Turner       Linda       T.              │
│ J   Blue Max Computers   Lennox       Paul        J.              │
│ R   Alpha Freight Lines  Long         Alfred      H.              │
│ R   Henry's Hair Hut     Harte        Henry       M.              │
│ R   Sangster Insurance   Sangster     Robert      M.              │
│ S   Chicken Chef Supreme Bailey       William     B.              │
│ S   Big Top Lanes        Smiley       Sharon      L.              │
│ S   Hidden Resorts       Comfort      Rex         T.              │
│ S   Ace Airplanes, Inc.  Eager        Charlie     Y.              │
│ S   Signal Plumbing      Moore        Sarah       G.              │
│                                                                ▼  │
│ ⌐Help ⌐Index ⌐Exit ⌐First ⌐Prev ⌐Next ⌐Search ⌐New ⌐Switch ⌐PullDn│
└─────────────────────────────────────────────────────────────────┘
```

Fig. 19.11

CUSTOMER.DBF
database sorted
by the default
sort field.

NOTE Accessories actually stores records in the database file on
disk in the same order that you added the data. In the
records file (REC) for every database, the program maintains an index that keeps track of the order of the records
when they are sorted by the sort field. Accessories uses this
index to display or print database records in order by the
values in the sort field.

Sometimes, you may want to rearrange the records. You might want to sort the CUSTOMER.DBF database by last name, for example. To change the sort field, display the Databases Edit menu and select the Sort Database option. Accessories displays the Sort Field Select dialog box (see fig. 19.12).

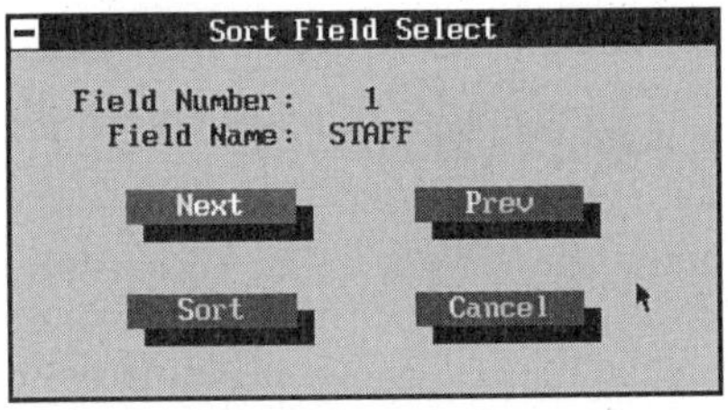

Fig. 19.12

The Sort Field
Select dialog
box.

```
┌─────────────────────────────────────┐
│ ─        Sort Field Select           │
│                                      │
│     Field Number:   1                │
│     Field Name:  STAFF               │
│                                      │
│       ┌──────────┐   ┌──────────┐    │
│       │   Next   │   │   Prev   │    │
│       └──────────┘   └──────────┘    │
│                                      │
│       ┌──────────┐   ┌──────────┐    │
│       │   Sort   │   │  Cancel  │  ▶ │
│       └──────────┘   └──────────┘    │
└─────────────────────────────────────┘
```

The Sort Field Select dialog box initially lists the field number and field name of the current sort field. In the CUSTOMER.DBF example, because field number 1—the default sort field—is the STAFF field, the STAFF field is listed in the Sort Field Select dialog box.

Accessories displays four command buttons in the Sort Field Select dialog box: Next, Prev, Sort, and Cancel. To choose a different sort field, select the Next command button to move between fields in the database structure. If you overshoot a sort field, you can use the Prev command button to move back through the fields one at a time. After the Field Number and Field Name entries at the top of the dialog box display the number and name of the new sort field, select the Sort command button. If you decide to leave the sort field unchanged, press Esc (Exit), select the Cancel command button, or click the close box at the top left corner of the dialog box.

To sort CUSTOMER.DBF by the LAST_NAME field, first display the Sort Field Select dialog box. Select the Next command button four times until LAST_NAME is listed. To complete the selection, select the Sort command button. Accessories shuffles the records on-screen so that they appear in alphabetical order by the last names (see fig. 19.13).

Every time you add a record, edit a sort field value, or change the sort field, Accessories must sort the index again. To maintain quick performance during data entry, Accessories sorts the index in memory and does not store the most current index to disk (to the record file) until you exit from the database window. In rare cases, particularly when the size of the sort field is large, the number of records you can enter in the database might be limited to fewer than the normal limit of 10,000 records. If Accessories displays a message indicating that you have reached the record-number limit, and you know that the total number of records is less than 10,000, the index might be the problem.

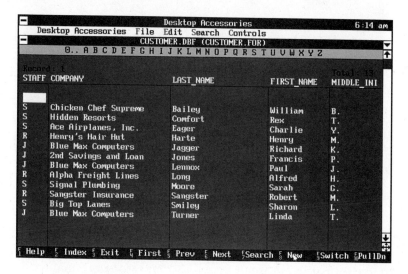

Fig. 19.13

CUSTOMER.DBF database sorted by last name.

To remedy this problem, press Esc (Exit) or F3 (Exit) to close the window; then load the database file again. You should be able to add more records.

Occasionally, you may want to sort more than one field, but Accessories sorts on only one field at a time. By using the **S**ort Database and Select **R**ecords commands in tandem, you can approximate sorting two fields. Suppose, for example, that you want to sort the CUSTOMER.DBF file first by the STAFF field (so that all records in each STAFF are listed together) and then by COMPANY (the records within every STAFF are in order by company name). First, use the **S**ort Database command to make COMPANY the sort field. Then choose Select **R**ecords to select records according to the STAFF field. Every time you select a different STAFF, Accessories displays all records in the STAFF sorted by COMPANY (see fig. 19.14).

T I P

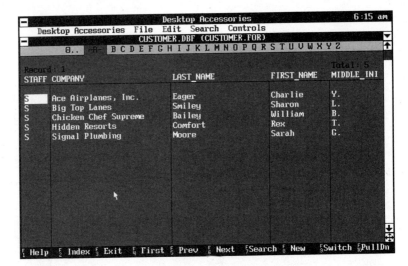

Fig. 19.14

STAFF S (Sally)
sorted by the
COMPANY
name.

Searching a Database

Often, the primary purpose of a database is to store information so that it can be found and displayed easily. The options on Accessories Databases' Search menu assist you in this way.

At first glance, searching the database might seem similar to using the Select **R**ecords command. The Search menu options, however, do not create a subset of records. Rather, these options provide a convenient method for moving the cursor quickly to a particular record that meets a specific criterion.

Accessories enables you to search all fields at one time for a particular character string or to search just the sort field. Accessories also enables you to display a record by specifying its record number.

Searching Fields

To search a database for a record that contains a specific character string in any field, select the **S**earch menu from the horizontal menu bar. The menu offers you the following choices: **F**ind Text in All Fields and Find **T**ext in Sort Field.

To search only the sort field, select Find **T**ext In Sort Field. Because Accessories maintains an index for the sort field, the fastest way to locate a record in a large database is through the sort field. When you search this field, Accessories searches only the index and does not have to search the entire database.

Accessories displays a dialog box that contains a text box, labeled Search Data, and three option buttons: Search All Records, Search Selected Records, and Search from Current Record. By default, the Search Selected Records option button is selected. This dialog box also includes two command buttons: **S**earch and **C**ancel.

> Use the F7 (Search) key to open the Search Sort Field dialog box directly. Whether you start a search from the Search Sort Field or the Search All Fields dialog box, you can use F7 to search for the next occurrence. Pressing F7 for the next occurrence reopens the search dialog box that was used to initiate the original search.

T I P

Type the appropriate text, called the *search string*, in the Search Data text box. (Search is not case sensitive.) To search all records—including hidden records—for the search string, select the Search All Records option button. If you want Accessories to search only the records that are selected, choose the Search Selected Records option button. (Searching selected records usually is faster because Accessories has to search fewer records.) To search from the current record, choose Search from the Current Record.

After you select the appropriate option button, select the **S**earch command button. Accessories starts at the first record in the database and begins searching all the sort fields for the search string. The program then moves the cursor to the first character in the field of the first record that contains the search string.

To continue the search, press F7 (Search) and again select the **S**earch command button. Accessories resumes the search with the current record and displays the next record that contains the search string.

Suppose, for example, that you want to search the database for a contact whose first name is Sarah. Choose **S**earch and select **F**ind Text in All Fields. In the Search All Fields dialog box, type **SARAH** in the Search Data text box and select the **S**earch command button (see fig. 19.15). Accessories moves the cursor to the first record that contains the search string *Sarah*.

If this is not the Sarah you want to call, press F7 (Search) and select **S**earch again, and Accessories displays the next record with the string *Sarah*, if another one exists. Continue the procedure until you find the record you want or you reach the end of the database.

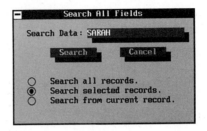

Fig. 19.15

Using the Search
All Fields dialog
box.

The Find Text in All Fields command finds the search string anywhere within the field. In CUSTOMER.DBF, you can type **ch** to search for Richard, and the Find Text In All Fields command stops on every field that contains the string *Richard* but stops also on every field that contains *ch*, including fields containing these values:

3217 S. S**ch**ool Ave.

Chicken Chef Supreme

Charlie

As with the Select **R**ecords command, you do not have to match the field entry exactly for Accessories to find the record. The longer and more precise the search string, however, the fewer false matches result.

T I P

Creative use of the space bar can help focus your search. Searching for the word *air* in the data shown in fig 19.13, for example, results in a match with *airplane* and *hair*. Press the space bar before typing *air* in the Search Data text box, and the search finds only *airplane*. Pressing the space bar after *air* finds *hair*. Inserting a space before *and* after *air* results in no matches found.

Use the Find Text In Sort Field command whenever possible. Because of the fewer number of items through which the program must search, this command is much faster than the Find Text in All Fields command.

If Accessories cannot find a match, the following message appears:

    No records were found that match the search string.

Select the **OK** command button to return to the Databases window.

Using Goto To Search by Record Number

The final method of moving quickly to a certain record is to use the Goto Record command. Every active record in the database has a record number that indicates the relative position of the record in the database's current sorted order. If you sort on a different field or add another record, however, the record number of a particular record may change, and you may have difficulty remembering specific record numbers.

You may have some idea, however, about the approximate area of the database you want to display. The database might contain 500 records, for example, and you want to move near the midpoint. Rather than use the mouse or the cursor-movement keys, you can use the Goto Record command to position the cursor in record 250.

To move to a specific record, choose Search and then select Goto Record. The Goto Records dialog box appears. This dialog box contains a text box labeled Record Number and two command buttons: Goto and Cancel. Type the record number of the target record in the text box (or click the provided arrows to increase or decrease the value) and select the Goto command button. Accessories moves the cursor to the target record.

Using Form Files

Every time you define a database structure in Accessories Databases, the program automatically creates a corresponding input form. This form is stored on disk in the form file, which has the same file name as the database but a different file name extension (FOR). This form file is the *default form file*.

The Default Form File

A form file is a Notepads file. The default form file CUSTOMER.FOR, for example, is shown in a Notepads window in figure 19.16. Field names are used as labels down the left side of the form. Every field value is represented by the field name typed within brackets. These bracketed field names are replaced with the number of spaces you indicated as the size of each field or with the data you have entered previously in the database file (see fig. 19.17). Notice that Accessories lists the name of the default form file next to the database name on the title bar.

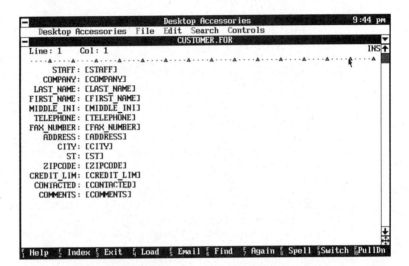

Fig. 19.16

The default form file in a Notepads window.

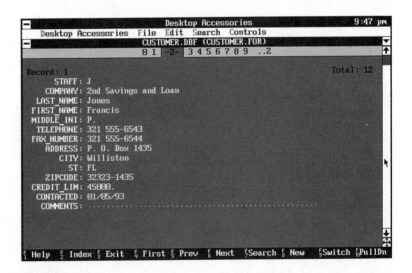

Fig. 19.17

Data using the default form file in Edit mode.

Desktop Accessories not only automatically creates the default form file but also automatically updates the default form file whenever you modify the database structure with the **Edit Fields** command on the **Edit** menu.

> **CAUTION:** Although you can modify the default form file by using Notepads, you may run into trouble. If you modify the default form file and later use the **E**dit Fields command to modify the database structure, Accessories, without warning, overwrites your customized version of the default form. Any changes you made to the original default form file are gone.

Custom Form Files

Along with the default form file, the program enables you to create one or more custom form files by using Notepads. You then can load a custom form file into a Databases window for data entry in Edit mode or as a template for custom-designed reports (printouts).

To create a form file, you first must open a Notepads window. You can either create a new form from scratch (use the file name extension FOR when you name the file) or load a copy of the default form file (use PC Tools Desktop or DOS to create a copy of the file under a different file name). Refer to Chapter 16, "Using PC Tools Notepads," for information about working with Notepad files.

Accessories form files are made up of two types of elements: fields and form text. *Fields* determine where you can enter data during data entry in Edit mode and where field values are printed in a report. To locate a field within a form file, type the field name within brackets. *Form text*, on the other hand, is everything you type in a form that is not a field. A form file can contain any text or other characters you want to display in a Databases window or print in a report.

For example, you can locate in a form file the STAFF field from CUSTOMER.DBF by typing **[STAFF]**. To show the data-entry person where to type a STAFF value during data entry, type the word **STAFF:** to the left of the STAFF field in the form file.

When you are designing an input form, think in terms of how the form will look on-screen. Sometimes form text is needed for explaining the type of data that should be entered in each field, but explanatory form text is not always necessary. The form file NEW.CUST.FOR depicted in figure 19.18, for example, is an input form for adding and editing data in the CUSTOMER.DBF database file. This form file includes form text only when necessary to elicit appropriate input during data entry in Edit mode.

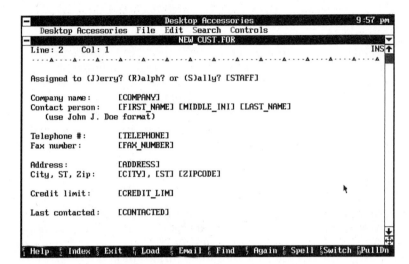

Fig. 19.18

A custom
form file,
NEW_CUST.FOR.

T I P   If you set tabs or employ other page layout options in the custom
form file, remember to specify Desktop Format when saving the
form. You lose all formatting if the file is saved in ASCII format.

After you create and save a custom form file, you must load the form
file into a Databases window to use the file. First, display the database
file in Edit mode. To load the form, select File and then Load Form to
display the Load Form dialog box (see fig. 19.19). Finally, select the
form file from the list of forms in the dialog box and select the Load
command button. Accessories displays the current record in the newly
loaded form.

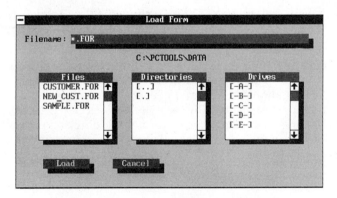

Fig. 19.19

The Load Form
dialog box.

Figure 19.20 shows how NEW_CUST.FOR is displayed after selecting F8 (New) to add a new customer to the database. Notice that Accessories displays the name of the loaded form file next to the database name in the title bar. Data entry is easy. Type the information required and press Enter to move to the beginning of the next entry. When you finish entering data, press F8 (New) for another blank form, or ESC (Exit) or F3 (Exit) to return to the menu system. If you exit from the database window while a custom form is loaded, Accessories stores the name of the form in the records file (REC) and loads the same form again the next time you load the database.

A blank data entry form after loading NEW_CUST.DBF and pressing F8 (New).

Desktop Accessories enables you to open as many as 15 application windows at one time. As you are designing a form file, you may find it convenient to load a form file into a Notepads window while the same form file is also loaded in an open Databases window. Whenever you want to make an adjustment to the form file, press F9 (Switch) to move to the Notepads window. After making the modification, press F9 (Switch) again to move back to the Databases window. Accessories immediately reflects in the Databases window any changes to the form file in the Notepads window. This procedure is much easier and faster than frequently opening and closing Notepads and Databases windows.

You can use form files as templates for printing information from a database, often called *report formats*. A typical example of a report format is a form letter. Figure 19.21 illustrates a form letter, HOLIDAY.FOR, which is intended for use with data from the CUSTOMER.DBF database and which you might send to business associates as a holiday greeting.

When you create the report format, remember to supply any punctuation (such as the commas after [CITY] and Dear [FIRST_NAME], for example), spaces, and formatting required.

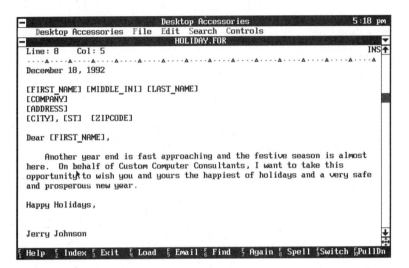

Fig. 19.21

A custom
form file,
HOLIDAY.FOR,
for use in printing
data from
CUSTOMER.DBF.

Form files most typically are used as input forms in Edit mode or as report formats for printing data. By loading a form file, you can control which fields are displayed and the order of columns (fields) in Browse mode. For example, to display in Browse mode a list from the CUSTOMER.DBF file that shows only first name, last name, and telephone number, you can create and load a custom form, PHONE.FOR, that includes only the fields [FIRST_NAME], [LAST_NAME], and [TELE-PHONE]. Load this form file into a Databases window that contains CUSTOMER.DBF; Accessories displays a list of these fields, sorted by first name. A similar form can be created that displays the fax number instead of the regular phone number. Use FAX.FOR when you want to use the autodialer to send fax messages. Figure 19.22 shows an example of these forms.

You can use a custom form to control the order of columns in Browse mode. The order of the bracketed field names you list in the form file determines the order in which Accessories displays fields in Browse mode. For example, you can rearrange fields in PHONE.FOR so that the fields are in the order [TELEPHONE], [FIRST_NAME], and [LAST_NAME]. The next time you display CUSTOMER.DBF in Browse mode, Accessories displays the columns (fields) of the database table in this new order.

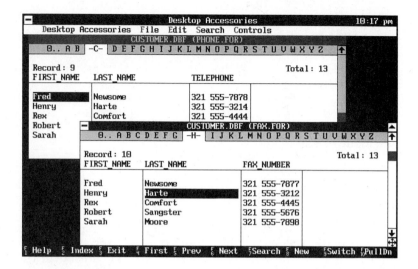

Fig. 19.22

Using custom
form files to
control the fields
displayed in
Browse mode.

CAUTION: Do not modify the structure of a database while a custom form file is loaded. If you load a custom form and then use the Edit Fields command to modify the database structure, Accessories renames the database file to that of the custom form and replaces the custom form with a new default form file. Before making a change to the database structure, first reload the default form file. Then you can proceed safely with the structure modification. If you add or delete a field or change the name of a field, you must use Notepads to make appropriate modifications to any custom form files you use with the database. After you save the new structure to disk and Accessories rebuilds the default form file to match the new structure, you can again load a custom form file into the Databases window.

For Related Information

◄◄ "Entering Text," p. 569.

▶▶ "Using Autodial," p. 841.

FROM HERE...

Printing a Database

With many database programs, figuring out how to print information from your database can be a difficult task. When you use the Desktop Accessories Databases application, however, printing a portion of your database (called a *report*) is as easy as displaying database records on-screen. With Accessories, you can print database records from either Browse mode or Edit mode.

Printing from Browse Mode

When you want to print data from the database in columns, you can use Browse mode. Accessories prints all active records and prints only fields visible in the Databases window. To maintain control over which records and fields are printed in Browse mode, take these preparatory steps:

1. If the columns are not already listed in the desired order, design and load a form file that includes the fields you want to print, listed in the proper order.

2. Adjust window size so that the window border surrounds only the columns (fields) you want included in the report.

3. Use the Select Records command to specify the records you want to print. If you want, use the Sort Database command to sort records in a different order.

After you complete these steps, you are ready to print the report. Select File from the horizontal menu bar and choose Print to display the Print dialog box, which contains six option buttons: LPT1, LPT2, LPT3, COM1, COM2, and Disk file. The dialog box also contains two command buttons: Print and Cancel, and three text boxes: Number of Copies, Line Spacing, and Starting Page Number.

The first three option buttons (LPT1, LPT2, and LPT3) represent parallel ports. Because a parallel printer probably is connected to LPT1, the first parallel port on your computer, select the first option button. Accessories can send output to a printer connected to LPT2 or LPT3 if your computer has these ports.

Occasionally, your printer may be connected to one of your computer system's serial ports. Laser printers, for example, sometimes are connected to a serial port. When you use the COM1 or COM2 option button in the Print dialog box, Accessories sends output to a serial printer connected to COM1 or COM2.

Occasionally, you may not want to send your report to a printer, preferring instead to create a file containing a copy of the report to be transferred to another program or printed later. This type of file is called a *print file*. To send the report to a file on disk, select the Disk File option button in the Print dialog box.

After you select the correct output port and type the proper values in the text boxes, select the **P**rint command button. Accessories displays a dialog box with this message:

    Now printing. Press escape to cancel.

If you selected a parallel or serial port, Desktop sends the report to the printer. Accessories prints the data from the selected fields and records in columns, with field names as column headings across the top of every page of the report. Figure 19.23 depicts a report printed from the one of the Browse mode Databases windows shown in figure 19.22.

If you select the Disk File option button in the Print dialog box, Accessories creates on the disk a file with the same name as the report form but with the file name extension PRT. This print file contains only ASCII characters. Because most popular word processing, spreadsheet, and database programs—including Desktop Notepads—can read ASCII files, you may be able to use the file with other software. You can later send an ASCII file to the printer by using the file COPY command in either PC Tools Desktop or DOS. Just copy the file to an appropriate output device name. For example, to send a CUSTOMER.DBF report file, CUSTOMER.PRT, to the parallel printer port LPT1, you can type this DOS command:

    COPY CUSTOMER.PRT LPT1

If you intend to create more than one print file from the same database, be sure to rename the first print file before creating a second. Otherwise, Accessories replaces the first print file with the second print file.

Printing from Edit Mode

Although columnar reports generated from Browse mode sometimes are appropriate, they are inflexible because you can print only in columns. Consequently, Accessories enables you to print from Edit mode, using a form file as a template or report format.

Occasionally, you may want to print database records by using the default form file as a format. The default form file generates a report with every field of a record in a separate line and every record on a separate page. More often, however, you will design a custom report format. Two typical examples are form letters and mailing labels.

To prepare the database for printing from Edit mode, follow these steps:

1. Design a form file that includes the fields and form text you want to print in the report. When you design the form file in Notepads, set page-layout settings such as margins, paper size, and line spacing. If you do not want page numbers, use the Header/Footer command on the Notepads Controls menu to delete the default number symbol (#) from the footer.

2. Load the form into the Databases window by selecting **D**atabases from the Main menu, then selecting the database file. Next, select **F**ile from the menu bar. Then select **L**oad Form. Select the form you need from the Load Form dialog box.

3. Use the Select **R**ecords command from the **E**dit menu to specify the records you want to print.

4. If necessary, use the **S**ort Database command in the **E**dit menu to change the order of the records.

Then select **F**ile on the horizontal menu bar, and select **P**rint to display the Print Selection dialog box. In addition to the two command buttons, **P**rint and **C**ancel, this dialog box also contains these option buttons:

- Print Selected Records
- Print Current Record
- Print Field Names

Most often, you will want to print the selected records, so select the Print Selected Records option button in the dialog box. To print a single record, select the Print Current Record option button. Choose the Print Field Names option button when you want Accessories to print a copy of the database structure for your records. The report generated by this option contains four columns with these headings:

FIELD

NAME

TYPE

SIZE

DEC

Beneath every column heading, Accessories lists the corresponding values from the database structure.

After you select the appropriate option button in the Print Selection dialog box, select the **P**rint command button. Accessories displays the Print dialog box, which functions identically in Browse and Edit modes.

After selecting a print device from the Print dialog box and typing the proper values in the text boxes, select the **P**rint command button. Accessories prints the report. If you send the report to a file with the Disk file option button, Accessories sends the output to a file with the name of the loaded form file but with the file name extension PRT.

To print a Christmas letter to Henry's Hair Hut, for example, follow these steps:

1. Load CUSTOMER.DBF into a Databases window in Edit mode.

2. Load the form file HOLIDAY.FOR into the database window (refer to fig. 19.21).

3. Make current the record that contains the information about Henry's Hair Hut.

4. Select **P**rint from the **F**ile menu.

5. Indicate the appropriate output device and select the **P**rint command button. Figure 19.24 depicts the generated letter.

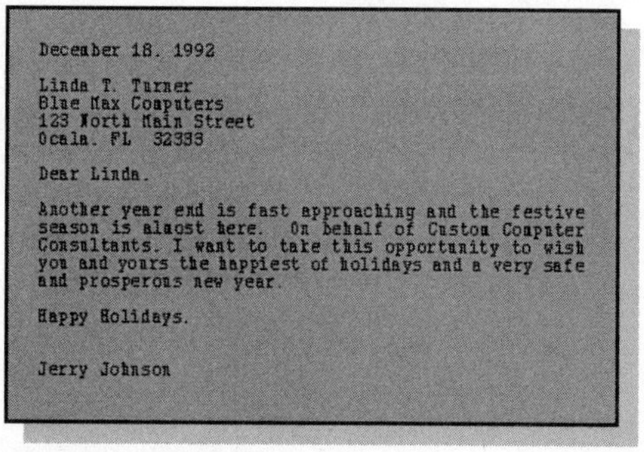

```
December 18, 1992

Linda T. Turner
Blue Max Computers
123 North Main Street
Ocala, FL  32333

Dear Linda,

Another year end is fast approaching and the festive
season is almost here.  On behalf of Custom Computer
Consultants, I want to take this opportunity to wish
you and yours the happiest of holidays and a very safe
and prosperous new year.

Happy Holidays,


Jerry Johnson
```

Fig. 19.24

A letter generated from the form letter HOLIDAY.FOR.

You can use Edit mode to print mailing labels that are only one label per row (sometimes called *1-up mailing labels*). Figure 19.25 illustrates a form file, LABEL.FOR, for printing names and addresses on 1-inch mailing labels, using data from CUSTOMER.DBF. Notice that the Page Layout dialog box is displayed for indicating the layout settings you might want to use. You must also select the **H**eader/Footer option from the Notepads Controls menu and delete the number symbol (#) from the footer to prevent page numbers from printing (see Chapter 16, "Using PC Tools Notepads," for more information about page-layout settings, headers, and footers).

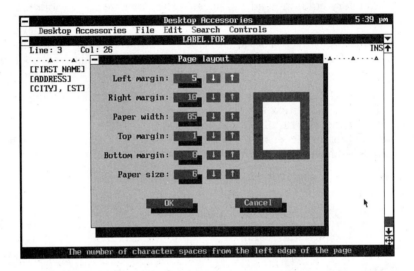

Fig. 19.25

A form file, LABEL.FOR, for printing 1-up mailing labels.

FROM HERE...

For Related Information

◀◀ "Printing a Notepads File," p. 589.

▶▶ "Using Macros for Printer Control," p. 735.

Transferring and Appending Records

Two of the most convenient features of Desktop Accessories Databases are the similar capabilities of transferring and appending data from one database file to another. The Transfer command enables you to add all selected records from a database in an open Databases window to the end of another database file on the disk. With the Append command, you can add all records from another database file on the disk to the end of the database file in the current Databases window.

Transferring Records

Occasionally, you may need to extract or transfer a portion of the data in your database file to another database. When you want to transfer records between two database files that have identical field names, load into a Databases window the database that contains the records to be extracted—the *source database*. Use the Select Records command to select only the records you want to transfer to the destination database.

After you select the appropriate records from the source database, select File from the horizontal menu bar. Then select Transfer from the pull-down menu to see the Transfer dialog box (see fig. 19.26). Type the name of the *destination database* (the database to which you are transferring the data) in the Filename text box or select the database from the list boxes; then choose the Select command button.

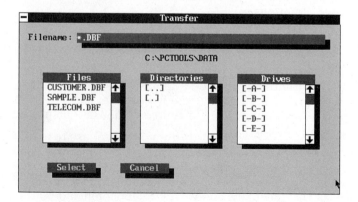

Fig. 19.26

The Transfer dialog box.

If the fields in the source and destination databases have exactly the same names, Accessories immediately proceeds with the transfer and displays the message `Please wait transferring records.`

Desktop adds all selected records from the source database to the end of the destination database. The next time you load the destination file in a Databases window, the records are displayed in order by the sort field (rather than at the end of the file).

The Accessories transfer operation copies data only between fields from the source and destination databases that share the same field name. For example, you might want to extract the "Jerry" records (STAFF J) from the CUSTOMER.DBF file and transfer them to JERRY.DBF, a database of names and addresses used to complete the HOLIDAY.FON letter for all the customers of Jerry Johnson.

To transfer STAFF J records from CUSTOMER.DBF to HOME_FON.DBF, first display CUSTOMER.DBF in a Databases window and use the Select Records command to locate all records with the STAFF field value of J. Select File from the horizontal menu bar, and then select Transfer. In the Transfer dialog box, type **JERRY.DBF** in the text box or select JERRY.DBF from the list boxes; then choose the Select command button.

Accessories displays the message `Please wait transferring records` as it proceeds with the record transfer. The next time you display JERRY.DBF in a database window, the file includes the STAFF J records from CUSTOMER.DBF.

Appending Records

Although appending records is similar to transferring records, two significant distinctions exist:

- The Append command adds all records from the source database to the destination database; Transfer copies only the selected records.

- You perform the Append operation from within a Databases window that displays the destination database; you perform the Transfer operation while the source database is displayed.

When you want to append records from one database to another, first display the destination database in a Databases window. Then display the File menu and select Append. In the Append dialog box, type in the text box the name of the source database or select the source database from the list boxes. Finally, choose the Select command button.

In appending records, Accessories compares the field names of the source and destination files and adds all the records from the source file to the existing records in the destination file. Even records marked as hidden in the source file are added to the destination file. During the append process, Accessories displays the message `Please wait transferring records`.

After all records are appended, Accessories returns to the Databases window and displays the destination database file, including the newly added records sorted according to the current sort field.

Chapter Summary

This chapter covers the Desktop Accessories Databases application. In this chapter, you learned how to define and modify the structure of a database file, add data to a database file, edit and sort data, and search a database file for specific data. You also learned how to create custom forms for entering, displaying, and printing information in a database file, as well as how to transfer data between Desktop database files.

Now that you have completed this chapter, you can appreciate how your personal computer can help you manage the information explosion. Turn to Chapter 20, "Managing Your Appointment Schedule," to learn how Accessories' Appointment Scheduler can help you better manage your time.

Managing Your Appointment Schedule

Whatever your position in the business world, time—especially your own time—is a precious commodity that seems always in short supply. You might be lucky enough to have a good executive secretary to help you manage your personal schedule efficiently, but if you don't, this chapter teaches you how to use the PC Tools Desktop Appointment Scheduler to squeeze every minute from every day, possibly even leaving some time for play and relaxation.

This chapter shows you how to use the Appointment Scheduler to maintain daily, weekly, and monthly appointment schedules. You learn how to make single appointments, make recurring appointments, set alarms, delete appointments, edit scheduled appointments, and add notes to appointment entries. The chapter describes how to use the Appointment Scheduler to find instantly a previously scheduled appointment and to find the next free time for an appointment. You learn how to print daily, weekly, and monthly schedules, as well as how to display a graph that depicts five days' worth of appointments at a glance.

In addition to scheduling appointments, you can use the Appointment Scheduler to create and maintain an ongoing list of tasks you want to accomplish—a list commonly called a *to-do list*. In this chapter, you learn how to use the Desktop Accessories Appointment Scheduler to create daily, weekly, and monthly prioritized to-do lists. You learn how to make, delete, and edit items in the lists and even how to create entries for items that recur annually. As with appointments, you learn how to attach an optional note to every entry in a to-do list.

After reading this chapter, you should be able to use the PC Tools Desktop Accessories Appointment Scheduler to help you manage every minute of your business day (or the entire day, if you want) and to keep your daily priorities in order. The Appointment Scheduler helps you put an end to forgotten appointments and missed deadlines because you simply lost track of time; you no longer will let a low-priority task prevent you from completing the job your boss assigned as the top priority.

Opening an Appointment Scheduler Window

As with most other Accessories applications, such as Notepads, the first step to using Appointment Scheduler is to open an application window and to load a file. When you want to open an Appointment Scheduler window, you first must display the **D**esktop Accessories main menu and select **A**ppointment Scheduler. Accessories displays the Appointment Scheduler File Load dialog box (see fig. 20.1).

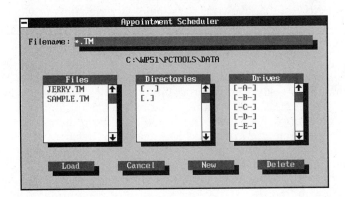

Fig. 20.1

The Appointment Scheduler File Load dialog box.

Loading a Schedule File

Use the File Load dialog box to load or delete an existing schedule file
or to create a new schedule file. The File Load dialog box works in essentially the same manner in Appointment Scheduler as it works in
Notepads. (Refer to Chapter 16, "Using PC Tools Notepads," for instructions on how to use the File Load dialog box.) After you create a new
schedule file or load an existing file, Accessories displays an Appointment Scheduler window. Figure 20.2 shows a schedule file named
JERRY.TM loaded into an Appointment Scheduler window.

Monthly
calendars

To-Do list

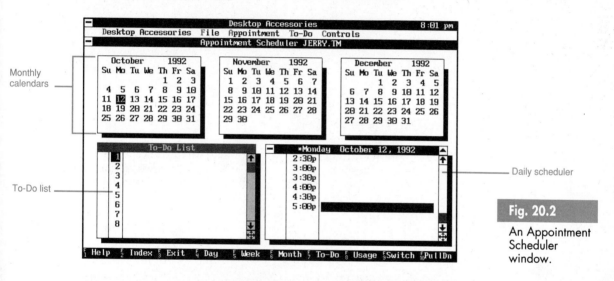

Daily scheduler

Fig. 20.2

An Appointment
Scheduler
window.

When you first install PC Tools, Desktop Accessories uses TM as the
default file name extension for schedule files. You can assign another
default directory to hold schedule files, but you cannot assign a
different extension. Refer to Chapter 16, "Using PC Tools Notepads,"
for instructions on how to change the default directory.

T I P

T I P   You can make Accessories automatically display the Appointment
Scheduler window every time you start your computer. In your
computer's AUTOEXEC.BAT file, include the parameter /RA in the
start-up command for Desktop Accessories. Then, every time you
reboot the computer, Accessories loads itself and displays an Appointment Scheduler window. If you create more than one schedule
file in the default Appointment Scheduler directory, Accessories
loads the last schedule file you loaded in an Accessories session.
See Appendix A, "Installing and Configuring PC Tools," for more information about parameters you can add to the Accessories start-up
command.

Examining the Appointment Scheduler Window

An Appointment Scheduler window exhibits some of the typical attributes of most Accessories application windows. As always, the top
line of the screen is the horizontal menu bar, and the bottom line is the
message bar. A window border, which has a close box in its upper left
corner, surrounds the Appointment Scheduler window. To close the
window, you can click the close box. In addition, Accessories enables
you to use the System Control pull-down menu options to change
screen colors or to move the window around the screen.

An Appointment Scheduler window normally consists of three regions:
the Monthly Calendars, the Daily Scheduler, and the To-Do List (refer to
fig. 20.2).

The Monthly Calendars region of an Appointment Scheduler window is
the upper half of the window. This portion of the window depicts a
perpetual calendar that displays three months at a time. By default, the
first monthly calendar displays the current month as determined by
your computer's system date. Accessories displays the month name as
a heading above the calendar. A highlighted block or cursor on the
calendar indicates the current date. Figure 20.2 shows the months of
October, November, and December of 1992. The cursor is on October
12. You can press the cursor-movement keys to move the cursor
around within the first month and to scroll through the calendars to
other months (see the section "Moving around the Appointment
Scheduler Window" later in this chapter).

The Daily Scheduler region is on the lower right side of the Appointment Scheduler window. The top of the Daily Scheduler displays the day of the week and the date highlighted in the Monthly Calendars. When you first open the Appointment Scheduler window, the highlighted date is the current date. Figure 20.2 displays the date Monday, October 12, 1992. Because this date is a holiday (Columbus Day), an asterisk appears in front of it.

Below the date, the Daily Scheduler lists appointment times, each in a separate row. By default, the first appointment time is 8:00a. Subsequent appointment times are 30 minutes apart, and the last appointment time is 5:00p. The start time, stop time, and increment between appointments are settings you can change. When you first open an Appointment Scheduler window, Desktop scrolls the Daily Scheduler so that the highlighted bar rests on the next appointment time for that day. For example, if you open an Appointment Scheduler window at 10:16 A.M. and appointment times start every 30 minutes, Desktop scrolls the highlighted bar so that the bar rests on the 10:30a appointment line.

The To-Do List region is the bottom left quarter of the Appointment Scheduler window. When you first open an Appointment Scheduler window, the To-Do List highlights the number 1 at the top left. This entry is the first one in the list. Accessories enables you to add as many as 80 items to this list.

You can adjust the layout of the Appointment Scheduler window to display one, two, or all three regions in one of five ways (designated A through E). To choose a new layout, select Controls from the horizontal menu bar to display the Controls pull-down menu (see fig. 20.3). Then select Schedule Layouts to display the Scheduler Layouts dialog box.

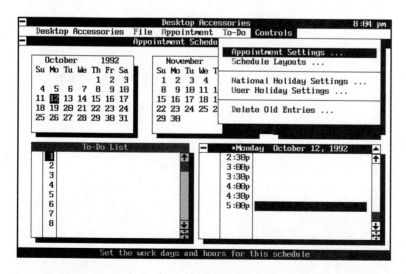

Fig. 20.3

The Controls pull-down menu.

In the Scheduler Layouts dialog box, Accessories uses display option B by default, indicating that the Appointment Scheduler window has all the regions displayed. Select the option for the new layout pattern you want. (A diagram on the right side of the screen illustrates the various selections.) Choose the **OK** button to use the new layout. Figure 20.4 shows an Appointment Scheduler window using an option other than the default.

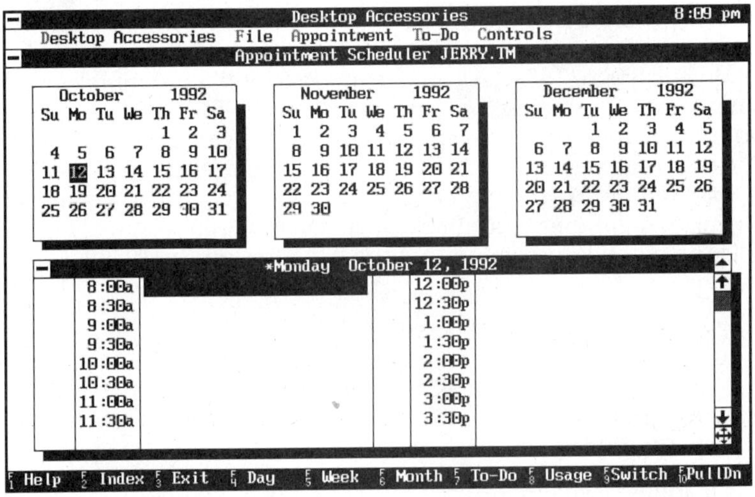

Fig. 20.4

An alternative layout for the Appointment Scheduler window.

When you want to return to the default Appointment Scheduler layout, execute the same commands again, and select option B from the Scheduler Layouts dialog box.

Loading Another Appointment Schedule

From time to time, you may need to load a different schedule file into an Appointment Scheduler window. More than one person may use your computer, for example, and every person may want to keep an individual appointment list on the computer. Or perhaps you have been given the task of using Appointment Scheduler to track the appointments of more than one person. Desktop provides three ways of loading additional appointment schedules:

- You can exit from the current Appointment Scheduler window and then load a schedule file into a new Appointment Scheduler window. To exit from the first Appointment Scheduler window, press Esc (Exit) or F3 (Exit), or click the window's close box. To open the second Appointment Scheduler window, choose **A**ppointment Scheduler from the **D**esktop Accessories main menu. Accessories displays the File Load dialog box, from which you can choose the schedule file you want to load.

■ You can open a second Appointment Scheduler application window. From the initial Appointment Scheduler window, select **D**esktop Accessories on the horizontal menu bar. Select **A**ppointment Scheduler from the menu, and then load the other schedule file from the File Load dialog box. Accessories opens the second Appointment Scheduler window by using the second schedule file. You can switch between the windows by pressing the shortcut command F9 (Switch) or Ctrl+Esc.

■ You can load a different schedule file into the current Appointment Scheduler window. From within the Appointment Scheduler window, select **F**ile on the horizontal menu bar and then select **L**oad. Accessories displays the File Load dialog box. Select the schedule file you want, and Accessories loads the file into the current Appointment Scheduler window, saving and closing the previous file on which you were working.

Several people acting as a work group can have their Appointment Scheduler configured so that you can set group appointments that will appear on each member's schedule. This feature is particularly useful if the members have access to a network, but group scheduling can also be managed on a single computer. Refer to the section "Making Group Appointments" later in this chapter for information on creating groups and setting up schedules.

Moving around the Appointment Scheduler Window

To use the Appointment Scheduler effectively, learn how to move among and within all three regions of an Appointment Scheduler window. Table 20.1 lists the cursor-movement keys available for moving around the Appointment Scheduler window.

Table 20.1 Appointment Scheduler Cursor-Movement Keys

Region	Key	Moves cursor to
All	Tab	Next region (clockwise)
	Shift+Tab	Next region (counterclockwise)
Calendars	→	Next day
	←	Preceding day
	↑	Same day of the week in preceding week
	↓	Same day of the week in next week
	PgUp	Same day of preceding month
	PgDn	Same day of next month
	Home	Today's date
	Ctrl+PgUp	Next year
	Crtl+PgDn	Previous year
Daily Scheduler	→	Same time next day
	←	Same time preceding day
	↑	Preceding appointment time
	↓	Next appointment time
	PgUp	Moves to top of list or up the number of rows the window displays
	PgDn	Moves to bottom of list or down the number of rows the window displays
To-Do List	→	Same entry, next day
	←	Same entry, preceding day
	↑	Preceding entry
	↓	Next entry
	PgUp	Moves to top of list or up the number of rows the window displays
	PgDn	Moves to bottom of list or down the number of rows the window displays

The date highlighted in the Monthly Calendars and displayed at the top of the Daily Scheduler links all regions of an Appointment Scheduler window. Whenever you move the cursor to a different date in the Monthly Calendars, for example, Accessories changes the Daily Scheduler heading accordingly and displays the appointment schedule and To-Do list for the new date.

Using the Mouse

You can also use the mouse to move around an Appointment Scheduler window. This section explains how to use the mouse in all three window regions.

To activate the Monthly Calendars and to move the cursor to a particular date in the current month, position the mouse pointer on the target date and click the left or the right mouse button.

To display a calendar of the preceding month, in the Monthly Calendars region of the window, position the mouse pointer on the left triangle (◄) that Accessories displays in the upper right corner of the first calendar, and click the left or the right mouse button. To display a calendar of the next month, position the mouse pointer on the right triangle (►) in the upper right corner of the first calendar, and click the left or right mouse button.

You can use the mouse to select an appointment time in the Daily Scheduler and to select an entry in the To-Do List. If the target appointment or entry is displayed in the window, position the mouse pointer at the entry you want and click the left or right mouse button. If you select an appointment time, Accessories opens the Make Appointment dialog box (described later in this chapter). If you select an entry in the To-Do List, Accessories displays the New To-Do Entry dialog box (also described later in this chapter).

Occasionally, you may not be able to see the specific appointment time or the target to-do entry displayed in the current window. To scroll the list of appointment times, you can use the mouse and the vertical scroll bar on the right side of the Daily Scheduler region of the Appointment Scheduler window. Similarly, you can scroll the To-Do List region by clicking the vertical scroll bar on the right side of the window.

Customizing the Appointment Scheduler

The primary purpose of the Daily Scheduler is to manage your appointments. To do so, you may have to tailor the program's settings to match your daily routine. This section describes how to set the Daily Scheduler for your normal workweek, daily work hours, typical appointment length, and observed holidays. This section shows you how to change the default date and time format displayed in the window.

Adjusting the Appointment Settings

Before you begin scheduling appointments with the Appointment Scheduler, check to see that the program's default settings match your normal work habits. To display a listing of these settings, open an Appointment Scheduler window and select Controls on the horizontal menu bar. Choose Appointment Settings from the Controls menu to display the Appointment Settings dialog box (see fig. 20.5).

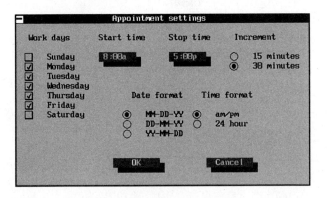

Fig. 20.5

The Appointment Settings dialog box.

The Appointment Settings dialog box enables you to set six settings that affect how the Appointment Scheduler operates: Work Days, Start Time, Stop Time, Increment, Date Format, and Time Format. The paragraphs that follow examine how to use these settings.

After you have made your changes in the Appointment Settings window, select the OK command button to save the changes and return to the Appointment Scheduler window. To return to the Appointment Scheduler window without saving changes to appointment settings, select the Cancel command button.

Setting the Work Days

The Work Days setting consists of seven check boxes, one for every day of the week. These check boxes determine which days of the week are included in your normal workweek.

By default, Accessories assumes the workweek to be five days: Monday through Friday. If your workweek differs, however, you can use the check boxes to indicate your actual workweek. Toggle the check mark on and off by pressing the space bar or Enter, or by clicking the box. If you work Saturday but not Wednesday, for example, remove the check mark in the Wednesday check box and add a check mark to the Saturday check box.

After you save the settings and begin making appointments, Desktop denotes nonworkday schedules by displaying an asterisk (*) to the left of the date heading in the Daily Scheduler region.

Setting Appointment Start Time, Stop Time, and Increment

In the Start Time section, Desktop displays a text box containing the time of day your appointments start—the beginning of your workday. The default value is 8:00a. To edit this setting, move the cursor to the Start Time text box and type a new time, using one of these formats:

H:MMa or HH:MMp

HH:MM

HHMM

H

In every format, H represents hours and M represents minutes. The last three formats are 24-hour formats. To change the start time to 9 A.M., for example, you can type *9:00a*, *9:00*, *900*, or just *9*. When you save the appointment settings, Desktop converts your entry to the current time format.

In the Stop Time section, Desktop displays a text box containing the time of day your appointments end—the end of your workday. The default value is 5:00p. Use a procedure similar to the one described for the Start Time text box to make any change to this setting.

The Desktop Appointment Settings dialog box lists two option buttons in the Increment section:

15 minutes

30 minutes

By default, Desktop uses a 30-minute appointment duration or *increment*. In other words, the Daily Scheduler lists a separate entry for every 30-minute interval, beginning with the start time up to, and including, the stop time. To decrease this interval to 15 minutes, select the 15 minutes option button.

T I P   When you set the appointment increment to 30 minutes and use any window layout except B, the Daily Scheduler can display 8 hours on one screen (8:00a to 4:00p, for example). With this display, you may not have to scroll the screen to see all your appointments.

Setting Date Format and Time Format

In the Date section, Desktop lists these option buttons:

MM-DD-YY

DD-MM-YY

YY-MM-DD

Every option represents a format Desktop uses to display dates in the Appointment Scheduler window. In every format, DD represents the day of the month, MM represents the month, and YY represents the year. By default, Desktop uses the MM-DD-YY format.

To change this setting, press one of the two option buttons not already selected. For example, a military user or European user might select the DD-MM-YY format. A date in this format is displayed as Friday 16 October 1992.

The Appointment Settings dialog box lists these two option buttons in the Time section:

am/pm

24 hour

The default format is am/pm. For example, 8 o'clock in the morning is denoted as 8:00a, and noon is 12:00p. If you routinely use a 24-hour clock, choose the 24-hour option.

 The Time format setting determines how appointment times are formatted in the left column of the Daily Scheduler. The format you use to enter Start and Stop time data does not change the final display format.

Assigning Holidays

Business people rarely make appointments on holidays. Consequently, Accessories enables you to specify which days during the year you observe as holidays. Accessories maintains a list of ten major holidays, and you can assign as many as nine additional holidays. Accessories alerts you to holiday schedules by placing an asterisk (*) to the left of the date.

To display the built-in holidays, select Controls on the horizontal menu bar and select National Holiday Settings from the Controls pull-down menu. Accessories displays the National Holiday Settings dialog box (see fig. 20.6). This box contains 10 check boxes, each representing a major holiday. A check mark in a check box activates the corresponding holiday. By default, all 10 holidays are active. If your company doesn't observe a particular holiday, you can deactivate it by removing the check mark from the holiday's check box.

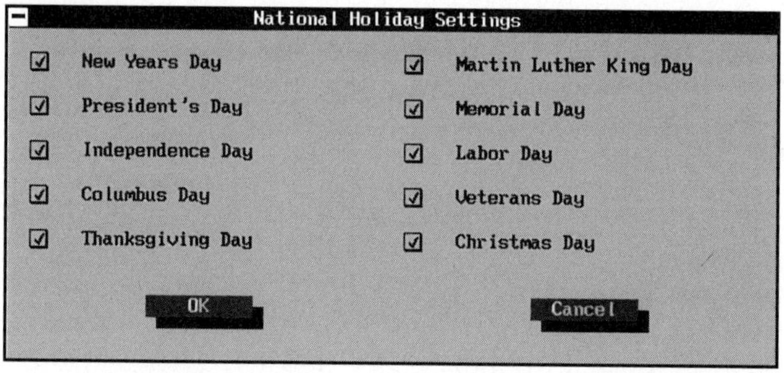

Fig. 20.6

The National Holiday Settings dialog box.

After you make any necessary adjustments to the National Holiday Settings dialog box, select OK to save the changes and return to the Appointment Scheduler window. Select Cancel to return to the Appointment Scheduler window without saving the changes.

Check the National Holiday Settings dialog box to be sure these dates are set for the day you plan to celebrate. November 11, 1992, for example, was observed as Veterans' Day at most workplaces, yet the Monday holiday rule followed by Appointment Scheduler resulted in November 9, 1992, being marked as the observed holiday.

T I P

To display a list of additional holiday settings, select **C**ontrols on the horizontal menu bar, and then select **U**ser Holiday Settings to display the User Holiday Settings dialog box. This dialog box contains nine text boxes. You can use these text boxes to specify additional dates you want included as holidays. For example, your company may have election day off, or perhaps you want to include your scheduled vacation in the list of holidays.

To add a user-defined holiday, press Tab or use the mouse to move the cursor to an empty text box; then type the date of the holiday, using the current date format. To add November 11, 1992, as a holiday, for example, move the cursor to one of the text boxes and type **11-11-91** (assuming that the current date format is MM-DD-YY). Save this change. The next time you display the Daily Scheduler for November 11, 1992, Accessories displays an asterisk to the left of the date to indicate that it is a holiday.

After you make necessary adjustments to the User Holiday Settings dialog box, select **O**K to save the changes and return to the Appointment Scheduler window. Select **C**ancel to return to the Appointment Scheduler window without saving the changes.

T   I   P   If you set up a recurring appointment (discussed later in the section "Establishing Recurring Appointments"), Accessories uses the list of holidays to skip meetings that otherwise would occur on one of the active holidays.

Now that you have adjusted the appointment settings and holiday settings, you are ready to start making appointments.

Making a New Appointment

One of the two major functions of the Appointment Scheduler is to manage your appointment schedule. Using the Daily Scheduler region of an Appointment Scheduler window, you can schedule, delete, edit, and add notes to appointments. This section describes how to accomplish all these tasks.

First, display the target date for the scheduled appointment. By default, Accessories opens an Appointment Scheduler window to the current date (as determined by the system clock). To display the date on which you want to make an appointment, you can use the mouse or the cursor-movement keys.

> **T I P**
>
> Make sure that your system clock is set correctly. Most newer computers have battery-maintained system clocks that don't have to be reset every time you start the computer. However, such clocks can sometimes gain or lose time, or the battery can run down. You can use either PC Tools Desktop or the DOS TIME command to set the time.

After you display the date, you can activate the Daily Scheduler region of the window, move the highlighted bar to the target appointment time, and display the Make Appointment dialog box, shown in figure 20.7, by using one of these methods:

- Position the mouse pointer on the target appointment time and click the left or the right mouse button.

- Press the Tab key to make the Daily Scheduler the active region, press the up- and down-arrow keys to move the highlighted bar to the appointment time, and then press Enter.

- Press the Tab key to make the Daily Scheduler the active region, press the up- and down-arrow keys to move the highlighted bar to the appointment time, select **A**ppointment, and select **M**ake.

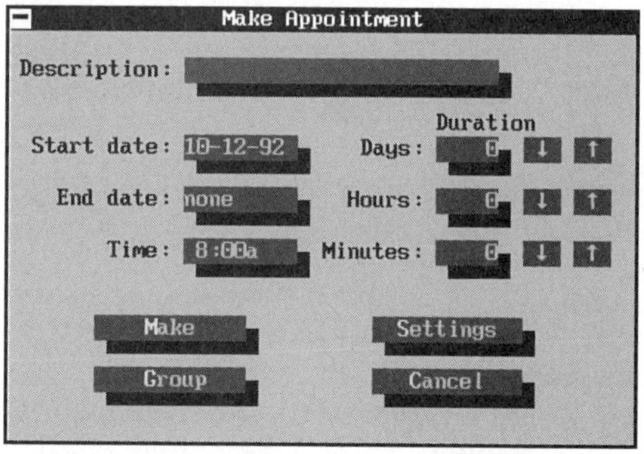

Fig. 20.7

The Make Appointment dialog box.

Suppose, for example, that you have scheduled a breakfast meeting with your marketing vice president for 8:20 A.M., December 2, 1992. You want to add this appointment to your appointment schedule. First, display an Appointment Scheduler window, and then click December 2 to display it in the monthly calendar. Accessories displays the schedule and to-do list for that date. Finally, click the 8:00a appointment line in the Daily Scheduler region of the window. Accessories displays the Make Appointment dialog box (refer to fig. 20.7).

T I P   If you attempt to make an appointment on a day earlier than the current date, Desktop displays this message:

```
In the past warning--You are making an appointment on
a day prior to the current date. Do you still want to
make the appointment?
```

Usually, this message means that you made a mistake. If so, select the Cancel command button. In the event that you do want to schedule the appointment (perhaps to create a record of a meeting that has occurred already), select the **OK** command button.

Entering a Description and Assigning Appointment Type

When Desktop Accessories first opens the Make Appointment dialog box, a highlighted bar is on the Description text box. Type a description of the appointment in this space. The description can be as long as 24 characters. After you save the Make Appointment dialog box, Accessories displays this description in the Daily Scheduler appointment entry and, if you choose to set an alarm, uses the description as the message that alerts you when the appointment time arrives.

In the Start Date text box, enter the first date on which you want a recurring appointment to appear in the Daily Scheduler. The default entry is the current date. Do not enter a date earlier than the current date.

An entry in the End Date text box is optional. The entry is not needed unless you are establishing a recurring entry (see the section "Establishing Recurring Appointments" later in this chapter). When you are establishing a recurring appointment, type the last date on which the appointment should appear in the Daily Scheduler. If you accept the default entry of None and establish a recurring appointment, Accessories schedules the appointment to recur indefinitely. You can use the Delete command on the Appointment menu to cancel an indefinitely recurring appointment; see the section "Deleting an Appointment" later in this chapter.

Setting the Appointment Starting Time and Duration

In the Time text box, type the actual scheduled starting time of the appointment. The default value is the time displayed in the appointment line when you activated the Make Appointment dialog box. This initial time value, however, is determined by the increment setting (15 minutes or 30 minutes) and might not always correspond exactly to the real time your appointment is scheduled to start.

For example, the appointment line initially might read 8:00a, but your appointment is scheduled to start at 8:20 A.M. You can edit the value in the Time text box. After you save the dialog box settings, Accessories changes the time listed in the appointment line to the value you entered in the text box.

In the Duration section of the Make Appointment dialog box, Accessories lists three text boxes: Days, Hours, and Minutes. Optionally, you can use these text boxes, individually or together, to set the projected appointment length in days, hours, and minutes. After you save the Make Appointment dialog box settings, Accessories indicates the duration of the appointment by drawing a line down the left side of the Daily Scheduler region, from the scheduled starting time of the appointment to the projected completion time. If you expect your breakfast meeting to last 40 minutes every morning, for example, type **40** in the Minutes text box.

The default value in all three text boxes is 0, which means that Accessories assumes that the appointment will be concluded by the beginning of the next appointment time listed in the Appointment Scheduler window.

Establishing Recurring Appointments

Much of your business week can be spent in meetings and appointments that recur at regular intervals. These meetings—breakfast meetings, staff meetings, sales meetings, board meetings, and so on—probably occur at the same time every day, every week, or perhaps every month. Consequently, Desktop enables you to use the Daily Scheduler to establish recurring appointments.

To establish the frequency of the recurring appointment, select the **S**ettings command button on the Make Appointment dialog box. The Special Appointment Settings dialog box appears (see fig. 20.8).

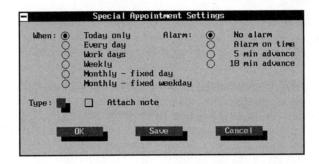

Fig. 20.8

The Special
Appointment
Settings dialog
box.

Select one of these six option buttons in the When section:

- *Today Only* (the default). Leave this option selected when the appointment does not recur at daily, weekly, or monthly intervals.

- *Every Day.* Select this option when the appointment is a daily routine, such as lunchtime.

- *Work Days.* Select this option to establish the appointment as a recurring appointment every day of the workweek (as defined in the Appointment Settings dialog box). Every weekday at 8:20 A.M., for example, you might have a breakfast meeting with your marketing vice president.

- *Weekly.* Select this option to create an appointment that recurs at the same time and on the same day, week after week.

- *Monthly—Fixed Day.* Select this option when you want Desktop to schedule the appointment on the same day of every month (on the 8th, for example), regardless of the day of the week.

- *Monthly—Fixed Weekday.* Select this option when you want Desktop to schedule the appointment once a month and on the same day of the week every month (on the second Friday of every month, for example).

Assigning a Type

Optionally, you can categorize your appointments by including a single character in the Type text box of the Special Appointment Settings dialog box. Marketing appointments can be designated as type M, sales-related appointments as type S, personal appointments as type P, group appointments as type G, and so on. You then can use the Find Appointment command to search for appointments by the description, the appointment type, or both. Refer to this chapter's "Finding an Appointment" section for more information about how to use the Find Appointment command.

Setting an Alarm

Even the best-organized personal schedule is worthless if you don't remember to attend the scheduled events. Desktop Accessories can take advantage of your computer's built-in clock and, in effect, turn your computer into a "smart" alarm clock.

The Special Appointment Settings dialog box lists these four option buttons in the Alarm section:

- *No Alarm.* By default, Accessories sounds no alarm when the appointment time arrives.

- *Alarm on Time.* Accessories interrupts any program you are using (assuming that the computer is on) and displays a message dialog box reminding you of the appointment.

- *5 Min Advance.* Accessories alerts you of the appointment 5 minutes before the scheduled start time.

- *10 Min Advance.* Accessories alerts you of the appointment 10 minutes before the scheduled start time.

After you save the dialog box settings, Accessories indicates that an alarm is set by displaying a double musical-note symbol to the left of the appointment time.

Suppose, for example, that you want an alarm to alert you a few minutes before your breakfast meeting. Assuming that you have set an alarm, when the appointment time arrives (or 5 or 10 minutes before the appointment time in the case of advance alarms), Accessories interrupts any program that is running (if Desktop Accessories has been loaded as a TSR).

As soon as Accessories is fully loaded into memory, Accessories displays a message dialog box containing the text description you typed in the Description text box, as well as two command buttons: **S**nooze and **OK**. Select **S**nooze to clear the message box from the screen and to have Accessories sound the alarm again in five minutes. Select **OK** to turn off the alarm. For additional information about how to use the alarm feature to start a program, load a file, or run a macro at a predetermined time, see Chapter 21, "Automating Your PC Using PC Tools Macros."

Attaching a Note

Sometimes the 24-character maximum length of the Description text box doesn't provide adequate room for you to annotate the purpose or plan for a scheduled appointment. Suppose, for example, that you have established an agenda for your breakfast meeting with the marketing vice president and you want Accessories to store this agenda with the meeting appointment. You can do so by attaching a Notepad file to any appointment in the Daily Scheduler.

To attach a Notepad file, check the Attach Note check box in the Special Appointment Settings dialog box. When you return to the Make Appointment dialog box and try to save these settings, Accessories does not return immediately to the Appointment Scheduler window but runs a *macro* (a series of recorded commands) to open a Notepad window and load a Notepad file. Accessories gives the notepad the same name as the schedule file but adds a unique file name extension.

> **NOTE**   Accessories adds a file name extension made up of three digits, such as 019. If the complete DOS path and file name for the note file exceeds 30 characters, the macro that loads the file does not work properly but displays a message that the file is not found. For example, C:\PCTOOLS\SCHEDULE\TERRY.029 just fits, but C:\PCTOOLS\SCHEDULE\TERRYSCD.029 is too long. If this happens, shorten the name of the schedule file or shorten the name of the working directory.

Accessories displays the appointment note in a Notepads window on top of the Appointment Scheduler window. The first line of the file lists the start date and start time of the appointment, as well as the appointment description (the Description text box entry from the Make Appointment dialog box). Then you can type any text you want—for example, an agenda for your breakfast marketing meeting—to be attached to the appointment (see fig. 20.9).

When you finish typing the note, press Esc or F3 (Exit) or click the close box to close the Notepads window. Desktop saves the appointment note and returns to the Appointment Scheduler window. Desktop places the letter *N* to the left of the appointment time in the Daily Scheduler region of the window so that you can tell at a glance which appointments have a note attached. To view a note you added to an appointment, highlight the appointment line and select **A**ttach Note from the **A**ppointment menu.

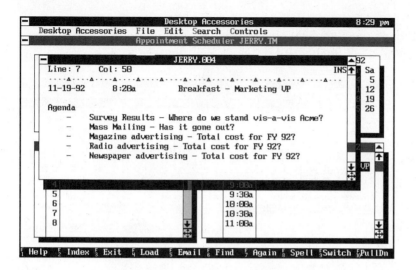

Fig. 20.9

An appointment
note.

> Although you can attach notes to group appointments, the note only
> attaches to your schedule and is not included in the Appointment
> Scheduler window of the other group members.
>
> **T I P**

Saving the Appointment

After you finish making entries and selections in the Special Appointment Settings dialog box, select the **O**K button to return to the Make
Appointment dialog box. Select the **M**ake command button to save the
settings and return to the Appointment Scheduler window. Accessories
adds the entry to the Daily Scheduler appointment list (see fig. 20.10).
To return to the Appointment Scheduler window without saving the
appointment, select **C**ancel.

Desktop helps you detect scheduling conflicts. If you attempt to schedule an appointment that overlaps another appointment, Desktop displays a message dialog box containing this message:

    Schedule conflict with an appointment on *date*

    Do you still want to make the appointment?

This message means that you are trying to schedule two appointments
for the same period. Select **C**ancel and resolve the conflict before trying
to save the new appointment again. Desktop permits you to make the

appointment, however, by choosing the **OK** command button, even though the command conflicts with one or more other appointments. Two appointments with the same time are displayed.

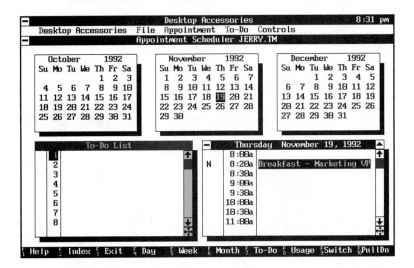

Fig. 20.10

A new appointment.

Using Group Appointments

If several people use your computer to enter their appointments, or if you and others have access to a network, you can create groups in Appointment Scheduler. Any time the group is scheduled for a joint appointment, the appointment information appears on the schedule of each group member. Group members can make personal appointments, as well as group appointments.

Creating Local Groups

Any member of a group having access to a stand-alone computer can create a group. Suppose the salespeople Jerry, Ralph, and Sally are working together to increase sales in 1993. To create the group, select **Groups** from the **File** pull-down menu. The Subscribe to a Group dialog box opens with both a list box of groups you have joined and the command buttons New, Edit, Delete, and Cancel. Select the **New** command button to open the Group Membership dialog box shown in figure 20.11.

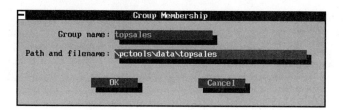

Fig. 20.11

The Group
Membership
dialog box.

To name the group TOPSALES, type **topsales** in the Group Name text box. In the Path and Filename text box, type the full path and file name to create the group file; then select **OK**. Desktop Accessories adds the extension DAT to the group file name. You can use the path \PCTOOLS\DATA, where your other data files are stored, or create a directory for group files. The specific directory is not important, but entering a path and the file name is mandatory.

The group name need not be the same as the group file name. You can choose a nickname for the group that is easy to remember. However, each group name must have a separate group file.

T   I   P

Group members then join the group from their personal Scheduler window, using the same procedure. After the members join, or subscribe, all group appointments are added to the schedules of every member as each appointment is made. Desktop provides OK, Local, and Cancel command buttons. To make a change on your schedule only, select **Local**. If you are unable to attend a group meeting, for example, you can use Local to delete the group meeting from your schedule but leave the meeting on the schedules of the other group members.

Creating Network Groups

Setting up a group that can operate on a network requires the creation of a directory on the network drive, such as H:\PCTOOLS\GROUPS, that all members of the group can access. The network administrator can create this directory and assign access privileges to group members. To make appointments, group members need to have read/write access to this directory. If only one member is responsible for entering the group appointments, all other members need only have read privileges to pick up the appointments made for the group.

To create the group, select **G**roups from the **F**ile pull-down menu. The Subscribe to a Group dialog box opens with a list box of groups you have joined and New, Edit, Delete, and Cancel command buttons. Select the **N**ew command button to open the Group Membership box (refer to fig. 20.11). Enter the group name in the Group Name text box and then a path and file name in the Path and Filename box. Select **O**K to save the new group file.

After the network group is created, each member of the group must subscribe to, or join, the group.

Making Group Appointments

To make an appointment for a group, select the date and time in the Daily Scheduler region of the window. Open the Make Appointment dialog box by pressing Enter or clicking the appointment time. Fill in the necessary information, including information in the Special Appointment Settings dialog box.

T I P   When others make group appointments, you receive notice of the new appointment when you open your Appointment Scheduler window. You are not, however, given any information about the appointment. You can use the Find command to find group appointments if the appointments are assigned a type, such as G. All members of the group should decide on a type and make the type assignment every time a group appointment is made.

To finalize the appointment, select the **G**roup command button to open the Select Group dialog box (see fig. 20.12). Highlight the appropriate group in the list box and select **M**ake to add the appointment to the group schedules.

After you make a group appointment, you can edit or delete it like any other appointment. When a group appointment is selected, Desktop displays a message advising you that any changes you make affect the entire group.

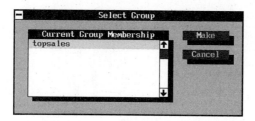

Fig. 20.12

The Select Group
dialog box.

For Related Information

◀◀ "Using Multiple Windows," p. 544.

◀◀ "Entering Text," p. 569.

◀◀ "Copying and Moving Text," p. 577.

▶▶ "Setting Smart Alarms," p. 744.

FROM HERE...

Deleting an Appointment

Occasionally, you may want to cancel an appointment you have already added to your appointment schedule. To do so, you remove the appointment from the Daily Scheduler.

When you want to delete an appointment, first load the schedule file containing the appointment. Next, use the Monthly Calendar to move the cursor to the month and day containing the target appointment. Finally, select the appointment by using one of these methods:

- Position the mouse pointer on the target appointment time and click the left or right mouse button.

- Press Tab to make the Daily Scheduler the active region. Press the up- and down-arrow keys to move the highlighted bar to the appointment time, and press Enter.

Desktop displays a message dialog box containing this message:

```
Do you want to Edit or Delete this entry?
```

The message box also contains four command buttons: Delete, Edit, Alter Note, and Cancel. Select the **D**elete command button. Press the up- and down-arrow keys to move the highlighted bar to the appointment time (or press Tab to make the Daily Scheduler the active region). Select **A**ppointment on the horizontal menu bar, and then select **D**elete (see fig. 20.13).

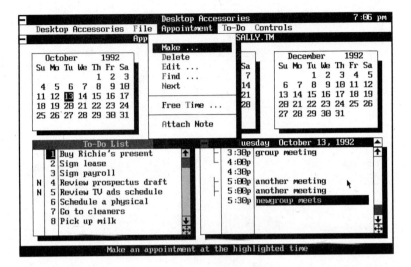

Fig. 20.13

The Appointment
pull-down menu.

When the appointment you are deleting is a recurring appointment,
Desktop does not immediately delete the entry. Rather, Desktop displays a dialog box with this message:

> The appointment you wish to delete is a recurring ap-
> pointment. Do you want to delete it everywhere, or just
> once?

This message dialog box contains three command buttons: All!, Today,
and Cancel. To delete all occurrences of the appointment, select the
All! command button. To delete only the current appointment and
leave other recurring appointments intact, select the Today command
button. To return to the Appointment Scheduler window without deleting any appointments, select Cancel.

After an appointment time has passed, you rarely need to keep a record
of the appointment in the schedule file. In fact, if you let the schedule
file grow too large, the size of the file decreases the performance of the
Appointment Scheduler. Make a practice, therefore, of routinely deleting old appointments from the file.

To delete old appointments, select Controls on the horizontal menu bar
and then select the Delete Old Entries command. Desktop displays the
Delete Old Entries dialog box (see fig. 20.14).

In the Cutoff Date text box, type the date before which you want Desktop to delete all appointments. After you specify the cutoff date, select
the Delete command button. Desktop deletes all appointments for
dates before the cutoff date and recovers the space on the disk that
had been used by those appointments.

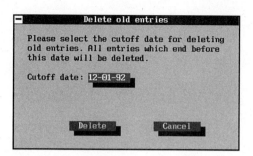

Fig. 20.14

The Delete Old Entries dialog box.

T I P

To keep a permanent record of old appointments for tax or other purposes, print the schedule and keep the hard copy rather than leave the appointments in the schedule file. Alternatively, make a backup copy of the TM file before you delete old entries.

Editing an Appointment

As with a word processing file or a database record, occasionally you may want to edit an appointment. You may want to change the description displayed in the Daily Scheduler region of the Appointment Scheduler window, or you may want to change the duration of an appointment. With Accessories, you can edit any setting you initially established in the Make Appointment and Special Appointment Settings dialog boxes. The program enables you to add a note file attached to an appointment or to edit an existing note.

Editing the Appointment Dialog Boxes

To edit an appointment, you first load the schedule file containing the appointment into an Appointment Scheduler window. Next, in the Monthly Calendars region of the window, move the cursor to the month and day containing the appointment you want to edit. Finally, select the appointment by using one of these methods:

■ Position the mouse pointer on the target appointment time and click the left or right mouse button.

■ Press the Tab key to make the Daily Scheduler the active region. Press the up- and down-arrow keys to move the highlighted bar to the appointment time, and press Enter.

■ Press the Tab key to make the Daily Scheduler the active region. Press the up- and down-arrow keys to move the highlighted bar to the appointment time. Select **A**ppointment on the horizontal menu bar; then select **E**dit.

If you use the first two methods, a message box containing the message `Do you want to Edit or Delete this entry?` appears. Choose **E**dit. Accessories displays the Make Appointment dialog box for the appointment. Now you can change any setting displayed in the Make Appointment dialog box or in the accompanying Special Appointment Settings dialog box. Refer to the "Making a New Appointment" section earlier in this chapter for guidelines on the various options displayed in these dialog boxes.

T I P   To reschedule a meeting to another time or date, you don't have to delete the initial appointment and reenter all the settings in the new appointment line. Instead, display the Make Appointment dialog box and edit the appropriate entries in the Time and Start Date text boxes. Then select the **M**ake command button; Accessories moves the appointment to the correct time and date.

When you finish making changes to the appointment settings, select **M**ake to save the changes to disk and return to the Appointment Scheduler window.

Adding a Note to an Existing Appointment

The Attach Note check box in the Special Appointment Settings dialog box determines whether Accessories attaches a note to a particular appointment. If you select this option while you are initially making the appointment, Accessories enables you to type the note immediately. Occasionally, however, you may decide to add a note after you have already added the appointment to the Daily Scheduler appointment list.

Desktop provides two ways to attach a note after the appointment has been made:

■ While you are editing the appointment in the Make Appointment dialog box, select the **S**ettings command button. Then select the Attach Note check box. Select the **O**K button to return to the Make

Appointment dialog box. Select **M**ake to save the settings. Desktop saves the settings and opens a Notepad window containing a new note file.

■ Press the Tab key to make the Daily Scheduler the active region. Press the up- and down-arrow keys to move the highlighted bar to the appointment time. Select **A**ppointment on the horizontal menu bar and select **A**ttach Note.

After Accessories opens the new Notepads window, you can type the note and close the Notepad window. Accessories returns to the Appointment Scheduler window. If you add a note to a group appointment, the note appears in your Scheduler window only.

Editing and Detaching a Note

From time to time, you may want to edit a note already attached to an appointment. Maybe you want to add an item to your meeting agenda or perhaps jot down a few notes about a telephone conversation you just had about the meeting. Accessories provides two ways to access an existing appointment note so that you can edit it:

■ Use the cursor-movement keys or the mouse to select the appointment to which the note is attached and, when the dialog box containing the message Do you want to Edit or Delete this entry? appears, select the **A**lter Note command button.

■ Press the Tab key to make the Daily Scheduler the active region. Press the up- and down-arrow keys to move the highlighted bar to the appointment time. Then select **A**ttach Note from the **A**ppointment menu.

Accessories opens a Notepad window on top of the Appointment Scheduler window and loads the notepad attached to the current appointment. When you finish editing the note and want to close the Notepad window, press Esc (Exit) or F3 (Exit) or click the close box. Desktop returns to the Appointment Scheduler window.

To detach a note, remove the check mark from the Attach Note check box in the Special Appointment Settings dialog box. Select the **M**ake command button. Desktop returns to the Appointment Scheduler window.

For Related Information

◄◄ "Entering Text," p. 569.

◄◄ "Inserting and Deleting Text," p. 575.

FROM HERE...

Using Appointments

In preceding sections, you learned how to use Desktop's Appointment Scheduler to record your appointments, to schedule recurring appointments, and to avoid conflicting appointments. But making appointments is only half the story. This section examines how to use the Desktop Appointment Scheduler to search for and locate particular appointments by description, type, date, or time; how to quickly find the next free appointment time; and how to display a graphical depiction of your appointments, free time, and conflicting appointments over a specific five-day period.

You can accomplish a number of the features by using shortcut-key commands. Table 20.2 lists all these commands, as well as all other keystroke commands available in the Appointment Scheduler.

Table 20.2 Keystroke Commands Available in the Appointment Scheduler		
Key	**Name**	**Function**
F1	Help	Displays context-sensitive help facility
F2	Index	Displays help facility index
F3 or Esc	Exit	Cancels current process or application
F4	Day	Displays or hides Daily Scheduler window
F5	Week	Displays or hides Weekly Appointment Display window
F6	Month	Displays or hides Monthly Calendar window
F7	To-Do	Displays or hides To-Do List window
F8	Usage	Displays Time Usage Graph window

Key	Name	Function
F9 or Ctrl+Esc	Switch	Switches active window
F10 or Alt	Menu	Activates horizontal menu bar
Alt+space bar	System Control	Displays System Control pull-down menu
Ins	Insert	Toggles between overtype mode and insert mode
Del	Delete	Deletes character or space at cursor

Finding an Appointment

Busy people often have many appointments. The more you use the Appointment Scheduler to keep your appointments, the more likely you are to forget precisely when you scheduled a particular appointment. The Appointment Scheduler's find feature enables you to search through the schedule file for appointments according to the description, type, date, and time of the appointment.

To find a particular appointment in an Appointment Scheduler window, load the appropriate schedule file in the window. Select **A**ppointment on the horizontal menu bar, and then select **F**ind Appointment. Accessories displays the Find Appointment dialog box (see fig. 20.15).

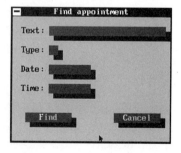

Fig. 20.15

The Find Appointment dialog box.

The Find Appointment dialog box contains four text boxes into which you can enter search criteria:

■ *Text.* In this text box, type a character string (as many as 24 characters long) that occurs in the description (the Description text box in the Make Appointment dialog box) of the target appointment. To find a sales meeting, for example, you can type **sales** in this text box. Whether you type the search string in upper- or lowercase letters is irrelevant. Accessories treats upper- and lowercase letters the same.

- *Type.* To limit the search to a specific type of appointment, enter a single character in this text box. Remember that the appointment type is an optional user-defined value; the value is stored in the Type text box in the Special Appointment Settings dialog box. In this text box, the case of the entry is significant. Note whether the entry is an upper- or lowercase letter.

- *Date.* You can limit the search to one day's appointment list by typing a date in this text box. You can use this text box alone to go directly to the first appointment on a particular date.

 NOTE Accessories searches only in ascending chronological order; consequently, you cannot use a search date that is earlier than the date of the displayed appointment list.

- *Time.* To limit the appointment time of the search, type a value in this text box. Used alone, this text box causes Accessories to stop at the first appointment list that contains an appointment which either begins on or is in progress during the specified time.

After you type the values you want, select the **F**ind command button. Accessories starts at the displayed Daily Scheduler appointment list and searches through the schedule file for a match. Accessories searches for appointments with descriptions containing the character string you typed in the Text box and limits the search to any appointment type, date, and time you specified in the other three text boxes.

Accessories uses the Daily Scheduler to display the appointment list containing a matching appointment but also continues to display the Find Appointment dialog box. You then can look at the matching appointment to determine whether the appointment is indeed the one for which you are searching. If necessary, you can refine the search by modifying the entry in the Find Appointment dialog box text boxes.

To continue with the search, select the **F**ind command button again. If you find the target appointment before Accessories locates it, select **C**ancel or click the close box to terminate the search and remove the Find Appointment dialog box from the screen. If Accessories doesn't find a match, a beep sounds and the Find Appointment dialog box disappears.

Suppose, for example, that you want to find an appointment you made with your stockbroker. If you search for *stock* (by entering **stock** in the Text text box, as shown in figure 20.16), Desktop finds the first appointment whose description includes the word *stock* but does not remove the Find Appointment dialog box. Continue to select **Find** until Accessories locates the appointment for which you are searching.

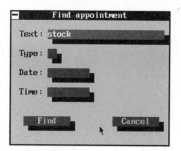

Fig. 20.16

The Find Appointment dialog box containing a search string.

The Find command is especially useful if you make group appointments. If you assigned a type to your group appointments, as explained earlier in the section "Making a New Appointment," you can enter in the Type text box the letter assigned to the group and then select the **Find** command button. You may need to repeat the **Find** command until you locate the new appointment.

Displaying the Next Appointment

Probably the most frequently asked question of the Appointment Scheduler is "What is my next appointment today?" Accessories provides a way for you to find the answer to this question.

Whenever you want Accessories to highlight the day's next scheduled appointment, display the Appointment pull-down menu and select the **Next** option. Accessories scans today's appointments in chronological order and highlights the next one.

Finding Free Time

When you are scheduling appointments, another frequently asked question is "When is my next free appointment?" With Desktop, you can answer this question instantly by selecting a menu option.

To display your next free appointment time, select **A**ppointment from the horizontal menu bar; then select the Free **T**ime command. Accessories displays the Find Free Time dialog box (see fig. 20.17)

Use the dialog box to specify the time of day, the duration of the desired appointment time, and whether the appointment must be on a workday (defined when you establish the appointment settings). The default search criteria is for a one-hour appointment between 8 A.M. and 5 P.M. on workdays.

You can modify the search criteria, if necessary, and then select the **F**ind command button. Accessories highlights the first appointment time that meets the search requirements.

Showing Time Usage

A unique feature of the Appointment Scheduler is its capacity to graphically depict how you schedule your time over a five-day period. At a glance, you can determine whether you are using your time efficiently. In addition, Appointment Scheduler can show you where appointments conflict.

To create a graph displaying five days of time usage, press F8 (Usage). Accessories displays a dialog box similar to the one shown in figure 20.18.

This dialog box shows the current day's time use, as well as the full week in which it falls (beginning on Sunday). You can press the up- and down-arrow keys to scroll the dates forward and back by one day. Press the PgDn and PgUp keys to move forward and back a week at a time. Press the Home key to return to the original five-day Time Usage Graph dialog box.

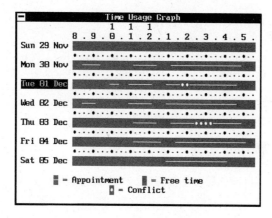

Fig. 20.18

The Time Usage
Graph dialog
box.

Accessories denotes scheduled appointments in the time-usage dialog box by a band of thin lines; free time is noted as the absence of any symbols. If you have conflicting appointments (scheduled appointments that overlap), the period of the overlap is denoted by dots.

The example in figure 20.18 shows substantial blocks of free time on Saturday morning and all day Sunday. The example indicates also that a scheduling conflict exists between 1:45 P.M. and 2 P.M. on Tuesday, December 1 and between 2:30 P.M. and 3:15 P.M. on Thursday, December 3.

Using the To-Do List

Although getting to meetings and appointments on time is certainly important, most people probably are not tied up in meetings all day. Fortunately, Accessories' Appointment Scheduler can help you schedule and remember tasks—exactly the purpose of Appointment Scheduler's To-Do List region.

Business time-management experts advise that you tackle tasks and goals in order of importance rather than from easiest to hardest. Doing so requires that you first clearly describe your tasks and goals and then prioritize them. This two-step analysis is easy to perform in Accessories' To-Do List.

The discussion that follows describes how to list each of your tasks and goals as an entry in the To-Do List, as well as how to rank your tasks and goals in order of importance. The discussion describes also how to edit and delete an entry and add a note to a To-Do List entry.

Creating a New Entry

The first step in analyzing your work is to describe every task or goal you want to accomplish. The To-Do List provides a space for typing a brief description. (Desktop also enables you to add a separate word processing file, a Notepad file, to every entry.) The second step in analyzing your assignments is to give every entry in the list a priority ranking. This section examines how to accomplish both of these steps, using the New To-Do Entry dialog box (see fig. 20.19).

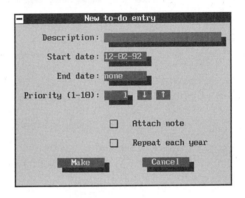

Fig. 20.19

The New To-Do
Entry dialog box.

When you want to add a new entry, use one of the following procedures to display the New To-Do Entry dialog box:

- Position the mouse pointer on the next empty entry line in the To-Do List region of the Appointment Scheduler window, and click the left or right mouse button.

- Press the Tab key to make the To-Do List the active region. Press the up- and down-arrow keys to move the highlighted bar to the next empty entry, and then press Enter.

- Press the Tab key to make the To-Do List the active region. Press the up- and down-arrow keys to move the highlighted bar to the next empty entry, and then select **M**ake from the **To**-Do menu (see fig. 20.20).

Type a short description (as many as 24 characters) of your task or goal in the Description text box of the New To-Do Entry dialog box. Make the description specific enough to identify the task. If you need additional space to completely describe the job, you can attach a note file.

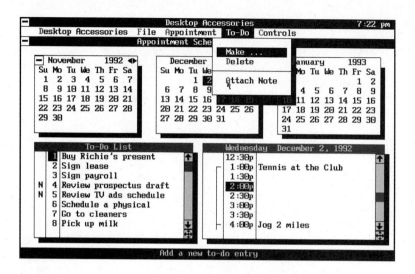

Fig. 20.20

The To-Do
pull-down menu.

Next, in the Start Date text box, indicate the first date on which you
want the task to appear in the To-Do List. The default value is the current date displayed in the Appointment Scheduler window. Similarly, in
the End Date text box, specify the final date that the entry should appear in the To-Do List. The default value for this second text box is
None, which means that the entry appears indefinitely (for dates after
the start date), until you delete the entry from the list.

Probably the easiest way to use the To-Do List is to routinely leave
the Start Date and End Date text boxes at the default values. After
you complete a task, simply delete the task from the list. As long as
the To-Do List displays an entry, you know that you haven't completed the task. By looking at the start date, you can quickly determine how long the entry has been pending.

T I P

After you indicate a start date and end date, type an integer from 1 to
10 in the Priority text box. This number denotes the level of importance
you place on the task or goal, regardless of the order in which you add
an entry to the list. (A value of 1 indicates the highest priority.) If all
entries are the same priority level, Desktop lists them in the order that
you add them to the list.

The New To-Do Entry dialog box also contains the Attach Note and
Repeat Each Year check boxes. Select the Attach Note check box to
attach a Notepads file to the To-Do entry. This action enables you to
type a longer description of the task or goal, as well as to record notes

about how you plan to solve the problem. After you save the entries in the New To-Do Entry dialog box, Accessories opens a Notepads window, enabling you to use all the word processing features described in Chapter 16, "Using PC Tools Notepads." Close the Notepads window, and Accessories returns to the Appointment Scheduler window. The letter *N* denotes any to-do entry to which a note is attached.

T I P   You can easily attach a note to a to-do entry after you save the new entry and the entry appears in the To-Do List. Using the mouse or cursor-movement keys, scroll the highlighted bar to the entry to which you want to attach the note. Then select **A**ttach Note from the **T**o-Do pull-down menu.

Choose the Repeat Each Year check box in the New To-Do Entry dialog box when the task is related to an anniversary, birthday, or other annual event. Desktop then automatically adds the time to the To-Do List every year on the same date.

T I P   When you select the Repeat Each Year check box, specify both start and end dates. Otherwise, the entry appears in the To-Do List all year.

Finally, select the **M**ake command button to add, in the order of its priority, the entry to the list and to return to the Appointment Scheduler window. To return to the Appointment Scheduler window without adding the entry, select the **C**ancel command button.

By following this procedure, you can add as many as 80 entries to the To-Do List. If you add more items than can be displayed in the To-Do List window, the list scrolls to make room for more entries.

Editing an Entry

To make any change to a to-do entry, follow one of these two procedures:

■ Position the mouse pointer on the entry you want to edit, and click the left or right mouse button.

■ Press the Tab key to make the To-Do List the active region. Press the up- and down-arrow keys to move the highlighted bar to the target entry, and press Enter.

Accessories displays a dialog box containing the following message:

```
Do you want to Edit or Delete this entry?
```

The dialog box contains four command buttons: Delete, Edit, Alter Note, and Cancel. Select the **E**dit command button. Desktop displays the New To-Do Entry dialog box containing the values for that entry. You then can make changes as necessary.

After you make all desired modifications, select the **M**ake command button to save the changes and return to the Appointment Scheduler window. To return to the Appointment Scheduler window without making any changes, select the **C**ancel command button.

Deleting an Entry

The only way you can indicate that a to-do entry has been accomplished is to delete the entry. Every time you complete a task or reach a goal you have added to the To-Do List (except yearly entries), you can use one of these methods to delete the entry:

■ Use the mouse or the cursor-movement keys to select the target entry. In the dialog box that appears, select the Delete command button.

■ Press the Tab key to make the Daily Scheduler the active region. Press the up- and down-arrow keys to move the highlighted bar to the appointment time. Select **T**o-Do on the horizontal menu bar and select **D**elete.

For Related Information

◄◄ "Entering Text," p. 569.

FROM HERE...

Printing

Accessories provides a number of alternatives for printing your schedule and to-do list. Accessories enables you to print daily, weekly, and monthly schedules and to-do lists.

To print the current day's schedule and list of things to do, you first must display the schedule in the Daily Scheduler region of the Appointment Scheduler window. Next, select **Print** from the **File** menu. Desktop displays the Print dialog box (see fig. 20.21).

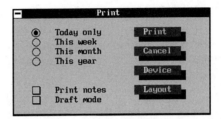

Fig. 20.21

The Print dialog box.

The Print dialog box contains these four option buttons:

■ *Today Only* (the default). Select this option to print the information for the day that is displayed (see fig. 20.22).

■ *This Week.* Desktop prints all the appointments for the next seven days. The report looks similar to the report shown in figure 20.23.

■ *This Month.* Desktop prints the information for the current month.

■ *This Year.* Desktop prints lists of all the scheduled daily appointments for the next year.

```
    December 2, 1992        Wednesday        December 2, 1992

                                '----------------------`
    Su Mo Tu We Th Fr Sa      ¦    ¦    ¦                        ¦
            '-`               ¦    ¦    ¦                        ¦
        1 ¦2¦ 3  4  5          ¦    ¦    ¦                        ¦
            '-'               ¦  '¦ 8:20a¦Breakfast—Marketing V  ¦
    6  7  8  9 10 11 12        ¦  +---+------------------¦
                                ¦  '¦ 9:00a¦                       ¦
                                ¦    ¦    ¦                        ¦
   13 14 15 16 17 18 19        ¦    ¦    ¦                        ¦
                                ¦  +---+------------------¦
                                ¦  ¦10:00a¦                       ¦
   20 21 22 23 24 25 26        ¦    ¦    ¦                        ¦
                                ¦    ¦    ¦                        ¦
```

Fig. 20.22

The current day's schedule and to-do list.

```
                                !     +— — —+— — — — — — — — — —!
     27 28 29 30 31             !     '!11:00a!Meeting re Personnel  !
                                !     !     !                        !
  '  — — — — — — — — —`  !     !     !                        !
  ! ! !                         ! +— — —+— — — — — — — — — —!
  ! ! 1!Buy Richie's present    !'!12:00p!                        !
  ! ! !                         ! !     !                        !
  ! ! 2!Sign lease              ! !     !                        !
  ! ! !                         ! +— — —+— — — — — — — — — —!
  ! ! 3!Sign payroll            ! ! 1:00p!Tennis at the Club      !
  ! ! !                         ! !     !                        !
  !N! 4!Review prospectus draft! !     !                        !
  ! ! !                         ! +— — —+— — — — — — — — — —!
  !N! 5!Review TV ads schedule  ! ! 2:00p!                        !
  ! ! !                         ! !     !                        !
  ! ! 6!Schedule a physical     ! !     !                        !
  ! ! !                         ! +— — —+— — — — — — — — — —!
  ! ! 7!Go to cleaners          ! ! 3:00p!                        !
  ! ! !                         ! !     !                        !
  ! ! 8!Pick up milk            ! !     !                        !
  ! ! !                         ! +— — —+— — — — — — — — — —!
  ! ! 9!                        ! ! 4:00p!Jog 2 Miles             !
  ! ! !                         ! !     !                        !
  ! !10!                        !'!     !                        !
  ! ! !                         ! +— — —+— — — — — — — — — —!
  ! !11!                        ! ! 5:00p!                        !
  ! ! !                         ! !     !                        !
  ! !12!                        ! !     !                        !
  ! ! !                         ! !     !                        !
  ! !13!                        ! !     !                        !
  ! ! !                         ! !     !                        !
  | |14|                        | |     |                        |
  | | |                         | |     |                        |
  | |15|                        | |     |                        |
  | | |                         | |     |                        |
  | |16|                        | |     |                        |
  '_____, '_____,'
```

Fig. 20.22

Continued.

```
    Monday November 30, 1992      Friday December 4, 1992
'_____`'_____`

|N% | 8:20a|Breakfast—Marketing VP||N% | 8:20a|Breakfast—Marketing VP|

|    |11:00a|Meeting re Personnel  ||   |11:00a|Meeting re Personnel   |

|    | 1:00p|Tennis at the Club    ||   | 1:00p|Tennis at the Club     |

|    | 4:00p|Jog 2 Miles           ||   | 4:00p|Jog 2 Miles            |

|    | 5:15p|Pick up children      ||   | 5:30p|Pick up children       |

|    |      |                      ||   |      |                       |

|    |      |                      ||   |      |                       |

|    |      |                      ||   |      |                       |

|    |      |                      ||   |      |                       |

|    |      |                      ||   |      |                       |
'_____''_____`


    Tuesday December 1, 1992     *Saturday December 5, 1992
'_____`'_____`'_____`

|N% | 8:20a|Breakfast—Marketing VP||  | 1:00p|Tennis at the Club     |

|    |10:00a|Conference Call—Japan ||  |      |                       |

|    |11:00a|Meeting re Personnel  ||  |      |                       |

|    | 1:00p|Tennis at the Club    ||  |      |                       |

|    | 1:45p|Conference Call       ||  |      |                       |

|    | 4:00p|Jog 2 Miles           ||  |      |                       |

|    |      |                      ||  |      |                       |

|    |      |                      ||  |      |                       |

|    |      |                      ||  |      |                       |

|    |      |                      ||  |      |                       |
'_____''_____`
```

Fig. 20.23

A weekly
schedule.

```
Wednesday December 2, 1992      *Sunday December 6, 1992

'_____`'_____`
¦                          ¦¦                          ¦
¦   ¦ 8:20a¦Breakfast—Marketing VP¦¦   ¦   1:00p¦Tennis at the Club   ¦
¦                          ¦¦   ¦                  ¦
¦   ¦11:00a¦Meeting re Personnel   ¦¦   ¦        ¦
¦                          ¦¦   ¦                  ¦
¦   ¦ 1:00p¦Tennis at the Club    ¦¦   ¦        ¦
¦                          ¦¦   ¦                  ¦
¦   ¦ 4:00p¦Jog 2 Miles           ¦¦   ¦        ¦
¦                          ¦¦   ¦                  ¦
¦   ¦ 4:45p¦Pick up children      ¦¦   ¦        ¦
¦   ¦      ¦                ¦¦   ¦        ¦
¦   ¦      ¦                ¦¦   ¦        ¦
¦   ¦      ¦                ¦¦   ¦        ¦
¦   ¦      ¦                ¦¦   ¦        ¦
¦   ¦      ¦                ¦¦   ¦        ¦
'_____''_____`

  Thursday December 3, 1992

'_____`_____`
¦N% ¦ 8:20a¦Breakfast—Marketing VP¦
¦                          ¦
¦   ¦11:00a¦Meeting re Personnel   ¦
¦                          ¦
¦   ¦ 1:00p¦Tennis at the Club    ¦
¦                          ¦
¦   ¦ 2:15p¦Meeting-Product Manager¦
¦                          ¦
¦   ¦ 4:00p¦Jog 2 Miles           ¦
¦   ¦      ¦                ¦
¦   ¦      ¦                ¦
¦   ¦      ¦                ¦
¦   ¦      ¦                ¦
¦   ¦      ¦                ¦
'_____`
```

Fig. 20.23

Continued.

In addition to these option buttons, the Print dialog box contains these check boxes:

- *Print Notes.* Accessories prints any notes attached to appointments or To-Do List entries. The notes are printed on separate sheets of paper.

- *Draft Mode.* Your printer prints in its fastest mode. (Not all printers support this option.)

The Scheduled Print dialog box contains these command buttons:

- *Print.* Accessories prints the schedule.

- *Cancel.* Accessories returns to the Appointment Schedule window without printing.

- *Device.* Accessories displays the Select Printer dialog box. Select an appropriate printer driver and an output device (LPT1, LPT2, LPT3, COM1, COM2, or Disk file), and select the **OK** button to return to the Schedule Print dialog box.

- *Layout.* Accessories displays the Schedule Printout Options dialog box (see fig. 20.24). Select a Form type (US Legal, US Letter, Half-Page, or Pocket). Select Mirror Image if you want to switch information on the left and right sides of the page. Select a Print Layout option (Daily: style A–Weekly Schedule). When all the options you want have been selected, choose the **OK** button to return to the Schedule Print dialog box.

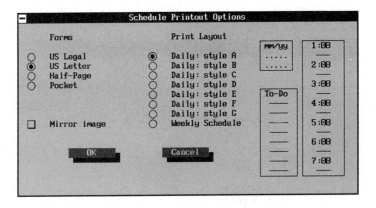

Fig. 20.24

The Schedule Printout Options dialog box.

After you make the appropriate settings, select the **Print** command button. Accessories sends the report to the specified device.

Saving the Schedule File

As in other Desktop Accessories application windows, file saving is normally automatic in an Appointment Scheduler window. Whenever you exit from the Appointment Scheduler window by pressing Esc (Exit) or F3 (Exit) or by clicking the close box, Accessories first saves the schedule file to disk.

As you work in an Appointment Scheduler window, making and editing appointments and adding, changing, and deleting to-do entries, Accessories saves the active schedule file every five minutes by default, regardless of whether you have made any changes. This feature is called *Autosave*. You can change this time interval between saves or even turn off Autosave.

To modify the save interval or to toggle off this feature, select **F**ile from the horizontal menu bar and then choose **A**utosave. Desktop displays the Automatic File Save dialog box (see fig. 20.25).

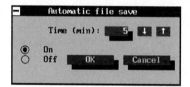

Fig. 20.25

The Automatic File Save dialog box.

To change the time interval between automatic saves, type a different number in the text box (the default entry is 5) and select the **OK** command button. To turn off the Autosave feature, select the Off option button and select the **OK** command button. Select **C**ancel to remove the dialog box without making any changes to the Autosave feature.

Accessories enables you to explicitly save a schedule file rather than wait for Autosave. Select **F**ile on the horizontal menu bar, and then choose **S**ave. Accessories displays the Save File to Disk dialog box (see fig. 20.26). Select the **S**ave command button. Accessories saves the file and returns to the Appointment Scheduler window.

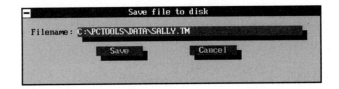

Fig. 20.26

The Save File to
Disk dialog box.

Exiting from Appointment Scheduler

To exit from an Appointment Scheduler window (which is the same as closing an Appointment Scheduler window), press Esc (Exit) or F3 (Exit), or click the application close box. Desktop saves any changes you have made and closes the window.

You also can use the Exit option on the **D**esktop Accessories menu to close a Notepads window; however, this option closes all open Accessories application windows.

Chapter Summary

This chapter examines how to use the Appointment Scheduler to maintain daily, weekly, and monthly appointment schedules. You learned how to make single and recurring appointments, set alarms, delete appointments, edit scheduled appointments, and add a note to an appointment entry. You also learned how to use the Appointment Scheduler to find previously scheduled appointments, the next appointment, and the next free appointment. In addition, you learned how to print daily, weekly, and monthly schedules, as well as how to display a graph that depicts five days' worth of appointments at a glance.

In addition to learning how to use the Appointment Scheduler for scheduling appointments, you learned how to use the program to create and maintain daily, weekly, and monthly prioritized to-do lists. And, as with appointment schedules, you learned how to print these lists.

You are now ready to use PC Tools Desktop Accessories Appointment Scheduler to help you manage your business day and keep your daily priorities in order. The next chapter examines how to use PC Tools macros.

Automating Your PC Using PC Tools Macros

Whenever you discover that you repeatedly perform a particular task on your computer, you should look for ways to get the computer to do more of the work. Without making mistakes, your computer can perform most tasks faster than you can. The Desktop Accessories Macro Editor enables you to take advantage of your computer's capacity to perform repetitive tasks quickly and correctly. Rather than type your return address every time you write a letter, for example, you can have your computer type the address for you.

A major selling point of stand-alone, single purpose programs is the wide variety of features and enhancements accessible with a single keystroke or special hot-key combinations. The Macro Editor enables you to create those same customized hotkeys—bold text by pressing Ctrl+B, for example—as well as other hotkeys customized for your unique tasks.

A *keyboard macro* is a string of characters that represents keystrokes. Every macro is stored, along with other macros, in a file on the disk and is available to be "played" by the press of a single key or key combination. This chapter examines how to define, activate, and deactivate keyboard macros intended for use with any program you run on your computer (assuming that PC Tools Desktop Accessories is running memory resident). This chapter explains how to use PC Tools macros to apply special printer attributes when you're printing from Accessories and how to automate tasks at a specific time by using macros with the Appointment Scheduler.

Defining a Macro

Creating a macro for later use in Desktop Accessories applications or other DOS programs is a two-step process. You first must define the macro in a Macro Editor file by typing, or recording, all the keystrokes that the macro will play. Then, you must "activate" the Macro Editor file or files that contain the macro definitions you want to use.

Desktop enables you to define keyboard macros in two ways:

■ You can type the macro keystrokes in a Macro Editor window.

■ You can use the Macro Editor's *learn mode* if you want Desktop to record your keystrokes automatically in a Macro Editor file.

 NOTE   Desktop macros are compatible with ProKey (Version 4.0 and later) macros, with the following qualifications:

■ *Supported keystrokes.* Not all keystrokes supported by ProKey are supported by Desktop. In other words, some keystrokes that can be used in ProKey cannot be stored for later playback in a Desktop keyboard macro.

■ *Redefinition of keyboard.* Desktop's Macro Editor cannot redefine the entire keyboard.

■ *Guarding macros.* Desktop does not support guarding macros or unique macro names, features found in ProKey.

Because Desktop Accessories must be resident in memory to play macros in other applications, you cannot play Accessories macros in Windows applications. Also, because you must make decisions during the operation of many PC Tools disk utilities, Accessories macros cannot be played in other PC Tools applications, except as discussed later in this chapter in the section "Setting Smart Alarms."

Understanding the Macro Editor Window

Before you can type a macro definition, you first must open a Macro Editor window. Display the **D**esktop Accessories main menu and choose **M**acro Editor. Accessories displays the File Load dialog box. Choose **N**ew to open a new file window or highlight the file you want to open and choose **O**K. The Macro Editor file appears in the Macro Editor window.

 NOTE Macro Editor files are actually Notepads files; however, these files use the file name extension PRO rather than TXT. (You cannot use a different file name extension for Macro Editor files.) Macro Editor's basic editing and file-saving features are the same as Notepads' features, including cut-and-paste and Autosave.

A Macro Editor window is similar in appearance to a Notepads window (see fig. 21.1). You can control the size and position of a Macro Editor window by using the same procedures you use to size and position a Notepads window. The only difference between a Macro Editor window and a Notepads window is the list of shortcut keys in the message bar. Table 21.1 lists the shortcut keys and other keystroke commands available in the Macro Editor.

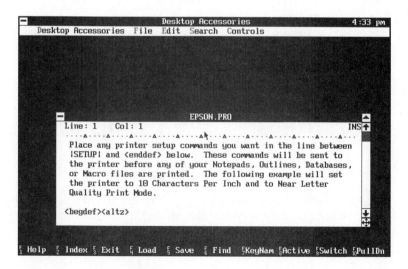

Fig. 21.1

A Macro Editor window containing the file EPSON.PRO.

Table 21.1 Keystroke Commands Available in the Macro Editor

Key	Name	Function
F1	Help	Displays the context-sensitive Help facility
F2	Index	Displays the Help facility index
F3	Exit	Cancels the current process or application (same as Esc)
F4	Load	Loads another Macro Editor window
F5	Save	Saves the current Macro Editor file to disk
F6	Find	Activates the find-and-replace feature
F7	KeyNam	Inserts the keystroke code of the following keystroke
F8	Active	Displays the Macros Active dialog box
F9	Switch	Switches the active window
F10 or Alt	PullDn	Activates the horizontal menu bar
Alt+Shift+=		While in learn mode, begins recording a macro definition
Alt+minus (-)		While in learn mode, ends recording a macro definition
Alt+space bar	System Control	Displays System Control pull-down menu
Esc	Cancel	Cancels current process or application (same as F3)

Understanding the Components of a Macro

A Macro Editor file can contain any number of macro definitions, limited only by the size of a Notepads file (about 60,000 characters). Every keyboard macro definition consists of the these four elements, described in the paragraphs that follow, in the order listed:

The <begdef> command

The macro key

The script

The <enddef> command

These components of a macro are explained in the following sections.

The <begdef> Command

The <begdef> command, which means "begin definition," starts every Macro Editor keyboard macro in a Macro Editor window and must begin in the first column of the window. You can type the command yourself or press Alt+plus (+)—the plus sign on the main keyboard, not on the numeric keypad—to enter the command.

The actual keystroke pattern for Alt+plus (+) requires that you hold down the Alt key, hold down the Shift key, and press =. *Do not simply press Alt and the plus sign from the numeric keypad.* To alleviate any confusion that this might cause, the key combination used to start a macro is conveyed as Alt+Shift+= throughout this chapter.

The Macro Key

The first *keystroke* listed after the <begdef> command is the one to which the macro is assigned; this keystroke is also called the *macro key*. You can assign a macro to any key on the keyboard; however, you cannot use the Shift, Alt, or Ctrl key alone. You can assign a macro to most keys pressed in combination with the Shift, Alt, or Ctrl keys (see table 21.2 for a complete list).

> When creating macros, the word *keystroke* means a single key or a combination of keys pressed together in a sequence.
>
> **T I P**

Some keys are displayed on-screen when you press them, and others are not. When you press the letter *A*, for example, Accessories displays an A on-screen. When you press the F1 key, however, Accessories does not display F1; rather, Accessories displays a help screen. To use a displayable keyboard character as a macro key, you must enclose the character in left and right angular brackets (<a>, for example).

Accessories uses special codes to represent keystrokes that don't normally display characters on-screen. Pressing Ctrl+E in Accessories Notepads, for example, doesn't cause a character to be displayed. To assign a macro to the Ctrl+E key combination, you must insert the special code <ctrle> immediately after the <begdef> command. The available codes are listed in table 21.2.

Table 21.2 Keystroke Codes Valid in Accessories Keyboard Macros			
Key Alone	**With Shift**	**With Alt**	**With Ctrl**
From the Main Keypad			
a	A	<alta>	<ctrla>
b	B	<altb>	<ctrlb>
c	C	<altc>	
d	D	<altd>	<ctrld>
e	E	<alte>	<ctrle>
f	F	<altf>	<ctrlf>
g	G	<altg>	<ctrlg>
h	H	<alth>	<ctrlh>
i	I	<alti>	<ctrli>
j	J	<altj>	<ctrlj>
k	K	<altk>	<ctrlk>
l	L	<altl>	<ctrll>
m	M	<altm>	<ctrlm>
n	N	<altn>	<ctrln>
o	O	<alto>	<ctrlo>
p	P	<altp>	<ctrlp>
q	Q	<altq>	
r	R	<altr>	<ctrlr>
s	S	<alts>	
t	T	<altt>	<ctrlt>
u	U	<altu>	<ctrlu>
v	V	<altv>	<ctrlv>
w	W	<altw>	<ctrlw>

Key Alone	With Shift	With Alt	With Ctrl
x	X	<altx>	<ctrlx>
y	Y	<alty>	<ctrly>
z	Z	<altz>	<ctrlz>
1	!	<alt1>	
2	@	<alt2>	<ctrl2>
3	#	<alt3>	
4	$	<alt4>	
5	%	<alt5>	
6	^	<alt6>	<ctrl6>
7	&	<alt7>	
8	*	<alt8>	
9	(	<alt9>	
0	)	<alt0>	
F1	<shiftf1>	<altf1>	<ctrlf1>
F3	<shiftf3>	<altf3>	<ctrlf3>
F4	<shiftf4>	<altf4>	<ctrlf4>
F5	<shiftf5>	<altf5>	<ctrlf5>
F6	<shiftf6>	<altf6>	<ctrlf6>
F7	<shiftf7>	<altf7>	<ctrlf7>
F8	<shiftf8>	<altf8>	<ctrlf8>
F9	<shiftf9>	<altf9>	<ctrlf9>
<desk>	<shiftf10>	<altf10>	<ctrlf10>
-	_	<enddef>	<vfld>
=	+	<begdef>	
[	{		<ctrl[>
]	}		<ffld>
;	:		
'	"		
\	|		<ctrl\>
,	<		
.	>		

continues

Table 21.2 Continued

Key Alone	With Shift	With Alt	With Ctrl
/	?		
<esc>			
<tab>	<shifttab>		
<bks>			<ctrlbks>
<enter>			<ctrlenter>
*			<ctrlprt>
<home>			<ctrlhome>
<up>			
<pgup>			<ctrlpgup>
<lft>			<ctrlleft>
<rgt>			<ctrlrgt>
<end>			<ctrlend>
<dn>			
<pgdn>			<ctrlpgdn>
<ins>			
<del>			
From the Numeric Keypad			
<k9>			
<k8>			
<k7>			
<k6>			
<k5>			
<k4>			
<k3>			
<k2>			
<k1>			
<k0>			
<k.>			
<k+>			
<k->			

T I P

You can assign several macros to the same keystroke combination, such as Ctrl+E, if each macro is in a separate Macro Editor file and only one of those files is active at a time.

The Script

The *script* is the set of actual keystrokes you want Accessories to execute when you run the macro. Simply type the displayable keyboard characters, and for nondisplayable characters, use the keystroke codes listed in table 21.2 to represent the keystrokes you want the macro to execute.

Although you can type the keystroke codes, Accessories provides an easier method. Just press the keystroke itself; Accessories inserts the proper code. This feature doesn't work, however, for the Alt key, for the function keys (F1 through F10), or for a keystroke that performs a Macro Editor function. For these keys, you first press F7 (KeyNam) and then press the keystroke you want included in the macro. For example, pressing Enter normally moves the cursor to the next line of the Macro Editor file. If you are defining a macro and want to include the keystroke code for Enter, first press F7 (KeyNam) and then press Enter. Desktop types the code <enter> in the script.

T I P

No harm is done if you press F7 unnecessarily. If you are not sure whether a keystroke will appear, press F7.

The <enddef> Command

The <enddef> command marks the end of every keyboard macro definition. You can type the command or press Alt+ minus (-)—the minus sign on the main keyboard, not on the numeric keypad—to enter the command automatically.

Typing a Macro

You can type as many macros in a file as you want—as many as about 60,000 characters per file. Every macro definition must begin in the first column of the Macro Editor window. Accessories enables you to create multiple Macro Editor files, and any or all of them can be active together, as you learn later.

> **T I P**
>
> Try grouping all macros relating to the same type of task in a single Macro Editor file. If you create macros to enter repetitive text in a database of customers and the items they purchase, for example, keep all those text macros in one file.

Suppose that you want to create a macro that types the name Englebert Humperdink and presses Enter every time you press Ctrl+E. To create this macro, follow these steps:

1. Open a Macro Editor file and press Alt+Shift+= to enter the command <begdef>. Alternatively, type **<begdef>**.

2. Press Ctrl+E. Desktop inserts the code <ctrle> to the right of the <begdef> command.

3. Type **Englebert Humperdink**.

4. To add the <enter> code to the definition, press F7 (KeyNam) and then press Enter.

5. Press Alt+minus (-) to enter the command <enddef>, which ends the definition. Alternatively, type **<enddef>**.

The completed macro definition is shown in figure 21.2.

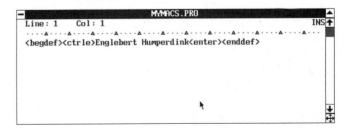

Fig. 21.2

Typing a macro definition.

Not all keystrokes can be used in an Accessories macro. You cannot, for example, use the hotkey for activating Accessories (Ctrl+space bar) or the hot key for activating PC Tools Desktop (Ctrl+Esc). A special macro code, <desk>, is provided, however, for invoking Desktop Accessories. Include this code in a macro when you want the macro to display the Desktop Accessories main menu. When you are recording a macro, Accessories records pressing the F10 key as <desk>. The keystrokes in table 21.2 represent the text and the keystrokes you can include in an Accessories macro. These keystrokes work in the active DOS or Accessories application.

NOTE To include a keystroke code that does not automatically appear on-screen—<pgdn>, for instance—you can type the angular brackets and keystroke name as listed in Table 21.2, or you can press F7 (KeyNam) and then press the key or keystroke combination.

T I P

Feel free to type explanations, instructions, or any other helpful annotations for your macros before or after you type the actual macro definition. Accessories looks for the macro to begin in the first column with <begdef> and runs the macro until encountering <enddef>. Any other text is ignored. Accessories also ignores carriage returns and tabs within the macro. Use these elements to space your macros so that they are easier to understand.

Thoughtful planning and adequate testing are two key elements in creating effective keyboard macros. Have a clear idea of the task you want the macro to perform before typing the macro. Writing down the keystrokes you want to include in the macro, especially if it is lengthy, is also recommended. Occasionally, a misplaced macro keystroke can have disastrous results, so after you define and activate the macro, test it on a sample file—not on real data.

Recording a Macro by Using Learn Mode

Assuming that Accessories is running memory-resident, you can automate the macro-definition process by recording macro keystrokes as you perform the operation you want the macro to execute. Sometimes this procedure is called *teaching* the macro how to perform the operation. Desktop calls this procedure *learn mode*.

To activate learn mode, open an Accessories Macro Editor window, select Controls from the horizontal menu bar, and then select Learn Mode from the Controls pull-down menu. Accessories returns to the Macro Editor window. The next time you display the Controls menu, Accessories displays a check mark next to the Learn Mode option. Then, even though you may close the Macro Editor window, the Accessories Macro Editor is still in learn mode. After you turn on learn mode, this mode remains active as you run Accessories, other PC Tools programs, and other DOS programs. Desktop does not, however, begin recording macros automatically.

To start recording a macro, press Alt+Shift+=, and then press the keystroke to which you want the macro assigned. This macro keystroke must be a function key or a keystroke combination using Alt or Ctrl. Refer to table 21.2 for the list of possible macro keys. Desktop begins to record your keystrokes in a memory buffer.

NOTE   If the cursor in the application you're running appears as an underline, Desktop changes the cursor to a block shape, indicating that Desktop is recording a macro.

NOTE   Most of the DOS applications you use regularly include a macro feature. The advantage of using the Accessories Macro Editor whenever possible is that you need only learn one macro editor rather than a different macro feature for each program.

Next, execute the operation or command you want the Macro Editor to learn. Accessories records the keystroke code for every keystroke you press. Keep in mind that most, but not all, keystrokes are supported by the Macro Editor (refer to table 21.2). Accessories ignores unsupported keystrokes. When you're finished, press Alt+minus (–) to turn off the recorder and hot key back into Accessories.

Accessories copies the recorded macros into a Macro Editor file named LEARN.PRO. To toggle off learn mode, open a Macro Editor window, select Controls from the horizontal menu bar, and select Learn Mode from the Controls pull-down menu. Accessories turns off learn mode and returns to the Macro Editor window. You can open a Macro Editor window and display the LEARN.PRO file. Then use the Clipboard to cut and paste the newly recorded macros to a new or existing Macro Editor file.

T I P

The Alt+Shift+= keystroke used to begin recording a macro in learn mode is interpreted by WordPerfect 5.1 for DOS as Alt+=, the command that Accesses the pull-down menus. If you need to use learn mode to record a macro in WordPerfect, press Alt+Shift+= before you launch WordPerfect. Execute your task in WordPerfect, and then end the macro by pressing Alt+minus (-). Return to Desktop Accessories and open the LEARN.PRO file to view your new macro. Edit the macro to remove the unnecessary keystrokes at the beginning, including WP, <enter>, and any others not needed for the task.

Suppose, for example, that you are working in Lotus 1-2-3 and want to create a macro, Alt+S, that saves a worksheet file to disk and replaces an existing file on the disk by the same name. First, hot key into Accessories and display a Macro Editor window. Select **C**ontrols, and then select **L**earn Mode. Hot key back to 1-2-3. You are ready to begin recording the macro.

To start recording a macro, press Alt+Shift+=. The cursor becomes block shaped. Then press Alt+S, the keystroke to which you want to assign the macro. Accessories begins to record your keystrokes in a memory buffer. Press the necessary keystrokes for saving a worksheet file to disk when a file by the same name already exists on the disk. Finally, to stop the recorder, press Alt+minus (-).

After you turn off the keystroke recorder, return to Accessories and display the Macro Editor file LEARN.PRO. This file then contains the Alt+S macro you recorded from within 1-2-3 (see fig. 21.3).

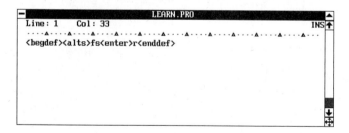

Fig. 21.3

The LEARN.PRO file containing the Alt+S macro.

NOTE

If you use learn mode to create a macro to use in Desktop Accessories, you must exit then restart Accessories if you want the learned macro to be recorded in the LEARN.PRO file.

T I P Some keystrokes are not recorded in the LEARN.PRO file even though you were able to successfully complete the task in the DOS application. This problem may occur if you need to use the Esc key, for example. Try typing the missing keystrokes directly into the macro in the LEARN.PRO file.

Be sure to save the macros you create using learn mode into another Macro Editor file. The next time you use learn mode, the macros you create are added to the LEARN.PRO file. You cannot create another macro assigned to the same macro key until the first macro is deleted.

Activating and Deactivating Macro Files

After you type or record macro definitions in a Macro Editor file, you must activate the file before you can use the macros. When the file you want to activate is displayed, press the shortcut key F8 (Active) or select **F**ile from the horizontal menu bar and then **M**acro Activation. Accessories displays the Macros Active dialog box (see fig. 21.4).

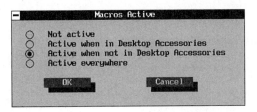

Fig. 21.4

The Macros Active dialog box.

The Macros Active dialog box contains the following options:

- *Not Active.* This option is the default for every Macro Editor file. While this option is selected, the macros in the file are not active; pressing the respective macro keys does not play the macros in the file.

- *Active When in Desktop Accessories.* Choose this option to activate macros intended for use only in Desktop Accessories. For example, the printer-control macro files included on the PC Tools distribution disks (discussed more fully later in the chapter) contain macro definitions intended for use only in Accessories applications. When you select this option, Accessories activates the macros while you are using Desktop, but the program turns them off when you hot key back to a DOS application or run another PC Tools program.

■ *Active When Not in Desktop Accessories.* Choose this option for macros you want to use in another PC Tools program or DOS application but not in an Accessories application. The Alt+S macro defined in the section "Recording a Macro By Using Learn Mode," for example, is intended for use in only a 1-2-3 spreadsheet. This macro cannot perform its intended function if you execute it from an Accessories application.

■ *Active Everywhere.* Choose this option for macros that can be used in Accessories applications and in other programs. A macro to type your name, for example, is useful in any application in Accessories, in another word processor, in a spreadsheet program, and so on.

> You can use Accessories macros in other DOS applications only if Desktop is running as memory resident.   **T I P**

After you choose the desired option, select the **OK** button. Accessories returns to the Macro Editor window. To return to the Macro Editor window without making any changes in the Macros Active dialog box, select **C**ancel.

After you activate a Macro Editor file, the macros in the file are saved in memory and are available for your use. Each time you start Accessories, any Macro Editor files designated as active are again saved into memory. To use the Alt+S macro, for example, press Alt+S while working in a 1-2-3 worksheet file. To cancel the execution of a macro before it is completed, press Esc.

> If your macro does not run after activating the Macro Editor file, return to the Macro Editor window and select **D**eactivate All Macros from the **C**ontrols menu, and then follow the instructions to activate the Macro Editor file again.   **T I P**

Activated Macro Editor files remain active until you deactivate them. You can deactivate an individual Macro Editor file by using the Not Active option in the Macros Active dialog box. To deactivate all active Macro Editor files, open a Macro Editor window, select **C**ontrols from the horizontal menu bar, and then select **D**eactivate All Macros. Accessories turns off all active Macro Editor files.

T I P   You can have several Macro Editor files active at the same time. When you work with multiple files, however, be sure the files do not contain macros that use the same macro key. If the same macro key is used in more than one file, the macro in the file activated first is the macro that works.

The **D**eactivate All Macros command does not erase any Macro Editor files from the disk. Instead, this command erases the active macros held in the Accessories macro memory buffer.

Adjusting Playback Delay

By default, Accessories plays macros with a 1/18-second delay between keystrokes. This time between keystrokes is called the *playback delay*. Occasionally, the default playback delay is too fast for a particular application to process. The application may seem to ignore a portion of the macro or may cause your computer to beep unexpectedly while the macro plays. If such a problem occurs, check first to be sure that the macro contains the correct keystrokes. After you determine that the macro is correct, resolve the problem by increasing the playback delay.

To change the playback delay, follow these steps:

1. Display a Macro Editor window, select **C**ontrols from the horizontal menu, and then choose **P**layback Delay. Accessories displays the Macro/Clipboard Playback Delay dialog box (see fig. 21.5).

Fig. 21.5

The Macro/ Clipboard Playback Delay dialog box.

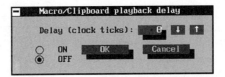

2. In the Delay text box, type a number representing the additional number of 1/18-second periods you want to elapse between keystrokes. The default value, 0, indicates a 1/18-second delay. Press 1 for a 2/18-second delay, press 2 for a 3/18-second delay, and so on.

3. Select the ON option to turn on the additional playback delay.

4. Select the **O**K button to save the new setting to disk. The next time you run a macro, Accessories uses the new playback delay time between keystrokes.

Using Special Macro Techniques

You can assign virtually any task to macros. This section describes a few ways to take advantage of Accessories macros, including how to use Accessories macros for printer control, how to start other programs by using macros, and how to run tasks at preset times by using macros with the Desktop Appointment Scheduler.

Desktop Accessories enables you to use a number of special techniques in the program's macros. You can link or chain macros, access the system date and time, add timed delays to macros, and create fill-in-the-blank forms. This section also describes how to use these techniques.

Using Macros for Printer Control

Most IBM PC-compatible printers can enhance printed characters in a number of ways. Dot-matrix printers, for example, usually can print characters underlined, in boldface type, in italics, in near-letter-quality print, and in different typeface sizes. Laser printers offer many additional features, such as the capacity to print various fonts (Courier, Times Roman, or Helvetica, for example). Accessories macros enable you to make use of these special printing attributes when you print Notepads files, Outlines files, or Databases reports. Macros that control special printing attributes are *printer-control macros.*

Controlling your printer through Desktop macros involves four steps:

1. Create a Macro Editor file containing printer-control macros capable of sending the appropriate software commands to your printer in order to turn print enhancements on and off.

2. Activate the Macro Editor file that contains the printer control macros.

3. Use the printer-control macros to embed in the Notepads, Outlines, or Databases form file special codes that invoke the correct printer-control commands during printing.

4. Print the file from Notepads, Outlines, or Databases.

Desktop provides two methods for creating a Macro Editor file that contains the printer-control macros for your printer: you can define every printer-control macro yourself, or you can customize one of the sample Macro Editor files distributed on the PC Tools program disks. The easier of the two methods is simply to modify a sample file.

PC Tools 8 is distributed with four sample Macro Editor files, each containing printer-control macros and each intended for use with a particular brand of printer:

Macro Editor file	Printer Group
EPSON.PRO	Epson dot-matrix printers
HPLJF.PRO	Hewlett-Packard LaserJet series laser printers
PANA.PRO	Panasonic dot-matrix printers
PROPTR.PRO	IBM Proprinter dot-matrix printers

These four groups represent the majority of printers used with personal computers. If you have another type of printer, it probably is capable of emulating a printer in one of these four groups. Even within these groups, however, different printer models support a variety of attributes. Accessories, therefore, enables you to customize printer-control macros to meet the exact specifications of the printers connected to your system.

To customize one of the provided Macro Editor files, load the file into a Macro Editor window. Figure 21.6, for example, shows a portion of the PANA.PRO Macro Editor file, which contains printer-control macros intended for use with Panasonic dot-matrix printers.

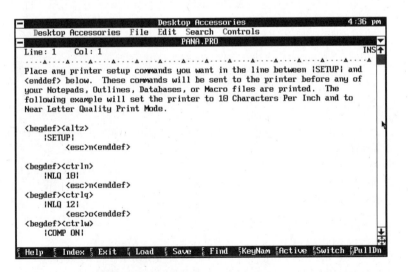

Fig. 21.6

Several of the macros in the PANA.PRO file.

Consult your printer's user manual for a list of the software commands that turn printing attributes on and off. Every command consists of a string of ASCII characters sent to the printer. Most such commands begin with the Esc character (ASCII decimal 27) and often are referred to as *escape codes*.

Accessories printer-control macros have the following special format:

<begdef><*macrokey*>|*attribute*|*printer command*<enddef>

Replace *macrokey* with the keystroke you want to use to turn on or off the printing attribute. Replace *attribute* with text you want to appear in the file whenever you press the macro keystroke. (This chapter refers to this text as the *attribute name*.) Replace *printer command* with the software command that turns on or off the desired printer attribute. The following line, for example, defines a macro you can use to turn on a Panasonic printer's NLQ mode at ten characters per inch:

<begdef><ctrln>|NLQ 10|<esc>n<enddef>

The preceding sample macro begins when you press Ctrl+N (<begdef><ctrln>). Near letter-quality 10 cpi text (|NLQ 10|) is desired. This command is transmitted to the printer by the escape code sequence, Esc N (<esc>n), and then the macro ends (<enddef>).

This macro is defined in the Macro Editor file PANA.PRO. Table 21.3 provides a complete list of the macros included in the PANA.PRO Macro Editor file. (**Note:** This list is representative of the macros included in the other three Macro Editor files provided with PC Tools 8. The comments added to the right of every macro explain that macro's purpose.) The discussions that follow assume that you have a Panasonic printer and have activated the Macro Editor file PANA.PRO, which contains these macros.

Table 21.3 Macros Included in the PANA.PRO Macro Editor File

Macro Code	Description
<begdef><altz>|SETUP|<esc>n<enddef>	* Printer setup
<begdef><ctrln>|NLQ 10|<esc>n<enddef>	* NLQ mode, 10 cpi
<begdef><ctrlq>|NLQ 12|<esc>o<enddef>	* NLQ mode, 12 cpi
<begdef><ctrlw>|COMP ON|<ctrlO><enddef>	* Compressed on
<begdef><ctrlv>|COMP OFF|<ctrlR><enddef>	* Compressed off
<begdef><ctrlx>|EXP ON|<esc>W1<enddef>	* Wide on
<begdef><ctrlz>|EXP OFF|<esc>W0<enddef>	* Wide off
<begdef><ctrle>|12 DFT|<esc>M<enddef>	* Draft mode, 12 cpi

continues

Table 21.3 Continued

Macro Code	Description
\<begdef>\<ctrlp> |10 DFT| \<esc>P\<enddef>	* Draft mode, 10 cpi
\<begdef>\<ctrlb> |BOLD ON| \<esc>E\<enddef>	* Bold on
\<begdef>\<ctrlh> |BOLD OFF| \<esc>F\<enddef>	* Bold off
\<begdef>\<ctrll> |DBL ON| \<esc>G\<enddef>	* Double on
\<begdef>\<ctrlk> |DBL OFF| \<esc>H\<enddef>	* Double off
\<begdef>\<ctrls> |SUP ON| \<esc>S0\<enddef>	* Superscript on
\<begdef>\<ctrla> |SUP OFF| \<esc>T\<enddef>	* Superscript off
\<begdef>\<ctrlt> |SUB ON| \<esc>S1\<enddef>	* Subscript on
\<begdef>\<ctrlr> |SUB OFF| \<esc>T\<cnddef>	* Subscript off
\<begdef>\<ctrlu> |UND ON| \<esc>-1\<enddef>	* Underline on
\<begdef>\<ctrly> |UND OFF| \<esc>-0\<enddef>	* Underline off
\<begdef>\<ctrli> |ITL ON| \<esc>4\<enddef>	* Italics on
\<begdef>\<ctrlj> |ITL OFF| \<esc>5\<enddef>	* Italics off
\<begdef>\<ctrlf> |PRO ON| \<esc>p1\<enddef>	* Proportional on
\<begdef>\<ctrlg> |PRO OFF| \<esc>p0\<enddef>	* Proportional off

The first macro in this list includes a setup command to initialize your printer (that is, to send printer-control commands to your printer to activate the printing attributes you want to use for normal text). Accessories automatically sends to the printer any software commands included in the setup macro every time you print a file in Notepads, Outlines, or Databases. Accessories sends the printer-control command before sending any text to the printer. (You don't need to include the setup attribute name |SETUP| in the document you are printing.) If you decide that you want to modify the setup command, place the appropriate printer-control command between |SETUP| and \<enddef>. The setup command shown in this list causes a Panasonic printer to turn on Near Letter Quality (NLQ) at 10 characters per inch.

The second step in using printer-control macros is to activate the Macro Editor file that contains them. Display the file in a Macro Editor window, select File from the horizontal menu, and then select Macro Activation to display the Macros Active dialog box (refer to fig. 21.4). Select the second option, Active When in Desktop Accessories.

After you activate the Macro Editor file that contains the printer-control macros for your printer, you are ready to put the macros to use. Open a Notepads, Outlines, or Databases Form file, and position the cursor where you want the printing attribute to begin. Then execute the corresponding macro. Accessories inserts the attribute name into the file at the cursor. Later, when you send the file to your printer, Desktop replaces the attribute name with software commands that cause the printer to apply the attribute. The attribute name is not printed.

Suppose, for example, that you created the Notepads file SALES.TXT, shown in figure 21.7. When printing the file, you want the printer to print in compressed mode (17 characters per inch [cpi]). You also want the printer to underline the column headings.

```
┌─────────────────────────── SALES.TXT ──────────────────────────▲▶
│ Line: 1    Col: 1                                            INS│
│····▲···▲···▲···▲···▲···▲···▲···▲···▲···▲···▲···▲···▲···▲··     │
│     Annual Report - Fiscal Year 1992                           │
│     Custom Computer Consultants, Inc.                          │
│                                                                │
│            1st Quarter    2nd Quarter    3rd Quarter    4th Quarter │
│                                                                │
│     Joe      $19,250       $18,211       $20,345       $15,987 │
│     Sally    $22,345       $21,567       $18,432       $16,765 │
│     Ralph    $21,888       $23,555       $17,988       $17,232 │
│                                                                │
│              $63,483       $63,333       $56,765       $49,984 ▼│
└────────────────────────────────────────────────────────────────┘
```

Fig. 21.7

The Notepads file SALES.TXT.

To print in compressed mode, bold the report title, and underline the column headings, follow these steps:

1. Position the cursor on the first character in the file and press Ctrl+W, the macro that turns on compressed mode. Accessories inserts |COMP ON|.

2. Turn off compressed mode at the end of the file. Move the cursor to the right of the last character in the file and press Ctrl+V; Accessories inserts |COMP OFF|.

3. To bold the report title, move to the beginning of the file and press Ctrl+B to invoke the begin-bold macro (see the preceding list of macros contained in PANA.PRO). Accessories inserts |BOLD ON|.

4. Press End to move to the end of the title and turn bold off by pressing Ctrl+H. Accessories inserts |BOLD OFF|.

5. To underline the column headings in SALES.TXT, position the cursor at the first column heading, and press Ctrl+U to invoke the begin-underline macro. Accessories inserts |UND ON| at the cursor.

6. Position the cursor to the right of the heading and press Ctrl+Y, the stop-underline macro. Accessories inserts ¦UND OFF¦.

7. Continue turning underline on and off at the beginning and end of each month name across the top of the columns.

Figure 21.8 shows the document after printer-control characters have been added.

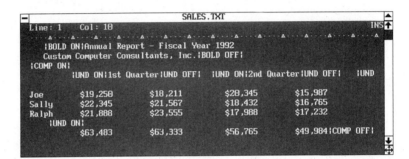

T I P   Accessories relates margins to number of characters. Using compressed text does not change the number of characters. You must change the margins by choosing **C**ontrols and then **P**age Layout, and then enter the number of compressed characters you want printed on each line. An easy way to calculate the new number is to multiply the number of 10 cpi characters by 1.5 for compressed characters.

The last step in printing with special attributes is to send the file to the printer. Figure 21.9 depicts a printout of the Notepads file SALES.TXT shown in figure 21.8.

Annual Report - Fiscal Year 1992

Custom Computer Consultants, Inc.

	1st Quarter	2nd Quarter	3rd Quarter	4th Quarter
Joe	$19,250	$18,211	$20,345	$15,987
Sally	$22,345	$21,567	$18,432	$16,765
Ralph	$21,888	$23,555	$17,988	$17,232
	$63,483	$63,333	$56,765	$49,984

Overriding an Active Macro

When activated, Accessories macros normally override all other commands that use the same keystrokes. Many DOS programs, for example,
use the F1 key to summon on-line help. If you assign an Accessories
macro to F1, pressing this key invokes the macro rather than on-line
help. Occasionally, you may want to turn off an active Accessories
macro temporarily so that the keystrokes to which you assigned the
macro revert to their original function without your needing to deactivate the entire Macro Editor file. This action is called *overriding* an active macro.

To override an active macro, simply type the accent grave (`) charac-
ter just before pressing the keystroke or keystrokes to which the macro
is assigned. (The accent-grave character shares a key with the tilde [~]
character.) If you follow this procedure, you still can use F1 to access a
program's on-line help even though you have defined and activated a
macro assigned to F1. Each time you want to use F1 to access Help, you
must first press the ` key.

If you need to type an ` while a Macro Editor file is active, press the
key twice.

T I P

For Related Information

◀◀ "Setting the Page Layout," p. 589.

◀◀ "Printing a Notepads File," p. 589.

◀◀ "Printing an Outline," p. 623.

◀◀ "Printing a Database," p. 664.

FROM HERE...

Linking Macros

Occasionally, you might create a macro that incorporates keystrokes
already existing in another macro. Rather than retyping the same keystrokes, you can include in the script of the second macro the keystroke that invokes the first macro. You might think of this process as
embedding one macro inside another macro.

For example, you may have already created the macro Ctrl+E that types *Englebert Humperdink* and presses Enter. Now, suppose that you are creating the macro Ctrl+H to type the following:

Englebert Humperdink
President, Chief Executive Officer

Use the following macro definition:

<begdef><ctrlh><ctrle>President, Chief Executive Officer<enddef>

Enter the macro key within angular brackets wherever you want it to execute. You cannot, however, invoke another macro from within a printer-control macro. Make sure that all linked macros are activated.

Inserting System Date and Time

Occasionally, you may want to retrieve the current date and time from your computer system. Perhaps your word processor doesn't already possess this feature, or it is too cumbersome to use.

To display the system date in the format *dd-mm-yy*, include the macro code <date>. To display the system time in the format *hh:mm* A.M. or P.M., include the macro code <time>. The following macro, for example, assigns the system date to the keystroke Alt+D:

<begdef><altd><date><enddef>

Pausing a Macro

Sometimes, you may want a macro to pause for a specified amount of time before continuing. For example, you might want to create a demo that displays a series of screens on your computer. You can use a Desktop macro to orchestrate this demo, pausing for a specified number of seconds at every screen. To cause an Accessories macro to pause, add this code at the point in the macro where the pause should occur:

<cmd>d*n*<enter>

The <cmd> code instructs Accessories to treat the next entries as commands instead of keystrokes. Replace *n* with the amount of time you want the macro to pause, and type the time in the format *hh:mm:ss.t* (hours, minutes, seconds, and tenths of seconds). When you type numbers without a colon, Accessories assumes that you mean seconds (rather than hours or minutes).

You must type the code <cmd>; no keystroke command is available for generating this code.

The following macro (invoked when you press Ctrl+D) displays a series of three text screens and pauses for 30 seconds on every screen:

```
<begdef><ctrld>type screen1.txt<enter>
<cmd>d30<enter>type screen2.txt<enter>
<cmd>d30<enter>type screen3.txt<enter><enddef>
```

Creating Fill-in-the-Blanks Macros

In addition to inserting a timed pause, with Desktop you can insert a delay in a macro for the purpose of accepting input from the user. For example, you might want to create a questionnaire that types itself out on the screen and pauses whenever a response must be typed. Desktop's fill-in-the-blanks macros enable you to create such a tool. You can create *fixed-length* blanks or *variable-length* blanks. The next two sections explain these two types of fill-in-the-blanks macros.

Fixed-Length Blanks

To create a fixed-length blank in a macro, insert this code:

```
<ffld>example<ffld>
```

When you are defining a fixed-length blank, you can type **<ffld>** (fixed-field), or you can press Ctrl+] to enter the code automatically. Replace *example* with a string of characters equal in number to the field length you want the macro to accept. Which characters you use isn't important; only the number of characters is significant.

When you run a macro that contains a fixed-length blank, Accessories pauses at the blank until the user types the same number of characters found in the *example*. After the user types the appropriate number of characters, the macro continues.

Variable-Length Blanks

You can create variable-length blanks in a similar manner to fixed-length blanks. Type the following code:

```
<vfld>..<vfld>
```

The code causes the macro to pause and accept characters typed by the user. Unlike fixed-length blanks, which pause until the user types a certain number of characters, variable-length fields pause until the user presses Enter.

When you are defining a variable-length blank, you can type the code <*vfld*> (variable-field) or press Ctrl+minus (–) to enter the code automatically.

Setting Smart Alarms

In Chapter 20, "Managing Your Appointment Schedule," you learned how to use your computer as a "smart" alarm clock to help you remember scheduled appointments. This section explains how to set a smart alarm, an alarm that causes Accessories to run a program, load a file, or run a macro at a preset time.

Running a Program at a Preset Time

To run a program at a preset time on a particular date, first open an Appointment Scheduler window and display in the Daily Scheduler the list of appointments for the date in question. Use the cursor-movement keys or the mouse to move the highlighted bar into the Daily Scheduler portion of the window, and highlight the appointment line nearest to the time at which you want to run the program. Press Enter or click the mouse button. Accessories displays the Make Appointment dialog box.

Fill in the Make Appointment dialog box as described in Chapter 20, with one exception. When you type the entry in the Description text box, use the following format:

note | program parameters

Replace *note* with any text you want to display when the alarm goes off if you want Accessories to pause for input from you. Replace *program* with the file name and path specification of the executable program or batch file you want Accessories to run (include the EXE, COM, or BAT file name extension). Replace *parameters* with any start-up parameters needed to run the specified program. Select the **M**ake command button to save the appointment settings and return to the Appointment Scheduler window.

When the appointment time arrives, Accessories causes the computer to sound an alarm and displays a box that contains this message:

```
note: Press [OK] to run program
```

In this message, *note* is the text you typed in the note section of the Description text box, and *program* is the file name you typed in the program section of the Description text box. The message box contains three command boxes: Snooze, OK, and Cancel. Select **OK** to run the program. Select **S**nooze to clear the message box from the screen and cause Desktop to sound the alarm again in five minutes. Select **C**ancel to turn off the alarm.

If you leave blank the note section of the Description text box, Accessories runs the program at the appointed time without displaying the message dialog box.

Suppose, for example, that you want to back up the contents of your hard disk to your tape drive every night at midnight (refer to Chapter 7, "Protecting Your Data with Central Point Backup," for a complete discussion of CP Backup). Load your schedule file into an Appointment Scheduler window and highlight the appointment nearest midnight. Type **12:00a** in the Time text box. Assuming that CPBACKUP.EXE is stored in the PCTOOLS directory on drive C and that you have created a setup file for Central Point Backup named DAILY, type this entry in the Description text box:

    |CPBACKUP.EXE DAILY

Select the Every Day and Alarm On Time options. Select **M**ake to save these settings.

After you set the alarm to run Central Point Backup at midnight, you can leave your computer running and go to bed. When 12 a.m. arrives, Desktop runs CP Backup, using the parameters found in DAILY. CP Backup backs up your hard disk as you sleep. ***Note:*** you can schedule backups from within CP Backup. (Refer to Chapter 7 for more details.)

Loading a File into a Notepad at a Preset Time

In addition to running a program at a preset time, you can load a Notepads file at a preset time. For example, you might set an alarm that alerts you to a meeting and displays the meeting's agenda on-screen. Display the Make Appointment dialog box. Set an alarm as described in Chapter 20, "Managing Your Appointment Schedule," and type an entry in the Description text box. Use the following format:

    note|*filename*

Replace *note* with any text you want to display when the alarm goes off. Replace *filename* with the file name of the Notepads file you want Desktop to load when the alarm goes off. If the appointment has an attached note, you can leave the *filename* section blank, and Accessories loads the attached file. Select **M**ake to save the settings and return to the Appointment Scheduler window.

When the appointment time arrives, Desktop sounds an alarm and displays a message box that contains this message:

```
note: Press [OK] to load filename
```

In this message, *note* is the text you typed in the note section in the Description text box, and *filename* is the name you typed in the file name section in the Description text box. The message box contains three command boxes: Snooze, OK, and Cancel. Select **OK** to load the Notepads file. Select **S**nooze to clear the message box from the screen and cause Accessories to sound the alarm again in five minutes. Select **C**ancel to turn off the alarm.

If you leave blank the note section of the Description text box, Accessories loads the Notepads file at the appointed time without displaying the message dialog box.

Using Macros in the Appointment Scheduler

You can create a "smart" alarm a third way. Using a macro in an appointment line, you can cause a macro to run at a preset time. You might, for example, create a macro to run a demo. Using the Appointment Scheduler, you can run the demo periodically at a predetermined time. First, open an Appointment Scheduler window and display in the Daily Scheduler the list of appointments for the date in question. Use the cursor-movement keys or the mouse to move the highlighted bar into the Daily Scheduler portion of the window, and highlight the appointment line nearest to the time at which you want to run the macro. Press Enter or click the mouse button. Accessories displays the Make Appointment dialog box.

Fill in the Make Appointment dialog box as described in Chapter 20, with one exception. When you type the entry in the Description text box, use the following format:

note|*macro*

Replace *note* with any text you want to display when the alarm goes off. Replace *macro* with the code representing the keystroke required to invoke the macro you want to run at the preset time. The macro must be defined and active for this feature to work. Select **M**ake to save the settings and return to the Appointment Scheduler window.

When the appointment time arrives, Desktop sounds an alarm and displays a message box that contains this message:

```
note: Press [OK] to execute the attached macro
```

In this message, *note* is the text you typed in the note section of the Note text box. The message box contains three command boxes: Snooze, OK, and Cancel. Select **OK** to run the macro. Select **S**nooze to clear the message box from the screen and cause Accessories to sound the alarm again in five minutes. Select **C**ancel to turn off the alarm.

If you leave blank the note section in the Description text box, Desktop runs the macro at the appointed time without displaying the message dialog box.

Chapter Summary

In this chapter, you learned how to perform repetitive tasks quickly and correctly by using the Accessories keyboard macro facility. This chapter explains how to define, activate, and deactivate keyboard macros intended for use with any DOS program you run on your computer. This chapter also explains how to use PC Tools macros to apply special printer attributes when you are printing from Accessories and how to automate tasks at a specific time through combined use of macros and the Appointment Scheduler.

You now have the know-how to use PC Tools macros to customize the operation of any program you run on your computer. Turn to Chapter 22 to examine Accessories' four powerful electronic calculators.

Using the Calculators

Although personal computers are becoming increasingly common in the workplace, many businesspeople still rely on their electronic calculators and adding machines to perform important computations. Often, users need to compute an interest rate or perform a scientific computation and have neither the time nor patience to design a spreadsheet for that purpose.

Years before the personal computer was introduced, high-technology companies such as Hewlett-Packard were producing advanced electronic calculators customized for use by mathematicians, scientists, businesspeople, and programmers. PC Tools Desktop Accessories brings you the best of both worlds by providing four electronic calculators, three of which emulate many functions of popular Hewlett-Packard calculators.

This final chapter of Part IV, "Using the Desktop Manager," introduces you to the four calculators in PC Tools Desktop Accessories: the Algebraic Calculator, the Financial Calculator (which emulates the HP-12C), the Programmers Calculator (which emulates the HP-16C), and the Scientific Calculator (which emulates the HP-11C).

Opening and Closing a Calculator Window

To use any of the four available calculators, select **C**alculators from the **D**esktop Accessories main menu to display the Calculators submenu (see fig. 22.1).

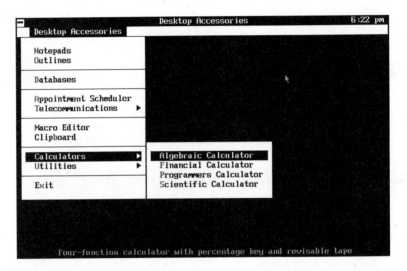

Fig. 22.1

The Calculators
submenu.

To access a calculator, select an option from this submenu. The sections that follow explain how to use each of these four electronic calculators. Accessories enables you to have as many as four calculator windows—one of each type—open at the same time. You cannot, however, open more than one calculator window of the same type (for example, you cannot open two Algebraic Calculators).

When you finish using an Accessories calculator, press Esc (Exit) or F3 (Exit), or click the close box in the upper left corner of the calculator window.

Using the Algebraic Calculator

To display the Algebraic Calculator, choose **C**alculators from the **D**esktop Accessories menu, and then select **A**lgebraic Calculator from the Calculators submenu. Accessories displays the window shown in figure 22.2.

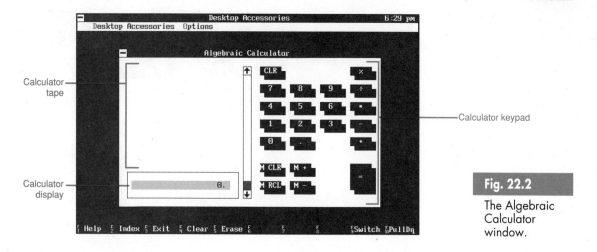

Fig. 22.2

The Algebraic Calculator window.

As in all Accessories windows, the top line of the screen contains the horizontal menu bar. When an Algebraic Calculator window is active, the menu bar displays **D**esktop Accessories and **O**ptions. The Options pull-down menu, shown in figure 22.3, features commands unique to the Algebraic Calculator.

The message bar at the bottom of the screen lists the available shortcut keys. The shortcut keys and other keystroke commands available in the Algebraic Calculator window are described in table 22.1.

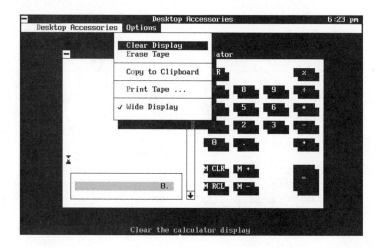

Fig. 22.3

The Options pull-down menu.

Table 22.1 Keystroke Commands Available in the Algebraic Calculator

Key	Name	Function
F1	Help	Displays context-sensitive Help facility.
F2	Index	Displays Help facility index.
F3	Exit	Exits from calculator (same as Esc).
F4 or C	Clear	Clears calculator display.
F5	Erase	Erases contents of calculator tape.
F9 or Ctrl+Esc	Switch	Switches active window.
F10 or Alt	PullDn	Activates horizontal menu bar.
Esc	Cancel	Exits from calculator (same as F3).
Alt+space bar	System Control	Displays System Control pull-down menu.
,	Comma Toggle	Toggles display of commas in calculator display and calculator tape.
D	Decimal	Pressing D followed by a number displays that fixed number of decimal places; pressing D followed by a period or decimal (.) returns the display to a floating decimal point.

In the lower left half of the Algebraic Calculator window, you see a text box, called the calculator display. Above the calculator display is the calculator tape. As many as 12 lines of numbers can be displayed in the calculator tape.

As you use the calculator, the tape scrolls from the calculator display. When the window is full, lines of the tape begin to scroll out the top of the window and disappear. Although a portion of the tape scrolls out of view, you can print the entire tape (up to a maximum of approximately 1,000 lines). Accessories even enables you to scroll portions of the tape back to the screen for viewing and editing. To scroll back, use the button or arrows on the vertical scroll bar at the right side of the tape.

The right half of the window contains a depiction of a calculator keypad. You can "push" a key by positioning the mouse pointer on the key and clicking the left or the right mouse button. You also can use your keyboard to push a key. A list of the calculator keypad keys and their equivalents on the computer keyboard are provided in table 22.2.

Table 22.2 Keyboard Keys Mapped to Calculator Keypad

Keyboard Key	Calculator Key	Function
0-9	0-9	Digits 0 through 9
C	CLR	Clear
%	%	Percentage
/	/	Divide
* or x	*	Multiply
–	–	Subtract
M C	M CLR	Memory clear
M R	M RCL	Memory recall
M+	M +	Add to memory
M–	M–	Subtract from memory
+	+	Add
= or Enter	=	Total or equal

You use the Algebraic Calculator as you use a common business calculator or adding machine with a memory register and paper tape printout. The Algebraic Calculator enables you to add, subtract, multiply, and divide numbers, save subtotals in a memory register, and store a complete record of all computations.

The output generated by this calculator is virtually identical in purpose and appearance to paper tapes produced by typical business calculators and adding machines, but each line of tape holds more characters. One major advantage of Accessories' Algebraic Calculator over its stand-alone Accessories counterparts is that you can edit its tape.

Toggling Wide Display

Accessories provides an alternative to the default Algebraic Calculator window display. When you want to see more of the screen "behind" the calculator, you can hide the calculator keypad, displaying only the calculator tape.

To hide the calculator keypad as shown in figure 22.4, select **O**ptions and then **W**ide Display. Removing the check marks toggles off the wide display. This slimmer version of the Algebraic Calculator window operates the same way as before; however, because the calculator keypad does not appear, you can use only the keyboard keys listed in table 22.2 to press calculator keys.

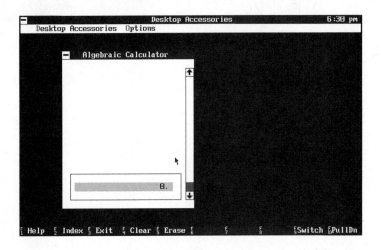

Fig. 22.4

The Algebraic Calculator with the calculator keypad hidden.

You can move this narrow Algebraic Calculator window around the screen to expose a portion of another file in which you are interested. Use the mouse to drag the Algebraic Calculator window, or use the System Control pull-down menu to move the window to the position you want.

Accessories continues to display the Algebraic Calculator window with the calculator keypad hidden until you toggle on the wide display by again selecting **W**ide Display from the **O**ptions pull-down menu.

Performing a Simple Calculation

To perform a calculation, enter numbers and operators in the order they would appear in an ordinary mathematical calculation, also referred to as an *algebraic expression*. As you type a number, Accessories displays the number in the calculator display. If you make a mistake, press the Backspace key to erase the error.

When you have typed a number correctly, press an *operator* key (any calculator key except the numbers 0 to 9 and the decimal). The number you typed appears in the calculator tape, followed by the operator symbol. Continue this procedure for every number in the algebraic expression. Whenever you press an operator key, Accessories adds the number to the bottom of the tape, scrolling the previously entered numbers up the screen.

After you type the final number in an expression, press Enter or the equal (=) key. Accessories displays this last number, followed by an equal sign (=), below the previously entered numbers on the tape. Accessories then displays a total line across the tape. Below the total line, Accessories displays the final result of the algebraic expression, followed by the letter T to indicate that this number is the total.

To compute the expression 1,276 + 495 + 258, for example, follow these steps:

1. Type **1276** and press the plus (+) key.

2. Type the second number, **495**, and again press the plus (+) key.

3. Type the third number, **258**, and press Enter or the equal (=) key.

   Accessories scrolls the tape up three lines and displays the numbers as shown in figure 22.5.

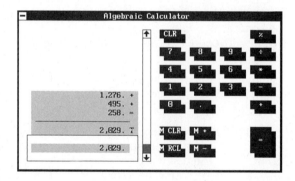

Fig. 22.5

Performing
a simple
calculation.

Typing a comma (,) toggles the display of commas in both the calculator display and tape. While you are entering numbers, type commas *only* when you want to toggle the display of commas.

The Algebraic Calculator's *automatic constant* feature is activated when you press any two operators without typing an intervening number. For example, if you type **111**, press the plus (+) key twice, and press Enter to obtain the total, the calculator adds 111 twice, and then adds the total to 111, as shown in the following calculation:

```
111  +
111  +
222  =
───
333  T
```

Intended to save keystrokes, this feature can result in an inaccurate calculator tape. To avoid this automatic-constant feature, never press two operators in sequence without typing an intervening number.

After you complete a calculation, you can use the total in the calculator display as the first entry of another algebraic expression by pressing the appropriate operator key. To multiply the answer 333 obtained in the preceding example by 15, press x, type **15**, and press the equal sign (=) or Enter.

Performing Calculations by Using the Memory Register

At times, you may want to compute and temporarily save a value for use in later computations. Accessories' Algebraic Calculator enables you to perform this procedure by storing the information in an area called the *memory register*.

By default, the memory register has a value of zero. When the memory register holds a nonzero value, Accessories displays the letter M in the first line above the calculator display.

After you type a number or complete a calculation, press the M+ key to add the contents of the calculator display to the memory register. To subtract the contents of the calculator display from the memory register, press the M–key. When you want to use the contents of the memory register in a calculation or display the contents, press the M CLR key. To clear the memory register and return its value to zero, press M RCL. Accessories no longer displays the letter M above the calculator display.

Suppose, for example, that you want to perform the following calculation:

$$(342 \times 5) + (42 \times 12)$$

To perform the first calculation, enter the following line in the Algebraic Calculator:

342*5

> If you plan to use the memory register during a calculation, press
> M CLR to clear the memory register before starting to enter
> numbers.

T I P

Press Enter or the equal (=) key. Accessories computes and displays
the product (1,710). To place this first product in the memory register,
press the M+ key. Again, 1,710 is displayed in the calculator tape, this
time with the annotation M+ to its right. The letter M is displayed also
to the left of the calculator tape, indicating that a nonzero value is
stored in the memory register.

To perform the second multiplication, type this line:

42*12

Press Enter or the equal (=) key. Accessories computes and displays
the product 504. To add this product to the memory register, press M
and then the plus (+) key.

To display the sum of the two products, press M RCL. Accessories displays 2,214. Figure 22.6 shows the entire sequence of calculations, as
displayed on the calculator tape.

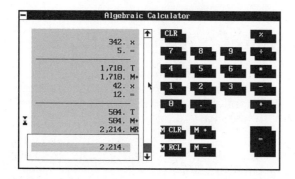

Fig. 22.6

Using the
Memory
Register.

Editing the Tape

A significant advantage of Accessories' Algebraic Calculator over a
typical electronic calculator is that you can recompute a calculation
without retyping all the entries. When you edit the numbers displayed
in the calculator tape, Accessories automatically recalculates the
answer.

To edit an entry on the calculator tape, scroll the tape (by using
the keys listed in table 22.3) until the entry you want to change is

displayed. You can edit your entries only; you cannot edit a calculated number (a number with a T, M+, M–, MR, or MC to its right).

Table 22.3 Algebraic Calculator Tape-Scrolling Keys	
Key	**Scroll Tape**
↑	Up one entry
↓	Down one entry
Home	To first (top) entry in calculator tape
End	To last entry in calculator tape
PgDn	12 entries up
PgUp	12 entries down

When the entry you want to change appears in the calculator display, you need only type the correct entry.

After you make the changes you want, Accessories automatically recomputes the total, using the edited entries. Scroll the tape, if necessary, until you can see the revised total.

Printing and Copying the Tape

Occasionally, you may want to print a hard copy of the calculator tape. You also may want to transfer the results of your calculations to another Accessories application or even to another DOS program. Accessories makes both tasks easy to perform.

To print the calculator tape, select **O**ptions, and then choose **P**rint Tape from the Options pull-down menu. Accessories displays the Print dialog box shown in figure 22.7.

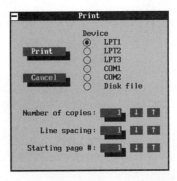

Fig. 22.7

The Print dialog box.

To send the calculator tape to your printer, determine the port to which your printer is connected and select the appropriate option button (for parallel printers, choose LPT1, LPT2, or LPT3; for serial printers, choose COM1 or COM2). When you want to create a disk file that can be used to send output to a printer later, select the Disk File option button.

By default, Accessories prints only one copy of each document. Occasionally, however, you may want to print several copies of a document. To print more than one copy type in the Number of Copies box the number of copies you want Accessories to print.

 Although Line Spacing and Starting Page # appear in the Print dialog box, these options are ignored when printing a calculator tape. Only Number of Copies is operational.

To begin printing the calculator tape, select the **P**rint command button. Accessories prints the number of copies indicated. If you decide not to print, choose **C**ancel from the dialog box. To interrupt printing, press Esc.

When printing to a file, Accessories creates an ASCII text file named CALC.PRT. You can print this file later by using the COPY command (either the DOS COPY command or the PC Tools Desktop **C**opy command) or the PRINT command (either DOS PRINT or the PC Shell **P**rint command). Just copy the file to the device named PRN. To print CALC.PRT by using the DOS COPY command, for example, type the following line at the DOS command line:

COPY CALC.PRT PRN

Printing an entire 1,000-line tape may not be what you have in mind. To print only a portion of the tape, you can retrieve CALC.PRT into a Notepads window, or you can copy the tape to the Clipboard. To copy the tape to the Accessories Clipboard, choose **O**ptions, and then select **C**opy to Clipboard. Accessories copies to the Clipboard the entire tape, to a maximum of 4,000 characters (approximately the last 160 lines). You then can use the Clipboard to paste all or part of the figures from the tape into another Accessories application window or even into another DOS program.

Erasing the Tape

Just as the paper tape in a business calculator doesn't self-destruct, the Accessories Algebraic Calculator calculator tape does not erase itself. Even if you close the calculator window, Accessories remembers the contents of the tape and redisplays it the next time you use the Algebraic Calculator.

To erase the contents of the calculator tape, press F5 (Erase) or select **O**ptions and then **E**rase Tape. Accessories erases the entire tape and clears the calculator display, returning it to zero.

FROM HERE...

For Related Information

◀◀ "Understanding Desktop Accessories Windows," p. 534.

◀◀ "Pasting Text from the Clipboard," p. 603.

Using the Financial Calculator

When you analyze financial data, you frequently must perform complex computations. Accessories' Financial Calculator, the second calculator listed in the Calculators menu, helps make the process easy. You can use the Financial Calculator, for example, to compute the monthly payment on a house mortgage. Or you can determine the amount of savings you will accumulate over a certain number of years by depositing a set amount of money every month. The Accessories Financial Calculator is designed to look and operate much like the Hewlett-Packard model HP-12C (without the HP-12C's programming capabilities).

This section explains how to use the Financial Calculator for simple financial calculations. For more detailed information about using the Financial Calculator, you may want to obtain the *HP-12C Owner's Handbook and Problem Solving Guide*, published by Hewlett-Packard.

To display the Financial Calculator window, shown in figure 22.8, select **F**inancial Calculator from the **C**alculators menu.

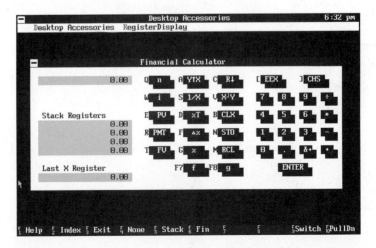

Fig. 22.8

The Financial Calculator window.

The horizontal menu bar contains the options Desktop Accessories and RegisterDisplay, and the Financial Calculator window's message bar lists shortcut keys. The shortcut keys and other keystroke commands available in the window are listed in table 22.4.

Table 22.4 Keystroke Commands Available in the Financial Calculator

Key	Name	Function
F1	Help	Displays context-sensitive Help facility
F2	Index	Displays Help facility index
F3	Exit	Exits from calculator application (same as Esc)
F4	None	Removes all registers from display
F5	Stack	Displays contents of stack registers
F6	Fin	Displays contents of financial registers
F7	f	Activates f-key set of calculator functions (this key is not listed in the message bar)
F8	g	Activates g-key set of calculator functions (this key is not listed in the message bar)
F9 or Ctrl+Esc	Switch	Switches active window
F10 or Alt	PullDn	Activates horizontal menu bar
Esc	Cancel	Cancels current process or application (same as F3)
Alt+space	System Control	Displays System Control pull-down menu bar

The Financial Calculator fills almost the entire screen. The calculator display is located in the upper left corner. Directly beneath the calculator display are the register displays (stack, financial, or data). The calculator keypad occupies the rest of the screen.

Using the Financial Calculator Keypad

The Financial Calculator keypad is labeled in the same manner as the HP-12C. Many of the calculator keys serve double- or triple-duty. You can use the mouse or the keyboard to "push" these buttons.

In the first set of functions, referred to in this chapter as the *primary functions*, each function is displayed on a calculator key. To execute a primary function, click the appropriate calculator key or use your keyboard to press the key listed to the left of the calculator key. This group of commands is listed in table 22.5.

Table 22.5 Primary Keyboard Keys Mapped to Financial Calculator Keypad

Keyboard Key	Calculator Key	Function
Q	n	Enter or calculate number of periods
W	i	Enter or calculate interest rate
E	PV	Enter or calculate present value
R	PMT	Enter or calculate payment
T	FV	Enter or calculate future value
A	Y↑X	Y to the Xth power
S	1/X	Reciprocal of X
D	%T	Percentage of total
F	Δ%	Percentage difference
G	%	Percentage
C	R↓	Roll down stack register
V	X↔Y	Exchange values in X and Y
B	CLX	Clear X register
F7	f	Prefix key to activate f-key set of functions
F8	g	Prefix key to activate g-key set of functions
N	STO	Store number in register
M	RCL	Recall stored number from register
]	CHS	Change sign

Keyboard Key	Calculator Key	Function
[	EEX	Enter exponent; preceded by STO, toggles c annunciator indicating continuous compounding
0-9	0-9	Digits 0-9
/	÷	Divide
*	*	Multiply
—	—	Subtract
+	+	Add
.	.	Decimal point
&	&+	Accumulate statistics: "The sum of"
Enter	Enter	Enter

Every command in the f-key category of Financial Calculator commands appears on the keys after that mode has been activated. These functions are referred to as the f-key set of calculator functions (see table 22.6). To execute one of these commands, you first must press a prefix key—the f calculator key. Click the f calculator key, or press the F7 function key on your keyboard. Accessories displays the same keypad, but the keys now have different labels and functions (see fig. 22.9).

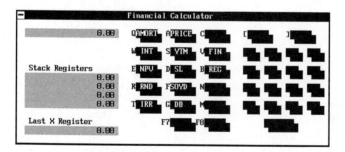

Fig. 22.9

The Financial Calculator after selecting the f calculator key.

When the keyboard is in f-key mode, you can press calculator keys by clicking a calculator key or by pressing on your keyboard the key listed to the left of the calculator key. Accessories executes the function listed on the calculator key. If you end up in f-key mode accidentally, you can return to normal mode by pressing the Enter key. Otherwise, the calculator is turned to normal mode after executing the function you selected.

Table 22.6 F-Prefix Keyboard Keys Mapped to Financial Calculator Keypad

Keyboard Key	Calculator Key	Function
Q	AMORT	Amortize (X=interest, Y=principal)
W	INT	Calculate simple interest
E	NPV	Net present value
R	RND	Round to display setting
T	IRR	Internal rate of return
A	PRICE	Bond price
S	YTM	Bond yield to maturity
D	SL	Straight-line depreciation
F	SOYD	Sum-of-year's-digits depreciation
G	DB	Declining-balance depreciation
X	Σ	Clear statistics registers (R0 through R5)
V	FIN	Clear financial registers
B	REG	Clear stack and data registers

You can use the f key not only to activate the f-key set of calculator functions but also to display numbers in scientific notation (select the f calculator key, and then press a decimal point) to change the number of decimal places displayed (the default is two decimal places). If you select f and then type an integer from 0 to 9, Accessories displays all values in the calculator display rounded to the number of decimal places specified. The numbers still are stored internally to the number of decimal places you entered (to a total of 12 significant digits).

T I P   You cannot press the F key on the computer keyboard to get f-key mode, nor can you press the G key to get g-key mode. These modes can be selected by pressing F7 for f-key mode or F8 for g-key mode, or by clicking the f or g keys at the bottom of the calculator keypad.

Every function in the g-key group of Financial Calculator commands appears on the keys when that mode is active. This group of functions is referred to here as the g-key set of functions (see table 22.7). To execute one of these functions, you first must press another prefix key, the g calculator key. Click the g calculator key, or press the F8 function key on the keyboard.

Accessories displays the same keyboard, but again the keys have different labels and functions. If you click the appropriate calculator key or press on your keyboard the key listed to the left of the calculator key, Accessories executes the command listed on the calculator key. (If you press F8 and enter g-key mode accidentally, press Enter to return to normal mode. Otherwise, the calculator is returned to normal mode after executing the g-key mode function you selected.)

Table 22.7 G-Prefix Keyboard Keys Mapped to Financial Calculator Keypad

Keyboard Key	Calculator Key	Function
Q	12X	Multiply by 12 and insert in financial register n
W	12÷	Divide by 12 and insert in financial register i
E	CFo	Initial cash flow
R	CFj	Amount of cash flow
T	Nj	Number of cash flows
A	=√x	Square root
S	EXP	Natural logarithm-e (approximately 2.718281828) to the power of value in X
D	LN	Natural logarithm—logarithm to base e
F	FRC	Leave fractional portion of number; truncate integer portion
G	INT	Leave integer portion of number; truncate fractional portion
]	DAT	Change date in Y by the number of days in X, and display date and day of week
7	BEG	Payments made at beginning of time period
8	END	Payments made at end of time period

continues

Table 22.7 Continued

Keyboard Key	Calculator Key	Function
[	ΔDY	Computes number of days between dates in Y and X
4	DMY	Toggles Day.Month.Year date format for bond calculations
5	MDY	Toggles Month.Day.Year date format for bond calculations
6	xw	Weighted mean
Enter	LST	Display contents of LSTX register
1	x,r	Linear estimate
2	y,r	Linear estimate (y) and correlation coefficient (r)
3	n!	Factorial
0	x	Mean (average)
.	s	Standard deviation
&	&–	Subtract last accumulation entry

Suppose, for example, that you want to perform one of the three functions (PMT, RND, and CFj) associated with the fourth calculator key from the top in the first column. You perform one of the following:

- To execute the primary function, PMT, press R or click this key.

- To perform the f-key function, RND, first click the f calculator key or press F7 to display the f-key set of functions on the keyboard. Then press R or click the calculator key.

- To execute the g-key function, CFj, first click the g calculator key or press F8 to display the g-key group of functions. Then press R or click the calculator key.

In the rest of this discussion about the Financial Calculator, each function is referenced by its label on the Financial Calculator keypad.

Performing a Simple Calculation

The Financial Calculator is capable of performing straightforward algebraic calculations and sophisticated financial calculations. Before you can understand how to enter a complex financial formula, familiarize yourself with the basics of entering simple formulas.

For entering a formula, Accessories' Financial Calculator uses a system called *Reverse Polish Notation* (RPN). The difference between this method and the more traditional *Infix Notation* approach used in the Algebraic Calculator (and in most pocket calculators) lies primarily in the order in which you enter mathematical operators and operandi. In the traditional method (Infix Notation), you type an operator (+, −, *, and so on) *between* operandi (the numbers on which an operator performs its function). In Reverse Polish notation, however, you type the first operand, press Enter, type the second operand, and then type the operator.

To illustrate the difference between Infix Notation and Reverse Polish Notation, suppose that you want to add the numbers 1,276 and 495. If you use Accessories' Algebraic Calculator with its traditional Infix Notation, you type **1276 + 495** and then press Enter or =. Accessories adds the two numbers. To add the same two numbers by using the Financial Calculator's Reverse Polish Notation, however, you type **1276**, press Enter, and then type **495 +**.

As you learn to perform more complex financial calculations, some options you select appear immediately under the calculator display as you toggle each on and off (see fig. 22.10). These options are beg, d.my, and c, which perform the following functions:

■ When *beg* is active, any loan or annuity calculation is based on each payment being made at the beginning of a payment period. When beg is not displayed, payments are assumed to be made at the end of the payment period. To toggle this feature, select g, and then select the BEG or the END key.

■ The option *d.my* indicates the required format for entering a calendar date. If d.my is not displayed, the required format for a date is Month.DayYear. To toggle between date formats, select g, and then select the DMY or the MDY key.

■ The option *c* indicates that continuous compounding is in effect during calculations involving partial periods. To turn continuous compounding off, select STO, and then select EEX on the calculator keypad.

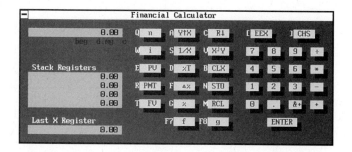

Fig. 22.10

The financial calculator with beg, d.my, and c indicators displayed.

Whenever you activate another Accessories window or exit the Desktop Accessories, the beg, d.my, and c options in the Financial Calculator are toggled off automatically.

Understanding the Financial Calculator Registers

The Financial Calculator uses five automatic-memory registers (called *stack registers*, which are named X, Y, Z, T, and LSTX, for last X). All five registers have a value of zero when you first open a Financial Calculator window.

Accessories enables you to display the contents of all five registers simultaneously so that you can review the intermediate steps in a complex computation. Press the F5 (Stack) shortcut key or select **R**egister-Display, and then select **S**tack Registers. You can see the stack registers in the register display area. Figure 22.11 shows the contents of the five registers after you type **1**, **2**, and **3**, pressing Enter after each number.

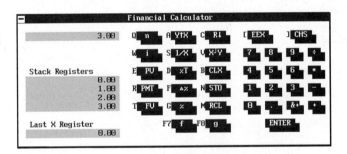

Fig. 22.11

The Stack
Registers display.

By using Reverse Polish Notation and automatic-memory stack registers, Accessories enables you to perform complicated mathematical calculations. Suppose, for example, that you want to calculate this expression:

$$(342 \times 5) + (42 \times 12)$$

To perform the first calculation, type **342**, press Enter, and type **5***. Accessories displays the produc 1,710 in the calculator display.

To perform the second calculation, type **42**, press Enter, and type **12***. Accessories displays the product 504 in the calculator display. Press the plus (+) key, and Accessories adds 1,710 (the product of the first operation) to 504 (the product of the second operation) and places the sum 2,214 in the calculator display.

In addition to the stack registers, the Financial Calculator has 20 *data registers* you can use to store numbers, which you can use later in calculations. Some of the Financial Calculator's built-in functions, such as the statistical functions, use several of these registers to hold the results of calculations.

The data registers are named R0, R1, R2, R3, R4, R5, R6, R7, R8, R9, R.0, R.1, R.2, R.3, R.4, R.5, R.6, R.7, R.8, and R.9. To store in one of the registers the value displayed in the calculator display, press the STO calculator key and then the number of the register. To store the number 34.78 in register R5, for example, first type **34.78** in the calculator display. Then press the STO calculator key and press 5. You see nothing on the screen to indicate this number is stored. To recall a value from one of the data registers to the calculator display, press the RCL key, and then type the number of the register.

To display the data registers so that you can determine the values stored there, select **R**egisterDisplay from the horizontal menu bar, and then select **D**ata Registers R0-R9 or Data **R**egisters R.0-R.9. Accessories displays the requested data registers (see fig. 22.12).

The Data Registers display.

To clear all values from the data registers (and from the stack registers) and return them to zero, select the f calculator key and then the REG key.

Performing a Financial Calculation

The primary purpose of the Financial Calculator is to perform financial calculations. In performing these calculations, you use the following memory registers, known as the *financial registers*:

■ The *Number of Months* (*n*) register holds the total number of time periods (usually months or years) covered by the investment or loan.

- The *Interest Rate* (*i*) register holds the interest rate of the investment or loan for one time period (usually months or years).

- The *Present Value* (*PV*) register holds the present value of the investment or loan. For a loan, this is the amount of money loaned or borrowed.

- The *Payment* (*PMT*) register holds the payment per single time period (usually months or years).

- The *Future Value* (*FV*) register holds the future value, the value of the investment or loan at the end of the term. For a loan, this value is zero unless a balloon payment is made at the end of the term. If you are calculating an investment, the future value is your financial goal.

The default value of all these registers is zero. To insert a new value, type a number in the calculator display, and then press the associated calculator function key (n, i, PV, PMT, or FV—refer to table 22.5). To insert 10,000 as the present value or amount of a loan, for example, type **10000** in the calculator display, and then press the PV calculator key or press E on the keyboard. Accessories inserts 10,000 in the PV register.

You can display the contents of these registers one by one or all together. To display the contents of one financial register, press the RCL calculator key and then the calculator key for the parameter you want to display. To display the current contents of the PV register, for example, press the RCL key and then the PV key.

When you want to display the contents of all five financial registers at one time, press the F6 (Fin) shortcut key or select Financial Registers from the RegisterDisplay menu. Accessories displays the financial registers in the register display area (see fig. 22.13).

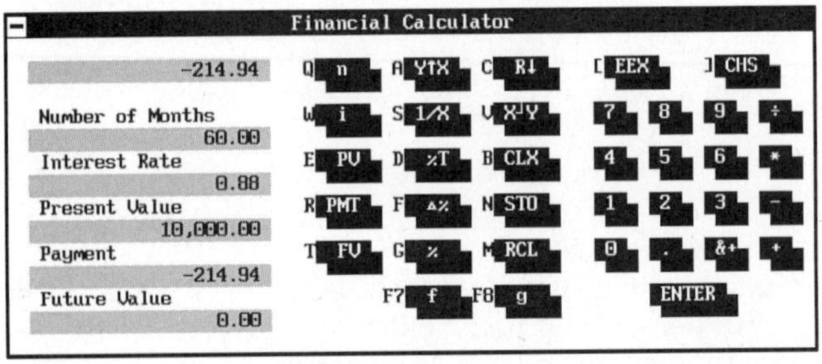

Fig. 22.13

The Financial Registers display.

To clear all values in the financial registers and return them to zero, select f, and then select the FIN calculator key (which appears after you select f).

To calculate a value for any one of the five financial registers, insert a value in each of the other registers, and press the function key for the parameter you want to find. Suppose, for example, that you want to determine the monthly payment for a loan of $10,000, at 10.5 percent per year, to be paid back in exactly 5 years. To solve this problem, complete the following steps:

1. Press 5, the term of the loan in years. Select the g calculator key. Then press the 12X calculator key to convert the term to months and to insert the value into the n register.

2. Type **10.5**, the yearly interest rate. Select the g calculator key. Then press the 12÷ key. This function divides 10.5 by 12, to yield a monthly interest rate (.88) and inserts this rate into the i register. (***Note***: The calculator recognizes any entry in the i register as *percent*.)

3. Type **10000** and press the PV key. This action inserts the loan amount, $10,000, into the PV register.

4. Because the goal is to pay off the loan, the FV register can remain at a value of zero.

5. To calculate the monthly payment, press the PMT calculator key. Accessories briefly displays the message `Calculating` and then displays the payment amount –214.94 in the calculator display. To see all financial registers at one time, press F6 (Fin) (refer to fig. 22.13).

Be sure to use the same unit of time to determine the values for each register. To figure a monthly payment in register PMT, for example, the values in registers n and i also must be based on a one-month time period.

Using the Programmers Calculator

The third calculator listed on the Calculators menu is the Programmers Calculator. This calculator helps you perform complex programming-related calculations. Personal computers and the programs that run on them often use numbers stored in a number base other than the commonly used decimal (base 10) number base. When programmers are designing software, they frequently must use numbers in base 16 (hexadecimal), base 8 (octal), or base 2 (binary) to perform calculations. To facilitate these calculations, the Programmers Calculator enables you easily to perform at one time simple or complex calculations in all these number bases.

The Programmers Calculator in PC Tools 8 is designed to look and operate like a Hewlett-Packard model HP-16C Calculator (but without the HP-16C's programming capabilities). This section introduces you to the Programmers Calculator but does not go into detail about its many uses. Programming and programming-related topics are beyond the scope of this book. For more detailed information about using the Programmers Calculator, you may want to obtain the *HP-16C Computer Scientist Owner's Handbook*, published by Hewlett-Packard.

To display the Programmers Calculator, select **P**rogrammers Calculator from the **C**alculators menu. Accessories displays the Programmer's Calculator window. Shortcut keys for the Programmers Calculator are listed in the message bar. Table 22.8 lists the shortcut keys and other keystroke commands available in this window.

Table 22.8 Keystroke Commands Available in the Programmer's Calculator Window

Key	Name	Function
F1	Help	Displays context-sensitive Help facility
F2	Index	Displays Help facility index
F3	Exit	Exits from the calculator (same as Esc)
F4	Stack	Displays contents of stack registers
F6	Data	Displays contents of data registers
F7	f	Activates f-key set of functions
F9 or Ctrl+Esc	Switch	Switches active window
F10 or Alt	PullDn	Activates horizontal menu bar
Esc	Cancel	Exits from the calculator (same as F3)
Alt+space bar	System Control	Displays System Control pull-down menu

The Programmer's Calculator window fills almost the entire screen. The calculator display area is located in the upper five lines of the window. Numbers displayed in this area of the screen are listed simultaneously in four number bases: hexadecimal (base 16), octal (base 8), decimal (base 10), and binary (base 2). Every number base is in a separate line of the calculator display. The fifth line displays the ASCII-character equivalent of the numbers in the other lines. A triangular pointer indicates the current number base.

In figure 22.14, for example, you see the number 97 expressed in five ways in the calculator display. The current number base for entering numbers and for displaying values in registers is base 16 (hexadecimal), as indicated by the triangular pointer in the HEX line of the calculator display.

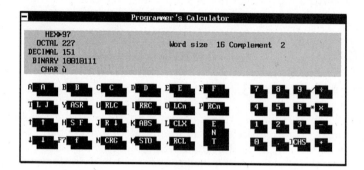

Fig. 22.14

Different expressions for the number 97 in the Programmer's Calculator window.

In the right portion of the calculator display, Accessories indicates the current word size (a number between 1 and 64) and the current number representation mode (Complement 1 for 1's Complement mode, Complement 2 for 2's Complement mode, or Complement U for Unsigned mode). Word size and number representation mode are of interest to programmers.

Accessories also displays one or more of the following system flags in the calculator display, to the right of the mode indicator, when appropriate:

■ Z. This flag, also known as *flag 3*, indicates that Accessories adds leading zeros to the left of the highest nonzero digit to fill up the word. To activate leading zeros, press ZER or press SF, and then type **3**. To clear the Leading Zero Control, press ZER or press CL, and then type **3**.

■ C. This flag, also known as *flag 4*, denotes the *carry condition*, which means that a carry-over number remains from an arithmetic operation or bit shifting. This condition is triggered automatically whenever an operation results in a carry-over number. To clear the carry flag, press CF (Clear Flag), and then type **4**.

■ G. This flag, also known as *flag 5*, means that the result of a calculation cannot be represented in the current mode and word size. To clear this flag, continue with another calculation or press CF, and then type **5**.

NOTE The Accessories Programmers Calculator does not use flags 0, 1, and 2. These flags are used in the HP-16C to control program execution; Accessories' version of the calculator is not programmable.

■ *P.* This flag is a prompt for more input. The flag appears, for example, when you press STO (Store) or RCL (Recall) but before you input the appropriate register, or when you press CL to clear a flag but before you type the flag number.

Using the Programmers Calculator Keypad

Below the calculator display, the calculator keypad fills the remainder of the window. Although the Programmers Calculator keypad is labeled in much the same way as that of the HP-16C, the two keypads are not the same, primarily because the Programmers Calculator is not programmable.

Most of the keys on the Programmers Calculator keypad serve double duty. In the first set of functions—referred to here as the *primary functions*—every function is listed on a calculator key. To execute a primary function, click the calculator key or press on your keyboard the key listed to the left of the calculator key. This group of commands is listed in table 22.9.

Table 22.9 Primary Keyboard Keys Mapped to Programmers Calculator Keypad

Keyboard Key	Calculator Key	Function
A	A	A-hex only (10 decimal)
B	B	B-hex only (11 decimal)
C	C	C-hex only (12 decimal)
D	D	D-hex only (13 decimal)
E	E	E-hex only (14 decimal)
F	F	F-hex only (15 decimal)
0-9	0-9	0-1: binary; 2-9: binary, hex, octal, and decimal

Keyboard Key	Calculator Key	Function
/	÷	Divide
T	LJ	Left-justify word in X, place in Y
Y	ASR	Arithmetic shift right-shift bits in X one place to right, replicate sign bit on left
U	RLC	Rotate left through carry-rotate bits in X one place to left through carry bit
I	RRC	Rotate right through carry-rotate bits in X one place to right through carry bit
O	LCn	Rotate left through carry n number of bits
P	RCn	Rotate right through carry n number of bits
*	X	Multiply
↑	↑	Move up one line in display to change number base
H	SF	Set flag
J	R↓	Roll stack registers down
K	ABS	Absolute value
L	CLX	Clear X register to zero
–	–	Subtract
↓	↓	Move down one line in display to change number base
F7	f	Prefix key to activate f-key set of Programmers Calculator functions
N	CRG	Clear data registers
M	STO	Store value in X to register
,	RCL	Recall value in register to X
.	.	Decimal
]	CHS	Change sign
+	+	Add
Enter	LST	Copy LSTX to X

Every command in the f-key category of Programmers Calculator commands, referred to here as the *f-key* set of calculator functions, appears on the keyboard keys after that mode has been activated. To execute one of these commands, you first must press the f prefix key on the calculator keypad. Click the f calculator key, or press the F7 function key on your keyboard. Accessories displays the letter f, referred to as the *f annunciator*. If you press the f calculator key by accident or simply change your mind before executing an f-key function, you can clear this prefix by pressing the CPX key.

When the f annunciator is displayed, click the calculator key on which the function name appears, or press the keyboard key listed to the left of this calculator key. Accessories executes the function listed on the calculator key. Every function in the f-key set, along with a short description of its purpose, is listed in table 22.10.

Table 22.10 F-Prefix Keyboard Keys Mapped to Programmers Calculator Keypad

Keyboard Key	Calculator Key	Function
A	SL	Shift bits in X one place to left
B	SR	Shift bits in X one place to right
C	RL	Rotate left-rotate bits in X one place to left
D	RR	Rotate right-rotate bits in X one place to right
E	RLn	Rotate left n number of bits
F	RRn	Rotate right n number of bits
7	MKL	Mask left-create left-justified set of mask bits
8	MKR	Mask right-create right-justified set of mask bits
9	RMD	Remainder after division- $|y|MOD|x|$
/	XOR	Exclusive OR
T	#B	Number of bits in X
Y	DBR	Double remainder
U	DB÷	Double divide
I	DBX	Double multiply
O	=√x	Square root of X

Keyboard Key	Calculator Key	Function
P	1/X	Reciprocal of X
4	SB	Set bit
5	CB	Clear bit
6	ZER	Leading zeros
*	AND	Logical (Boolean) product
↑	RST	Restore start-up state
H	CF	Clear flag
J	R↑	Roll registers up
K	X↔Y	Exchange values in X and Y
L	BSP	Backspace (same as Backspace key on keyboard)
Enter	LST	Copy LSTX to X
1	1s	Set 1's complement mode
2	2s	Set 2's complement mode
3	UNS	Set unsigned mode
-	NOT	Logical (Boolean) NOT
N	CPX	Clear prefix (clear f annunciator)
M	WSZ	Word size
,	PRC	Precision
+	OR	Logical (Boolean) OR

A table of the ASCII characters available in PC Tools and their hex and decimal equivalents is available in Desktop Accessories. Refer Chapter 15, "Navigating the Desktop Accessories," for information about accessing the ASCII table.

Understanding the Programmers Calculator Registers

The Programmers Calculator, like the Financial Calculator, uses Reverse Polish Notation and several memory registers, including five automatic-memory registers called *stack registers*. These registers—X, Y, Z, T, and LSTX (for last X)—work similarly to those in the Financial

Calculator. Refer to the "Performing a Simple Calculation" section in the discussion of the financial calculator earlier in this chapter for a detailed discussion of Reverse Polish Notation and stack registers.

NOTE   Rather than clear the stack registers in the Programmers Calculator when you close the window, Accessories remembers the register values and reloads them the next time you use the Programmers Calculator.

To display the contents of all five registers at one time, press the F4 (Stack) shortcut key or select **R**egisterDisplay and then **S**tack Registers. On the screen's left side, Accessories displays the Stack box, which lists the five registers and their contents. Accessories displays the contents of every register in the current number base.

In addition to the stack registers, Accessories' Programmers Calculator has 10 data registers in which you can store numbers. These data registers are named R0, R1, R2, R3, R4, R5, R6, R7, R8, and R9. To store in one of these registers the value displayed in the calculator display, press the STO calculator key and then the register's number. When you want to recall to the calculator display a value from one of the data registers, press the RCL calculator key, and then type the register's number.

To review the contents of the data registers simultaneously, press the F6 (Data) shortcut key or select **R**egisterDisplay and then **D**ata Registers. Accessories displays the Data box with the contents of each register in the current number base (see fig. 22.15).

To clear all values in the data registers and return them to zero, press the CRG calculator key. (This command does not clear the stack registers.)

Fig. 22.15

The contents of each data register listed in the Data box.

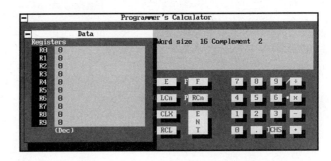

For Related Information

◀◀ "Displaying the ASCII Table" p. 552.

FROM HERE...

Using the Scientific Calculator

The last calculator listed on the Calculators menu, the Scientific Calculator, helps you perform the complex computations that frequently are needed when you analyze scientific data.

The Accessories Scientific Calculator is designed to look and operate like a Hewlett-Packard model HP-11C Calculator (but without the HP-11C's programming capabilities). This section introduces you to the Scientific Calculator but does not go into detail about its many uses. For more detailed information about using the calculator to perform scientific calculations, you may want to obtain the *HP-11C Owner's Handbook and Problem Solving Guide*, published by Hewlett-Packard.

To display the Scientific Calculator, select **S**cientific Calculator from the **C**alculators menu. Accessories displays the Scientific Calculator window (see fig. 22.16).

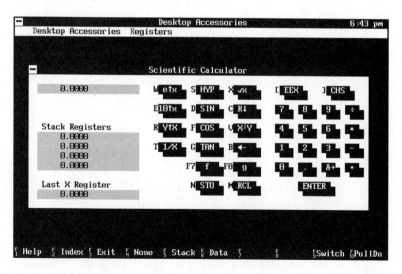

Fig. 22.16

The Scientific Calculator window.

The Scientific Calculator window is surrounded by a window border with a close box in its upper left corner. The horizontal menu bar contains the options Desktop Accessories and Registers. Shortcut keys are listed in the Scientific Calculator window's message bar. Table 22.11 lists the shortcut keys and other keystroke commands available in the window.

Table 22.11 Keystroke Commands Available in the Scientific Calculator

Key	Name	Function
F1	Help	Displays context-sensitive Help facility
F2	Index	Displays Help facility index
F3	Exit	Exits from calculator (same as Esc)
F4	None	Removes all registers from display
F5	Stack	Displays contents of stack registers
F6	Data	Displays contents of data registers
F7	f	Activates f-key set of calculator functions (this key is not listed in message bar)
F8	g	Activates g-key set of calculator functions (this key is not listed in message bar)
F9 or Ctrl+Esc	Switch	Switches active window
F10 or Alt	PullDn	Activates horizontal menu bar
Esc	Cancel	Exits from calculator (same as F3)
Alt+space bar	System Control	Displays System Control pull-down menu

The Scientific Calculator window fills almost the entire screen. The calculator display is located in the window's upper left corner. Directly beneath this area is the register display area (stack or data). The calculator keypad occupies the remainder of the screen.

Using the Scientific Calculator Keypad

Although the Scientific Calculator's keypad is labeled much like that of the HP-11C, the two keypads are not the same, primarily because the Scientific Calculator is not programmable.

Many of the Scientific Calculator keys serve a dual or triple purpose. In the first set of functions, referred to here as the *primary functions*, every function is listed on a calculator key. To execute a primary function, click the calculator key or press on your keyboard the key listed to the left of the calculator key. This group of commands is listed in table 22.12.

Table 22.12 Primary Keyboard Keys Mapped to Scientific Calculator Keypad

Keyboard Key	Calculator Key	Function
W	e↑X	Natural antilogarithm—raise e to the power of the number in X
E	10↑X	Common antilogarithm—raise 10 to the power of the number in X
R	Y↑X	Raise number in Y to the power of the number in X
T	1/X	Reciprocal of X
S	HYP	Hyperbolic (use with SIN, COS, and TAN)
D	SIN	Sine
F	COS	Cosine
G	TAN	Tangent
X	=√x	Square root
C	R↓	Roll down stack register
V	X↔Y	Exchange values in X and Y
B	←	Clear digit or digits
F7	f	Prefix key to activate f-key set of functions
F8	g	Prefix key to activate g-key set of functions
N	STO	Store number in register
M	RCL	Recall stored number from register
]	CHS	Change sign
/	÷	Divide
[	EEX	Enter exponent; preceded by STO, toggles c annunciator indicating continuous compounding
0-9	0-9	Digits 0-9
*	*	Multiply
Enter	Enter	Enter
−	−	Subtract
.	.	Decimal point

continues

Table 22.12 Continued

Keyboard Key	Calculator Key	Function
&	&+	Accumulate statistics
+	+	Add

In the second category of Scientific Calculator commands, referred to in this chapter as the f-key set of calculator functions, every command is listed on a keyboard key when that mode has been activated. To execute one of these commands, you first must press the f prefix key on the calculator keypad. Click the f calculator key, or press the F7 function key on your keyboard. If you press F7 by mistake, press Enter to return to normal mode. Otherwise, selecting a key completes the operation and returns to normal mode.

When the program is in f-key mode, click the appropriate calculator key or press the keyboard key listed on the calculator key. Accessories executes the function. Table 22.13 lists each of these functions and a short description of its purpose.

Table 22.13 F-Prefix Keyboard Keys Mapped to Scientific Calculator Keypad

Keyboard Key	Calculator Key	Function
X	Σ	Clear statistics registers (R0 through R5)
V	REG	Clear stack and data registers
B	PREFIX	Clear prefix (clear f or g annunciator)
N	FRAC	Leave fractional portion of number; truncate integer portion
]	Pi	Place value of pi (3.141592654) in X
7	FIX	Set fixed-point display mode
8	SCI	Set scientific-notation display mode
9	ENG	Set engineering-notation display mode
1	Pyx	Calculate number of permutations—Y items X at a time
2	HMS	Convert decimal hours to hours, minutes, and seconds, or convert decimal degrees to degrees, minutes, and seconds

Keyboard Key	Calculator Key	Function
3	RAD	Convert degrees to radians
0	x!	Factorial or Gamma function
.	y,r	Linear estimate (y) and correlation coefficient (r)
&	L.R.	Calculate linear regression

Every function in the third group of Scientific Calculator commands, referred to as the g-key set of functions, appears on the keyboard keys after that mode has been activated. To execute one of these functions, you first must press the g prefix key. Click the calculator keypad's g prefix key, or press the F8 function key on your keyboard. Click the desired calculator key or use your keyboard to press the key listed on the calculator key. Accessories executes the command listed. Table 22.14 lists these g-key commands. If you press F8 by mistake, press Enter to return to normal mode. Otherwise, selecting a key completes the operation and returns to normal mode.

Table 22.14 G-Prefix Keyboard Keys Mapped to Scientific Calculator Keypad

Keyboard Key	Calculator Key	Function
W	LN	Natural logarithm—logarithm to base e
E	LOG	Common logarithm (base 10) of X
R	%	Percentage
T	Δ%	Percentage difference
S	AHYP	Inverse hyperbolic—use with SIN, COS, and TAN
D	ASIN	Arcsine of X
F	ACOS	Arccosine of X
G	ATAN	Arctangent of X
X	x^2	X squared
C	R↑	Roll registers up
V	RND	Round to display setting
B	CLX	Clear X register
N	INT	Leave integer portion of number; truncate fractional

continues

Table 22.14 Continued

Keyboard Key	Calculator Key	Function
]	ABS	Absolute value of X
7	DEG	Set display mode to degrees
8	RAD	Set display mode to radians
9	GRD	Set display mode to grads
1	Cyx	Calculate number of combinations of Y items X at a time
2	H	Convert hours, minutes, and seconds to decimal hours; convert degrees, minutes, and seconds to decimal degrees
3	DG	Convert radians to degrees
Enter	Enter	Copy LSTX to X
0	x	Mean (average)
.	s	Standard deviation
&	&–	Subtract last accumulation

Understanding the Scientific Calculator Registers

The Scientific Calculator (like the Financial and Programmers Calculators) uses Reverse Polish Notation and several memory registers, including five automatic-memory stack registers. These stack registers— X, Y, Z, T, and LSTX (for last X)—work in a manner similar to those in the Financial and Programmers Calculators. Notice that Accessories does not clear the Scientific Calculator's stack registers when you close the window. As in the Programmers Calculator, Accessories remembers and reloads the register values the next time you use the Scientific Calculator.

In addition to the stack registers, Accessories' Scientific Calculator has 20 data registers (named R0 through R9 and R.1 through R.9) in which you can store numbers. To store in one of these registers the value shown in the calculator display, press the STO calculator key and then the register's number. When you want to recall to the calculator display a value from one of the data registers, press the RCL calculator key, and type the register's number.

To clear all values in the data registers and return them to zero, press the f calculator key and then the CRG calculator key. (This command does not clear the stack registers.)

Chapter Summary

This chapter, the last in Part IV, "Using the Desktop Manager," introduces the four PC Tools Accessories calculators: the Algebraic, Financial, Programmers, and Scientific Calculators. Now that you have been introduced to PC Tools Accessories, you are ready to become a more efficient and productive PC user.

Chapter 23, which starts Part V, "Communicating by Modem, Fax, or Local Area Network," teaches you how to use PC Tools as a telephone-dialer telecommunications program and a fax mailbox.

PART

V

OUTLINE

Communicating by Modem, Fax, or Local Area Network

Using PC Tools Telecommunications

Using Electronic Mail

Sending and Receiving Fax with Fax Telecommunications

Controlling a PC Remotely with CP Commute

Using PC Tools Telecommunications

I n general, one of the most frequent uses of computers has been to transmit and receive data electronically over telephone lines, an activity often referred to as *telecommunications*. Before the advent of the personal computer, telecommunications provided the primary access to computers for businesses that could not justify the expense of buying and operating a computer system. More recently, however, as the cost of owning computers has come down, telecommunications has become an activity used primarily for electronically transferring files and correspondence between two computers and for electronically retrieving information from large commercial databases. With PC Tools Desktop, using your computer's capacity to communicate with other computers over phone lines is easy.

This chapter first discusses how to use the features of the Desktop Modem Telecommunications module. The chapter explains how to work with phone directories, dial and connect to another computer, and send and receive computer files. The chapter also explains how to automate telecommunications tasks by using scripts provided with PC Tools.

To use your computer for telecommunications, you must have a peripheral device called a *modem* attached to (or installed in) your computer. Among other things, this device can automate the dialing of telephone numbers. This chapter explains how you can take special advantage of this autodial capability of your modem to create an electronic telephone book. The chapter describes also how the program enables your modem to dial any telephone number on-screen, whether in a spreadsheet, a word processing file, or any other type of file.

Opening the Modem Telecommunications Window

The first step in using PC Tools Desktop and your computer to connect to another computer over telephone lines is to open the Modem Telecommunications window. Display the Desktop main menu, and select **A**ccessories. To display the Modem Telecommunications window, choose **M**odem Telecommunications. Desktop displays a screen similar to the one shown in figure 23.1.

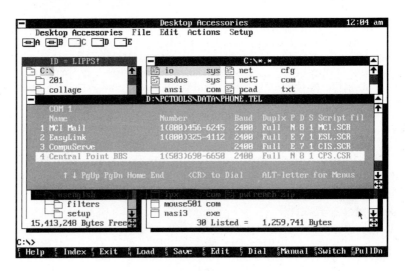

Fig. 23.1

The Modem Telecommunications window.

Examining the Telecommunications Window

Table 23.1 lists the available shortcut commands and other keystroke commands available in Modem Telecommunications. Each command listed in table 23.1 is examined in the chapter.

Table 23.1 Keystroke Commands Available in the Modem Telecommunications Window

Key	Name	Function
F1	Help	Displays context-sensitive Help facility
F2	Index	Displays Help facility index
F3	Exit	Cancels current process, application, or dialog box (same as Esc)
F4	Load	Loads another phone directory file
F5	Save	Saves the current phone directory file to disk
F6	Edit	Edits highlighted phone directory entry
F7	Dial	Dials highlighted phone directory entry
F8	Manual	Displays the terminal screen for manual dialing
F9 or Ctrl+Esc	Switch	Switches active window
F10 or Alt	Menu	Activates horizontal menu bar
Esc	Cancel	Cancels current process or application (same as F3)
Alt+space bar	Window Control	Displays Window Control dialog box
Ins	Insert	Toggles between overtype mode and insert mode when you are editing an entry

The title bar displays the name of the default phone directory file, PHONE.TEL. Desktop loads this file automatically when you open the Modem Telecommunications window. The file can contain as many as 60 entries. You can use the Load command on the File menu to access other phone directory files (see the section "Loading a New or Existing Phone Directory" later in this chapter).

At the left end of the top line of the Modem Telecommunications window, Desktop lists the serial port to which you have attached your modem, as specified during installation or start-up (see Appendix A, "Installing and Configuring PC Tools"). Figure 23.1, for example, indicates that the computer's modem is attached to COM1.

The second line in the Modem Telecommunications window contains labels for the column headings of the phone directory. The Name column contains the name or short description of the computer system to which you want to connect your computer. The Number column contains the telephone number of each system. The other columns explain the baud rate, duplex, parity, data bits, and stop bits settings, which are explained later in the chapter. A full discussion of creating a new phone directory is included later in this chapter.

The remainder of the Modem Telecommunications window contains the actual phone-directory entries. Each row in the tabular format represents one computer system to which you may want to connect.

Desktop can store a maximum of 60 entries in a Desktop phone directory file. By default, even before you add any entries to the phone directory, Desktop already has partially filled in four dialing directory entries. The included entries are three electronic-mail services (MCI Mail, EasyLink, and CompuServe) and the Central Point Software electronic bulletin board system, highlighted in figure 23.1.

Desktop enables you to easily move the highlighted bar up and down within the window, by using the cursor-movement keys ($\uparrow$, $\downarrow$, Home, End, PgDn, and PgUp). You can also use the mouse to move the highlighted bar: Click the vertical scroll bar to display the portion of the directory that contains the entry you want to use. Then, using either the left or right mouse button, click the target entry to highlight it. Double-clicking dials the entry, which is explained later in this chapter.

Loading a New or Existing Phone Directory

In addition to providing the default phone directory, PHONE.TEL, Desktop enables you to create any number of additional phone directories for use in the Modem Telecommunications window. For example, you might live in an area such as Washington, DC, which boasts a large number of electronic bulletin boards—too many to fit within a single Desktop phone directory. You might want to create separate directories for the District of Columbia, Virginia, and Maryland.

When you want to create a new directory, display the Modem Telecommunications window, and then press the shortcut command F4 (Load). Alternatively, select **F**ile to display the File menu, as shown in figure 23.2, and then choose **L**oad from the File pull-down menu. Desktop displays the File Load dialog box (see fig. 23.3).

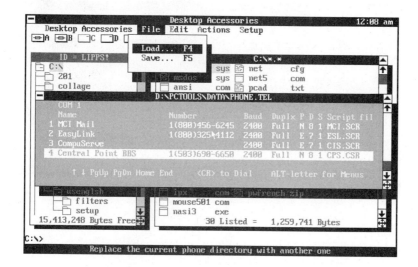

Fig. 23.2

The Modem Telecommunications File menu.

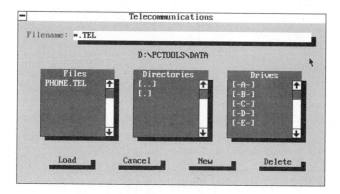

Fig. 23.3

The File Load dialog box.

Type a valid DOS file name in the Filename text box and select the **New** command button. (*Note:* You do not have to type a file name extension.

Desktop adds the TEL extension by default.) Suppose, for example, that you want to name files DC.TEL, VA.TEL, and MD.TEL for phone directories containing Washington, DC, Virginia, and Maryland phone numbers, respectively. When you select New, Desktop creates a new phone directory file with the name you specify—DC.TEL, for example—and loads the new file into the Modem Telecommunications window (see fig. 23.4).

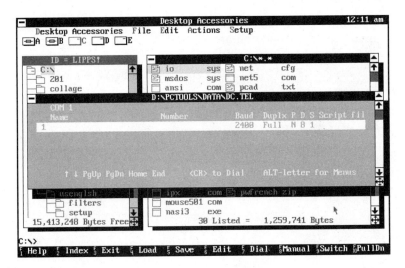

Fig. 23.4

A new phone directory file.

After Desktop loads a new directory, you can create entries. Refer to the following sections for more information about adding entries to a phone directory.

Using the Modem Telecommunications File Load dialog box, you can also load an existing phone directory. Open the Modem Telecommunications window and display the File Load dialog box by pressing F4 (Load) or choosing Load from the File menu. Desktop lists all available phone directory files in the list box. Use the cursor-movement keys or the mouse to select the directory you want Desktop to load. Choose the Load command button, double-click the entry, or press Enter. Desktop loads the directory into the Modem Telecommunications window and replaces the previous directory.

NOTE   When you load a new or existing directory, Desktop replaces the directory on-screen with the specified directory; however, it does not save any changes you may have made to the previous directory. Make a habit of saving any changes before loading another directory.

Managing a Phone Directory

The first step toward communicating with another computer over telephone lines is to dial the telephone number. The most obvious purpose of the Desktop Modem Telecommunications phone directory is to help you dial the number.

Dialing phone numbers is not the only purpose of the phone directory, however. The phone directory also helps you take care of several other chores necessary for successful PC telecommunications. Through the phone directory, Desktop enables you to match the communications settings (such as transmission speed) of the computer to which you are connecting. Without matching settings, you cannot communicate with the other computer.

This section of the chapter describes how to create entries in a phone directory, as well as how to edit or remove entries from a directory.

Creating an Entry

A Desktop Modem Telecommunications phone directory can contain as many as 60 entries. Every entry represents a different computer to which you might want to connect. PC Tools supplies four entries in the default phone directory, PHONE.TEL, but you probably want to add more. You may want to add an entry for the electronic bulletin board of your local PC users' group, for example.

Suppose, for instance, that you want to create an entry to dial the Capital PC User Group Member Information eXchange (CPCUG MIX). To add an entry, open the Modem Telecommunications window and select **E**dit to display the Edit menu, shown in figure 23.5; then select **C**reate New Entry. Desktop displays the Edit Phone Directory dialog box, shown in figure 23.6.

The Edit Phone Directory dialog box is made up of two screens. The first screen, shown in figure 23.6, contains eight text boxes and three command buttons. Select **N**ext Screen to display the second Edit Phone Directory dialog box screen (see fig. 23.7). The second screen contains nine sets of option buttons. In each text box, you can type an optional value, as discussed in the paragraphs that follow.

After you make the necessary entries and selections in the Edit Phone Directory dialog box, as explained in the sections that follow, select the **O**K command button. Desktop adds the new entry as the last row in the phone directory and returns to the Modem Telecommunications window. To quit from the dialog box without adding the new entry, select the **C**ancel command button.

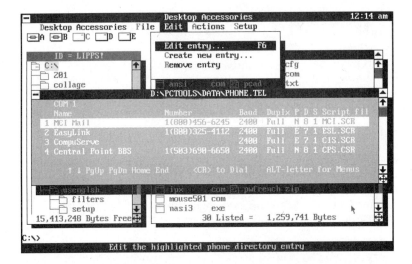

Fig. 23.5

The Modem Telecommunications Edit menu.

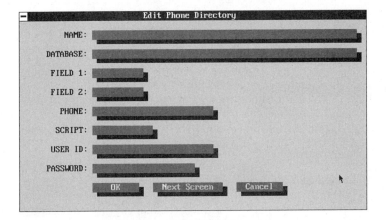

Fig. 23.6

The first screen in the Edit Phone Directory dialog box.

Figure 23.8 shows the selections for the Capital PC User Group Member Information eXchange (CPCUG MIX). Figure 23.9 shows this entry added to the phone directory.

Specifying the Name

In the NAME text box of the Edit Phone Directory dialog box, type a name or description of the computer system to which you want to connect. The value you type in this text box appears in the NAME column of the Modem Telecommunications window. The name value can contain as many as 50 characters.

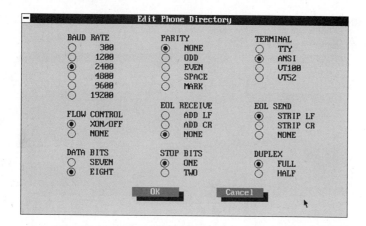

Fig. 23.7

The second screen in the Edit Phone Directory dialog box.

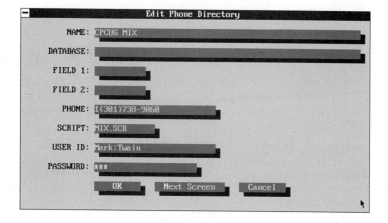

Fig. 23.8

A completed Edit Phone Directory dialog box for the new CPCUG MIX entry.

Specifying a Database

The script language of PC Tools Desktop includes the DATABASE command, which enables a script to access data stored in as many as two fields in a Desktop database file. For this command to work, however, you must provide file information. In three text boxes in the Edit Phone Directory dialog box, you must indicate the name of the database file and the name of the two fields.

When you plan to use the DATABASE command in a script, type the file name of the target database in the DATABASE text box; in the FIELD 1 text box, type the name of the first field that the script will use; and in the FIELD 2 text box, type the field name of the second field the script will use.

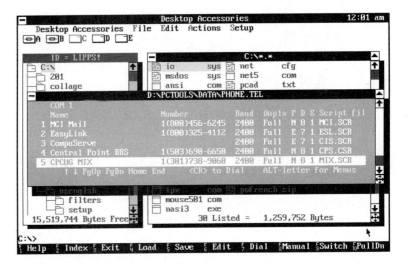

Fig. 23.9

The phone directory after adding an entry for CPCUG MIX.

If you don't plan to use a script with the DATABASE command, leave these fields blank. For a complete discussion of the DATABASE command, see the section "Variables and Variable-Manipulation Commands" later in this chapter.

Specifying a Phone Number

In the PHONE text box, type the telephone number of the remote computer system. Be sure to include all digits required to dial the computer on the other end. Many business phone systems, for example, require that you first dial 9 to get an outside line. In such a case, you must include the 9 in the PHONE text box. The telephone number can contain up to 25 characters.

T I P

If you have call waiting, you may want to disable this service so that your telecommunications will not be interrupted. In most cases, including *70 at the beginning of an entry turns off call waiting; however, contact your local phone company to find the number you should use.

Listing a Script File

As you become experienced in using the Modem Telecommunications application, you may begin to get bored with typing your user ID and password every time you log on to a system. Desktop provides a feature known as the *script facility* to automate such tasks as signing on to an electronic-mail system or bulletin board system. Desktop scripts are actually small programs that can even automate the transfer of files to and from other systems. With PC Tools 8, Central Point Software distributes several scripts that enable you to easily log on to your favorite commercial electronic-mail service, send mail, receive mail, and even send fax with a minimum of typing on your part.

Desktop lists four script files in the Script file column of the Modem Telecommunications window: MCI.SCR, ESL.SCR, CIS.SCR, and CPS.SCR (refer to fig. 23.1). Each script assists you in signing on to the respective computer system by typing your user ID and password and then helping you navigate the particular service.

A later section in this chapter teaches you how to create and use scripts. After you create a script, you must add the name of the script to the system's entry in your phone directory. Type the complete file name of the script (including the file name extension SCR) in the SCRIPT text box in the Edit Phone Directory dialog box.

Supplying User ID and Password

Virtually all computer systems that allow access by telephone lines limit that access to authorized users. Without specific authorization, you are not permitted to use the system. Typically, authorized users of computer systems are identified by a *user ID* and *password*. Each of the four scripts listed in the Script file column in figure 23.1 automate signing on to a computer system if you first supply a user ID and a password.

Commercial systems, such as MCI Mail and CompuServe, assign your initial user ID and password. You must obtain these items *off-line* (that is, by telephone or mail) before you are permitted to sign on to the system for the first time.

By contrast, a private electronic bulletin board system (or BBS) usually permits you to choose your own user ID and password. The majority of bulletin boards operate as *open systems*; in other words, you indicate during your first call a user ID and password that you intend to use in the future. When you connect on subsequent occasions, you use the same user ID and password to sign on.

When you intend to use a script that will employ your user ID or password in automating the sign-on procedure for a particular computer system, you must add these items to the Edit Phone Directory dialog box. Type the user ID (up to 25 characters) in the USER ID text box. Type the password (up to 21 characters) in the PASSWORD text box. When you are not using a script file, however, you can leave both of these boxes blank.

NOTE After you save the dialog box and then redisplay it during a later session for the purpose of making a change, Desktop hides the password by displaying solid squares in the PASSWORD text box.

NOTE The USER ID and PASSWORD fields are *case-sensitive*, meaning that capitalization is important; be careful to enter your user ID and password exactly as you do when you call the system.

Later sections give more information about how to use your user ID and password in a script.

Setting Line Parameters

On the second Edit Phone Directory dialog box screen, which you access by clicking the **Next Screen** button, you use the four groups of option buttons to set parameters that determine serial port line settings: *baud*, *parity*, *data bits*, and *stop bits*. For telecommunication by modem between two computers to be effective, each parameter must be set to the same value on both ends; in other words, both computers must use the same settings.

Baud Rate

The BAUD RATE option buttons represent six available transmission rates: 300, 1200, 2400, 4800, 9600, and 19200. The term *baud* typically is used to mean *bits per second*. In Desktop's Modem Telecommunications application, the term *baud* refers to the data-transmission rate between the computer and the modem. Select the appropriate transmission speed by choosing the appropriate option button. The speed you choose for an entry must match the transmission speed used by the computer to which you intend to connect.

Parity

The PARITY option buttons indicate the parity-checking method you want to employ (the default setting is NONE, indicating no parity checking). *Parity checking* is a method of screening for transmission errors. An error in transmission of even a single bit can completely change the meaning of the byte that included the bit. To help detect errors as they occur, some computers use the eighth bit of every byte as a *parity bit*. The parity of an integer (whole number) indicates whether the integer is odd or even. Four ways for using a parity bit are available: odd, even, space, and mark.

When the computer is using the *even parity* method, the computer sets the value of the parity bit to 1 or 0 so that the total of all eight bits is even. Similarly, the *odd parity* method assigns the value of the parity bit so that the sum of all digits in every byte is an odd number. In *space parity*, the parity bit is always set to 0. Conversely, the *mark parity* method always sets the parity bit to 1.

For PC-to-PC communication—including connection to bulletin boards—use NONE (no parity). In connecting to an on-line service such as MCI Mail or CompuServe, you usually must use the EVEN option.

Data Bits

The DATA BITS option buttons indicate the number of data bits (seven or eight). The default option is the EIGHT option button. The personal computer uses eight bits at a time to represent a byte of data. Many other types of computers, however, including mainframes used by on-line services, use only seven data bits per byte. For every entry in the Modem Telecommunications phone directory, you specify whether data occupies the first seven bits of every byte or all eight bits. Desktop calls this specification the number of *data bits*. Some programs use the term *word length* or *character length* to mean the same thing.

You may occasionally use your computer to communicate with another computer that needs eight data bits per byte. At other times you may communicate with a computer that can use only seven data bits per byte. The only way to know for sure which one you need is to ask the operator of the other computer.

A simple rule of thumb is to use eight data bits for PC-to-PC or PC-to-bulletin-board connections. All personal computers need 8-bit bytes to represent the full IBM character set, as well as for transmission of program files. When you are calling an on-line service (such as Compu-Serve) or another mainframe-based system, use seven data bits because most of these systems are run on computers that typically use only seven data bits per byte.

Stop Bits

You use the STOP BITS options to indicate the number of stop bits (one or two) to be included at the end of every byte of transmitted data. Data sent through a serial port comes out as a single-file stream of bits, but each bit means nothing by itself. Because a computer stores information in bytes, each made up of eight bits, the receiving computer must be capable of reconstructing the bytes of data from the stream of bits in order to make sense of the transmission.

Computers use two methods to clearly identify every byte of data sent through a serial port: *synchronous* and *asynchronous* transmission. Personal computers use the asynchronous method to send data through a serial port. The sending computer marks the beginning of every byte that will be transmitted with a *start bit*. This start bit informs the receiving computer that a byte of data follows. Then, to mark the end of the byte, the computer sends either one or two *stop bits* (the number of stop bits is a user option). The stop bits inform the receiving computer it has just received the entire byte. Using this procedure, timing is not critical.

When you set up PC communication software, such as Desktop Modem Telecommunications, to communicate with another computer, you must specify whether to use one or two stop bits (an option specified by the RS232 standard). The number of stop bits used on your end must match the number used by the computer on the other end.

When in doubt, use one stop bit, which is the default choice in the Edit Phone Directory dialog box. You seldom see two stop bits used by another computer.

Selecting Terminal Emulation

Terminals are special devices you use to connect to host computers for entering and retrieving data. When Desktop *emulates* a particular type of terminal, it "impersonates" the terminal to communicate with a host computer that expects only terminals to be connected. Desktop can emulate four types of terminals:

TTY

ANSI

VT100

VT52

Use the TERMINAL option buttons in the Edit Phone Directory dialog box to select an appropriate terminal emulation for every entry.

The most generic and least capable of Desktop's terminal emulations is TTY. Use this emulation only as a last resort. For commercial electronic-mail systems, use either VT100 or VT52, two popular types of terminals manufactured by Digital Equipment Corporation (DEC). Both of these DEC emulations provide the host system better screen control than TTY.

When you are creating an entry for connecting to a BBS, choose the ANSI option. This emulation enables bulletin board systems to display characters, line graphics, and animation in color.

Activating Flow Control

Many remote systems, including most on-line services and bulletin boards, support a flow-control method known as *XON/XOFF* (or *software pacing*). These systems stop transmitting information when they receive an ASCII character that is referred to as the *XOFF* character. This character is the same one generated when you press Ctrl+S on your keyboard. When the remote system receives another ASCII character known as *XON*, the remote system continues transmission. The XON character is the same character generated when you press Ctrl+Q.

You can use the following FLOW CONTROL option buttons to control whether Desktop activates the XON/OFF feature:

- Choose the *XON/OFF* option button to suspend the transmission of characters to a remote computer when XOFF is received and to resume transmission when XON is received.

- Select the *NONE* option to turn off the XON/OFF feature.

Choosing End-of-Line Processing

EOL RECEIVE and EOL SEND include option buttons that fall into the more general category of end-of-line processing. These options determine how Desktop handles the ASCII characters that cause *carriage returns* (moving the cursor to the beginning of the line) and *line feeds* (moving the cursor to the next line on the screen). The EOL RECEIVE option buttons determine how Desktop handles line-feed and carriage-return characters received by your computer during a telecommunications session. The EOL SEND options control how Desktop handles line-feed and carriage-return characters sent by your computer to a remote computer.

For you to be able to read more than one line of text on-screen during a telecommunications session, something analogous to the typewriter's line feed and carriage return must occur at the end of every line. Each action is represented by a specific ASCII character sent or received by your computer. The carriage return (CR) symbol is ASCII decimal 13, and line feed (LF) is ASCII decimal 10.

The following option buttons are listed beneath EOL RECEIVE in the Edit Phone Directory dialog box:

- *ADD LF.* Select this option if you want Desktop to add a line feed (LF) to every carriage return (CR) received from the computer on the other end.

- *ADD CR.* Select this option button if you want Desktop to add a carriage return to every line-feed character received from the remote computer.

- *NONE* is the default option. Choose this option if you don't want Desktop to add a carriage return or a line feed to incoming carriage-return and line-feed characters.

Most host computers, such as commercial electronic-mail services and BBSs, already add a line feed to every carriage return. If Desktop also adds a line feed, everything on-screen is double-spaced. Therefore, use the NONE option in most cases.

The EOL SEND option buttons are listed in the following:

- *STRIP LF.* Select this option button if you want Desktop to strip LF characters from ASCII text sent by your computer to the remote computer. This option is the default.

- *STRIP CR.* Select this option button if you want Desktop to remove CR characters from ASCII text sent by your computer to the remote computer.

- *NONE.* Choose this option button if you don't want Desktop to remove line feeds or carriage returns from ASCII text sent by your computer to another computer.

Most host computers, such as those accessed when you use on-line services and bulletin boards, add a line feed to every carriage return. If Desktop also adds a line feed, everything on-screen is double-spaced; therefore, leave the EOL SEND option set to the STRIP LF option in most cases.

Selecting Duplex

The last group of option buttons in the Edit Phone Directory are used with the DUPLEX option. *Duplex* refers to the capability of a modem to send and receive information at the same time. A modem capable of simultaneously sending and receiving data is called a *full-duplex* modem. *Half-duplex* modems, on the other hand, operate like a one-lane bridge. When a half-duplex modem is receiving data, the modem cannot send data. When the modem is sending data, the modem cannot receive data. The modem continually switches from send to receive and from receive to send to communicate with another modem.

When your computer is connected as a terminal to a host computer (such as an on-line service or bulletin board) via a full-duplex modem, the computer at the other end typically *echoes* to your screen any character you type on your keyboard. This action provides a crude but effective way to confirm that the other computer received the character you typed. In Desktop, *full-duplex* refers to this echo feature rather than to whether you are using a full-duplex modem. Because the remote computer is echoing characters, Desktop does not display characters to your screen as you type them.

By contrast, *half-duplex* means that the remote computer does not echo the characters you type. For you to see what you are typing, your computer must display text to the screen as you type.

The available DUPLEX option buttons are FULL and HALF. Select the appropriate option button for the entry. The default setting is FULL. Just as other communication settings must match at both ends of the PC communication line, the duplex mode must match the computer on the other end. Otherwise, one of two problems occurs:

■ When the computer on the other end is echoing the characters you send back to your screen but you have set Desktop Modem Telecommunications to half-duplex, you see double characters. You type "Hello," for example, and "HHeelllloo" appears on your screen.

To remedy this problem, you must switch the Duplex setting from half-duplex mode to full-duplex mode.

■ If the other computer is not echoing characters you transmit back to your screen but you have set Desktop Modem Telecommunications to full-duplex mode, you cannot see the characters you type. The remedy is to change the Duplex setting to half-duplex.

Editing an Existing Entry

From time to time as you use Desktop for telecommunication, you may need to modify one or more settings of a phone-directory entry. Perhaps you need to change a phone number, edit your password, or change the terminal emulation.

When you want to edit a phone-directory entry, use the mouse or the cursor-movement keys to move the highlighted bar to the entry you want to modify. Press the shortcut key F6 (Edit) or select Edit from the horizontal menu bar and then Edit Entry. Desktop displays the Edit Phone Directory dialog box containing the settings from the highlighted entry.

While Desktop displays the Edit Phone Directory dialog box, you can make changes to the values in the text boxes or select different option buttons in the same manner used to create the entry. When you finish making modifications, select the **OK** command button. Desktop saves the changes and returns to the Modem Telecommunications window. To quit without saving modifications, select the **Cancel** command button.

Deleting an Entry

Occasionally, you may need to delete one or more entries from a Modem Telecommunications phone directory. First, display the directory in the Modem Telecommunications window, and then use the mouse or the cursor-movement keys to highlight the entry you want to delete. Select **Edit** and then the **Remove** entry option. Desktop permanently deletes the entry from the phone directory and moves all subsequent entries up one line.

> **CAUTION:** Because you will not be prompted for confirmation before the entry is deleted, use this command with caution.

Saving the Phone Directory

As is the case in most Desktop applications, Desktop automatically saves information to disk. Changes such as additions, changes, and deletions to a phone directory are saved whenever you close the application window. Desktop does not automatically save the directory, however, if you use the **Load** command to load a different phone directory. Desktop provides an alternative method of saving a phone directory to disk.

To save the currently displayed phone directory to disk, press the shortcut key F5 (Save). Alternatively, select **File**, and then choose **Save** from the File pull-down menu. Desktop displays the Save File to Disk dialog box, similar to the one shown in figure 23.10. The dialog box includes the file name of the current phone directory. To save the directory, select the **S**ave command button. Desktop saves the file and returns to the Modem Telecommunications window.

Fig. 23.10

The Save File to Disk dialog box.

You can also save the currently displayed phone directory to disk with a new name. Simply erase the phone directory name in the Save File to Disk dialog box and substitute the name you want to use. Then select the **S**ave command button.

Connecting to Another Computer

When you use Desktop to connect to another computer, your computer normally does the calling. When the computer you intend to call has placed its modem in autoanswer mode, the next step is for you to instruct your modem to place the call. This section examines how to set up your modem for use with Desktop, as well as how to use Desktop to call another computer. Additionally, you will learn how to set up your computer so that your modem answers a call from another modem.

Occasionally, you may be talking to someone on the telephone and decide that you want to connect your computers over the same phone line. This portion of the chapter also explains the steps for accomplishing this connection.

Configuring Your Modem

Although your modem was initially configured when you installed PC Tools 8, you can change the COM port, initialization strings, connect strings, and dialing method from the Modem Setup dialog box.

To display the Modem Setup dialog box, shown in figure 23.11, select **S**etup from the Modem Telecommunications window, and then choose **M**odem setup.

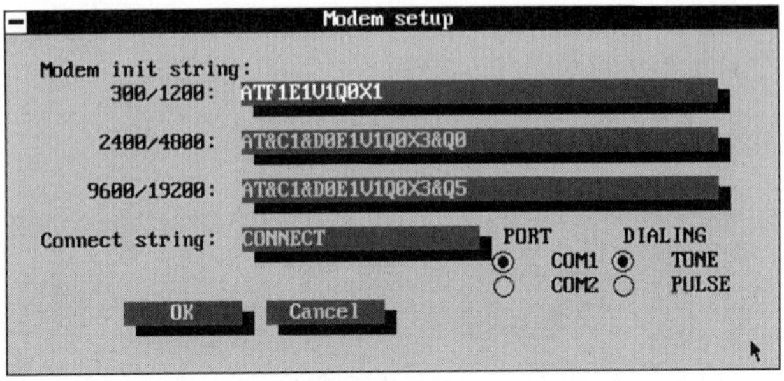

Fig. 23.11

The Modem Set-up dialog box.

The Modem initialization strings are grouped by modem baud rate; the string that Desktop uses depends on the baud rate you selected in the Edit Phone Directory dialog box. The default strings should work for most AT command modems; if your modem requires a different initialization string, refer to your modem manual for more information.

The Connect string should correspond to the response sent by your modem to your computer when it successfully connects. Again, use the default in almost all cases; if your modem doesn't accept standard AT commands, refer to your modem manual.

Desktop supports COM1 through COM4 for a modem or null-modem connection; because COM1 and COM2 cover almost all cases, COM3 and COM4 appear only if you specified the /C3 or /C4 command line options when starting from DOS. Finally, the last group of option buttons allows you to choose between touch-tone and pulse dialing.

To save any changes you made, select **OK**. To exit the dialog box without making any changes, press **C**ancel.

Using an Entry To Dial a Phone Number

From the Modem Telecommunications window, you can use one of the following methods to call another computer:

- Using the left or right mouse button, double-click the phone-directory entry for the computer system you want to call.

- Use the mouse or cursor-movement keys to move the highlighted bar to the phone-directory entry for the computer system you want to call, and then press F7 (Dial).

- Use the mouse or cursor-movement keys to move the highlighted bar to the phone-directory entry for the computer system you want to call, and then press Enter.

■ Type the entry number of the phone-directory entry for the computer system you want to call, and then press Enter.

■ Use the mouse or cursor-movement keys to move the highlighted bar to the phone-directory entry for the computer system you want to call; select **A**ctions from the horizontal menu bar, and then select the **D**ial option (see fig. 23.12).

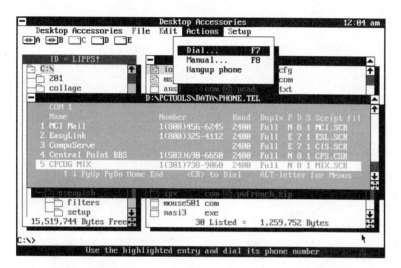

Fig. 23.12

The Actions menu.

Desktop sends to your modem a software command instructing the modem to begin dialing the phone number listed in the highlighted entry. While the modem is dialing the number, Desktop displays the following message in the message bar:

```
Dialing-Press ESC to Cancel
```

When the modem on the other end answers, the modems begin to communicate. Desktop first displays the message Connected in the message bar and then displays the on-line screen, similar to the screen shown in figure 23.13.

Understanding the On-Line Screen

The Modem Telecommunications on-line screen is a little different in appearance from other Desktop application windows. If you press F10, Desktop displays a horizontal menu bar. By default, the screen displays shortcut keys in the message bar. The shortcut keys listed in the message bar are not the same as those listed at the bottom of the Modem

Telecommunications window (the phone directory window). Table 23.2 lists the shortcut key commands and other keystroke commands available in the on-line window.

```
-                                Telecommunications      ALT-ESC Off  12:14 am
CONNECT 2400
Welcome to CPCUG MIX - Node 6

You have reached the Capital PC User Group Member Information Exchange (CPCUG
MIX).  Full access is limited to CPCUG members and others specifically granted
access.  All callers are expected to use their real names.

If you have not already done so, you will be asked supply information to
verify that you are a member of CPCUG.  Just answer the questions with the
information that is shown on your Capital PC User Group membership card or the
mailing label from a recent issue of the Monitor. If you have any question
about your membership, please ask it in the MEMBER conference.  Note that you
will be given limited access even if you are not a member.  Limited access
means 20 minutes per day (instead of 2 hours), no downloading, and no use of
doors other than the membership verification door. See Bulletin 1 for
information on how to join CPCUG.

Members, please visit the NOTICE conference to get updated information about
events and to pick up any changes to the schedule published in the Monitor.


What is your First Name?
       Connected        |      Send      |      Receive    | 2400 N81 | FDX | ANSI
1 Help  2 Index 3 Exit  4 ASCII 52modem 6 ASCII 72modem 8Hangup 9Switch 0PullDn
```

Fig. 23.13

The on-line screen after connecting to CPCUG MIX.

Table 23.2 Keystroke Commands Available in the Modem Telecommunications Window On-line Screen

Key	Name	Function
F1	Help	Displays context-sensitive Help facility
F2	Index	Displays Help facility index
F3	Exit	Cancels current process, application, or dialog box (same as Esc)
F4	ASCII	Sends a file with the ASCII file-transfer protocol
F5	Varies	Sends a file with the default binary transfer protocol (XMODEM, ZMODEM, or KERMIT)
F6	ASCII	Receives a file with the ASCII transfer protocol
F7	Varies	Receives a file with the default binary transfer protocol (XMODEM, ZMODEM, or KERMIT)

Key	Name	Function
F8	Hangup	Disconnects, signals the modem to go *on-hook* (hangs up the phone line), and returns to phone directory
F9 or Ctrl+Esc	Switch	Switches active window
F10 or Alt	Menu	Activates horizontal menu bar
Esc	Cancel	Cancels current process or application (same as F3)
Alt+space bar	Window Control	Displays Window Control dialog box
Ins	Insert	Toggles between overtype mode and insert mode when you are editing an entry

Just above the message bar, the on-line screen includes a bar not found in other types of Desktop screens. This chapter refers to the bar as the *telecommunications status bar*. The remainder of the screen displays characters sent between your computer and the computer at the other end of the phone line. Unlike other Desktop screens, this window does not include a window border, resize box, or zoom feature.

If you prefer a "cleaner" screen during an on-line session, you can suppress the message bar and telecommunications status bar. Select the Full Online Screen option on the Modem Telecommunications window's Setup menu. This action adds a check mark to the left of this option and turns off the message bar and telecommunications status bar when Desktop displays the on-line screen.

The telecommunications status bar is divided into six sections. At the left end, the first section of the telecommunications status bar is referred to in this chapter as the *line status*. This section informs you whether the computer is connected to another computer. When you are communicating with another computer, the line status indicates Connected (refer to fig. 23.13). If you display the on-line screen before dialing another computer, as discussed in the section "Using Manual Dial" later in this chapter, Desktop displays the message Not Connected (see fig. 23.14).

Fig. 23.14

The terminal screen indicating that the computers are not connected.

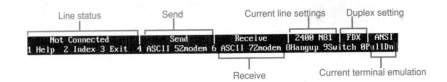

Line status   Send   Current line settings   Duplex setting

```
   Not Connected          Send          Receive     2400 N81   FDX   ANSI
1 Help  2 Index 3 Exit  4 ASCII 5Zmodem 6 ASCII 7Zmodem 8Hangup 9Switch 0PullDn
```

Receive   Current terminal emulation

> **NOTE**
>
> If the first message in the telecommunications status bar always displays Connected—even when your computer is not connected to another computer—then the Carrier Detect (CD) setting on your modem is probably set so that Desktop thinks that a modem carrier signal is always present. Change this modem setting so that the modem monitors the existence of a carrier and raises the CD signal high when carrier is detected; this tells Desktop that you are actually connected. For some modems, you can change this setting through a dipswitch setting; for other modems, you must use a command like AT&C1. Consult your modem manual for more information.

The Send section of the on-line screen's telecommunications status bar contains two shortcut keys: F4 (ASCII) and F5 (either XMODEM, ZMODEM or KERMIT). You use these two shortcut commands to send files. The Receive section of the telecommunications status bar contains two shortcut keys, F6 (ASCII) and F7 (either XMODEM, ZMODEM or KERMIT), which you use to receive files.

The next section of the telecommunications status bar shows the current line settings—the transmission speed setting and the current parity, data bits, and stop bits settings. The section to the right of the current line settings indicates the duplex setting—whether Desktop is set to full duplex (FDX) or to half-duplex (HDX). The status bar shown in figure 23.14 indicates that the duplex setting is full duplex.

The last section on the status line displays the current terminal emulation. Figure 23.14, for example, indicates that Desktop is using ANSI terminal emulation.

The telecommunications status bar and message bar occupy two lines of the on-line screen. Desktop enables you to turn off the telecommunications status bar and the message bar, increasing the available number of lines by two. Display the Modem Telecommunications window (at the phone-directory screen, not the on-line screen) and select **S**etup to display the Setup menu; then select **F**ull Online Screen. The next time Desktop displays the on-line screen, the telecommunications status bar and the message bar will be hidden.

All the shortcut keys listed in the status bar and message bar of the on-line screen continue to work, even if they are not listed at the bottom of the screen.

Understanding the Alternate Keyboards

When Desktop is emulating a DEC VT52 or DEC VT100 terminal, the keyboard operates differently than normal. To remind you that this alternate keyboard is active, Desktop displays the message ALT-ESC On near the right end of the horizontal menu bar. When the terminal emulation is TTY or ANSI, this message is ALT-ESC Off to indicate that the alternate keyboard is not active. You can toggle between the standard Modem Telecommunications on-line keyboard and the alternate VT52/VT100 keyboard by pressing the Alt+Esc keystroke combination. Table 23.3 describes the keys that are different on the two keyboards.

Table 23.3 The Standard and VT52/VT100 Alternate Keyboards

PC Key	Alternate Keyboard On	Alternate Keyboard Off
F1	PF1	Help
F2	PF2	Index
F3	PF3	Exit
F4	PF4	Send ASCII
F5		Send with Binary Protocol
PC Key	Effect with Alt+Esc on	Effect with Alt+Esc off
F6		Receive ASCII
F7		Receive with Binary Protocol
F8		Hangup
F9		Swap
F1		Activates horizontal menu bar (same as Alt)
Shift+F1	Help	PF1
Shift+F2	Index	PF2
Shift+F3	Exit	PF3
Shift+F4	Send ASCII	PF4

continues

Table 23.3 Continued

PC Key	Alternate Keyboard On	Alternate Keyboard Off
Shift+F5	Send with Binary Protocol	
Shift+F6	Receive ASCII	
Shift+F7	Receive with Binary Protocol	
Shift+F8	Hangup	
Shift+F9	Swap	
Shift+F10	Activates horizontal menu bar	
Alt		Activates horizontal menu bar (same as F10)
Alt+space bar	Window Control	Window Control
Ins		Toggles between overtype mode and insert mode when you are editing an entry
Esc	Send Esc to modem	Exit to Modem Telecommunications window (phone directory)
Shift+Esc	Exit to Modem	Send Esc to Modem Telecommunications window (phone directory)
Ctrl+End	Break	

Using Manual Dial

In addition to dialing another computer via the phone directory, you can dial a phone number manually, without first creating a phone-directory entry. First, display the dialing directory. Then use the mouse or cursor-movement keys to position the highlighted bar on an entry containing the communication parameters required to communicate with the computer system you want to dial. Finally, press the shortcut key F8 (Manual) or select **A**ctions on the horizontal menu bar and then **M**anual from the Actions menu. Desktop displays the on-line screen (refer to fig. 23.14). Notice that the line-status section of the telecommunications status bar displays Not Connected, which means that your computer is not communicating with another computer.

After Desktop displays the on-line screen, you can manually issue the software command that causes your modem to dial the phone number of the target computer system. The requisite software command for Hayes-compatible modems is the following:

   ATDT *phone number*

Replace *phone number* with the actual telephone number of the computer system to which you want to connect (for pulse phones, replace ATDT with ATDP). To dial the number 555-1234, for example, type the command **ATDT5551234** and press Enter.

> **NOTE**
>
> Do not be concerned if the command and number do not appear on-screen as you type. With the full-duplex setting, this situation is normal. The modem still responds properly and dials the phone. If you are not confident that you can type the correct command without seeing what you are typing, type **ATE1** and press Enter.
>
> In Hayes-compatible modems, this command, which has no effect on the duplex setting, causes the modem to echo the commands that the modem receives in command mode. The commands are echoed to the screen. The modem sends the message OK to the screen. You then can type the command to dial the remote computer, and the modem echoes your keystrokes to the screen.

Your modem dials the phone number, and the remote computer's line begins to ring. The remote modem answers the call, and the two computers begin communicating. To alert you to the connection, your modem sends a message, such as CONNECT 2400, to the screen. Desktop changes the line-status message at the left end of the telecommunications status bar to Connected (refer to fig. 23.13).

You can use another method to dial a number manually from the keyboard. Create an entry and leave the Phone text box blank. Whenever you want to dial a number manually, select this entry. Desktop displays a dialog box containing a Phone Number text box and two command buttons: OK and Cancel. Type the number you want the modem to dial, and select the **OK** command button. Desktop instructs your modem to dial the number.

T I P   To make manual dialing more convenient, set up one or more generic entries with blank numbers. If, for example, you create an entry
called "2400 No Parity" and set the appropriate line parameters but
leave the number blank, you can use this entry for all 2400 8-N-1 dialing. Other generic entries might feature 7 data bits and even parity
or different baud rates.

Receiving a Call

Because you may be on the receiving end of a connection, you need to
understand the actions required to set up Desktop Modem Telecommunications and your modem for that role. When the phone rings, you are
expected to answer the phone. When another computer's modem is
calling, however, you want your modem to answer and connect with
the calling modem. To do so, you first send your modem the proper
command to place the modem in *autoanswer mode*.

If you can dedicate a telephone line to use for your computer, you can
set Desktop so that every time you use the program, Desktop places
your modem in autoanswer mode so that the modem is ready to answer the line whenever another computer's modem calls.

However, when your modem's telephone line is used for both voice
communication and computer communication, you cannot always
leave the modem in autoanswer mode because, in this mode, any incoming call—from a modem or not—gets an earful of the modem's carrier signal. Therefore, place your computer's modem in autoanswer
mode only when you expect another modem to call your number.

In autoanswer mode, the modem being called picks up the ringing line
and says "hello" with a carrier signal. Assuming that the calling modem
and your modem are compatible, the two modems *shake hands* and
begin a communication session. You then can use Desktop to send and
receive information to and from the remote computer.

   For the connection to be successful, your baud rate, data
bits, stop bits, and parity settings must match the settings
used by the remote computer.

Whenever you expect that someone is going to use his or her computer's modem to call, place your modem in autoanswer mode. Press
F8 (Manual) or select **A**ctions on the horizontal menu bar, and then

select **M**anual from the Actions menu. Desktop displays the on-line screen with the message Not Connected displayed in the line-status portion of the telecommunications status bar. Type the following command and press Enter:

ATS0=n

Replace the n with a positive whole number that equals the number of rings you want the modem to wait before answering the call. If you want the modem to answer after the first ring, for example, type **ATS0=1**, and then press Enter. (One ring is the recommended value.)

After you type this command, your modem sends the message OK to the screen, indicating that the modem has accepted the command and is ready to answer the next call.

To turn off autoanswer mode, type **ATS0=0** in the on-line screen and press Enter. The modem again sends the response OK to the screen, indicating that the modem has turned off autoanswer mode. The modem no longer answers the phone.

Connecting during a Voice Call

Occasionally, you and an associate may be talking on the phone and decide to connect your computers. For example, you might want to send your associate a copy of the spreadsheet file being discussed.

Ideally, each of you has a second telephone line, separate from the one on which you are talking. If so, you can use the preceding discussions to make the connection. More typically, however, your computers' modems and your telephones share the same line. Although you can hang up and use the modems to place and answer the call again, making the connection without hanging up is more convenient (and more economical if the call is a toll call).

Compare your line parameters before you continue so that you can be sure that the parameters are identical.

T I P

To connect computers over the same phone line used by your voice call (when you are using Hayes-compatible modems), both parties first must activate Desktop Modem Telecommunications and be at the on-line screen. Decide which one of your computers will act as the *originate* computer. The other computer acts as the *answer* computer. The operator of the answer computer must type the following command and press Enter:

ATA

This command places the modem in answer mode and forces the modem to begin transmitting the carrier signal.

In the meantime, the operator of the originate computer must type this command and press Enter:

ATD

This command places the modem in originate mode. The modem is "listening" for a carrier signal from an answer-mode modem.

After each operator enters the proper command, and as soon as the answer modem emits a carrier signal, both operators must immediately hang up the telephone. The modems keep the lines open and communicate.

Using a Direct Connection

When two computers are physically close enough to be connected by a 50-foot (or shorter) cable, using a modem isn't necessary. Instead, connect the computers by a *null-modem cable*. Connect the cable to the serial port you designated when you installed Desktop.

With a null-modem cable connected between two computers, establishing a communication connection is easy. Open the Modem Telecommunications window and press F8 (Manual) or select the **M**anual command on the **A**ctions menu to display the on-line screen. You can tell whether the two computers are connected properly if you can type in the on-line screen of one computer and see the results in the on-line screen of the other computer. If you see nothing or you see different characters than what you are typing, make sure that you have all communications parameters set properly.

After the two computers are connected, you can transmit files between the two computers. Refer to Chapter 26, "Controlling a PC Remotely with CP Commute," for a discussion about how to transfer files. This feature enables you to, among other things, transmit files between two computers connected by a special null-modem cable, which you can usually find at your local computer store.

Ending a Connection

The last step in any communication session is to hang up the line. When you are connected to an on-line service or bulletin board, issue the sign-off command appropriate for that system. The host computer usually drops the line first. You may see a few meaningless characters on-screen followed by the message NO CARRIER, indicating that the modems are disconnected.

Sometimes you must disconnect the line from your end. At the on-line screen, press F8 (Hangup). Alternatively, select Actions, and then choose Hangup Phone from the Actions menu. Desktop briefly displays the message Disconnecting in the message bar as the program sends to your modem the signal to hang up the telephone line. Desktop then returns to the Modem Telecommunications window and the phone directory.

> **CAUTION:** If you press Esc, F3 (Exit), or the Desktop hot key to exit from the Modem Telecommunications window, Desktop does not hang up the line. Be careful not to forget that you still are connected (especially if you are connected to a commercial system that charges by the minute).

For Related Information

▸▸ "Transferring Files," p. 902.

FROM HERE...

Sending and Receiving Files

In concept, transferring a file from one computer to another is nearly the same as copying a file from one disk drive to another. You make an electronic duplicate or copy of the original file and then place the copy in a different location (from the user's perspective). File transfer between computers, however, is significantly more complicated than file transfer between disk drives.

This section shows you how to perform this operation by using Desktop Modem Telecommunications. You will learn the basic steps for sending or receiving a file between your computer and a *remote computer* (the computer on the other end of the telephone line) by using Desktop's four available file-transfer protocols: ASCII, XMODEM, ZMODEM, and KERMIT. A *protocol* is simply a set of agreed-upon rules for file transfer that ensures data is sent and received accurately.

Selecting the Binary Transfer Options

Of the four file-transfer protocols offered by PC Tools 8, three are called *binary* protocols. Unlike ASCII—which can only send and receive standard text files—the XMODEM, ZMODEM, and KERMIT protocols can also send programs and data files. These binary protocols also include error-detection routines that retransmit data garbled by telephone static.

The Binary Transfer Options dialog box, shown in figure 23.15, enables you to control the defaults for all file transfers using any of the three binary protocols. To open the dialog box, display the Modem Telecommunications window, select **S**etup, and then choose **B**inary transfer options.

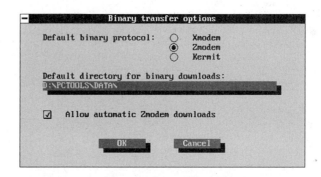

Fig. 23.15

The Binary Transfer Options dialog box.

The Default Binary Protocol option buttons determine which binary protocol is activated when you select the shortcut keys F5 (Send Binary) and F7 (Receive Binary) from the on-line screen. The labels for these keys change to reflect the default you choose. You learn more about these protocols and how to use them later in this chapter.

As a rule, select ZMODEM if the services you call support ZMODEM transfers. ZMODEM is the fastest of the three binary protocols, it supports *batch* transfers (where multiple files are received at one time), and it's the most reliable. ZMODEM has become the "protocol of choice" on most bulletin board systems.

KERMIT is also a reliable batch transfer protocol, but it's much slower than ZMODEM. KERMIT is most often used to connect with mainframe or minicomputer systems.

If the system you're calling doesn't support ZMODEM or KERMIT, the system likely will support XMODEM, still the most widely used binary protocol. Although not as fast or as reliable as ZMODEM or KERMIT, XMODEM does offer error-detection and binary capability that the ASCII protocol doesn't support.

The Default Directory for Binary Downloads field in the Binary Transfer Options dialog box tells Desktop where to save the files you download (receive from other computers) using one of the binary transfer protocols. Type the entire path of the directory, which should already exist on the destination disk. The default directory is your \PCTOOLS directory or the location specified during installation.

You may find storing program and data files in a separate directory from ASCII files (like copies of your electronic mail or stock quotes) convenient.

T I P

The last option in this dialog box is a check box that specifies whether to enable or disable ZMODEM automatic downloading. Normally, you want to enable this feature, which allows Desktop to begin receiving a file with the ZMODEM protocol without requiring you to use the Receive shortcut key or menu command. Instead, the remote computer sends a series of characters that Desktop recognizes as the beginning of a file transfer, which it automatically begins to receive. To begin the ZMODEM receive process manually, turn this check box off.

Using the ASCII File-Transfer Protocol

ASCII—short for *American Standard Code for Information Interchange*— forms the lowest common denominator between the countless programs that run on a personal computer and between the many different types of computers that proliferate high-tech society. Virtually every word processing, spreadsheet, and database program—including Desktop Notepads—that runs on a personal computer can create an ASCII file. And every computer with which you communicate can handle ASCII characters. Despite all this, the primary reason you need to know how to use the ASCII file-transfer protocol is that most electronic-mail systems can display only ASCII characters.

Many PC programs are character-based (with the notable exception of programs that run under graphics-based programs like Microsoft Windows and OS/2). Every character or symbol displayed on-screen is represented in memory by 1 of 256 codes referred to collectively as the *IBM extended ASCII character set*, or just the *IBM character set*.

Sending a File Using ASCII

Suppose that you created an ASCII file and want to transmit the file to an electronic-mail system. Before you begin sending the file, you must instruct the remote computer to begin its ASCII receive procedure; if you are sending text for a message on an electronic-mail system, you want the remote computer to begin this procedure when the system expects you to type your message. Issue the proper command to the host or bulletin board to prepare it to receive ASCII text.

T I P   Because the remote computer cannot tell whether Desktop is sending the ASCII characters from a file or whether you are typing the characters at the keyboard, prepare as much mail off-line as possible. Following this procedure is much more convenient and can save money.

When the remote system is ready for you to begin transmitting the file, press F4 (ASCII) or select **S**end from the horizontal menu bar, and then select **A**SCII from the Send menu. Desktop displays the Send ASCII dialog box. With the exception of its title bar, this dialog box is identical to the File Load dialog box. By default, Desktop lists the file names from the current DOS directory in the list box of the Send ASCII dialog box (see Chapter 1, "Navigating the Desktop," for information about changing to a different directory). Figure 23.16 shows the Send ASCII dialog box after the directory has been changed to D:\PCTOOLS\DATA.

After Desktop displays the directory containing the file you want to send, use the cursor-movement keys or the mouse to highlight the file name in the list box. Select the **L**oad command button. Desktop begins sending the ASCII file. Character by character, line by line, Desktop types the file in the on-line screen as though you were typing the characters yourself.

As Desktop sends the file, the program indicates in the message bar the name of the file being sent, as well as the number of lines of characters already sent. Desktop displays the message ESC ends. After the file has been sent, your computer displays the message Transfer complete.

Type the command expected by the host system to save the file (and send it to the addressee, if you are sending electronic mail).

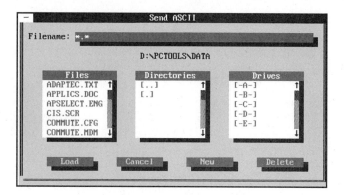

Fig. 23.16

The Send ASCII dialog box.

Receiving a File Using ASCII

When you want to use the ASCII file-transfer protocol to receive a file, you must initiate the download procedure on your end before the remote computer begins sending the file. To begin the process, press F6 (ASCII) or select ASCII from the Receive menu. Desktop displays the Save File to Disk dialog box (see fig. 23.17).

Fig. 23.17

Receiving a file by using the ASCII file-transfer protocol.

Type a valid DOS file name in the Filename text box and select the **S**ave command button. If you are reading your electronic mail from June 14, 1992, for example, you may want to type the name *mail0614.txt* in the text box and select the **S**ave command button. From this point, Desktop saves to the specified file all characters received during the session until you execute a command to end the transfer.

> **CAUTION:** Desktop does not warn you if you type a file name that is the same as an existing file's. The program just replaces the contents of the existing file with the data received during the ASCII file transfer.

As Desktop receives characters, the program indicates in the message bar the file name to which characters are being saved, as well as the number of lines of characters that have been received. Desktop also displays the message ESC ends.

After the host system displays the characters that you want to save in the disk file, you are ready to end the transfer. Press Esc or F3 (Exit) or select **E**nd Transfer on the **A**ctions menu. Desktop closes the ASCII file and stops saving incoming characters.

A common practice when you read electronic mail on a long-distance system (or a system that bills for its use) is to activate the ASCII receive feature so that Desktop saves all incoming characters to a specified file. Then instruct the host system to display all your mail as fast as possible. When all mail has been displayed, end the ASCII transfer and quit from the host system. You can then read your mail off-line at your leisure, without worrying about mounting connect costs.

You can use the Desktop Clipboard to capture as much as a screenful of information (see Chapter 2, "Controlling the Desktop," and Chapter 17, "Using PC Tools Clipboard," for more information about how to use the Clipboard).

Using the XMODEM File-Transfer Protocol

The most widely available PC-based file-transfer protocol is XMODEM. Like so many other communications terms, XMODEM can mean different things to different people, so you should understand the background of this protocol, as well as how Desktop Modem Telecommunications uses the term.

As it is most broadly used, XMODEM refers to a file-transfer protocol included in the program MODEM2. This file-transfer protocol was originally called the MODEM protocol and was intended to transfer files between computers running the CP/M operating system. Since 1979, however, the MODEM file-transfer protocol has become known as XMODEM and has been implemented in countless communications programs for use in transferring files between computers running many different operating systems. Virtually all popular communications programs for IBM PC types of computers include an implementation of XMODEM. Since the protocol's original introduction, several "new and improved" versions have appeared under various names, such as YMODEM and WXMODEM.

The original XMODEM used the *checksum error-checking* scheme. This method of detecting errors is adequate for low-speed data transmission

(1200 bps or less) but can miss errors that are more likely to occur when data is sent at higher transmission speeds (2400 bps or faster). One popular variation of XMODEM adds the CCITT CRC-16 error-checking scheme, which is much more reliable than the checksum method at the higher transmission rates.

The CRC-16 version of XMODEM is often called XMODEM/CRC, but Desktop Modem Telecommunications refers to it simply as XMODEM. Desktop's use of the name in this manner leads to no problems, however, because the CRC-16 version is *backward compatible* with the checksum version. In other words, you can use Desktop's XMODEM to send or receive a file to or from a computer that uses the original checksum version of XMODEM or the newer CRC-16 version. When you are communicating with a host computer that gives you a choice between XMODEM and XMODEM/CRC, always choose XMODEM/CRC.

Always choose XMODEM, ZMODEM, or KERMIT over the ASCII file-transfer protocol when you are sending any type of file other than a *pure ASCII file* (a file containing nothing but ASCII characters). In other words, use these more advanced protocols to send spreadsheet files, formatted word processing files, database files, and executable program files. These non-ASCII files sometimes are referred to collectively as *binary* files.

Sending a File Using XMODEM

When you want to use the XMODEM file-transfer protocol to send a file, first connect to a host system and inform the host program that you intend to upload a file by using XMODEM (the exact command depends on the host program with which you are communicating). When the host instructs you to begin your transfer procedure, you are ready to begin the Desktop XMODEM file-transfer procedure.

To begin the transfer, press the shortcut key F5 (XModem) or select **S**end and then **XMODEM** from the Send menu. Desktop displays the Send XMODEM dialog box. With the exception of its title bar, this dialog box is identical to the File Load dialog box. By default, Desktop lists the file names from the current DOS directory in the list box of the Send XMODEM dialog box.

After Desktop displays the directory that contains the file you want to send, use the cursor-movement keys or the mouse to highlight the file name in the list box. Select the **L**oad command button. Desktop begins sending the file.

As Desktop sends a file by using XMODEM, the program displays the Transfer Status dialog box (see fig. 23.18). This dialog box lists the file name of the file you are sending, the time that has elapsed since the transfer began, the number of bytes of data that have been transferred, the error-checking method (CRC or checksum), an error count, and the last message generated by the XMODEM protocol.

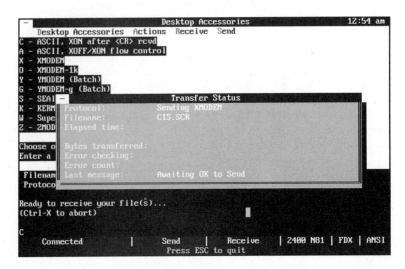

Fig. 23.18

The Transfer Status dialog box as it appears when Desktop sends a file.

You can abort the file-transfer process by pressing Esc or by selecting End Transfer from the Actions menu.

When Desktop successfully completes the XMODEM file-transfer operation, the program displays the message *** COMPLETED *** in the last line of the Send dialog box. The following message also appears in the message bar:

    Transfer Completed-Press any key to Continue

Receiving a File Using XMODEM

In addition to sending a file by using the XMODEM file-transfer protocol, you can receive a file by using XMODEM. You first must be connected to the remote computer and at the on-line screen. When you are connected to a host system—an on-line service like CompuServe or a PC bulletin board, for example—you usually inform the host program that you intend to download a file by selecting an appropriate menu option or command. Type the name of the file you are going to download and select XMODEM as the file-transfer protocol. When the host instructs you to begin your transfer procedure, begin the receive XMODEM procedure.

To begin the transfer, press the shortcut key F7 (XModem) or select **XMODEM** from the **R**eceive menu. Desktop displays the Save File to Disk dialog box. In the Filename text box, type the file name you want Desktop to use for the file it receives. To avoid overwriting existing data, use a file name that does not already exist on the disk. Select **OK**; Desktop begins receiving the file.

As Desktop receives a file using XMODEM, the program displays the Transfer Status dialog box shown in figure 23.19. This dialog box lists the name of the file you are receiving, the time that has elapsed since the transfer began, the number of bytes of data that have been transferred, the error-checking method (CRC or checksum), an error count, and the last message generated by the XMODEM protocol.

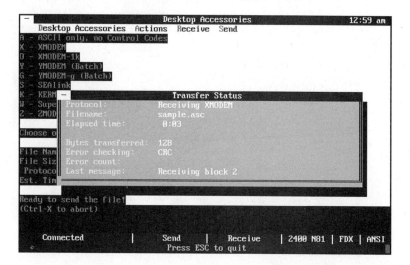

Fig. 23.19

The Transfer Status dialog box as it appears when Desktop receives a file.

You can abort the file-transfer process by pressing Esc or F3 (Exit).

When Desktop successfully completes the XMODEM file-transfer operation, the program displays the message *** COMPLETED *** in the last line of the Receive dialog box. The following message appears in the message bar:

    Transfer Complete-Press any key to Continue

Using the ZMODEM File-Transfer Protocol

ZMODEM is the only protocol offered in PC Tools 8 that allows automatic downloading, a handy feature that can help reduce both keystrokes and errors while receiving files. ZMODEM is also the fastest of the three binary protocols. Unlike XMODEM and KERMIT, which must wait for the receiving computer to acknowledge each incoming packet of data, ZMODEM sends data continuously. This transfer method is called *streaming*, and it accounts for the protocol's efficiency.

Sending Files Using ZMODEM

The first steps in sending one or more files with ZMODEM are similar to those you use for an XMODEM transfer: connect to the host system and inform the remote computer that you intend to upload a file with ZMODEM. When the host instructs you to begin your transfer procedure, you are ready to begin the Desktop ZMODEM file-transfer procedure.

If you selected ZMODEM as the default binary transfer in the Binary Transfer Options dialog box, you can simply press the shortcut key F5 (Zmodem); if ZMODEM is not your default protocol, select **Z**MODEM from the **S**end menu. Desktop displays the Send Zmodem dialog box. By default, Desktop lists the file names from the current DOS directory in the list box of the Send Zmodem dialog box (see fig. 23.20).

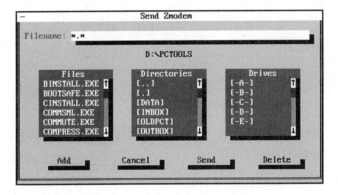

Fig. 23.20

The Send Zmodem dialog box.

After Desktop displays the directory that contains the file(s) you want to send, use the cursor-movement keys or the mouse to highlight a file name in the list box. Select the **A**dd command button.

Note that the transfer does not begin immediately, as it would for an XMODEM protocol transfer, because you can send up to 15 files at one time using ZMODEM or KERMIT. Therefore, you can now select another file to send—Desktop keeps track of the files in a separate list. Don't take too much time in selecting your files, though; the host system's

ZMODEM receive program will eventually *time out* if the transfer doesn't begin within a number of seconds. When you finish selecting files, choose **S**end.

Desktop now displays the Verify File List dialog box, which contains the file names you specified for the transfer (see fig. 23.21). If the names are correct, select **OK** to send the files. If the file list is in error, select **Can**cel; the program returns to the on-line screen.

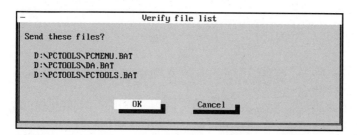

```
┌─                    Verify file list                        ┐
│                                                             │
│  Send these files?                                          │
│                                                             │
│     D:\PCTOOLS\PCMENU.BAT                                   │
│     D:\PCTOOLS\DA.BAT                                        │
│     D:\PCTOOLS\PCTOOLS.BAT                                   │
│                                                             │
│                                                             │
│              ┌    OK    ┐        ┌  Cancel  ┐               │
└─                                                            ┘
```

Fig. 23.21

The Verify File List dialog box.

Desktop displays the Transfer Status dialog box during the transfer (refer to fig. 23.18). As before, you can abort the file-transfer process by pressing Esc or by selecting **E**nd Transfer from the **A**ctions menu.

When Desktop successfully completes the ZMODEM file-transfer operation, the program displays the message *** COMPLETED *** in the last line of the Send dialog box. The following message appears in the message bar:

```
Transfer Completed-Press any key to Continue
```

Receiving Files Using ZMODEM

To receive one or more files with the ZMODEM file-transfer protocol, initiate the ZMODEM download process on the remote computer by specifying the file name(s) and selecting ZMODEM as the file-transfer protocol.

If you enabled the Allow Automatic Zmodem Downloads check box in the Binary Transfer Options dialog box, you need do nothing more. When the host instructs you to begin your transfer procedure, the host sends a string of characters that instruct Desktop to begin a ZMODEM download. The Transfer Status dialog box appears within a few seconds.

If you disabled automatic ZMODEM downloading, press the shortcut key F7 (Zmodem) or select **Z**MODEM from the **R**eceive menu. Because the ZMODEM protocol doesn't require a file name, Desktop doesn't prompt you for one. Again, the Transfer Status dialog box appears within a few seconds (refer to fig. 23.19). As before, you can abort the file-transfer process by pressing Esc or selecting End Transfer from the Actions menu.

When Desktop successfully completes the ZMODEM file-transfer operation, the program displays the message *** COMPLETED *** in the last line of the Receive dialog box. This following message appears in the message bar:

```
Transfer Complete-Press any key to Continue
```

Using the KERMIT File-Transfer Protocol

KERMIT is a popular public-domain protocol that supports the batch transfer of multiple files in one session. KERMIT is also widely supported throughout the mainframe and minicomputer world. You may find KERMIT on many computers that do not support ZMODEM, and its reliability is superior to that of the XMODEM protocol.

Sending Files Using KERMIT

The first steps in sending one or more files with KERMIT are similar to those you use for a XMODEM transfer: connect to the host system and inform the remote computer that you intend to upload a file with KERMIT. When the host instructs you to begin your transfer procedure, you are ready to begin the Desktop KERMIT file-transfer procedure.

If you selected KERMIT as the default binary transfer in the Binary Transfer Options dialog box, you can simply press the shortcut key F5 (KERMIT). If KERMIT is not your default protocol, select KERMIT from the Send menu. Desktop displays the Send Kermit dialog box, which is similar to the Send Zmodem dialog box. By default, Desktop lists the file names from the current DOS directory in the list box of the Send Kermit dialog box.

After Desktop displays the directory that contains the file(s) you want to send, use the cursor-movement keys or the mouse to highlight a file name in the list box. Select the Add command button.

Like ZMODEM, the KERMIT protocol can send up to 15 files at one time, so you can select another file now. Make sure that you don't take too much time in selecting your files, though; the host system's KERMIT receive program will eventually time out if the transfer doesn't begin within a number of seconds. When you finish selecting files, choose Send.

Desktop now displays the Verify File List dialog box, which contains the file names you specified for the transfer. If the names are correct, select **OK** to send the files. If the file list is in error, select **C**ancel; the program returns to the on-line screen.

Desktop displays the Transfer Status dialog box (refer to fig. 23.18) during the transfer. As before, you can abort the file-transfer process by pressing Esc or selecting **A**ctions and then **E**nd Transfer from the Actions menu.

When Desktop successfully completes the KERMIT file-transfer operation, the program displays the message `*** COMPLETED ***` in the last line of the Send dialog box. The following message appears in the message bar:

    Transfer Completed-Press any key to Continue

Receiving Files Using KERMIT

To receive one or more files with the KERMIT file-transfer protocol, initiate the KERMIT download process on the remote computer by specifying the file name(s) and selecting KERMIT as the file-transfer protocol.

Next, press the shortcut key F7 (KERMIT) or select **K**ermit from the **R**eceive menu. Because the KERMIT protocol doesn't require a file name, Desktop doesn't prompt you for one. Again, the Transfer Status dialog box appears within a few seconds (refer to fig. 23.19). As before, you can abort the file-transfer process by pressing Esc or by selecting **E**nd Transfer from the **A**ctions menu.

When Desktop successfully completes the KERMIT file-transfer operation, the program displays the message `*** COMPLETED ***` in the last line of the Receive dialog box. This following message appears in the message bar:

    Transfer Complete-Press any key to Continue

Using Scripts To Automate Telecommunications

As you become an experienced telecommunicator, you soon will notice that you continually perform tasks that require similar (if not identical) keystrokes. Every time you log on to a particular computer system, you must type the same user ID and password. Similarly, you type the same keystrokes every time you check your electronic mail on the electronic-mail service to which you subscribe. Fortunately, Desktop provides a simple programming language for automating these repetitive tasks.

Programs created in this language are known as *scripts*. These scripts are used in conjunction with entries in the Modem Telecommunications phone directory. As soon as you dial and connect to a remote computer system through use of a phone-directory entry, Desktop runs the script specified in the entry's Script text box in the Edit Phone Directory dialog box.

The Desktop Modem Telecommunications script language is a high-level communications programming language suitable for use in developing simple communications applications. Although extensive coverage of this programmable side of Desktop Modem Telecommunications is beyond the scope of this book, this section helps you develop a feel for the overall capabilities of the script language and an understanding of the scripts supplied with PC Tools 8. This section examines how to create a script, explains the syntax of the script commands, and presents an example script that demonstrates the use of various commands.

Creating a Script File

A Desktop script file consists of a series of lines of ASCII characters (alternatively, scripts can be saved in PC Tools Desktop format); you can create scripts with any ASCII text editor or Notepads. Each line contains one command from the Desktop Modem Telecommunications script language. Desktop executes script commands one by one, from top to bottom, unless the program encounters a command that causes execution to branch to some other portion of the script. Any text or characters that appear on a line to the right of an asterisk (*) are ignored when Desktop executes the script. This text is used to place comments, often called *internal documentation*, in the script for your reference.

Script commands do not have to begin at the left margin. Indenting is permitted. Thus, you can create scripts that show program structure by the level of indention.

You can use Desktop's Outlines application to write scripts. This practice makes writing the script in modules easier by enabling you to expand and collapse individual sections of the script at will. (Refer to

Chapter 18, "Using the Outliner," for more information about using the Desktop Outlines application.)

A Desktop script file must be stored in ASCII or PC Tools Desktop format. Desktop Notepads, therefore, is well suited for creating such a script. You can, however, use any word processor or text editor that can save a file in ASCII format. A convenient procedure is to make a copy of an existing script file (by using DOS or PC Shell), and then modify the file to work with a different remote computer system. (Refer to Chapter 16, "Using PC Tools Notepads," for more information about how to use the Notepads application to create and save a file, as well as to edit existing files.)

You can use any valid DOS file name for a Desktop script; however, the scripts supplied in PC Tools Version 8 by Central Point Software use the file name extension SCR. Place scripts in the \PCTOOLS or \PCTOOLS\DATA directories. Always specify the full file name, including file name extension, when you supply the script name in the SCRIPT text box in the Edit Phone Directory dialog box.

You can also run a script directly from the on-line screen **Actions** menu; select **R**un Script, and Desktop displays the Run Script dialog box. Enter the name of the script file (the SCR extension is not required), and select **OK**. The script must be present in the \PCTOOLS or \PCTOOLS\DATA directories.

Understanding the Script Commands

Desktop provides 18 script commands you can use to develop scripts. These commands can be classified into five groups:

■ Variable manipulation commands

■ Communication commands

■ Program control and branching commands

■ Display commands

■ Script debugging commands

In the following discussion of commands, parameters separated by a pipe character (|) are alternatives; parameters in **bold** are mandatory; parameters in *italics* are optional; parameters in UPPERCASE letters must be spelled exactly as indicated; and parameters in lowercase letters must be substituted with values you provide.

Variables and Variable-Manipulation Commands

This group of commands enables you to create and use temporary fields called *variables*. Desktop permits you to create as many as six variables—v1, v2, v3, v4, v5, or v6. (Variables 4 through 6 are new with Version 8.0.) Desktop Modem Telecommunications variables exist only in memory (RAM) and are used in scripts to temporarily hold information used by the script.

Desktop enables you to use two special variables in scripts: *userid* and *password*. These variables correspond to the USER ID and PASSWORD text boxes in the Edit Phone Directory dialog box. When you use either variable in a script, Desktop substitutes the corresponding value from the current entry's Edit Phone Directory dialog box settings. If you later change the password or user ID, you do not have to modify the script. Just edit the phone-directory entry and change the appropriate value in the Edit Phone Directory text box.

You can use the commands that follow to create and manipulate variables in scripts. These commands enable the script to read information from an input file and accept input typed on-screen.

DATABASE V1 | V2 *V2*

You can use this command in conjunction with the DATABASE, FIELD 1, and FIELD 2 text boxes in the Edit Phone Directory dialog box to assign a value to variable v1, variable v2, or both. Field 1 corresponds to v1, and Field 2 corresponds to v2. When Desktop encounters this command in the script, the program opens a Desktop Databases window and loads the database file specified in the DATABASE text box of the Edit Phone Directory dialog box for the current phone-directory entry. Desktop displays the database in browse mode. Position the highlighted bar on the record that contains the values you want inserted in v1 and v2. To select the record, press Enter or click the left or right mouse button. Desktop inserts into variable v1 the values in Field 1; it inserts into variable v2 the values in Field 2.

INPUT V1 | V2 | V3 | V4 | V5 | V6

Use the INPUT command to accept characters typed at your computer system's keyboard. Desktop stores as many as 80 characters in the specified variable. When Desktop executes this command during script processing, the program displays a question mark at the left side of the on-line screen. You then can type a value, up to 80 characters long, and press Enter. Desktop stores the value typed in the variable that was specified in the command. The script then can use that value in further processing.

Communication Commands

Desktop Modem Telecommunications provides commands specifically involved in the communication of data between your computer and a remote computer. These commands transfer data to or from a remote computer, disconnect your computer from a remote computer, and enable you to transfer files in the background:

> DOWNLOAD ASCII I XMODEM I ZMODEM I KERMIT
>
> HANGUP
>
> RECEIVE
>
> SEND
>
> UPLOAD

DOWNLOAD ASCII I XMODEM "file name" I ZMODEM I KERMIT I V1 I V2 I V3 I V4 I V5 I V6

Use this command to receive a file using the specified file-transfer protocol. Desktop saves the file to disk by using the file name indicated in the command or contained in the specified variable. DOWNLOAD ASCII is equivalent to F6, and DOWNLOAD XMODEM I ZMODEM I KERMIT is equivalent to F7.

HANGUP

This command terminates the connection between your computer and the remote computer. HANGUP is equivalent to F8 (Hangup).

RECEIVE V1 I V2 I V3 I V4 I V5 I V6

This command causes Desktop to store in the specified variable the next characters sent by the remote computer, up to the first carriage return or line-feed character. Desktop can store as many as 80 characters in the variable. If nothing is received within 10 seconds, the variable is set to null (nothing).

SEND V1 I V2 I V3 I V4 I V5 I V6 I USERID I PASSWORD I "string";

When Desktop encounters this script command, the program transmits to the remote computer the characters contained in the variable or in the specified string, followed by a carriage return. The effect is equivalent to typing the characters at the keyboard. Type character strings in quotation marks. Many on-line services and bulletin boards use Ctrl+key combinations—such as Ctrl+C, Ctrl+X, Ctrl+S, and Ctrl+Q, for example—to enable you to manually control the flow of information across your screen or to cancel an operation in midstream.

To incorporate these keystroke combinations into a character string for transmission by the SEND command, use the caret symbol (^) to represent the Ctrl key. Table 23.4 lists Ctrl+key combinations often used by on-line services and bulletin boards. In general, you can create any Ctrl+key combination by typing the caret symbol (^) followed by a letter (from A to Z in upper- or lowercase) or by one of these characters:

[ ] \ ^ -

Several of the control codes in table 23.4 translate into keystrokes that you would not normally expect. For example, ^M sends a carriage return to the remote computer. In other words, whenever you want the SEND command to transmit a carriage return, use the code ^M.

Table 23.4 Control Codes

Code	Keystroke Executed by the Macro
^C	Ctrl+C
^S	Ctrl+S
^Q	Ctrl+Q
^X	Ctrl+X
^M	Enter
^H	Backspace
^I	Horizontal tab (Tab key)
^K	Vertical tab (up arrow)
^[	Esc
^]	Left arrow

If the SEND statement is followed by a semicolon (;), the carriage return is not appended. Using semicolons may be necessary for bulletin boards and online services that use "single keystroke" commands, where no carriage return is required.

UPLOAD ASCII | XMODEM | ZMODEM | KERMIT "file name" | V1 | V2 | V3 | V4 | V5 | V6

Use this command to send a file by using the specified file-transfer protocol. Desktop sends the file specified by the file name or variable contained in the command. This command is equivalent to the commands found in the Send menu. UPLOAD ASCII is equivalent to F4, and

UPLOAD XMODEM | ZMODEM | KERMIT is equivalent to F5. (ZMODEM and KERMIT are new parameters for the UPLOAD command in Version 8.0.)

Program-Control and Branching Commands

Program-control commands enable you to establish conditions for performance of particular commands in the script. A branching command enables you to control the sequence in which script commands are executed. These two types of commands are often used together.

You can use program-control commands to cause the script to perform a group of commands based on the occurrence of a specified condition. You can use program-control commands to stop processing script commands temporarily until a specified time or until the occurrence of a specified event. The branching command GOTO causes execution of the script to branch to another line in the script. Program-control commands and branching commands include the seven in the remainder of this section:

:label

This command identifies a location in the script to which the program can branch (using a GOTO command or IF command). Type a colon (:) followed immediately by a label (a name with a maximum of eight characters).

GOTO label

This command causes Desktop to jump to the line in the script designated by the label and continue processing the script commands from that point toward the end of the script.

GOSUB label

This command causes Desktop to temporarily jump to the line in the script designated by the label and continue processing the script commands from that point. Unlike GOTO, however, script execution returns to the line after the GOSUB when a RETURN command is reached. The GPSUB command enables you to use *subroutines* in your scripts; a subroutine can be executed many times to perform a certain task as often as needed.

RETURN

This command causes Desktop to exit a GOSUB subroutine; script execution resumes at the next line following the GOSUB statement.

IF V1 | V2 | V3 | V4 | V5 | V6 = | <> | *CONTAINS* **"string" GOTO label**

This command causes Desktop to compare the value of the specified variable to the string. When the comparison statement is true, Desktop branches processing to the line in the script identified by the label. When the comparison statement is false, processing continues to the next line after the IF statement.

PAUSE *n*

Use this command to cause Desktop to suspend processing for a set length of time. When no time is specified, Desktop pauses the script for one second. Optionally, you can follow the command with a positive integer indicating the number of seconds you want the script to pause.

WAITFOR "string"

Use this command if you want Desktop to temporarily stop processing the script until the remote computer sends the characters contained in the string. WAITFOR and SEND often are used in tandem to cause Desktop to send the appropriate response to a known prompt. The case of the target string doesn't matter.

Display Commands

The commands in this category enable you to take charge of the information that Desktop Modem Telecommunications displays on-screen.

PRINT V1 | V2 | V3 | V4 | V5 | V6 | "string";

Use this command if you want to display in your computer's on-line screen the contents of the specified variable or string. This command is often used for creating a screen prompt that informs a user to enter data (normally followed by the INPUT command). By default, Desktop issues a carriage return at the end of the string. As with the SEND command, you can add a semicolon (;) at the end of the command when you want Desktop to suppress the carriage return.

ECHO ON | OFF

By default, Desktop does not display characters that are being received by the computer while the script is processing. Sometimes you want all incoming characters to be displayed on your screen, even if the script is waiting for a specific prompt. To turn on the display of all incoming characters, use the command ECHO ON. To turn off the display of incoming characters, later in the script, use the command ECHO OFF.

TRON

This command (short for *trace on*) is a diagnostic tool that causes every script command to be displayed in the message bar as the command is executed. Use this command to help determine the effect of every command in the script (especially when your script is not operating as you expected). Press the space bar to execute the command and Esc to abort the script.

TROFF

Use this command to turn *trace off*, thus causing Desktop to quit displaying script commands in the message bar as the commands are executed.

Looking at an Example

Central Point Software distributes ten sophisticated script files, including the following four, with PC Tools Version 8:

- *MCI.SCR.* This script file automates log-on to MCI Mail and then displays a menu that enables you to choose between reading your electronic mail, sending electronic mail, sending electronic mail as a facsimile (fax), or exiting from the script and entering MCI command mode.

- *ESL.SCR.* This script automates connection and use of Western Union's EasyLink. After you are logged on to the system, the script displays a menu that provides options for reading electronic mail, sending electronic mail, sending electronic mail as a facsimile (fax), sending electronic mail as a Telex, and entering EasyLink command mode.

- *CIS.SCR.* Use this script to automate logging on and using the on-line service CompuServe. The script automates connection and log-on and then displays a menu containing options for reading electronic mail, sending electronic mail, sending mail as fax, connecting to *PC Magazine*'s PC MagNet, and exiting to CompuServe command mode.

- *CPS.SCR.* This script file automates log-on to Central Point Software's electronic BBS.

These scripts make use of nearly all the available script commands; consequently, they serve as excellent examples for learning how to create your own scripts.

Each one of the first three scripts—MCI.SCR, ESL.SCR, and CIS.SCR—make special use of the database file TELECOM.DBF (provided also with PC Tools 8). For example, in this database file you can store the CompuServe user ID number for all individuals with whom you communicate. Then, when you want to send electronic mail to one of your colleagues, you don't have to search your notes to find the right

CompuServe ID number. The CIS.SCR script uses the DATABASE command to display the TELECOM.DBF database file. You just select the appropriate record from the screen, and the script does the rest.

The scripts supplied with PC Tools are too lengthy and involved for coverage in this chapter. Rather, this chapter presents the following simple script for logging on to a local electronic bulletin-board system, the CPCUG MIX. Because the log-on procedures for most bulletin boards are similar, only a few modifications to this script are required if you want to use it to log on to a BBS in your area.

```
* Sample script MIX.SCR for logging on to the CPCUG MIX
*
* Display message to user explaining what's going on.
PRINT "Connecting to the MIX."

* Send two carriage returns to cause BBS to display
*  log-on prompt.
SEND "^M^M"

* Wait for the log-on prompt
WAITFOR "FIRST Name?"

* Type the user ID stored in the User ID text box in the
*  Edit Phone Directory dialog box.
SEND userid

* Wait for the password prompt.
WAITFOR "word"

* Type the password stored in the Password text box in the
*  Edit Phone Directory dialog box.
SEND password

* Inform user that log-on is completed.
PRINT "You are logged on to the MIX."
```

By using this simple script and scripts provided with PC Tools 8 as examples, you can create scripts that automate much of the repetition that is otherwise obligatory in PC telecommunications.

FROM HERE...

For Related Information

◄◄ "Editing an Outline," p. 617.

◄◄ "Collapsing and Expanding Headlines," p. 620.

Using Autodial

One of the primary conveniences of Hayes-compatible modems is their capacity to dial the telephone. Desktop's Autodialer feature enables you to take advantage of this feature even when you are only making a voice call. PC Tools enables you to integrate Desktop Databases with features from Desktop Modem Telecommunications to create an electronic phone book you can use to speed-dial telephone numbers. If you loaded Desktop as a memory-resident program, PC Tools even enables the Autodial feature to "grab" a telephone number from any PC screen, regardless of what program you are using, and have your modem dial the number.

Configuring Autodial

Before you can use Autodial in a Databases window or from within another DOS program, you must configure Autodial for use with your computer system and modem.

To configure Autodial, first load a database file in a Databases window. Select **C**ontrols and then select **C**onfigure Autodial. Desktop displays the Configure Autodialer dialog box (see fig. 23.22).

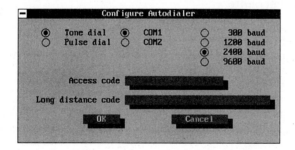

Fig. 23.22

The Configure Autodialer dialog box.

In this dialog box, you use the first set of option buttons to indicate whether the telephone system to which the modem is connected supports tone dial or pulse dial. Next, indicate the serial port to which your modem is connected. Then choose the transmission rate that matches the capability of your modem.

In the Access Code text box, enter any access code that you must dial to access an outside line. For example, some PBX systems require you to dial 9 before dialing the regular telephone number. By including the code in this screen, you don't have to include the access code in the database file that contains the telephone numbers. A comma (,) pauses two seconds before dialing, and you can use more than one comma if necessary.

In the Long Distance Code text box, type the number required to access your long-distance service (such as the number 1).

After you make any necessary adjustments to the Configure Autodialer dialog box settings, select the **OK** command button. Desktop returns to the Databases window. (To quit to the Databases window without saving the changes you made, select the **C**ancel command button.)

Dialing a Number from within Desktop Databases

After you configure Autodial, dialing a number is simple. First, load a Desktop database file into a Databases window. Next, use the cursor-movement keys or the mouse to display the record containing the phone number you want Autodial to dial (in browse mode, move the highlighted bar to the target record). Select **C**ontrols, and then select **A**utodial. Desktop searches the current record for a field value that looks like a telephone number. When a number is found, Desktop begins the dial process. If you have multiple numbers, Autodial dials the first number encountered.

Desktop enables you to specify a long-distance code for Autodial, but not all phone calls require use of this code. To dial a local call, for example, you don't have to dial the number 1 first. When Autodial is dialing a number that includes an area code, it knows to dial the long-distance code first. Desktop dials the number and displays the Disconnect Modem dialog box. When the phone begins to ring, pick up the telephone handset and press Esc or the Enter key to disengage the modem. You then can hear the phone ring (or indicate busy) through the handset.

If you are dialing a number that does not include an area code, Desktop displays a dialog box similar to the one shown in figure 23.23. Select **L**ocal if you want Desktop to dial the number without adding the long-distance code. Select **D**istant when you want Desktop to precede the telephone number with the long-distance code. Select **C**ancel to return to the Databases window without dialing the number.

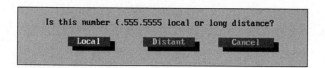

Fig. 23.23

Choosing
between local
and long
distance.

Dialing a Number from within Another DOS Program

If you installed Desktop as a memory-resident program, Desktop enables you to use your modem to dial a telephone number from any DOS screen.

When the number you want to dial is displayed, press Ctrl+O. Desktop first loads itself into memory and then scans the screen for the first string of three or more consecutive numbers. Desktop assumes that this number is the phone number you want to dial, displays a dialog box which indicates that Desktop is ready to dial, and displays the number Desktop has found (see fig. 23.24).

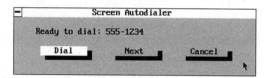

Fig. 23.24

Dialing a number
from a DOS
screen.

Because the first phone number in the screen might not be the phone number you want to dial, Desktop doesn't begin dialing immediately. To dial the number, select the **D**ial command button in the dialog box. If the displayed number is not the one you want to dial, select the **N**ext command button until the appropriate number appears. Then select **D**ial to dial the number. You can select **C**ancel to return to the DOS application without dialing a number.

When you select the **D**ial command button, Desktop sends a command to the modem to dial the chosen number. Desktop displays a dialog box that instructs you to pick up the telephone handset and press Esc or Enter as soon as the telephone begins to ring. Desktop returns to the DOS application screen.

Chapter Summary

This chapter examines how to use the features in the Desktop Modem Telecommunications module. You learned how to work with phone directories, dial and connect to another computer, and send and receive computer files. The chapter explains how to use scripts to automate your use of the Modem Telecommunications application, and you learned how to use the Autodial feature capability. You should now be aware of the full breadth of PC Tools' impressive communications capabilities.

Turn to Chapter 24, "Using Electronic Mail," to learn how to use Desktop to send and receive electronic mail.

Using Electronic Mail

O ne of the most popular uses of PC telecommunications is to connect to commercial on-line services such as MCI Mail, CompuServe, EasyLink, GEnie and Prodigy, to name just a few. Each service offers some form of electronic mail through which subscribers can correspond. Through its Desktop program, PC Tools 8 helps automate the process of sending and receiving mail on three of the most widely used services: MCI Mail, CompuServe, and EasyLink. This chapter describes how to take advantage of PC Tools' Electronic Mail feature.

Understanding PC Tools' Electronic Mail

PC Tools' Electronic Mail facility is actually a series of Desktop Modem Telecommunications scripts that you access through the Desktop menus (refer to the discussion of scripts in Chapter 23, "Using PC Tools Telecommunications"). Through these scripts, Desktop acts as your

personal electronic mail carrier. The program can log on to a specified
on-line service, send or download electronic mail, and then log off. You
can even establish an electronic mail schedule for Desktop so that, at
preset times, the program automatically logs on to the specified service
and sends or downloads mail. When you want to send electronic mail,
you type a message in a Notepads window and press a shortcut key. To
check your electronic mail, you just display the Desktop. The program
alerts you if messages are waiting for you to read.

To use the Desktop Electronic Mail feature, you must have a modem
connected to or installed in your computer. For the electronic mail
scheduling feature to work, Desktop must be loaded as a TSR program
rather than as a stand-alone program. See Appendix A, "Installing and
Configuring PC Tools," for a complete discussion of how to install PC
Tools and how to load Desktop as a TSR program.

To start Electronic Mail, start Desktop and display the Desktop screen.
Select **A**ccessories from the Desktop menu bar, and then choose
Electronic Mail from the submenu. (If you're running the stand-alone
Desktop Accessories, the Electronic Mail option appears on the Tele-
communications submenu.) Desktop displays the Electronic Mail
screen, which initially displays the Inbox window (see fig. 24.1).

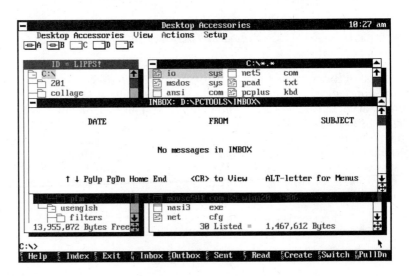

The Inbox window lists any electronic mail messages that you received
but did not delete. The first time you use Electronic Mail, the Inbox
window displays the message No messages in INBOX.

The horizontal menu bar of the Electronic Mail screen contains the
following options: Desktop Accessories, View, Actions, and Setup. In

the message bar, Desktop lists the function-key commands, which are described in table 24.1.

Table 24.1 Keystroke Commands Available in the Inbox, Outbox, and Sent Screens

Key	Name	Function
F1	Help	Displays context-sensitive Help facility
F2	Index	Displays Help facility index
F3	Exit	Cancels current process, application, or dialog box (same as Esc)
F4	Inbox	Displays Inbox window, which lists messages received
F5	Outbox	Displays Outbox window, which lists files you want Desktop to send via Electronic Mail
F6	Sent	Displays the Sent window, which lists messages Desktop has transmitted to the electronic mail service
F7	Read	Connects to electronic mail service and downloads any mail addressed to you
F8	Create	Opens a Notepads window in which you can create a message that will be sent via electronic mail
F9 or Ctrl+Esc	Switch	Switches active window
F10 or Alt	PullDn	Activates horizontal menu bar
Esc	Cancel	Cancels current process or application (same as F3)
Alt+space bar	Window Control	Displays Window Control dialog box

The Outbox and Sent windows are similar in appearance to the Inbox window. To see a list of messages you have scheduled for sending, press F5 (Outbox). Desktop switches to the Outbox window box. To see a list of messages that Desktop has already mailed, press F6 (Sent). Desktop displays the Sent window.

FROM HERE...

For Related Information

◄◄ "Creating an Entry," p. 795.

◄◄ "Using Scripts To Automate Telecommunications," p. 831.

Setting Up Electronic Mail

The first step in using Desktop's Electronic Mail is to configure the application. Before you can send or receive electronic mail, you must specify the on-line electronic mail service to which you are a subscriber and then specify the directories that will hold incoming and outgoing messages. You can specify schedules for automatically sending and receiving mail between your computer and the electronic mail service. The following sections describe the configuration procedure.

Selecting an Electronic Mail Service

Desktop can automate the sending and receiving of electronic mail between your computer and three electronic mail services: MCI Mail, CompuServe, and EasyLink. You must specify which service you want the program to use. Display the Outbox, Inbox, or Sent window, and then select **S**etup from the menu. When Desktop displays the Setup menu, shown in figure 24.2, choose the **M**ail Service option. Desktop displays the Electronic Mail Service dialog box (see fig. 24.3).

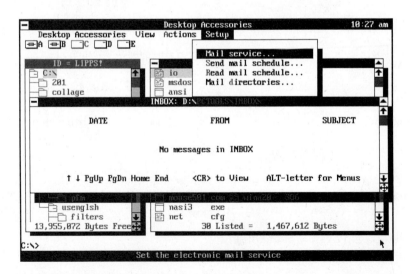

Fig. 24.2

The Electronic Mail Setup menu.

Fig. 24.3

The Electronic
Mail Service
dialog box.

Desktop displays the following option buttons:

■ *MCI Mail.* This option specifies the MCI Mail electronic mail
service.

■ *CompuServe.* This option specifies the CompuServe on-line service, which offers an electronic mail service as one of its features.

■ *EasyLink.* This option specifies the EasyLink electronic mail
service.

■ *No Service.* This option disables the sending and downloading of
electronic mail messages.

After you select the service you want to use, you may need to configure
dialing and connection options for the service. If you have already configured an entry for this service in the Modem Telecommunications
window, Desktop uses the same entry to connect to the service for the
purpose of sending electronic mail. Select the **OK** command button in
the Electronic Mail Service dialog box to return to the Electronic Mail
screen.

If you have not created a Modem Telecommunications entry for the
electronic mail service, you need to do so now. Select the desired service, and then choose the Configure command button in the Electronic
Mail Service dialog box. Desktop displays the Configure Mail dialog box
for the service you selected. The dialog box in figure 24.4, for example,
appears when you select CompuServe.

In the Phone Number text box, type the number that Desktop must dial
to connect to the electronic mail service. If you are calling from a business phone system, be sure to include any access number required to
access an outside line. The number can be up to 25 characters long.

In the User ID text box, type your user identification number for the
service. The number must be obtained from the electronic mail service
or from a subscription kit that you purchased or that was included
with hardware or software you purchased. The ID can be up to 25
characters long.

Fig. 24.4

The Configure
Mail dialog box
for CompuServe.

Type your password in the Password text box. The password is visible
as you enter it, but the next time you display the Configure Mail screen
for this electronic mail service, the password is hidden. The password
can be up to 21 characters long.

> **NOTE** If you change the password you use to log on to the elec-
> tronic mail service, don't forget to change the password in
> the Electronic Mail Configure Mail dialog box or the Modem
> Telecommunications Edit Phone Directory dialog box for
> this on-line service.

Select the appropriate choices from these groups of option buttons in
the Configure mail dialog box:

- *Baud Rate* determines the maximum transmission rate—300, 1200,
  2400, 4800, 9600, or 19200—between your computer and the modem. Usually, you choose the modem's fastest setting. Check your
  modem's documentation for the optimum setting.

- *Dialing* determines whether the modem dials a phone number by
  using tones or pulses. If you have a touch-tone phone, choose
  Tone. If you have a rotary phone, choose Pulse.

- *Port* indicates the serial port—COM1, COM2, COM3, or COM4—to
  which the modem is attached.

After you complete all the necessary entries in the Configure Mail window, select the **O**K command button. Desktop returns to the Electronic
Mail screen.

Specifying Directories

During installation of PC Tools 8, Install, the installation program, creates several directories. By default, Install creates on drive C a directory named \PCTOOLS. Install also creates six subdirectories including three mail directories: C:\PCTOOLS\INBOX, the default directory for incoming electronic mail; C:\PCTOOLS\OUTBOX, the default directory for outgoing electronic mail; and C:\PCTOOLS\SENT, the default directory for outgoing messages that have been mailed.

To assign different mail directories or to confirm that Install has assigned these directories as the mail directories, select **S**etup from the horizontal menu bar and choose Mail **D**irectories. Desktop displays the Electronic Mail Directories dialog box (see fig. 24.5).

Fig. 24.5

The Electronic Mail Directories dialog box.

The Electronic Mail Directories dialog box includes three text boxes— one for each mail directory. To specify different directories, move the highlight to every text box you want to modify, and then enter the necessary changes. After you confirm that the correct directories are listed, select the **OK** command button to return to the Electronic Mail screen.

For Related Information

◄◄ "Connecting to Another Computer," p. 807.

FROM HERE...

Creating an Electronic Mail Message

To create a message you intend to send by Desktop's Electronic Mail, display the Electronic Mail screen; then press F8 (Create) or select **C**reate Mail Message from the **A**ctions menu. Desktop displays a new Notepads window with a message header already typed. If you specified MCI Mail as the electronic mail service, Desktop types the following header:

```
TO:
CC:
SUBJECT:
ATTACH:
```

NOTE   Attachments of files for all services and MCI Forwarding are new to PC Tools Version 8.

You can also specify two optional labels in an MCI Mail message header between the TO and CC lines. These labels follow:

EMS:

MBX

These labels enable you to forward the message through MCI Mail to another electronic mail service. EMS should be followed by the mail service name, and MBX precedes the addressee's ID on that service. You can have multiple MBXs, indicating multiple users on one electronic mail service.

If you selected CompuServe as the electronic mail service, Desktop adds this header:

```
TO:
FROM:
SUBJECT
ATTACH:
```

If you selected EasyLink as the electronic mail service, Desktop uses this header:

```
TO:
SUBJECT:
ATTACH:
```

Each header is designed to meet the requirements of the particular electronic mail service. In any of the three header formats, you must specify in the TO line the identification number of the message addressee. Other entries are optional. Type the message below the header. Refer to Chapter 16, "Using PC Tools Notepads," if you need information about typing and editing text in a Notepads window.

> **WARNING:** Do not edit the header supplied by Desktop; any change you make may prevent your mail from being delivered properly by the service.

NOTE Desktop recognizes up to 10 optional ATTACH lines in any of the three header formats. An *ATTACH line* specifies a full path and file name of a file to be sent with the electronic mail message.

Desktop enables you to create electronic mail messages in a Notepads window. The Desktop Notepads application is covered in detail in Chapter 16, "Using PC Tools Notepads." You can send any Notepads file from any Notepads window by using the F5 (Email) command. When you use this method, however, Desktop does not automatically provide the header format. For this reason, creating all electronic mail messages from the Electronic Mail screen is the most convenient method.

Suppose, for example, that you selected CompuServe as your electronic mail service and that you want to send a message to Joe Green. Display the Electronic Mail screen and press F8 (Create). Desktop displays a Notepads window similar to the one shown in figure 24.6. Type Joe's user identification number in the TO line. Type the subject of the message in the SUBJECT line, and type your name in the FROM line. Because a file will not be attached, leave the ATTACH line blank. Start your message below the ATTACH line.

When you are sending mail via CompuServe, you can type the user's name in the TO line, if you prefer; in that case, you must include the user ID number in brackets([ ]). To include Joe Green's name in the TO line, use this format:

Joe Green [12345,6789]

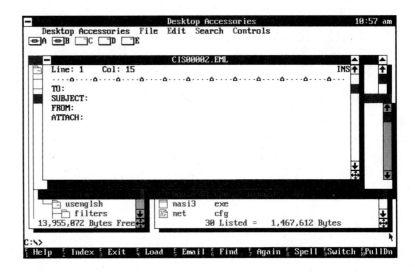

Fig. 24.6

Creating an electronic mail message.

FROM HERE...

For Related Information

◄◄ "Entering Text," p. 569.

◄◄ "Inserting and Deleting Text," p. 575.

◄◄ "Copying and Moving Text," p. 577.

Sending Electronic Mail

After you type the message, press F5 (Email) or select Send Electronic Mail from the File menu. Desktop displays the Send Electronic Mail Options dialog box (see fig. 24.7).

Fig. 24.7

The Send Electronic Mail Options dialog box.

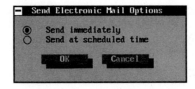

Select one of the following option buttons:

■ *Send Immediately.* This option immediately dials and connects to the electronic mail service and transmits the message to the addressee (see fig. 24.8).

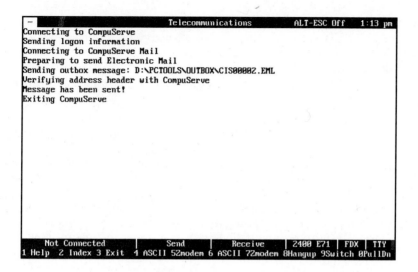

```
─                    Telecommunications        ALT-ESC Off   1:13 pm
Connecting to CompuServe
Sending logon information
Connecting to CompuServe Mail
Preparing to send Electronic Mail
Sending outbox message: D:\PCTOOLS\OUTBOX\CIS00002.EML
Verifying address header with CompuServe
Message has been sent!
Exiting CompuServe
```

```
    Not Connected    │    Send    │   Receive   │ 2400 E71 │ FDX │ TTY
1 Help  2 Index 3 Exit  4 ASCII 52modem 6 ASCII 72modem 8Hangup 9Switch 0PullDn
```

Fig. 24.8

Sending an electronic mail message.

■ *Send at Scheduled Time.* This option places the message in the Outbox directory. The next time Desktop connects to the electronic mail service according to the schedule you established for sending messages, the program transmits your message to the specified addressee and logs off automatically.

Select an option button; then select the **OK** command button. Press Esc to cancel.

You can use the computer to perform other tasks, with Desktop or other DOS programs, while Desktop still is connected. Be careful, however, not to use a program that attempts to control the serial port to which your modem is connected—and don't turn off your computer until the transmission is over!

Reading Electronic Mail

As explained earlier in this chapter, you can cause Desktop to log on periodically to the selected electronic mail service to check your mail. If you load Desktop as memory-resident, the program handles most of the connection and message-downloading procedure in the background so that you can use the computer for other purposes. If Desktop has downloaded a message in the background, the program displays the message You have new Electronic Mail the next time you display the Desktop window.

At times, however, you may not want to wait for the scheduled mail-reading event. Desktop enables you to easily connect to the on-line service and look for electronic mail. To connect to the previously selected electronic mail service and check your mail, display the Electronic Mail screen and press F7 (Read), or choose **R**ead Mail Now from the **A**ctions menu.

When Desktop connects to the electronic mail service, the program logs on to the service, downloads any messages, and logs off. Unless you loaded Backtalk, Desktop displays its progress on-screen, as shown in figure 24.9. If you load Backtalk in memory before starting Desktop, Desktop briefly interrupts your work to connect to the electronic mail service and then handles the remainder of the message downloading in the background. Desktop alerts you that an electronic mail session is in progress by displaying a flashing letter B in the upper right corner of the screen. Desktop removes the B and your computer beeps when the session is complete.

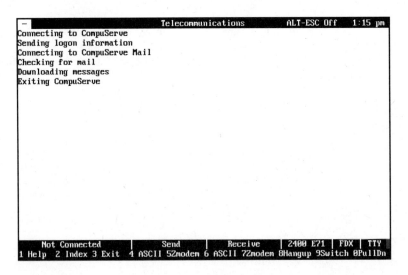

Downloading
electronic mail.

To read a message that Desktop has downloaded to your Inbox directory, perform one of the following actions:

- Highlight the entry in the Inbox window and press Enter.

- Highlight the entry in the Inbox window; then choose **V**iew Highlighted Message from the **A**ctions menu.

- Double-click the message entry with the mouse.

Desktop opens a Notepads window and displays the message. Press the cursor-movement keys to move through the file.

While the Notepads window is displayed, Desktop lists eight function-key commands in the message bar. These function key commands are listed in table 24.2.

Table 24.2 Function Key Commands Available When Reading Electronic Mail

Key	Name	Function
F1	Help	Displays context-sensitive Help facility
F2	Index	Displays Help facility index
F3	Exit	Cancels current process or application (same as Esc)
F4	Delete	Deletes displayed message
F5	Reply	Creates and sends an electronic mail message to the person from whom you received the displayed message
F8	Next	Displays next message
F9 or Ctrl+Esc	Switch	Switches active window
F10 or Alt	PullDn	Activates horizontal menu bar
Esc	Cancel	Cancels current process or application (same as F3)
Alt+space bar	Window Control	Displays Window Control dialog box

When you are finished reading the message, you can take one of the following actions:

- Save the file for future reference.
- Delete the file.
- Send a reply to the person who sent you the displayed message.

To save the message, follow these steps:

1. Select File to display the File menu, and then select Save. Desktop displays the Save File to Disk dialog box.

2. Type a different file name in the Filename text box.

3. Select the **S**ave command button. Desktop saves the file to disk and returns to the Notepads window.

4. Press Esc or F3 (Exit) to return to the Electronic Mail screen.

To delete rather than save the message, press F4 (Delete) or choose **A**ctions from the horizontal menu bar to display the Actions menu, and then select **D**elete Highlighted Message. Desktop deletes the file from disk, removes the message from the screen, and returns to the Electronic Mail screen.

To send a reply to the individual who sent the displayed message, follow these steps:

1. Press F5 (Reply). Desktop opens another Notepads window with a mail message header. Desktop has already filled in the TO line with the information that was in the FROM line in the original message. The SUBJECT line also is filled in with the SUBJECT line information from the original message.

2. Type your reply and press F5 (Email). The Send Electronic Mail Options dialog box appears.

3. Select Send Immediately or Send at Scheduled Time.

4. Select the **O**K command button. Desktop returns to the Electronic Mail screen and sends the reply at the time you specified.

You can also view messages in your Inbox, Outbox, and Sent directories directly from the Electronic Mail screen. To view these messages, select **V**iew from the menu and then choose View **I**nbox (F4), View **O**utbox (F5), or View **S**ent (F6).

For Related Information

◀◀ "Moving around the Notepad," p. 574.

FROM HERE...

Using Electronic Mail's Scheduling Feature

Electronic mail services can be an efficient way to transmit information quickly over long distances. A potential weakness in this method of communication is the likelihood that you cannot check your electronic mailbox in a timely manner. PC Tools provides a solution to this problem. By using Desktop's Electronic Mail application, you can schedule the periodic unattended reception of electronic mail. In addition, you can create several messages to be sent by electronic mail and then have Desktop send the accumulated messages at set intervals.

 Desktop must be running memory-resident (as a TSR) for the scheduling feature to work.

Scheduling Automatic Reading

To schedule a time for Desktop to check your electronic mail, display the Electronic Mail screen. Then choose Setup from the horizontal menu bar and choose Read Mail Schedule. Desktop displays the Read Mail Schedule dialog box (see fig. 24.10).

Fig. 24.10

The Read Mail Schedule dialog box.

In the Every text box, type a number that indicates how often you want Desktop to check your electronic mailbox on the electronic mail service. The default value of 1 causes Desktop to log on to the electronic mail service every hour to check your mail.

You may expect electronic mail to be sent to you only during business hours. Use the Start and End text boxes to specify a range of hours during the day when Desktop periodically will check the electronic mail service for mail addressed to you. The default values for Start and End are 9:00a and 5:00p, respectively. Type times in 12-hour format (type **a** or **p** after the time to denote A.M. or P.M..) or in 24-hour format (indicating A.M. or P.M. is not necessary).

Select the Every Day option button if you want Desktop to check mail all week long. Choose the Work Days option button if you want Desktop to check electronic mail only during the workweek. Refer to Chapter 20, "Managing Your Appointment Schedule," for more information about controlling which days Desktop considers workdays.

For Related Information

◄◄ "Customizing the Appointment Scheduler," p. 682.

◄◄ "Setting the Work Days," p. 683.

◄◄ "Making a New Appointment," p. 686.

After you have made all necessary entries and changes, select the **OK** button. Desktop returns to the Electronic Mail screen. As long as your computer is turned on and Desktop is loaded as memory-resident, Desktop checks your electronic mail at the designated intervals, even if you are running another program. If someone sends you a message, Desktop automatically downloads the message. The next time you display the Desktop window, the program alerts you that you have electronic mail.

Scheduling Automatic Sending

To schedule a time for Desktop to send your electronic mail, display the Electronic Mail screen; then choose **S**etup from the menu and **S**end Mail Schedule from the Setup menu. Desktop displays the Send Mail Schedule dialog box, which is similar in appearance to the Read Mail Schedule dialog box (refer to fig. 24.10).

In the Every text box, type a number that indicates how often you want Desktop to connect to the electronic mail service for the purpose of sending your messages. (*Note:* Desktop does not dial and connect to the service unless you created messages that have not been sent yet.) The default value in the Every text box is 2, which causes Desktop to log on every two hours to the electronic mail service to send your outgoing mail.

Use the Start and End text boxes to specify a range of hours during the day when Desktop periodically will check to see whether you have placed files in the Outbox directory for sending to the electronic mail service. The default values for Start and End are 9:30a and 5:30p, respectively. Type times in 12-hour format (type **a** or **p** after the time to denote A.M. or P.M.) or in 24-hour format.

Finally, select the Every Day option button if you want Desktop to send outgoing mail all week long. Choose the Work Days option button if you want Desktop to send mail only during the workweek. (Refer to Chapter 20, "Managing Your Appointment Schedule," for more information about controlling which days Desktop considers workdays.)

After you make all necessary entries and changes, select the **OK** command button in the Send Mail Schedule dialog box. Desktop returns to the Electronic Mail screen. As long as your computer is turned on and Desktop is loaded as memory-resident, Desktop checks the Outbox directory for outgoing electronic mail at the designated intervals, even if you are running another program.

Chapter Summary

This chapter explains how to use the Desktop Electronic Mail facility to send and receive messages between your computer and an on-line electronic mail service. The chapter discusses how to set up Electronic Mail, select an electronic mail service, specify directories, create an electronic mail message, send mail, and read mail. This chapter also discusses how to schedule automatic reading and sending of electronic mail.

Turn to Chapter 25, "Sending and Receiving Fax with Fax Telecommunications," to learn how PC Tools can enable you to send facsimile (fax) transmissions from your computer.

Sending and Receiving Fax with Fax Tele- communications

One unique feature in PC Tools is support for sending and receiving facsimile (fax), a form of telecommunications. Although most businesses continue to use stand-alone facsimile machines, PC Tools enables you to send and receive facsimile transmissions directly from your computer, without a separate fax machine, if your computer system meets one of the following requirements:

- The system has a Connection CoProcessor board from Intel PCEO (Hillsboro, Oregon), a SatisFAXtion board from Intel, or a Personal Link board from SpectraFax Corporation (in Naples, Florida).

- The system has a fax board compliant with the DCA/Intel Communicating Application Standard (CAS).

- The system is connected to a Novell NetWare network that contains one of these boards.

In fact, Desktop's Fax Telecommunications application enables you to send and receive fax transmissions even while you are using your computer to perform other tasks. This chapter explains how to use this impressive capability of PC Tools.

Understanding What You Need

PC Tools 8 Fax Telecommunications has been tested by Central Point Software and is certified to work with the SatisFAXtion board or Connection CoProcessor board from Intel PCEO and with the Personal Link board from SpectraFax Corporation, all of which comply with the CAS standard. For convenience, this chapter refers to these boards as *CAS boards*, but neither Que Corporation, the author, nor Central Point Software warrants that any boards other than the SatisFAXtion board, Connection CoProcessor, and Personal Link boards will operate with PC Tools 8. Testing by the author was performed on the Connection CoProcessor from Intel PCEO. Before you purchase a fax board for the purpose of using the board with PC Tools, check with your dealer or the board's manufacturer to determine whether the board is compatible with PC Tools 8 for the purpose of sending fax.

Assuming that you have a compatible board installed in your computer—or in a computer on a Novell local area network to which your computer is attached—PC Tools 8 enables you, from within any PC program, to send text in a Notepads file to a CCITT Group 3-compliant facsimile machine or to another computer equipped with a fax board capable of receiving Group 3 fax transmissions. You can even transfer binary files at a rate of 9,600 bps from one CAS board to another. You also can use PC Tools Desktop to check your fax log to determine what transmissions have been sent or received.

The remaining portion of the chapter describes how to use Desktop to send files by using an internal CAS fax board and how to check your fax log for fax messages and files sent or received by your board.

FROM HERE...

For Related Information

▶▶ "Meeting Basic System Requirements," p. 910.

Configuring Fax Telecommunications

Before you can use Desktop's Fax Telecommunications application, you must configure PC Tools for use with your CAS fax board. See Appendix A, "Installing and Configuring PC Tools," for information on installing the memory-resident program ITLFAX.EXE distributed with PC Tools 8. The remainder of the chapter assumes that your computer or local area network contains a properly installed CAS fax board.

After the fax board is installed, display the Desktop main menu and select **D**esktop Accessories. To display a window from which you can send a text message or file via your fax board, choose the **F**ax option. Desktop displays the Send FAX Directory window (see fig. 25.1).

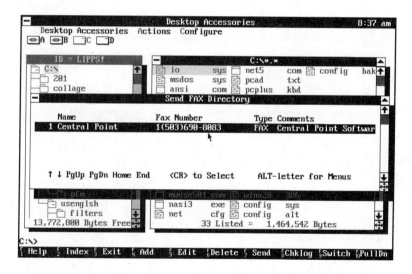

Fig. 25.1

The Send FAX Directory window.

To configure Desktop for use with the fax board, select **C**onfigure (see fig. 25.2) from the menu bar. The Configure menu lists the five options described in the following paragraphs.

Choose the **F**AX Drive option to indicate the drive and directory in which you want Desktop to create the files that will be sent by the fax-board software. This drive and directory can be assigned by Install during installation (see Appendix A, "Installing and Configuring PC Tools"). When you choose this option, Desktop displays a dialog box containing the prompt Enter the FAX drive letter and path where Desktop will place fax files. Type the drive and directory name—for example, C:\PCTOOLS\FAX—in the text box below this prompt. After you specify the drive and directory, select the **OK** command button. Desktop returns to the Fax Telecommunications window.

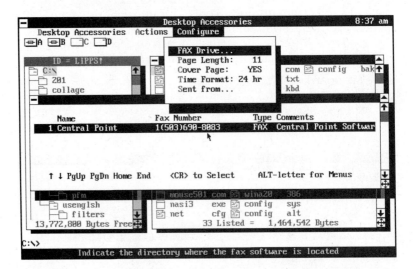

Fig. 25.2

The Configure menu.

NOTE If Fax Telecommunications has been installed on your network, your network administrator should have already created a directory in which all users are to store their fax files; enter this drive and directory in the text box. The "global" directory allows a single fax board installed in a network workstation to send faxes for all Desktop users.

Choose the **P**age Length option to set the page length (in inches) of fax messages. Desktop displays a dialog box in which you can type a one- or two-digit number. The default page length is 11 inches. This length causes the receiving fax machine to cut letter-size messages. You can increase or decrease this number whenever you want the receiving fax machine to cut pages of a different size. When you are sending a short message, for example, you can shorten the page-length number to conserve paper at the receiving end. After you type the desired number, select the **OK** command button. Desktop returns to the Fax Telecommunications window.

Choose the **C**over Page option to specify that you normally want Desktop to add a cover page in front of the message you are sending. Desktop displays a dialog box containing the Cover Page check box. Select this check box to enable the cover page feature. A cover page customarily is used for indicating routing information such as the recipient's name, the sender's name, the date, and the total number of pages in the message. If you mark the Cover Page check box, Desktop gives you the option of sending a cover page every time you send a fax. The cover page automatically includes routing information and provides space for a logo and for you to type optional text. If you do not mark this box, Desktop does not add a cover page. After marking the check box, select **OK** to return to the Fax Telecommunications window.

Choose the **T**ime Format option to indicate whether you want Desktop to print the time on each fax in 24-hour format or in A.M./P.M. format at the top of each fax page. Select the format you want; then select the **OK** command button. Desktop returns to the Fax Telecommunications window.

Choose the **S**ent From option to specify the name you want Desktop to show as the sender of each fax. Type the sender name that you want to appear on every fax (up to 30 letters); then select the **OK** command button. Desktop returns to the Fax Telecommunications window. Desktop includes the sender's name on the cover page (if you use one) and prints the name in the middle of the top line of every page of the fax message.

> **T I P**
>
> Use the same name in the **S**ent From configuration that you used when you set up your CAS fax board. By using the same name, you enable Desktop to correctly identify fax messages and files addressed to you. For example, the setup program that comes with the Intel Connection CoProcessor is SETUPCC.EXE. Use the same name in the Desktop Fax Telecommunications configuration that you used in the Name setting when you ran SETUPCC. Alternatively, you can use SETUPCC (or the program that came with your CAS board, if you are not using the Connection CoProcessor) to change the Name setting to match the name you are using in the configuration of Desktop Fax Telecommunications.

After you configure Fax Telecommunications, you are ready to learn how to send a fax to fax machines and to other CAS boards, as well as how to read your fax log.

Examining the Send Fax Directory Window

The Send FAX Directory screen is similar in appearance to the Modem Telecommunications screen; it contains a Directory window and menu selections. The FAX Directory Window can contain a maximum of 99 entries (refer to fig. 25.1).

The menu bar at the top of the screen contains the options **D**esktop Accessories, **A**ctions, and **C**onfigure. The message bar at the bottom of the screen lists 10 shortcut keys. Table 25.1 lists the functions of these and other keystroke commands available in the Send FAX Directory screen.

Table 25.1 Keystroke Commands Available in a Send Fax Window		
Key	**Name**	**Function**
F1	Help	Displays context-sensitive Help facility
F2	Index	Displays Help facility index
F3	Exit	Cancels current process, application, or dialog box (same as Esc)
F4	Add	Adds an entry to Send FAX Directory
F5	Edit	Edits highlighted entry in Send FAX Directory
F6	Delete	Deletes highlighted directory entry
F7	Send	Sends a fax or file to system listed in highlighted directory entry
F8	Chklog	Displays FAX log
F9 or Ctrl+Esc	Switch	Switches to FAX Log window (if it is already open)
F10 or Alt	PullDn	Activates horizontal menu bar

Key	Name	Function
Esc	Cancel	Cancels current process or application (same as F3)
Alt+space bar	Window Control	Displays Desktop System Control dialog box
Ins	Insert	Toggles between overtype mode and insert mode when you are editing an entry

Sending a Fax or File

Desktop enables you to use your CAS fax board to send a text message to a fax machine or a non-CAS fax board. Desktop also enables you to use your CAS fax board to transmit any type of disk file—but only to another CAS fax board. Before you can send a fax or file, you first must create a directory entry.

Open the Send FAX Directory window. If you are sending a message to an individual or business for the first time, press the shortcut key F4 (Add) or select Add a New Entry from the Actions menu (see fig. 25.3). Desktop displays the Fax Details dialog box (see fig. 25.4).

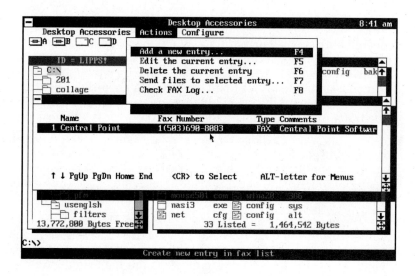

Fig. 25.3

The Actions menu.

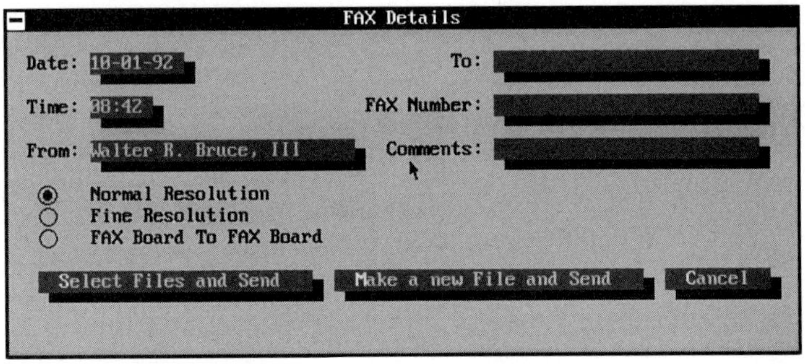

Fig. 25.4

The FAX Details
dialog box.

> **NOTE** If an entry already is listed for the system you want to call,
> type the entry number; you also can use the cursor-move-
> ment keys or the mouse to position the highlight bar on the
> entry. Press Enter or position the mouse pointer on the en-
> try and click either mouse button. Desktop displays the FAX
> Details dialog box with the text boxes filled in.

The Fax Details dialog box contains six text boxes (three are already
filled in):

- *Date.* The entry in this text box determines the date that the fax or
  file is sent. By default, Desktop fills in the current date, but you
  can schedule your fax to be sent at a future date by typing that
  date here.

- *Time.* This text box determines when the fax or file is sent. The
  default entry is the current time. When the value in this text box is
  the current or a past time, the fax or file is sent immediately. You
  can send the message or file at a later time by typing the desired
  transmission time in this text box. Your CAS board delays the
  transmission until the specified time arrives and then completes
  the transmission (assuming that your computer is still turned on).

- *From.* This text box indicates the sender's name. Desktop uses the
  name you specified during configuration, using the **S**ent From
  command on the Configure menu. Desktop prints this name in the
  center of the top line of every page of a fax message. This name
  can contain no more than 32 characters.

- *To.* The cursor appears in this text box when Desktop displays the
  Fax Details dialog box. Type the name of the addressee here (up
  to 32 characters). Desktop prints this name at the top left of every
  page in a fax message. Desktop displays this name in the Name
  column of the directory displayed in the Send Fax Directory window (refer to fig. 25.1).

■ *FAX Number.* In this text box, type the telephone number of the facsimile machine, fax board, or CAS fax board to which you want to transmit a fax or file. Desktop displays this number in the FAX Number column of the directory displayed in the Send Fax Directory window. The number can contain up to 32 characters.

■ *Comments.* Use this text box to type a short description of the types of messages or files normally sent to the specified recipient. Desktop displays the contents of this text box in the Comments column of the directory displayed in the Send FAX Directory window, but no entry is required in this text box.

When you are sending a fax long distance, you may want to delay transmission until late in the evening, when toll rates are lowest. Use the Time text box for this purpose. If you delay the time until after midnight, however, you also must change the entry in the Date text box to the following day. In addition, you must remember to leave your computer running.

T I P

Below the six text boxes in the Fax Details dialog box, Desktop lists the following option buttons:

■ *Normal Resolution.* Resolution is measured in dots per inch (dpi). Select this option to send a fax at *normal resolution* (200 dpi horizontally by 100 dpi vertically). The option, which is the default, is usually sufficient for transmission of text and is also faster than the Fine Resolution option. When this option is selected for an entry, Desktop displays FAX in the Type column of the Send FAX Directory window.

■ *Fine Resolution.* Choose this option to send a fax or graphics file at *fine resolution* (200 dpi horizontally by 200 dpi vertically). When this option is selected for an entry, Desktop displays FAX in the Type column in the Send FAX Directory window.

■ *FAX Board to FAX Board.* Use this option when you want to send, via your CAS board, any type of disk file to another CAS board. This capability is equivalent to sending a file by using Modem Telecommunications and a binary file-transfer protocol such as ZMODEM or XMODEM. The advantage of using the CAS board-to-CAS board method is the board's speed, which is 9,600 bits per second (bps). Most popular modems transmit data at a slower rate: usually 2,400 bps. When this option is selected for an entry, Desktop displays File in the Type column in the Send FAX Directory window.

Selecting a File

After you fill in the text boxes and select the appropriate option button, you must select one of three command buttons listed along the bottom of the Fax Details dialog box: Select Files and Send, Make a New File and Send, or Cancel.

Occasionally, you may want to type a message from scratch and then send the message. Select the **M**ake a New File and Send command button to cause Desktop to open a Notepads window. Type your message and press Esc (Exit) or F3 (Exit), or click the close box.

After you type the file or files you want to send or if you want to send files from CAS board to CAS board, choose the **S**elect Files and Send command button. If this is the first time you have sent a fax or file using the current entry, Desktop displays the Files to Select dialog box (see fig. 25.5). This dialog box lists the default Notepads directory in the Files list box. You can specify one or more files to be sent by repeatedly typing file names in the text box and pressing Enter or by selecting multiple file names from the Files list box.

Fig. 25.5

The Files to Select dialog box.

> **NOTE** When you are sending to a fax machine or to a non-CAS fax board, all files you choose must be Notepads files. If you are sending to another CAS board, you can select any type of file.

Select as many as 20 files. As you select each file name, Desktop builds a list of files in the Files to Send dialog box, which is not visible until the Files to Select dialog box disappears from the screen. When you finish selecting files to be sent, select the **S**end command button in the Files to Select dialog box. Desktop displays the Files to Send dialog box, as shown in figure 25.6. If the correct files are listed, select the **S**end command button to forward the files to the CAS board. If a file is listed that you don't want to send or if a file name is missing, select the **C**hoose Different Files command button in the Files to Send dialog box to return to the Files to Select dialog box.

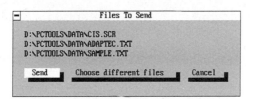

Fig. 25.6

The Files to Send
dialog box.

For second and subsequent uses of a Send FAX directory entry, Desktop displays the Files To Send dialog box, which lists the last file or files sent to this particular recipient. At the bottom of the dialog box, Desktop lists three command buttons: Send, Choose Different Files, and Cancel. Choose Send to send the same messages or files again. Select Choose Different Files when you want to send from 1 to 20 other files. Desktop displays a File Load box and enables you to select files, as described in the preceding paragraphs. When you finish selecting files to be sent, select the Send command button.

Including a Cover Page

Assuming that you configured Fax Telecommunications to include a cover page, after you select the Send command button in the Files To Send dialog box, Desktop displays a message dialog box that asks whether you want to include a cover page with the current transmission (see fig. 25.7).

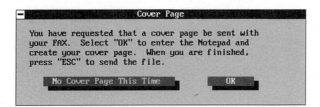

Fig. 25.7

The Cover Page
message box.

Select OK when you want to include a cover page. Desktop then opens a Notepads window to a notepad named COVER.TXT. In the bottom half of the fax message's cover page, type the message you want to be printed. When you finish typing the message, press Esc (Exit) or F3 (Exit), or click the close box.

When your CAS board sends a cover page, the page is formatted so that a logo occupies the top four inches of the cover page. The default logo is the one on the cover of the PC Tools documentation. This logo is stored on the disk in a file named PCTOOLS.PCX. You can use a graphics editor program such as PC Paintbrush (or another program that creates files in PCX format) to edit this file or to create your own logo file. If you create your own logo, you must save the logo in PCX format under the file name PCTOOLS.PCX, and the file must be stored in the same directory as the PC Tools program files. The logo portion of the cover page is not sent when you are transferring a file between CAS boards. The logo is sent only when you are transmitting text as a facsimile.

The middle portion of the cover page shows routing information you specified in the Fax Details dialog box. This section of the page lists the name of the recipient you specified in the To text box, the name of the sender specified in the From text box, and the date of the fax transmission specified in the Date text box. This section also indicates the total number of pages in the fax.

The lower 5 1/2 inches of the cover page incorporates the text you typed in the cover file COVER.TXT.

Sending the Message or File

When you finish typing the cover message or if you configured Desktop so that a cover page isn't included, Desktop transfers the message or file to your CAS board for transmission to the recipient's system and displays the following message:

```
Processing FAX submission now... please wait...
```

When the transfer of control is complete, Desktop displays the message Your request has been routed to your FAX card. Select the **OK** command button to confirm this message and to return to the Send FAX Directory window. If this is the first time you have sent a file to this recipient, Desktop adds an entry for this recipient to the Send Fax directory.

Your CAS board operates in the *background*, which means that after Desktop transfers the messages or files to the board for transmission (along with the telephone number, date and time for transmission, and other pertinent information), the CAS board can complete the procedure without further action on your part or on the part of your computer's main CPU (central processing unit). You can continue working with Desktop, or you can return to any other program on your computer. You do not need to wait for the transmission to be completed.

> **CAUTION:** Do not turn off your computer until you are sure that the CAS board has completed its transmissions. If you interrupt a fax transfer by rebooting or switching off your PC, the fax currently being sent will not be completed successfully and will have to be resent.

If the message or file is sent immediately and your FAX board's speaker is on, you first hear the dial tone, and then you hear the CAS board dial the destination telephone number. The CAS board generates a continual beep. Then you hear the phone ring, the remote system answer, and a high-pitched tone called a *carrier signal*. When the two machines begin to communicate, the CAS board turns off the speaker. When the transmission is complete, the CAS board causes your computer to beep, signaling that the transfer is finished.

Receiving Fax

Desktop's Fax Telecommunications application doesn't facilitate receiving fax messages. The nature of CAS fax boards, however, allows you to use the board to receive a fax message from a fax machine or fax board and even to receive a file from another CAS fax board while you are using Desktop or any other DOS program. Refer to the documentation that came with your CAS board to determine how to set the board to automatically answer incoming calls from other fax machines, fax boards, or CAS boards. You must use your CAS board-supplied software to read and print fax messages you receive and to move received files to a directory in which you can use them.

The next section examines how to check the Fax Log to determine whether you have received a fax message or a file transmitted by a CAS board.

Using the Fax Log

Although your CAS fax board operates independently in the background, you need a way to determine whether a fax has been transmitted successfully. The software included with your CAS board maintains a log of all incoming and outgoing fax events. Desktop's Fax Telecommunications application provides two convenient ways to view this log.

To check the status of an outgoing fax or to check whether you have received any fax messages or files or to abort a fax transmission, use one of the following methods to display Desktop's Fax Log window:

■ Choose **T**elecommunications from the **D**esktop Accessories menu; then choose **C**heck the Fax Log from the Telecommunications submenu.

■ Display a Send FAX Directory window and press the shortcut key F8 (Chklog) or select **A**ctions; then select **C**heck FAX Log from the Actions menu.

Desktop displays the FAX Log window (see fig. 25.8). The default size and position of this window are the same as that of the Send FAX Directory window. If you were viewing the Send FAX Directory window when you issued the command to check the FAX log, the Send FAX Directory window remains open and hidden behind the Fax Log window. The FAX Log window contains the same window elements as other Desktop application windows: title bar, close box, zoom arrow, move box, resize box, and scroll bars.

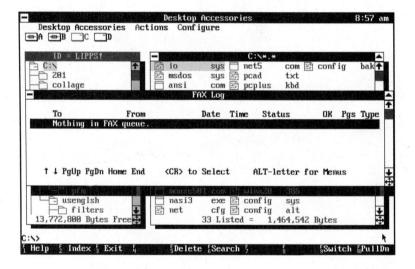

Fig. 25.8

The FAX Log window.

The Fax Log window contains eight columns listing information about transmitted and received fax messages and files:

■ The *To* column lists the intended recipient of the fax.

■ The *From* column lists the sender of the fax or file.

■ The *Date* column lists the date that the transmission was attempted.

■ The *Time* column shows the time of attempted transmission.

■ The *Status* column indicates the status of the transmission (Dialing, Sending, Sent, Receiving, Received, and Aborted) and certain error messages.

■ The *OK* column displays Yes when the transmission is error-free and No if you aborted the transfer or if an error occurred that prematurely halted transmission.

■ The *Pgs* column indicates the number of pages in the fax message (including the cover page). The number in this column is always 1 when a file is transmitted between CAS fax boards.

■ The *Type* column displays FAX when the transmission was a normal fax transmission and File when the transfer of a file was between CAS boards.

When the Fax Log window is the active window, Desktop provides a different set of menu options and shortcut keys. Table 25.2 lists the available shortcut keys and their functions, as well as the other keystroke commands available in the Fax Log window.

Table 25.2 Keystroke Commands Available in a FAX Log Window

Key	Name	Function
F1	Help	Displays context-sensitive Help facility
F2	Index	Displays Help facility index
F3	Exit	Cancels current process, application, or dialog box (same as Esc)
F5	Delete	Deletes current entry
F6	Search	Searches fax log
F9 or Ctrl+Esc	Switch	Switches to Send FAX Directory window (if it is open)
F10 or Alt	PullDn	Activates horizontal menu bar
Esc	Cancel	Cancels current process or application (same as F3)
Alt+space bar	System Control	Displays Desktop's System Control menu
Ins	Insert	Toggles between overtype mode and insert mode when you are editing an entry

Deleting an Entry or Aborting a Transmission

After a transmission is completed, you may have no reason to continue listing the transmission in the log. To delete the entry, use the cursor-movement keys or the mouse to position the highlight bar at the entry; then press the shortcut key F5 (Delete) or select **D**elete the Selected Entry from the **A**ctions menu. Desktop displays a message box asking you to confirm the deletion. Select **O**K to delete the log entry.

Occasionally, you may want to abort a transmission before it is completed. To abort a transmission, display the Fax Log dialog box and press the F5 (Delete) key or select the **D**elete the Selected Entry option from the **A**ctions menu to delete the entry. Desktop displays a message asking whether you want to abort the transmission. To abort the transmission, select **O**K.

Adjusting AutoUpdate

While the Fax Log window is the active Desktop window, Desktop rechecks, by default, the status of the fax log every 60 seconds and refreshes the contents of the screen. Using this feature, you can continually monitor the progress of a transmission. You can change the amount of time that passes between checks, however, by selecting **C**onfigure from the horizontal menu bar and then selecting **A**utoUpdate. Desktop displays this message:

```
Enter an autoupdate time in seconds or 0 to disable
```

The default value is 60 seconds. Type a larger number to reduce the frequency with which Desktop checks the status of the fax log; type a smaller number to increase the frequency.

The AutoUpdate feature is effective only while the Fax Log window is the active window. If the Fax Log window is displayed but not active, Desktop does not continually check the status of the fax log and update the screen. In this case, you must press F9 (Swap) to make the Fax Log window active if you want Desktop to update the information.

Chapter Summary

This chapter examines how to use the features of the Desktop Fax Tele-communications module and explains what hardware you need to send fax, using PC Tools. You learned how to use the Send FAX Directory window and the Check FAX Log window to send a facsimile or a file to a fax machine or a PC with a fax board. You also learned how to check for incoming files and fax messages.

Now turn to Chapter 26, "Controlling a PC Remotely with CP Commute," to learn how you can use your PC to control another PC across a LAN or over telephone lines.

Controlling a PC Remotely with CP Commute

This chapter introduces the most commonly used features of Central Point Commute, the PC Tools 8 utility that enables you to control a PC remotely over a modem connection, Novell NetWare local area network (LAN), or a direct connection. The chapter first describes the steps you must take to connect with another computer running Central Point Commute. The chapter then describes how you can use Central Point Commute to start and use DOS and Windows applications on the remote PC. Next, you learn how to use Central Point Commute's Chat windows when you want to type a message to the operator of the computer at the other end of the connection. The chapter also covers how to use Commute to transfer files between two computers. Finally, the chapter describes how to terminate the connection between a Central Point Commute take-control PC and a give-control PC.

Starting Commute

To start Central Point Commute, type **commute** at the DOS command line, and then press Enter. If you choose to have Install install applications in the PC Shell program-list menus, you can start Commute by displaying the PC Tools Main menu and selecting **C**ommute.

You can also use a version of Commute that requires less memory while resident; the program COMMSML.EXE can be used on PCs with no high memory or a smaller amount of conventional memory. COMMSML uses the same set of commands, so you can substitute it freely for COMMUTE; however, do not use COMMSML with Windows. To exit a COMMSML session, type **exit** from DOS.

Getting Set Up

The first time you start Commute, the program displays the Commute User Name dialog box (see fig. 26.1). Type a Commute user name in the text box and select the **OK** command button. The name can be up to 20 characters long and can include spaces. This name identifies you when you call other PCs that are running Commute.

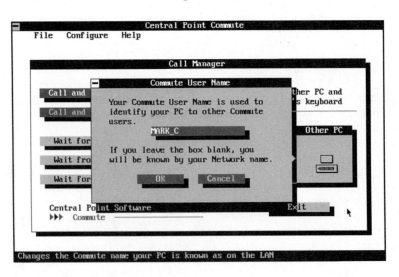

Fig. 26.1

The Commute User Name dialog box.

If you plan to use Commute to connect over a Novell NetWare LAN, using your assigned network user name is convenient but not mandatory. If you are logged in to the network when you run Commute for the first time, Commute automatically displays your network user name in the text box. If you are not logged in but plan to use Commute over a Novell network, you can leave the user name blank; Commute then automatically uses your network user name when you make a Commute connection over the network. If you use a modem or direct connection, enter a name to identify you to other Commute users. After you enter a name or if you decide to accept the default name, select the **OK** command button.

NOTE   If you plan to use Commute to take control of another PC that has established a Give Control list, as discussed later in this chapter, your Commute user name must match the name assigned to you in the other PC's Give Control list.

After you select the **OK** command button, Commute displays the Connection Type dialog box (see fig. 26.2).

Fig. 26.2

The Connection Type dialog box.

Select one of the following option buttons from the Connection Type dialog box:

■ *Connect by Modem.* Select this option when you plan to connect your printer most frequently to the remote PC through a modem over the telephone system.

■ *Connect by LAN.* Select this option when you think you most often will connect to the remote PC over a Novell NetWare LAN.

■ *Direct Connection.* Select this option if you plan to usually connect your computer to the remote computer by null-modem cable.

NOTE   A *null-modem* cable is a special type of serial cable you can connect to the respective serial (COM) ports of two computers so that data can be transferred between the computers.

Selecting a Modem

When you choose the Connect by Modem option in the Connection Type dialog box, Commute displays the Modem List dialog box, which displays two columns of option buttons (see fig. 26.3). Each option button represents a particular brand and model of modem. The modems are listed in alphabetical order by manufacturer. If you don't see your modem on the first screen, press PgDn or select the Next command button. You can choose from six pages of modems.

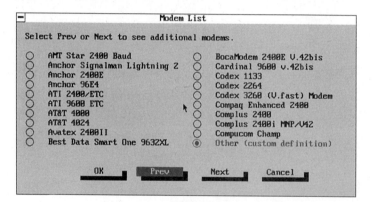

Fig. 26.3

The Modem List dialog box.

If your modem is not listed, choose a brand and model of modem that is compatible with your modem—a good choice is the Hayes-compatible (2400 baud)—or choose the Other (custom-definition) option button on the final page of modems. Then select OK. Commute displays the Edit Modem Commands dialog box (see fig. 26.4). Refer to your modem's documentation for help, and modify the Initialization String, Dial String, Answer String, and Hangup String, as necessary; then select the OK command button.

Selecting a COM Port

After you select a modem for the Connect by Modem connection type or if you select Direct Connection as the connection type, Commute displays the COM Port dialog box (see fig. 26.5). This dialog box lists four option buttons: COM1, COM2, COM3, and COM4. Choose the option button that corresponds to the serial (COM) port to which your modem or null-modem cable is attached. If you have a nonstandard serial port installed in your machine, select the Edit command button to display a dialog box that lists the current IRQ (interrupt request line) and input/output address. Refer to the documentation from your computer to determine the values for these text boxes. Select the OK command button to continue.

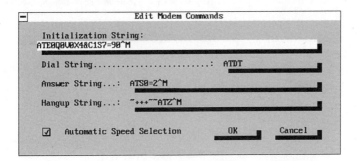

Fig. 26.4

The Edit Modem Commands dialog box.

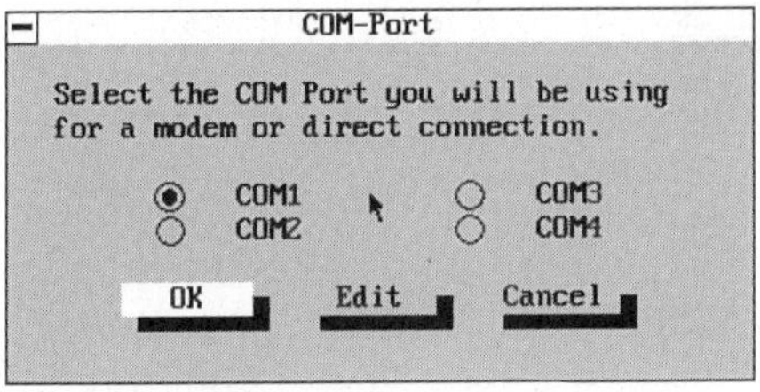

Fig. 26.5

The COM-Port dialog box.

After you specify your Commute user name, select a connection type, specify a modem model, and select a COM port, Commute displays the Call Manager window, shown in figure 26.6. Commute now is set up and ready to use.

 Selecting a modem model and COM port is not required when you choose the Network connection type.

Creating a Private Call List

The first step in communicating with another computer over telephone lines—whether next door, across town, or across the country—is to dial the telephone number. Because you will probably want to use

Commute to connect to the same remote computers on a regular basis, the program enables you to build a list of telephone numbers, called the *Private Call List*, that you can use when you are placing a call with Commute. Also, because Commute enables you to connect to other computers over Novell NetWare LANs, as well as directly by null-modem cable, you can list LAN users and direct connections in the Private Call List.

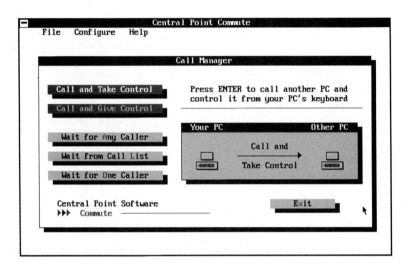

Fig. 26.6

The Call Manager window.

The first phase of every Commute communications session is the connection phase. When you use Commute to connect to another PC to take control of that computer, you are operating the *take-control PC*, and your computer does the calling. The remote PC is the *give-control PC*.

To create a Private Call List, follow these steps:

1. Display the Call Manager window and select **F**ile from the horizontal menu bar; then choose **P**rivate Call List from the File menu. Commute displays the Private Call List dialog box (see fig. 26.7).

   By default, the Private Call list includes two entries:

   ■ MANUAL CALL displays the Manual Call dialog box, which enables you to dial any telephone number or make a LAN or direct connection without having to predefine an entry.

   ■ LAN USER LIST displays the LAN Server List dialog box, which lists available network servers. After you select a server, Commute displays the LAN User List, which enables you to select the LAN user to whom you want to place a call.

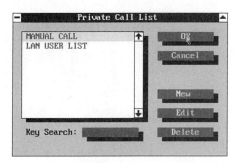

2. Select the **New** command button. Commute displays the Edit Call List dialog box (see fig. 26.8).

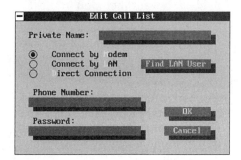

3. Select the type of connection that this entry requires: Connect by **M**odem, Connect by **L**AN, or **D**irect Connection. Then, in the Private Name text box, type a name that reminds you whom this entry will call.

4. If you want to specify a LAN user but don't remember the user's network name, select the **F**ind LAN User command button. Commute displays the LAN Server List dialog box. Select the server to which the Commute user is assigned. Commute then searches the network for active Commute users. If any Commute users are found, Commute displays their names in the LAN User List dialog box, as shown in figure 26.9. If no Commute user is logged on to the server and waiting for a call, Commute cannot find a Commute user and displays an error message instead.

In the LAN User List dialog box, you can select **S**how Commute Users Only to display only those LAN users running Commute and awaiting a call, or you can select Show All LAN Users to display a complete list of LAN users, who may or may not be running Commute (in fact, these users don't even have to be logged on). If you choose the latter, a successful connection may not be possible.

Fig. 26.9

The LAN User List
dialog box
showing a
Commute user.

5. Select the **OK** command button. Commute displays the LAN User List with all network users listed.

6. Select the user name you want included in this Call List entry, and then select the **OK** command button.

7. In the Phone Number text box of the Edit Call List dialog box (refer to fig. 26.8), type the phone number for the remote PC.

   If you selected the Connect by LAN option button, Commute displays the Commute User Name text box in place of the Phone Number text box. Type the user's log-in name in this text box.

   If you used the Find LAN User command button to fill in the dialog box, Commute has already entered the user's name in the Commute User Name text box.

8. If the give-control PC requires a password, type the password in the Password text box.

9. Select the **OK** command button. Commute returns to the Private Call List dialog box and adds the new entry to the list box.

Repeat this procedure for every entry you want to add. To edit an entry, highlight the name in the list box and select the **E**dit command button. Commute displays the Edit Call List dialog box (refer to fig. 26.8). Make the desired modifications and select **OK** to return to the Private Call List dialog box.

To delete an entry, highlight its name and select **D**elete.

When you finish adding, editing, and deleting entries in the Edit Call List dialog box, select **OK** to save all changes. Commute returns to the Call Manager window. The Private Call List is ready for use.

When Commute displays the Private Call List, you can expand the dialog box by pressing F8. In addition to the Private Name, Commute lists the phone number (for modem connections) or the LAN user name (for LAN connections).

Creating a Give-Control List

Every time you permit someone to connect to and take control of your computer through Commute, you are exhibiting a significant amount of confidence in the operator's competence and good intentions. Consequently, you may want to maintain strict control over which callers are given access. Commute's Give Control List provides the needed security by enabling you to assign user passwords and take other security precautions.

With the Give Control List dialog box, you can require every Commute user who calls and connects with your system to enter a password. After Commute confirms that the caller has entered the valid password, the program checks for a *callback* phone number and for file-transfer privileges. A callback phone number determines whether the give-control PC, for security purposes, hangs up the telephone line and immediately calls back the phone number stored in the Phone Number field of the caller's Give Control List entry. Two check boxes in the Give Control List entry determine whether the caller is permitted to transfer files between the calling computer and your computer during the Commute session.

To create a Give Control List, follow these steps:

1. Display the Call Manager window and select **F**ile from the menu. Then choose Give Control List from the File menu. Commute displays the Give Control List dialog box.

2. To add a new entry to the list, select the **N**ew command button. Commute displays the Edit Give Control List dialog box (see fig. 26.10).

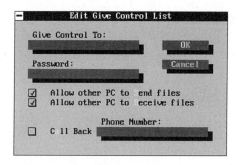

Fig. 26.10

The Edit Give Control List dialog box.

3. In the Give Control To text box, type the Commute user name for the take-control PC. This name must be the same as the Commute user name for the take-control PC.

4. To require a password, type the password in the Password text box. The remote user types the same password in the Take-Control Private Call List entry that calls your PC.

5. Check the Allow Other PC to **S**end Files check box to permit the take-control PC to transfer files to your computer. Check the Allow Other PC to **R**eceive Files check box to permit the take-control PC to transfer files from your computer to the remote computer.

> **NOTE** The Call-back field in the Edit Give Control List dialog box is used only for modem connections.

6. After you enter a name and optionally enter a password or call-back number, select the **OK** command button. Commute returns to the Give Control List dialog box with the new entry added to the list.

7. Select the **OK** command button. Commute saves all additions to the Give Control List.

Repeat this procedure for every entry you want to add.

To edit an entry, highlight the name in the list box and select the **E**dit command button. Commute displays the Edit Give Control dialog box. Make the modifications you want, and select **OK** to return to the Give Control List dialog box.

To delete an entry, highlight its name and select **D**elete.

When you finish adding, editing, and deleting entries in the Give Control List dialog box, select **OK** to save all changes. Commute returns to the Call Manager window. The Give Control List is ready for use.

When Commute displays the Give Control List, you can expand the dialog box by pressing F8. In addition to the Private Name, Commute lists the phone number (for modem connections) or the LAN user name (for LAN connections).

For Related Information

◀◀ "Using a Direct Connection," p. 818.

Connecting

Commute enables you to connect a take-control PC to a give-control PC over telephone lines or a local area network. You can also connect to a give-control PC by direct connection over a null-modem cable.

Preparing the Give-Control PC To Answer a Call

Before accepting a phone call, the give-control PC must be ready to receive a call by modem or null-modem cable or over a network. The operator of the give-control PC must select one of the following command buttons from the Call Manager window to place the computer in a waiting-for-call mode (refer to fig. 26.6):

- *Wait for Any Caller.* Choose this command if you want Commute to accept a call from any take-control PC. You load Commute automatically in this mode by adding the command COMMUTE /R to your PC's AUTOEXEC.BAT file.

- *Wait from Call List.* This command causes Commute to accept a call from only take-control PCs in the Give Control List. When the operator selects this command, Commute displays the Connection Type dialog box. Choose the desired connection type and select OK. You load Commute automatically in this mode by adding the command COMMUTE /RL to your PC's AUTOEXEC.BAT file.

- *Wait for One Caller.* This command causes Commute to accept a call from only a specified take-control PC in the Give Control List. When the operator selects this command, Commute displays the Give Control List. The operator selects the name of the user from whom the call is expected. Commute then displays the Connection Type dialog box. The operator selects Connect by Modem, Connect by LAN, or Direct Connection, and then selects the OK command button. If you choose the Connect by Modem option, Commute briefly displays a dialog box that contains the message Preparing to Wait for Call. Please wait...

NOTE You can call an entry from your Private Call list or another user on your network by running Commute from DOS with the appropriate command-line switches. For more information on these options, run Commute by using the command line COMMUTE/?.

Finally, Commute is ready to answer a call, with a portion of the program memory-resident. Commute returns to the DOS command line and displays the following message on the DOS screen, just above the DOS command line:

```
Commute V2.0
_Copyright 1991,1992 Central Point Software, Inc.
Commute Both Resident Modes Installed
```

This message indicates that Commute is waiting in the background for a caller. The operator of this PC can continue to use the computer as usual until the take-control PC calls. If the Commute session will take place over a modem connection, however, avoid using the COM port being monitored by Commute. Likewise, the take-control PC operator must avoid running any application on the give-control PC that uses the same COM port; following this procedure prevents two programs from "locking" your PC by trying to use the same COM port.

Initiating the Call from the Take-Control PC

In most cases, Commute sessions are initiated by the operator of the take-control PC, after the operator of the give-control PC has instructed Commute to wait for a call. When you know that the give-control PC is waiting and you are ready to place a call, display the Call Manager window; then select the Call and **T**ake Control command button. Commute displays the Private Call List dialog box (see fig. 26.11).

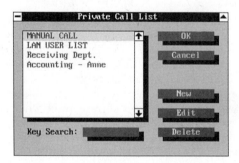

If you have already defined an entry in the Private Call List for the PC you want to call, use the mouse to double-click the entry; alternatively, use the cursor-movement keys to highlight the entry, and then press Enter.

If you have not defined an entry for the destination PC, you can do so now and then select the entry, or you can use the MANUAL CALL entry (for a modem connection) or the LAN USER LIST entry (for a LAN connection), as explained in the following:

■ To use MANUAL CALL, double-click the entry, or highlight the entry and press Enter. Commute displays the Manual Call dialog box (see fig. 26.12). Select the connection type and, in the Dial text box, enter the phone number (for a modem connection) or the Commute User Name for the PC you want to call. Select the **OK** command button to place the call.

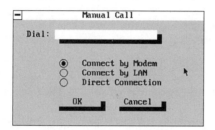

Fig. 26.12

The Manual Call dialog box.

■ To use the LAN USER LIST entry, double-click the entry, or highlight the entry and press Enter. Commute displays the LAN Server List dialog box (refer to fig. 26.9), which lists available network servers. After you select a server, Commute displays a list of Commute users who are logged on to the selected server. Select a user, and select the **OK** command button to place the call.

Commute displays the Commute Call in Progress dialog box, which informs you of the progress of the call (see fig. 26.13).

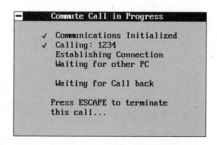

Fig. 26.13

The Commute Call in Progress dialog box.

As the program accomplishes each step, it displays a check mark to the left of each message. Commute displays the number the modem is dialing. If you are connecting by network, Commute replaces the message in the second line with the message `Call Answered - LAN`.

When you call by modem—depending on the brand and model of your modem—you probably first hear a dial tone and then the modem dialing the telephone number of the remote PC. Most modems turn the speaker on before dialing and turn the speaker off after the modem begins to communicate with the receiving modem.

After the two PCs begin to communicate, Commute displays the following message:

```
Connection established in the Commute Call in Progress
dialog box.
```

If you are prompted to do so, type your Commute user name and the password assigned to you by the operator of the give-control PC. The give-control PC checks your name and password against its Give Control List and determines whether the list contains a call-back number for your system.

If, for an added level of security, a call-back is required, the give-control PC disconnects the line and calls you back. Your screen displays a check mark next to the message Waiting for Call Back. When the give-control PC's modem returns the call, your computer's modem answers the call and reestablishes the connection.

When the connection is complete, Commute clears the Call Manager window from the screen and displays whatever screen happens to be displayed on the give-control PC.

Initiating the Call from the Give-Control PC

You may occasionally be operating the give-control PC and want to place a call to the take-control PC. Perhaps you are having a problem operating a new feature in your accounting program and want to call your technical-support expert for assistance. You start Commute on your computer and select Wait for Any Caller in the Call Manager window. When Commute displays the Connection Type dialog box, select the connection type you intend to use (most likely, the Connect by Modem type) and select OK. Commute displays the DOS command line. From the DOS command line, start your accounting program.

The operator of the take-control PC—your tech-support expert in this example—starts Commute and selects the Wait for Any Caller command button and the connection type. When the take-control PC displays the DOS command line, the stage is set for you to call from your give-control PC to the take-control PC.

At the give-control PC keyboard, press Alt+Right Shift (hold the Alt key and press the Shift key on the right side of the keyboard). Commute displays the Call Manager window. To place the call, select the Call and **G**ive Control command button. Commute displays the Private Call List.

From this point, you use the same process described in the preceding section to initiate the call.

After the connection is made, the screens on both the take- and give-control PCs display your accounting program.

Running an Application on the Give-Control PC

During a Commute *session*, the period in which a Commute data link is active between two PCs, the operator of the take-control PC can run virtually any DOS or Windows program on the give-control PC. All text or graphics displayed on the give-control PC's screen are also displayed on the take-control PC's screen. The take-control PC does not need a copy of the application software running on the give-control PC.

In many circumstances, the give-control PC operator is someone who needs assistance with a software-related problem, and the take-control PC operator is attempting to provide the assistance. Perhaps you are learning a new database program and cannot get a certain procedure to work. You have a friend who is an expert user of this database program, but she lives 50 miles away. By using Commute, you can link your PCs so that she can show you how to resolve your difficulty.

In other cases, the take-control PC operator wants to connect to the give-control PC to access software or data on the give-control PC. Or the take-control PC operator may want to gain access to a network to which the give-control PC is connected. Suppose, for example, that you are on a business trip in Chicago. You are preparing to call a client and realize that you forgot to check your database for the status of the client's last order. You have your laptop computer with you, but the data you need is stored on your office desktop computer. Luckily, you left your desktop computer running with Commute memory-resident, waiting for a call. By using Commute on your laptop computer, you can call your office computer, run the database program, and find the information you need.

By using Commute, you can even take control of another PC on a LAN. Perhaps you are a PC technical-support specialist for a Fortune 500 company. Users continually call you with software questions that require you to run all over your company's 10-story building. You decide to install Commute on every user's system. When a user calls with a problem, you can establish a Commute session with the user's PC over the network and diagnose and resolve the problem without leaving your office.

Chapter 25, "Sending and Receiving Fax with Fax Telecommunications," describes how to use PC Tools Desktop to send facsimile transmissions over a LAN, through a CAS fax board. Desktop does not have a facility for reading incoming fax messages, but you can use Commute to take control of the network workstation in which the CAS fax board resides. By running the fax board software on the computer that holds the fax board, you can view and print over the network any fax message that the board has received.

Starting the Application

For the take-control PC operator to be able to run a DOS application during a Commute connection (including Microsoft Windows programs), the give-control PC operator must start Commute on the give-control PC before starting the application program.

When Commute is waiting for a call (and is memory-resident), the give-control PC operator can start the application program and then establish a Commute data link. Alternatively, either PC operator can establish the data link and then start the application. Whether the link is established first or the application is started first is irrelevant. Also unimportant is which operator initiates the call or executes the commands on the give-control PC to run the application program. (*Note:* The application software must be located on the give-control PC.)

During a Commute session, the keyboards and screens on both the take- and give-control PCs are in *lock step*; input from either keyboard affects the applications program in the same way. Both screens are identical. Either PC operator, therefore, can start the program and execute commands in the application program.

> **NOTE** Because the take-control and give-control PCs' keyboards are equally effective, be careful that the operators of both PCs do not attempt to type at the same time.

Suppose, for example, that your brother has asked for your help in fine-tuning a spreadsheet that compares the costs of two mortgages. Because your brother lives 150 miles away, you want to use Commute to link your PCs and run 1-2-3 remotely on your brother's PC. Your brother starts Commute on his computer, and you start Commute on yours. Follow the procedure described in the section "Connecting" earlier in this chapter to initiate a Commute session. After connecting, both screens display the DOS prompt.

At the DOS prompt, either you or your brother executes the necessary commands to start 1-2-3. You may, for example, type these commands and press Enter after each one:

    CD \LOTUS

    123

As you type, the command appears on your brother's screen and on your screen. Similarly, when the program runs, 1-2-3 displays a blank worksheet on both screens. Then either you or your brother can execute 1-2-3 commands, and the result of each command appears simultaneously on both computer screens.

Running Windows on the Give-Control PC

If you elect to include Windows support during the installation of PC Tools 8, Windows 3.0 and 3.1 run on the give-control PC like any other program. However, be aware of the following facts when running Windows under Commute:

- The transmission of graphical Windows screens may slow your Commute session considerably. A high-speed, error-correcting modem of 9600 baud or faster is recommended for optimum performance.

- If your PC is running Windows and you receive a call from another Commute user, Commute displays a dialog box alerting you that a Commute connection is requested. You can choose to accept or reject the incoming call from the dialog box.

- Install modifies several Windows files; a PC Tools program group is generated in PROGMAN.INI, and new keyboard and mouse drivers are substituted in SYSTEM.INI. To restore these original files, copy PROGMAN.CP8 and SYSTEM.CP8 over PROGMAN.INI and SYSTEM.INI, respectively.

- Instead of using the Commute Automatic Disconnect feature, exit Windows as you normally would with the Exit command from the Program Manager's File menu.

For Related Information

◄◄ "Understanding What You Need," p. 864.

◄◄ "Configuring Fax Telecommunications," p. 865.

◄◄ "Sending a Fax or File," p. 869.

Displaying the Commute Session Manager Window

Occasionally, while the application is running on the give-control PC, you may want to send messages to the remote PC operator, exchange files, control your printer, and so on. Commute enables the operator of the take-control PC to perform these and other operations through the Commute Session Manager.

The take-control PC operator can display the Commute Session Manager, shown in figure 26.14, by pressing Alt+Right Shift.

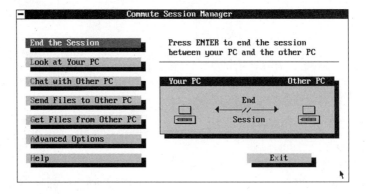

Fig. 26.14

The Commute Session Manager window.

The Commute Session Manager window contains the following command buttons:

■ *End the Session* disconnects from the give-control PC.

■ *Look at Your PC* temporarily returns your PC to the state it was in before you started Commute (see the section "Accessing the DOS Command Line on the Take-Control PC" later in this chapter).

- *Chat with Other PC* displays a Chat window on both the take- and give-control PCs (see the section "Using the Chat Window" later in this chapter).

- *Send Files to Other PC* displays the Send Files to Other PC dialog box, which enables you to transfer files from your computer's disks to the disks on the give-control PC (see the section "Transferring Files" later in this chapter).

- *Get Files from Other PC* displays the Get Files from Other PC dialog box, which enables you to transfer files from the disk drives on the give-control PC to the disk drives on the take-control PC (see the section "Transferring Files" later in this chapter).

- *Advanced Options* displays the Commute Advanced Options window (see the section "Using the Advanced Options" later in this chapter).

- *Help* displays the context-sensitive Help facility (same as F1).

- *Exit* returns to the give-control PC's application.

You execute a command from the Commute Session Manager window by selecting a command button. Every command button listed in this window is discussed in a later section in this chapter. When you finish using the Session Manager, select the **Exit** command button or press Esc or F3. Commute returns you to the give-control PC's application screen (the 1-2-3 screen in the example).

Accessing the DOS Command Line on the Take-Control PC

During a Commute session, you may want to access DOS temporarily on the take-control PC. Perhaps you want to execute a DOS command such as DIR (which lists files in a DOS directory), or maybe you want to run another program quickly without losing the current Commute connection.

To access DOS on the take-control PC, display the Commute Session Manager window and select the **Look at Your PC** command button. Commute clears the screen and displays the DOS prompt. Now you can execute nearly any DOS command or run a DOS program. To see a list of the files in the current directory, for example, type **dir** and press Enter. DOS displays a list of file names and again displays the DOS prompt.

If you run a DOS application program, keep in mind that some of the take-control PC's memory is occupied by Commute (the amount varies, depending on whether you're using a memory manager), DOS, and any memory-resident programs that may be loaded. Some programs are too big to run in this manner.

> **CAUTION:** Do not execute a command or run a program that affects the take-control PC's communication (COM or serial) ports or that is memory-resident. Attempting to use a COM port might result in disconnection from the remote PC, and loading a memory-resident program may make returning to Commute without rebooting the take-control PC impossible.

After you finish with the DOS command or DOS program, type **exit** at the DOS prompt and press Enter. Commute returns to the give-control PC's application program.

Keep in mind that you must use the **L**ook at Your PC command button from the take-control PC's Session Manager to execute DOS commands, access files, and access directories on the take-control PC. If you do not use this option, all DOS commands, file references, and directory references during a Commute session apply to the give-control PC, not to the take-control PC.

Using the Chat Window

During a Commute session, you may occasionally want to converse with the operator of the remote PC. In an office environment, you may have enough telephone lines to talk over one line and connect your computers over another. Commute provides a method of conversing, however, that doesn't require a second telephone line: the Chat window, shown in figure 26.15. Commute enables the operator of either PC in a Commute session to open the Chat window.

How you access the Chat window depends on whether your computer is the give-control or take-control PC. To display the Chat window from the take-control PC, display the Commute Session Manager window and select the **C**hat with Other PC command button. To display the Chat window from the give-control PC, press the Commute hotkey (Alt+Right Shift).

The upper half of the Chat window displays characters you type on your PC's keyboard. Any characters typed by the operator at the other end of the connection appear on your screen in the lower half of the Chat window.

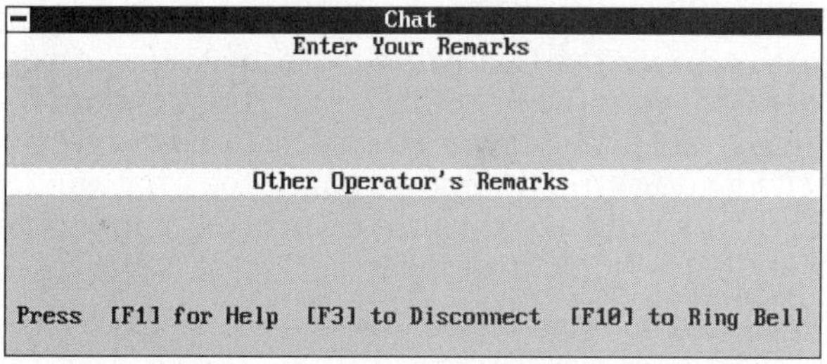

```
┌─────────────────────────────────────────────────────────┐
│ ■                         Chat                            │
│                     Enter Your Remarks                    │
│                                                           │
│                                                           │
│                                                           │
│                   Other Operator's Remarks                │
│                                                           │
│                                                           │
│                                                           │
│ Press  [F1] for Help  [F3] to Disconnect  [F10] to Ring Bell │
└─────────────────────────────────────────────────────────┘
```

Fig. 26.15

The Chat
window.

You may, for example, use Commute to connect to your brother's computer to work on a spreadsheet that computes the cost of a home mortgage. During the session, you decide that you need to ask your brother a question about the spreadsheet. Press Alt+Right Shift to display the Commute Session Manager. Select the Chat with Other PC command button to display the Chat window.

While the Chat window is displayed, either operator can use any of the function key commands listed in table 26.1.

Table 26.1 Function Key Commands Available in the Chat Window

Key	Name	Function
F1	Help	Displays the context-sensitive Help facility
F3	Disconnect	Terminates the Commute session
F10	Bell	Sounds a bell on the take- and give-control PCs

Your side of the conversation—the messages that you type—appears in the upper half of your Chat window and in the lower half of the remote PC's Chat window. As you type, characters fill in the upper half of your Chat window from left to right. To erase characters, press the Backspace key. The arrow keys are ineffective while you are typing in the Chat window.

When you press the Enter key or type past the right end of a line, Commute moves the cursor down one line and to the left side of the screen. If the section fills and you move the cursor to the next line, the information in the top line scrolls off the screen and out of sight.

Characters typed by the remote PC operator appear in the Other Operator's Remarks section of your Chat window. When the section fills and still another line is received, the information at the top scrolls off the screen and out of sight.

When you finish your conversation with the remote PC operator, press Esc. Commute removes the Chat window. If the take-control PC operator caused the Chat window to be displayed, the Commute Session Manager window still is displayed. Press Esc or F3 to return to the application. If the give-control operator caused the Chat window to be displayed, both PCs return to the give-control PC's application screen as soon as the Chat window disappears.

Transferring Files

Commute enables the take-control PC operator to transfer files quickly and easily between the take-control and give-control PCs. Suppose, for example, that you want to copy a 1-2-3 spreadsheet file named HOUSE.WK1 from the LTSDAT directory on the give-control PC's drive C to the LFILES directory on the local drive C.

Press the hotkey, Alt+Right Shift, to display the Commute Session Manager window. Select the **G**et Files from Other PC command button. Commute displays the Receive Files from Other PC dialog box (see fig. 26.16).

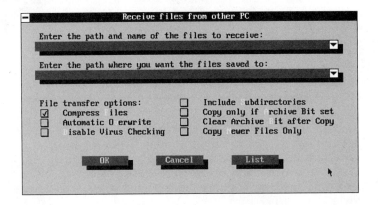

Fig. 26.16

The Receive Files from Other PC dialog box.

The Receive Files from Other PC dialog box contains two text boxes, seven check boxes, and two command buttons. In the first text box, type the complete directory path and file specification for the files you want to transfer to your computer. For example, to copy HOUSE.WK1 from the give-control PC's drive C and LTSDAT directory, type the following specification in the first text box:

    C:\LTSDAT\HOUSE.WK1

The second text box in the Receive Files from Other PC dialog box indicates the destination drive and directory on your computer. Type the full drive, directory, and file specification. To copy the spreadsheet file HOUSE.WK1 into the LFILES directory on drive C, for example, type the following in the second text box:

C:\LFILES\HOUSE.WK1

 Commute enables you to use the wild-card characters * and ? in either file specification.

In the lower half of the dialog box, Commute displays the following file-transfer options:

■ *Compress Files* compresses and decompresses files automatically to decrease transmission time. This box is checked by default. Note that compression is not effective in reducing transfer time if the file is an *archive* because archive files are usually compressed already. Most download files offered by bulletin boards and on-line services have already been compressed into archives.

■ *Automatic Overwrite* overwrites existing files of the same name as a transferred file without alerting you. By default, this box is not checked. Commute normally displays a warning and requires confirmation before it replaces any existing file.

■ *Disable Virus Checking* turns off the feature that scans all incoming files for viruses. By default, this box is not checked, which means that virus checking occurs on every file transferred from the give-control PC.

■ *Include Subdirectories* causes Commute to automatically include all files from subordinate directories that meet the file specification typed in the first text box. By default, this box is not checked.

■ *Copy Only if Archive Bit Set* copies only files that have been modified or created since the last backup operation. By default, this box is not checked.

■ *Clear Archive Bit after Copy* clears the archive bit for every file that is copied. You normally use this option with the preceding option when you are backing up the give-control PC's disk. By default, this box is not checked.

■ *Copy Newer Files Only* copies only files that are newer than files by the same name that exist already on the local disk. By default, this option is not checked.

After you check any boxes you want to use, select the **OK** command button. Commute transfers the files you specify, using the selected options. Commute depicts the progress of the file transfer in the dialog box.

Commute enables you to send files to the give-control PC from the take-control PC. Display the Commute Session Manager window and choose **S**end Files to Other PC. Commute displays the Send Files to Other PC dialog box, which is nearly identical to the Receive Files from Other PC dialog box. Type values in the text boxes, and select the check boxes you want. When you select the **OK** command button, Commute transfers the designated files.

Using the Advanced Options

In addition to the options listed in the Commute Session Manager window, Commute provides several advanced options. Display the Commute Session Manager window, and select the **A**dvanced Options command button. Commute displays the Commute Advanced Options dialog box (see fig. 26.17).

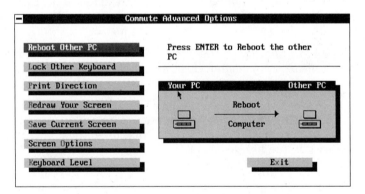

Fig. 26.17

The Commute
Advanced
Options dialog
box.

The Commute Advanced Options dialog box displays the following command buttons:

■ *Reboot Other PC* causes the give-control PC to reboot. This command is most useful for ensuring that no one else, after you are finished, can call in and initiate a Commute session. If Commute is loaded in the give-control PC's AUTOEXEC.BAT, this option *resets* the give-control PC after every call.

■ *Lock Other Keyboard* suspends input temporarily from the other PC's keyboard so that you do not need to worry about both operators typing simultaneously.

■ *Print Direction* displays the Print Direction dialog box, which contains these options: Your PC, Other PC, Both PCs, and Neither. Each option determines the destination of any printing generated by the application running on the give-control PC.

■ *Redraw Your Screen* refreshes your screen. Try this option if unusual characters fill your screen.

■ *Save Current Screen* saves the current screen shot to a named file.

■ *Screen Options* displays the Screen Options dialog box in which you can select maximum screen resolution, screen-refresh rate, and number of screen colors.

■ *Keyboard Level* toggles the standard and enhanced keyboard levels.

■ *Exit* returns to the Commute Session Manager window.

Ending a Session

When you are ready to end the Commute session, the take-control PC operator or the give-control PC operator can terminate the link.

If you are the take-control PC operator and want to end the session, follow these steps:

1. Press Alt+Right Shift. The Commute Session Manager appears on the take-control PC.

2. Select End the Session from the Commute Session Manager window. Commute warns you that you are about to disconnect the communications link.

3. Select OK to end the Commute session.

If you are the give-control PC operator and want to end the session, follow these steps:

1. Press Alt+Right Shift. The Chat window appears.

2. Press F3 (Disconnect) from the Chat window. Commute warns you that you are about to disconnect the communications link.

3. Select OK to end the Commute session.

Chapter Summary

This chapter introduces the most commonly used features of Central Point Commute. The chapter describes the steps you must take to connect with another computer running Central Point Commute and then describes how you can use Commute to start and use a DOS application on the remote PC. You learned how to use Central Point Commute's Chat windows when you want to type a message to the operator of the computer at the other end of the connection and how to transfer files and terminate the connection between a Central Point Commute take-control PC and a give-control PC.

By now, you have had the opportunity to try the many tools in PC Tools 8. You are well on your way to becoming a PC Tools expert. This book has introduced you to the ins and outs of the most comprehensive, yet easiest-to-use, software tools available for the personal computer. Whatever the task, you now can decide when to use one of the PC Tools, which tool to select, and how best to use it. Whether you use your PC for business or for personal use, for profit or for pleasure, put PC Tools 8 to work. Use what you have learned in this book to get the most out of this incredible collection of useful programs.

Appendixes

O U T L I N E

Installing and Configuring PC Tools

Using PC Tools from within
  Microsoft Windows

Installing and Configuring PC Tools

T his appendix explains how to run the PC Tools 8 Install program on a stand-alone computer system. The appendix also describes the PC Config program that you use to customize your PC Tools Desktop setup. If you are installing PC Tools Desktop to or from a network environment, refer to the PC Tools documentation accompanying your software for more complete instructions.

All the programs and utilities in PC Tools 8 are Windows-aware, meaning that they are optimized to run as both stand-alone DOS applications and DOS Applications in the Windows environment. Two Windows-specific programs are included on the distribution disks if you select the Access PC Tools In Windows option at the beginning of the install process.

PC Tools 8 programs provide a number of parameters to assist you in the initial process of installing the programs. With all PC Tools programs, you may type the program name followed by /? to see the available start-up switches for each program. To see what switch parameters are available for PC Tools Desktop, for example, type **pctools /?** at the DOS command line and press Enter. PC Tools displays the available command-line options.

NOTE   In prior versions of Central Point software, you invoked the programs by typing DESKTOP or SHELL at the DOS prompt. In this release, to provide backward compatibility with prior versions, you can invoke PC Tools Desktop in one of three ways:

Type	Action
pctools	PC Tools Desktop loads from the batch file PCTOOLS.BAT in your \PCTOOLS directory.
pcshell	PCSHELL, which provides backward compatibility, loads PC Tools Desktop.
desktop	PC Tools loads only the Desktop Accessories module (see the section "Configuring PC Tools Desktop and Desktop Accessories" later in this chapter for more about Desktop Accessories).

Meeting Basic System Requirements

Your computer must meet certain minimum requirements to successfully install and run the PC Tools programs. To run PC Tools Desktop on a single-user (*stand-alone*) computer, your system must have 512K of system memory (RAM), at least one floppy drive, and a hard drive with between 5 and 9M of free disk space. If you plan to run the PC Tools programs in memory-resident mode, you should have at least 640K of system memory (RAM). Your system must be running DOS 3.3 or later.

A mouse is optional, but the PC Tools Desktop programs are designed to make good use of one. If you use an older mouse, you may need to obtain new drivers from the manufacturer to take full advantage of your mouse with the PC Tools Desktop applications, especially in memory-resident mode. PC Tools supports the Microsoft Mouse driver Version 6.14 and later, as well as the Logitech/Dexxa Mouse Version 3.4 and later.

To use the PC Tools Fax application software, your fax board must be installed and configured prior to installing PC Tools Desktop. PC Tools supports the Intel Connection CoProcessor and SatisFAXtion fax boards, as well as the SpectraFax fax board. Other boards capable of emulating these fax boards may work with PC Tools. Consult the PC Tools documentation or Central Point Software for additional fax boards that may be supported.

You can install PC Tools Desktop on a Novell NetWare server (running Novell NetWare Version 2.12 or later), an IBM PC LAN server, or other NetBios-compatible networks. After the network administrator has installed PC Tools programs on the network server, network users may run PC Tools programs from the server, install and configure their own workstations, or install PC Tools programs from the server to their own workstation hard disks. (Each user on the network must have his or her own license.)

Running Install

Use the PC Tools 8 Install program to install PC Tools Desktop on your hard disk; refer to figure A.1 for an example of the PC Tools Install screen. Most of the programs on the distribution disks are compressed and will not work until Install uncompresses them as they are copied to the hard disk. Install performs several setup tasks such as adding start-up commands to your AUTOEXEC.BAT file, scanning your hard disk for application programs, and adding application programs to the PC Shell Applications menu.

To run Install, insert the first distribution disk (labeled INSTALL) into drive A. Type **a:** at the DOS command line and press Enter. Next, type **install** at the DOS command line and press Enter. The screen shown in figure A.1 appears.

 NOTE If you are installing to a black-and-white monitor, type **in-stall /bw** and press Enter. If you are installing to an LCD display, type **install /lcd** and press Enter. For a list of other available options, type **install /?** and press Enter.

Choosing an Installation Type

One of the first things Install does after checking the integrity of your hard disk and scanning for possible viral infection is provide you with a menu from which you select a type of installation.

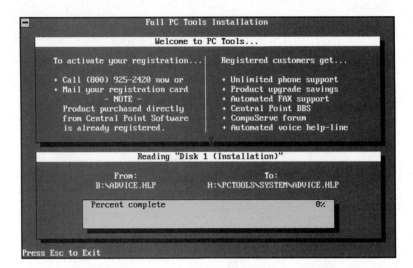

The PC Tools
Install screen.

First, Install checks your system to determine the type of video controller installed and then prompts you to choose Color, Monochrome, LCD,
or B/W (black and white), as shown in figure A.2. Select the appropriate
monitor type to match your computer's display.

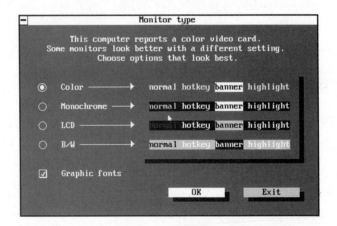

Fig. A.2

The Monitor type
dialog box.

PC Tools can create special graphic screen fonts that give the PC Tools
screens a Windows-like appearance. The default for VGA monitors, for
example, is to have the **G**raphics Fonts box checked. Check the **Graphics Fonts** check box to use the special fonts, and then select **OK**.

Next, Install displays a warning screen telling you to exit Install if you
need to run Undelete to recover erased files, run DiskFix to repair a

damaged disk, run Unformat to unformat a disk, or run FileFix to recover damaged files (see fig. A.3). Do not continue with Install if you
need to perform any of these actions. Instead, exit Install by selecting
Exit, repair any damage to your files or disks, and then repeat the installation procedures. If you do not need to perform any of these repairs, select **OK** to continue.

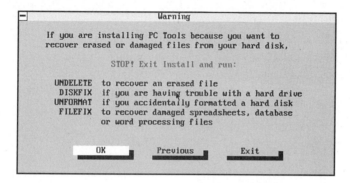

Fig. A.3

The Warning
dialog box.

PC Tools Install has been enhanced from Version 7 to provide more
choice in what—and how—you install the various programs on the
distribution disks. Four different installation options, shown in figure
A.4, are provided: Full, Minimal, Laptop, and Custom. An Uninstall
option is also presented as a menu choice, although it is initially inaccessible if you have not previously installed PC Tools. (If you have
installed PC Tools 8 already, the only available menu choice is
Uninstall.)

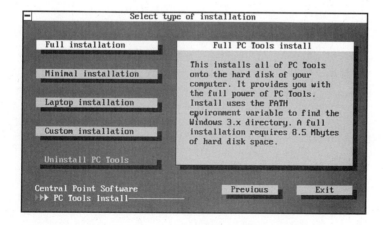

Fig. A.4

The Select Type
of Installation
dialog box.

When highlighted, each installation option displays a brief description in a box on the right side of the screen. This description explains the type of installation each option provides. On-line, context-sensitive help, which more fully explains each of the installation options, is available when you press F1. The four installation methods are discussed briefly in the following paragraphs.

Full installation installs all the PC Tools 8 programs included on the distribution disks to your computer system.

Minimal installation installs the most frequently installed PC Tools programs. These programs include the following:

PC Tools Desktop	File Viewer
Central Point Anti-Virus	Installation
Central Point Backup	Mirror
Compress	PC-Cache
Menus	PC Config
Data Monitor	DriveMap
DiskFix	Program Scheduler
Build Emergency Disk	RAMBoost
FileFind	System Information
Undelete	

Laptop installation installs programs most appropriate for laptop computer users. These programs include the following:

PC Tools Desktop	Build Emergency Disk
Central Point Anti-Virus	DiskFix
Central Point Backup	FileFind
Central Point Commute	File Viewer
Compress	Installation
Menus	Mirror
Data Monitor	PC-Cache
PC Config	DriveMap
Program Scheduler	RAMBoost
System Information	Undelete

Custom installation provides you with complete control over which programs are installed and where and how those programs are installed. Network administrators who install PC Tools programs on the network server should use this installation choice.

Continuing with Install

Install displays a dialog box asking you to confirm the drive and directory into which you want to install the PC Tools programs (see fig. A.5). The default is C:\PCTOOLS, but you may change this to the drive and directory of your choice. Type in the drive and directory, or select **OK** to continue. If the directory you typed does not exist, Install asks whether you want the program to create the directory for you. Select **Yes**, and then select **OK** to confirm the path you have chosen.

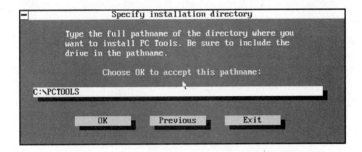

Fig. A.5

The Specify Installation Directory dialog box.

Install asks whether you want to access PC Tools applications from Windows, prompting you for the drive and directory where your Windows programs and files are installed. If you do not have Windows installed or do not choose to use your PC Tools programs in Windows, select **S**kip to continue. Otherwise, type in the drive letter and directory name you want to use; then select **OK** to continue with the installation.

After you select the appropriate options, PC Tools checks the integrity of your hard disk to determine whether enough space is available to install the program files; if so, PC Tools begins installing the program files. Screens appear, depending on the type of installation you chose. These screens ask for information as the installation progresses and inform you of its activities during the process.

Creating an Emergency Disk

PC Tools Install automatically runs the Create Emergency Disk utility during the installation process so that, in the event of a failure of some kind, you can reboot your system and work with the recovery programs to restore your system to a functional state. Figure A.6 displays an example of the Build Emergency Disk dialog box that appears when you begin creating your Emergency Disk.

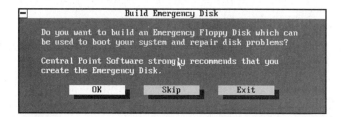

Fig. A.6

The Build Emergency Disk dialog box.

Choose the Create Disk option to begin the Create Emergency Disk process. After PC Tools analyzes your system, it prompts you to remove any installation disks from your drive and insert a blank disk to hold the Emergency Disk files (see fig. A.7). You can configure the Emergency Disk to hold certain files that are important to you by selecting Configure Disk in the dialog box to view suggestions of files to include.

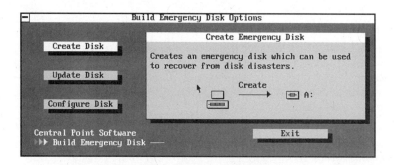

Fig. A.7

The Build Emergency Disk Options dialog box.

You can perform the emergency disk process as many times as you like after the installation process is complete; however, do *not* skip the process during installation. Instead, run EDISK program in your \PCTOOLS directory after Install is completed to prepare a *second* emergency disk, which you can put away for safe-keeping in case your first disk becomes lost or damaged.

The emergency disk contains at least the following files necessary to boot your system from drive A:

- The DOS hidden system files required to boot from your hard disk: IO.SYS and MSDOS.SYS (or IBMBIO.COM and IBMDOS.COM)

- A copy of COMMAND.COM, the DOS command interpreter

- A copy of your AUTOEXEC.BAT file and a specialized version of your CONFIGURES file containing the following lines:

  FILES=35
  BUFFERS=35

- A copy of your hard disk partition file (named PARTNSAV.FIL on the emergency disk) especially created by PC Tools' MIRROR program during the installation process and information about your computer's CMOS data

- SYS.COM, the program DOS uses to install the DOS system files and command interpreter to a disk to make it bootable

- DOS's FDISK program to display, create, and remove partitions from your hard disk

- MI.COM, PC Tools Memory Information utility

- UNFORMAT and UNDELETE, PC Tools programs that help you undo an accidental disk format and recover erased files on a disk

- PCFORMAT, PC Tools' disk format utility

- PC Tools' DiskFix, which enables you to diagnose, troubleshoot, and repair a variety of problems you may encounter on your system

Using a preformatted disk for the emergency disk procedure is not required; PC Tools uses its own PCFORMAT program to prepare the disk for you. Central Point recommends that you use the highest capacity disk available for your drive A so that more recovery utilities can fit on the disk.

After you create the Emergency Disk, Install gives you the following options, as shown in figure A.8:

- Rename your existing FORMAT.COM program to FORMAT!.COM, and then install a batch file that runs PCFORMAT each time you type **format** at the DOS command line.

■ (DOS 5.0 only) Rename your existing UNDELETE.EXE to UNDELET!.EXE, and then install a batch file that runs PC Tools' UNDEL program when you type **undelete** at the DOS command line.

You can select **OK** or **SKIP** to move on to the next install option.

Fig. A.8

The Use PC Format? dialog box.

If you chose to install the Scheduler to perform operations at scheduled times, Install provides you with the opportunity to schedule CPBackup, DiskFix, Compress, and Central Point Anti-Virus (see fig. A.9). Fill in the times you want these utilities scheduled to execute, pressing Tab to move from option to option, and select **OK** to continue.

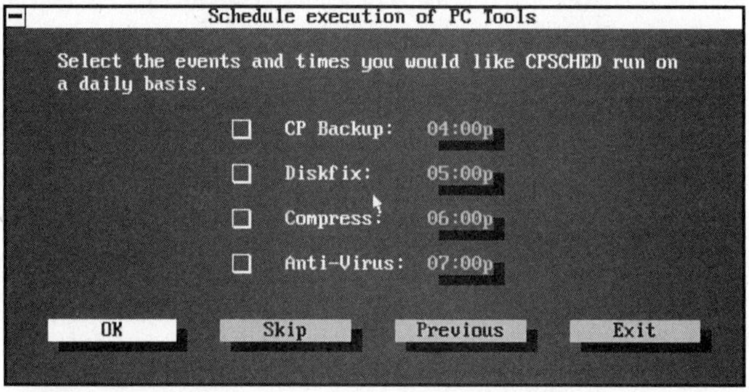

Fig. A.9

The Schedule Execution of PC Tools dialog box.

If you have set up PC Tools programs initially to run under Windows, Install displays an additional install dialog box, shown in figure A.10, asking whether you want to load the Windows Scheduler. Select **OK** if you plan to run PC Tools programs under Windows; choose **S**kip to move to the next install option.

Install asks whether you want to convert setup files from backup programs such as Norton Backup or FastBack Plus for use with CPBackup, presenting you with a dialog box containing your logical drives (see fig. A.11). Deselect those drives that have no setup files for these programs and select **OK** to continue; select **S**kip to bypass this option.

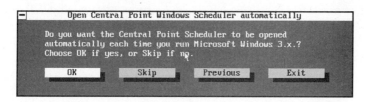

Fig. A.10

The Open
Central Point
Windows
Scheduler
Automatically
dialog box.

Fig. A.11

The Convert
Backup File
Formats to CP
Backup dialog
box.

Install gives you an option to convert any menu formats you may have created from Fifth Generation's DirectAccess Menu program, presenting you with a dialog box from which you choose drives like the Backup Formats option provided (see fig. A.12). If you use DirectAccess, select the drives for Install to search and select **O**K to search and convert your menu file formats; otherwise, select **S**kip to bypass this option and continue with the customizing portion of the installation.

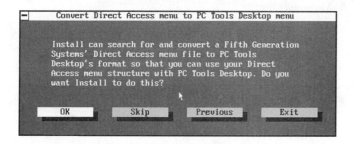

Fig. A.12

The Convert
Direct Access
Menu options
dialog box.

Configuring PC Tools Desktop and Desktop Accessories

PC Tools Desktop is the shell from which you can access and use all the PC Tools programs utilities. From PC Tools Desktop, you also can

access your favorite utilities and applications by pressing F10 for
a custom menu. PC Tools creates this menu for you later in the
installation.

Desktop accessories such as the Notepads, Databases, Appointment
Scheduler, Macro Editor, Clipboard, and Calculators, as well as Modem
Telecommunications, Electronic Mail, and fax utility programs, are all
available directly from the Desktop.

NOTE   In previous versions, Desktop Manager contained the accessories, and Shell contained the utilities. Now, all utilities and
programs are contained in one program called PC Tools
Desktop.

When the basics are completed, Install runs PC Config, the program
you use to configure (or reconfigure) your startup program options, as
shown in figure A.13, and the individual programs you want PC Tools to
load each time you run PC Tools Desktop.

Fig. A.13

The Configure
Startup Programs
dialog box.

To change your setup, the startup programs list, and other features of
the program, you can run PC Config from PC Tools Desktop's Configure
menu at any time.

Selecting Startup Options

When PC Config has begun, you're nearly finished installing and configuring PC Tools. The next step in the installation process involves telling
PC Tools about your display preferences (colors, screen lines); your

mouse and keyboard (compatibility, speed); Startup Programs you want to run each time you run PC Tools Desktop; and Passwords for specific portions of PC Tools. The PC Config window displays the command buttons shown in figure A.14.

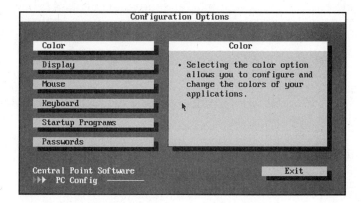

Fig. A.14

The PC Config Configurations options menu.

Setting Screen Colors

To select a different set of screen colors for use by PC Tools programs, choose the **C**olor command button in the PC Config window. PC Tools displays the Color Options screen as shown in figure A.15.

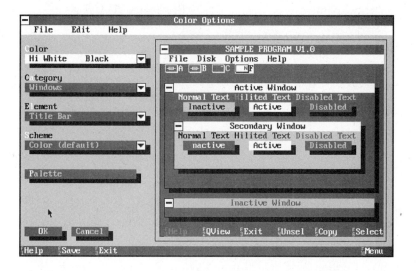

Fig. A.15

The Screen Color Options dialog box.

The Color Options screen displays seven command buttons on the left side of the screen and the Sample Program window on the right side of the screen. The following list describes the command buttons:

- *Color* displays the Color drop-down list box. Use this command button to set the background and foreground colors for the current screen element. You can display the Color drop-down list box by clicking the target screen element in the sample program window.

- *Category* displays the Category drop-down list box. Use this command to choose from the following groups of screen elements displayed in the sample window on the right side of the Color Options screen:

Windows	Help Window
Menu	Misc. Items
Backdrop	Graph Colors
Dialog & Wait Box	List Boxes
Error & Caution Box	File/Tree List Boxes

- *Element* displays the Element drop-down list box. Use this command to select a screen element from those available in the current category.

- *Scheme* displays the Scheme drop-down list box. Use this command to choose from among the following predefined color schemes, as well as any you have defined and saved:

Monochrome	Bordeaux VGA/EGA
LCD (default)	Arizona VGA/EGA
Black/White (default)	Windows VGA/EGA
Color (default)	Ocean VGA/EGA
PCTools V6 Colors	Rugby VGA/EGA
PCTools V7 Colors	Wing Tips VGA/EGA
Zenith Minisport	Pastel VGA/EGA
Zenith Supersport	The Blues VGA/EGA
Toshiba Gas Plasma	DESQView
LCD #1	Veddy Lite
LCD #2	4th of July
LCD #3	Classic Gray
LCD #4	Mediterranean

- *Palette* displays the Palette Change dialog box in place of the Sample Program window. Use this dialog box to change the screen colors used in all screen-color categories. Select a color to edit, and then choose **E**dit Palette to display the Palette Table dialog box. Choose the new color and select **OK** to return to the Palette Change dialog box. Select **OK** again to return to the Color Options screen.

■ *Windows Attributes* enables you to change the Background Matte, the Borders, and the Button Arrows much like those you can change through the control panel in Windows. This option also shows you a rough representation of what the Matte backgrounds will look like on your display.

If you make changes to a predefined color scheme, save the custom scheme for future use. To use the current scheme name, press F2 (Save). Alternatively, select **F**ile from the horizontal menu bar and choose **S**ave Scheme. When PC Config displays the Save Scheme dialog box, select the **OK** command button. To save the custom scheme with a new name, select **F**ile from the horizontal menu bar, and then Save Scheme **A**s. When PC Config displays the Save Scheme As dialog box, type the new scheme name in the Scheme Name text box and select **OK**.

When you finish making changes in the Color Options window, select **OK** to save the modifications and return to the PC Config window.

Configuring the Display

PC Config enables you to change several settings that determine whether PC Tools uses the special PC Tools graphics characters. You also can determine the number of lines of characters displayed on-screen. To set these options, select the **D**isplay command button in the PC Config window. PC Config displays the Display Options dialog box shown in figure A.16.

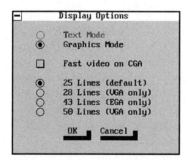

Fig. A.16

The Display Options dialog box.

Select the **T**ext Mode option button from the Display Options dialog box to prevent PC Tools from using its unique graphics-character font. This action may be necessary if the characters do not display properly. Choose **G**raphics Mode to turn on the special font (the default setting).

If the video display adapter in your computer is compatible with the IBM Color Graphics Adapter (CGA), check the **F**ast Video on CGA check box. Although your screen will paint faster, you may see some screen flicker or specks of white color on-screen.

Choose from among the listed display-mode option buttons. By default, the screen shows 25 lines of text per screen. On EGA and VGA screens, you can display more lines per screen.

Select the **OK** command button when you finish making changes to the display options.

Configuring the Mouse

PC Config enables you to customize the way the program responds to your mouse. From the PC Config window, select **M**ouse to display the Mouse Options dialog box, shown in figure A.17; then check any of the following options:

■ *Fast Mouse **R**eset* gives you the best mouse performance. You may need to turn off this feature if you use a PS/2 mouse port and Windows. This option is enabled by default.

■ *Left Handed Mouse* exchanges the mouse buttons to benefit left-handed users.

■ *Disable Mouse* turns off the mouse. Use this option only if your mouse driver is not compatible with PC Tools.

■ *Graphics **M**ouse* causes PC Tools to display the mouse pointer as an arrow rather than as a block. This option, checked by default, is available on EGA and VGA systems.

Select **OK** to save your changes and return to the PC Config window.

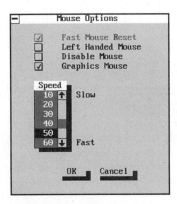

Fig. A.17

The Mouse Options dialog box.

Configuring the Keyboard

Select **K**eyboard from the PC Config window to display the Keyboard Options dialog box (see fig. A.18). Check the **E**nable Keyboard Speed check box to turn on the PC Tools facility for controlling keyboard rate and keyboard delay. Keyboard *rate* is the speed at which a keystroke is repeated if you hold down the key. Keyboard *delay* is the time you must hold down a key before it starts to repeat.

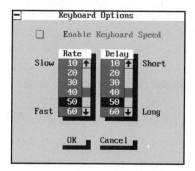

Fig. A.18

The Keyboard Options dialog box.

Select **OK** to save any changes and return to the PC Config window.

Selecting Startup Programs

Select **S**tartup Programs from the PC Config window to display a list of the PC Tools Desktop programs you can set up to run each time you load PC Tools Desktop (see fig. A.19).

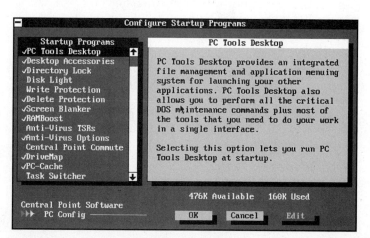

Fig. A.19

The Configure Startup Programs dialog box.

As you configure PC Tools Desktop's programs and utilities, PC Tools keeps you informed of your memory status and warns you when your memory falls below 512K of RAM.

If you plan to load the new RAMBoost utility or you are using a third-party memory manager, do not be overly concerned with the memory values as you begin this configuration process. You can always change the configuration later and allow PC Tools to optimize your system for you.

You can configure these applications at any time by running PC Config at the DOS command line (or from within PC Tools Desktop by selecting **C**onfigure Startup Pr**o**grams from the menu bar). Each of these program setup options is briefly discussed in the following paragraphs.

On-line, context-sensitive help is available throughout each installation selection if you need additional information about a program's functions and features. The help screens can trace you forward and backward, and each screen can be printed so that you can easily reference it during installation. Following is a list of the Startup programs:

- *Directory Lock* simply and effectively locks a specific directory (or directories) from modification or access by other individuals without the proper password.

- *Disk Light* provides you with visible hard disk activity lights in the upper right corner of your display. Disk Light's primary purpose is to provide an on-screen indicator of your hard disk activity for computers that may be in another room, where seeing any disk activity light on the front of the computer is difficult, or where no activity light can be seen at all (that is, the activity light is burned out or disconnected, for example).

- *Write Protection*, like Directory Light, uses the Data Monitor program to prevent important files from being changed or deleted. With protection enabled, you are prompted with a dialog box asking you for confirmation when a write or a delete action is about to take place.

- *Delete Protection* turns on the Delete Sentry and/or Delete Tracker program—depending on how you configure protection—to save deleted files in a hidden directory or to track deleted files for later restoration. Delete Sentry is the more powerful of the two utilities and gives you the greatest protection against accidentally deleting important or necessary files.

- *Screen Blanker* enables PC Tools to blank your screen after a period of inactivity. When you activate Screen Blanker, a floating message appears randomly while Screen Blanker is active. Pressing any key restores your screen. Screen Blanker is configurable inside PC Tools with 11 patterns from which you can choose.

■ *RAMBoost* is a new utility to the PC Tools suite of programs. Much like Quarterdeck's OPTIMIZE program, RAMBoost arranges and rearranges your program loading order at boot time to provide the maximum amount of free conventional memory possible.

During installation, RAMBoost automatically takes your system through a series of configuration steps to learn how your system is configured and how it can best load the programs you need in a minimum amount of memory. Each time you reconfigure your system, RAMBoost again organizes your system configuration files for optimum performance.

See the section "Setting Up RAMBoost" later in this chapter for more information on the RAMBoost Program.

■ *Anti-Virus TSRs and Options.* PC Tools comes with two levels of protection against viral infection: VSafe and VWatch.

VSafe is a memory-resident program that, when loaded from your AUTOEXEC.BAT file, scans your system for viral infections of all kinds and watches in the background for any sign of potential viral infection. VSafe also removes viral infections from your system.

VWatch also is a memory-resident program that watches in the background for potential viral infection. If an infection is found, VWatch stops all disk operation so that you can run the VSafe program to check your system and remove any infection.

■ *Commute* runs as a memory-resident utility and enables one computer to control another computer via telephone lines, LAN hardware, or null modem cables. Manual and automatic "remote control" processing capabilities are available.

■ *DriveMap* is a peripheral control utility that enables you to control printing devices and physical devices (hard drives, floppy drives, and so on) over a network or by using serial and parallel cables that connect two or more computers together.

See the section "Setting Up DriveMap" later in this chapter for additional information on using this utility.

■ *PC-Cache* is a disk and memory-caching utility that stores the most frequently accessed information in your computer in faster RAM to speed loading the information for your application. PC-Cache can be run in Windows, in DOS, or both, and can utilize conventional, extended, and expanded memory in your computer.

■ *Task Switcher* is comparable to other program switching utilities available, such as DesqView and Headroom. Task Switcher enables you to switch easily between one or more programs with hotkeys.

■ *Program Scheduler for DOS* and *Scheduler for Windows* perform in nearly the same way. You can configure each Scheduler to perform specific tasks at certain times of the day or night. Programs such as Compress, CPBackup, DiskFix, and Anti-Virus can be run at specified times of the day.

See Appendix B for additional information about setting up PC Tools programs in Windows.

■ *Mirror* backs up the File Allocation Tables (FAT) of your hard drives, as well as the Partition Tables (if you configure it to do so). With the files that Mirror creates on your system, you stand a much better chance of recovering from an accidental format or from a damaged disk.

■ *Fax Driver*. PC Tools Desktop supports several fax boards and provides its own software for use with DOS. With the Fax Driver loaded, you can send and receive faxes from a local computer or from a remote workstation.

■ *Setting Password Options*. PC Tools enables you to configure several of the Desktop programs with passwords to prevent unauthorized access. This feature is particularly helpful for network administrators to use. One password is allowed to be set for Anti-Virus, Compress, DiskEdit, DiskFix, PCFormat, Undelete, and Program Configuration.

Remember that you can change all the setup options for these features after you install PC Tools Desktop. Run PC Config from the DOS Prompt (or choose **C**onfigure from the PC Tools Desktop horizontal menu bar) and select Startup Programs to change your installed setup options.

Setting Up RAMBoost

RAMBoost's purpose is to help you gain as much free conventional memory as possible by arranging and rearranging the loading order of your device drivers, TSRs, and other programs into an order that makes the best use of your available resources.

If you selected RAMBoost as one of the programs to automatically run when you boot your system, the Install program automatically configures your program selections in your AUTOEXEC.BAT and CONFIG.SYS files to prepare your system for testing configurations to achieve the maximum free memory.

RAMBoost is designed to work in conjunction with and to complement the performance of your current memory management software (QEMM, 386Max, and DOS 5 programs, for example), not to replace them. Although RAMBoost is designed to work with DOS 5 and Windows' EMM386 drivers, it performs equally well with QEMM and 386Max.

RAMBoost analyzes your system and configuration files first, running in learn mode the first time to determine resources, loading order, and so on. RAMboost then runs again, in active mode on the second reboot, after it configures your system for optimum performance.

Each time your CONFIG.SYS or AUTOEXEC.BAT file is changed, RAMBoost sees the archive file attributes on these files and triggers a new learn mode, again optimizing the loading order of your programs, device drivers, and TSRs to ensure maximum performance for your system.

In order for RAMBoost to run, it requires the following minimum system configuration:

- An 80386 or 80486 CPU

- MS-DOS 3.3 or higher, or DR-DOS 6.0

- EMS 4.0 compatible hardware and/or software

Refer to the PC Tools Manual for additional information on running RAMSETUP and configuring RAMBoost; fine-tuning RAMBoost using the Options Editor, command line options, and troubleshooting techniques; and for additional information about changing your system configuration files manually.

Setting Up DriveMap

Sharing printers, hard disks, and other peripherals with other computers can be achieved by using PC Tools' DriveMap utility. Peripherals can be easily protected from access by other users through the global password protection feature. *DriveMap* is a memory-resident communication program enabling computers and printers to be shared among a group of users through simple serial or parallel cables or through network adapters and software. *Mapping* means assigning the drive letter or port number to another computer's drive or port, enabling your computer and others that are connected to share a device as if it were a single device.

The first time you run the DriveMap configuration program, you are asked for a user name (to tell other users which system they are attached to) and a password (to protect your sensitive files from access by others). Selecting Next takes you to the Control Panel where you can select Local Port links that you want to enable for parallel and serial ports, as well as network BIOS communications.

After you select the physical ports you want to link to, select **OK** to return to the Device Manager window where you can choose the local drives to which you want to enable links. The Device Manager window displays a list of all the local drives and ports it has found. In this window, you can enable or disable mapping to a drive or device, whether the device is on your own computer or another computer currently attached by a cable or a network adapter.

For additional information on Mapping, Unmapping, Protecting and Unprotecting, and troubleshooting DriveMap, refer to the PC Tools Documentation.

Using Install Command Line Options

Table A.1 lists command line options you can use to run Install. Command instructions for BINSTALL and CINSTALL are detailed in the PC Tools manual.

Table A.1 Install Command Line Options	
Option	**Action**
/?	Displays command line options on-screen.
/BPD:*n*	Generates a beep every *n* milliseconds. The default is 100 milliseconds.
/BPF:*n*	Generates a beep for a specific sound level, in Hertz (Hz).

Option	Action
/LIMIT:n	Limits the number of bytes to be written to a 360K disk, where n is the number of bytes.
/VIDEO	Shows command line help for video and mouse options.
/FL	(For network administrators) Creates master floppy directories while installation is in process to be used by others on the network for installation.
/UNINSTALL	Removes PC Tools programs you already have installed.
/DISKREQ	Shows you how much disk space is required for individual functions in the Select Tools to Install dialog box.

Summary

Installing PC Tools 8 is explained well in the manuals accompanying the software, and individual options discussed in this appendix are covered in more depth in other chapters of the book. Refer to the index for more detailed information about the options presented here and their uses.

Using PC Tools from within Microsoft Windows

One of the most significant features of PC Tools 8 is the capability to operate most PC Tools utilities from Microsoft Windows 3.x. This appendix gives you an overview of running PC Tools 8 from Windows.

PC Tools 8 includes two programs designed for use exclusively from Microsoft Windows: Central Point Scheduler and TSR Manager. Chapter 7, "Protecting Your Data with Central Point Backup," describes how to use Central Point Scheduler.

Although you can use nearly all other PC Tools programs—Anti-Virus, Desktop, Commute, and so on—from DOS, you also can access these programs from Windows. This chapter explains how you can use Windows as a platform for PC Tools programs.

Starting Windows 3.x

Several ways exist to start Microsoft Windows. Depending on your computer, you can start Windows at the DOS prompt, through a menu, or automatically through the AUTOEXEC.BAT file. The normal start-up command is to type **win** at the DOS prompt.

Windows starts in one of three modes—real, standard, or enhanced—depending on what CPU your computer has and what version of Windows you use, as explained in the following:

- *Real mode.* Windows starts in real mode if your computer has an Intel 8088 or 8086 CPU chip. If you have a 8088 or 8086 chip, you cannot run Windows 3.1. Real mode can run any Windows program written specifically for Windows 2.0 through Windows 3.0; real mode is not available in Windows 3.1. In Windows' real mode, you can run a Windows-specific program in its own sizable and movable window; however, DOS programs run only in full screen. You can force Windows 3.0 to start in real mode by typing the command **win /r** at the DOS prompt.

- *Standard mode.* Windows automatically starts in standard mode if your computer uses an 80286 CPU. In standard mode, non-Windows applications run only in full screen; however, you can switch between multiple applications programs. All other programs are suspended when you switch to a non-Windows program. If your computer has an Intel 80386 CPU, you may obtain improved performance by forcing Windows to start in standard mode by typing the command **win /s** at the DOS prompt. You may want to test your applications in standard versus enhanced mode to see if a significant difference exists between them.

- *Enhanced mode.* The default mode for an Intel 80386-based computer is enhanced mode. In enhanced mode, Windows can run Windows programs and non-Windows programs simultaneously. Non-Windows programs, like Windows programs, can be run in sizable windows, as well as in full screen. The default setting for DOS-based PC Tools applications is for the programs to run in full screen windows.

After you type the Windows start-up command and press Enter, Windows displays its logo and begins to load. If you chose to have the PC Tools installation program cause Windows to load the TSR Manager and the Central Point Scheduler automatically, icons for running applications appear in the lower left corner of the Windows desktop.

Depending on how you configured Windows, certain *groups*, or collections of applications, may be open. When you exit Windows and have the **S**ave Settings on Exit option selected on the **O**ptions menu (this setting is the default setting), Windows remembers which groups are open for the next session. The Main program group is displayed in the Program Manager window (see fig. B.1). If necessary, click the minimize button to minimize the Main program group and any other groups you have open. Windows displays all program-group icons (see fig. B.2).

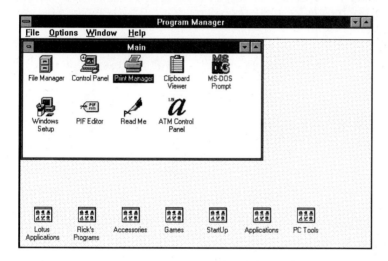

Fig. B.1

The Main
Program group.

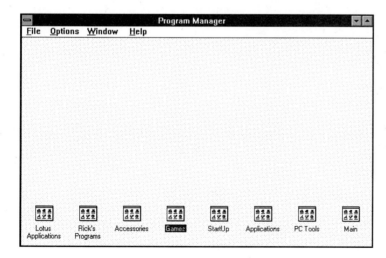

Fig. B.2

The Program
Manager
showing all
program groups.

Running PC Tools Programs in Windows

When you install PC Tools and its Windows utilities, the installation program automatically creates a Windows program group named PC Tools (refer to fig. B.2). To run a PC Tools program from within Windows, double-click the PC Tools icon. Windows opens the PC Tools program group and displays the program icons (see fig. B.3).

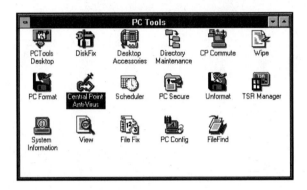

Fig. B.3

The PC Tools Program Group icons.

The PC Tools program group displays icons for these programs:

DiskFix

PC Tools Desktop

Desktop Accessories

Directory Maintenance

CP Commute

Wipe

File Fix

System Information

PC Config

FileFind

TSR Manager

PC Format

View

Unformat

PC Secure

Scheduler

Central Point Anti-Virus

Windows displays a name below each icon. To start a program, you can double-click the program's icon, or you can press the arrow keys to move the highlight to the name of the program you want to start and then press Enter.

If the program is designed to run in Windows, such as the programs Central Point Scheduler and the TSR Manager, the program opens in its own movable window. Figure B.4, for example, shows the Central Point Scheduler window. Programs designed to run from the DOS command line, however, run in full-screen mode and have the same appearance as if they were run directly from DOS.

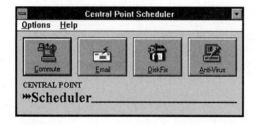

Fig. B.4

The Scheduler window.

By default, when you run a PC Tools program from within Microsoft Windows in full-screen mode, the mouse pointer appears as a block rather than an arrow. (***Note:*** The mouse pointer is not displayed at all in a PC Tools program displayed inside a Windows window. The pointer you see is the Windows pointer.) To see the arrow-shaped pointer, edit the PIF file for every utility and add the parameter /BT in the **O**ptional Parameters line in the PIF file. Figure B.5 shows the DISKFIX.PIF file with the /BT Optional Parameter.

You can run a PC Tools utility in a window rather than in a full screen. You can use PC Config (see Appendix A, "Installing and Configuring PC Tools," for a discussion of PC Config) to change the Display Options setting to text mode. You also can edit the PIF file for the PC Tools utility to include /NF on the **O**ptional Parameters line.

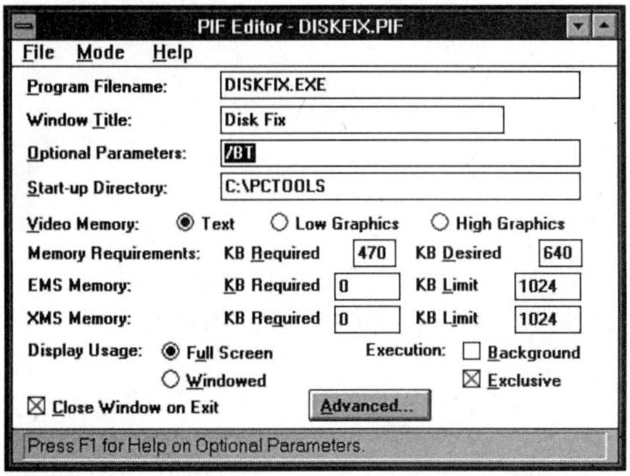

Fig. B.5

The DISKFIX.PIF
in the PIF Editor
(Windows in
Enhanced mode).

If you want Windows 3.1 to display a PC Tools DOS program in a window, you also can use one of these procedures:

■ Edit the Windows PIF Editor to modify the PIF (Program Information File) for the PC Tools utility to specify **W**indowed as the Display Usage option. In figure B.5, the Display Usage option shows that the DiskFix utility will be full screen rather than windowed. Start the program from the PC Tools program group in the Program Manager.

■ Display the program full screen and press Alt+Enter to switch to windowed mode.

The PIF files are located in the WINDOWS directory. Following are the names of the PIF files for each of the PC Tools programs:

Program	PIF File
DiskFix	DISKFIX.PIF
PCTools Desktop	PCSHELL.PIF
Desktop Accessories	DESKTOP.PIF
Directory Maintenance	DM.PIF
CP Commute	COMMUTE.PIF
Wipe	WIPE.PIF
File Fix	FILEFIX.PIF
System Information	SI.PIF
PC Config	PCCONFIG.PIF
FileFind	FF.PIF

Program	PIF File
PC Format	PCFORMAT.PIF
View	VIEW.PIF
Unformat	UNFORMAT.PIF
PC Secure	PCSECURE.PIF
Central Point Anti-Virus	CPAV.PIF

Because the Scheduler and TSR Manager are not DOS-based programs, no PIF files exist for these applications.

Working with PC Tools Applications under Windows

The sections that follow describe special considerations to keep in mind whenever you run other PC Tools programs from Microsoft Windows. After you open the application from the PC Tools group, the procedure you use to open the programs is generally the same as if you started the program without using Windows. You cannot use Microsoft Windows to start some programs (such as Compress), however.

Commute

The remote-control program Commute, discussed fully in Chapter 26, "Controlling a PC Remotely with CP Commute," enables you to use your PC to take control of another PC via telephone line or local area network (LAN), even if the remote computer is running Microsoft Windows 3.x. The remote computer, however, must have special mouse and keyboard drivers installed for the Commute session to give you control over a Windows session.

When you install PC Tools Commute on a computer that has Windows 3.x, Install copies the mouse, keyboard, and display drivers COMMMOU.DRV, COMMKBD.DRV, and COMMDIS.DRV to the WINDOWS directory and replaces the appropriate lines in the SYSTEM.INI file with the new drivers. If Commute does not work properly, you may need to make further adjustments for enhanced mode, for memory manager programs, or for Novell Networks. Some of these adjustments are described in the following.

- *386 Enhanced mode.* To enable someone working on a computer that is connected to your computer with Commute to run Windows in 386 Enhanced mode, copy the driver COMMVXD.386 from the \PCTOOLS\SYSTEM directory (or the directory in which you installed PC Tools) to the \WINDOWS\SYSTEM directory. Edit the SYSTEM.INI file to add the line **device=commvxd.386** to the [386Enh] section of SYSTEM.INI.

- *Memory Manager Programs.* If you experience lockups or system errors when running Windows remotely and have a memory manager program, you may need to exclude a segment of high memory when using Commute. Change the CONFIG.SYS file to exclude the memory segment B000.BFFF. See your memory manager's documentation for specific instructions.

- *Novell Network.* If you have problems with Commute while running Windows on a Novell Network, try loading Commute memory-resident before starting Windows.

The Windows TSR Manager must be loaded for Commute to answer incoming calls while you are working in a Windows session.

Compress

Compress does not run from within Windows. If you attempt to run Compress, Compress displays the Compress Execution Error message box, stating Compress cannot be run from within a multitasking environment. Select **OK** to return to Windows. Exit from Windows, and then run Compress. See Chapter 8, "Speeding Up Your Hard Disk with Compress," for information about how to use the Compress utility.

Data Monitor

The Data Monitor's Write Protection, Directory Lock, Delete Tracker, and Delete Sentry features remain effective while you run Microsoft Windows 3.x. You must be running the TSR Manager, however, for Data Monitor to be capable of displaying the warning messages that appear if you attempt to delete or modify a file in a protected directory. If the TSR Manager is not running, you hear an alarm but see no warning.

NOTE By default, the PC Tools 8 installation program adds the TSR Manager to the Windows configuration file WIN.INI so that the TSR Manager starts automatically every time you begin a Windows session. The TSR Manager enables Data Monitor and other PC Tools memory-resident utilities to display messages, when necessary, in the Microsoft Windows environment.

If the TSR Manager is running and you attempt to access a locked directory, Data Monitor displays a dialog box that prompts you to enter a password. If the TSR Manager is not running, you hear an alarm but see no dialog box, and you cannot enter a password, effectively locking you out of the directory.

See Appendix A, "Installing and Configuring PC Tools," for a brief discussion of the Data Monitor.

DiskFix

You can run DiskFix (discussed fully in Chapter 11, "Recovering Damaged or Formatted Disks") from Windows for the purpose of analyzing the condition of a drive and generating a report about a drive. If you attempt to use DiskFix to make a repair to a disk while you still are running Windows, however, DiskFix displays the message This operation cannot be done while running Windows. To make a repair, you first must exit Windows.

PC-Cache

PC-Cache, the PC Tools disk-caching program, can speed disk access by providing in memory a buffer for the most frequently accessed data on the disk. The installation of PC-Cache is covered in Appendix A.

Another disk-caching program, SMARTDRV.SYS, is distributed with Windows 3.x. Do not use SMARTDRV.SYS and PC-Cache together. Given the choice between the two programs, use PC-Cache because it can adjust its use of your computer's memory automatically for DOS programs and Windows 3.x.

If you plan to run Windows 3.x on your computer, start PC-Cache with the /WIN parameter. When you start Windows, PC-Cache automatically shrinks to provide more memory for Windows. PC-Cache also turns off the write-delay feature. As soon as you exit from Windows, PC-Cache returns the cache to its original size and turns on the write-delay feature.

Unless you used the /WIN parameter in the start-up command, PC-Cache does not adjust its size but does turn off write-delay when you start Windows. When you exit from Windows, turn on write delay again by typing **pc-cache/write:on**.

If you configured PC-Cache to create a cache larger than 300K in expanded (LIM EMS) memory, the cache is disabled automatically when you start Windows. To start PC-Cache again when you exit Windows, type **pc-cache /on**.

PC Tools Desktop

When you run PC Tools Desktop from within Windows, the program runs as a stand-alone program, not as a TSR. Windows' multitasking capabilities, however, enable you to use the program much as you would if it were resident in memory.

After you start the program in a window, press Ctrl+Esc to display the Windows Task List. Select another program from the list. Windows switches to the other program. You can also hold down the Alt key and press Tab until the Desktop program name appears. When you want to return to the PC Tools program, press Alt+Tab or Ctrl+Esc and select the program from the Task List.

Because Desktop does not run as a TSR from within Windows, Desktop cannot monitor any electronic-mail reading and sending schedule you may have established (see Chapter 24, "Using Electronic Mail"). The Scheduler, however, takes over this task. The following section, "Scheduler," provides more information about this feature.

For more information on PC Tools Desktop, see Part I, "Using the Desktop."

Scheduler

By default, the PC Tools 8 installation program adds the Scheduler to the Windows configuration file WIN.INI so that the Scheduler starts automatically every time you begin a Windows session. The Scheduler enables Central Point Backup, Commute, Desktop Electronic Mail and appointment alarms, and DiskFix to perform the scheduled events at the appointed times. If the Scheduler is not running in Windows, none of your scheduled events are carried out.

When you run the Scheduler from real or standard mode, the scheduled event interrupts the current application, runs the task, and returns to the interrupted application. When you run the Scheduler from enhanced mode, an icon appears on the desktop screen when the event is running. In either case, a dialog box appears if necessary to prompt you for information.

You can schedule events from within the respective programs—CP Backup, Commute, Desktop, or DiskFix—but you also can adjust the schedules from the Scheduler. Select the Scheduler icon from the Windows desktop to display the Scheduler window (see fig. B.6).

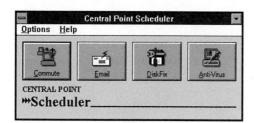

The Central Point Scheduler window and its command buttons.

The Schedule window displays the following command buttons:

- *Commute* displays the Commute Schedule dialog box (refer to Chapter 26, "Controlling a PC Remotely with CP Commute").

- *Email* displays the Create E-Mail Schedule dialog box (refer to Chapter 24, "Using Electronic Mail").

- *DiskFix* displays the Create DiskFix Schedule dialog box (refer to Chapter 11, "Recovering Damaged or Formatted Disks").

- *Anti-Virus* displays the Create Anti-Virus Schedule dialog box (refer to Chapter 14, "Protecting Your System with CP Anti-Virus").

After you make any adjustments you want to a schedule, select the **OK** command button to return to the Scheduler window. Then click the minimize button in the upper right corner of the Scheduler window to minimize the Scheduler.

TSR Manager

By default, the PC Tools 8 installation program adds the TSR Manager to the Windows configuration file WIN.INI so that the TSR Manager starts automatically every time you begin a Windows session if you have a PC Tools TSR running. The TSR Manager enables Data Monitor,

VSafe, and other PC Tools memory-resident utilities to display messages, when necessary, in the Microsoft Windows environment.

The TSR Manager enables you to display the status of VDefend and to configure Data Monitor from within Microsoft Windows. Select the TSR Manager icon from the Windows desktop to display the TSR Manager window (see fig. B.7).

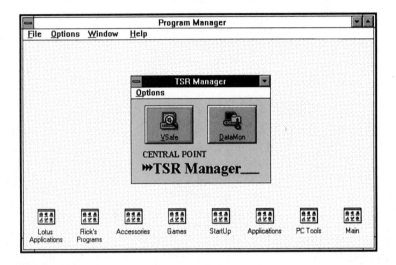

Fig. B.7

TSR Manager
with VSafe and
DataMon
buttons.

If TSRs are loaded into memory, the TSR Manager window displays command buttons of any TSRs loaded:

- **VWatch** displays a dialog box which states that VWatch is running. If VWatch detects a computer virus, VWatch alerts you with a dialog box. Select **OK** to return to the TSR Manager. See Appendix A, "Installing and Configuring PC Tools," for instructions for adding VWatch to AUTOEXEC.BAT.

- **VSafe** displays a dialog box that enables you to change settings for virus warning and protection options. See Appendix A for instructions for adding VSafe to AUTOEXEC.BAT. You will see only one of the two VWatch or VSafe command buttons.

- **DataMon** displays the Central Point Data Monitor dialog box. If you configured Data Monitor so that the Directory Lock or the Write Protect feature is enabled, the Data Monitor dialog box displays a check box through which you can toggle the respective feature. You also can select **R**un Data Monitor to run Data Monitor itself to configure all the program's options. See Appendix A for more information about configuring Data Monitor. Select the **OK** command button to return to the TSR Manager window.

■ *Commute* displays the Central Point Commute dialog box. Select the **R**un Commute button to run the Commute program in full-screen mode. When a call comes in and you have Commute loaded, PC Tools will interrupt your current Windows application. If you want to cancel the call, press Esc. See Chapter 26, "Controlling a PC Remotely with CP Commute."

Click the minimize button in the upper right corner of the TSR Manager window to minimize the window.

Summary

This appendix gives you an overview of running PC Tools 8 from Windows and explains how to start Windows on different systems and how to start PC Tools utilities from Windows. The appendix also discusses special considerations you must follow when running the various PC Tools utilities through Windows.

Symbols

– (minus sign) directory
   icons, 229
* (asterisk) key
   Expand Branch (Tree
     window), 232
   wild-card character, 67,
     136, 370
+ (plus sign), directory
   icons, 230
.. (parent directory), 561
→ key, cursor-movement
   CP Backup, 277
   Desktop applications, 41
   File Editor screen, 155
   Sector Edit screen, 160
↓ key, cursor-movement
   Compress File Allocation
     Analysis, 320
   CP Backup, 277
   Desktop applications, 41
   File Editor screen, 155
   Sector Edit screen, 160
← key, cursor-movement
   CP Backup, 277
   Desktop applications, 41
   File Editor screen, 155
   Sector Edit screen, 160
↑ key, cursor-movement
   Compress File Allocation
     Analysis, 320

   CP Backup, 277
   Desktop applications, 41
   File Editor screen, 155
   Sector Edit screen, 160
/? (display command-line
   options) Install program
   option, 930
? (question mark) wild-card
   character, 67, 136
… (ellipsis), 42
1st Copy of FAT (DiskEdit's
   Select menu) command,
   444-445
2nd Copy of FAT (DiskEdit's
   Select menu) command,
   444-445
386 Enhanced mode, 940

A

aborting fax transmissions, 878
About (Help menu)
   command, 49
accessing pull-down menus, 27
Accessories
   databases
     files, 626
     window, 627
   keyboard macros, 724-726
   Notepads files, 626
   PC Tools Desktop, 919-928

Save File to Disk dialog
box, 595
scripts, 727
Actions menu (FAX Log
window) commands
Add a New Entry, 869
Delete the Selected Entry, 878
activating
macro files, 732-734, 741
PC Tools Desktop, 910
active windows, 534-535
Activity Log (CP Anti-Virus' Scan
menu) command, 507-508
Activity Log dialog box, 507-508
Add a New Entry (Actions
menu) command, 869
Add Directory (Directory
Maintenance submenu)
command, 235-236
Add to Exception List dialog
box, 500
adding
fax cover pages, 867
keystroke codes, 729
addresses
clusters, deleted files, 383
memory, listing, 352
adjusting playback delay in
macros, 734
Advanced Options Commute
Session Manager window
command button, 899
Advanced Program Item
Information dialog box, 113-117
Advice (DiskFix Main menu)
command, 424
alarms, smart, 744-747
alert messages, creating for
viruses, 510
Algebraic Calculator, 750-760
automatic constant, 755
calculations, 754-756
keyboard keys, 753
tapes
copying, 758-759
editing, 757-758

erasing, 759-760
printing, 758-759
tape-scrolling keys, 758
algebraic expressions, 754
All Files Compare dialog
box, 284
allocation codes, mapping
disk, 361
file, 361
Alt key (Menu)
Compress, 315
CP Backup, 273
Desktop applications, 29-31
Notepads DA, 567
alternate keyboards, 813-814
American Standard Code for
Information Interchange, see
ASCII
ANSI terminals, 802
answer computer, 817
answering calls, 891-892
Anti-Virus
Scheduler program command
button, 943
TSRs and Options Startup
program, 927
Append (Desk Accessories' File
menu) command, 669-671
appending records, 670-671
Application Colors (Desktop
Accessories' System Control
menu) command, 536
Application Search (Menu
window File menu) command,
96
application windows, 534
applications
give-control PC
executing, 895-898
starting, 896-897
Outlines scripts, 832
windows, 534
Appointment Scheduler, 673-674
appointment settings, 682
date and time formats, 684
increments, 684

Start Time section, 683
Stop Time section, 683
Work Days, 683
appointments, 686-688
  alarms, 691
  annotating, 692-693
  deleting, 697-699
  descriptions, 688
  duration, 689
  editing, 699-702
  finding, 703-705
  group, 696-697
  recurring, 689-690
  saving, 693-694
  starting time, 689
  types, 688-691
  upcoming, 705
cursor-movement keys, 680
entries
  creating, 708-710
  editing, 710-711
exiting, 718
files
  loading, 675-679
  saving, 717
free time, 705-706
groups, 694
  local, 694-695
  network, 695-696
holidays, assigning, 685-686
keystroke commands, 702-703
macros, 746-747
notes
  detaching, 701-703
  editing, 701-703
  existing appointments,
    700-701
printing schedules, 711-716
time usage, 706-707
windows
  attributes, 676-678
  Daily Scheduler region, 677
  exiting, 678
  layout, 677
  Monthly Calendars
    region, 676

mouse movement, 681
navigating, 679-681
opening, 674
To-Do List region, 677, 707
see also Desktop Accessories
Appointment Scheduler
  (Desktop Accessories' main
  menu) command, 525, 529
Appointment Settings
  Appointment (Scheduler's
  Controls menu) command, 682
Appointment Settings dialog
  box, 682
archives, 903
  attribute bit, 161
  bits, 298
  files, 143-145
arrows, Zoom, 39, 534, 540
ASCII (American Standard Code
  Information Interchange)
  area, 159
  files
    receiving, 823-824
    sending, 822-825
  file-transfer protocol, 820-824
  tables, 552-554
  text
    editor, scripts, 832-833
    searching disks, 224-225
ASCII (Modem
  Telecommunications' Receive
  menu) command, 823-824
ASCII Table (Desktop
  Accessories' Utilities
  submenu) command, 553
associating files, specifying for
  program items, 114
asterisk (*) key
  Expand Branch (Tree
    window), 232
  wild-card character, 67, 136,
    370
asynchronous transmission, 802
Attach Note (Appointment
  Scheduler's Appointment
  menu) command, 692, 701, 710

Attribute (Change submenu)
command, 162
Attribute Exclusions (CP
Backup's Selection options
submenu) command, 304-305
attributes
directories, 241-242, 252
files, 161-164
excluding from backup,
304-305
names, 737
auto indent, 572-573
Auto Indent (Notepads' Controls
menu) command, 572
Auto View mode, 440
autoanswer mode, 816
Autodial, 841
configuring, 841-842
phone numbers
dialing from within
Desktop databases, 842
dialing from within DOS
programs, 843
Autodial (Databases' Control
menu) command, 842
AUTOEXEC.BAT file, displaying,
357
automatic
constant, 755
recovery, files, 396-397
speed search, 68
Automatic Search dialog box,
261
Autosave command
Appointment Scheduler's File
menu, 717
Notepads' File menu, 596
AutoUpdate feature, 878

B

Background Mat (Windows
menu) command, 37
Backspace key cursor-
movement
File Editor screen, 155
Sector Edit screen, 160

Backup Complete dialog box,
271-272
Backup Confidence Test dialog
box, 264, 290
Backup Directory dialog box,
275
Backup From (CP Backup's
Action menu) command, 275
Backup Method (CP Backup's
Options menu) command,
297-298
Backup Method dialog box,
297-298
Backup Progress window,
270-271
Backup Speed (CP Backup's
Configure menu), 289-290
Backup Speed dialog box,
289-290
backups
changing
devices, 288
methods, 297-298
speed, 289-290
user levels, 290
comparing/restoring data,
280-286
overwrite warnings, 302
compressing files, 299
correcting errors, 301
CP Backup window elements,
272-274
detecting viruses, 301
drive and media, 274
Emergency Disks, 409-412
excluding files by attribute,
304-305
FATs and root directories,
405-407
files
comparing to current
versions, 146-147
displaying in directory
trees, 305-306
selecting by date, 305
formatting media, 300-301
from setting, 260, 274-275

full, 269-272
history files, 301-302
Notepads DA files, 595-596
partition tables, boot sectors, and CMOS data, 407-408
reports, 298-299
scheduling, 125-131, 291-294
source drives, selecting, 274-275
specific directories, 276-278, 302-303
specific files, 278, 303-304
starting, 278-280
tape drives, 308
timing, 302
verifying data, 299-300
backward compatiblity of CRC-16 error-checking scheme, 825
bad sectors, 203
marking, 222-223
banners, 32, 240
batch files
checking for potential disk problems, 419-422
transfers, 820
baud rate, 800, 850
BBSs (Bulletin Board Systems)
control codes, 836
end-of-line processing, 804
ID and password, 799
<begdef> command, 723
Begin Compress (Compress menu) Compress command, 330-331
Bell (Commute Chat window) command, 901
benchmarks, 354-357
binary
number base, 772
protocols, 820-821
viewer, 194
Binary Transfer (Modem Telecommunications' Setup menu) command, 820-821
Binary Transfer Options dialog box, 820-821, 829

BIOS data, 352
bits
archive, 298
data, 801
start, 802
stop, 802
blanks, macros
fixed-length, 743
variable-length, 743
blocks of text
copying between DOS and Accessories programs, 601-603
marking, 578-579
pasting between DOS and Accessories programs, 603-606
Boot Record (DiskEdit's Select menu) command, 447
Boot Record Editor, 447-448
boot records
rebuilding, 412-419
viewing and editing, 447-448
boot sectors
checking for viruses at startup, 519-522
rebuilding with Emergency Disks, 409
saving backups, 407-408
bootable disks, 206, 211
booting from floppy disks, 409-411
BOOTSAFE command, 519-522
borders, window elements, 534
boxes
check, 46
Close, 534
close, 33, 543
list, 46
message, 547
program close, 26
Resize, 38-39, 534, 539-540
resize, 33
scroll, 34
text, 47
/BPD:n (generate beep) Install program option, 930

/BPF:n (generate beep/sound level) Install program option, 930

Branch Size (DM Directory Maintenance's Directory menu) command, 244-245

branches
expanding/collapsing, 228-232
script commands, 837-838

Browse mode, 632
cursor-movement keys, 635
databases, printing, 664-665
Edit mode, toggling, 633

buffers, 578

Build Emergency Disk
dialog box, 916
Disk menu command, 217-218
program, 914

Build Emergency Disk Options
dialog box, 217-218

Bulletin Board Systems, *see* BBSs

buttons
command, 47-48
confirmation, 43
grayed out, 267
option, 45

C

cables, null-modem, 818, 884

caching disks, 941-942

calculations
executing, 766-768
Algebraic Calculator, 754-756
financial, 769-771
memory registers, 756-757

Calculators
Algebraic, 750-760
Desktop Accessories menu command, 526, 530, 750
displaying, 752
Financial, 760-771
keypad, 753
hiding, 754
wide display, 754

menu commands
Financial Calculator, 760
Programmers Calculator (Calculators menu) command, 772
Scientific Calculator, 779
primary keyboard keys, 762-763, 774-775
Programmers, 771-779
keypad, 774-777
registers, 777-779
Scientific, 779-785
windows, 750
see also Desktop Accessories

calls
answering, 891-892
give-control PCs, 894-895
private lists, 885-888
take-control PCs, 892-894

carriage returns, 803-804

Carrier Detect (CD) setting, 812

carrier signals, 875

carry condition, 773

CAS fax boards, 864
background operation, 874
PC Tools, configuring, 865-867

cascading
menus, 93
windows, 85

case-sensitive, user ID and password, 800

Caution dialog box, 248

CD (CHDIR) command, 243

Central Point Anti-Virus program
activity log, 507-508
checksums
creating, 503-504
exceptions, 504-505
choosing objects to scan, 494-496
CPAV.PIF, 939
customizing, 501-503
exiting, 511-512
Express menu, 486-488
exiting, 491

full menus, 492-494
immunizing files, 498-500
infection reports, 507-508
passwords, 510-511
program, 914
scheduling to run
  automatically, 505-507
starting from DOS command
  line, 512-513
switching to full menus, 491
virus list, 508
  updating signatures, 509
viruses
  cleaning, 496-497
  creating alert messages
    for, 510
  detecting and cleaning, 490
  network notification
    messages, 509-510
  searching for, 488-489, 496
  searching for on different
    drives, 490-491
window elements, 492-494
Central Point Backup (CP
Backup) program, 914
  comparing/restoring data,
    280-286
  configuring
    initial startup, 261-266
    reconfiguring, 287-291,
      294-307
  full backups, 269-272
  scheduling backups, 291-294
  selective backups
    CP Backup window
      elements, 272-274
    source drives, selecting,
      274-275
    specific directories,
      276-278
    specific files, 278
    starting, 278-280
  starting, 260
    DOS command line,
      308-310
  tape drives, 308
  window elements, 272-274

Central Point Commute
(CP Commute) program
  calls
    answering, 891-892
    give-control PCs, 894-895
    private lists, 885-888
  Chat window, 900-904
  COM Port, 884-885
  COMMUTE.PIF, 938
  entries
    deleting, 888
    editing, 888
  give-control lists, 889-890
  Manager window, 898-905
  modems, 884
  PCs, connecting, 894
  program, 914
  sessions, 905
  starting, 882
  user names, 883
Central Point Software Copy II
PC, 212
  script files, 839-840
central processing unit, *see* CPU
CGA (Color Graphics Adapter),
  924
Change (File menu) command,
  69
Change Active Window dialog
  box, 546
Change Alert Message
  (CP Anti-Virus' Configure
  menu) command, 510
Change Colors dialog box,
  536-537
Change Directory dialog box,
  185
Change Drive (Disk menu)
  command, 227
Change File (File menu)
  command, 69, 475
Change Password (CP Anti-
  Virus' Configure menu)
  command, 511
Change Password dialog box,
  78-79, 511

characters
  control, 573
  deleting, 901
  fields, 629
    selection criteria, 648-650
  inserting and deleting, 576
  length, *see* data bits
  strings, 649
    searching disks, 223-225
Chat window
  Central Point Commute,
    900-902
  files, transferring, 902-904
Chat with Other PC Commute
  Session Manager window
  command button, 899
check boxes, 46
checksums
  creating, 503-504
  deleting, 504
  error-checking scheme, 824
  exceptions for, 504-505
Chklog (Fax
  Telecommunications)
  command, 876
Choose Compression Technique
  dialog box, 322-323
Choose Directories (CP
  Backup's Action menu)
  command, 277, 281-283
Choose Directory dialog box,
  281-283
Choose Drive (Compress'
  Compress menu) command,
  315
Choose Drive & Media (CP
  Backup's Configure menu)
  command, 288
Choose Drive & Media dialog
  box, 263-264, 288
Choose Ordering Method dialog
  box, 324-325
Choose Sort Method dialog box,
  328-329
Choose Tape Type dialog
  box, 261

CIS.SCR script file, 839
Clean (CP Anti-Virus' Scan
  menu) command, 497
cleaning viruses, 490, 496-497
clicking mouse, 27
Clipboard (Desktop
  Accessories' main menu)
  command, 530
Clipboard DA, 526, 578, 600
  copying between DOS and
    Accessories programs,
    601-603
  editing text, 609-611
  pasting
    between DOS and
      Accessories programs,
      603-606
    slowing playback, 612-613
  printing, 611-612
  using, 613-614
  window, 537, 606-609
  see also Desktop Accessories
Close (System Control menu)
  command, 52
Close box, 33, 534, 543
  program, 26
  windows, 40
Close Central Point Anti-Virus
  dialog box, 491, 511
Close dialog box, 506-507
Close PC Secure dialog box, 473
Close PC Tools Desktop dialog
  box, 52, 57
closing
  active tasks, 125
  Desktop, 52-53, 543
Cluster (DiskEdit's Select menu)
  command, 453
clusters, 158, 245
  analyzing map blocks, 321
  chains, 445
  deleted files
    addresses, 383
    scanning, 391-392
  lost, checking, 312-313
  mapping allocation,
    Compress, 316

<cmd> code, 742
CMOS (Complementary Metal-
  Oxide Semiconductor), 341
    data, saving backups, 407-408
    line (SI dialog box), 341-342
codes
    allocation
        disk mapping, 361
        file mapping, 361
    <cmd>, 742
    control, used by on-line
      services and BBSs, 836
    <desk>, 729
    escape, 737
    keystrokes, 729
Collapse (Tree menu)
  command, 230
Collapse Current (Outlines'
  Headlines menu) command,
  621
collapsing
    directory-tree branches,
      228-232
    outline headlines, 620-622
Color Graphics Adapter, *see*
  CGA
Color Options screen command
  buttons
    Color, 922
    Element, 922
    Palette, 922
    Scheme, 922
    Windows Attributes, 923
colors
    Desktop Accessories
      windows, 535-537
    foreground, 537
    screen, 921-923
Colors (Display Options
  submenu) command, 62-63
COM Ports, 807-808
    dialog box, 884
    selecting, 884-885
command buttons, 47-48
    Color Options screen
        Color, 922

Element, 922
Palette, 922
Scheme, 922
Windows Attributes, 923
Commute Session Manager
window
    Advanced Options, 899
    Chat with Other PC, 899
    End the Session, 898
    Exit, 899
    Get Files from Other PC,
      899
    Help, 899
    Look at Your PC, 898
    Send Files to Other PC, 899
Scheduler program
    Anti-Virus, 943
    Commute, 943
    DiskFix, 943
    Email, 943
TSR Manager, 944
    Commute, 945
    DataMon, 944
    VSafe, 944
    VWatch, 944
commands
    Add Directory (Directory
      Maintenance submenu),
      235-236
    adding to menus, 73-74
    Appointment Scheduler
        Appointment Settings
          (Controls menu), 682
        Attach Note (Appointment
          menu), 692, 701
        Attach Note (To-Do menu),
          710
        Autosave (File menu), 717
        Delete (Appointment
          menu), 688, 697
        Delete (To-Do menu), 711
        Delete Old Entries
          (Controls menu), 698
        Edit (Appointment menu),
          700
        Find Appointment
          (Appointment menu), 703

Free Time (Appointment menu), 706

Groups (File menu), 694-696

Make (Appointment menu), 687

Make (To-Do menu), 708

National Holiday (Controls menu), 685

Next (Appointment menu), 705

Print (File menu), 712

Save (File menu), 717

Schedule Layouts (Controls menu), 677

User Holiday Settings (Controls menu), 686

Attribute (Change submenu), 162

Background Mat (Windows menu), 37

<begdef>, 723

Build Emergency Disk (Disk menu), 217-218

Calculators menu
Financial Calculator, 760
Programmers Calculator (Calculators menu), 772
Scientific Calculator, 779

Change (File menu), 69

Change Drive (Disk menu), 227

Clipboard DA, 607
Copy to Clipboard (Copy/Paste menu), 602
Paste from Clipboard (Copy/Paste menu), 604
Print (File menu), 611
Set Playback Delay (Copy/Paste menu), 612

Close (System Control menu), 52

Collapse (Tree menu), 230

Colors (Display Options submenu), 62-63

Commands (Help menu), 49

Commute Chat window
Bell, 901
Disconnect, 905

Compare (File menu), 146-147

Compare Disk (Disk menu), 219-221

Compare Windows (Windows menu), 221

Compress
Begin Compress (Compress menu), 330-331
Choose Drive (Compress menu), 315
Compression Technique (Options menu), 322-323
Directory Order (Options menu), 326
Disk Statistics (Analysis menu), 317-319
File Fragmentation Analysis (Analysis menu), 319-320
File Sort Options (Options menu), 328-329
Files to Place First (Options menu), 326-327
Ordering Methods (Options menu), 324-325
Print Report (Options menu), 330
Show Files in Each Map Block (Analysis menu), 321
Unmovable Files (Options menu), 327-328

Confirmation (Configure menu), 60

Copy (File menu), 140

Copy Disk (Disk menu), 212-214

Copy Menu Item (File menu), 118

CP Anti-Virus
Activity Log (Scan menu), 507-508

Change Alert Message (Configure menu), 510

Change Password (Configure menu), 511

Clean (Scan menu), 497

Delete Checklist Files (Scan menu), 504

Detect & Clean (Express menu), 490

Detect (Express menu), 488

Detect (Scan menu), 496

Exit (Express menu), 491

Exit (Scan menu), 511

Full Menus (Express menu), 491

Immunization (Scan menu), 498

Immunization Exceptions (Configure menu), 500

Remove Immunization (Scan menu), 499

Select New Drive (Express menu), 490

Send Network Messages To (Configure menu), 509

Set Options (Options menu), 501

Verification Exceptions (Configure menu), 504-505

Virus List (Scan menu), 508

CP Backup, 260

Attribute Exclusions (Selection options submenu), 304-305

Backup From (Action menu) command, 275

Backup Method (Options menu), 297-298

Backup Speed (Configure menu), 289-290

Choose Directories (Action menu), 277, 281-283

Choose Drive & Media (Configure menu), 288

Compress (Options menu), 299

Date Range Selection (Selection options submenu), 305

Define Equipment (Configure menu), 288

Error Correction (Options menu), 301

Format Always (Options menu), 301

Include/Exclude Files (Selection options submenu), 303-304

Load Setup (File menu), 307

Long Format (Display options submenu), 306

Manual Subdirectory Inclusion (Selection options), 302-303

Media Format (Options menu), 300

Options menu, 294-296

Overwrite Warning (Options menu), 302

Reporting (Options menu), 298

Save as Default (File menu), 291, 306

Save History (Options menu), 301-302

Save Setup As (File menu), 307

Schedule Backups (Action menu), 291-292

Sort Options (Display options submenu), 306

Start Backup (Action menu), 278

Start Compare (Action menu), 283

Start Restore (Action menu), 285

Tape Tools menu, 308

Time Display (Options menu), 302

User Level (Configure
menu), 290
Verify (Options menu),
299-300
Virus Detection (Options
menu), 301
Cut Menu Item (File menu),
118
Data Protection (Configure
menu), 57
Databases window
Autodial (Controls menu),
842
Configure Autodial
(Controls menu), 841-842
Deactivate All Macros
(Controls menu), 733
Define Function Keys
(Configure menu), 44, 58
Delete (File menu), 150-151
Delete Directory (Directory
Maintenance submenu),
237-240
Delete Menu Item (File
menu), 106, 117
Desktop
Change File (File menu),
475
Disk Editor (Disk menu),
436
Display Options (Configure
menu), 190
Electronic Mail
(Accessories menu), 846
Electronic Mail (File
menu), 854
Locate (File menu), 173
Mail Directories (Setup
menu), 851
Mail Service (Setup menu),
848
Program Scheduler (Tools
menu), 127
Quick View (File
menu), 191

Startup Programs
(Configure menu), 126
System Information (Tools
menu), 334
Wipe Disk (Disk menu), 475
Wipe File (Change File
submenu), 475
Desktop Accessories
Append (File menu),
669-671
Application Colors (System
Control menu), 536
Ascii Table (Utilities
submenu), 553
Calculators, 750
Delete Record (Edit menu),
646
Edit Fields (Edit menu),
642-644, 658, 663
Find Text in All Fields
(Search menu), 654-656
Find Text in Sort Field
(Search menu), 654-656
Goto Record (Search
menu), 657
Hide Current Record (Edit
menu), 647-648
Hotkey Selection (Utilities
submenu), 552
main menu, 529-530
Maximize (System Control
menu), 540
Modify Data (File menu),
634-638
Move (System Control
menu), 538
Pack Database (Edit
menu), 646-647
Print (File menu), 664-668
Restore (System Control
menu), 540
Save Setup (Controls
menu), 541-542
Select All Records (Edit
menu), 648-654

Select Records (Edit menu), 648-654, 666

Size (System Control menu), 539

Sort Database (Edit menu), 652-653, 666

Switch To (System Control menu), 546

Transfer (File menu), 669-670

Undelete Record (Edit menu), 646

Unload Desktop Accessories (Utilities submenu), 555

Device Drives (Memory menu), 354

dialog boxes, 547
elements, 43-48

Directory Attributes (Directory Maintenance submenu), 241-242

Directory Maintenance (Disk menu), 234-235

Disk Info (Disk menu), 215

Disk Light (Display Options submenu), 63

Disk Optimization (Tools menu), 314

DiskEdit
1st Copy of FAT (Select menu), 444-445

2nd Copy of FAT (Select menu), 444-445

Boot Record (Select menu), 447

Cluster (Select menu), 453

Configuration (Tools menu), 440, 445, 451

Copy to Clipboard (Edit menu), 452

Directory (Select menu), 440

Drive (Select menu), 446

Drive Info (Info menu), 454

Hex (View menu), 448

Map of Object (Info menu), 443, 451

Mark Block (Edit menu), 452

Object Information (Info menu), 450

Partition Table (Select menu), 446

Paste from Clipboard (Edit menu), 452

Repeat Search (Tools menu), 454

Search (Tools menu), 453-454

Select Directory (View menu), 454

Split Screen (View menu), 450

Undo (Edit menu), 452

Write Object (Tools menu), 446, 455

DiskFix
Advice, 424

Configure Options, 424, 431-432

Repair a Disk, 423-426

Revitalize a Disk, 423, 429-431

Surface Scan, 423, 426-429

Undo a DiskFix Repair, 423, 426

Display Options (Configure menu), 62

DM Directory Maintenance
Branch Size (Directory menu), 244-245

Copy Tree (Directory menu), 249

Delete Directory (Directory menu), 248-249

Make Directory (Directory menu), 247

Modify Attributes (Directory menu), 252

Network Rights (Directory menu), 253

Print Tree (Volume menu), 252

Prune and Graft (Directory menu), 251

Rename Directory (Directory menu), 248

Rename Volume (Volume menu), 246-247

Reread Tree (Volume menu), 245

Show Files (Directory menu), 244

Tree Data Display (Volume menu), 245-246

DM Program (Directory Maintenance submenu), 242

DOS
  adding to Desktop menus, 76-77
  BOOTSAFE, 521-522
  CD (CHDIR), 243
  COMPRESS, 314, 324-325, 329-332
  CPAV, 512-513
  CPBACKUP, 260, 308-310
  CPTASK, 121-122
  DIR, 255
  DISKFIX, 422, 433-434
  DM, 242
  FF, 173
  FILEATTR, 163-164
  FILECHK, 313, 419-422
  FILEDATE, 164
  FORMAT, 202-204
  MIRROR, 404-405
  not freeing memory before executing, 70
  PCFORMAT, 208-210
  PCSECURE, 460
  SI, 334
  UNFORMAT, 413
  VIEW, 190
  VSAFE, 516-517
  VWATCH, 518
  XCOPY, 249

DOS Advice (Help menu), 49

DOS Session (Tools menu), 86

Drive Mapping (Configure menu), 58

Drives (FileFind), 172

Drop on Drive Copies to Root (Tree submenu), 234

Dual List Display (Windows menu), 80, 137

Edit (Change submenu), 153-154

Edit Pull-downs (Configure menu), 72

Edit Text (Change submenu), 69

Electronic Mail
  Create Mail Message (Actions menu), 852-854
  Read Mail Now (Actions menu), 856
  Read Mail Schedule (Setup menu), 859
  Send Mail Schedule (Setup menu), 860
  View Highlighted Message (Actions menu), 856

Encrypt (Secure submenu), 165

<enddef>, 727

Execution (Configure menu), 57

Exit PC Tools Desktop (File menu), 52

Expand All (Tree menu), 232

Expand Branch (Tree menu), 232

Expand One Level (Tree menu), 231

Expunge Directory (Directory Maintenance submenu), 238

Fax Telecommunications
  Add a New Entry (Actions menu), 869
  Chklog, 876
  Delete the Selected Entry (Actions menu), 878

File Display Options (Display Options submenu), 44, 64
File Editor (Configure Editors submenu), 69
File Information (Information submenu), 66
File Window (Windows menu), 40
FileFind
  Filters (Search menu), 180
  Find Duplicates (Search menu), 185
  Go to Directory (File menu), 176
  Groups (Search menu), 177
  Search Files (File menu), 187
  Selected Drives (Search menu), 184
  Start (Search menu), 175
  View File (File menu), 186
Find Deleted Files (File menu), 387
FORMAT, destructive versions, 405
Format (Disk menu), 204
grayed out, 267
Help menu, 48-49
Hex Edit (Change submenu), 157
Hide All Windows (Windows menu), 40, 85
Index (Help menu), 49-51
Information (File menu), 66
Keyboard (Help menu), 49
List Filter (Display Options submenu), 66
Load Pull-downs (Configure menu), 27, 71
Load Pull-downs (Special menu), 28
Local Tree (Tree submenu), 233
Make System Disk (Disk menu), 206, 211
Maps (Tools menu), 360

Maximize (System Control menu), 40
Menu window
  Application Search (File menu), 96
  Import Direct Access (File menu), 119
Menu Window (Windows menu), 40, 82, 91
Modem Telecommunications DA
  ASCII (Receive menu), 823-824
  ASCII (Send menu), 822-824
  Binary transfer (Setup menu), 820-821
  Create New Entry (Edit menu), 795-805
  Edit Entry (Edit menu), 806
  End Transfer (Actions menu), 824-826, 829-831
  Full Online Screen (Setup menu), 811
  Hangup Phone (Actions menu), 819
  KERMIT (Receive menu), 831
  KERMIT (Send menu), 830
  Manual (Actions menu), 814-818
  Remove (Edit menu), 806
  Run Script (Actions menu), 833
  Save (File menu), 806-807
  XMODEM (Receive menu), 827
  XMODEM (Send menu), 825
  ZMODEM (Receive menu), 829
  ZMODEM (Send menu), 828
Modem Telecomunications DA Manual (Actions menu), 817
Move (File menu), 142

Move (System Control menu), 38

moving within menu schemes, 73-74

New Menu Item (File menu), 107

Notepads DA
Auto Indent (Controls menu), 572
Autosave (Notepads' File menu), 596
Control Char Display (Controls menu), 573
Copy to Clipboard (Edit menu), 580
Cut to Clipboard (Edit menu), 580
Delete All Text (Edit menu), 577
Exit without Saving (Notepad's File menu), 577, 597
Find (Search menu), 584
Find Again (Search menu), 584
Goto (Edit menu), 575
Header/Footer (Controls menu), 591
Insert File (Edit menu), 577
Mark Block (Edit menu), 578
Overtype Mode (Controls menu), 576
Page Layout (Controls menu), 589
Paste to Clipboard (Edit menu), 581
Print (Notepad's File menu), 592
Replace (Search menu), 585
Save (Notepads' File menu), 595
Save Setup (Controls menu), 596

Tab Ruler Display (Controls menu), 586
Tab Ruler Edit (Controls menu), 587
Unmark Block (Edit menu), 579
Wordwrap (Controls menu), 571

Open (File menu), 94, 138

Outlines DA
Collapse Current (Headlines menu), 621
Demote (Headlines menu), 620
Exit Without Saving (File menu), 623
Expand All (Headlines menu), 622
Expand Current (Headlines menu), 622
Main Headline Only (Headlines menu), 621
Print (File menu), 623
Promote (Headlines menu), 619
Show Level (Headlines menu), 621

Password (Configure menu), 78-79

Paste Menu Item (File menu), 118

PC Secure
Compression (Options menu), 466
Decrypt File (File menu), 472
Delete Original File (Options menu), 467
Encrypt File (File menu), 468
Expert Mode (Options menu), 468
Full DES Encryption (Options menu), 465
Hidden (Options menu), 467

One Key (Options menu), 466

Quick Encryption (Options menu), 465

Read-Only (Options menu), 467

Print Directory (Print submenu), 168

Print File (Print submenu), 165-168

program-item start-up, 108

Properties (File menu), 106

Prune and Graft (Directory Maintenance submenu), 239-240

Quick Run (Execution submenu), 70

Re-Read Tree (Disk menu), 227

Rebuild, 404

Rename (File menu), 149-150

Rename Directory (Directory Maintenance submenu), 237

Rename Volume (Disk menu), 212

Reset Current Directory (Tree submenu), 234

Restore (System Control menu), 40

Return to Startup Directory (Tree submenu), 234

Run DOS Command (File menu), 86

Save Configuration (Configure menu), 56

Scheduler
Schedule Anti-Virus Scanning (Configure menu), 506-507

Screen Blanker (Display Options submenu), 63

Screen Size (Display Options submenu), 62, 63

script, 833
branching, 837-838
communications, 835-837
display, 838-839
program-control, 837-838
variable-manipulation, 834

Search Disk (Disk menu), 223-225

Secure Options (Configure menu), 58

Select All (File menu), 136, 137

Select Filter (Display Options submenu), 44, 136-137

selecting, 28-29

Single List Display (Windows menu), 81

Size (System Control menu), 39

Software Interrupts (System menu), 346

Sort Directory (Disk menu), 254-256

Speed (Configure menu), 58

Speed Search (Speed submenu), 68

Startup First Level (Tree submenu), 233

Startup Programs (Configure menu), 58

Tiled Windows (Display Options submenu), 85

toggling, 63

Topics (Help menu), 48-49

Tree (Configure menu), 57, 233-234

Tree Window (Windows menu), 40

Unzip Files (Compression submenu), 144-145

Upper Case (Display Options submenu), 34, 64

Verify (Information submenu), 148

Verify Disk (Disk menu), 222-223

View Window (Windows menu), 34-35, 40, 83

Wait on DOS (Execution submenu), 87

Wipe (Change submenu), 152-153

Zip Files (Compression submenu), 143-144

Commands (Help menu) command, 49

communications script commands, 835-837

Commute Advanced Options dialog box, 904-905

Commute Call in Progress dialog box, 893

Commute Chat window commands
    Bell, 901
    Disconnect, 905
    files, overwriting, 903
    subdirectories, 903

Commute remote-control program, 939

Commute Scheduler program command button, 943

Commute Session Manager window command buttons
    Advanced Options, 899
    Chat with Other PC, 899
    End the Session, 898
    Exit, 899
    Get Files from Other PC, 899
    Help, 899
    Look at Your PC, 898
    Send Files to Other PC, 899

Commute Startup program, 927

Commute TSR Manager command button, 945

Commute User Name dialog box, 882

COMMUTE.PIF file, 938

Compare (File menu) command, 146-147

Compare Disk (Disk menu) command, 219-221

Compare Windows (Windows menu) command, 221

comparing
    backups
        data, 280-286
        files to current versions, 146-147
    contents of directories or drives, 221
    contents of disks, 219-221

Complementary Metal-Oxide Semiconductor, *see* CMOS

Compress, 940
    analyzing disk allocation, 317-319
    elements, 314-317
    fragmented files, analyzing allocation, 319-320
    ordering methods for files and directories, 324-328
    printing reports, 329-330
    program, 914
    running from DOS command line, 324-325, 329-332
    sorting directories, 328-329
    starting, 314-317

Compress (CP Backup's Options menu) command, 299

COMPRESS command, 314, 324-325, 329-332

Compress File Settings dialog box, 143-144

Compress Options dialog box, 299

Compress Recommendation dialog box, 314

compressed mode, printing, 739

compressing files, 143-145, 299, 465-466, 903

Compression (File menu) command
    Unzip Files, 144-145
    Zip Files, 143-144

Compression (PC Secure's Options menu) command, 466

Compression Technique (Compress' Options menu) command, 322-323

CompuServe, 845, 848-849, 852
  user ID and password, 799
Computer panel (SI dialog box), 335-336
computers
  connecting
    directly, 818
    during voice calls, 817-818
    terminating, 819
  connecting to others, 807-816
  echoing, 805
  null-modem cables, 818
  receiving telephone calls, 816
  single-user, 910
  stand-alone, 910
  telecommunications files
    Autodial, 841-843
    scripts to automate, 831-840
    sending and receiving, 819-831
confidence tests (CP Backup), 264-265
Configuration (DiskEdit's Tools menu) command, 440, 445, 451
Configuration Changes dialog box, 440
Configuration Options dialog box, 480-481
Configure Autodial (Databases' Control menu) command, 841-842
Configure Autodialer dialog box, 841-842
Configure DiskFix dialog box, 431-432
Configure Emergency Disk dialog box, 218
Configure File Editor dialog box, 69, 870
Configure menu, 56-58, 920
Configure Options (DiskFix Main menu) command, 424, 431-432
configuring
  Autodial, 841-842

Central Point Backup (CP Backup)
  initial startup, 261-266
  reconfiguring, 287-291, 294-307
Desktop, 56-70
  PC Tools, 919-928
DiskEdit utility, 436-439
DiskFix utility, 431-432
Menu window, 95
modems, 807-808
mouse, 924
password protection for, 78-79
PC Tools with CAS fax board, 865-867
program startup, 920
Scheduler to run at startup, 126-127
screen display, 923-924
Task Switcher to run at startup, 120-122
Tree window, 233-234
VSafe program, 514-516
Wipe program, 480-481
Confirmation (Configure menu) command, 60
confirmation
  buttons, 43
  preferences 60-62
Confirmation Options dialog box, 60-62
connecting computers, 894
  directly, 818
  during voice calls, 817-818
  terminating, 819
Connection Type dialog box, 883, 891, 894
contents, displaying in registers, 778
context-sensitive help, 50-51
contiguous files, 311-312
Control Char Display (Notepads' Controls menu) command, 573
control
  characters, 573

control codes, used by on-line services and BBSs, 836
controlling printers with macros, 735-740
conventional, 350-352
    memory, freeing, 928-929
Conventional Memory Information dialog box, 351
converting menu formats, 919
Copy (File menu) command, 140
Copy dialog box, 141
Copy Disk (Disk menu) command, 212-214
Copy II PC (Central Point Software), 212
Copy Menu Item (File menu) command, 118
copy protected disks, 212
Copy to Clipboard commands
    Copy/Paste menu, 602
    DiskEdit's Edit menu, 452
    Notepads' Edit menu, 580
Copy Tree (DM Directory Maintenance's Directory menu) command, 249
copying
    Algebraic Calculator tape, 758-759
    between DOS and Accessories programs, 601-603
    directories, 240-241, 249-250
    discrepancies
        comparing directory/drive contents, 221
        comparing disk contents, 219-221
        verifying disks, 221-223
    disks, 212-214
    files, 139-141, 903
        with drag-and-drop, 32
    header database files, 371
    objects, 451-452
    text, 577-581

correcting error backups, 301
cover pages for fax, 873-874
    adding, 867
CP Backup, see Central Point Backup
CP Backup (Tools menu) command, 260
CP Commute, see Central Point Commute
CPAV command, 512-513
CPAV.PIF file, 939
CPBACKUP command, 260, 308-310
CPS.SCR. script file, 839
CPSCHED (Central Point Scheduler) memory-resident program, 291-294
CPTASK command, 121-122
CPU speed test, 355
CRC-16 error-checking scheme, 825
Create Custom Menu Item dialog box, 76-77
Create Emergency Disk utility, 916-919
Create Mail Message (Electronic Mail's Action menu) command, 852-854
Create New Entry (Modem Telecommunications' Edit menu) command, 795-805
create-file method of recovery, 399-400
creating
    call lists, private, 885-888
    emergency disks in PC Tools Install program, 916-919
    give-control lists, 889-890
criteria, selection, backup files, 303-304
cross-linked files, checking, 312-313
Ctrl+key combinations, 554
current
    directories, 41
    drives, Compress, 315

fields, 634
files, 41, 83
  displaying contents, 35
  versus selected files,
    134-135
records, 634
setup file, 274
cursor-movement keys
  Compress File Allocation
    Analysis, 320
  CP Backup, 277
  Desktop window, 41-42
  File Editor screen, 155
  modes
    Browse, 635
    Edit, 637
  Notepads DA, 574-575
  Sector Edit screen, 160
  tab ruler, 588
  View window, 194-196
Custom option (PC Tools 8
  Install program), 913-914
Cut Menu Item (File menu)
  command, 118
Cut to Clipboard (Notepads'
  Edit menu) command, 580

D

data bits, 801
data dictionary file (R:BASE),
  372
Data Monitor program, 384, 914,
  940-941
Data Protection (Configure
  menu) command, 57
data registers, 769, 785
  reviewing, 778
database files, 626
  deleting, 650-651
  form files, 657
    custom, 659-664
    default, 657-659
  headers, 371
  loading, 641-642

printing, 664
  from Browse mode,
    664-665
  from Edit mode, 666-668
repairing, 371-378
searching, 654-657
sorting, 651-653
databases
  acceptable entries, 636
  creating, 627-634
  decimals, 629-631
  Desktop, dialing phone
    numbers from, 842
  destination, 669
  exiting, 632-633
  field definitions
    adding, 643
    deleting, 643
    modifying, 634, 643-644
  fields, 628
    searching, 654-656
    sizes, 629-631
    types, 629-631
  file viewers, 193
  modes, toggling between, 633
  records
    adding, 634-638
    deleting, 645-646
    editing, 638
    hiding, 647-648
    packing, 646-647
    purging, 644-645
    selecting, 647-650
    undeleting, 645-646
  saving, 632-633
  source, 669
  specifying, 797-798
Databases (Desktop
  Accessories' main menu)
  command, 529
Databases DA, 525
  window size, 537
  see also Desktop Accessories
Databases File Load dialog box,
  628, 650
DataMon TSR Manager
  command button, 944

date fields, 630
   selection criteria, 648-650
Date Range Selection (CP
  Backup's Selection submenu)
  command, 305
Date Range Selection dialog box,
  305
dates
   fax, 870
   files, 870
     changing, 163-164
   format, 742
   selecting backup files, 305
dBASE files, 626
   repairing, 374-375
   repairing headers, 376-378
   zapped records, 374
DBF file name extension, 626
Deactivate All Macros (Controls
  menu) command, 733
deactivating
   learn mode, 730
   macros, 732-734
   virus protection, 903
decimal numbers, 554, 629-631,
  772
decompressing files, 903
Decrypt File (PC Secure's File
  menu) command, 472
decrypting files and directories,
  472
default form files, 657-659
Define Equipment (CP Backup's
  Configure menu) command,
  288
Define Equipment dialog box,
  262-263, 288
Define Function Keys (Configure
  menu) command, 44, 58
Define Function Keys dialog
  box, 44-45, 58-60
defining macros, 720
Del (One List) key, 31, 81
<DelayN> keyword, 111, 115
Delete (Scheduler) command
   Appointment menu, 688, 697
   To-Do menu, 711

Delete (File menu) command,
  150-151
Delete All Text (Notepads' Edit
  menu) command, 577
Delete an Item dialog box, 106,
  117
Delete Checklist Files (CP Anti-
  Virus' Scan menu) command,
  504
Delete Checklist Files dialog
  box, 504
Delete Directory (Directory
  Maintenance submenu)
  command, 237-240, 248-249
Delete Menu Item (File menu)
  command, 106, 117
Delete Old Entries
  (Appointment Scheduler's
  Controls menu) command, 698
Delete Original File (PC Secure's
  Options menu) command, 467
Delete Protection Startup
  program, 926
Delete Record (Desktop
  Accessories' Edit menu)
  command, 646
Delete Sentry protection
  program, 383
   purging files, 401-402
Delete the Selected Entry (FAX
  Log Actions menu) command,
  878
Delete Tracker protection
  program, 383
delete tracking, 404
deleting
   appointments, 697-699
   characters, 901
   checksums, 504
   Desktop Accessories, 555-556
   directories, 237-240, 248-249
   entries, 888
   fax entries, 878
   field definitions, 643-644
   file immunization, 498-499

files, 150-151
   database, 650-651
   Notepads DA, 594
   original, after encrypting,
    467
   recovering, 383-402
   scanning free clusters,
    391-392
  phone directory entries, 806
  program groups, 106
  program items, 117
  records, 645-646
  search groups (FileFind), 179
  text, 575-577
  VSafe program, 519
  VWatch program, 518
Demote (Outlines' Headlines
  menu) command, 620
demoting outline headlines,
  618-620
DES (Data Encryption Standard)
  encryption, 459, 465
description windows, 104
<desk> code, 729
Desktop
  background mat, turning
   off, 37
  closing, 52-53
  configuring, 56-58, 919-928
   password protection, 78-79
  confirmation preferences,
   setting, 60-62
  databases, dialing phone
   numbers from within, 842
  DOS command line, 86
  Electronic Mail, see
   Electronic Mail
  File window
   changing display of file
    information, 64-66
   filtering files, 66-68
  function-key commands,
   customizing, 58-60
  memory, not freeing, 70
  pausing before returning
   to, 112

PC Tools, 942
pull-down menus,
  customizing, 71-78
returning from DOS, 87
screen
  customizing display, 62-64
  elements, 36, 226-227
Search Files options, 172, 187
speed search, 68
text editors, selecting, 69
windows, 79
  hiding, 85
  Menu, displaying, 82-83
  toggling, 80-85
  View, displaying, 83-84
Desktop Accessories, 525-526,
919-928
  Appointment Scheduler, see
   Appointment Scheduler
  ASCII table, displaying,
   552-554
  Clipboard, see Clipboard DA
  databases, acceptable
   entries, 636
  dialog boxes, 547
  help, 547-550
  horizontal menu bar, 531
  hotkeys, 551-552
  installing, 526-529
  keyboard shortcuts, 532-533
  Modem Telecommunications,
   see Modem
   Telecommunications DA
  Notepads, see Notepads DA
  Outlines, see Outlines DA
  pull-down menus, 532
  returning to DOS, 556-557
  unloading, 555-556
  windows
   changing colors, 535-537
   closing, 543
   elements, 534-535
   maximizing, 540
   moving, 538
   multiple, 544-547
   opening, 529-530

resizing, 539-540
saving settings, 541-542
scrolling, 542-543
sizes, 537
Desktop Accessories program
(DESKTOP.PIF), 938
desktop platforms, 599
DESKTOP.PIF file, 938
destination
databases, 669
disks, 283
Detect & Clean (CP Anti-Virus'
Express menu) command, 490
Detect (CP Anti-Virus)
command
Express menu, 488
Scan menu, 496
detecting viruses, 301
device drivers, 354
Device Drivers Information
dialog box, 354
Device Drives (Memory menu)
command, 354
dialing phone numbers, 808-809
from within Desktop
databases with Autodial,
842
from within DOS programs,
843
manually, 814-816
dialog boxes, 42
Accessories Save File to Disk,
595
Activity Log, 507-508
Add to Exception List, 500
Advanced Program Item
Information, 113-117
All Files Compare, 284
Appointment Settings, 682
Automatic Search, 261
Backup Complete, 271-272
Backup Confidence Test, 264,
290
Backup from Directory, 275
Backup Method, 297-298
Backup Speed, 289-290

Binary Transfer Options,
820-821, 829
Build Emergency Disk, 916
Build Emergency Disk
Options, 217-218
Caution, 248
Change Active Window, 546
Change Colors, 536-537
Change Directory, 185
Change Password, 78-79, 511
Choose Compression
Technique, 322-323
Choose Directory, 281-283
Choose Drive & Media,
263-264, 288
Choose Ordering Method,
324-325
Choose Sort Method, 328-329
Choose Tape Type, 261
Close, 506-507
Close Central Point Anti-
Virus, 491, 511
Close PC Secure, 473
Close PC Tools Desktop, 52,
57
COM Port, 884
command, 547
Commute Advanced Options
dialog box, 904-905
Commute Call in Progress,
893
Commute User Name, 882
Compress File Settings,
143-144
Compress Options, 299
Compress Recommendation,
314
Configuration Changes, 440
Configuration Options,
480-481
Configure Autodialer, 841-842
Configure DiskFix, 431-432
Configure Emergency Disk,
218
Configure File Editor, 69
Confirmation Options, 60-62

Connection Type, 883, 891, 894
Conventional Memory Information, 351
Copy, 141
Create Custom Menu Item, 76-77
Databases File Load, 628, 650
Date Range Selection, 305
Define Equipment, 262-263, 288
Define Function Keys, 44-45, 58-60
Delete an Item, 106, 117
Delete Checklist Files, 504
Desktop Accessories applications, 547
Device Drivers Information, 354
Directory Add, 235-236
Directory Ordering, 326-328
Directory Prune and Graft, 239
Directory Rename, 237
Directory Sort, 255-256
Disconnect Modem, 842
Disk Compare, 220
Disk Copy, 213-214
Disk Information, 215
Disk Mapping, 361-362
Disk Options, 479-480
Disk Rename, 212
Disk Search, 223-225
Disk Statistics, 317-319
Disk Verify, 222
Display Options, 44, 64-66, 923
Drive Selection, 204-205, 315, 413, 424, 429, 476-479
Duplicate Search Filters, 186
Edit Call List, 887
Edit File, 153-154
Edit Menu Item, 75
Edit Modem Commands, 884
Edit Phone Directory, 795-808, 834, 850

Edit Search Groups, 177-179
Effective Rights, 253
Electronic Mail Configure Mail, 850
Electronic Mail Directories, 851-852
Electronic Mail Service, 848-850
elements, 43-48
Enter Password, 79
Enter Task to Run, 123-124
Expanded Memory Information, 353
Extended Memory Information, 352
Fax Details, 869-871
Field Editor, 628-634, 643-644
File Compare, 146-147
File Delete, 150-151
File Fragmentation Analysis, 319-320
File List Filter, 66-68
File Load, 379, 560-566, 577, 594, 627, 641, 675, 822-825
File Mapping, 360
File Options, 476-479
File Print, 165-168
File Rename, 149-150
File Select Filter, 44-45, 136-137
File Selection, 468-472
Files Did Not Compare, 284
Files DisImmunized, 499
Files Found on Drive C:, 414
Files in This Map Block, 321
Files to Place First, 326-327
Files to Select, 872
Files to Send, 872
Find, 584-585
Find and Replace, 585-586
Find Appointment, 703
Find Deleted Files, 387
Give Control List, 889
Go To, 575
Hardware Interrupt Information, 347

Hotkey, 552
Immunization Exceptions, 500
Include/Exclude Files, 303-304
Infection Report, 507-508
Key Input, 469-471
Keyboard Options, 925
Keyword List, 110-112
LAN Server List, 887
Load Form, 660
Load Setup File, 307
Logical Drive Information, 348
Macro/Clipboard Playback
  Delay, 612-613, 734
Macros Active, 732-733, 738
Make Appointment, 744-746
Make Directory, 247
Manual Call, 893
Master Key, 461
Media Format, 300
Menu Configuration Options,
  104
Menu Editor, 72-78
Menu Editor Options, 72-73,
  78
Menu Options Configuration,
  95
message, 42-43
Mirror Used?, 413
Modem List, 884
Modem Setup, 807-808
Modem Telecommunications
  File Load, 794
Modify Attributes, 252
Modify Directory Attributes,
  241-242
More File Information, 66
Mouse Options, 924
Name Backup Set, 269-270,
  279
Network Filters, 182-183
Network Messages, 509-510
New Menu Item, 102, 107
New To-Do Entry, 708
No Viewable Records, 645
Object Information, 450-451
Operating System
  Information, 337-338

Options Settings, 501-503
Overwrite Warning, 285-286
Page Header & Footer,
  591-592
Page Layout, 589-591
Partition Table Information,
  349
Password, 469
Pattern Testing Options, 426,
  431
Percent Completed, 480
Print, 592-593, 611-612, 664,
  712, 758
Print Selection, 666
Print Tree, 252
Printing Options, 358
Private Call List, 886
Program Group Information,
  102-106
Program Item Information,
  107-113, 117
Progress, 470-471
Prune and Graft, 251
RBase Repair Options, 372
Read Mail Schedule, 859
Receive, 827-831
Receive Files from Other PC,
  902-903
Rename Directory, 248
Report Options, 298
Reporting Options, 358
Run Script, 833
Save File to Disk, 807, 823, 827
Save Setup File, 307
Schedule or Edit an Event,
  128-130, 292, 506-507
Scheduled Print, 716-718
Scheduler Layouts, 678
Scheduler Options, 131, 292
Search Attributes, 183
Search Filters, 181-182
Search Groups, 177
Search Sort Field, 655
Select Drives/Directory,
  184-185
Select File to Fix, 370

Select Format Options, 205-207
Select Records, 648
Send, 826-831
Send ASCII, 822
Send Files to Other PC, 904
Send Kermit, 830
Send Mail Schedule, 860
Send XMODEM, 825
Send Zmodem, 828
SI (System Information), 335-336
Software Interrupt Information, 346
Sort Field Select, 652
Sort Options, 306
Special Appointment Settings, 689
Speed Search, 68
Text Search, 187-189
toggling options, 63
Transfer, 669
Transfer Status, 825-831
Tree Data Display, 245-246
Uncompress File Settings, 144-145
Unformatting, 415
Unmovable Files, 327-328
Use a New Menu File, 27, 71-72
User Level, 290
Verification Exceptions, 504-505
Verify File List, 829-831
Virus Found, 497
Virus List, 508
Viruses Detected and Cleaned, 489, 496
Wiping, 152-153
Word Misspelled, 582-583
Write Object, 455-456
DIR command, 255
<Dir> keyword, 110
<Dir\> keyword, 111
Direct Access Version 5, 119
direct connections, 818

Direct Memory Access (DMA) controller, 289
directories, 34, 225
  adding, 235-236, 247
  assigning default to Notepads DA, 562-563
  attributes, changing, 241-242, 252
  changing, 227-228
  comparing contents, 221
  comparing/restoring data, 280-286
  copying, 240-241, 249-250
  current, 41
  decrypting, 472
  deleting, 237-240, 248-249
  Electronic mail, 851
  encrypting, 470-471
  Install program, 915
  managing, 234-235
    on networks, 242-254
  moving, 239-241, 250-251
  ordering methods, 324-328
  parent, 561
  printing, 168-169
  program-item start-up, 109
  recovering, 400
  renaming, 237, 247-248
  root, 34, 225
    rebuilding, 412-419
    saving backups, 405-407
  searching, 183-185
    FileFind, 172
    with speed search, 68
  selected, 227
  selective backups, 276-278, 302-303
  sorting, 328-329
    files, 254-256
  undeleting, 238
  viewing and editing, 440-443
directories, phone, see phone directories
Directory (DiskEdit's Select menu) command, 440
Directory Add dialog box, 235-236

Directory Attributes (Directory
Maintenance submenu)
command, 241-242
Directory Editor (DiskEdit),
440-443
Directory Lock Startup program,
926
Directory Maintenance (Disk
menu) command, 234-235
Add Directory, 235-236
Delete Directory, 237-240
Directory Attributes, 241-242
DM Program, 242
Expunge Directory, 238
Prune and Graft, 239-240
Rename Directory, 237
Directory Maintenance program
(DM.PIF), 938
Directory Order (Compress'
Options menu) command, 326
Directory Ordering dialog box,
326-328
Directory Prune and Graft dialog
box, 239
Directory Rename dialog box,
237
Directory Sort dialog box,
255-256
Directory Tree panel (CP Anti-
Virus), 493
directory trees, 25
changing directories, 228, 245
data display, changing,
245-246
displaying backup files,
305-306
expanding/collapsing
branches, 228-232
printing, 251-252
refreshing, 227, 245
Disconnect (Commute Chat
window) command, 905
Disconnect Modem dialog box,
842
Disk Compare dialog box, 220
Disk Copy dialog box, 213-214

Disk Editor (Disk menu)
command, 436
disk files, ancillary, 626
Disk Info (Disk menu) command,
215
Disk Information dialog box, 215
Disk Light (Display Options
submenu) command, 63-64
Disk Light Startup program, 926
Disk Manager (On-Track)
program, 408
Disk Mapping dialog box,
361-362
Disk Optimization (Tools menu)
command, 314
Disk Options dialog box, 479-480
Disk Rename dialog box, 212
Disk Search dialog box, 223-225
Disk Statistics (Compress'
Analysis menu) command,
317-319
Disk Statistics dialog box,
317-319
Disk Verify dialog box, 222
DiskEdit utility
Boot Record Editor, 447-448
Directory Editor, 440-443
File Allocation Table Editor,
444-445
Hex Editor, 448
memory information,
displaying, 456
objects
displaying and mapping,
449-451
marking, copying, and
pasting, 451-452
Partition Table Editor,
445-447
repairing disks and files,
453-456
starting
and configuring, 436-439
from DOS command line,
457
versus technical support, 436

DISKFIX command, 422, 433-434
DiskFix Scheduler program
  command button, 943
DiskFix utility, 369, 422-424, 914,
  938-941
    configuring, 431-432
    exiting, 432
    repairing disks, 424-426
    revitalizing disks with low-
      level formats, 429-431
    scanning disk surfaces,
      426-429
    starting from DOS command
      line, 433-434
DISKFIX.PIF file, 938
/DISKREQ Install program
  option, 931
disks
    allocation, 317-319
      compression techniques,
        322-324
    bootable (system), 206, 211
    caching, 941-942
    changing and reading, 36
    checking for potential
      problems, 419-422
    comparing, 219-221
    copying, 212-214
    destination, 283
    displaying information
      about, 215
    emergency, 916-919
      creating, 216-219
    formatting, 202-210
      backup, 300-301
    immunizing, 498-500
    mapping, 361-362
    parking heads, 202
    preparing for use, 202
    rebuilding after accidental
      formats, 412-419
    repairing, 424-426, 941
      manually, 453-456
    revitalizing with low-level
      formats, 429-431
    scanning surfaces, 426-429

  scheduling maintenance
    events, 125-131
  searching, 223-225
  verifying, 221-223
  viruses
    cleaning, 496-497
    detecting and cleaning, 490
    protecting against, 492,
      513-519
    searching for, 488-489, 496
  volume labels
    changing, 246-247
    renaming, 212
  volume serial numbers, 208
  wiping, 479-480
  working, 495
display
  configuring, 923-924
  script commands, 838-839
Display Options (Configure
  menu) command, 62, 190
  File Display Options, 44
  Select Filter, 44, 136-137
  Upper Case, 34
Display options (CP Backup
  Options menu) command, 306
Display Options dialog box, 44,
  64-66, 923
Display Options submenu, 62
displaying
  AUTOEXEC.BAT file, 357
  calculators, 752-754
  Central Point Commute user
    names, 883
  drive information, 348-350
  files (system), 357-358
  memory information, 350-354
  register contents, 778
  SI, 334-347
DM command, 242
DM Directory Maintenance
  program, 234-235, 242-245
  changing tree data display,
    245-246
  directories
    adding, 247
    attributes, changing, 252

copying, 249-250
deleting, 248-249
moving, 250-251
printing trees, 251-252
renaming, 247-248
exiting, 254
network rights, displaying, 253
volume labels, changing, 246-247
DM.PIF file, 938
DMA (Direct Memory Access) controller, 289
DOS
command line, 86, 226
accessing on take-control PC, 899-900
BootSafe, starting, 521-522
Central Point Anti-Virus Express, starting, 486, 497
Central Point Anti-Virus, starting, 512-513
Compress, running, 324-332
CP Backup, starting, 260, 308-310
DiskEdit, starting, 457
DiskFix, starting, 433-434
FileCheck running, 313
FileFind, starting, 172
FileFix, starting, 370
parameters, keywords, 109-112
PC Format, running, 208-210
PC Secure, starting, 473-474
SI, 359
Undelete, starting, 384
VSafe, starting, 516-517
VWatch, starting, 518
Wipe, starting, 481-483
commands, 70
adding to Desktop menus, 76-77
exiting from Desktop to, 86
file attributes/dates, changing, 163-164
file protection, 383
moving directories, 239, 250
programs
copying/pasting between Accessories, 600-606
dialing phone numbers with Autodial, 843
returning to Desktop, 87, 556-557
DOS Advice (Help menu) command, 49
DOS Program Scheduler window, 292
DOS Session (Tools menu) command, 86
drag-and-drop, 32-33
copying/moving directories, 240-241
copying files, 141
launching files, 94, 115, 138
<Drag> keyword, 111
dragging windows, 538
Drive (DiskEdit's Select menu) command, 446
Drive Info (DiskEdit's Info menu) command, 454
<Drive> keyword, 110
drive line, 26, 226
CP Anti-Virus, 493
Drive Mapping (Configure menu) command, 58
drive maps
analyzing blocks, 321
Compress, 316
Revitalize a Disk, 431
Surface Scan, 427-428
Drive Selection dialog box, 204-205, 315, 413, 424, 429, 476-479
Drive Summary line (SI dialog box), 348
DriveMap Startup program, 914, 927-930

drivers
  device, 354
  XMS, 353
drives
  backups, 288, 308
  backup drive and media, 274
  changing, 227, 245
  comparing contents, 221
  displaying information,
    348-350
  hard disks
    partitions, 349
    speed test, 355-356
  icons, listing, 348
  Install program, 915
  logical, 275
  physical details, 349
  searching, 183-185
  source (backup-from setting),
    260, 274-275
  viruses, searching for,
    490-491
Drives (FileFind) command, 172
Drop on Drive Copies to Root
  (Tree submenu) command, 234
dual file lists
  comparing files, 146-147
  copying files between, 140
Dual List Display (Windows
  menu) command, 80, 137
dual-list window displays,
  toggling with one-list displays,
  80-82
duplex, *see* full- or half-duplex
  modems
Duplicate Search Filters dialog
  box, 186

E

EasyLink, 845-849, 852
echoing, 805
Edisk program, 217-219
Edit (Appointment Scheduler's
  Appointment menu) command,
  700

Edit (Change submenu)
  command, 153-154
Edit Call List dialog box, 887
Edit Entry (Modem
  Communications' Edit menu)
  command, 806
Edit Fields (Desktop
  Accessories' Edit menu)
  command, 642-644, 658, 663
Edit File dialog box, 153-154
Edit Menu Item dialog box, 75
Edit mode, 633
  cursor-movement keys, 637
  databases, printing, 666-668
  toggling between Browse
    mode, 633
Edit Modem Commands dialog
  box, 884
Edit Phone Directory dialog box,
  795-808, 834, 850
Edit Pull-downs (Configure
  menu) command, 72
Edit Search Groups dialog box,
  177-179
Edit Text (Change submenu)
  command, 69
editing
  entries, 888
  files
    ASCII, 153-156
    hexadecimal, 157-161
  menu items, 75-76
  menus, 72-78
  phone directory entries,
    805-806
  program group properties,
    106
  program items, 117
  records, 638
  search groups (FileFind),
    178-179
  tape, 757-758
  text (in Clipboard), 609-611
editors
  DiskEdit utility, 440
    Boot Record, 447-448
    Directory, 440-443

File Allocation Table,
444-445
Hex, 448
Partition Table, 445-447
File, 153-156
Hex, 157-161
effective rights, 253
Effective Rights dialog box, 253
electronic mail, 845-848
directories, 851
electronic mail services
CompuServe, 852
EasyLink, 852
end-of-line processing, 804
ID and password, 799
MCI Mail, 852
selecting, 848-850
reading, 855-858
receiving files
ASCII, 823-824
KERMIT, 831
XMODEM, 826-827
scheduling unattended
receipt, 858-861
sending files, 854-855
ASCII, 822
KERMIT, 830
XMODEM, 825
ZMODEM, 828
Electronic Mail (Desktop's File
menu) command, 854
Electronic Mail Configure Mail
dialog box, 850
Electronic Mail Directories
dialog box, 851-852
Electronic Mail Service dialog
box, 848-850
Element (Color Options screen)
command button, 922
ellipsis (...), 42
Email Scheduler program
command button, 943
emergency disks, 409-412
creating, 216-219, 916-919
emulating terminals, 802-803
Encrypt (Secure submenu)
command, 165

Encrypt File (PC Secure's File
menu) command, 468
encrypting files, 164-165, 459,
465-471
deleting originals, 467
files not to encrypt, 460
hiding, 467
End key
Compress File Allocation
Analysis, 320
CP Backup, 277
Desktop applications, 42
File Editor screen, 155
Sector Edit screen, 160
End the Session (Commute
Session Manager) command
button, 898
End Transfer (Modem
Telecommunications' Actions
menu) command, 824-832
end-of-line processing, 803-804
<enddef> command, 727
Enhanced mode, 934
Enter an autoupdate time in
seconds or 0 to disable
message, 878
Enter key
File Editor screen, 155
Select (CP Backup), 273
Enter Password dialog box, 79
Enter Task to Run dialog box,
123-124
entries
acceptable for databases, 636
deleting, 888
editing, 888
fax, deleting, 878
phone directories, 795-805
deleting, 806
dialing phone numbers,
808-809
editing, 805-806
saving, 806-807
EPSON.PRO Macro Editor file,
736
erasing Algebraic Calculator
tapes, 759-760

Error Correction (CP Backup's Options menu) command, 301
error-checking schemes, 824-825
errors
  correcting backups, 301
  FAT, 312-313
Esc key
  Cancel (Compress), 315
  Cancel (CP Backup), 273
  Cancel (FAX Log window), 877
  Cancel (Macro Editor), 722
  Cancel (PC Secure), 463
  Escape (Financial Calculator), 761
  Escape (Programmer Calculator), 772
  Escape (Scientific Calculator), 780
  Exit (Desktop applications), 31, 52
  Exit (Help window), 51
  Pauses (Central Point Anti-Virus), 488, 494
escape codes, 737
ESL.SCR script file, 839
even parity method, 801
events, 126
  preparing for occurence, 131
  scheduling, 127-130
executing
  applications, give-control PC, 895-898
  calculations, 766-768
    Algebraic Calculator, 754-756
    financial, 769-771
  PC Tools programs, 910-919
  preset time programs, 744-745
  Windows, on give-control PC, 897-898
Execution (Configure menu) command, 57
Exit (Commute Session Manager) command button, 899

Exit (CP Anti-Virus) command
  Express menu, 491
  Scan menu, 511
Exit PC Tools Desktop (File menu) command, 52
Exit without Saving command
  Notepads' File menu, 577, 597
  Outlines' File menu, 623
exiting
  Appointment Scheduler, 718
  Central Point Anti-Virus, 511-512
  databases, 632-633
  Desktop, 86
  DiskFix utility, 432
  DM Directory Maintenance program, 254
  field entries, 639
  from records, 639-641
  Notepads DA, 596-597
  Outlines DA, 623
  PC Secure utility, 473
  programs, pausing after, 112
  windows (Appointment Scheduler), 678
Expand All (Outlines' Headlines menu) command 622
Expand All (Tree menu) command, 232
Expand Branch (Tree menu) command, 232
Expand Current (Outlines' Headlines menu) command, 622
Expand One Level (Tree menu) command, 231
expanded memory, 350-354
Expanded Memory Information dialog box, 353
expanding
  directory-tree branches, 228-232
  outline headlines, 622
Expert mode, 468
Expert Mode (PC Secure's Options menu) command, 468

Express Backup window, 266
  Backup From list, 275
  Compare/Restore command
    buttons, 281
  elements, 266-269
  full backups, 269-272
Express menu (Central Point
  Anti-Virus), 486-488
  exiting, 491
Express mode, 266-267
  turning off, 272
expressions, algebraic, 754
Expunge Directory (Directory
  Maintenance submenu)
  command, 238
<Ext> keyword, 111
extended memory, 350-353
  BIOS data, 352
  plain, 352
  XMS, 352
Extended Memory Information
  dialog box, 352
extended partitions, 445

F

f annunciator, 776
F-prefix keyboard keys
  Financial Calculator, 764
  Programmer Calculator,
    776-777
  Scientific Calculator, 782-783
FATs (File Allocation Tables),
  928
  cluster chains, 445
  comparing copies, 317-319
  errors, checking for, 312-313
  rebuilding, 412-419
  saving backups, 405-407
  viewing and editing, 444-445
fax
  boards, 911
  cover pages, 867, 873-874
  date sent, 870
  deleting entries, 878
  page length, 866

receiving, 875
resolution, 871
sending messages, 869-875
telephone numbers, 871
time, 870
transmissions
  aborting, 878
  AutoUpdate feature, 878
  logging, 875-878
  monitoring, 878
Fax Details dialog box, 869-871
Fax Driver Startup program, 928
Fax Log window, 876-877
Fax Telecommunications,
  Chklog command, 876
FF command, 173
FF.PIF file, 938
Field Editor dialog box, 628-634,
  643-644
fields, 628-629
  character, selection criteria,
    648-650
  date, selection criteria,
    648-650
  definitions
    adding, 643
    deleting, 643
    modifying, 634, 643-644
  exiting entries, 639
  logical, selection criteria,
    648-650
  numeric, selection criteria,
    648-650
  saving entries, 639
  sizes, 629-631
  types, 629-631
File Allocation Table Editor,
  444-445
File Allocation Tables, *see* FATs
file associations, specifying, 114
File Attribute window, 162-163
File Compare dialog box,
  146-147
File Delete dialog box, 150-151
File Display Options (Display
  Options submenu) command,
  44, 64

File Editor, 153-156
File Editor (Configure Editors submenu) command, 69
File Fragmentation Analysis (Compress' Analysis menu) command, 319-320
File Fragmentation Analysis dialog box, 319-320
File Information (Information submenu) command, 66
File Information panel (CP Anti-Virus), 493
<File> keyword, 111
File List Filter dialog box, 66-68
File Load dialog box, 379, 560-566, 577, 594, 627, 641, 675, 822-825
File Mapping dialog box, 360
file names
    assigning default to Notepads DA, 562
    DBF, 626
    locating deleted files, 387-389
    OUT, 615
    PRT, 594
File Options dialog box, 476-479
File Print dialog box, 165-168
file protection, 383-384
    DOS, 383
    programs
        Delete Sentry, 383
        Delete Tracker, 383
        Netware 386, 383
        VWatch, 384
File Rename dialog box, 149-150
File Repair window, 370
File Select Filter dialog box, 44-45, 136-137
File Selection dialog box, 468-471, 472
File Sort Options (Compress' Options menu) command, 328-329
File Viewer program, 914
file viewers, 189-194
    binary, 194
    databases, 193

PCX files, toggling, 194
    spreadsheets, 193
    word processors, 192-193
File Window (Windows menu) command, 40
File windows, 33, 226-227
    dual-list displays, toggling with one-list displays, 80-82
    file information, changing display of, 64-66
    filtering files, 66-68
    listing files (Undelete utility), 385-386
file-transfer protocols, 820
    ASCII, 821-824
    KERMIT, 830-832
    XMODEM, 824-827
    ZMODEM, 827-830
FILEATTR command, 163-164
FileAttr utility, 163-164
FileCheck program, 312-313, 419-422
FILECHK command, 313, 419-422
FILEDATE command, 164
FileDate utility, 164
FileFind utility, 171-172, 914, 938
    directories, locating, 172
    search groups, 172-174
    searching for files
        by file name, 174-176
        finding duplicates, 185-187
        selecting drives and directories for, 183-185
        with filters, 180-183
        with predefined search groups, 176-180
    searching for text, 187-189
    starting, 172-173
FileFind window, 173
FileFix utility, 367-382, 938
    database files, 371
        dBASE, 374-387
        Paradox, 373-374
        R:BASE, 372-373
    quitting, 382
    spreadsheet files, 379-380
    starting, 370

FILEFIX.PIF file, 938
<Filename> keyword, 111
files
   Accessories Notepads, 626
   analyzing map blocks, 321
   ancillary disk, 626
   Appointment Scheduler
     loading, 675-679
     saving, 717
   archiving, 143-145
   attributes, changing, 161-164
   AUTOEXEC.BAT, *see*
   AUTOEXEC.BAT file
   backups
     comparing/restoring data,
       280-286
     comparing to current
       versions, 146-147
     compressing, 299
     displaying in directory
       trees, 305-306
     excluding by attribute,
       304-305
     full, 269-272
     history, 271, 280-283
     saving, 301-302
     selecting by date, 305
     selective, 278, 303-304
   batch, 419-422
   checksums
     creating, 503-504
     exceptions, 504-505
   compressing, 143-145,
     465-466, 903
   CONFIG.SYS, *see* CONFIG.SYS
   file
   contiguous, 311-312
   copying, 139-141, 903
     with drag-and-drop, 32
   cross-linked, checking for,
     312-313
   current, 41, 83
     displaying contents, 35
     setup, 274
   database, *see* database files
   date, 870
     changing, 163-164

dBASE
   repairing, 374-375
   zapped records, 374
dBASE-compatible, 626
decompressing, 903
decrypting, 472
deleted
   locating by file name,
     387-389
   locating by predefined
     search groups, 390-391
   scanning free clusters,
     391-392
deleting, 150-151
deselecting, 137
editing
   ASCII, 153-156
   hexadecimal, 157-161
encrypting, 164-165, 468-471
   deleting originals, 467
   hiding, 467
   types of encryption, 465
filtering, 66-68
footers, 591-592
form, 657
   custom, 659-664
   default, 657-659
fragmented, 311, 360
   analyzing allocation,
     319-320
   checking for, 312-313
   compression techniques,
     322-324
   ordering methods, 324-328
headers, 591-592
   database files, 371
immunizing, 498-500
information, changing display
   of, 64-66
inserting contents into text,
   576
launching, 115, 137-139
   from Menu window, 94-95
listing, 34, 244
   Undelete File window,
     385-386

Macro Editor, 736
macros
   activating, 732-734
   deactivating, 732-734
mapping, 360-361
mirror-image
   recovering from accidental
     formats, 412-415
   saving system information,
     405-407
MIRROR.FIL, 405-407
moving, 139, 142
   with drag-and-drop, 33
networks, recovering, 400-401
Notepads DA
   creating, 563-565
   deleting, 594
   loading, 565-566, 745-746
   saving, 595-596
Outlines DA
   printing, 623
   saving, 623
overwriting, 903
page layout, 589-591
Paradox, repairing, 373-374
printing, 165-168, 592-594
   from Clipboard DA, 611-612
R:BASE, repairing, 372-373
read-only, 467
receiving
   ASCII, 823-824
   KERMIT, 831
   XMODEM, 826-827
recovering, 383-402
   automatically, 396-397
   create-file method, 399-400
   manually, 397-399
   selecting, 394-395
renaming, 149-150
repairing
   manually, 453-456
   selecting, 370-371
reports, 358
RTF (Rich Text Format), 178
script, 799
   creating, 832-833

searching for, 171
   by file name, 174-176
   excluding files from
     search, 174
   finding duplicate names,
     185-187
   selecting drives and
     directories, 183-185
   text, 187-189
   with filters, 180-183
   with search groups, 172,
     176-180
   with speed search, 68
sectors, 360
selecting, 872-873
   filtering with wild-card
     characters, 136-137
   multiple, 136
   single, 135
   versus current files,
     134-135
sending, 869-875
   ASCII, 822-823
   KERMIT, 830-831
   XMODEM, 825-826
   ZMODEM, 828-829
setup, 306-307
sorting in directories, 254-256
spreadsheets, repairing,
   379-380
swap, 122
system, *see* system files
telecommunications
   scripts to automate,
     831-840
   sending and receiving,
     819-831
time, 870
   changing, 163-164
transferring, 902-904
undeleting, 151-152
unmovable, 327-328
verifying readability, 148
viewing
   PCX format, 171
   View utility, 171

viruses
  cleaning, 490, 496-497
  protecting against, 492,
    513-519
  searching for, 488-490, 496
wiping, 152-153, 476-479
WordPerfect, repairing,
  380-382
Files Did Not Compare dialog
  box, 284
Files DisImmunized dialog box,
  499
Files Found on Drive C: dialog
  box, 414
Files in Current Directory panel
  (CP Anti-Virus), 493
Files in This Map Block dialog
  box, 321
Files to Place First (Compress'
  Options menu) command,
  326-327
Files to Place First dialog box,
  326-327
Files to Select dialog box, 872
Files to Send dialog box, 872
fill-in-the-blank macros, 743-744
Filter option (FileFind utility),
  172
filtering
  file lists, 66-68
  files with wild-card
    characters, 136-137
  see also search filters
Filters (FileFind's Search menu)
  command, 180
financial
  calculations, executing,
    769-771
  registers, 769-771
Financial Calculator, 760-771
  F-prefix keyboard keys, 764
  G-prefix keyboard keys,
    765-766
  primary keyboard keys,
    762-763

registers, 768-771
  data, 769
  stack, 768-769
Financial Calculator (Calculator
  menu) command, 760
Find (Notepads' Search menu)
  command, 584
Find Again (Notepads' Search
  menu) command, 584
Find and Replace dialog box,
  585-586
Find Appointment
  (Appointment Scheduler's
  Appointment menu) command,
  703
Find Appointment dialog box,
  703
Find Deleted Files (File menu)
  command, 387
Find Deleted Files dialog box,
  387
Find dialog box, 584-585
Find Duplicates (FileFind's
  Search menu) command, 185
Find Text in All Fields (Desktop
  Accessories' Search menu)
  command, 654-656
Find Text in Sort Field (Desktop
  Accessories' Search menu)
  command, 654-656
finding files, see searches
fine resolution, 871
fixed-length blanks, 743
fixed-length macros, 743
/FL (create master floppy)
  Install program option, 931
floppy disks, booting from,
  409-411
flow-control, 803
footers, 591-592
FOR form files, 626
foreground color, 537
form files, 657
  custom, 659-664
  default, 657-659

report formats, 661
templates, 661
Format (Disk menu) command, 204
Format Always (CP Backup's Options menu) command, 301
FORMAT command, 202-204
destructive versions, 405
formats
date, 742
files, directory-tree display, 306
long, 306
menus, converting, 919
report, 661
time, 742
formatting
backup media, 300-301
disks, 202-210
Notepads DA files, 595-596
fragmentation, 360
fragmented files, 311
analyzing allocation, 319-320
checking for, 312-313
compression techniques, 322-324
ordering methods, 324-328
Free Time (Appointment Scheduler's Appointment menu) command, 706
freeing conventional memory, 928-929
full backups, 269-272
Full DES Encryption (PC Secure's Options menu) command, 465
Full Menus (CP Anti-Virus Express menu) command, 491
Full Online Screen (Modem Telecommunications' Setup menu) command, 811
Full option (PC Tools 8 Install program), 913-914
full-duplex modem, 805
function key commands, 30, 752
customizing, 58-60

F1 (Help), 31-32, 50-51
F2
AppSrch (Menu window), 101
Drive (Central Point Anti-Virus), 487-490, 494
Index (Algebraic Calculator), 752
Index (Clipboard DA), 608
Index (Compress), 315
Index (Databases), 640
Index (DiskEdit), 439
Index (Electronic Mail), 857
Index (FAX Log window), 877
Index (Financial Calculator), 761
Index (Help window), 51
Index (hex editor File Edit screen), 158
Index (Inbox, Outbox, and Sent screens), 847
Index (Macro Editor), 722
Index (Modem Telecommunications DA), 791, 810
Index (Notepads DA), 567
Index (Outlines DA), 616
Index (PC Secure), 463
Index (Programmer Calculator), 772
Index (Scientific Calculator), 780
Index (Sector Edit screen), 160
Index (Send Fax window), 868
Info (View window), 196
Print (SI), 358
Print (System Information), 335
QView (CP Backup), 273
QView (Desktop), 31, 190-192

Reread (DM Directory Maintenance), 243-245
Save (File Editor screen), 156
F3
Disconnect (Commute Chat window), 905
Exit (Algebraic Calculator), 752
Exit (CP Backup), 273
Exit (Central Point Anti-Virus), 488-494
Exit (Desktop applications), 31-32, 52
Exit (DM Directory Maintenance), 243-244, 254
Exit (FAX Log window), 877
Exit (File Editor screen), 156
Exit (FileFix), 382
Exit (Financial Calculator), 761
Exit (Help window), 51
Exit (hex editor File Edit screen), 158
Exit (Macro Editor), 722
Exit (Programmer Calculator), 772
Exit (Scientific Calculator), 780
Exit (Sector Edit screen), 160
Exit (Send Fax window), 868
Exit (SI), 339
Exit (Undelete), 402
F4
Add (Send Fax window), 868
ASCII (hex editor File Edit screen), 158
ASCII (Modem Telecommunications DA), 810, 822
Auto (System Information), 335

Begin (Compress), 315, 330
Clear (Algebraic Calculator), 752
Delete (Electronic Mail), 857
Desel (Desktop applications), 31, 137
Detect (Central Point Anti-Virus), 488, 494-496
Encrypt (PC Secure), 463, 468
Files (View window), 197
First (Databases), 640
Hex (DiskEdit), 439, 448
Inbox (Inbox, Outbox, and Sent screens), 847
Launch (View window), 197
Load (Macro Editor), 722
Load (Modem Telecommunications DA), 791
Load (Notepads DA), 565-567
Load (Outlines DA), 616
Make (DM Directory Maintenance), 243, 247
New (Menu window), 101-102
None (Financial Calculator), 761
None (Scientific Calculator), 780
NxtDriv (CP Backup), 273-276
Search (File Editor screen), 156
Stack (Programmer Calculator), 772
Topics (Help window), 51
View (Undelete), 386
F5
Analyze (Compress), 315-317
Backup (CP Backup), 273, 278

Clean (Central Point Anti-Virus), 488-490, 494-497

Config (System Information), 335

Copy (Desktop applications), 31, 140

Decrypt (PC Secure), 463, 472

Delete (FAX Log window), 877

Edit (Menu window), 101, 106, 117

Edit (Send Fax window), 868

Email (Electronic Mail), 854

Email (Notepads DA), 567

Email (Outlines DA), 616

Erase (Algebraic Calculator), 752

GoBack (Help window), 51

Goto (View window), 197

Hex (hex editor File Edit screen), 158

KERMIT (Modem Telecommunications DA), 830

Outbox (Inbox, Outbox, and Sent screens), 847

Prev (Databases), 640

Rename (DM Directory Maintenance), 243, 248

Replace (File Editor screen), 156

Reply (Electronic Mail), 857

Save (Macro Editor), 722

Save (Modem Telecommunications DA), 791

Save (Sector Edit screen), 160

Send Binary (Modem Telecommunications DA), 820

Stack (Financial Calculator), 761

Stack (Scientific Calculator), 780

Text (DiskEdit), 439-442

Varies (Modem Telecommunications DA), 810

XModem (Modem Telecommunications DA), 825

ZModem (Modem Telecommunications DA), 828

F6

ASCII (Modem Telecommunications DA), 810, 823

Config (Desktop applications), 95

Config (Menu window), 101

CPU (System Information), 335

Data (Programmer Calculator), 772

Data (Scientific Calculator), 780

Delete (DM Directory Maintenance), 243, 248

Delete (Send Fax window), 868

Dir (DiskEdit), 439

Display (Desktop applications), 31, 44, 64, 254

Edit (Modem Telecommunications DA), 791

Find (Clipboard DA), 608

Find (Financial Calculator), 761

Find (Macro Editor), 722

Find (Notepads DA), 567, 585

Find (Outlines DA), 616

Immune (Central Point Anti-Virus), 494, 498

Next (Databases), 641

Print (Help window), 51
Restore (CP Backup), 273, 285
Search (FAX Log window), 877
Sector (hex editor File Edit screen), 158
Select (File Editor screen), 156
Sent (Inbox, Outbox, and Sent screens), 847
Technique (Compress), 315, 322
Unselect (Undelete), 395
Viewer (View window), 197
F7
Again (Notepads DA), 567, 584
Again (Outlines DA), 616
Cut (File Editor screen), 156
Cut (Menu window), 101, 106, 117-118
Edit (hex editor File Edit screen), 158
FAT (DiskEdit), 439
Device (CP Backup), 273, 288
Dial (Modem Telecommunications DA), 791
Disk (SI), 355
Disk (System Information), 335
f-key (Financial Calculator), 761
f-key (Scientific Calculator), 780
Find (Undelete), 387
KERMIT (Modem Telecommunications DA), 831
KeyNam (Macro Editor), 722
LitKey, 114
Locate (Desktop applications), 31

Locate (Desktop), 173
Log (Central Point Anti-Virus), 488, 494, 508
Methods (Compress), 315, 324
Prev (Help window), 51
Prune/Graft (DM Directory Maintenance), 243, 251
Read (Electronic Mail), 856
Read (Inbox, Outbox, and Sent screens), 847
Receive Binary (Modem Telecommunications DA), 820
Search (Databases), 641
Search (View window), 198
Send (Send Fax window), 868
Tree (Undelete), 389
Varies (Modem Telecommunications DA), 810
XModem (Modem Telecommunications DA), 827
ZModem (Modem Telecommunications DA), 829
F8
Active (Macro Editor), 722
ASC/hx (Sector Edit screen), 160
Chklog (Fax Telecommunications), 876
Chklog (Send Fax window), 868
Copy (File Editor screen), 156
Copy (Menu window), 101, 118
Create (Electronic Mail), 852
Create (Inbox, Outbox, and Sent screens), 847
DirOrdr (Compress), 315, 326

Express (Central Point Anti-Virus), 494

Files (DM Directory Maintenance), 243-244

g-key (Scientific Calculator), 780

g-key set, 761

Hangup (Modem Telecommunications DA), 811, 819

Keywrd, 110-111, 115

Manual (Modem Telecommunications DA), 791, 818

Menus (Central Point Anti-Virus), 488-491

New (Databases), 641

Next (Electronic Mail), 857

Next (Help window), 51

Partn (DiskEdit), 439

Setup (CP Backup), 273, 288

Soft (System Information), 335, 346

Spell (Notepads DA), 567, 582

Spell (Outlines DA), 616

Undel (Undelete), 396

Zoom (Desktop applications), 31, 40

Zoom/Unzoom (View window), 190, 198

F9

Boot (DiskEdit), 439

Compare (CP Backup), 273, 283

Copy (DM Directory Maintenance), 243, 249

Hard (SI), 347

Hard (System Information), 335

List (Central Point Anti-Virus), 488, 494, 508

Manuals (Help window), 51

Paste (File Editor screen), 156

Paste (Menu window), 101, 118

PrvFle (View window), 198

Select (Desktop applications), 31, 44

Sort (Compress), 315, 328

Switch (Algebraic Calculator), 752

Switch (Clipboard DA), 608

Switch (Databases), 641

Switch (Electronic Mail), 857

Switch (FAX Log window), 877

Switch (Financial Calculator), 761

Switch (Inbox, Outbox, and Sent screens), 847

Switch (Macro Editor), 722

Switch (Modem Telecommunications DA), 791, 811

Switch (Notepads DA), 567

Switch (Outlines DA), 616

Switch (Programmer Calculator), 772

Switch (Send Fax window), 868

F10

Bell (Commute Chat window), 901

Desktop (Menu window), 101

Menu (Central Point Anti-Virus), 494

Menu (Compress), 315

Menu (CP Backup), 273

Menu (Databases), 641

Menu (Desktop applications), 31, 83-85, 91, 101

Menu (DiskEdit), 439

Menu (DM Directory Maintenance), 243

Menu (Modem Telecommunications DA), 791, 811

Menu (System Information), 335
NextFle (View window), 198
PullDn (Algebraic Calculator), 752
PullDn (Clipboard DA), 608
PullDn (Electronic Mail), 857
PullDn (FAX Log window), 877
PullDn (Financial Calculator), 761
PullDn (Inbox, Outbox, and Sent screens), 847
PullDn (Macro Editor), 722
PullDn (Notepads DA), 567
PullDn (Outlines DA), 616
PullDn (Scientific Calculator), 780
PullDn (Send Fax window), 868
Show (File Editor screen), 156
Future Value (FV) register, 770

G

g-prefix keyboard keys
Financial Calculator, 765-766
Scientific Calculator, 783-784
General Information window (SI), 336
Get Files from Other PC (Commute Session Manager) command button, 899
Give Control List dialog box, 889
give-control lists, 889-891
give-control PCs, 886
applications
executing, 895-898
starting, 896-897
calls, 894-895
Go To dialog box, 575
Go to Directory (FileFind's File menu) command, 176

Goto (Notepads' Edit menu) command, 575
Goto Record (Desktop Accessories' Search menu) command, 657
grafting directories, 239-240, 250-251
grayed out commands, 267
Groups (Appointment Scheduler's File menu) command, 694-696
Groups (FileFind's Search menu) command, 177
guarding macros, 720

H

half-duplex modem, 805
Hangup Phone (Modem Telecommunications' Actions menu) command, 819
hard disks
full backups, 269-272
map blocks, 321
partitions, 349
speed, testing, 355-356
viruses, checking for, 519-522
Hardware Interrupt Information dialog box, 347
hardware interrupts, 347
Hayes-compatible modems, 815-817
Autodial, 841-843
Header/Footer (Notepads' Controls menu) command, 591
headers, 591-592
database files, 371
dBASE files, repairing, 376-378
headlines
collapsing, 620-622
creating, 617-618
expanding, 622
promoting and demoting, 618-620
heads, parking, 202

Help (Commute Session Manager) command button, 899
help
    context-sensitive, 50-51
    Desktop Accessories, 547-550
Help menu commands, 48-49
Hex (DiskEdit's View menu) command, 448
Hex Edit (Change submenu) command, 157
Hex Editor, 157-161, 448
Hex mode, 442
hexadecimal area, 159
hexadecimal master keys, 462
hexadecimal numbers, 553-554, 772
    searching for, 187, 223-225
Hidden (PC Secure's Options menu) command, 467
hidden attribute bit, 161
hidden files, unmovable, 327-328
Hide All Windows (Windows menu) command, 40, 85
Hide Current Record (Desktop Accessories' Edit menu) command, 647-648
hiding
    calculator keypad, 754
    Desktop windows, 85
    encrypted files, 467
    records, 647-648
    View window, 35
    windows, 40-41
high memory, 26, 351
history files, backups, 271, 280
    saving, 301-302
    selecting, 281-283
Home key
    Compress File Allocation Analysis, 320
    CP Backup, 277
    Desktop applications, 42
    File Editor screen, 155
    Sector Edit screen, 160
horizontal menu bars, see menu bars

Hotkey dialog box, 552
Hotkey Selection (Desktop Accessories' Utilities menu) command, 552
hotkeys, 24, 63
    Desktop Accessories, 551-552
    editing, 75
    program groups, 103
HP-11C Owner's Handbook and Problem Solving Guide, 779
HP-12C Owner's Handbook and Problem Solving Guide, 760
HP-16C Computer Scientist Owner's Handbook, 772
HPLJF.PRO Macro Editor file, 736
hypertext links, 50-51

I

I/O ports line SI dialog box, 339-340
IBM extended ASCII character set, 822
icons
    drives, listing, 348
    program group, 93
    program item, 92
IDs, user, 799-800
Immunization (CP Anti-Virus' Scan menu) command, 498
Immunization Exceptions (CP Anti-Virus' Configure menu) command, 500
Immunization Exceptions dialog box, 500
immunizing files, 498-500
imploding files, 144
Import Direct Access (Menu window File menu) command, 119
importing Direct Access Version 5 menus, 119
Inbox window (electronic mail), 846

Include/Exclude Files (CP
Backup Selection options
menu) command, 303-304
Include/Exclude Files dialog
box, 303-304
increments, 684
indenting, auto, 572-573
Index (Help menu) command,
49, 51
index files (R:BASE), 372
Infection Report dialog box,
507-508
infection reports, 507-508
Information (File menu)
command, 66
Verify, 148
Ins key
Dual Lists (Desktop
applications), 31, 80
Ins (Insert mode) key, 75
Insert (FAX Log window), 877
Insert File (Notepads' Edit
menu) command, 577
Insert mode, 75, 576, 638
Install program, 914
directories, 915
drives, 915
executing, 911-919
options
/? (display command-line
options), 930
/BPD:n (generate beep),
930
/BPF:n (generate beep/
sound level), 930
Custom, 913-914
/DISKREQ, 931
/FL (create master floppy),
931
Full, 913-914
Laptop, 913-914
/LIMIT:n (limit bytes), 931
Minimal, 913-914
/UNINSTALL, 931
/VIDEO (video/mouse
options), 931

installing
Desktop, 911
Desktop Accessories, 526-529
VSafe and VWatch programs,
514
Intel Connection CoProcessor
fax board, 911
Interest Rate (i) register, 770
internal documentation, scripts,
832
interrupt request line (IRQ), 347
interrupts
hardware, 347
software, 345-346
IRQ (interrupt request line), 347

J-K

KERMIT file-transfer protocol,
820-821, 830-832
KERMIT, files
receiving, 831
sending, 830-831
KERMIT (Modem
Telecommunications)
command
Receive menu, 831-832
Send menu, 830-832
Key Input dialog box, 469, 471
Keyboard (Help menu)
command, 49
keyboard macros, 719, 724-726
Keyboard Options dialog box,
925
keyboard shortcuts
all Desktop applications,
532-533
Alt+Esc (Task Switcher), 120
Alt+F4 (Close) (Desktop
applications), 52
Alt+space bar
Menu (DiskEdit), 439
System Control (Desktop
applications), 38, 536
System Control (Notepads
DA), 567

Alt+Tab (next task) (Task Switcher), 120
Clipboard DA, 608-609
Compress, 315
creating for program items, 114-116
Ctrl+Alt+Del (boot), 219, 411
Ctrl+Alt+drive letter (dual-list display), 81
Ctrl+Del (Clipboard Copy), 551
Ctrl+drive letter
    change dual-list display drive, 81
    Read Disk (Desktop applications), 36
Ctrl+Enter (Open File) (Menu window), 94
Ctrl+Esc
    Desktop, 24, 52
    Switch (Electronic Mail), 857
    Switch (Modem Telecommunications DA), 791, 811
    Switch (Notepads DA), 567
Ctrl+F2 (Speed Search), 68
Ctrl+Ins (Clipboard Paste), 551
Ctrl+O (Screen Autodial), 551
Ctrl+space bar (Desktop Accessories), 551
Desktop applications (table), 31-32
File Editor, 156
hex editor File Edit screen, 158
hotkeys, 24, 63
    Desktop Accessories, 551-552
    editing, 75
    program groups, 103
Sector Edit screen, 160
Shift+6 (caret), 75
Shift+Tab (moving between windows), 35

View window, 196-198
    see also cursor-movement keys; function-key commands
Keyboard/Mouse line (SI dialog box), 340-341
keyboards
    alternate, 813-814
    delay, 925
    primary keys, 781-782
    rate, 925
    redefining, 720
keypads
    Calculator, 753
    Programmers Calculator, 774-777
    Scientific Calculator, 780-784
keys
    * (Expand Branch) (Tree window), 232
    Alt, 29, 567
        Menu (Modem Telecommunications DA), 791, 811
    cursor-movement
        Browse mode, 635
        CP Backup, 277
        Desktop window, 41-42
        Edit mode, 637
        File Editor screen, 155
        Notepads DA, 574-575
        Sector Edit screen, 160
        tab ruler, 588
        View window, 194-196
    Del (One List), 81
    Esc
        Cancel (PC Secure), 463
        Exit (Desktop applications), 52
        Exit (Help window), 51
        Pauses (Central Point Anti-Virus), 488, 494
    function, see function-key commands
    Ins
        Dual List, 80
        Insert mode, 75

macro, 723-727
master, 461-463
    disabling, 468
one per session, 466
operators, 754
Tab, 35
keystroke codes
    Accessories, keyboard
        macros, 724-726
    adding, 729
    supported, 720
Keyword List dialog box,
    110-112
keywords, 109-112
    <DelayN>, 115
    <Dir\>, 111
    <Filename>, 111
    <NL>, 115
    <Path>, 115
    <Typein>, 115-116

L

labels, renaming disk volumes,
    212
LAN (local area network), 939
LAN Server List dialog box, 887
Laptop option (PC Tools 8
    Install program), 913-914
Last Action panel (CP Anti-
    Virus), 493
launching files, 115, 137-139
    from Menu window, 94-95
learn mode, 720
    deactivating, 730
    macros, recording, 729-732
Legend box (Compress
    window), 315
/LIMIT:n (limit bytes) Install
    program option, 931
line feeds, 803-804
line status, 811
linking macros, 741-742
list boxes, 46
List Filter (Display Options
    submenu) command, 66

<ListFile> keyword, 111
listing
    files, 34
        Undelete File window,
            385-386
    hardware interrupts, 347
    icons, drives, 348
    memory addresses, 352
    PC Tools 8 options, 911
lists
    call, private, 885-888
    give-control, 889-890
    To-Do, 674
Load Form dialog box, 660
Load Pull-downs command
    Configure menu, 27, 71
    Special menu, 28
Load Setup (CP Backup's File
    menu) command, 307
Load Setup File dialog box, 307
loading
    Appointment Scheduler files,
        675-679
    database files, 641-642
    new or existing phone
        directories, 792-794
    Notepad files, 565-566,
        745-746
    Version 6- or Version 7-
        compatible pull-down
        menus, 71-72
    Windows Scheduler, 918
local area network (LAN), 939
Local Tree (Tree submenu)
    command, 233
Locate (File menu) command,
    173
Located Files window, 175
lock step, 896
logging fax transmissions,
    875-878
Logical Drive Information dialog
    box, 348
logical drives, 275
logical fields, 630
    selection criteria, 648-650

long format, 306
Long Format (CP Backup's Display options submenu) command, 306
Look at Your PC (Commute Session Manager) command buttons, 898
lost clusters, 312-313
low-level formatting, 429-431

M

Macro Editor, 720
  files, 736
Macro Editor (Desktop Accessories' main menu) command, 529
Macro Editor DA, 526
  window size, 537
Macro Editor window, 721-722
macro key, 723-727
Macro/Clipboard Playback Delay dialog box, 612-613, 734
macros, 692
  active, 741
  Appointment Scheduler, 746-747
  defining, 720
  files
    activating, 732-734
    deactivating, 732-734
  fill-in-the-blank, 743-744
  fixed-length, 743
  guarding, 720
  keyboard, 719
  linking, 741-742
  PANA.PRO Macro Editor File, 737
  pausing, 742-743
  playback delay, 734
  printers, controlling, 735-740
  recording, 731
    learn mode, 729-732
  typing, 728-734
  variable-length, 743-744

Macros Active dialog box, 732-733, 738
Mail Directories (Desktop's Setup menu) command, 851
Mail Service (Desktop's Setup menu) command, 848
Main Headline Only (Outlines' Headlines menu) comm, 621
Main program group, 98
Make (Appointment Scheduler) command
  Appointment menu, 687
  To-Do menu, 708
Make Appointment dialog box, 744-746
Make Directory (DM Directory Maintenance Directory menu) command, 247
Make Directory dialog box, 247
Make System Disk (Disk menu) command, 206, 211
Manager window (Central Point Commute), 898-905
manual file recovery, 397-399
Manual (Modem Telecommunications Actions menu) command
Manual Call dialog box, 893
Manual Subdirectory Inclusion (CP Backup Selection options menu) command, 302-303
Map of Object (DiskEdit's Info menu) command, 443, 451
mapping, 930
  disks, 361-362
  files, 360-361
  memory, 363
  objects, 449-451
Maps (Tools menu) command, 360
margins, 590-591
Mark Block command
  DiskEdit's Edit menu, 452
  Notepads' Edit menu, 578
mark parity method, 801

marking
    bad sectors, 222-223
    blocks of text, 578-579
    objects, 451-452
Master Key dialog box, 461
master keys, 461
    disabling, 468
    entering, 461-463
Maximize (Desktop Accessories'
    System Control menu)
    command, 40, 540
maximizing windows, 39-40, 540
MCI Mail, 845-852
    user ID and password, 799
MCI.SCR. script file, 839
Media Format (CP Backup's
    Options menu) command, 300
Media Format dialog box, 300
memory, 70
    addresses, listing, 352
    conventional, 350-352
        freeing, 928-929
    displaying information,
        350-354, 456
    expanded, 350-354
    extended, 350-353
    high, 26, 351
    mapping, 363
    registers, 756-757, 784-785
    requirements, 910
    reserved, 26, 351
    unloading
        Desktop Accessories,
            555-556
        VSafe program, 519
        VWatch program, 518
    upper, 26, 312, 351
    VSafe and VWatch program
        requirements, 513-514
Memory Information (MI), 333
Memory Manager programs, 940
Memory panel (SI dialog box),
    336, 350
memory-resident mode, 910
menu bars, 26
    CP Anti-Virus, 492

Desktop Accessories, 531
    SI window, 351, 335
Menu Configuration Options
    dialog box, 104
Menu Editor dialog box, 72-78
Menu Editor Options dialog box,
    72-73, 78
Menu Options Configuration
    dialog box, 95
Menu window, 33
    building system, 96-100
    configuring, 95
    displaying, 82-83, 90-91
    elements, 92-94
    function-key commands,
        100-102
    importing Direct Access
        Version 5 menus, 119
    launching files with
        programs, 94-95
    program groups, adding and
        editing, 102-106
    program items
        adding and editing, 107-112
        moving within and
            between program groups,
            117-118
    saving changes, 118
Menu Window (Windows menu)
    command, 40, 82, 91
Menu window only mode, 95
menus, 27-33, 914
    cascading, 93
    commands, moving and
        adding, 73-74
    Configure, 56-58, 920
    Direct Access Version 5,
        importing into Menu
        window, 119
    Display Options submenu, 62
    DOS commands, adding,
        76-77
    editing, 72-76
    Express (Central Point Anti-
        Virus), 486-488
    formats, converting, 919

main, 528
PC Shell Applications, 911
pull-down, 532
saving schemes, 77-78
short, 72
switching to Version 6- or
Version 7-compatible, 71-72
message bars, 27
CP Anti-Virus, 494
Desktop Accessories, 531
message boxes, 547
message dialog boxes, 42-43
messages
Enter an autoupdate time in
seconds or 0 to disable, 878
ERROR- Invalid path or path
not found, 561
fax, sending, 874-875
network virus notification,
509-510
note: Press [OK] to load
filename, 746
note: Press [OK] to run
program, 744
Processing FAX submission
now... please wait..., 874
Sector not found, 426, 429
MI (Memory Information), 333
MI.COM program, 363-364
Minimal option (PC Tools 8
Install program), 913-914
minus sign (–), 229
MIRROR command, 404-405
Mirror program, 404-408, 914
Mirror Startup program, 928
Mirror Used? dialog box, 413
mirror-image files
recovering from accidental
formats, 412-415
saving system information to,
405-407
MIRROR.FIL file, 405-407
Modem List dialog box, 884
Modem Setup dialog box,
807-808

Modem Telecommunications DA
connecting to other
computers, 807-816
files, sending and receiving,
819-831
phone directories
loading new or existing,
792-794
managing, 795-807
scripts, 831-840
window
elements, 791-792
opening, 790
Modem Telecommunications
File Load dialog box, 794
modems, 790
configuring, 807-808
full- and half-duplex, 805
Hayes-compatible, 815-817
Autodial, 841-843
receiving telephone calls, 816
selecting, 884
modes
386 Enhanced, 940
Auto View, 440
autoanswer, 816
Browse, 632
cursor-movement keys,
635
printing databases, 664-665
toggling between Edit and
Browse, 633
compressed, printing, 739
dual-list display, 81
Edit, 633
cursor-movement keys,
637
printing databases, 666-668
toggling between Browse
mode, 633
Enhanced, 934
Expert, 468
Express, 266-267
turning off, 272
Hex, 442

Insert, 75, 576, 638
learn, 720
memory-resident, 910
Menu window only, 95
overtype, 576, 638
Read Only, 436
Real, 934
Standard, 934
test, 75-76
Text, 442
Modify Attributes (DM Directory Maintenance Directory menu) command, 252
Modify Attributes dialog box, 252
Modify Data (Desktop Accessories' File menu) command, 634-638
Modify Directory Attributes dialog box, 241-242
monitoring fax transmissions, 878
More File Information dialog box, 66
mouse, 910
    clicking, 27
    configuring, 924
    drag-and-drop, 32-33
Mouse Options dialog box, 924
Move (Desktop Accessories' System Control menu) command, 538
Move (File menu) command, 142
Move (System Control menu) command, 38
moving
    between windows, 35
    commands within menu schemes, 73-74
    Desktop Accessories application windows, 538
    directories, 239-241, 250-251
    files, 139-142
        with drag-and-drop, 33
    program items, 117-118
    text, 577-581

windows, 37-38
    within windows, 41-42
multiple files, selecting, 136

N

Name Backup Set dialog box, 269-270, 279
National Holiday Settings (Appointment Scheduler's Controls menu) command, 685
navigating windows (Appointment Scheduler), 679-681
Near Letter Quality (NLQ), 738
Netware 386 file protection, 383
Network Filters dialog box, 182-183
Network line (SI dialog box), 342-345
Network Messages dialog box, 509-510
Network Rights (DM Directory Maintenance's Directory menu) command, 253
networks
    directories, managing, 242-254
    files, recovering, 400-401
    performance testing, 357
    rights, displaying, 253
    search filters, 182-183
    virus notification messages, 509-510
New Menu Item (File menu) command, 107
New Menu Item dialog box, 102, 107
New To-Do Entry dialog box, 708
Next (Appointment Scheduler's Appointment menu) command, 705
<NL> keyword, 111, 115
NLQ (Near Letter Quality)), 738
No Viewable Records dialog box, 645

normal resolution, 871
note: Press [OK] to load
  filename message, 746
note: Press [OK] to run program
  message, 744
Notepads (Desktop Accessories'
  main menu) command, 529
Notepads DA, 69, 525
  cursor-movement keys,
    574-575
  directories, assigning default,
    562-563
  exiting, 596-597
  files
    assigning default
      extensions, 562
    creating, 563-565
    deleting, 594
    form, 657-664
    headers and footers,
      591-592
    loading, 565-566, 745-746
    page layout, 589-591
    printing, 592-594
    saving, 595-596
  scripts, 832-833
  Spellcheck, 581-583
  tab ruler, 586-589
  text
    auto indent, 572-573
    copying and moving,
      577-581
    displaying control
      characters, 573
    entering, 569-570
    inserting and deleting,
      575-577
    searching for, 584-585
    searching for and
      replacing, 585-586
    wordwrap, 570-572
  window, 852-854
    elements, 566-569
    opening, 560-561
    size, 537
Novell Network, 911, 940

null-modem cables, 818, 884
number bases
  binary, 772
  decimal, 772
  hexadecimal, 772
  octal, 772
Number of Months (n) register,
  769
numbers
  decimal, 554
  hexadecimal, 553-554
    searching disks for,
      223-225
numeric fields, 630

O

Object Information (DiskEdit's
  Info menu) command, 450
Object Information dialog box,
  450-451
objects
  DiskEdit, 440
  displaying and mapping,
    449-451
  marking, copying, and
    pasting, 451-452
octal number base, 772
odd parity method, 801
offset area, 158-159
offsets, 158
on-line screens, 809-813
on-line services, control codes,
  836
One Key (PC Secure's Options
  menu) command, 466
Open (File menu) command, 94,
  138
open systems, bulletin boards,
  799
opening windows
  Appointment Scheduler, 674
  Calculator, 750
  Desktop Accessories,
    529-530, 544

Modem Telecommunications DA, 790
Notepads DA, 560-561
Operating System Information dialog box, 337-338
Operating System line (SI dialog box), 337-338
operators, keys, 754
option buttons, 45
options
  command line (SI), 359
  Desktop (Search Files), 172, 187
  FileFind (Filter), 172
  Install program
    /? (display command-line options), 930
    /BPD:n (generate beep), 930
    /BPF:n (generate beep/ sound level), 930
    /DISKREQ, 931
    /FL (create master floppy), 931
    /LIMIT:n (limit byte), 931
    /UNINSTALL, 931
    /VIDEO (video/mouse options), 931
  listing, 911
  startup, 920-921
Options menu, CP Backup, 294-296
Options Settings dialog box, 501-503
Ordering Methods (Compress' Options menu) command, 324-325
ordering methods for files and directories, 324-328
orientation (View window), 190
originate computer, 817
OUT file extension, 615
Outlines (Desktop Accessories' main menu) command, 529
Outlines DA, 525
  exiting, 623

headlines
  collapsing, 620-622
  creating, 617-618
  expanding, 622
  promoting and demoting, 618-620
printing files, 623
saving files, 623
scripts, 832
versus Notepads DA, 617
window
  elements, 615-617
  size, 537
overriding macros, 741
overtype mode, 576, 638
Overtype Mode (Notepads' Controls menu) command, 576
Overwrite Warning (CP Backup's Options menu) command, 302
Overwrite Warning dialog box, 285-286
overwriting files, 903

P

Pack Database (Desktop Accessories' Edit menu) command, 646-647
packing records, 646-647
Page Header & Footer dialog box, 591-592
Page Layout (Notepads' Controls menu) command, 589
Page Layout dialog box, 589-591
pages, fax
  cover, 873-874
  length, 866
Palette (Color Options screen) command button, 922
PANA.PRO Macro Editor File, 736-737
Paradox
  files, repairing, 373-374
  records, recovering, 373

parameters, 800-802
see also switches
parent
    directories, 561
    groups, 92, 98-100
parity, 801
Park utility, 202
parking heads, 202
Partition Table (DiskEdit's
  Select menu) command, 446
Partition Table Editor, 445-447
Partition Table Information
  dialog box, 349
partition tables, 445
    rebuilding with Emergency
      Disks, 409
    saving backups, 407-408
    viewing and editing, 445-447
    viruses, 519-522
partitions, 349, 407
    extended, 445
Password (Configure menu)
  command, 78-79
Password dialog box, 469
password variable, 834
passwords
    configuration protection,
      78-79
    for Central Point Anti-Virus
      functions, 510-511
    for function key lists, 59
    master keys, disabling, 468
    PC Secure master keys,
      461-466
    program groups, 103
    program items, 109
    user, 799-800
Paste from Clipboard command
  Clipboard's Copy/Paste
    menu, 604
  DiskEdit's Edit menu, 452
Paste Menu Item (File menu)
  command, 118
Paste to Clipboard (Notepads'
  Edit menu) command, 581

pasting, 451-452, 581
    between DOS and
      Accessories programs,
      603-606
    slowing playback, 612-613
<Path> keyword, 110, 115
Pattern Testing Options dialog
  box, 426, 431
pausing
    after exiting programs, 112
    macros, 742-743
Payment (PMT) register, 770
PC Config program 914
    PCCONFIG.PIF, 938
PC Format, 939
    running
      from DOS command line,
        208-210
      from PC Tools Desktop,
        204-208
    versus DOS FORMAT
      command, 203-204
PC Secure utility, 165, 939
    compressing files, 465-466
    decrypting files and
      directories, 472
    deleting original files, 467
    encrypting files, 468-471
      files not to encrypt, 460
      hiding, 467
      types of encryption, 465
    exiting, 473
    keys
      master, disabling, 461-463,
        468
      one per session, 466
    read-only files, 467
    saving configurations, 468
    screen elements, 463-464
    starting, 460-461
      from DOS command line,
        473-474
PC Shell Applications menu, 911
PC Tools
    configuring with CAS fax
      board, 865-867

Desktop, 942
  accessories, 919-928
  activating, 910
  configuring, 919-928
  installing on Novell
    NetWare server, 911
  Install program
    Custom, 913-914
    directory, 915
    drive, 915
    emergency disks, 916-919
    executing, 911-919
    Full, 913-914
    Laptop, 913-914
    Minimal, 913-914
    options, 930-931
  options, listing, 911
  programs
    executing, 910, 939-945
    in Windows, 936-939
  screen elements, 26-27
  starting, 24-25, 920-921
PC Tools Desktop program, 914
PC-Cache program, 914, 941-942
PC-Cache Startup program, 927
PCCONFIG.PIF file, 938
PCFORMAT command, 208-210
PCFORMAT.PIF file, 939
PCs
  connecting, 894
  give-control, 886
    calls, 891-895
  take-control, 886
    calls, 892-894
PCSECURE command, 460
PCSECURE.PIF file, 939
PCSHELL.PIF file, 938
PCTools Desktop program, 938
PCX files, viewing, 171
Percent Completed dialog box,
  480
performance testing networks,
  357
peripherals, protecting, 929
PgDn key, cursor-movement
  Compress File Allocation
    Analysis, 320

CP Backup, 277
Desktop applications, 42
File Editor screen, 155
Sector Edit screen, 160
PgUp key, cursor-movement
  Compress File Allocation
    Analysis, 320
  CP Backup, 277
  Desktop applications, 42
  File Editor screen, 155
  Sector Edit screen, 160
phone directories
  entries, 795-805
    deleting, 806
    dialing phone numbers,
      808-809
    editing, 805-806
    saving, 806-807
  loading new or existing,
    792-794
  managing, 795
phone numbers, 798
  dialing, 808-809
    manually, 814-816
    with Autodial, 841-843
PIF files, 938-939
PkUnzip utility, 143-145
PkZip utility, 143
plain extended memory, 352
plus sign (+), 230
point-and-shoot method of
  selecting commands, 29, 531
ports
  COM, 807-808
  serial, 850
Present Value (PV) register, 770
preset times, 744-747
primary functions, 762, 774, 780
primary keyboard keys
  Financial Calculator, 762-763
  Programmer Calculator,
    774-775
Print (Desktop Accessories' File
  menu) command, 664-668
Print (Appointment Scheduler's
  File menu) command, 712

Print (Clipboard's File menu)
  command, 611
Print (File menu) command
    Print Directory, 168
    Print File, 165-168
Print (Notepads' File menu)
  command, 592
Print (Outlines' File menu)
  command, 623
Print dialog box, 592-593,
  611-612, 664, 712, 758
Print Directory (Print submenu)
  command, 168
Print File (Print submenu)
  command, 165-168
print files, 665
Print Report (Compress'
  Options menu) command, 330
Print Selection dialog box, 666
Print Tree (DM Directory
  Maintenance Volume menu)
  command, 252
Print Tree dialog box, 252
printer-control macros, 735
printers, controlling, 735-740
printing
    Algebraic Calculator tape,
      758-759
    compressed mode, 739
    database files, 664
      from Browse mode,
        664-665
      from Edit mode, 666-668
    directories, 168-169
      trees, 251-252
    files, 165-168, 592-594
    from Clipboard DA, 611-612
    Outlines DA files, 623
    page layout for, 589-591
    reports
      compress operations,
        329-330
      SI, 358
Printing Options dialog box, 358
Private Call List dialog box, 886
processing, end-of-line, 803-804
Processing FAX submission, 874

program close boxes, 26
Program Group Information
  dialog box, 102-106
program groups, 92-94
    adding items, 107
    creating, 102-103
    deleting, 106
    descriptions, adding, 104-106
    Main, 98
    moving program items within
      and between, 117-118
    properties, editing, 106
    searching for programs to
      add, 96-100
Program Item Information dialog
  box, 107-113, 117
program items, 92-94
    adding to groups, 107
    commands, keywords for
      parameters, 109-112
    controlling execution, 116-117
    creating, 97
    deleting, 117
    descriptions, adding, 112
    editing, 117
    file associations, 114
    keyboard shortcuts, creating,
      114-116
    moving within and between
      program groups, 117-118
    passwords, 109
    pausing after exiting, 112
    start-up commands, 108
    start-up directories, 109
    titles, 108
    user prompts, 113-114
Program Scheduler (Tools
  menu) command, 127
Program Scheduler Startup
  program, 914, 928
Program Scheduler window, 128
program-control script
  commands, 837-838
Programmer Calculator
    F-prefix keyboard keys,
      776-777
    keypad, 774-777

primary keyboard keys, 774-775
registers, stack, 777-779
Programmers Calculator (Calculators menu) command, 772
programs
Appointment Scheduler, 673-718
BootSafe, 519-522
Build Emergency Disk, 914
Central Point Anti-Virus, 486-513, 914
Central Point Backup, 914
Central Point Commute, 914
Central Point Software Copy II PC, 212
Compress, 914, 940
copy protected, 212
CPSCHED (Central Point Scheduler), 291-294
Create Emergency Disk, 916-919
Data Monitor, 914, 940-941
Desktop Accessories, 525-557
Direct Access Version 5, 119
Disk Manager (On-Track), 408
DiskEdit, 436-439, 453-457
DiskFix, 369, 422-434, 914, 941
DM Directory Maintenance, 234-235, 242-254
DOS, dialing phone numbers, 843
DriveMap, 914, 929-930
Edisk, 217-219
executing, preset time, 744-745
File Viewer, 914
FileAttr, 163-164
FileCheck, 312-313, 419-422
FileDate, 164
FileFind, 171-189, 914
FileFix, 367-382
Installation, 914
launching files, 115, 137-139
from Menu window, 94-95

Memory Manager, 940
Menus, 914
MI.COM, 363-364
Mirror, 404-408, 914
Park utility, 202
pausing after exiting, 112
PC Config, 914
PC Format, 203-208
PC Secure, 165, 460-474
PC Tools Desktop, 914
PC-Cache, 914, 941-942
PkUnzip utility, 143-145
PkZip utility, 143
Program Scheduler, 914
RAMBoost, 914
recovery, 369
remote-control (Commute), 939
running, 122-124
Scheduler, 125-131, 942-943
searching for, 96-100
SMARTDRV.SYS, 941
SpeedStor (Storage Dimensions), 408
starting, 937
Startup
Anti-Virus TSRs and Options, 927
Commute, 927
Delete Protection, 926
Directory Lock, 926
Disk Light, 926
DriveMap, 927
Fax Driver, 928
Mirror, 928
PC-Cache, 927
Program Scheduler, 928
RAMBoost, 927
Screen Blanker, 926
Setting Password Options, 928
Task Switcher, 928
VSafe, 927
VWatch, 927
Write Protection, 926
startup, configuring, 920

switching between, 124
System Information, 914
Task Switcher, 120-125
terminate-and-stay-resident (TSR), 526-527
TSR Manager, 943-945
Undelete, 383-402, 914
Unformat, 412-419
View, 171, 189-198
viruses, detecting, 301
VSafe, 513-519
VWatch, 513-514, 518
Wipe, 152-153, 475-483
Progress dialog box, 470-471
Promote (Outlines' Headlines menu) command, 619
promoting outline headlines, 618-620
prompts, user, 113-114
properties
    program groups, 103, 106
    program items, 107-109
Properties (File menu) command, 106
PROPTR.PRO Macro Editor file, 736
protecting
    anti-viral protection, 927
    files, 383-384, 513-519
        Delete Sentry program, 383
        Delete Tracker program, 383
        DOS, 383
        encrypting, 164-165
        Netware 386, 383
        VWatch program, 384
    peripherals, 929
protocols
    binary, 820-821
    file-transfer, 820-821
        ASCII, 821-824
        KERMIT, 830-832
        XMODEM, 824-827
        ZMODEM, 827-830
PRT file extension, 594

Prune and Graft (Directory Maintenance submenu) command, 239-240, 251
Prune and Graft dialog box, 251
pruning directories, 239-240, 250-251
pull-down menus, 27-33
    Desktop Accessories, 532
    short, 72
    switching to Version 6- or Version 7- compatible, 71-72
purging Delete Sentry files, 401-402

Q

question mark (?) wild-card character, 67, 136
Quick Encryption, 465
Quick Encryption (PC Secure's Options menu) command, 465
Quick Run (Execution submenu) command, 70
Quick View (File menu) command, 191
quitting
    FileFix, 382
    Undelete, 402

R

R:BASE
    data files, 372
    index files, 372
    repairing files, 372-373
radio buttons, see option buttons
RAM (random-access memory), 910
RAMBoost, 914, 928-929
random-access memory (RAM), 910
RBase Repair Options dialog box, 372

Re-Read Tree (Disk menu) command, 227
Read Mail Now (Electronic Mail's Actions menu) command, 856
Read Mail Schedule (Electronic Mail's Setup menu) command, 859
Read Mail Schedule dialog box, 859
read only attribute bit, 161
Read Only mode, 436
Read-Only (PC Secure's Options menu) command, 467
read-only files, 467
reading Electronic Mail, 855-860
Real mode, 934
Rebuild command, 404
REC record files, 626
Receive dialog box, 827-831
Receive Files from Other PC dialog box, 902-903
receiving
　fax, 875
　files
　　ASCII, 823-824
　　KERMIT, 831
　　telecommunications, 819-840
　　XMODEM, 826-827
record numbers, searching by, 657
recording macros, 731
　learn mode, 729-732
records
　adding to databases, 634-638
　appending, 670-671
　boot, rebuilding, 412-419
　deleting, 645-646
　editing, 638
　exiting from, 639-641
　hiding, 647-648
　packing, 646-647
　Paradox, recovering, 373
　purging, 644-645

selecting, 647-650
transferring, 669-670
undeleting, 645-646
recovering
　directories, 400
　files, 383-402
　　automatically, 396-397
　　create-file method, 399-400
　　manually, 397-399
　　networks, 400-401
　from hard disk disasters, 216-219
　records (Paradox), 373
recovery utilities, 369
redefining keyboards, 720
refreshing directory trees, 227, 245
registers, 777-779
　contents, displaying, 778
　data, 769, 785
　　reviewing, 778
　financial, 769-771
　Financial Calculator, 768-771
　Future Value (FV), 770
　Interest Rate (i), 770
　memory, 756, 784-785
　Number of Months (n), 769
　Payment (PMT), 770
　Present Value (PV), 770
　stack, 768-769, 777-779, 784-785
Registers, Scientific Calculator, 784-785
Relative Performance panel SI dialog box, 336
Relative Performance panel (SI dialog box), 354
remote computers, telecommunications files, 820-831
remote-control programs Commute, 939
Remove (Modem Communications' Edit menu) command, 806

Remove Immunization (CP Anti-Virus' Scan menu) command, 499
Rename (File menu) command, 149-150
Rename Directory (Directory Maintenance submenu) command, 237, 248
Rename Directory dialog box, 248
Rename Volume (Disk menu) command, 212
Rename Volume (DM Directory Maintenance's Volume menu) command, 246-247
renaming
    directories, 237, 247-248
    disk volume labels, 212
    files, 149-150
Repair a Disk (DiskFix Main menu) command, 423-426
Repair Drive window, 424-425
repairing
    disks, 424-426, 941
        manually, 453-456
    files
        database, 371-378
        dBASE, 374-375
        manually, 453-456
        Paradox, 373-374
        R:BASE, 372-373
        selecting, 370-371
        spreadsheets, 379-380
        WordPerfect, 380-382
    headers
        database files, 371
        dBASE files, 376-378
Repeat Search (DiskEdit's Tools menu) command, 454
Replace (Notepads' Search menu) command, 585
report formats, 661
Report Options dialog box, 298
Reporting (CP Backup's Options menu) command, 298

Reporting Options dialog box, 358
reports
    backup, 298-299
    compress operations, 329-330
    infection, 507-508
    sending to files, 358
    SI, printing, 358
requirements, memory, 910
Reread Tree (DM Directory Maintenance's Volume menu) command, 245
reserved memory, 26, 351
Reset Current Directory (Tree submenu) command, 234
Resize box, 38-39, 534, 539-540
resize boxes, 33
resizing
    Desktop Accessories application windows, 539-540
    windows, 38-39
resolution, 871
Restore (Desktop Accessories' System Control menu) command, 540
Restore (System Control menu) command, 40
restoring
    backup data, 280-286, 302
    partition tables/boot sectors, 521
    windows, 40
Return to Startup Directory (Tree submenu) command, 234
returns, carriage, 803-804
Reverse Polish Notation (RPN), 767-768
Revitalize a Disk (DiskFix Main menu) command, 423, 429-431
Revitalize a Disk disk map, 430-431
rights, network, 253
root directories, 34, 225
    rebuilding, 412-419
    saving backups, 405-407

RPN (Reverse Polish Notation), 767-768
RTF (Rich Text Format) files, 178
ruler, tab, 586-589
Run DOS Command (File menu) command, 86
Run Script (Modem Telecommunications' Actions menu) command, 833
Run Script dialog box, 833

S

SatisFAXtion fax board, 911
Save (Appointment Scheduler's File menu) command, 717
Save (Modem Communications' File menu) command, 806-807
Save (Notepads' File menu) command, 595
Save as Default (CP Backup's File menu) command, 291, 306
Save Configuration (Configure menu) command, 56
Save File to Disk dialog box, 807, 823, 827
Save History (CP Backup's Options menu) command, 301-302
Save Setup (Desktop Accessories' Controls menu) command, 541-542
Save Setup (Notepads' Controls menu) command, 596
Save Setup As (CP Backup's File menu) command, 307
Save Setup File dialog box, 307
saving
    Appointment Scheduler files, 717
    autosave, 596
    backups
        partition tables, boot sectors, and CMOS data, 407-408
        history files, 301-302

CP Backup configuration settings, 291, 306
databases, 632-633
Desktop Accessories windows settings, 541-542
FATs and root directories, 405-407
field entries, 639
menu schemes, 77-78
Menu window changes, 118
Notepads DA files, 595-596
Outlines DA files, 623
partition tables, 520
PC Secure configurations, 468
phone directory entries, 806-807
scanning disk surfaces, 426-429
Schedule Anti-Virus Scanning (Scheduler's Configure menu) command, 506-507
Schedule Backups (CP Backup's Action menu) command, 291-292
Schedule Layouts (Appointment Scheduler's Controls menu) command, 677
Schedule or Edit an Event dialog box, 128-130, 292, 506-507
Scheduled Print dialog box, 716
Scheduler, 125-126, 942-943
    Central Point Anti-Virus, running, 505-507
    changing schedules, 130
    command buttons, 943
    configuring to run at startup, 126-127
    customizing, 130-131
    preparing for scheduled events, 131
    scheduling events, 127-130
    Windows, loading, 918
Scheduler Layouts dialog box, 678
Scheduler Options dialog box, 131, 292
scheduling backups, 291-294

Scheme (Color Options screen)
    command button, 922
Scientific Calculator, 779-785
    keyboard, 780-784
    keypad
        f-prefix keyboard keys,
            782-783
        g-prefix keyboard keys,
            783-784
    Registers, 784-785
Scientific Calculator (Calculator
    menu) command, 779
screen
    color, 921-923
    display, configuring, 923-924
Screen Blanker (Display Options
    submenu) command, 63
Screen Blanker Startup
    program, 926
Screen Size (Display Options
    submenu) command, 62-63
screens
    CP Backup Welcome, 261
    Desktop, customizing display,
        62-64
    Directory Maintenance
        elements, 242-243
    File Editor, 154-156
    hex editor File Edit, 157-161
    moving within, 41-42
    on-line, 809-813
    PC Secure utility elements,
        463-464
    PC Tools Desktop elements,
        36
    PC Tools elements, 26-27
    Sector Edit, 159-161
script commands, 833
    branching, 837-838
    communications, 835-837
    display, 838-839
    program-control, 837-838
    variable-manipulation, 834
script files, 799
    Central Point Software,
        839-840
    creating, 832-833

scripts, 727
    automating
        telecommunications,
            831-840
scroll arrows, 34
scroll bars, 27, 34, 534
scroll boxes, 34
scrolling
    Desktop Accessories
        windows, 542-543
    View window, 190
Search Attributes dialog box,
    183
Search Disk (Disk menu)
    command, 223-225
Search (DiskEdit's Tools menu)
    command, 453-454
Search Files (FileFind's File
    menu) command, 187
Search Files option (Desktop),
    172, 187
search filters, 180-181
    on networks, 182-183
    stand-alone systems, 181-182
Search Filters dialog box,
    181-182
search groups, 174, 179-180
    creating, 178
        by file name, 174
    deleting entries, 179
    editing entries, 178-179
    FileFind, 172
    locating deleted files, 390-391
    predefined, 176-180
Search Groups dialog box, 177
Search Sort Field dialog box, 655
search strings, 187, 223, 388, 655
searches
    canceling, 389
    database files, 654-657
    deleted files
        locating by file name,
            387-389
        locating by predefined
            search groups, 390-391
    disks, 223-225

fields, 654-656
FileFind directories, 172
files, 171-172
  by file name, 174-176
  duplicate names, 185-187
  excluding files from
    search, 174
  on hard disks, 172-187
  selecting drives and
    directories for, 183-185
  with filters, 180-183
  with predefined search
    groups, 176-180
for programs, 96-100
for text, 187-189, 584-586
for viruses, 488-489, 496
  and cleaning, 490
  choosing objects to scan,
    494-496
  in partition tables, 520
  on different drives, 490-491
hexadecmal numbers, 187
with speed search, 68
Sector Edit screen, 159-161
sectors, 158
  bad, 203
    marking, 222-223
  boot
    checking for viruses at
      startup, 519-522
    rebuilding with Emergency
      Disks, 409
    saving backups, 407-408
  files, 360
Secure (File menu) command,
  165
Secure Options (Configure
  menu) command, 58
Select All (File menu) command,
  136-137
Select All Records (Desktop
  Accessories' Edit menu)
  command, 648-654
Select Directory (DiskEdit's
  View menu) command, 454
Select Drives/Directory dialog
  box, 184-185

Select File to Fix dialog box, 370
Select Filter (Display Options
  submenu) command, 44,
  136-137
Select Format Options dialog
  box, 205-207
Select New Drive (CP Anti-Virus'
  Express menu) command, 490
Select Records (Desktop
  Accessories' Edit menu)
  command, 648-654, 666
Select Records dialog box, 648
selected directories, 227
Selected Drives (FileFind's
  Search menu) command, 184
selected files, versus current
  files, 134-135
selecting
  COM Port, 884-885
  files, 872-873
    for repair, 370-371
    recovering, 394-395
  modems, 884
  records, 647-648
  rows, 336
  startup options, 920-921
selection bar, 569
selection criteria, 648-650
selection lists, changing, 303-304
Selection options (CP Backup's
  Options menu) command
  Attribute Exclusions, 304-305
  Date Range Selection, 305
  Include/Exclude Files, 303-304
  Manual Subdirectory
    Inclusion, 302-303
selective backups
  CP Backup window elements,
    272-274
  source drives, selecting,
    274-275
  specific directories, 276-278
  specific files, 278
  starting, 278-280
Send ASCII dialog box, 822
Send dialog box, 826-831

Send Fax window, 868-869
Send Files to Other PC
    (Commute Session Manager)
    command button, 899
Send Files to Other PC dialog
    box, 904
Send Kermit dialog box, 830
Send Mail Schedule (Electronic
    Mail Setup menu) command,
    860
Send Mail Schedule dialog box,
    860
Send Network Messages To
    (CP Anti-Virus' Configure
    menu) command, 509
Send XMODEM dialog box, 825
Send Zmodem dialog box, 828
sending
    electronic mail, 854-855
        automatically, 860-861
    fax files, 869-875
    files, 869-875
        ASCII, 822-823
        KERMIT, 830-831
        telecommunications,
            819-840
        XMODEM, 825-826
        ZMODEM, 828-829
        see also transmission
Sent From (Configure menu)
    command, 870
serial numbers, disk volumes,
    208
serial ports, 850
sessions, ending (Central Point
    Commute), 905
Set Options (CP Anti-Virus'
    Options menu) command, 501
Set Playback Delay (Clipboard's
    Copy/Paste menu) command,
    612
Setting Password Options
    Startup program, 928
setup files, 306-307
shaking hands, 816
short pull-down menus, 72

Show Files (DM Directory
    Maintenance's Directory
    menu) command, 244
Show Files in Each Map Block
    (Compress' Analysis menu)
    command, 321
Show Level (Outlines' Headlines
    menu) command, 621
shrinking files, 144
SI command, 334
SI dialog box, 335-336
    CMOS line, 341-342
    Computer panel
        selecting rows, 336
    Conventional, 351
    Drive Summary line, 348
    I/O ports line, 339-340
    Keyboard/Mouse line, 340-341
    Memory panel, 336, 350
    Network line, 342-345
    Operating System
        Information, 337
    Operating System line,
        337-338
    Relative Performance panel,
        336, 354
    System Type line, 336-337
    Video Adapter line, 338-339
SI (System Information), 333,
938
    command line options, 359
    displaying, 334-347
    General Information window,
        336
    reports, printing, 358
    running from DOS command
        line, 359
SI.PIF file, 938
signals, carrier, 875
Single List Display (Windows
    menu) command, 81
single-user computer, 910
Size (Desktop Accessories'
    System Control menu)
    command, 539
Size (System Control menu)
    command, 39

smart alarms, 744-747
SMARTDRV.SYS program, 941
Software Interrupt Information
  dialog box, 346
software interrupts, 345-346
Software Interrupts (System
  menu) command, 346
software pacing, *see* XON/XOFF
  flow control
Sort Database (Desktop
  Accessories' Edit menu)
  command, 652-653, 666
Sort Directory (Disk menu)
  command, 254-256
Sort Field Select dialog box, 652
sort fields, 639, 651-653
Sort Options (CP Backup's
  Display options submenu)
  command, 306
Sort Options dialog box, 306
sorting
    directories, 328-329
    files, 254-256
        database, 651-653
        in directory trees, 306
        in File window, 64-65
source databases, 669
source drives, 260
    selecting, 274-275
space
    parity, 801
    storage, directory branchs,
    244-245
Special Appointment Settings
  dialog box, 689
SpectraFax fax board, 911
speed
    backup, changing, 289-290
    CPU, testing, 355
    hard disks, testing, 355-356
Speed (Configure menu)
  command, 58
Speed Search (Speed submenu)
  command, 68
Speed Search dialog box, 68
SpeedStor (Storage Dimensions)
  program, 408

Spellcheck, 581-583
Split Screen (DiskEdit's View
  menu) command, 450
spreadsheets
    file viewers, 193
    files, repairing, 379-380
stack registers, 768-769, 777-779,
784-785
stand-alone systems, 910
    search filters, 181-182
Standard mode, 934
Start (FileFind's Search menu)
  command, 175
Start Backup (CP Backup's
  Action menu) command, 278
start bits, 802
Start Compare (CP Backup's
  Action menu) command, 283
Start Restore (CP Backup's
  Action menu) command, 285
start-up commands, 108
start-up directories, 109
start-up switches, viewing, 909
starting
    applications, 896-897, 937
    BootSafe program, 521-522
    Central Point Anti-Virus,
    512-513
    Central Point Anti-Virus
    Express, 486, 497
    Central Point Backup,
    260-269, 308-310
    Central Point Commute, 882
    Compress, 314-317
    DiskEdit utility, 436-439, 457
    DiskFix utility, 433-434
    FileFind utility, 172-173
    FileFix, 370
    PC Secure utility, 460-461,
    473-474
    PC Tools, 24-25
    selective backups, 278-280
    Undelete utility, 384
    VSafe program, 516-517
    VWatch program, 518
    Windows, 934-935
    Wipe program, 481-483

startup
  options, 920-921
  programs
    Anti-Virus TSRs and
      Options, 927
    Commute, 927
    configuring, 920
    Delete Protection, 926
    Directory Lock, 926
    Disk Light, 926
    DriveMap, 927
    Fax Driver, 928
    Mirror, 928
    PC-Cache, 927
    Program Scheduler, 928
    RAMBoost, 927
    Screen Blanker, 926
    Setting Password Options,
      928
    Task Switcher, 928
    VSafe, 927
    VWatch, 927
    Write Protection, 926
  Scheduler, configuring,
    126-127
  Task Switcher, configuring,
    120-122
  viruses, 519-522
Startup First Level (Tree
  submenu) command, 233
Startup Programs (Configure
  menu) command, 58, 126
status bar, 811-813
Status box (Compress window),
  315
status lines, 34
stop bits, 802
storage space
  directory branchs, 244-245
  disks, displaying information,
    215
strings
  search, 223
  searching for on disks,
    223-225
subdirectories, 34
  including, 903

submenus, 29
Surface Scan (DiskFix Main
  menu) command, 423-429
Surface Scan drive map, 427-428
swap files, 122
Switch To (Desktop
  Accessories' System Control
  menu) command, 546
switches
  BOOTSAFE command,
    521-522
  COMPRESS command,
    324-325, 329-332
  CPAV command, 512-513
  CPBACKUP command,
    308-310
  CPTASK command, 121-122
  DiskEdit utility, 457
  DISKFIX command, 433-434
  FILEATTR command, 163-164
  FILECHK command, 313,
    419-422
  FILEDATE command, 164
  MIRROR command, 404-408
  PC Secure utility, 473-474
  PCFORMAT command,
    208-210
  start-up, 909
  VSAFE command, 516-517
  VWATCH command, 518
  Wipe program, 481-483
switching
  between Desktop Accessories
    application windows,
    545-546
  between tasks, 124
synchronous transmission, 802
system attribute bit, 161
system disks, 206, 211
system files
  displaying, 357-358
  see also AUTOEXEC.BAT file;
    CONFIG.SYS file
system information, saving to
  mirror-image files, 405-407
System Information (Tools
  menu) command, 334

System Information, *see* SI
System Type line (SI dialog
box), 336-337

T

Tab key
Tree/Files (CP Backup), 273
Tree/Files (Desktop
applications), 32-35
tab ruler, 586-589
Tab Ruler Display (Notepads'
Controls menu) command, 586
Tab Ruler Edit (Notepads'
Controls menu) command, 587
tables, partition, 519-522
take-control PCs, 886
calls, 892-894
DOS command lines,
accessing, 899-900
tape
copying (Algebraic
Calculato), 758-759
editing, 757-758
erasing (Algebraic
Calculator), 759-760
formatting, 300-301
printing (Algebraic
Calculator), 758-759
tape drives, backups, 308
Tape Tools menu (CP Backup),
308
tape-scrolling keys (Algebraic
Calculator), 758
Task Switcher, 120, 928
closing active tasks, 125
configuring to run at startup,
120-122
running programs, 122-124
switching between tasks, 124
telecommunications
Autodial, 841-843
see also Modem
Telecommunications

Telecommunications (Desktop
Accessories' main menu)
command, 530
Telecommunications DA,
525-526
telecommunications files
scripts to automate, 831-840
sending and receiving,
819-831
telecommunications status bar,
811-813
telephone calls
connecting computers
during, 817-818
receiving, 816
see also phone numbers
templates, form files, 661
terminal emulation
ANSI, 802-803
TTY, 802-803
VT100, 802-803
VT52, 802-803
terminate-and-stay-resident
(TSR) programs, 526-527
terminating computer
connections, 819
test mode, 75-76
testing
confidence tests (CP
Backup), 264-265
emergency disks, 219
text
attributes, names, 737
auto indent, 572-573
copying, 577-581, 601-603
deleting, 569-570
displaying control
characters, 573
editing, 609-611
inserting, 569-570, 575-577
pasting, 603-606
searching for, 187-189,
584-586
spell checking, 581-583
wordwrap, 570-572
text boxes, 47

text editors
    ASCII scripts, 832-833
    selecting, 69
Text mode, 442
Text Search dialog box, 187-189
Tiled Windows (Display Options
    submenu) command, 85
tiling windows, 85
time
    display, 531
    fax, 870
    files, 163-164, 870
        preset, 744-747
    format, 742
Time Display (CP Backup's
    Options menu) command, 302
time out, electronic mail, 829
timing backups, 302
title bars, 26-27, 33, 534
titles
    program groups, 103
    program items, 108
to-do lists, 674
toggling, 24, 63
    between Edit and Browse
        modes, 633
Topics (Help menu) command,
    48-49
tracking, 404
Transfer (Desk Accessories' File
    menu) command, 669-670
Transfer dialog box, 669
Transfer Status dialog box,
    825-831
transferring
    files, 902-904
    records, 669-670
transfers, batch, 820
transmissions
    asynchronous, 802
    fax
        aborting, 878
        AutoUpdate feature, 878
        logging, 875-878
        monitoring, 878
    synchronous, 802

Tree (Configure menu)
    command, 57, 233-234
Tree Data Display (DM
    Directory Maintenance's
    Volume menu) command,
    245-246
Tree Data Display dialog box,
    245-246
Tree window, 225-226
    as part of Desktop screen,
        226-227
    configuring, 233-234
    directories
        adding, 236
        attributes, changing,
            241-242
        copying, 240-241
        deleting, 237-238
        moving, 239-241
        renaming, 237
    directory trees
        changing directories, 228
        expanding/collapsing
            branches, 228-232
        refreshing, 227
    disks/drives, changing, 227
    dual-list displays, toggling
        with one-list displays, 80-82
Tree Window (Windows menu)
    command, 40
tree windows, 33
TSR Manager program, 943-945
TTY terminals, 802
<Typein> keyword, 111, 115-116
typing macros, 728-734

U

UMB memory, 351
Uncompress File Settings dialog
    box, 144-145
Undelete Record (Desktop
    Accessories' Edit menu)
    command, 646

Undelete utility, 383-402, 914
  commands, 385
  deleted files, locating, 387-392
    by file name, 387-389
    by predefined search
      groups, 390-391
  File window, listing files,
    385-386
  quitting, 402
  selecting files, 394-395
  starting, 384-386
undeleting
  directories, 238
  files, 151-152
  records, 645-646
Undo (DiskEdit's Edit menu)
  command, 452
Undo a DiskFix Repair (DiskFix
  Main menu) command, 423-426
UNFORMAT command, 413
Unformat program, 412-419, 939
UNFORMAT.PIF file, 939
Unformatting dialog box, 415
/UNINSTALL Install program
  option, 931
Unload Desktop Accessories
  (Desktop Accessories' Utilities
  menu) command, 555
unloading
  Desktop Accessories, 555-556
  VSafe program, 519
  VWatch program, 518
Unmark Block (Notepads' Edit
  menu) command, 579
Unmovable Files dialog box,
  327-328
Unmovable Files (Compress'
  Options menu) command,
  327-328
Unzip Files (Compression
  submenu) command, 144-145
updating
  emergency disks, 218
  virus signatures, 509
Upper Case (Display Options
  submenu) command, 34, 64

upper memory blocks, 26, 312,
  351
Use A New Menu File dialog box,
  71-72
Use a New Menu File dialog box,
  27
User Holiday Settings
  (Appointment Scheduler's
  Controls menu) command, 686
user IDs and passwords,
  799-800, 849
user interface, 526
User Level (CP Backup's
  Configure menu) command,
  290
User Level dialog box, 290
user levels, 267
  backup, changing, 290
user id variable, 834
users
  effective rights, networks, 253
  names, displaying, 883
  prompts, 113-114
utilities, see programs
Utilities (Desktop Accessories'
  main menu) command, 530
Utilities DA, 526
  ASCII table, displaying,
    552-554
  hotkeys, 551-552

V

variable-length blanks, 743-744
variable-manipulation script
  commands, 834
variables, script commands, 834
Verification Exceptions (CP
  Anti-Virus' Configure menu)
  command, 504-505
Verification Exceptions dialog
  box, 504-505
Verify (Information submenu)
  command, 148
Verify (CP Backup's Options
  menu) command, 299-300

Verify Disk (Disk menu)
command, 222-223
Verify File List dialog box,
829-831
verifying
backup data, 299-300
disks, 221-223
file readability, 148
/VIDEO (video/mouse options)
Install program option, 931
Video Adapter line (SI dialog
box), 338-339
VIEW command, 190
View File (FileFind's File menu)
command, 186
View Highlighted Message
(Electronic Mail's Actions
menu) command, 856
View program, 171, 939
View window, 33
cursor-movement keys,
194-196
displaying, 34, 83-84, 189-192
file viewers, 189-194
databases, 193
spreadsheets, 193
word processors, 192-193
hiding, 35
keyboard shortcuts, 196-198
orientation, 190
scrolling, 190
View Window (Windows menu)
command, 34-35, 40, 83
VIEW.PIF file, 939
viewing
files, 171
start-up switches, 909
virtual machines, 527
Virus Detection (CP Backup's
Options menu) command, 301
Virus Found dialog box, 497
Virus Information panel (CP
Anti-Virus), 493
Virus List (CP Anti-Virus' Scan
menu) command, 508
Virus List dialog box, 508

viruses
checking for, 519-522
cleaning, 490, 496-497
creating alert messages
for, 510
deactivating protection, 903
detecting, backups, 301
immunizing files/disks
against, 498-500
listing, 508
network notification
messages, 509-510
protection, 492, 513-519, 927
searching for, 488-489, 496
choosing objects to scan,
494-496
on different drives, 490-491
updating signatures, 509
Viruses Detected and Cleaned
dialog box, 489, 496
volume labels
changing, 246-247
renaming, 212
volume serial numbers, 208
VSAFE command, 516-517
VSafe program, 513, 927
configuring, 514-516
installing, 514
memory requirements,
513-514
starting from DOS command
line, 516-517
unloading from memory, 519
VSafe TSR Manager command
button, 944
VT52 terminals, 802
alternate keyboard, 813-814
VT100 terminals, 802
alternate keyboard, 813-814
VWATCH command, 518
VWatch protection program,
384, 513, 927
installing, 514
memory requirements,
513-514

starting from DOS command
line, 518
unloading from memory, 518
VWatch TSR Manager command
button, 944

W

Wait on DOS (Execution
submenu) command, 87
wide display, calculator keypad,
754
wild-card characters, 67, 649
* (asterisk), 370
selecting files, 136-137
Windows
executing 897-898
modes, 934
PC Tools, 936-939
executing, 939-945
starting, 934-935
windows, 27
Accessories Databases, 627
active, 534-535
application, 534
Appointment Scheduler
attributes, 676-678
Daily Scheduler region, 677
exiting, 678
layout, 677
Monthly Calendars region,
676
mouse movement, 681
navigating, 679-681
opening, 674
To-Do List region, 677
Backup Progress, 270-271
Calculator, 750
cascading, 85
Central Point Anti-Virus
elements, 492-494
Central Point Commute
Chat, 900-902
Manager, 898-905

Clipboard DA, 606-609
Commute program, 939-940
Compress, 314-317, 940
Data Monitor program,
940-941
description, 104
Desktop program, 79, 942
hiding, 85
Menu, displaying, 82-83
toggling, 80-85
View, displaying, 83-84
Desktop Accessories
changing colors, 535-537
closing, 543
elements, 534-535
maximizing, 540
moving, 538
multiple, 544-547
opening, 529-530
resizing, 539-540
saving settings, 541-542
scrolling, 542-543
sizes, 537
DiskFix program, 941
DOS Program Scheduler, 292
elements, 33-35
Express Backup, 266-269, 275,
281
Fax Log, 876-877
File, 226-227
File Attribute, 162-163
FileFind, 173
File Repair, 370
General Information (SI), 336
hiding, 40-41
Inbox (electronic mail
message), 846
Located Files, 175
Macro Editor, 721-722
Menu, see Menu window
Modem Telecommunications
DA, 790-791
moving, 37-38
moving around in, 41-42
moving between, 35

Notepads DA, 852-854
    elements, 566-569
    opening, 560-561
Outlines DA, 615-617
PC-Cache program, 941-942
Program Scheduler, 128
Repair Drive, 424-425
resizing, 38-39
Scheduler, 942-943
    loading, 918
Send Fax, 868-869
SI (System Information), 335
tiling, 85
Tree, 225-232
TSR Manager program,
    943-945
View, 189-198
zooming, 39-40
Windows Attributes (Color
Options screen) command
button, 923
Windows-aware, 909
Wipe (Change submenu)
command, 152-153
Wipe Disk (Disk menu)
command, 475
Wipe File (Change File
submenu) command, 475
Wipe program, 475-476, 938
    configuring, 480-481
    starting, 481-483
WIPE.PIF file, 938
wiping
    disks, 479-480
    files, 152-153, 476-479
Wiping dialog box, 152-153
word length, *see* data bits
Word Misspelled dialog box,
    582-583
word processors, file viewers,
    192-193
WordPerfect files, repairing,
    380-382
wordwrap, 570-572

Wordwrap (Notepads' Controls
menu) command, 571
working disks, 495
Write Object (DiskEdit's Tools
menu) command, 446, 455
Write Object dialog box, 455-456
Write Protection Startup
program, 926

X-Z

XCOPY command, 249
XMODEM file-transfer protocol,
    820-827
    receiving files, 826-827
    sending files, 825-826
XMODEM (Modem
Telecommunications)
command
    Receive menu, 827
    Send menu, 825-827
XMS driver, 353
XMS memory, 352
XON/XOFF flow control, 803

Zip Files (Compression
submenu) command, 143-144
zipping files, 143-145
ZMODEM file-transfer protocol,
    820-821, 827-830
    sending files, 828-829
ZMODEM (Modem
Telecommunications)
command
    Receive menu, 829-830
    Send menu, 828-830
zoom arrows, 33, 39, 534, 540
zooming windows, 39-40